CULTURAL ANTHROPOLOGY

CULTURAL ANTHROPOLOGY

FIFTH EDITION

BARBARA MILLER
George Washington University

Prentice Hall
Upper Saddle River London Singapore
Toronto Tokyo Sydney Hong Kong Mexico City

Editor in Chief: Dickson Musslewhite
Editor in Chief of Development: Rochelle Diogenes
VP/Editorial Director: Leah Jewell
Publisher: Nancy Roberts
Editorial Assistant: Nart Varoqua
Development Editor: Monica Ohlinger
Director of Marketing: Brandy Dawson
Marketing Manager: Lindsey Prudhomme
Marketing Assistant: Craig Deming
Managing Editor (Production): Maureen Richardson
Project Manager: Marianne Peters-Riordan
Permissions Researcher: Jane Scelta
Operations Specialist: Maura Zaldivar
Senior Art Director: Nancy Wells
Art Director: Anne Bonanno Nieglos
Interior and Cover Design: Anne DeMarinis
Cover Photos: Bede Girl: GMB Akash/Panos Pictures; Lace: grivet/Shuttershock; Water Jar: Lotus Sculpture; Water Droplets: Tony Sweet/Digital Vision/ Getty Images, Inc.
AV Project Manager: Maria Piper
Manager, Rights and Permissions: Zina Arabia
Manager, Visual Research: Beth Brenzel
Manager, Cover Visual Research & Permissions: Karen Sanatar
Image Permission Coordinator: Fran Toepfer
Photo Researcher: Kathy Ringrose
Composition/Full-Service Project Management: Jill Traut/ Macmillan Publishing Solutions
Printer/Binder: Courier Companies
Cover Printer: Phoenix Color Corp.

This book was set in 10/13 Adobe Caslon.

Credits and acknowledgments borrowed from other sources and reproduced, with permission, in this textbook appear on the appropriate page within the text or on pages 422–423.

Library of Congress Cataloging-in-Publication Data

Miller, Barbara D.
Cultural anthropology / Barbara Miller.—5th ed.
p. cm.
ISBN-13: 978-0-205-68329-1 (pbk.)
ISBN-10: 0-205-68329-0 (pbk.)
1. Ethnology. I. Title.
GN316.M49 2009
306—dc22

2008043583

10 9 8 7 6 5 4 3 2

Prentice Hall
is an imprint of

www.pearsonhighered.com

Student ISBN-13: 978-020-568329-1
ISBN-10: 020-568329-0
Exam ISBN-13: 978-020-568330-7
ISBN-10: 020-568330-4

brief CONTENTS

CONTENTS

10 POLITICS AND LEADERSHIP 241

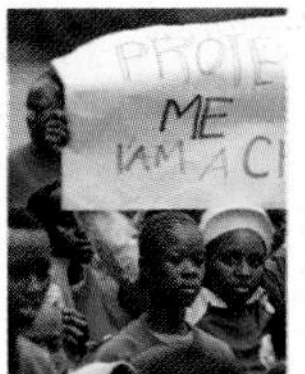

11 SOCIAL CONTROL AND SOCIAL CONFLICT 265

PART IV SYMBOLIC SYSTEMS 289

12 COMMUNICATION 291

ME

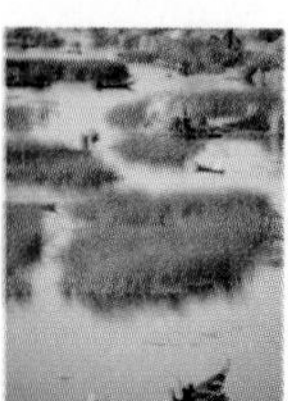

16 PEOPLE DEFINING DEVELOPMENT 395

boxed FEATURES

LESSONS applied

everyday ANTHROPOLOGY

CRITICAL thinking

CULTURAMA

eye on the ENVIRONMENT

Maps

PREFACE

"I had no idea all those cultures were out there," said one of my students after taking my introductory cultural anthropology course. Another commented, "I'm a business major, but I am going to keep the books from this course because they will help me in my career. I need to understand people."

Cultural anthropology opens up whole new worlds. Not just "out there," but here, there, and everywhere. The subject matter of cultural anthropology may seem distant, exotic, and "other"—jungle drumbeats and painted faces, for example. This book helps students to encounter those faraway cultures and also to realize that their culture has its own versions of jungle drumbeats and painted faces. "Making the strange familiar" is essential learning in a globalizing world where cultural diversity may equal cultural survival for all of us. "Making the familiar strange" is a priceless revelation because it reduces the divide between "us" and the "other." "We" become "other" through the insights of cultural anthropology.

To achieve its goals, *Cultural Anthropology*, Fifth Edition, delivers rich and exciting information about the world's cultures and promotes critical thinking and reflective learning. Students will find many points at which they can connect with the material, view their own culture as a culture, and make connections between anthropology and their everyday life in, for example, hairstyles, food symbolism, sleep deprivation, doctor–patient dialogues, racism and sexism, and the meaning of gestures.

Knowledge of the world's cultures and how they are changing relates to careers in our increasingly globalized world. The need to understand people (including ourselves) and cultures is critical to any endeavor in the short term and to the survival of humanity in the long run. The study of the world's cultures involves learning new words and analytical categories, but this effort will pay off in terms of bringing the world's peoples and cultures closer to you. If this book achieves my aspirations, anyone who reads it will live a life that is more culturally aware, enriched, and tolerant.

HOW THIS BOOK IS ORGANIZED

The book's organization and pedagogical features are all designed to help ensure student engagement. The chapters are organized in five parts.

Part I, Introduction to Cultural Anthropology, includes three chapters that provide the foundation for the rest of the book. They describe what anthropology is, the evolution of culture, and how cultural anthropologists do research. Chapter 2, on the evolution of humanity and culture, is new to this edition. It includes material on nonhuman primate culture, hominin evolution, and the Neolithic revolution. This new chapter provides a bridge to the rest of the book's discussion of contemporary human cultures.

Part II, Cultural Foundations, includes chapters that explain how people make a living, how they reproduce and raise children, and how different cultures deal with the inevitabilities of illness, suffering, and death. A revised Chapter 6, Reproduction and Human Development, combines two previously separate chapters and efficiently covers the important topics of each.

Part III, Social Organization, provides chapters about how people around the world organize themselves into groups based on kinship and other forms of social ties, how they form political alliances, and how they deal with conflict and the need for order.

Part IV, Symbolic Systems, presents chapters on communication and language, religion, and expressive culture and art.

Part V, Contemporary Cultural Change, looks at two of the most important topics shaping cultural change in our times: migration and international development. These chapters explicitly put culture into motion and show how people are both affected by larger structures, such as globalization or violence, and exercise agency in attempting to create meaningful and secure lives.

SIGNIFICANT CHANGES IN THE FIFTH EDITION

New Chapter, The Evolution of Humanity and Culture (Chapter 2) This chapter provides carefully selected material in biological anthropology and archaeology to describe the highlights of modern humanity's evolution from our early hominin origins to the rise of cities and states following the Neolithic revolution. It provides a useful context for the understanding of human culture, its distinctiveness and importance. For students whose only anthropology class is a course in cultural anthropology, this chapter offers more exposure to biological anthropology and archaeology than Chapter 1 provides. This new chapter is unique, compared to counterpart chapters in other cultural anthropology textbooks, because it goes beyond biological evolution to discuss cultural evolution during and following the Neolithic revolution.

New Box, Eye on the Environment These boxes provide material that links culture with some aspect of the environment. Examples include Neanderthal adaptations to the cold, Inuit place names and environmental knowledge, eagle protection among the Hopi Indians, and environmental destruction from oil drilling in Nigeria. These new boxes, along with many in-text references to how culture and the environment interact, enable students to make new connections and think critically.

New and Updated Maps The author has designed several new maps to provide complementary information for the textual material without distracting the reader with unnecessary details.

New Photographs The new photographs are carefully chosen to enliven the textual material and to be thought provoking. Photographs arranged in pairs or trios, with linked captions, offer a mini-photo essay for students to ponder.

CONTINUED FEATURES

Several continuing features make this textbook distinctive and effective.

Anthropology Works Each of the book's five parts opens with a profile of an applied anthropologist, someone who uses his or her anthropology training in a professional career. Profiles include a business anthropologist, a medical anthropologist, a forensic anthropologist, a development anthropologist, and a federal relations anthropologist.

Culturama All chapters, except for Chapter 2, include a one-page profile of a cultural group accompanied by a mini-panorama of two photographs and a map with captions. These brief summaries provide an enticing glimpse into the culture. MyAnthroLab includes a list of resources (readings, videos, and websites) about each culture, offering avenues for those who want to learn more.

In-Text Glossary Definitions for the Key Concepts are provided on the page where the concept is first mentioned and defined. A paginated list of the Key Concepts appears at the end of each chapter. The Glossary at the end of the book contains the complete list with definitions.

THINKING OUTSIDE THE BOX

Listen to the interview on the Web with French paleoanthropologist Jean-Jacques Hublin about Neanderthals and their fate: www.pbs.org/wgbh/evolution/library/07/3/text_pop/l_073_02.htm. What is Hublin's position?

Thinking Outside the Box The Thinking Outside the Box feature provides 3 or 4 thought-provoking questions in each chapter, displayed at the bottom of the page. These questions prompt readers to relate an issue to their own cultural experiences or provide an avenue for further research. They can promote class discussion and serve as a basis for a class project.

The Big Questions Three Big Questions are posed at the beginning of each chapter to alert readers to the chapter's overarching themes. They are carried through in the chapter outline as the three major headings. At the end of the chapter, The Big Questions Revisited provides a helpful review of the key points related to each Big Question.

BOXED FEATURES

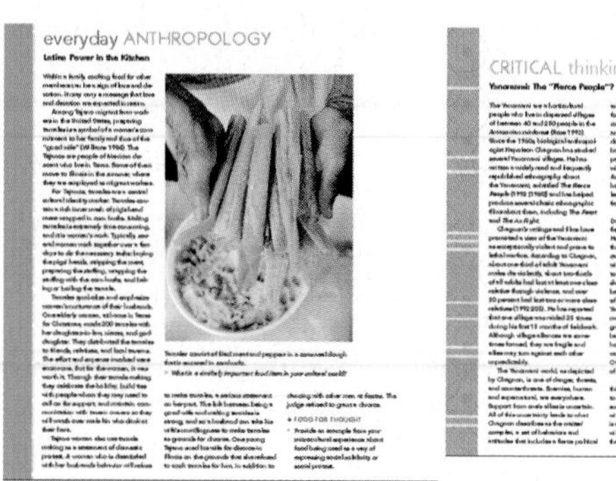

Everyday Anthropology boxes present cultural examples that connect to everyone's lives and prompt reflective learning. Critical Thinking boxes introduce an issue and show how it has been studied or analyzed from different anthropological perspectives. These boxes provide tie-ins to the major theoretical debates in cultural anthropology presented in Chapter 1. Although students may appreciate the interesting material that cultural anthropology offers, they are still likely to ask, "Does this knowledge have any practical applications?" Lessons Applied boxes highlight how applied anthropologists work and the relevance of anthropology in addressing social problems.

COMMITMENT TO CULTURAL SURVIVAL

In confirming our commitment to the sustainability of the world's cultures, especially of endangered indigenous peoples, the author and the publisher donate a portion of the royalties from sales of new copies of this book to the organization called Cultural Survival (see its Mission Statement on the inside front cover). Cultural Survival helps support indigenous people worldwide in achieving and maintaining their preferred lifestyles and environment. Back issues of the journal *Cultural Survival Quarterly* are available on the Web at www.cs.org.

THE IMPORTANCE OF NAMES

Since the beginning of modern humanity, people have been naming each other, naming other groups, and naming features of the places they inhabit. People of earlier times often referred to themselves in terms that translate roughly into "The People." As far as they were concerned, they were The People: the only people on earth.

Things are more complicated now. European colonialism, starting in the fifteenth century, launched centuries of rapid contact between Europeans and thousands of indigenous groups around the world. The Europeans named and described these groups in their European languages. The names were not those that the people used for themselves, or if they were, the transliteration into a European language altered local names into something very different from the original.

The Spanish explorers' naming of all the indigenous peoples of North America as Indians is a famous example of a misnomer. Beyond just being wrong by thinking they had reached India, the Spanish conquerors who renamed thousands of people and claimed their territory simultaneously erased much of the indigenous people's heritage and identity.

The challenge of using the preferred names for people and places of the world faces us today as people worldwide wrestle with the issue of what they want to be called. Until recently, indigenous peoples of the present-day United States preferred to be called Native Americans, rejecting the pejorative term "Indian." Now, they are claiming and recasting the term "Indian." In Canada, preferred terms are "First Nations," "Native Peoples," and "Northern Peoples." From small-scale groups to entire countries, people are attempting to revive precolonial group names and place names. Bombay is now Mumbai. Group names and place names are frequently contested. Is someone Hispanic or Latino? Is it the Persian Gulf or the Arabian Gulf? Is it Greenland or Kalaallit Nunaat? Does it matter? The answer is yes, resoundingly, yes.

This book strives to provide the most currently accepted names for people, places, objects, activities, and ideas. By the time it is printed, however, some names and their English spellings will have changed. It is an ongoing challenge to keep track of such changes, but such is part of our job as citizens of a transforming world.

THE COVER IMAGE

In this photograph, a Bede (bay-day) girl of Bangladesh carries water to her home for drinking and cooking. The Bede, referred to in English as "water gypsies," are a marginalized ethnic group who live on boats and move from place to place to make a living. Because "gypsy" is a derogatory term, it is preferable to use the people's own preferred name. The water this girl is carrying is drawn from a tubewell, of which many thousands were constructed in Bangladesh in recent decades in the hope of providing clean water for drinking, cooking, and bathing. Unfortunately, over 80 percent of Bangladesh's tubewells are polluted with arsenic, which can cause cancer, skin lesions, reproductive problems in women, and hypertension. The only option to well water is ground water, which carries the risk of infectious diseases. Clean water is an increasingly scarce resource in Bangladesh and worldwide.

IN THANKS

The breadth, depth, and quality of this edition are the result of many people's ideas, comments, corrections, and care. For the first edition, four anthropologists carefully reviewed multiple drafts of the book. I will always be grateful to them for their monumental contribution that helped make this book what it is today: Elliot Fratkin, Smith College; Maxine Margolis, University of Florida; Russell Reid, University of Louisville; and Robert Trotter II, University of Arizona.

My biological anthropologist colleague at George Washington University, Chet Sherwood, gave the first two sections of new Chapter 2 a close reading and offered many ways to improve them. Thanks, Chet.

The cultural anthropologists who served as reviewers for the second, third, fourth, and fifth editions helped me move the book forward in many ways: Warren D. Anderson, Southeast Missouri State University; Jason Antrosio, Albion College; Diane Baxter, University of Oregon; Monica L. Bellas, Cerritos College; Barbara Bonnekessen, University of Missouri–Kansas City; Peter Brown, University of Wisconsin, Oshkosh; Howard Campbell, University of Texas, El Paso; (the late) Charles R. de Burlo, The University of Vermont; Elizabeth de la Portilla, University of Texas at San Antonio; William W. Donner, Kutztown University; Lisa Pope Fischer, Santa Monica College; Pamela J. Ford, Mount San Jacinto College; Mary Kay Gilliland, Pima Community College; Nancy Gonlin, Bellevue Community College; Jeanne Humble, Bluegrass Community & Technical College; Ann Kingsolver, University of South Carolina; Leslie Lischka, Linfield College; William M. Loker, California State University, Chico; Martin F. Manalansan IV, University of Illinois; Corey Pressman, Mt. Hood Community College; Ed Robbins, University of Wisconsin; Jacquelyn Robinson, Albany State University; Harry Sanabria, University of Pittsburgh; Kathleen M. Saunders, Western Washington University; G. Richard Scott, University of Nevada, Reno; Wesley Shumar, Drexel University; David Simmons, University of South Carolina; Kimberly Eison Simmons, University of South Carolina; Lori A. Stanley, Luther College; Jim Wilce, Northern Arizona

University; Peter Wogan, Willamette University; and Katrina Worley, Sierra College.

Many anthropologists and others have provided encouragement, suggestions, feedback, references, and photographs: Lila Abu-Lughod, Abigail Adams, Vincanne Adams, Catherine Allen, Joseph Alter, Matthew Amster, Myrdene Anderson, Donald Attwood, Christopher Baker, Isabel Balseiro, Nancy Benco, Marc Bermann, Alexia Bloch, Elson Boles, Lynne Bolles, John Bowen, Don Brenneis, Alison Brooks, Judith K. Brown, D. Glynn Cochrane, Jeffery Cohen, Carole Counihan, Brian Craik, Liza Dalby, Loring Danforth, Patricia Delaney, Alexander Dent, Linus Digim'rina, Timothy Earle, Daniel Everett, Johannes Fabian, Ilana Feldman, Elliot Fratkin, Martin Fusi, Maris Boyd Gillette, Richard A. Gould, David Gow, Richard Grinker, Daniel Gross, (the late) Marvin Harris, Tobias Hecht, Cornelia Mayer Herzfeld, Michael Herzfeld, Barry Hewlett, Danny Hoffman, Michael Horowitz, (the late) Robert Humphrey, Lanita Jacobs-Huey, Vicki Jensen, Anstice Justin, Barry D. Kass, Patty Kelly, Laurel Kendall, David Kideckel, Diane E. King, Stuart Kirsch, Dorinne Kondo, Conrad Kottak, Jennifer Kramer, Donald B. Kraybill, Ruth Krulfeld, Joel Kuipers, Takie Lebra, David Lempert, Lamont Lindstrom, Susan Orpett Long, Luisa Maffi, Beatriz Manz, Samuel Martínez, Catherine McCoid, Leroy McDermott, Kimber Haddox McKay, Jerry Milanich, Laura Miller, Madhushree Mukerjee, Kirin Narayan, Sarah Nelson, Gananath Obeyesekere, Ellen Oxfeld, Hanna Papanek, Michael G. Peletz, Deborah Pellow, Gregory Possehl, David Price, Joanne Rappaport, Jennifer Robertson, Nicole Sault, Joel Savishinsky, David Z. Scheffel, Nancy Scheper-Hughes, Pankaj Sekhsaria, Bob Shepherd, Richard Shweder, Jennie Smith-Pariola, Chunghee Soh, Kate Spilde Contreras, Anthony Stocks, Patricia Tovar, Sita Venkateswar, Martha Ward, James (Woody) Watson, Rubie Watson, Van Yasek, and Kevin Yelvington.

For this edition, I have been fortunate to work with a team of excellent publishing professionals. I am grateful to Nancy Roberts, my new publisher at Pearson/Prentice Hall, for her support of this revision and to Monica Ohlinger, my development editor who is the head of Ohlinger Publishing Services in Columbus, Ohio, for her contributions and care throughout the revision process.

I thank the Millers—my parents, siblings, aunts and uncles, and nieces and nephews—for their interest and support. My father's two comments about the book were that it has an awful lot of long words, and how do I know so much about sex? "From reading, Dad," was my truthful reply. I am grateful to the Heatons—my former in-laws, including my ex-husband, (late) parents-in-law, brothers- and sisters-in-law, and nieces and nephews—for their enduring friendship.

I thank, especially, my son, Jack Heaton. He was a superb traveling companion on our trip around the world with the Semester at Sea Program in 1996, when I wrote much of the first edition. He continues to be excellent company during our time together in DC. This book is dedicated to him.

Barbara Miller
Washington, DC

SUPPORT FOR INSTRUCTORS AND STUDENTS

This book is accompanied by an extensive learning package to enhance the experience of both instructors and students. The author is personally responsible for the material in the Instructor's Resource Manual, MyTest, and the PowerPoint slides.

Instructor's Resource Manual with Tests (0-205-68331-2) For each chapter in the text, this valuable resource provides a detailed outline, list of objectives, discussion questions, and suggested readings and videos. In addition, test questions in multiple-choice, true/false, fill-in-the-blank, and short-answer formats are available for each chapter; the answers are page-referenced to the text. For easy access, this manual is available within the instructor section of MyAnthroLab for *Cultural Anthropology, Fifth Edition,* or at www.pearsonhighered.com.

MyTest (0-205-68364-9) This computerized software allows instructors to create their own personalized exams, edit any or all of the existing test questions, and add new questions. Other special features of this program include random generation of test questions, creation of alternate versions of the same test, scrambling question sequence, and test preview before printing. For easy access, this software is available within the instructor section of MyAnthroLab for *Cultural Anthropology, Fifth Edition,* or at www.pearsonhighered.com.

PowerPoint Presentation for Cultural Anthropology (0-205-68332-0) These PowerPoint slides combine text and graphics for each chapter to help instructors convey anthropological principles in a clear and engaging way. For easy access, they are available within the instructor section of MyAnthroLab for *Cultural Anthropology, Fifth Edition,* or at www.pearsonhighered.com.

Strategies in Teaching Anthropology (0-13-603466-7) Unique in focus and content, this book focuses on the "how" of teaching anthropology across all four fields and provides a wide array of associated learning outcomes and student activities. It is a valuable single-source compendium of strategies and teaching "tricks of the trade" from a group of seasoned teaching anthropologists, working in a variety of teaching settings, who share their pedagogical techniques, knowledge, and observations.

PEARSON myanthrolab MyAnthroLab is an interactive and instructive multimedia site designed to help students and instructors save time and improve results. It offers access to a wealth of resources geared to meet the individual teaching and learning needs of every instructor and student. Combining an e-book, video, audio, multimedia simulations, research support, and assessment, MyAnthroLab engages students and gives them the tools they need to enhance their performance in the course. Please see your Pearson sales representative for more information about **MyAnthroLab**, or visit www.myanthrolab.com.

Student Field Guide
and
Workbook
EthnoQuest
An Interactive Multimedia Simulation for Cultural Anthropology Fieldwork
Version 3.0
Frances F. Berdan • Edward A. Stark
Carey Van Loon

EthnoQuest® (0-13-185013-X) This interactive multimedia simulation includes a series of 10 ethnographic encounters within the culture of a fictional Mexican village set in a computer-based learning environment. It provides students with a realistic problem-solving experience and is designed to help students experience the fieldwork of a cultural anthropologist. Please see your Pearson sales representative for more information about **EthnoQuest®.**

about the AUTHOR

"***Cultural anthropology*** is exciting because it **CONNECTS** with everything, from **FOOD** to **ART**. And it can help prevent or **SOLVE** world problems related to ***social inequality*** and injustice."

BARBARA D. MILLER

Barbara Miller is Professor of Anthropology and International Affairs and Director of the Culture in Global Affairs (CIGA) Research and Policy Program at The George Washington University. She received her Ph.D. in anthropology from Syracuse University in 1978. Before coming to GW in 1994, she taught at the University of Rochester, SUNY Cortland, Ithaca College, Cornell University, and the University of Pittsburgh. For thirty years, Barbara's research has focused mainly on gender-based inequalities in India, especially the nutritional and medical neglect of daughters in northern regions of the country. In addition, she has conducted research on culture and rural development in Bangladesh, on low-income household dynamics in Jamaica, and on Hindu adolescents in Pittsburgh. Her current interests include continued research on gender inequalities in health in South Asia, the role of cultural anthropology in informing policy issues, and cultural heritage and public policy, especially as related to women, children, and other disenfranchised groups. She teaches courses on introductory cultural anthropology, medical anthropology, development anthropology, culture and population, health and development in South Asia, and migration and mental health. In addition to many journal articles and book chapters, she has published several books: *The Endangered Sex: Neglect of Female Children in Rural North India,* 2nd ed. (Oxford University Press, 1997); an edited volume, *Sex and Gender Hierarchies* (Cambridge University Press, 1993); and a co-edited volume with Alf Hiltebeitel, *Hair: Its Power and Meaning in Asian Cultures* (SUNY Press, 1998). In addition to *Cultural Anthropology,* fifth edition, she is the author of *Anthropology,* second edition (Pearson/Allyn & Bacon 2008 and *Cultural Anthropology in a Globalizing World,* first edition (Pearson/Allyn & Bacon 2008).

CULTURAL ANTHROPOLOGY

1  ANTHROPOLOGY AND THE STUDY OF CULTURE

2  THE EVOLUTION OF HUMANITY AND CULTURE

3  RESEARCHING CULTURE

PART I
INTRODUCTION TO CULTURAL ANTHROPOLOGY

ANTHROPOLOGY works

Susan Squires, a business anthropologist, is one of the brains behind the General Mills breakfast food, Go-Gurt®. During its first year of production in 1991, Go-Gurt generated sales of $37 million. Squires, who earned a Ph.D. in cultural anthropology from Boston University, is one of the growing number of anthropologists who use their knowledge of anthropology in the business world.

Research into the development of Go-Gurt took Squires and an industrial designer into the homes of American families to observe their breakfast behavior and food choices. On their first day of research, they arrived at a residence at 6:30 a.m., laden with video cameras and other equipment, prepared to have breakfast with a family they had never met.

General Mills had learned from focus group studies that mothers want their families to eat whole-grain breakfast foods. Squires, in contrast, found a wide range of preferences and behavior related to individual hunger patterns and the need to leave home early for work or school.

She realized that the ideal breakfast food should be portable, healthy, fun, and come in a disposable container. The answer: yogurt packaged so that it does not require a spoon and can be frozen or refrigerated. One mother said that her daughter thinks she is eating a popsicle when she has Go-Gurt for breakfast.

The work of Susan Squires demonstrates how cultural anthropology can benefit the business world and the everyday lives of consumers. Two assets of cultural anthropology in the business world are, first, its attention to everyday life and, second, its attention to cultural variation, which exposes differences in preferences, values, and behavior.

Young boys on an outrigger canoe near one of the islands of New Ireland province in the northeastern part of Papua New Guinea. A preferred food source is shark, and some men are adept at "shark calling," which draws the shark near the boat so it can be speared and netted.

ANTHROPOLOGY AND THE STUDY OF CULTURE

the BIG questions

- What is anthropology?
- What is cultural anthropology?
- How is cultural anthropology relevant to a career?

OUTLINE

A member of the Dani people, Irian Jaya, New Guinea, holding a stone adze, photographed in the 1990s.

Old bones, Jurassic Park, cannibalism, hidden treasure, *Indiana Jones and the Temple of Doom*. The popular impression of anthropology is based mainly on movies and television shows that depict anthropologists as adventurers and heroes. Many anthropologists do have adventures and discover treasures such as ancient pottery, medicinal plants, and jade carvings. But most of their research is not glamorous. Some anthropologists spend years in difficult physical conditions searching for the earliest fossils of our ancestors. Others live among people in Silicon Valley, California, and study first-hand how they work and organize family life in a setting permeated by modern technology. Some anthropologists conduct laboratory analyses of the contents of tooth enamel to reveal where an individual once lived. Others study designs on prehistoric pottery to learn what the symbols mean, or observe nonhuman primates such as chimpanzees or orangutans in the wild to learn how they live.

Anthropology is the study of humanity, including prehistoric origins and contemporary human diversity. Compared to other disciplines that study humanity (such as history, psychology, economics, political science, and sociology), anthropology is broader in scope. Anthropology covers a much greater span of time than these disciplines and it encompasses a broader range of topics.

anthropology the study of humanity, including prehistoric origins and contemporary human diversity.

biological anthropology or **physical anthropology** the study of humans as biological organisms, including evolution and contemporary variation.

archaeology or **prehistory** the study of past human cultures through their material remains.

linguistic anthropology the study of human communication, including its origins, history, and contemporary variation and change.

cultural anthropology or **social anthropology** the study of living peoples and their cultures, including variation and change.

culture people's learned and shared behavior and beliefs.

applied anthropology or **practicing anthropology** or **practical anthropology** the use of anthropological knowledge to prevent or solve problems or to shape and achieve policy goals.

◆◆◆

Introducing Anthropology

In North America, anthropology is divided into four fields (see Figure 1.1) that focus on separate, but connected, subject matter related to humanity:

- **Biological anthropology** (or physical anthropology)—the study of humans as biological organisms, including evolution and contemporary variation.
- **Archaeology** (or prehistory)—the study of past human cultures through their material remains.

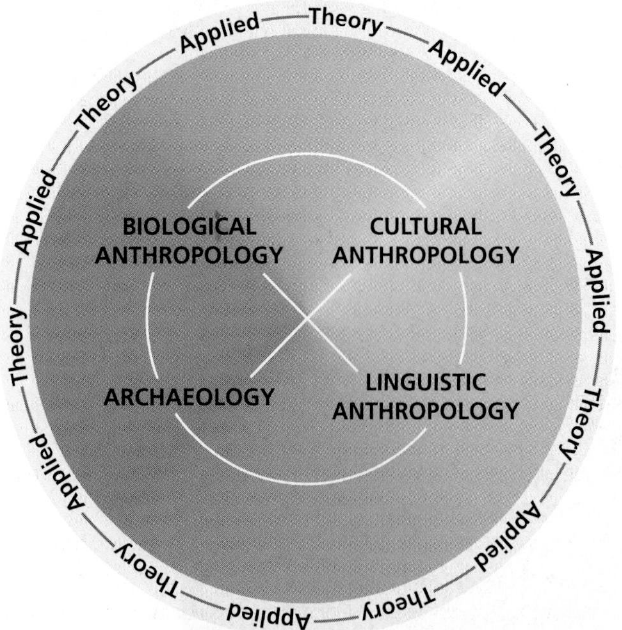

FIGURE 1.1 The Four Fields of Anthropology

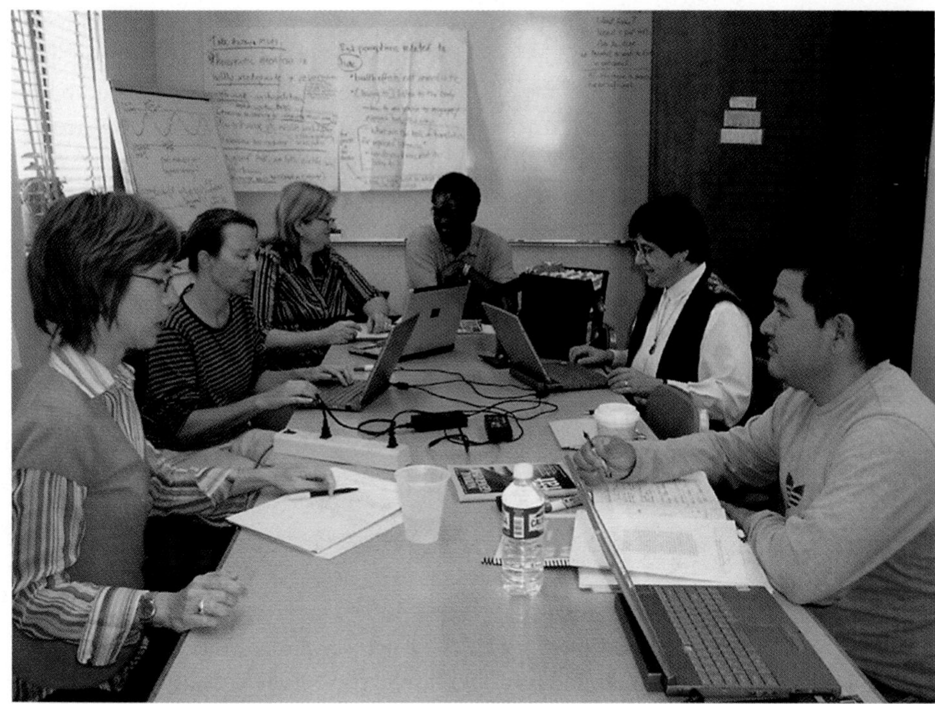

A team of anthropologists and students discuss their research project on Silicon Valley culture.

▶ *If you were given a grant to conduct anthropological research, where would you go and what would you study?*

- **Linguistic anthropology**—the study of human communication, including its origins, history, and contemporary variation and change.
- **Cultural anthropology** (or social anthropology)—the study of living peoples and their cultures, including variation and change. **Culture** refers to people's learned and shared behaviors and beliefs.

Some anthropologists argue that a fifth field, applied anthropology, should be added. **Applied anthropology** (also called *practicing anthropology* or *practical anthropology*) is the use of anthropological knowledge to prevent or solve problems or to shape and achieve policy goals. The author of this book takes the position that the application of knowledge, just like theory, is an integral part of each of the four fields and should be integrated within each of them.

BIOLOGICAL OR PHYSICAL ANTHROPOLOGY

Biological anthropology encompasses three subfields. The first, *primatology*, is the study of the nonhuman members of the order of mammals called primates, which includes a wide range of animals from very small, nocturnal creatures to gorillas, the largest members. Primatologists study nonhuman primates in the wild and in captivity. They record and analyze how the animals spend their time, collect and share food, form social groups, rear offspring, develop leadership patterns, and experience conflict and conflict resolution. Primatologists are alarmed about the decline in numbers, and even extinction, of nonhuman primates. Many apply their knowledge to nonhuman primate conservation.

The second subfield is *paleoanthropology*, the study of human evolution on the basis of the fossil record. One important activity is the search for fossils to increase the amount and quality of the evidence related to the way human evolution occurred. Discoveries of new fossils provide "aha!" moments and arresting photographs for the covers of popular magazines. A less glamorous but equally important activity in paleoanthropology is dating and classifying new fossils.

The third subfield is the study of *contemporary human biological variation*. Anthropologists working in this area define, measure, and seek to explain differences in the biological makeup and behavior of contemporary humans. They study such biological factors as DNA within and across populations, body size and shape, human nutrition and disease, and human growth and development.

ARCHAEOLOGY

Archaeology means, literally, the "study of the old," but "the old" is limited to human culture. Therefore, the time-depth of archaeology goes back only to the beginnings of *Homo sapiens*, between 300,000–160,000 years ago when they first emerged in Africa. Archaeology encompasses two major areas: *prehistoric archaeology*, which concerns the human past before written records, and *historical archaeology*, which deals with the human

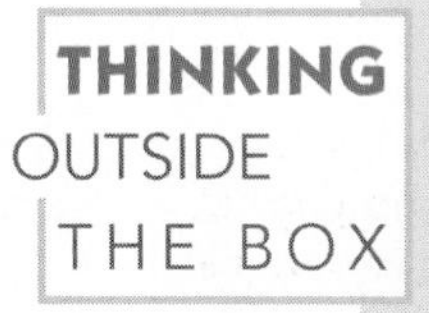

What are your impressions of anthropology? How did you acquire them? Make notes of these impressions and review them at the end of the course.

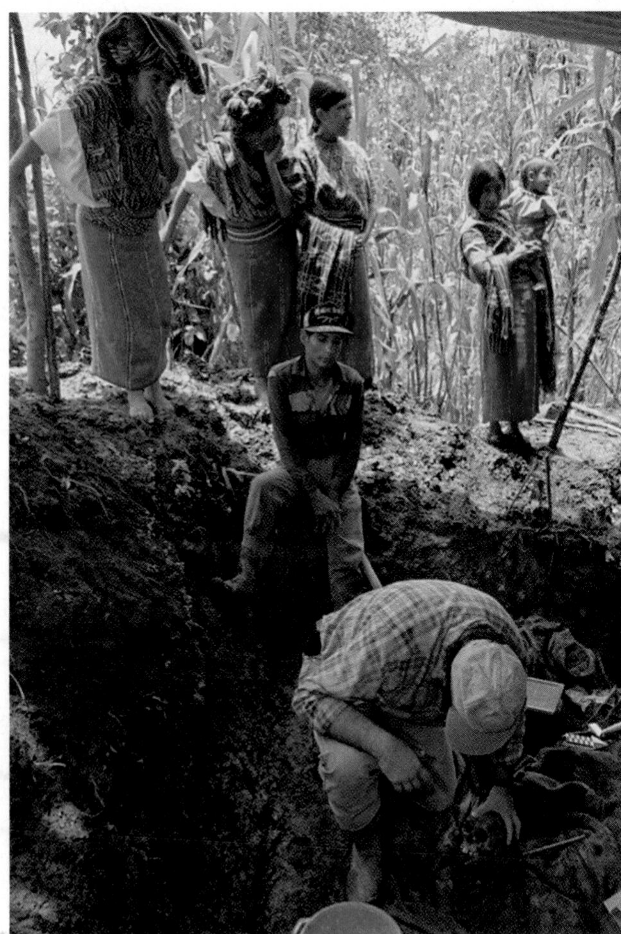

Maya people watch as forensic anthropologist Francisco de Leon conducts an exhumation of more than 50 bodies in a highland Guatemalan village in 1997.

▶ *Are courses in forensic anthropology offered at your school?*

past in societies that have written documents. Prehistoric archaeologists often identify themselves with broad geographic regions, studying, for example, Old World archaeology (Africa, Europe, and Asia) or New World archaeology (North, Central, and South Americas).

Another set of specialties within archaeology is based on the context in which the archaeology takes place. For example, *underwater archaeology* is the study of submerged archaeological sites. Underwater archaeological sites may be from either prehistoric or historic times. Some prehistoric sites include early human settlements in parts of Europe, such as household sites discovered in Switzerland that were once near lakes but are now submerged.

The archaeology of the recent past is another important research direction. *Industrial archaeology* focuses on changes in material culture and society during and since the Industrial Revolution. It is especially active in Great Britain, home of the Industrial Revolution. There, industrial archaeologists study such topics as the design of iron bridges, the growth and distribution of china potteries, miners' housing, and cotton mills. An important role of industrial archaeology is the conservation of industrial sites, which are more likely to be neglected or destroyed than are sites that have natural beauty or cultural glamour attached to them.

An example of what could be called the *archaeology of contemporary life* is the "Garbage Project" conducted by archaeologists at the University of Arizona at Tucson (Rathje and Murphy 1992). They have excavated part of the Fresh Kills landfill on Staten Island, near New York City. Its mass is estimated at 100 million tons and its volume at 2.9 billion cubic feet. Thus, it is one of the largest human-made

Stephen Lubkemann, trained as a cultural anthropologist and an underwater archaeologist, documents the remains of the hull of DRTO-036, a vessel that wrecked in the Dry Tortugas in the mid-nineteenth century. The vessel lies within Dry Tortugas National Park in the Florida Keys.

▶ *You can access UNESCO's Convention on the Protection of Underwater Heritage on the Internet.*

Iron Bridge, England, is an important site of industrial archaeology. Considered the "birthplace of industry," the site includes the world's first iron bridge and remains of factories, furnaces, and canals.

▶ *Take a virtual tour of the site by going to http://www.ironbridge.org.uk/.*

structures in North America. Excavation of pop-top can tabs, disposable diapers, cosmetics containers, and telephone books reveals much about recent consumption patterns and how they affect the environment. One surprising finding is that the kinds of garbage people often blame for filling up landfills, such as fast-food packaging and disposable diapers, cause less serious problems than paper. Newspaper, especially, is a major culprit because of sheer quantity. This information can improve recycling efforts worldwide. The Fresh Kills landfill continues to grow rapidly due to everyday trash accumulation and other, less common sources of debris, such as the remains from the World Trade Center in Manhattan following the 9/11 attack.

LINGUISTIC ANTHROPOLOGY

Linguistic anthropology is devoted to the study of communication, mainly (but not exclusively) among humans. Linguistic anthropology has three subfields: *historical linguistics,* the study of language change over time and how languages are related; *descriptive linguistics,* or structural linguistics, the study of how contemporary languages differ in terms of their formal structure; and *sociolinguistics,* the study of the relationships among social variation, social context, and linguistic variation, including nonverbal communication.

New directions in linguistic anthropology are connected to important current issues. First is a trend to study language in everyday use, or *discourse,* and how it relates to power structures at local, regional, and international levels (Duranti 1997a). In some contexts, powerful people speak more than less powerful people, whereas sometimes the more powerful people speak less. Power relations may also be expressed through intonation, word choice, and such nonverbal forms of communication as posture and dress. Second is increased attention to the role of information technology in communication, especially the Internet and cell phones. Third is attention to the increasingly rapid extinction of indigenous languages and what can be done about it. These topics are discussed in depth in Chapter 12.

CULTURAL ANTHROPOLOGY

Cultural anthropology is the study of contemporary people and their cultures. It considers variations and similarities across cultures and how cultures change over time. Cultural anthropologists learn about culture by spending extended periods of time living with the people they study (discussed in Chapter 3).

Prominent areas of specialization in cultural anthropology include economic anthropology, psychological anthropology, medical anthropology, political anthropology, and international development anthropology (the study of the effects and patterns of international development policies and plans in cross-cultural perspective). The rest of this book covers these and other topics.

APPLIED ANTHROPOLOGY: SEPARATE FIELD OR CROSS-CUTTING FOCUS?

In the United States, applied anthropology emerged during and after World War II. Its first concern was with improving the lives of contemporary peoples and their needs, and so it was more closely associated with cultural anthropology than with the other three fields.

Many anthropologists feel that applied anthropology should be considered a fifth field of anthropology, standing on its own. An alternative position is that the application of knowledge to solve problems, just like theory, should be part of each field (see Figure 1.1). This is the author's position, and

LESSONS applied

Orangutan Research Leads to Orangutan Advocacy

Primatologist Biruté Galdikas (beer-OOH-tay GAL-dee-kas) first went to Indonesia to study orangutans in 1971 (Galdikas 1995). She soon became aware of the threat to the orangutans from local people who, as a way of making money, capture them for sale to zoos around the world. The poachers separate the young from their mothers, often killing the mothers in the process.

Orangutan juveniles are highly dependent on their mothers, maintaining close bodily contact with them for at least two years and nursing until they are around 8 years old. Because of this long period of orangutans' need for maternal contact, Galdikas set up her camp to serve as a way station for orphans. She became the maternal figure. Her first "infant" was an orphaned orangutan, Sugito, who clung to her as though she were his own mother for years.

The survival of orangutans on Borneo and Sumatra (their only habitats worldwide) is critically endangered by massive commercial and illegal logging, population resettlement programs, plantations, and other pressures on the rainforests where the orangutans live. A rainforest is an environment found at mid-latitudes, of tall, broad-leaf evergreen trees, with annual rainfall of 400 centimeters (or 60 inches) and no dry season.

Galdikas is focusing her efforts on orangutan preservation. She says, "I feel like I'm viewing an animal holocaust and holocaust is not a word I use lightly. . . . The destruction of the tropical rainforest is accelerating daily" (Dreifus 2000:D3). Across all ranges, it is estimated that during the twentieth century the orangutan population experienced a huge decrease, from 315,000 in 1900 to 44,000 in 2000 (IUCN/SSC Conservation Breeding Specialist Group 2004). Aerial surveys (Ancrenaz et al. 2005) and DNA analysis of living orangutans (Goossens et al. 2006) confirm recent and dramatic declines that, if not halted, will lead to extinction in the next few decades.

Galdikas has studied orangutans longer than anyone else. She links her knowledge of and love for the orangutans with applied anthropology and advocacy on their behalf. Since the beginning of her fieldwork in Borneo, she has maintained and expanded the Camp Leakey field site and research center (named after her mentor, Lewis

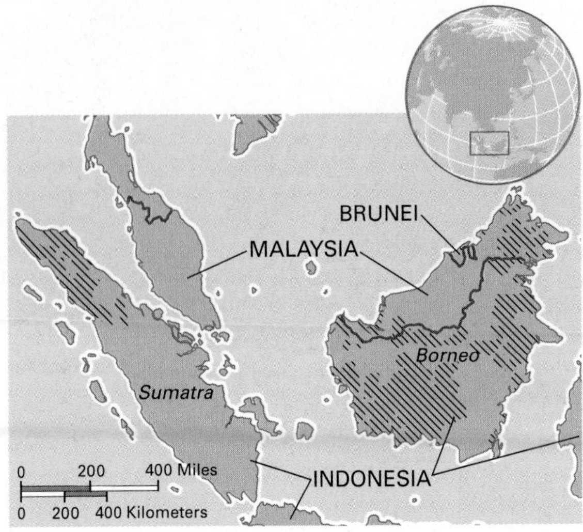

MAP 1.1 Orangutan Regions in Malaysia and Indonesia. Orangutans are the only great apes living outside Africa. Fossil evidence indicates that their habitats in the past extended throughout Southeast Asia and southern China. They are now limited to pockets of rainforest on the islands of Sumatra and Borneo.

therefore many examples of applied anthropology appear throughout this book.

Applied anthropology is an important thread that weaves through all four fields of anthropology:

- Archaeologists are employed in *cultural resource management (CRM)*, assessing the presence of possible archaeological remains before construction projects such as roads and buildings can proceed.
- Biological anthropologists are employed as *forensic anthropologists*, participating in criminal investigations through laboratory work identifying bodily remains. Others work in the area of primate conservation (see Lessons Applied box).
- Linguistic anthropologists consult with educational institutions about how to improve standardized tests for bilingual populations and conduct policy research for governments.
- Cultural anthropologists apply their knowledge to improve policies and programs in every domain of life, including education, health care, business, poverty reduction, and conflict prevention and resolution.

Applied roles of anthropologists are illustrated in the Anthropology Works profiles at the beginning of each of the five parts of this book and in the Lessons Applied boxes.

rainforest an environment, found at mid-latitudes, of tall, broad-leaf evergreen trees, with annual rainfall of 400 centimeters (or 60 inches) and no dry season.

(LEFT) Lowland rainforest in Borneo in the morning mist. (RIGHT) Biruté Galdikas has been studying orangutans in Borneo, Indonesia, for over three decades and is an active supporter of conservation of their habitat.

▶ *Learn about her work and the status of wild orangutans by searching on the Web.*

Leakey, who inspired her research on orangutans). In 1986, she co-founded the Orangutan Foundation International (OFI), which now has several chapters worldwide. She has published scholarly articles and given public talks around the world on her research. Educating the public about the imminent danger to the orangutans is an important part of her activism. Galdikas and other orangutan experts are lobbying international institutions such as the World Bank to promote forest conservation as part of their loan agreements.

Camp Leakey employs many local people in diverse roles, including anti-poaching guards. The OFI sponsors study tours to Borneo for international students and opportunities for them to contribute to conservation efforts.

The success of Galdikas's activism depends on her deep knowledge of orangutans. Over the decades, she has filled thousands of notebooks with her observations of orangutan behavior, along with such details about their habitat as the fruiting times of different species of trees. A donor recently gave software and funding for staff to analyze the raw data (Hawn 2002). The findings will indicate how much territory is needed to support a viable orangutan population. In turn, these findings will facilitate conservation policy and planning.

◆ FOOD FOR THOUGHT

- Some people claim that science should not be linked with advocacy because it will create biases in research. Others say that scientists have an obligation to use their knowledge for good causes. Where do you stand in this debate and why?

◆◆◆

Introducing Cultural Anthropology

Cultural anthropology is devoted to studying human cultures worldwide, both their similarities and differences. Cultural anthropology makes "the strange familiar and the familiar strange" (Spiro 1990). Therefore, it teaches us to look at ourselves from the "outside" as a somewhat "strange" culture. A good example of making the familiar strange is the case of the Nacirema, a culture first described in 1956:

> The Nacirema are a North American group living in the territory between the Canadian Cree, the Yaqui and the Tarahumara of Mexico, and the Carib and the Arawak of the Antilles. Little is known of their origin, though tradition states that they came from the east. According to Nacirema mythology, their nation was originated by a culture hero, Notgnihsaw, who is otherwise known for two great feats of strength—the throwing of a piece of wampum across the river Pa-To-Mac and the chopping down of a cherry tree in which the Spirit of Truth resided. (Miner 1965 [1956]:415)

The anthropologist goes on to describe the Nacirema's intense focus on the human body and their many private rituals. He provides a detailed account of a daily ritual performed within the home in a specially constructed shrine area:

> The focal point of the shrine is a box or chest which is built into the wall. In this chest are kept the many charms

> and magical potions without which no native believes he could live. These preparations are secured from a variety of specialized practitioners. The most powerful of these are the medicine men, whose assistance must be rewarded with substantial gifts. . . . Beneath the charm box is a small font. Each day every member of the family, in succession, enters the shrine room, bows his head before the charm-box, mingles different sorts of holy water in the font, and proceeds with a brief rite of ablution. (1965:415–416)

If you do not recognize this tribe, try spelling its name backwards. (*Note:* Please forgive Miner for his use of the masculine pronoun in describing Nacirema society in general; his writings are several decades old.)

This section provides an overview of cultural anthropology's history and theoretical foundations. It also introduces the concept of culture, important cultural categories, distinctive features of cultural anthropology, and three major debates in cultural anthropology.

A BRIEF HISTORY OF CULTURAL ANTHROPOLOGY

The beginning of cultural anthropology goes back to writers such as Herodotus (fifth century BCE; note: BCE stands for "Before the Common Era," a secular transformation of BC, or "Before Christ"), Marco Polo (thirteenth to fourteenth centuries), and Ibn Khaldun (fourteenth century), who traveled extensively and wrote reports about cultures they encountered. More recent conceptual roots are found in writers of the French Enlightenment, such as philosopher Charles Montesquieu, who wrote in the first half of the eighteenth century. His book *The Spirit of the Laws,* published in 1748 [1949], discussed the temperament, appearance, and government of various people around the world. He explained cultural differences as due to the different climates in which people lived (Barnard 2000: 22ff). European colonial expansion prompted Enlightenment thinkers to question the accuracy of the biblical narrative of human origins. The Bible does not, for example, mention the existence of people in the New World.

FIGURE 1.2 Key Contributors to Cultural Anthropology

Late Nineteenth Century	
Sir Edward Tylor	Armchair anthropology, first definition of culture
Sir James Frazer	Armchair anthropology, comparative study of religion
Lewis Henry Morgan	Insider's view, cultural evolution, comparative method
Early Twentieth Century	
Bronislaw Malinowski	Functionalism, holism, participant observation
Franz Boas	Cultural relativism, historical particularism, advocacy
Margaret Mead	Personality and culture, cultural constructionism, public anthropology
Ruth Benedict	Personality and culture, national character studies
Zora Neale Hurston	Black culture, women's roles, ethnographic novels
Mid- and Late Twentieth Century and Early Twenty-First Century	
Claude Lévi-Strauss	Symbolic analysis, French structuralism
Beatrice Medicine	Native American anthropology
Eleanor Leacock	Anthropology of colonialism and indigenous peoples
Marvin Harris	Cultural materialism, comparison, theory building
Mary Douglas	Symbolic anthropology
Michelle Rosaldo	Feminist anthropology
Clifford Geertz	Interpretive anthropology, thick description of local culture
Laura Nader	Legal anthropology, "studying up"
George Marcus	Critique of culture, critique of cultural anthropology
Gilbert Herdt	Gay anthropology
Nancy Scheper-Hughes	Critical medical anthropology
Leith Mullings	Anti-racist anthropology
Sally Engle Merry	Globalization and human rights

Two giants in the history of anthropology. (LEFT) Franz Boas emphasized the four-field approach and the principle of cultural relativism. (RIGHT) Margaret Mead, a student of Boas at Columbia University, moved the Boasian legacy forward by her pioneering research on the cultural construction of personality and gender.

In the second half of the nineteenth century, the discovery of the principles of biological evolution by Charles Darwin and others offered for the first time a scientific explanation for human origins. Biological *evolution* says that early forms evolve into later forms through the process of natural selection, whereby the most biologically fit organisms survive to reproduce while those that are less fit die out. Darwin's model is thus one of continuous progress of increasing fitness through struggle among competing organisms. The concept of evolution was important in the thinking of early cultural anthropologists.

The most important founding figures of cultural anthropology in the late eighteenth and early nineteenth centuries were Sir Edward Tylor and Sir James Frazer in England and Lewis Henry Morgan in the United States. Inspired by the concept of biological evolution, they developed a model of cultural evolution whereby all cultures evolve from lower to higher forms over time. This view placed non-Western peoples at a "primitive" stage and Euro-American culture as "civilization" and assumed that non-Western cultures would either catch up to the level of Western civilization or die out.

Polish-born Bronislaw Malinowski is a major figure in modern cultural anthropology (see photo, p. 66). In the first half of the twentieth century, he established a theoretical approach called **functionalism**: the view that a culture is similar to a biological organism, in which parts work to support the operation and maintenance of the whole. Religion and family organization, for example, contribute to the functioning of the whole culture. Functionalism is linked to the concept of **holism**, the view that one must study all aspects of a culture in order to understand it.

Franz Boas is considered the founder of North American cultural anthropology. Born in Germany and educated in physics and geography, he came to the United States in 1887 (Patterson 2001:46ff). He brought with him a skepticism toward Western science gained from a year's study with the Inuit, the indigenous people of Baffin Island (see Map 3.4 p. 76). He learned from the Inuit that people in different cultures may have different perceptions of even basic physical substances, such as "water." Boas came to recognize the individuality and validity of different cultures. He introduced the now widely known concept of **cultural relativism**, or the view that each culture must be understood in terms of the values and ideas of that culture and not be judged by the standards of

---

functionalism the theory that a culture is similar to a biological organism, in which parts work to support the operation and maintenance of the whole.

holism the perspective in anthropology that cultures are complex systems that cannot be fully understood without paying attention to their different components, including economics, social organization, and ideology.

cultural relativism the perspective that each culture must be understood in terms of the values and ideas of that culture and should not be judged by the standards of another.

another. According to Boas, no culture is more advanced than another. His position thus contrasted markedly with that of the nineteenth-century cultural evolutionists.

Margaret Mead is Boas's most famous student. She contributed to knowledge of South Pacific cultures, gender roles, and the impact of child-rearing practices on personality. Her scholarly works as well as her columns in popular magazines had wide influence on U.S. child-care patterns in the 1950s. Mead was thus an early *public anthropologist* who took seriously the importance of bringing cultural anthropology knowledge to the general public in order to create positive social change.

Following World War II, cultural anthropology in the United States expanded substantially in terms of the number of trained anthropologists and departments of anthropology in colleges and universities. Along with this growth came increased theoretical diversity. Several anthropologists developed theories of culture based on environmental factors. They suggested that similar environments (for example, deserts or tropical rainforests or mountains) would predictably lead to the emergence of similar cultures.

At the same time, French anthropologist Claude Lévi-Strauss was developing a quite different theoretical perspective, known as *French structuralism.* He maintained that the best way to understand a culture is to collect its myths and stories and analyze the underlying themes in them. French structuralism inspired the development of *symbolic anthropology,* or the study of culture as a system of meanings, which was especially prominent in the United States in the latter part of the twentieth century.

In the 1960s, Marxist theory emerged in anthropology, stating the importance of people's access to the means of production. It inspired the emergence of a new theoretical school in the United States called **cultural materialism**. Cultural materialism is an approach to studying culture by emphasizing the material aspects of life, especially the natural environment and how people make a living. Also arising in the 1960s was the theoretical position referred to as **interpretive anthropology, or intepretivism.** This perspective developed from both U.S. symbolic anthropology and French structural anthropology. It says that understanding culture should focus on what people think about, their ideas, and the symbols and meanings that are important to them. These two positions will be discussed further later in this section.

Since the 1990s, two other theoretical directions have gained prominence. Both are influenced by *postmodernism,* an intellectual pursuit that asks whether modernity is truly progress and that questions such aspects of modernism as the scientific method, urbanization, technological change, and mass communication. The first theory is termed **structurism** (the author coined this term), the view that powerful structures such as economics, politics, and media shape cultures, influencing how people behave and think, even when they don't realize it. The second theory emphasizes human **agency**, or free will, and the power of individuals to create and change culture by acting against structures. These two positions are revisited at the end of this section.

Cultural anthropology continues to be rethought and refashioned. Over the past few decades, several new theoretical perspectives have transformed and enriched the field. *Feminist anthropology* is a perspective that emphasizes the need to study female roles and gender-based inequality. In the 1970s, early feminist anthropologists realized that anthropology had overlooked women. To address this gap, feminist anthropologists undertook research that explicitly focused on women and girls, that is, half of the world's people. A related area is *gay and lesbian anthropology,* or *queer anthropology,* a perspective that emphasizes the need to study gay people's cultures and discrimination based on sexual identity and preferences. Findings from both these areas are presented in this book.

In North American anthropology, African American, Latino, and Native American anthropologists are increasing in number and visibility. Yet anthropology in North America and Europe remains one of the "whitest" professions (Shanklin 2000). Some steps for moving the discipline toward *anti-racist anthropology* include these (Mullings 2005):

- Examine and recognize anthropology's history of and implications with racism.
- Work to increase diversity of professors, researchers, staff, and students in the discipline.
- Teach about racism in anthropology classes and textbooks.

Worldwide, non-Western anthropologists are increasingly questioning the dominance of Euro-American anthropology and offering new perspectives (Kuwayama 2004). Their work provides useful critiques of anthropology as a largely Western-defined discipline and promises to lead it in new directions in the future.

---

cultural materialism a theoretical position that takes material features of life, such as the environment, natural resources, and mode of production, as the bases for explaining social organization and ideology.

interpretive anthropology or **interpretivism** the view that cultures can be understood by studying what people think about, their ideas, and the meanings that are important to them.

structurism a theoretical position concerning human behavior and ideas that says large forces such as the economy, social and political organization, and the media shape what people do and think.

agency the ability of humans to make choices and exercise free will even within dominating structures.

microculture a distinct pattern of learned and shared behavior and thinking found within larger cultures.

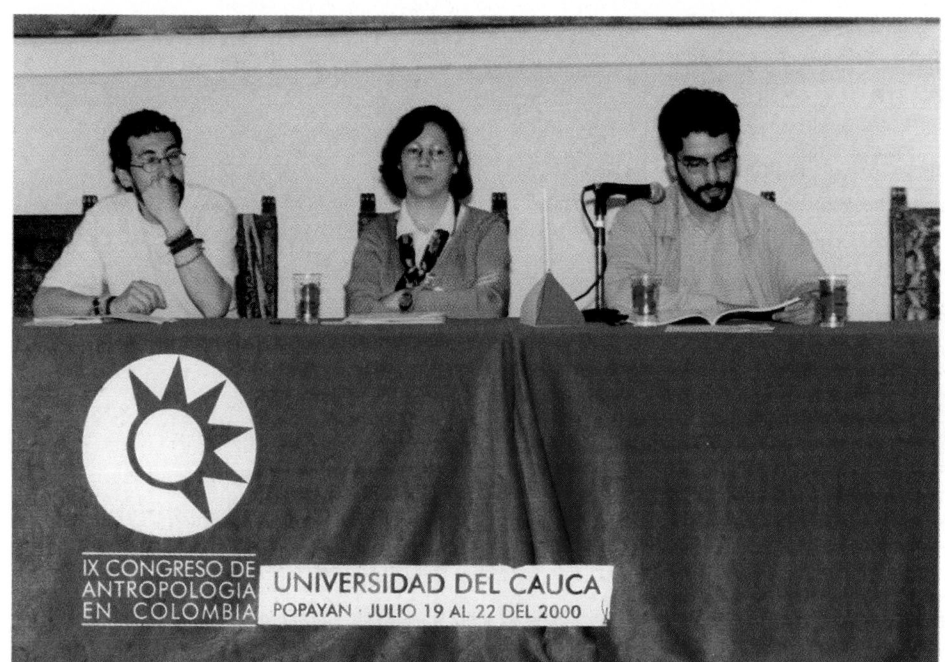

Colombian anthropologist Patricia Tovar (center) at an anthropology conference in Colombia. In Central and South America, applied anthropology is an integral part of cultural anthropology.

THE CONCEPT OF CULTURE

Although cultural anthropologists are united in the study of culture, the question of how to define it has been debated for decades. This section discusses definitions of culture today, characteristics of culture, and bases for cultural identity.

DEFINITIONS OF CULTURE Culture is the core concept in cultural anthropology, so it might seem likely that cultural anthropologists would agree about what it is. In the 1950s, an effort to collect definitions of culture produced 164 different ones (Kroeber and Kluckhohn 1952). Since then, no one has tried to count the number of definitions of culture used by anthropologists.

British anthropologist Sir Edward Tylor proposed the first definition in 1871. He stated, "Culture, or civilization . . . is that complex whole which includes knowledge, belief, art, law, morals, custom, and any other capabilities and habits acquired by man as a member of society" (Kroeber and Kluckhohn 1952:81). The phrase "that complex whole" has been the most durable feature of his definition. Two other features of Tylor's definition have not stood the test of time. First, most anthropologists now avoid using the word man to refer to all humans; instead, they use generic words such as *people* and humans. One may argue that the word man can be used generically according to its linguistic roots, but this usage can be ambiguous. Second, most anthropologists no longer equate culture with civilization. The word *civilization* implies a sense of "highness" versus noncivilized "lowness" and sets up a distinction placing "us" (people of the so-called civilized regions) in a superior position to "them."

In contemporary cultural anthropology, the cultural materialists and the interpretive anthropologists support two different definitions of culture. Cultural materialist Marvin Harris says, "A culture is the total socially acquired life-way or life-style of a group of people. It consists of the patterned repetitive ways of thinking, feeling, and acting that are characteristic of the members of a particular society or segment of society" (1975:144). In contrast, Clifford Geertz, speaking for the interpretivists, believes that culture consists of symbols, motivations, moods, and thoughts. This definition focuses on people's perceptions, thoughts, and ideas and does not include behavior as a part of culture. The definition of culture used in this book is that culture is learned and shared behavior and beliefs, and thus is broader than Geertz's definition. 

Culture exists among all human beings. It is something that all humans have. Some anthropologists refer to this universal concept of culture as *Culture* with a capital *C*. Culture also exists in a more specific way. The term **microculture**, or local culture, refers to distinct patterns of learned and shared behavior and ideas found in local regions and among particular groups. Microcultures are based on ethnicity, gender, age, and more.

THINKING OUTSIDE THE BOX

This brief history of cultural anthropology describes early contributions by anthropologists, most of whom were white, European or Euro-American, and male. Compare this pattern with the history of some other discipline you have studied. What are some similarities and differences?

Two prominent American cultural anthropologists of the twentieth century anthropology in North America. (LEFT) Marvin Harris argued for a cultural materialist/political economy perspective on understanding culture and an emphasis on deductive methods. Throughout the later twentieth century, Harris had frequent debates with Clifford Geertz (RIGHT), who championed a perspective on understanding culture informed by symbolic anthropology and an emphasis on meaning, text, and narrative and an inductive method.

CHARACTERISTICS OF CULTURE Understanding of the complex concept of culture can be gained by looking at its characteristics.

CULTURE IS NOT THE SAME AS NATURE The relationship between nature and culture is of great interest to cultural anthropologists in their quest to understand people's behavior and thinking. This book emphasizes the importance of culture.

Obviously, culture and nature are intertwined and often difficult to separate in terms of their effects. For example, certain aspects of biology affect people's behavior and lifestyle, such as being HIV-positive. But it is impossible to predict how a person who is HIV-positive will fare in Culture A versus Culture B. Different cultural contexts shape matters such as labeling and negative stereotypes and access to care and support. A good way to see how culture diverges from, and shapes, nature is to consider basic natural demands of life within different cultural contexts. Universal human functions that everyone must perform to stay alive are

- Eating
- Drinking
- Sleeping
- Eliminating

You may wonder about requirements for shelter and clothing. They vary, depending on the climate, so they are not included on this list. You may also wonder about sexual intercourse. It is not necessary for individual survival, so it is not included on this list, but it is discussed elsewhere in this book. Given the primary importance of these four functions in supporting a human being's life, it seems logical that people would fulfill them in similar ways everywhere. But that is not the case.

Eating Culture shapes what people eat, how they eat, when they eat, and the meanings of food and eating. Culture also defines foods that are acceptable and unacceptable. In China, most people think that cheese is disgusting, but in France, most people love cheese. Throughout China, pork is a widely favored meat. The religions of Judaism and Islam, in contrast, forbid consumption of pork. In many cultures where gathering wild plant foods, hunting, and fishing are important, people value the freshness of food. They would consider a package of frozen food on a grocery store shelf as way past its time.

Perceptions of taste vary dramatically. Western researchers have defined four supposedly universal taste categories: sweet, sour, bitter, and salty. Cross-cultural research disproves these as universals. For example, the Weyéwa people of the highlands of Sumba, Indonesia (see Map 1.2), define seven categories of flavor: sour, sweet, salty, bitter, tart, bland, and pungent (Kuipers 1991).

How to eat is also an important aspect of food behavior. Rules about proper ways to eat are one of the first things

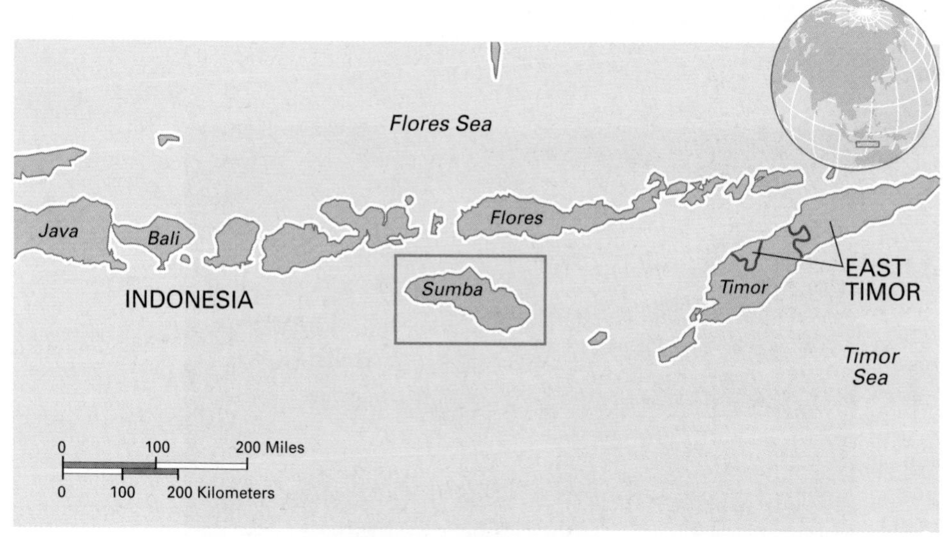

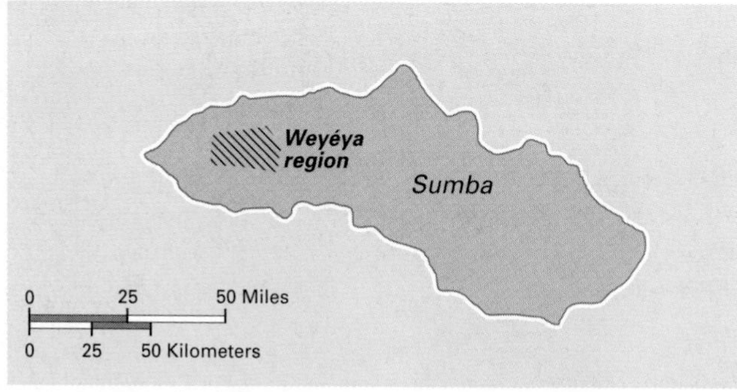

MAP 1.2 **Weyéwa Region in Indonesia.**
Sumba, one of Indonesia's many islands, is 75 miles long. The Weyéwa people number about 85,000 and live in small settlements on grassy plateaus in the western part of the island. They grow rice, maize, and millet, and they raise water buffaloes and pigs.

a person needs to learn when living in another culture. Dining rules in India require using only the right hand. The left hand is considered polluted because it is used for personal cleansing after elimination. A person's clean right hand is the preferred eating utensil. Silverware that has been touched by others, even though it has been washed, is considered unclean. In some cultures, it is important to eat only from one's own plate, whereas in others, eating from a shared central platter is considered proper.

Ethiopian women dining at an Ethiopian restaurant. The main meal consists of several meat and vegetable dishes, cooked with special spices and laid out on injera bread, a soft flat bread that is torn into small pieces and used to wrap bite-sized bits of meat and vegetables. The entire meal can be eaten without utensils.

▶ *How does this dining scene resemble or differ from a recent meal that you have had in a restaurant?*

Another area of cultural variation involves who is responsible for cooking and serving food. In many cultures, domestic cooking is women's responsibility, but cooking for public feasts is more often something that men do. Power issues may arise about who cooks what for whom (see Everyday Anthropology).

Drinking Cross-cultural variations related to drinking are also complex. Every culture defines the appropriate substances to drink, when to drink and with whom, and the meanings of the beverages and drinking occasions. French culture allows for consumption of relatively large amounts of table wine with family meals, including lunch. In the United States, water is generally served and consumed during family meals. In India, water is served and consumed at the end of the meal. Around the world, different categories of people drink different beverages. In cultures where alcoholic beverages are consumed, men tend to consume more than women.

Culture often defines the meaning of particular drinks and the style of drinking and serving them. Social drinking—whether the beverage is coffee, beer, or vodka—creates and reinforces bonds. Beer-drinking rituals in U.S. college fraternities

everyday ANTHROPOLOGY

Latina Power in the Kitchen

Within a family, cooking food for other members can be a sign of love and devotion. It may carry a message that love and devotion are expected in return.

Among Tejano migrant farm workers in the United States, preparing tamales is a symbol of a woman's commitment to her family and thus of the "good wife" (Williams 1984). The Tejanos are people of Mexican descent who live in Texas. Some of them move to Illinois in the summer, where they are employed as migrant workers.

For Tejanos, tamales are a central cultural identity marker. Tamales contain a rich inner mash of pig's head meat wrapped in corn husks. Making tamales is extremely time consuming, and it is women's work. Typically, several women work together over a few days to do the necessary tasks: buying the pigs' heads, stripping the meat, preparing the stuffing, wrapping the stuffing with the corn husks, and baking or boiling the tamale.

Tamales symbolize and emphasize women's nurturance of their husbands. One elderly woman, at home in Texas for Christmas, made 200 tamales with her daughters-in-law, nieces, and goddaughter. They distributed the tamales to friends, relatives, and local taverns. The effort and expense involved were enormous. But for the women, it was worth it. Through their tamale making, they celebrate the holiday, build ties with people whom they may need to call on for support, and maintain communication with tavern owners so they will watch over male kin who drink at their bars.

Tejano woman also use tamale making as a statement of domestic protest. A woman who is dissatisfied with her husband's behavior will refuse to make tamales, a serious statement on her part. The link between being a good wife and making tamales is strong, and so a husband can take his wife's unwillingness to make tamales as grounds for divorce. One young Tejano sued his wife for divorce in Illinois on the grounds that she refused to cook tamales for him, in addition to dancing with other men at fiestas. The judge refused to grant a divorce.

Tamales consist of fried meat and peppers in a cornmeal dough that is encased in cornhusks.

▶ *What is a similarly important food item in your cultural world?*

◆ **FOOD FOR THOUGHT**

- Provide an example from your microcultural experience about food being used as a way of expressing social solidarity or social protest.

are a good example. In an ethnographic film entitled *Salamanders,* filmed at a large university in the northeastern United States, the fraternity brothers run to various "stations" in the fraternity house, downing a beer at each (Hornbein and Hornbein 1992). At one point, a brother chugs a beer, turns with a stagger toward the next station, falls flat on his face, and passes out. The movie documents another drinking ritual in which both young men and women at fraternity parties swallow live salamanders, sometimes two or three at a time, with large gulps of beer (this practice is now forbidden by law).

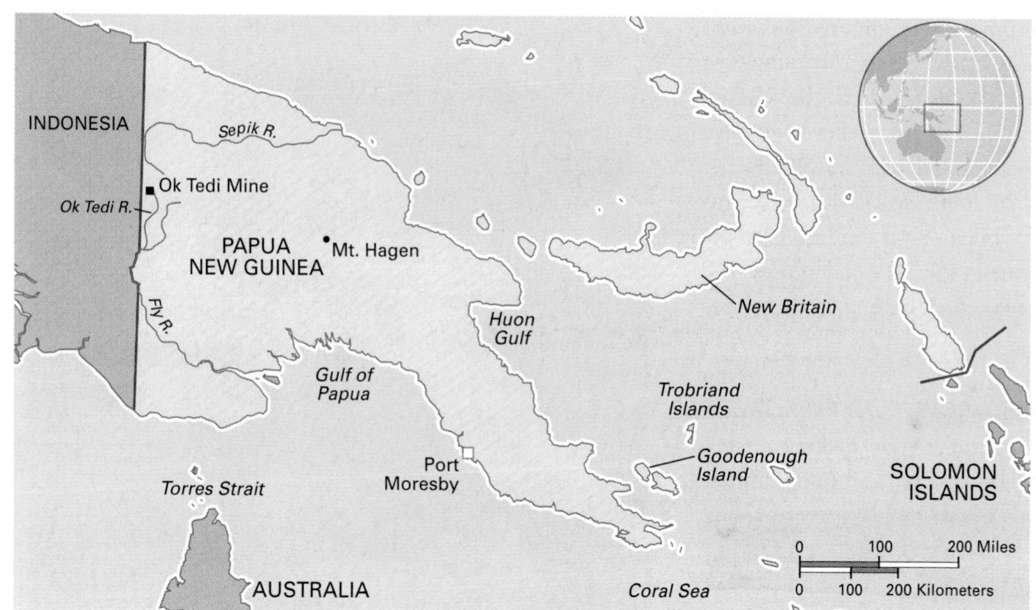

MAP 1.3 Papua New Guinea.
The Independent State of Papua New Guinea gained its autonomy from Australia in 1975. Mostly mountainous with coastal lowlands, PNG is richly endowed with gold, copper, silver, natural gas, timber, oil, and fisheries. Its population is around 5,700,000. Port Moresby, the capital, has a high rate of HIV/AIDS infection among the working-age population.

Sleeping Common sense might say that sleep is the one natural function that is not shaped by culture, because people tend to do it at least once every 24 hours, everyone shuts their eyes to do it, everyone lies down to do it, and most people sleep at night. Going without sleep for an extended period can lead to insanity and even death.

Sleep, however, is at least as much culturally shaped as it is biologically determined. Cultural influences on sleep include the questions of who sleeps with whom, how much sleep a person should have, and why some people have insomnia or what are called sleep disorders. Across cultures, marked variation exists in rules about where infants and children should sleep: with the mother, with both parents, or by themselves in a separate room? Among indigenous peoples of the Amazon region of South America, mothers and babies share the same hammock for many months, and breastfeeding occurs whenever the baby is hungry.

Culture shapes the amount of time a person sleeps. In rural India, women sleep fewer hours than men because they have to get up early to start the fire for the morning meal. In fast-track, corporate North America, "type A" males sleep relatively few hours and are proud of that fact—to sleep too much is to be a wimp. A disorder in Japan called *excessive daytime sleepiness* (EDS) is common in Tokyo and other large cities (Doi and Minowa 2003). Excessive sleepiness is correlated with more accidents on the job, more absenteeism, decreased productivity, deteriorated personal and professional relationships, and increased rates of illness and death. Women are almost twice as likely as men to experience EDS, and married women are especially vulnerable.

Eliminating Given its basic importance in cross-cultural experience, it is ironic that elimination receives little attention (in print) from anthropologists. Anyone who has traveled internationally knows that there is much to learn about elimination when in an unfamiliar context.

The first question is where to eliminate. Differences emerge in the degree to which elimination is a private act or can be done in more or less public areas. In many European cities, public options include street urinals for males but not for females. In most villages in India, houses do not have interior bathrooms. Instead, early in the morning, groups of women and girls leave the house and head for a certain field where they squat and chat. Men go to a different area. Everyone carries, in their left hand, a small brass pot full of water with which they splash themselves clean. Think about the ecological advantages: This system adds fertilizer to the fields and leaves no paper litter. Westerners may consider the village practice unclean and unpleasant, but village-dwelling people in India would think that the Western system is unsanitary because using toilet paper does not clean one as well as water, and they would find the practice of sitting on a toilet less comfortable than squatting.

In many cultures, the products of elimination (urine and feces) are considered polluting and disgusting. Among some groups in Papua New Guinea (see Map 1.3), people take great care to bury or otherwise hide their fecal matter for fear that someone will find it and use it for magic against them.

THINKING OUTSIDE THE BOX

Think about your everyday drinking patterns (no matter what the liquid) and then think about your drinking patterns on special occasions, including weekends, holidays, or special events such as weddings. What beverages do you consume, with whom, and what are the meanings and wider social implications involved?

A negative assessment of the products of elimination is not universal, however. Among some Native American cultures of the Pacific Northwest region of Canada and the United States, urine, especially women's urine, was believed to have medicinal and cleansing properties and was considered the "water of life" (Furst 1989). In some death rituals, it was sprinkled over the corpse in the hope that it might rejuvenate the deceased. People stored urine in special wooden boxes for ritual use, including for a baby's first bath (the urine was mixed with water).

CULTURE IS BASED ON SYMBOLS Our entire lives—from eating breakfast to greeting our friends, making money, creating art, and practicing religion—are based on and organized through symbols. A **symbol** is an object, word, or action with a culturally defined meaning that stands for something else with which it has no necessary or natural relationship. Symbols are arbitrary (bearing no necessary relationship to that which is symbolized), unpredictable, and diverse. Because symbols are arbitrary, it is impossible to predict how a particular culture will symbolize something. Although one might assume that people who are hungry would have an expression for hunger involving their stomach, no one could predict that in Hindi, the language of northern India, a colloquial expression for being hungry is saying that "rats are jumping in my stomach." The linguistic history of *Barbara*—the name of the author of this book—reveals that originally, in the Greek, it referred to people who were outsiders, "barbarians," and, by extension, uncivilized and savage. On top of that, the Greek term referred to such people as "bearded." The symbolic content of the American name Barbara does not immediately convey a sense of beardedness in its current context because symbolic meaning can change. It is through symbols, arbitrary and amazingly rich in their attributions, that culture is shared, stored, and transmitted over time.

CULTURE IS LEARNED Because culture is based on symbols that are arbitrary, culture must be learned anew in each context. Cultural learning begins from the moment of birth, if not before (some people think that an unborn baby takes in and stores information through sounds heard from the outside world). A large but unknown amount of people's cultural learning is unconscious, occurring as a normal part of life through observation. Schools, in contrast, are a formal way to learn culture. Not all cultures throughout history have been exposed to formal schooling. Instead, children learn appropriate cultural patterns through guidance from elders and by observation and practice. Hearing stories and seeing performances of rituals and dramas are other long-standing forms of learning.

symbol an object, word, or action with culturally defined meaning that stands for something else; most symbols are arbitrary.

globalization increased and intensified international ties related to the spread of Western, especially United States, capitalism that affect all world cultures.

localization the transformation of global culture by local cultures into something new.

class a way of categorizing people on the basis of their economic position in society, usually measured in terms of income or wealth.

In India, a white sari (women's garment) symbolizes widowhood. ▶ *What might these women think about the Western custom of a bride wearing white?*

CULTURES ARE INTEGRATED To state that cultures are internally integrated is to assert the principle of holism. Thus, studying only one or two aspects of culture provides understanding so limited that it is more likely to be misleading or wrong than more comprehensive approaches.

Consider what would happen if a researcher were to study intertribal warfare in highland Papua New Guinea (see Map 1.3) and focused only on the actual practice of warfare without examining other aspects of culture. A key feature of highland culture is the exchange of pigs at political feasts. To become a political leader, a man must acquire many pigs. Pigs eat yams, which men grow, but pigs are cared for by women. This division of labor means that a man with more than one wife will be able to maintain more pigs and rise politically by giving more feasts. Such feasting enhances an aspiring leader's status and makes his guests indebted to him. With more followers attracted through feasting, a leader can gather forces and wage war on neighboring villages. Success in war brings gains in territory. So far, this example pays attention mainly to economics, politics, and marriage systems. But other aspects

Clash of civilizations	Conflict model
McDonaldization	Takeover and homogenization model
Hybridization	Blending model
Localization	Local cultural remaking and transformation of global culture

FIGURE 1.3 Four Models of Cultural Interaction

of culture are involved, too. Supernatural powers affect the success of warfare. Painting spears and shields with particular designs is believed to increase their power. At feasts and marriages, body decoration (including paint, shell ornaments, and elaborate feather headdresses) is an important expression of identity and status. Looking at warfare without attention to its wider cultural context yields an extremely narrow view.

Cultural integration is relevant to applied anthropologists interested in proposing ways to promote positive change. Years of experience show that introducing programs for change in one aspect of culture without considering their effects in other domains is often detrimental to the welfare and survival of a culture. For example, Western missionaries and colonialists in parts of Southeast Asia banned the practice of head-hunting. This practice was connected to many other aspects of the people's culture, including politics, religion, and psychology (a man's sense of identity as a man sometimes depended on the taking of a head). Stopping head-hunting might seem like a good thing, but its cessation had disastrous consequences for the cultures in which it was practiced.

CULTURES INTERACT AND CHANGE Cultures interact with each other and change each other through contact such as trade networks, international development projects, telecommunications, education, migration, and tourism. **Globalization**, the process of intense global interconnectedness and movement of goods, information, and people, is a major force of contemporary cultural change. It has gained momentum through recent technological change, especially the boom in information and communications technologies.

Globalization does not spread evenly, and its interactions with and effects on local cultures vary substantially from positive change to cultural destruction and extinction. Four models of cultural interaction capture some of the variation (see Figure 1.3).

The *clash of civilizations* argument says that the spread of Euro-American capitalism and lifeways throughout the world has created disenchantment, alienation, and resentment among other cultural systems. This model divides the world into the "West and the rest."

The *McDonaldization* model says that, under the powerful influence of U.S.-dominated corporate culture, the world is becoming culturally homogeneous. "Fast-food culture," with its principles of mass production, speed, standardization, and impersonal service, is taken to be at the center of this new global culture.

Hybridization, also called *syncretism* and *creolization,* occurs when aspects of two or more cultures combine to form something new—a blend. In Japan, for instance, a grandmother might bow in gratitude to an automated banking machine. In the Amazon region and in the Arctic, indigenous people use satellite imagery to map and protect the boundaries of their ancestral lands.

A fourth pattern is **localization**, the transformation of global culture by local microcultures into something new. Consider the example of McDonald's restaurants. In many Asian settings, people resist the pattern of eating quickly and insist on leisurely family gatherings (Watson 1997). The McDonald's managers accommodate and alter the pace of service to allow for a slower turnover of tables. In Riyadh, Saudi Arabia, McDonald's provides separate areas for families and for heterosexual couples. Many other examples of cultural localization exist, throwing into question the notion that a form of Western "mono-culture" is taking over the entire world and erasing cultural diversity.

MULTIPLE CULTURAL WORLDS

Within large cultures, a variety of microcultures exist, as discussed in this section (see Figure 1.4). A particular individual in such a complex situation is likely to be a member of several microcultures. Microcultures may overlap or may be related to each other hierarchically in terms of power, status, and rights.

In discussing microcultures, the contrast between *difference* and *hierarchy* is important. People and groups can be considered different from each other in terms of a particular characteristic, but they may or may not be unequal on the basis of it. For example, people with blue or brown eyes might be recognized as different, but this difference does not entail unequal treatment or status. In other instances, such differences do become the basis for inequality.

CLASS **Class** is a category based on people's economic position in society, usually measured in terms of income or wealth and exhibited in terms of lifestyle. Class societies may be divided into upper, middle, and lower classes. Separate classes are, for example, the working class (people who trade their labor for wages) and the landowning class (people who

Class	Gender and sexuality
"Race"	Age
Ethnicity and indigeneity	Institution

FIGURE 1.4 Some Bases of Microcultures

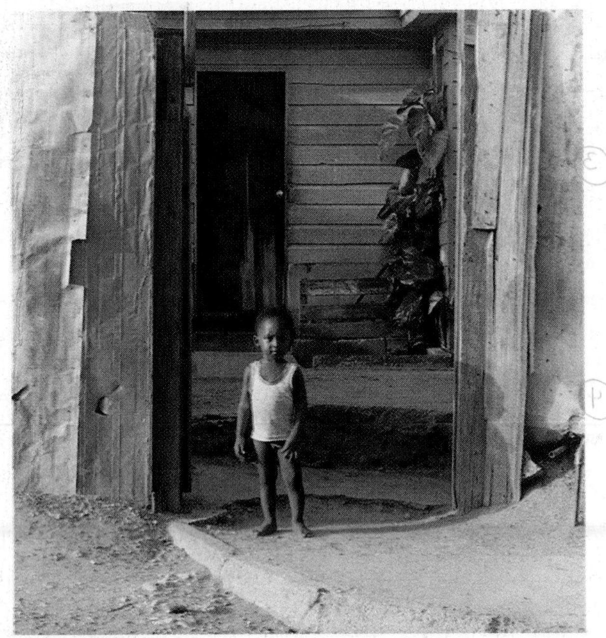

A view into the yard of a house in a low-income neighborhood of Kingston, Jamaica. People in these neighborhoods prefer the term "low-income" to "poor."

own land on which they or others labor). Classes are related in a hierarchical system, with upper classes dominating lower classes. Class struggle, in the classic Marxist view, is inevitable as those at the top seek to maintain their position while those at the bottom seek to improve theirs. People at the bottom may attempt to improve their class position by gaining access to resources and by adopting aspects of upper-class symbolic behavior, such as speech, dress, and leisure and recreation.

Class is a recent social development in human history, extending back in time for only about 10,000 years, and still not found in some remote local cultures. Among the few relatively undisturbed groups of indigenous peoples, everyone has equal wealth, and sharing food and other resources among the group is expected.

"RACE," ETHNICITY, AND INDIGENOUS PEOPLES

"Race" refers to groups of people with supposedly homogeneous biological traits. The term "race" is extremely complicated as it is used in diverse ways in different parts of the world and among different groups of people. Therefore, it makes sense to put the word in quotation marks in order to highlight its multiple meanings. In South Africa, as in the United States, "race" is mainly defined on the basis of skin color. In pre–twentieth-century China, body hair was the key biological basis for racial classification (Dikötter 1998). The "barbarian" races had more body hair than the "civilized" Chinese people. Chinese writers referred to bearded, male missionaries from Europe as "hairy barbarians." Into the twentieth century, some Chinese anthropologists divided humans into evolutionary stages on the basis of amounts of body hair.

Anthropological and other scientific research demonstrates that biological features do not explain or account for a person's behavior or lifestyle. Rather than being a biological category, racial classifications are cultural constructions. They are often associated with discrimination against and cruelty toward those "races" considered less worthy by those in power.

Ethnicity refers to a shared sense of identity among a group based on a heritage, language, or culture. Examples include African Americans and Italian Americans in the United States, the Croats of Eastern Europe, the Han of China, and the Hutu and Tutsi of Rwanda. This sense of identity may be expressed through political movements to gain or protect group rights and recognition or more quietly stated in how one lives one's daily life. Compared to the term "race," "ethnicity" appears to be a more neutral, less stigmatizing term. But it, too, has been, and still is, a basis for discrimination, segregation, and oppression. The "ethnic cleansing" campaigns conducted in the early 1990s by the Serbs against Muslims in the former Yugoslavia are an extreme case of ethnic discrimination. In China, Han ethnic domination over minority ethnic groups has been a reality for centuries. Han political repression of the Tibetan people prompted thousands of Tibetans to flee their homeland. Living in exile, they struggle to keep their ethnic heritage alive.

Indigenous people, following guidelines laid down by the United Nations, are defined as groups who have a long-standing connection with their home territory predating colonial or other societies that prevail in their territory (Sanders 1999). They are typically a numerical minority and often have lost the rights to their original territory. The United Nations distinguishes between indigenous peoples and *minority ethnic groups* such as the Roma, the Tamils of Sri Lanka, and African Americans. The San peoples of Southern Africa, and their several subgroups, are an important example of indigenous peoples whose way of life was dramatically affected first by colonialism and now by globalization (see Culturama).

GENDER **Gender** refers to culturally constructed and learned behaviors and ideas attributed to males, females, or sometimes a blended or "third" gender. Gender differs from

---

"race" a classification of people into groups on the basis of supposedly homogeneous and largely superficial biological traits such as skin color or hair characteristics.

ethnicity a shared sense of identity among a group based on a heritage, language, or culture.

indigenous people groups who have a long-standing connection with their home territory that predates colonial or outside societies that prevail in that territory.

gender culturally constructed and learned behaviors and ideas attributed to males, females, or blended genders.

CULTURAMA

San Peoples of Southern Africa

San is a cluster name for many groups of people in southern Africa who speak related languages that have glottal click sounds. Around 2000 years ago, the San were the only people living in southern Africa, but today they are restricted to scattered locations throughout the region. European colonialists referred to San people as "Bushmen," a derogatory term at the time but one that San people now prefer over what some locals call them. Some San also refer to themselves with the English term "First People."

For many centuries, the San supported themselves through collecting food such as roots and birds' eggs and by hunting eland, giraffe, and other animals. Now, pressure from African governments, farmers, ranchers, game reserves, diamond companies, and international tourism have greatly reduced the San's access to their ancestral land and their ability to survive. Some have been arrested for hunting on what they consider their land.

The Ju/'hoansi ("True People") are a subgroup of San who live in a region crossing the borders of Namibia and Botswana, and numbering between 10,000 and 15,000 people. As described by Richard Lee in the early 1960s, they were highly mobile food collectors and quite healthy (1979). Today, most have been forced from their homeland and live as poor, urban squatters or in government-built resettlement camps. Many work as farm laborers or in the international tourist industry, serving as guides and producing and selling crafts. Others are unemployed.

The specifics of the San people's situation depends on government policy toward indigenous people in the particular country where they live. Conditions are most difficult for San peoples, at this time, in Botswana due to forced sedentarization.

Transnational advocacy organizations, including Working Group of Indigenous Minorities in Southern Africa (WIMSA) and First People of the Kalahari (FPK), are making progress in protecting the rights of San peoples. Recently, WIMSA waged an international legal case with a large pharmaceutical company and succeeded in ensuring that the San receive a portion of the profits from the commercial development of hoodia (*Hoodia gordonia*). Hoodia is extracted from a cactus indigenous to the Kalahari region. An effective appetite suppressant, it is now widely available in North America and on the Internet as diet pills.

Thanks to Alison Brooks, George Washington University, for reviewing this material.

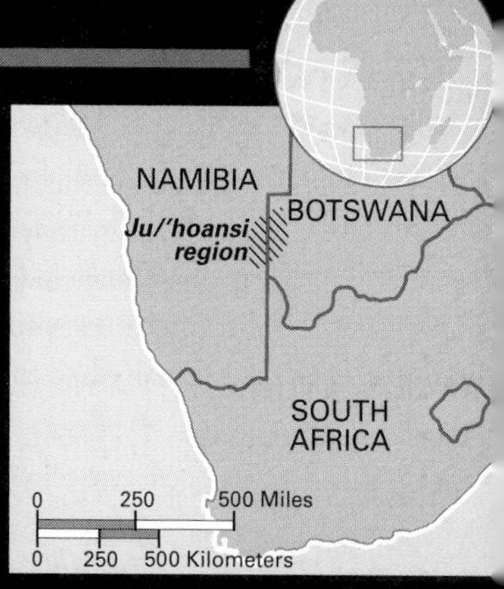

(LEFT) Richard Lee (wearing a shirt) asks Ju/'hoansi men about food plants of the Kalahari desert. This photograph was taken in 1968. Lee, and many other researchers affiliated with the Harvard Kalahari research project, learned to speak the Ju/'hoansi language.

(CENTER) San peoples have long consumed parts of the hoodia plant to suppress hunger and thirst when on long trips in the desert. (CENTER) Now they cultivate it

MAP 1.4 Ju/'hoansi Region in Namibia and Botswana. Before country boundaries were drawn, the Ju/'hoansi freely ranged across their traditional territory (shaded area), depending on the seasonal availability of food and water.

Huli men of the Mount Hagen region of highland Papua New Guinea in festive attire for a dance performance.

sex, which is based on biological markers such as genitals and hormones to define categories of male and female. Cultural anthropology shows that a person's biological makeup does not necessarily correspond to gender. Biology directly determines only a few roles and tasks, such as giving birth and nursing infants.

Cross-culturally, gender differences vary from societies in which male and female roles and worlds are similar or overlapping, to those in which genders are sharply differentiated. In much of rural Thailand (see Map 6.7, p. 157), men and women are about the same size, their clothing is similar, and their agricultural tasks are complementary and often interchangeable (Potter 1977). In contrast, among many groups in highland Papua New Guinea, extreme gender segregation exists in most aspects of life, including the kinds of food men and women eat (Meigs 1984). The men's house physically and symbolically separates the worlds of men and women. Men engage in rituals that purge them of female substances: nose or penis bleeding, vomiting, tongue scraping, sweating, and eye washing. Men possess sacred flutes, which they parade though the village from time to time. If women dare to look at the flutes, men traditionally had the right to kill them.

AGE The human life cycle, from birth to old age, takes people through cultural stages for which appropriate behavior and thinking must be learned anew. In many African herding societies, elaborate age categories for males define their roles and status as they move from being boys with few responsibilities and little status, to young men who are warriors and live apart from the rest of the group, to adult men who are allowed to marry, have children, and become respected elders. "The Hill," or the collective members of the United States Senate and the House of Representatives, is a highly age-graded microculture (Weatherford 1981). The Hill is a *gerontocracy* (a group ruled by senior members) in which the older politicians dominate younger politicians in terms of amount of time they speak and how much attention their words receive. It may take a junior member between 10 and 20 years to become as effective and powerful as a senior member.

ethnocentrism judging other cultures by the standards of one's own culture rather than by the standards of that particular culture.

INSTITUTIONS *Institutions,* or enduring group settings formed for a particular purpose, have their own characteristic microcultures. Institutions include hospitals, schools and universities, and prisons. Anyone who has entered such an institution has experienced a feeling of strangeness. Until you gain familiarity with the often unwritten cultural rules, you may do things that offend or puzzle people, that fail to get you what you want, and that make you feel marginalized and insecure.

Anthropologists who study educational institutions show that schools often replicate and reinforce stereotypes, power relations, and inequalities of the wider society. A study of middle schools in the southwestern Rocky Mountain region of the United States found a situation in which teachers marginalized Mexican immigrant girls (Meador 2005). In this school, Mexican immigrant students are labeled as ESL (English as a second language) students because they are not fluent in English and take special courses designed to improve their English. In addition, the teachers' mental model of a "good student" is a student who is:

- Motivated to do well in school and gets good grades
- An athlete
- Popular and has good students as friends
- Comes from a stable family

It is impossible for Mexican immigrant children to conform to this image. Mexicana girls are especially disadvantaged because most are not interested in, or good at, sports. The few Mexicana girls who are motivated to try to get good grades are consistently overlooked by the teachers, who instead call on students who are confident, bright, and popular, and who sit in front of the classroom and raise their hands eagerly.

DISTINCTIVE FEATURES OF CULTURAL ANTHROPOLOGY

Cultural anthropology has two distinct research goals and two distinct guiding concepts. Researchers and teachers in other disciplines have begun to adopt these goals and concepts in recent decades, so they are now found beyond cultural anthropology. Such cross-discipline contributions are something of which cultural anthropology can be proud.

CULTURAL RELATIVISM Most people grow up thinking that their culture is *the* way of life and that other ways of life are strange and inferior. Cultural anthropologists label this attitude **ethnocentrism**: judging other cultures by the standards of one's own culture rather than by the standards of other cultures. Ethnocentrism has fueled centuries of efforts to change "other" people in the world, sometimes through religious missionary work, sometimes in the form of colonial domination.

The opposite of ethnocentrism is **cultural relativism**, the idea that each culture must be understood in terms of its own values and beliefs and not by the standards of another culture. Cultural relativism assumes that no culture is better than any other. How does a person gain a sense of cultural relativism? The best way is to be able to spend substantial amounts of time living with people outside your own culture. Studying abroad and socially engaged travel help.

You can also experience aspects of other cultures by reading about them, learning about them in anthropology classes, doing Internet research, preparing and eating "foreign" foods, listening to "world music," reading novels by authors from other cultures, and making friends who are "different" from you.

One way that some anthropologists have interpreted cultural relativism is *absolute cultural relativism*, which says that whatever goes on in a particular culture must not be questioned or changed because it would be ethnocentric to question any behavior or idea anywhere (see Figure 1.5). The position of absolute cultural relativism, however, can lead in dangerous directions. Consider the example of the Holocaust during World War II in which millions of Jews, Roma, and other minorities in much of Eastern and Western Europe were killed as part of the German Nazis' Aryan supremacy campaign. The absolute cultural relativist position becomes boxed in, logically, to saying that because the Holocaust was undertaken according to the values of the culture, outsiders have no business questioning it. Can anyone feel comfortable with such a position?

Critical cultural relativism offers an alternative view that poses questions about cultural practices and ideas in terms of who accepts them and why, and who they might be harming or helping. In terms of the Nazi Holocaust, a critical cultural relativist would ask, "Whose culture supported the values that killed millions of people on the grounds of racial purity?" Not the cultures of the Jews, Roma, and other victims. It was the culture of Aryan supremacists, who were just one group among many. In other words, the situation was far more complex than a simple absolute cultural relativist statement suggests. Rather, it was a case of *cultural imperialism*, in which one dominant group claimed supremacy over minority cultures and took actions in its own interests and at the expense of the subjugated cultures. Critical cultural relativism avoids the trap of adopting a homogenized view. It recognizes internal cultural differences and winners/losers, oppressors/victims. It pays attention to the interests of various power groups. It can illuminate the causes and consequences of recent and contemporary conflict situations, such as those in Rwanda, Iraq, and Kenya.

Many cultural anthropologists seek to *critique* (which means to probe underlying power interests, not just to offer negative comments as in the general usage of the term "criticism") the behavior and values of groups from the standpoint of a set of generally agreed-on human rights and values. Two issues emerge in this endeavor. First, it is difficult if not impossible to generate a universal list of what all cultures would agree to as good and right. Second, as Claude Lévi-Strauss said, "No society is perfect" (1968:385), and so we have no perfect model of the best society.

VALUING AND SUSTAINING DIVERSITY Anthropologists value and are committed to maintaining cultural diversity throughout the world, as part of humanity's rich heritage. Many cultural anthropologists share their expertise and knowledge to support the survival of indigenous peoples and other small-scale groups worldwide.

In the United States, an organization called Cultural Survival helps indigenous peoples and ethnic minorities deal as equals in their interactions with outsiders. Cultural Survival's guiding principle is printed on the inside cover of this book. Cultural Survival sponsors programs to help indigenous peoples and ethnic minorities protect and manage their natural environment, claim land rights, and protect their cultural heritage.

Absolute Cultural Relativism	Whatever goes on within a particular culture cannot be questioned or changed by outsiders as that would be ethnocentric.
Critical Cultural Relativism ↳ less homogenized view	Anyone can pose questions about what goes on in various cultures, including their own culture, in terms of how particular practices or beliefs may harm certain members; follows Lévi-Strauss's comment that no society is perfect and that, therefore, all societies may be able to learn from others and improve.

FIGURE 1.5 **Cultural Relativism: Two Views**

Native American dancers perform at the annual Gateway Pow Wow in Brooklyn, New York.

▶ *Think of possible examples in your microculture of attempts to revitalize aspects of the culture.*

THREE THEORETICAL DEBATES IN CULTURAL ANTHROPOLOGY

Transitioning to theory, this section describes three debates in cultural anthropology that go to the heart of its basic questions about *how* people behave and think cross-culturally and *why* people behave and think the way they do. Introduced briefly here, they reappear throughout the book.

BIOLOGICAL DETERMINISM VERSUS CULTURAL CONSTRUCTIONISM **Biological determinism** seeks to explain why people do and think what they do by considering biological factors such as people's genes and hormones. Thus, biological determinists search for the gene or hormone that contributes to behavior such as homicide, alcoholism, or adolescent stress. They also examine cultural practices in terms of how they contribute to the "reproductive success of the species," or how they contribute to the gene pool of subsequent generations by boosting the number of surviving offspring produced in a particular population. In this view, behaviors and ideas that have reproductive advantages are more likely than others to be passed on to future generations. Biological determinists, for example, have provided an explanation for why human males apparently have "better" spatial skills than females. They say that these differences are the result of evolutionary selection because males with "better" spatial skills would have an advantage in securing both food and mates. Males with "better" spatial skills impregnate more females and have more offspring with "better" spatial skills.

Cultural constructionism, in contrast, maintains that human behavior and ideas are best explained as products of culturally shaped learning. In terms of the example of "better" male spatial skills, cultural constructionists would provide evidence that such skills are passed on culturally through learning, not genes. They would say that parents and teachers socialize boys and girls differently in spatial skills and are more likely to promote learning of certain kinds of spatial skills among boys. Though recognizing the role of biological factors such as genes and hormones, anthropologists who favor cultural construction and learning as an explanation for behaviors such as homicide and alcoholism point to childhood experiences and family roles as being perhaps even more important than genes or hormones. Most cultural anthropologists are cultural constructionists, but some connect biology and culture in their work.

INTERPRETIVE ANTHROPOLOGY VERSUS CULTURAL MATERIALISM Interpretive anthropology, or interpretivism, focuses on understanding culture by studying what people think about, their explanations of their lives, and the symbols that are important to them. For example, in understanding the eating habits of Hindus, interpretivists ask why Hindus do not eat beef. Hindus point to their religious beliefs, according to which cows are sacred and it is a sin to kill and eat them. Interpretivists accept this explanation as sufficient.

Cultural materialism attempts to learn about culture by first examining the material aspects of life: the natural

---

biological determinism a theory that explains human behavior and ideas mainly as shaped by biological features such as genes and hormones.

cultural constructionism a theory that explains human behavior and ideas mainly as shaped by learning.

(TOP) Traffic in the city of Varanasi (Banaras), northern India. Foreign visitors to India often comment that the presence of so many wandering cows is a sign of wastefulness and inefficiency. (BOTTOM) SUVs, trucks, and buses share the road in Los Angeles. SUVs are still popular in the United States in spite of their poor gas mileage.

▶ *If you were an energy policy maker, what lessons would you draw from this pair of photographs?*

environment and how people make a living within particular environments. Cultural materialists believe that these basic facts of life shape culture, even though people may not realize it. They use a three-level model to explain culture. The bottom level is *infrastructure,* a term that refers to basic material factors such as natural resources, the economy, and population. According to this model, infrastructure tends to shape the other two domains of culture: *structure* (social organization, kinship, and political organization) and *superstructure* (ideas, values, and beliefs). This book's chapters are organized roughly in terms of these three categories, but with recognition that the layers are not neat and tidy but rather have interconnections.

A cultural materialist explanation for the taboo on killing cows and eating beef involves the fact that cattle in India play a more important role alive than dead or carved into steaks (Harris 1974). The many cattle wandering the streets of Indian cities and villages look useless to Westerners. Closer analysis shows that the seemingly useless population of bovines serves many useful functions. Ambling along, they eat paper trash and other edible refuse. Their excrement is "brown gold," useful as fertilizer or, when mixed with straw and formed into dried patties, as cooking fuel. Most important, farmers use cattle to plow fields. Cultural materialists take into account Hindu beliefs about the sacred meaning of cattle, but they see its relationship to the material value of cattle, as symbolic protection keeping these extremely useful animals out of the meat factory.

Some cultural anthropologists are strong interpretivists, whereas some are strong cultural materialists. Many combine the best of both views.

INDIVIDUAL AGENCY VERSUS STRUCTURISM This debate concerns the question of how much individual will, or agency, affects the way people behave and think, compared with the power of forces, or *structures,* that are beyond individual control. Western philosophical thought gives much emphasis to the role of agency, the ability of individuals to make choices and exercise free will. In contrast, structurism emphasizes that free choice is an illusion because choices are structured by larger forces such as the economy, social and political organization, and ideological systems.

A prime example is the study of poverty. Those who emphasize agency focus their research on how individuals attempt to act as agents, even in situations of extreme poverty, in order to change their situation as best they can. Structurists would emphasize that the poor are trapped by large and powerful forces. They would describe how the political economy and other forces provide little room for agency for those at the bottom. An increasing number of cultural anthropologists seek to blend a structural perspective with attention to agency.

◆◆◆

Cultural Anthropology and Careers

Some of you reading this book may take only one anthropology course to satisfy a requirement. Others may become interested in the subject matter and take a few more. Some will decide to major or minor in anthropology. Just one course in anthropology may change your way of thinking about the world and your place in it. More than that, anthropology coursework may enhance your ability to get a job. Take a look at the inside of the back cover of this book for specific résumé builders.

MAJORING IN ANTHROPOLOGY

An anthropology B.A. is a liberal arts degree. It is not, however, a professional degree, such as a business degree or a degree in physical therapy. It provides a solid education relevant to many career directions that are likely to require further study, such as law, criminal justice, medicine and health services, social services, education, humanitarian assistance, international development programs, and business. Students interested in pursuing a B.A. major in anthropology should know that anthropology is at least as useful as other liberal arts majors for either graduate study or a professional career.

Anthropology has several clear advantages over other liberal arts majors, and employers and graduate schools are increasingly recognizing these features. Cultural anthropology provides knowledge about the world's people and diversity. It offers insights about a variety of specialized research methods. Cross-cultural awareness and communication skills are valuable assets sought by business, government, health-care providers, and nongovernmental organizations.

The recurrent question is this: Will it be possible to get a good job related to anthropology with a B.A. in anthropology? The answer is yes, but it takes planning and hard work. Do the following: Gain expertise in at least one foreign language, study abroad, do service learning during your undergraduate years, and conduct an independent research project and write up the results as a professional report or conference paper. Package these skills on your résumé so that they appear relevant to employers. Do not give up. Good jobs are out there, and coursework and skills in anthropology are increasingly valued.

Anthropology is also an excellent minor. It complements almost any other area of study by adding a cross-cultural perspective. For example, if you are majoring in music, courses about world music will enrich your primary interest. The same applies to subjects such as interior design, psychology, criminal justice, international affairs, economics, political science, and more.

GRADUATE STUDY IN ANTHROPOLOGY

Some of you may go on to pursue a master's degree (M.A.) or doctorate degree (Ph.D.) in anthropology. If you do, here is some advice. Be passionate about your interest but also be aware that full-time jobs as a professor or as a professional anthropologist are not easy to get. To expand possibilities of a good job, it is wise to consider combining a professional skill with your degree program in anthropology, such as a law degree, an M.A. degree in project management, a Master's of Public Health (M.P.H.), a certificate in disaster relief, or participation in a training program in conflict prevention and resolution.

Useful skills will make your anthropology degree more powerful. In biological anthropology, it may be coursework in anatomy that helps you get a job working in a forensics lab or teaching anatomy in a medical school. In archaeology, it may be your experience on a summer dig that helps you get a job with a firm in your home state that investigates building sites before construction begins, to check for the presence of fossils or artifacts. In cultural anthropology, cross-cultural experiences or knowledge of a foreign language may get you a position with an international aid organization. In linguistic anthropology, your knowledge of bilingualism means that you can help design a more effective program for teaching English to refugees.

LIVING AN ANTHROPOLOGICAL LIFE

Studying cultural anthropology makes for smart people and people with breadth and flexibility. In North America, college graduates are likely to change careers (not just jobs, but careers) several times in their lives. Because you never know where you are going to end up working, or in what endeavor, it pays to be broadly informed about the world. Cultural anthropology prompts you to ask original and important questions about the world's people and their relationships with one another, and it helps provide some useful answers.

Beyond career value, cultural anthroplogy will enrich your daily life by increasing your exposure to the world's cultures. When you pick up a newspaper, you will find several articles that connect with what you have learned in your anthropology classes. You will be able to view your own everyday life as culturally constructed in interesting and meaningful ways. You will be a different person, and you will live a richer life.

1

the BIG questions REVISITED

◆ What is anthropology?

Anthropology is an academic discipline, like history or economics. It comprises four interrelated fields in its attempt to explore all facets of humanity from its origins through the present. Biological or physical anthropology is the study of humans as biological organisms, including their evolution and contemporary variation. Archaeology is the study of past human cultures through their material remains. Linguistic anthropology is the study of human communication, including its origins, history, and contemporary variation and change. Cultural anthropology is the study of living peoples and their cultures, including variation and change. Culture refers to people's learned and shared behaviors and beliefs.

Each field makes both theoretical and applied contributions. The perspective of this book is that applied anthropology, just like theoretical anthropology, should be an integrated and important part of all four fields, rather than a separate, fifth field. Examples of applied anthropology in the four fields include forensic anthropology, nonhuman primate conservation, assisting in literacy programs for refugees, and advising businesses about people's preferences.

◆ What is cultural anthropology?

Cultural anthropology is the field within general anthropology that focuses on the study of contemporary humans. Culture is defined as learned and shared ways of behaving and thinking. It has several distinctive features that set it apart from the other fields of general anthropology and from other academic disciplines. Its two basic goals are ethnography and ethnology. Cultural relativism, attributed to Franz Boas, is a guiding principle that other disciplines have widely adopted. Cultural anthropology values and works to sustain cultural diversity.

Culture is the key concept of cultural anthropology. Some anthropologists define culture as learned and shared behavior and ideas, whereas others equate culture with ideas alone and exclude behavior as a part of culture. It is easier to understand culture by considering its characteristics: Culture is related to nature but is not the same as nature; it is based on symbols and it is learned; cultures are integrated within themselves; and cultures interact with other cultures and change. Four models of cultural interaction involve varying degrees of conflict, blending, and resistance. People participate in cultures of different levels, including local microcultures shaped by such factors as class, "race"/ethnicity/indigeneity, gender, age, and institutions.

Cultural anthropology has a rich history of theoretical approaches and changing topical focuses. Three important theoretical debates are biological determinism versus cultural constructionism, interpretive anthropology versus cultural materialism, and individual agency versus structurism. Each, in its own way, attempts to understand and explain why people behave and think the way they do and to account for differences and similarities across cultures.

◆ How is cultural anthropology relevant to a career?

Taking just one course in cultural anthropology expands awareness of the diversity of the world's cultures and the importance of cross-cultural understanding. Employers in many fields—such as public health, humanitarian aid, law enforcement, business, and education—increasingly value a degree in cultural anthropology. In today's diverse and connected world, being culturally informed and culturally sensitive is essential.

Graduate degrees in cultural anthropology, either at the M.A. or Ph.D. level, are even more likely to lead to professional positions that directly use your anthropological education and skills. Combining graduate coursework in anthropology with a professional degree, such as a master's degree in public health or public administration, or a law degree, is a successful route to a meaningful career outside academia. Cultural anthropology, beyond its career relevance, will enrich your everyday life with its insights.

KEY CONCEPTS

agency, p. 14
anthropology, p. 6
applied anthropology or **practicing anthropology** or **practical anthropology,** p. 7
archaeology or **prehistory,** p. 6
biological anthropology or **physical anthropology,** p. 6
biological determinism, p. 26
class, p. 21
cultural anthropology or **social anthropology,** p. 7
cultural constructionism, p. 26
cultural materialism, p. 14
cultural relativism, p. 13
culture, p. 7
ethnicity, p. 22
ethnocentrism, p. 25
functionalism, p. 13
gender, p. 22
globalization, p. 21
holism, p. 13
indigenous people, p. 22
interpretive anthropology, or **interpretivism,** p. 14
linguistic anthropology, p. 7
localization, p. 21
microculture, p. 15
"race," p. 22
rainforest, p. 10
structurism, p. 14
symbol, p. 20

SUGGESTED READINGS

Thomas J. Barfield, ed. *The Dictionary of Anthropology*. Malden, MA: Blackwell Publishing, 1997. This reference work contains hundreds of brief essays on concepts in anthropology, such as evolution, myth, functionalism, and applied anthropology, and on important anthropologists.

Stanley R. Barrett. *Anthropology: A Student's Guide to Theory and Method*. Toronto: University of Toronto Press, 2000. This book organizes the theoretical history of cultural anthropology into three phases and summarizes trends in each. The author discusses how to do research in cultural anthropology.

Mario Blaser, Harvey A. Feit, and Glenn McRae, eds. *In the Way of Development: Indigenous Peoples, Life Projects and Globalization*. New York: Zed Books, in association with the International Development Research Centre, 2004. Twenty chapters contributed by indigenous leaders, social activists, and cultural anthropologists address indigenous peoples' responses to capitalism and indigenous ideas about future change that is positive for them and for the environment.

Ira E. Harrison and Faye V. Harrison, eds. *African-American Pioneers in Anthropology*. Chicago: University of Illinois Press, 1999. This collection of intellectual biographies highlights the contributions of 13 African American anthropologists to the development of cultural anthropology in the United States.

Takami Kuwayama, ed. *Native Anthropology: The Japanese Challenge to Western Academic Hegemony*. Melbourne: Trans Pacific Press, 2004. The chapters in this book discuss various topics in Japanese anthropology, including "native anthropology," the marginalization of Asian anthropologists, folklore studies, and how U.S. anthropology textbooks present Japan.

James H. McDonald, ed. *The Applied Anthropology Reader*. Boston: Allyn and Bacon, 2002. This collection of over 50 brief essays explores topics in applied cultural anthropology, including ethics, methods, urban settings, health, international development, the environment, education, and business.

R. Bruce Morrison and C. Roderick Wilson, eds. *Native Peoples: The Canadian Experience*, 3rd ed. Toronto, Ontario: Oxford University Press, 2004. This sourcebook on Northern Peoples contains 26 chapters with sections divided by region. Chapters about various cultural groups provide historical context and updates on the current situation.

Thomas C. Patterson. *A Social History of Anthropology in the United States*. New York: Berg, 2001. This history of anthropology in the United States emphasizes the social and political context of the discipline and how that context shaped theories and methods.

Richard J. Perry. *Five Key Concepts in Anthropological Thinking*. Upper Saddle River, NJ: Prentice-Hall, 2003. The five key concepts are evolution, culture, structure, function, and relativism. The author raises thought-provoking questions about anthropology as being Eurocentric and about the appropriation of the culture concept beyond anthropology.

Pat Shipman. *The Evolution of Racism: Human Differences and the Use and Abuse of Science*. Cambridge, MA: Harvard University Press, 1994. This book offers a history of the "race" concept in Western thought from Darwin to contemporary DNA studies. The author addresses thorny issues such as racism in the United States and Nazi Germany's use of Darwinism.

Hominin footprints preserved at Laetoli, Tanzania, are about 3.6 million years old. These individuals were between 3 and 4 feet tall when standing upright. For a close-up view of one of the footprints and further information, go to the human origins section of the website of the Smithsonian Institution's National Museum of Natural History, www.mnh.si.edu/anthro/humanorigins/ha/laetoli.htm.

THE EVOLUTION OF HUMANITY AND CULTURE

the BIG questions

- What do living nonhuman primates tell us about human culture?
- What role did culture play during hominin evolution?
- How has modern human culture changed in the past 12,000 years?

OUTLINE

Substantial scientific evidence indicates that modern humans have evolved from a shared lineage with primate ancestors between 4 and 8 million years ago. The mid-nineteenth century was a turning point in European thinking about human origins as scientific thinking challenged the biblical narrative of human origins. Two British thinkers, Charles Darwin and Alfred Russel Wallace, independently discovered the principle of **natural selection**, the process by which organisms better adapted to the environment reproduce more effectively compared to less well-adapted forms. This principle, in turn, supported the acceptance of the concept of **evolution**, or inherited and cumulative change in the characteristics of a species, population, or culture. This scientific view conflicts with some religious perspectives, including Christian *creationism,* based on a literal understanding of biblical writings, that all animal species, including humans, date from the Day of Creation and have always existed in the physical form that they do now. The scientific view of human origins, however, does not conflict with all religious perspectives, including nonliteralist Christians and Buddhists.

Fossils (the preserved remains of a plant or animal of the past), **artifacts** (portable objects made or modified by humans), and new genetic analyses provide strong evidence that modern humans existed before the Christian Day of Creation, estimated to be 4004 BCE. The evidence also shows that human anatomy evolved over time from more ape-like to more human-like, and human cultural capabilities have changed dramatically. Many anthropologists, like other scientists, find ways to reconcile the scientific evidence with their personal religious beliefs.

This chapter accepts the scientific perspective on human evolution. It therefore begins with a discussion of the primates closest to humans and describes how they provide insights into what the lives of the earliest human ancestors might have been like. It then turns to a description of the main stages in evolution to modern humans. The last section covers the development of settled life, agriculture, and cities and states.

◆◆◆

Nonhuman Primates and the Roots of Human Culture

According to abundant evidence from genetics, anatomy, physiology, and behavior, humans are primates. This section describes primate characteristics in general and then situates humans within the group of primate with whom we are most closely related in order to provide some comparisons.

PRIMATE CHARACTERISTICS

The **primates** are an order of mammals that includes modern humans. Primates vary in size from several ounces to over 400 pounds. Some inhabit limited areas, and others range more widely. In defining primate characteristics, *morphology,* or physical form, is a basic consideration because it is related to behavior. Compared to the faces of other mammals such as dogs or cows, primate faces tend to be flat with reduced snouts. Relatedly, primates differ from other mammals in terms of being highly reliant on vision for dealing with their environment and social interactions. Primates have five digits on their hands and feet, opposable thumbs, and they can grasp with both their hands and feet. Primate brains are large in relation to body size. Because of their large brain size, primates take longer to mature than other mammals do. This extended

Members of a group of Hanuman langurs in India involved in social behavior. Most primates are highly social and interact with their group-mates in complex ways.

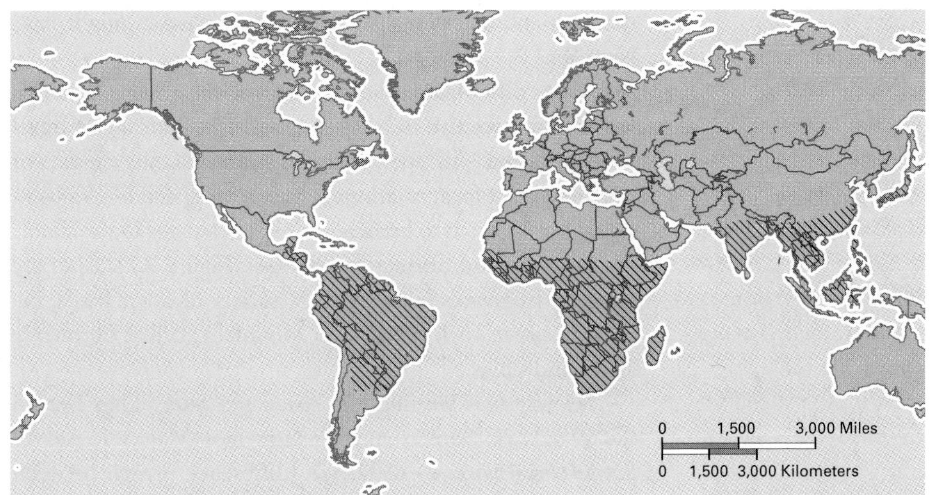

MAP 2.1 Where Nonhuman Primates Live Today.
The habitats of nonhuman primates are greatly reduced from what they were in prehistory, and they are increasingly threatened by human encroachment and environmental change.

developmental period, combined with the fact that most primate species are highly social, provides a context for the social molding of primate behavior.

In terms of environmental adaptations, most nonhuman primate species live in low-altitude areas of the tropics or subtropics (see Map 2.1). A few live in high altitudes in Africa, Nepal, and Japan. Most primate species are *arboreal* (tree-dwelling), *quadrupedal* (moving on all fours), and *diurnal* (active during the day), and most, like humans, have a high degree of **sociality**, or a preference for living in groups and interacting regularly with members of the same species.

All nonhuman primates in the wild provide for their food needs by **foraging**, or obtaining food available in nature through gathering, hunting, or scavenging. Species vary, however, in terms of the kinds of foods they prefer (Strier 2007). Five major dietary patterns of primates are based on their primary food sources:

- *Frugivores* eat mainly fruit. They have large front teeth, or incisors, to allow them to puncture the flesh of large fruits and transfer pieces into their mouths, like when you bite into an apple. Digestion of fruits occurs in the small intestine, so frugivores have a long small intestine.
- *Folivores* eat primarily leaves. Leaves are difficult to digest because of the chemicals, such as cellulose, in their walls. Folivores' chewing teeth are designed to help them break leaves into small pieces, and bacteria in their digestive systems break down the cell walls of leaves. Some folivores have an expanded large intestine (Milton 1984).
- *Insectivores* eat mainly insects. They have high, sharp cusps on their molar teeth to puncture and break up the insects' hard covering. The contents of insects are quite easy to digest, so insectivores have short and simple guts. Insects are difficult to catch, so the limited food sources mean that insectivores are small-bodied.
- *Gummivores* have a diet that relies on the gums and saps of trees. Some have protruding lower incisors that they use to gouge the outer layer of trees to start the flow of gums and saps. Many have large intestines to help them digest these food sources.
- *Omnivores* are generalists: many kinds of foods make up their diet. Therefore, they lack specialized dental or gut morphology. Humans are omnivores.

Most primates live in a *social group,* or collection of animals that interact regularly. Group life has advantages in terms of information sharing about food sources and protection against threats from other groups. The details of group organization vary. The most common social group among nonhuman primates, by far, is the *multi-male/multi-female (MM/MF) group*. This type of group contains adults of both sexes and the females' offspring. Females make up the core of the group and often have strong alliances with each other. Male membership in these groups is less stable. A rare subvariety is called a *fission-fusion group,* a large group of 50 or more individuals that regularly breaks up into much smaller subgroups for foraging. Although rare among nonhuman primate species overall, the fission-fusion pattern is important because it is found in chimpanzees and bonobos, the nonhuman primates most like humans. Thus it is possible that the early human ancestors may have had a fission-fusion form of social organization.

---

natural selection the process by which organisms better adapted to the environment reproduce more effectively compared with less well-adapted forms.

evolution inherited and cumulative change in the characteristics of a species, population, or culture.

fossil the preserved remains of a plant or animal of the past.

artifact a portable object made or modified by humans.

primates an order of mammals that includes modern humans.

sociality the preference for living in groups and interacting regularly with members of the same species.

foraging obtaining food available in nature through gathering, hunting, or scavenging.

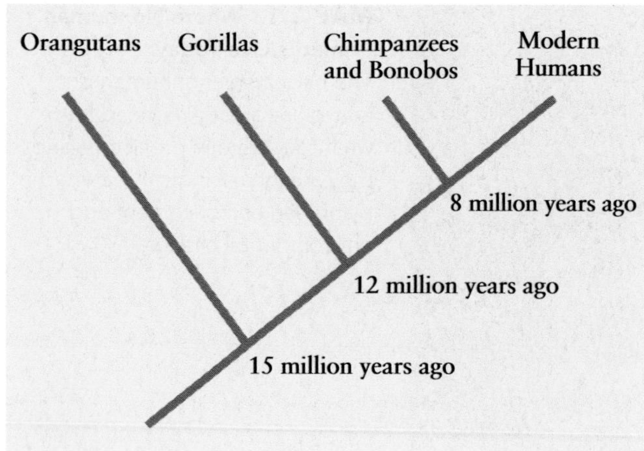

FIGURE 2.1 The Great Apes, Including Modern Humans.

Complex communication and signaling systems are another key feature of nonhuman primate behavior that enables individuals to exist in stable groups. Primates communicate through smell, touch, visual, and vocal channels. The facial muscles of most primates allow for a wider range of expressions compared to other mammals. Primates use facial expressions to communicate threats and fear and to facilitate courtship, play, grooming, and post-conflict reconciliation.

THE GREAT APES

According to genetic data, modern humans are closely related to the living great apes with whom we shared a *common ancestor* between 4 and 8 million years ago (see Figure 2.1). The term **great apes** refers to a category of large, tailless primates that includes the orangutans, gorillas, chimpanzees, bonobos, and humans All great ape species are considered to be endangered in the wild.

Since our last common ancestor with the other great apes, the human line diverged in two significant ways:

- Human anatomy evolved with an emphasis on habitual locomotion on two legs and much larger brains.
- Humans developed culture, including verbal language, to a more complex degree.

In spite of the many differences between humans and the other great apes, the great apes provide insights into what the lives and behavior of early human ancestors might have been like.

Apes differ from other primates in the absence of a tail, larger brains relative to body size, and the tendency to travel by brachiation. All apes, including humans, are capable of **brachiation**, a form of arboreal travel, using the forelimbs to swing from branch to branch, related to changes in the shoulder anatomy and distinct to apes (see Figure 2.2). Apes are typically frugivores but they eat a variety of other foods, including insects such as termites. Mountain gorillas eat mainly leaves and stalks.

Orangutans are the only Asian great ape. They live on the islands of Borneo and Sumatra (see Map 1.1, p. 10). *Sexual dimorphism* in body size (difference in size between males and females) is marked, with the weight of an adult male (175–200 pounds) roughly double that of an adult female (73–99 pounds). In spite of their large size, however, orangutans are mainly arboreal and are known for their "four-handed" mode of movement in the tree canopy. Orangutans are frugivorous and spend substantial amounts of time each day locating and consuming food. They are the least social, and by implication, the most solitary of the great apes. When ripe fruit is abundant, however, orangutans will congregate temporarily. The only constant social unit is that of a mother and her offspring. Mothers and offspring forage together, and mothers often transfer food to immature offspring who solicit food, especially food that is difficult to process (Jaeggi, van Noordwijk, and van Schaik 2008). In this way, offspring gain nutrition and also knowledge about food processing. Orangutans in Sumatra make simple tools from branches that they use for termite and ant fishing and to access seeds. An adult male's territory overlaps the home ranges of several females and is defended from other males. Adult males use large air sacs on their necks to make loud bellowing noises so that they can locate, and usually avoid, each other. The primate line leading to humans split with the orangutans about 15 million years ago.

Gorillas, the largest of the living primates, live in sub-Saharan Africa. Gorillas eat a wide variety of plants, up to 200 species, and supplement their plant diet with termites and ants. Like orangutans, gorillas have a high degree of sexual dimorphism in body size. In the wild, adult male gorillas weigh

FIGURE 2.2 Brachiation in Action.

between 350 and 400 pounds, whereas adult females weigh between 150 and 200 pounds. Gorillas often live in social groups composed of a single male and multiple females with the females' dependent offspring. Males compete with each other intensely for access to the females. Although they live primarily in dense forests, gorillas are largely terrestrial, adult males especially so because of their large body size. They are quadrupedal and travel using a locomotor pattern called **knuckle-walking**. Knuckle-walking is a form of terrestrial travel that involves walking flat-footed while supporting the upper body on the front of fingers bent beyond the knuckle. The human line split with the gorillas about 12 million years ago.

Chimpanzees and bonobos, who live in sub-Saharan Africa, are the great apes most closely related to humans. Chimpanzees are found in several locations in West, Central, and East Africa. Bonobos live only in the Democratic Republic of Congo. Several chimpanzee populations in conservation areas are somewhat protected from human hunting. Because no bonobo population has such protection, they are more heavily hunted and even more endangered.

Compared to orangutans and gorillas, chimpanzees and bonobos are smaller and exhibit less sexual dimorphism in body size. In the wild, adult males weigh between 75 and 150 pounds, adult females between 60 and 100 pounds. Chimpanzees and bonobos are more arboreal than gorillas, but like gorillas, they are knuckle-walkers when on the ground. They are frugivores

Orangutan mother and juvenile in Tanjung Puting National Park on the island of Borneo, Indonesia (see Map 1.1, p. 10). Many thousands of years ago, their habitat included mainland Asia and Southeast Asia. DNA evidence suggests that, if the continued loss of their habitat persists, orangutans may be extinct 50 years from now. The most immediate threats include the expansion of palm oil agriculture, illegal logging, and poaching.

An adult male silverback gorilla knuckle-walking.

▶ *Practice knuckle-walking across a room and consider the role of arm-to-leg length in this form of locomotion.*

great apes a category of large and tailless primates that includes orangutans, gorillas, chimpanzees, bonobos, and humans.

brachiation arboreal travel, using the forelimbs to swing from branch to branch, that is distinct to apes.

knuckle-walking a form of terrestrial travel that involves walking flat-footed while supporting the upper body on the front of fingers bent beyond the knuckle.

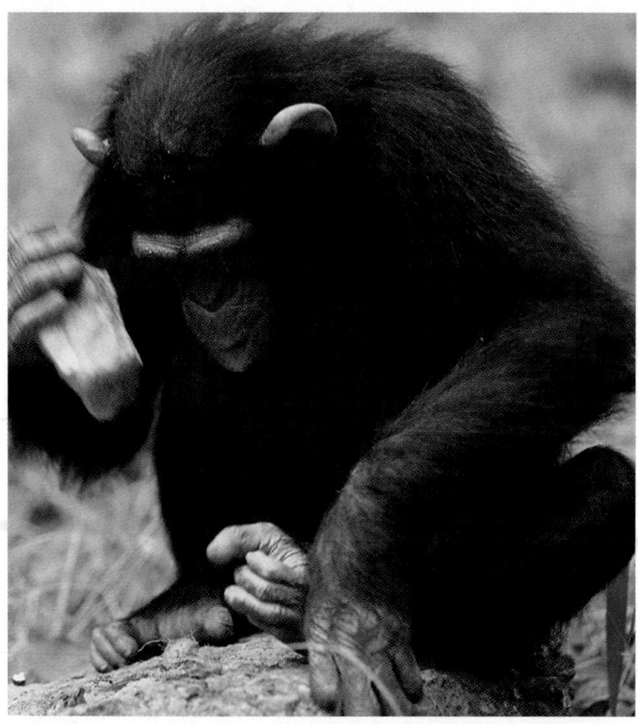

(LEFT) A chimpanzee using a stone hammer to crack open a nut. (RIGHT) A bonobo mother and her offspring show that leisure time and play are not limited to humans.

but occasionally eat other food, including insects, vegetation, and small animals such as monkeys. Chimpanzees in Senegal, for example, consume termites year round and derive substantial calories and nutrients from them (Bogart and Pruetz 2008), a finding that suggests the possibility of termites as an important part of the diet of early human ancestors.

Chimpanzees and bonobos spend 25 percent of their time in social interactions, compared with 10 percent for the other great apes, except for humans (Sussman and Garber 2004). Grooming is the major form of social interaction, with most of the interactions occurring between mothers and offspring.

Although chimpanzees and bonobos are alike in many ways, primatologists are also interested in the differences between them and which is the better model for the early human ancestors (see Figure 2.3). Bonobos are similar in size to chimpanzees, but they have less sexual dimorphism in body size, so they are more like humans in this respect. Bonobos use two-legged, upright locomotion more than chimpanzees, again appearing more like humans. In terms of diet, both chimpanzees and bonobos hunt and eat small animals, though bonobos hunt less frequently than chimpanzees. Given the diversity in human dietary preferences, which range from veganism to eating meat, it is impossible to speculate on which animal is the better model for early humans on this dimension. Evidence of animal carcass butchery during several stages of hominin evolution suggests that animal protein was an important part of the diet.

Chimpanzees live in large, fluid groups of 50 to 60 individuals, but the entire group is rarely, if ever, together in one area. Subgroups form, dissolve, and reform, sometimes with different members. Adult males often travel together, whereas adult females travel with their offspring. In contrast to many other primate species, chimpanzees are *patrilocal,* a residence pattern in which males stay in their birth group throughout their lives. Females leave their birth group at reproductive age, between 10 and 15 years, to join a new group. Therefore, the core of the large social group is biologically related males. Males often form "gangs" that, as a group, seek food or defend territory. In some instances, these males go beyond their home range to seek out and kill members of a neighboring group.

Like chimpanzees, bonobos are patrilocal, but a difference is that migrant bonobo females develop strong alliances with females in their new group, forming *matrifocal* social groups centered on one or more adult female. In contrast to chimpanzees, adult female bonobos dominate the control of food distribution, and males solicit their attention by offering them choice food items. Bonobo social organization is related to the fact that they eat more vegetation, which is common and abundant, than chimpanzees do. Females spend less time foraging and have more time to establish and maintain social ties.

Bonobos have the highest rates of sexual contact of all nonhuman primates. Sexual contact occurs among all possible sex and age combinations, although rarely between close relatives. Bonobo reproductive rates, nonetheless, are similar to those found among chimpanzees. Bonobos thus have high rates of social or recreational sex, and this pattern is related to lower rates of conflict compared to chimpanzees. Bonobos use sexual contact to prevent conflict and to resolve post-conflict situations.

Chimpanzees	Bonobos
Terrestrial and arboreal	Terrestrial, more erect posture
Frequent tool users	Little observed tool use
More hunting and meat-eating	Occasional hunting and meat-eating
Hunting by males	Hunting by males and females
Male dominance over females	Female dominance over males
Males share meat only	Females share fruit and sometimes meat
Infanticide documented	No infanticide observed
Frequent intergroup aggression	Infrequent intergroup aggression
Less frequent sexual behavior	Frequent sexual behavior
Male–female sexual interactions	Prolific sexual interactions between and among males and females

FIGURE 2.3 Chimpanzee/Bonobo Differences.

Source: derived from Stanford 1998 and comments by Frans B. M. de Waal, Barbara Fruth, Kano Takayoshi, and William C. McGrew

Attractive food, or almost anything of interest to more than one bonobo, sparks sexual interest. The two bonobos will suspend potential competition for the item of interest and briefly mount each other or participate in what primatologists refer to as *G-G rubbing*, or genital–genital rubbing (de Waal and Lanting 1997:109). G-G rubbing is unique to bonobos and may qualify as a cultural innovation. This activity appears to distract the two parties and reframe the relationship as one of alliance and cooperation rather than competition and conflict. In one example of conflict prevention, when one mother struck another mother's infant, the two females participated in intense G-G rubbing rather than hostility, and peace was the outcome.

The current genetic evidence indicates that chimpanzees and bonobos are equally close to modern humans. Considering behavioral evidence, some scholars argue that chimpanzees are the better model given human patterns of male dominance and high levels of intergroup violence (Wrangham and Peterson 1996). The bonobo model suggests, in contrast, that humanity's biological heritage includes a propensity for being sexually active, female-centric, and relatively peaceful. Neither the chimpanzee nor bonobo model applies neatly to all modern human cultures, no doubt because our lineages split between 4 and 8 million years ago, and much has happened since then in terms of human evolution.

NONHUMAN PRIMATE CULTURE

Culture has long been thought to be unique to humans and their recent ancestors. Increasing evidence, however, indicates that animals other than humans have aspects of culture. In primatology, *culture* is defined as behavior that is learned (not innate) and shared (not individual).

In the 1950s, Japanese primatologists first raised the possibility of nonhuman primate culture (Kawamura 1959). Their findings emerged from a long-term study of macaques, a variety of Old World monkeys, on the island of Koshima, Japan (see Map 3.2, p. 68). In order to lure the macaques into areas where they could be observed easily, the researchers provided sweet potatoes on the beach. Soon, an adult female monkey, whom they named Imo, began carrying the potatoes from the beach to a pool of fresh water to wash the sand from the potatoes before eating them. Some of Imo's relatives began to do the same thing, and the behavior spread throughout much of her group.

Later, the primatologists provisioned the monkeys with rice in order to keep them in open areas for longer periods of

A Japanese macaque washing a sweet potato. Sweet-potato-washing is an early example of a nonhuman primate cultural behavior studied by primatologists.

THINKING OUTSIDE THE BOX

What are the main forms of social groups in your microculture? What social groups do you belong to, how did you join, and what holds the group together?

time. They thought it would take the monkeys a long time to work out how to sort rice grains from beach sand. But Imo promptly started dropping handfuls of sandy rice into the fresh water pools. The sand sank and the rice floated, making it possible for her to collect sand-free rice grains. This practice, too, spread throughout much of the group, especially among younger individuals. The behaviors of Imo and her group, being learned and shared, conform to part of the definition of nonhuman primate culture. (Note that primatologists can study only behavior, not beliefs or symbol systems, so that part of the definition of culture is still reserved for humans.)

Comparative studies shed more light on the question of primate culture. Primatologists look for behavioral differences among primates of the same species at different field sites with similar environmental conditions. Comparison of data from seven chimpanzee research sites in East and West Africa revealed 39 differences in tool use, grooming, and other social behaviors that can be explained only as the result of cultural differences and social learning (Whiten et al. 1999). The tools include hammers and anvils for cracking open nuts, probes for ant-fishing, leaves to sit on, and sticks to fan away flies. Male chimpanzees in some groups in Uganda regularly use leaves to clean their penis after sexual intercourse (O'Hara and Lee 2006). Cultural variation in social interaction and communication includes the *grooming hand clasp,* or holding the arm of another individual over his or her head during grooming (McGrew 2004), and doing a slow bodily display, or "raindance," at the start of rain.

All great apes build sleeping nests. Comparison of nest-building patterns among chimpanzees in two sites in southeastern Senegal (see Map 16.4, p. 407), West Africa, reveals that this behavior is an adaptation to predator pressures (Pruetz et al. 2008). The natural environment in both study sites is similar, but the degree of threat from animal predators differs. In the site where the threat from predators is higher, the chimpanzees build tree nests at higher levels than in the area where predation is a lesser threat. Building a nest several feet high in a tree requires planning and dealing with problems such as finding materials, transporting them to the nest site, and making sure the nest structure will hold. Furthermore, it is prompted by risk-assessment that is informed by degrees of predation.

Young primates learn various cultural behaviors by watching adults. Beyond learning, however, invention also occurs. For 27 years, Japanese primatologists have been observing chimpanzees using tools in Bossou, Guinea, West Africa (Yamamoto et al. 2008). But it was only in 2003 that they saw one youthful male, named JJ, transfer his considerable skills at using a stick to retrieve ants on the ground to obtaining them in trees. For the new activity, JJ had to adapt his tools by using a shorter stick. No immigrant chimpanzees had come into the area, so JJ came up with this new approach on his own. Future research is needed to show whether JJ's innovation will spread to others in his group.

These intriguing examples suggest how the earliest human ancestors began to develop culture, through invention and sharing, as a key form of adaptation to various environments. In addition to a fruit-based diet, they may have regularly eaten insects such as termites. They may have developed the technique of building nests high in trees to protect themselves from predators. They probably lived in flexible social groups and experienced occasional within-group and across-group conflict.

◆◆◆

Hominin Evolution to Modern Humans

This section provides an overview of the several extinct species of early humans with attention to changes in anatomy (physical structure of the body) and culture. **Hominins** is a category of primates that includes modern humans and extinct species of early human ancestors that are more closely related to humans than to living chimpanzees and bonobos. The main hominin evidence includes fossils, artifacts, and new evidence from the growing field of DNA analysis.

THE EARLY HOMININS

In the first stage of separation from the other great apes, lasting from 8 million years ago until 3 million years ago, all the early hominins lived in Africa. These hominins are distinct from other apes in changes to the pelvis and lower limbs for habitual bipedalism, larger brains, and smaller teeth. **Bipedalism** is upright locomotion on two feet. These three anatomical characteristics were probably associated with other important changes including culture.

TWO EARLIEST SPECIES The oldest known hominin fossil is *Sahelanthropus tchadensis* (Brunet et al. 2002). Dated to between 7 and 6 million years ago, this fossil, discovered in Toros-Menalla in Chad, is important because it dramatically extends the regional pattern of fossil evidence for the early era beyond eastern and southern Africa into central/western Africa (see Map 2.2). The discovery of *S. tchadensis* means that the early hominins most likely occupied a much wider area of Africa than paleoanthropologists previously thought.

---

hominins a category of primates that includes modern humans and extinct species of early human ancestors that are more closely related to humans than to living chimpanzees and bonobos.

bipedalism upright locomotion on two feet.

australopithecines a category of several extinct hominin species found in East and Central Africa that lived between 4.5 and 3 million years ago.

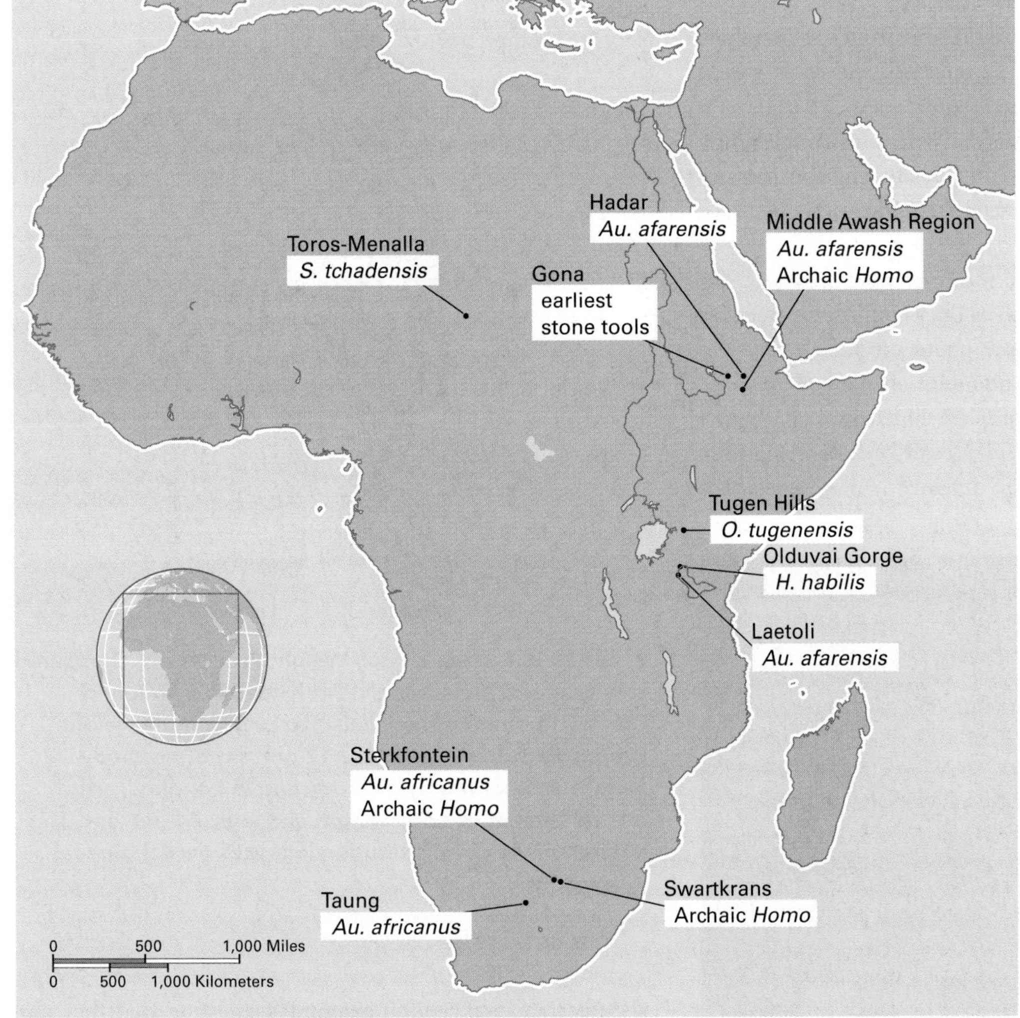

MAP 2.2 **Sites of Early Hominins and Archaic *Homo* in Africa Mentioned in This Chapter.**

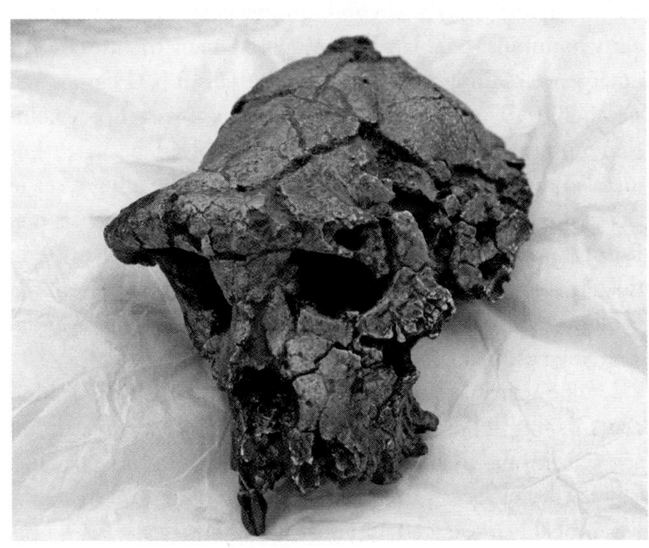

This fossil, discovered by a Chad-French team of paleoanthropologists, is nicknamed Toumaï, which means "a much-wanted child born after a long wait." The cranium of Toumaï is a mixture of features. Its dimensions suggest a chimpanzee-sized brain, but it has heavy brow ridges like hominins.

The second oldest primitive hominin species is *Orrorin tugenensis,* named for some fossils found in the Tugen Hills of Kenya that date to 6 million years ago (Senut et al. 2001). Although only a few fossils have been found for this species, the collection includes a femur (thighbone). Analysis of its shape and strength indicates bipedalism (Richmond and Jungers 2008).

THE AUSTRALOPITHECINES **Australopithecines** refers to a category of several extinct species of hominins found in East and Central Africa that lived between roughly 4 million and 2 million years ago. Abundant fossil evidence exists for this group. "Lucy," the most famous hominin fossil in the world, was found in Hadar, Ethiopia (Johanson 2004). She belongs to the species *Australopithecus afarensis,* which lived from 4.3 million to 3 million years ago. The 1974 discovery of Lucy made headlines because so much of her skeleton was preserved (see Figure 2.4).

The australopithecine era also provides the first artifacts, in the form of stone tools. The oldest stone tools, dating to 2.6 million years ago, are from Gona, Ethiopia (Semaw et al. 2003).

SUMMARY OF THE EARLY HOMININS The anatomy of these early species exhibits evolution away from ape-like characteristics to more human-like characteristics. Most would have been around 4 feet tall when standing upright and would have weighed around 100 pounds. Their arms were slightly longer than those of modern humans, and the shortness of their lower limbs would have made them look more like apes than like humans.

Orrorin tugenensis is the earliest fossil evidence for bipedalism, and later fossils such as Lucy confirm the trend, as do the footprints at Laetoli (see photo on p. 32). It is less clear, however, when the early hominins abandoned knuckle-walking or brachiation for complete bipedalism. Although early hominins such as Lucy had a lower body that was fully designed for bipedalism, they retained some aspects of shoulder and upper limb anatomy suggesting that they also brachiated to seek protection in trees. This combination could have given them a decisive advantage over other animals.

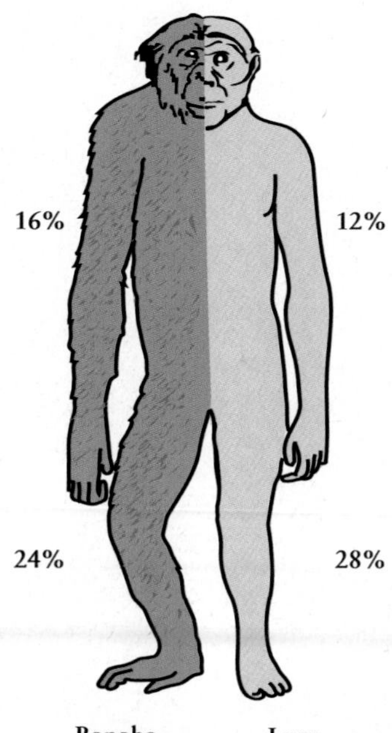

FIGURE 2.4 Lucy's Body Weight Proportions Compared to a Bonobo. Primatologist Adrienne Zihlman found that living bonobos are similar to Lucy in body weight proportions. Lucy's arms are 12 percent of her body weight and her legs are 28 percent. In bonobos, arms are 16 percent of body weight and legs, 24 percent. This pattern of weight distribution indicates partial bipedal locomotion.

Source: Adapted from an original drawing by Carla Simmons in Sussman 1984:197

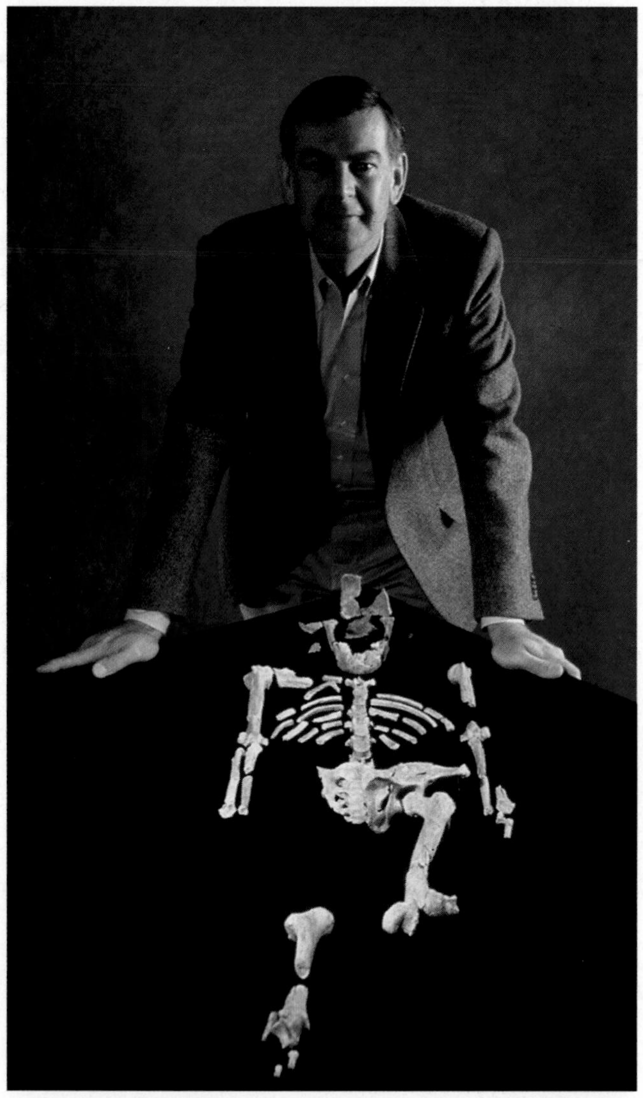

Lucy and Don Johanson, the paleoanthropologist who discovered her. Because they have fossils of about 40 percent of Lucy's skeleton, researchers can make fairly accurate estimates about her stature, body weight, and other characteristics.

Why did bipedalism and upright posture evolve among early hominins? Scholars have proposed many theories for the emergence of upright posture and bipedalism (O'Higgins and Elton 2007, Thorpe et al. 2007). One prominent theory holds that upright posture and bipedalism evolved because they enabled hominins to see other animals over the tall grasses in the more open areas, or savanna, compared to dense rain forests. A **savanna** environment consists of open plains with tall grasses and patches of trees; during this period of hominin evolution, the extent of rainforests was declining and savannas were increasing due to climate change.

The general pattern of early hominin food acquisition was foraging. The diet of the early hominins was mixed, not specialized, and included a wide variety of fruits, insects, nuts, tubers (fleshy roots of plants), and some animal meat which was probably scavenged rather than hunted.

The evidence of stone tools is an indication of culture. Some early hominins made and used simple stone tools. Given that stone tool-making traditions were likely to be learned and shared, the early hominins therefore possessed some elements of culture.

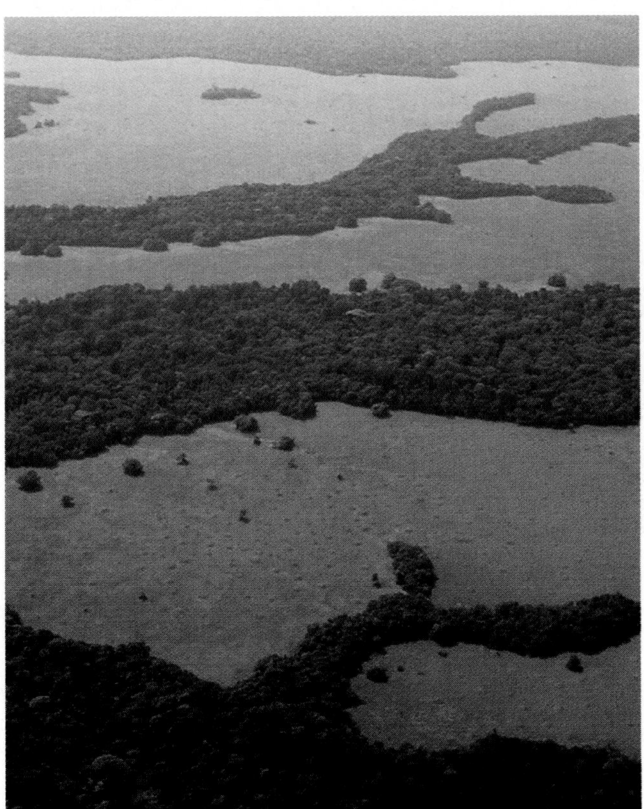

When the early hominins were evolving in Africa, the environment was changing from dense forest to patches of woodland interspersed with open grasslands.

▶ *How might this type of environment be related to the evolution of bipedalism?*

ARCHAIC *HOMO*

Archaic *Homo* is a category of extinct hominin species that lived from 2.4 million years to 19,000 years ago. Compared to the early hominins, these species have a more modern human-like body shape, larger brains, and smaller jaws and teeth. Stone tools are prominent in the culture of all archaic *Homo* species. These hominins migrated into much of the Old World. Paleoanthropologists argue about whether they are ancestors to modern humans. Some say they all died out whereas others say they interbred with later species. There is no conclusive proof to support either position at this time.

Homo habilis In Olduvai Gorge, Tanzania, in 1960, Louis and Mary Leakey discovered fossils representing a form they thought was human-like. They argued that the Olduvai evidence should be included in the genus *Homo* because it satisfied the accepted functional criteria of manual dexterity, upright posture, and fully bipedal locomotion. They argued for naming a new species called *Homo habilis* (literally "Handy Human") (Leakey et al. 1964). Associated with *H. habilis* are distinctive stone tools that are named Oldowan because they were first found in Olduvai Gorge. The **Oldowan tradition** is characterized by *core tools* and *flake tools*. Core tools are made from rounded stones that have had flakes chipped off them, either at one end or along one side. Flake tools are more numerous than core tools. Flake tools are the sharp pieces of stone that break off a core when it is struck. It is unlikely that Oldowan stone tools were the only tools used by their makers. Rather, they were the tools that survived in the archaeological record because they were made of hard stone (see the Critical Thinking box).

Homo erectus *Homo erectus* ("Upright Human") is the first hominin species that was widely distributed across the Old World. Although *H. erectus* was a highly successful species in terms of duration, around 2 million years, and in terms of its colonization of much of the Old World, if you met an *H. erectus* individual in the street, you would not mistake him for a modern human. His head would be smaller, his forehead lower, and no modern human would have such a pronounced brow ridge. The average brain size of *H. erectus* was about 1000 centimeters, or two-thirds the size of the average modern human brain.

H. erectus is associated with the emergence, around 1.7 million years ago, of a new stone tool tradition called the **Acheulian tradition**, characterized by the prevalence of handaxes (Toth and Schick 1993). A ***handaxe*** is a bifacial (two-sided) stone tool that is flat, pear-shaped, and flaked on all its edges and on both surfaces. The Acheulian tradition is named after a site in St. Acheul, France, where European archaeologists first discovered handaxes. The oldest Acheulian stone tools are from Ethiopia and Kenya. Acheulian tools, in contrast to Oldowan tools, were worked on both sides, more finely crafted, more consistently shaped, and therefore indicate more planning, skill, and manual dexterity.

ARCHAIC *HOMO* MOVES OUT OF AFRICA Around 2 million years ago, archaic *Homo* began to migrate out of Africa. The question of why archaic *Homo* left Africa remains unanswered. Three major hypotheses exist:

- Hominins had become meat-eaters, and their preference for meat led them to follow herds of animals as these moved out of Africa to new areas.

---

savanna an environment that consists of open plains with tall grasses and patches of trees.

archaic *Homo* a category of several extinct hominin species that lived from 2.4 million years to 19,000 years ago and is characterized by different stone tool traditions, depending on the species.

Oldowan tradition the oldest hominin toolkit, characterized by core tools and flake tools.

Acheulian tradition the toolkit of *H. erectus*, used from 1.7 million years ago to 300,000 years ago, and characterized by handaxes.

CRITICAL thinking

What Is Really in the Toolbox?

It is reasonable to assume that stone tools were not the only tools that archaic *Homo* used, given that it is likely that other materials were available for tools and that a wider variety of uses existed than the probable functions of core tools, flakes, and scrapers. This exercise asks you to do a mini-experimental study by imagining that you are living in an open woodland environment like that of archaic *Homo*. Imagine your daily life, including how you obtain food and where you sleep at night.

An experimental archaeologist uses a newly made stone tool to cut raw meat.

◆ **CRITICAL THINKING QUESTIONS**

- Make a list of the activities you would perform over a 24-hour period and what tools you might need for those activities.
- What materials in the savanna would provide useful tools for performing these activities?
- Assume you have 10 tools in your tool kit. Three of them are made from stone: one core tool and two flake tools. What are the other seven tools? What is the likelihood that these other seven tools would be preserved in the archaeological record available to future ages?

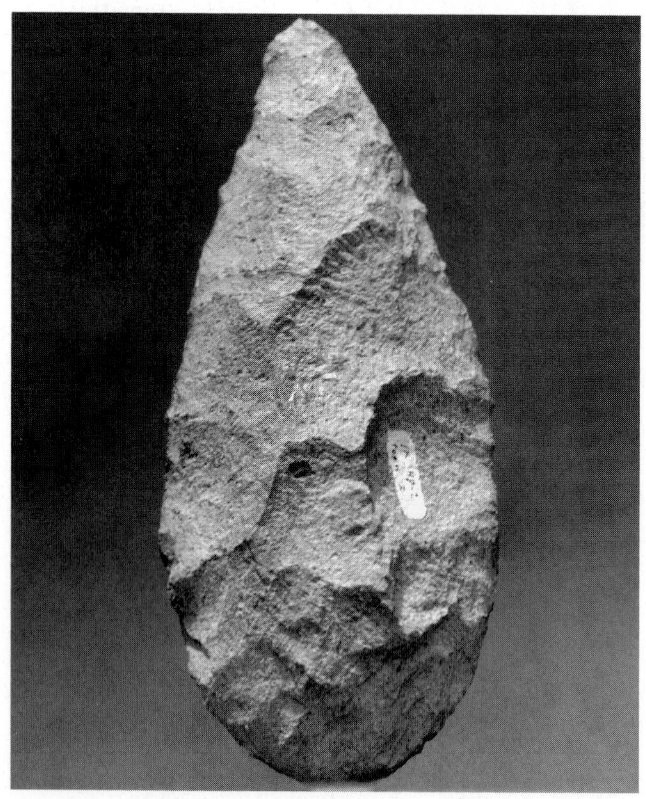

Acheulian handaxe from Tanzania.

▶ *Imagine that you are gripping the widest part in your hand, with the narrow part pointing horizontal or downward, cutting through tree bark or striking at an attacking hyena.*

- They were attracted by the cool and arid northern climate, where their ability to adapt to varied conditions gave them an advantage over other species.
- Humans are "natural" migrants—they just have to keep moving.

No matter what the reason for leaving Africa, the general direction of migration was north and east, out of Africa toward the Middle East and then on into Asia. The earliest fossil evidence of hominins outside Africa, dated at 1.8 million years ago, comes from the site of Dmanisi in the Caucasus region of the country of Georgia (Vekua et al. 2002) (see Map 2.3). Dmanisi hominins are small in stature, and their brains are also small, around 600 centimeters, or not much larger than the average brain size of the Australopithecines. Yet their limb proportions are more modern, and they obviously had the capacity for long-distance travel. The stone tools at Dmanisi are core and flake tools, similar to the Oldowan toolkit.

From Dmanisi, there is a large geographical gap as to where *H. erectus* went. Some evidence indicates that *H. erectus* reached Java, in Southeast Asia, as early as 1.8 million years ago (Swisher et al. 1994). How they got to Java is a mystery, because no evidence exists to explain their migration (see Map 2.4).

Homo floresiensis Another Asian puzzle is the recent discovery of a dwarf-sized species of hominins, nicknamed "the Hobbit," found on the island of Flores in Southeast Asia (see Map 2.4). The fossil evidence for this species consists of a

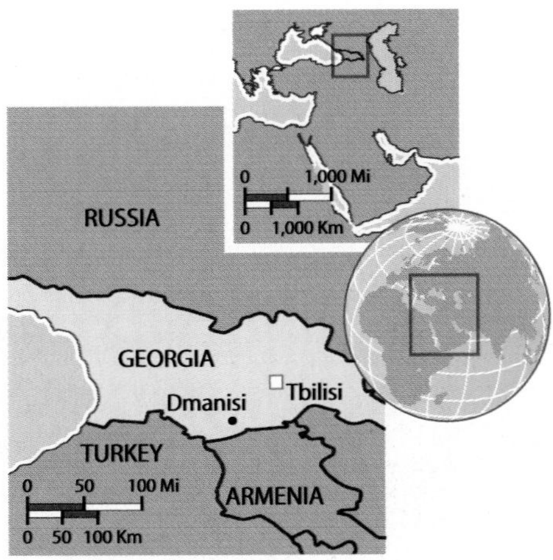

MAP 2.3 Dmanisi, Georgia.
The country of Georgia has the distinction of being the site of 1.7 million-year-old hominin fossils found at Dmanisi. Many thousands of years later, during the Neolithic era, modern humans first domesticated grapes and produced wine in this region. Given its location on the Black Sea, Georgia has long been involved in trade.

well-preserved skeleton from one individual, dated at 18,000 years ago, and a single tooth from another individual, dated at 40,000 years ago (Morwood et al. 2004, Brown et al. 2004). This hominin was just over 3 feet tall, stood upright, and was probably bipedal. Its brain size was small. Stone tools found with the fossils, however, are like those of modern humans who had much larger brains. Scientists continue to debate whether the Hobbit is a separate species of archaic *Homo* or whether it is a pathologically dwarfed modern human from the recent past. Ongoing research and more fossil and archaeological evidence will help resolve this debate. If the Hobbit proves to be a legitimate archaic *Homo* species, then these questions remain: How did a hominin with such a small brain get to Flores? How did it produce modern-style stone tools? How did it survive until recent times?

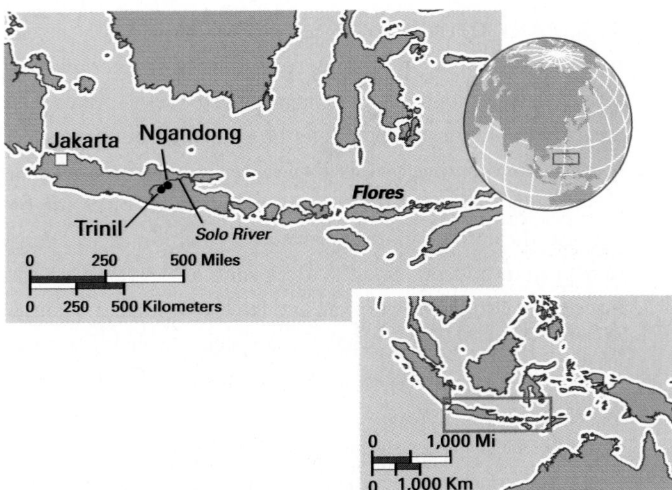

MAP 2.4 Hominin Sites on Islands of Indonesia.
Since the early twentieth century, paleoanthropologists and archaeologists have made important hominin discoveries at several island sites in Indonesia, including Java and Flores. This research demonstrates that early human ancestors were living in this part of the world earlier than anyone had suspected and had sophisticated nautical abilities.

THE NEANDERTHALS *Homo neanderthalensis*, informally referred to as Neanderthals, was first discovered in a site in Germany called Neanderthal. It is known from over a hundred sites spread across most of Europe, into what is now Israel and Iraq, and all the way into Siberia (see Map 2.5). The oldest Neanderthal sites are in Western Europe, where Neanderthal

Artist's impression, based on fossil remains, of *H. floresiensis*, nicknamed "the Hobbit."

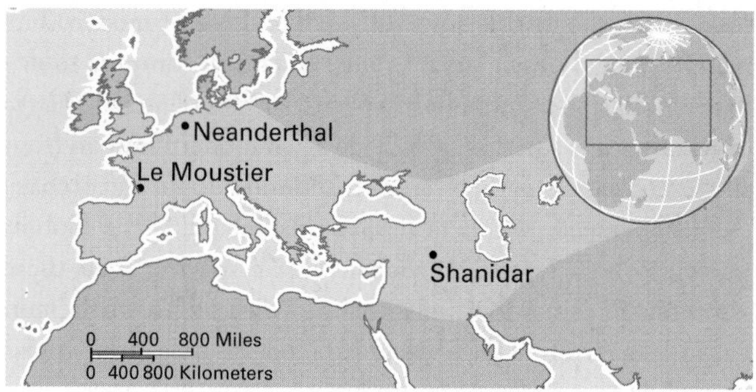

MAP 2.5 Neanderthal Sites and Distribution in the Old World.
The discovery of many Neanderthal sites across the Old World indicates that they occupied an extensive area. During their later period, they overlapped with modern humans in the Middle East and Europe. Whether Neanderthals and modern humans interbred is debated.

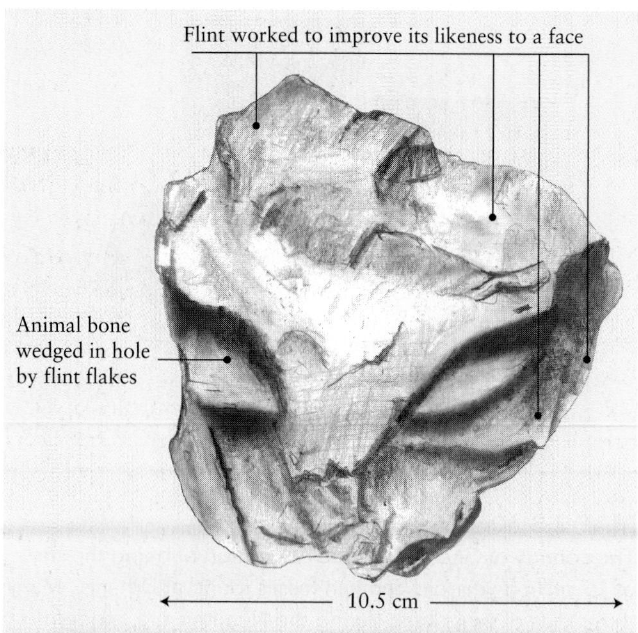

FIGURE 2.5 Worked Flint Found by the Loire River in Northern France. Dated to 35,000 years ago, this object was made by Neanderthals and is one of the earliest examples of sculpture.

remains are found mainly in rock shelters and caves. The Neanderthals survived from 400,000 to 30,000 years ago.

The Neanderthals are highly distinctive in terms of their morphology. Compared to modern humans, they had heavier limb bones, larger brains, and distinctive facial skeletons. Neanderthals were the only hominin species able to tolerate, over thousands of years, the cold temperatures that intermittently affected Europe and northern Asia. Although the distinctive morphology of the Neanderthals may be the result of biological adaptations to a very cold climate, it is likely that they may also have developed cultural adaptations to the cold, including clothing (see Eye on the Environment). Another cultural feature is that Neanderthals were the first hominins to bury their dead regularly, so the quality and quantity of their fossil records are better than for other archaic *Homo* species.

Most Neanderthal fossils are found in association with a stone tool kit referred to as the **Mousterian tradition**, named after the site of Le Moustier, France, where such tools were first described. Mousterian tool kits, compared to the Acheulian, are characterized by smaller, lighter, and more specialized flake tools such as points, scrapers, and awls. Neanderthals created material items other than tools that demonstrate their relatively advanced way of thinking and behaving. This book's definition of *expressive culture,* provided in Chapter 14, is behavior and beliefs related to art and leisure. The Neanderthals had elements of expressive culture including portable art, though of a simple sort (see Figure 2.5), and flutes. They may have had the capacity for verbal language, though this issue is debated. Another debated issue is whether the Neanderthals went extinct, perhaps wiped out by the incoming modern humans, or whether they interbred with modern humans and can be considered part of our direct lineage.

SUMMARY OF ARCHAIC *HOMO* Compared to the early hominins, the smaller chewing teeth and the smaller and more slender jaws of archaic *Homo* suggest that these species either ate different kinds of food or ate the same food but processed it outside the mouth, possibly by cooking. One way to improve dietary quality was to eat more animal meat, birds, or fish, because these food sources provide large amounts of energy-rich protein and fat. Food sources such as eggs, worms, and insects can also provide protein and fat, but in smaller quantities per mouthful. Evidence that these species probably ate meat comes from an unlikely source: tapeworms (Hoberg et al. 2001). The first evidence of tapeworm infection in hominins coincides with the emergence of archaic *Homo* in Africa, a finding that points to the likelihood that they ate substantial amounts of meat. No one knows for sure how such meat was obtained, but most thinking leans toward the view that it was scavenged from animals killed by other predators.

Archaic *Homo* species inhabited a wide variety of habitats including those with temperate climates and those with cold climates. An increasingly complex culture was key to surviving in such varied environments. Evidence that *H. erectus*

Mousterian tradition the toolkit of the Neanderthals characterized by the predominance of small, light, and more specialized flake tools such as points, scrapers, and awls.

Anatomically Modern Humans (AMH) or ***Homo sapiens*** or **modern humans** the species to which modern humans belong and also referred to by that term; first emerged in Africa between 300,000–160,000 years ago and then spread throughout the Old and New Worlds.

eye on the ENVIRONMENT

Clothing as a Thermal Adaptation to Cold and Wind

During the many thousands of years in which Neanderthals lived in Eurasia, the climate was mainly cold, and winds were likely strong. Neanderthals' biological and cultural adaptations allowed them to survive in latitudes up to 55 degrees N (Gilligan 2007). Their biological adaptations include a short, wide body with short limbs, a body type that allows for conservation of heat. Neanderthal cultural adaptations include cave dwelling and the use of fire to provide heat and light inside the caves. Their Mousterian toolkit, which includes scrapers, points, and awls, strongly suggests the likelihood that they made and wore clothing.

Among the many theories about the fate of the Neanderthals, Australian archaeologist Ian Gilligan offers a novel theory. His explanation for Neanderthal extinction involves climate change, Neanderthal morphology, and Neanderthal culture. Gilligan argues that the Neanderthals' biological and cultural adaptations were sufficient under normal and consistent cold regimes but insufficient during severe cold weather spikes that occurred near the end of their time on earth. Most importantly, he differentiates between two types of clothing: simple and complex, and their thermal effectiveness in situations of extreme cold.

- *Simple clothing* is loosely draped around the body and has only one layer.
- *Complex clothing* has multiple layers and the first layer, at least, is fitted to the body.

Simple clothing provides limited protection against cold and wind, whereas complex clothing can protect against severe cold and wind in polar environments.

No surviving remains of clothing from the Neanderthals exist, so archaeologists can only make inferences about the type of clothing they wore from their tools. Given the reasonable assumption that the basic material for Neanderthal clothing was animal hides, these would have required cleaning and scraping in order to make them usable as simple clothing. The Neanderthal Mousterian toolkit was able to perform these tasks, and thus it is likely that they had simple clothing.

Complex clothing, however, requires more careful preparation of the various layers and stitching pieces together to form a fitted layer. More specialized tools such as borers and needles are necessary. The Neanderthals did not possess such tools, but the modern humans who arrived in Eurasia did.

Gilligan's working hypothesis is that the biological adaptation of Neanderthals, along with their cultural ability to produce simple clothing, was effective over many thousands of years. But, in later times, cold temperatures spiked, and the Neanderthals lacked the ability to protect themselves with complex clothing and therefore succumbed to hypothermia. In contrast, the in-coming modern humans lacked biological adaptations to the extreme cold, but they did have the technology to produce complex clothing which allowed them to survive spikes of cold weather better than the Neanderthals could.

Using knowledge of temperature changes during the later Neanderthal era and inferences from the Neanderthal and modern human toolkits, it is possible to generate a reasonable scenario that Neanderthals died out because of their inability to survive extreme cold stress. Although Neanderthals survived for thousands of years in cold conditions, they did not extend their territory from inner Siberia further to Alaska and on into the New World, as did their modern human successors. Complex clothing could have made all the difference.

◆ **FOOD FOR THOUGHT**

- What is your experience, in extremely cold weather, with the effectiveness of close-fitting and layered clothing versus loose-fitting and nonlayered clothing?

had reached islands in Southeast Asia over 1 million years ago means that the species had devised a way to travel by water, presumably using some sort of raft or boat, and could cross substantial distances, at least 15 miles from island to island, on open sea. This achievement marks a major locomotive advance, enabling archaic *Homo* to migrate to and settle in a far wider range of places than are available by foot.

Archaic *Homo* species had some aspects of culture including stone tools. Neanderthal artifacts document the beginning of art and music. Neanderthals buried their dead and may have had a sense of supernaturalism or a belief in life after death. They may have had verbal language.

MODERN HUMANS

The term **anatomically modern humans (AMH)** refers to *Homo sapiens,* the species to which modern humans belong; this book uses the term "modern humans." This era is the

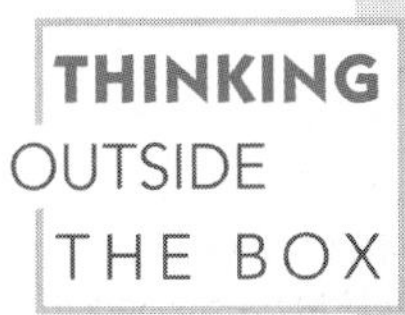

Listen to the interview on the Web with French paleoanthropologist Jean-Jacques Hublin about Neanderthals and their fate: www.pbs.org/wgbh/evolution/library/07/3/text_pop/1_073_02.htm. What is Hublin's position?

Blades from Kapthurin, Kenya, dated at 300,000 years ago. Many archaeologists say that these blades, and other early tools, indicate that humans had aspects of modern behavior far in advance of modern anatomy.

last period during which any evidence exists of significant morphological change. Compared to the Neanderthals, modern humans have steeper foreheads with smaller brow ridges, smaller faces, smaller incisor teeth, and thinner limb bones. Culture, in contrast, continues to become more elaborate and complex, as people alter how they interact with nature and with each other. In this relatively short period, the number of human species was reduced to one, and modern humans emerged as the only form of human life on the earth.

MODERN HUMAN ORIGINS IN AFRICA No one knows which, if any, of the earlier species may be a direct ancestor to modern humans. At this point, the fossil evidence does not indicate a clear line from any archaic *Homo* species to modern humans. Future fossil evidence may help fill in the gaps. The earliest fossil evidence for modern humans is from a site in Ethiopia and dates to 160,000 years ago. Archaeological evidence also supports the African origins theory of modern humans. Modern tools such as blades that may have been used on the tips of spears and arrows have been found in African sites dated to 300,000 years ago. Given the early date of the archaeological evidence for modernity, it is likely that future fossil discoveries in Africa will be from that time, too. Or, modern behavior may have preceded modern biological evolution.

Upper Paleolithic the period of modern human occupation in Europe and Eurasia (including the Middle East) from 45,000–40,000 years ago to 12,000 years ago, characterized by microlithic tools and prolific cave art and portable art.

Cro-Magnons the first modern humans in Europe, dating from 40,000 years ago.

Clovis culture New World population characterized by the Clovis point with the earliest site dated to 11,000 years ago in the Southwest United States.

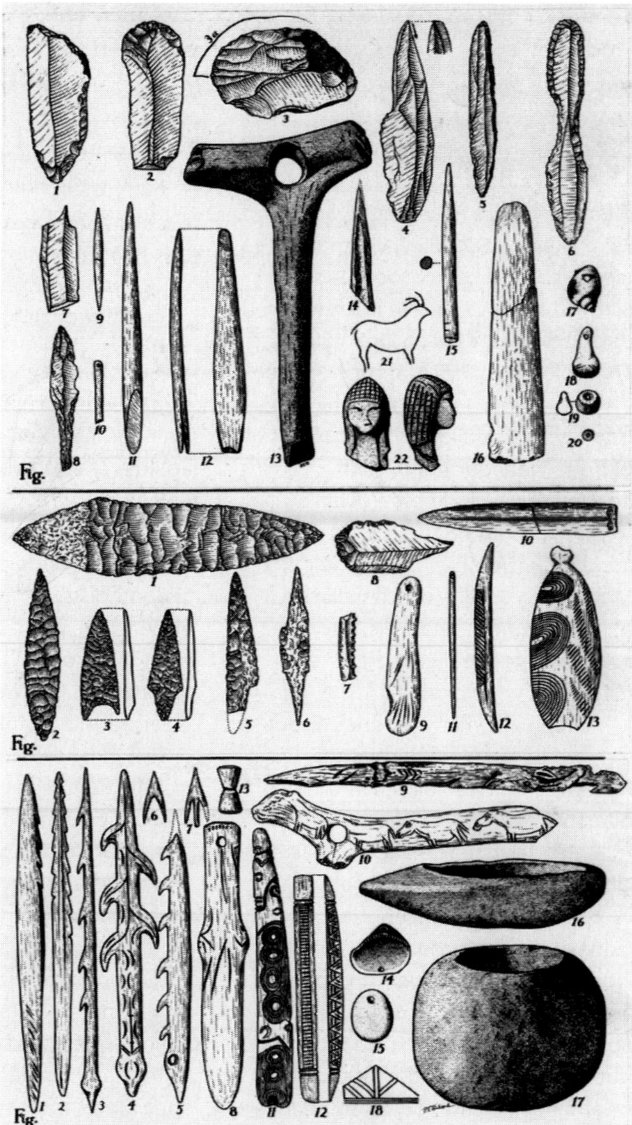

Upper Paleolithic artifacts. These artifacts were made by the earliest modern humans in Europe.

Genetic analysis indicates that all modern humans are descended from a common ancestral population that lived in Africa at least 200,000 years ago (Ingman et al. 2000, Quintana-Murci et al. 1999). There are more different versions of genes in contemporary modern human populations in Africa than in all the rest of the world put together (Tishkoff and Verrelli 2003). This finding is consistent with the view that Africa has been the dominant source of the novel genes and gene combinations of modern humans. Many novel versions of genes originated in African populations and then spread into the Middle East, Asia, and Europe (Pääbo 2003).

MODERN HUMANS DURING THE UPPER PALEOLITHIC IN THE OLD WORLD The **Upper Paleolithic** is the period of modern human occupation in Europe and Eurasia (including the Middle East) 45,000 years ago to 12,000 years ago. During this period, *microliths* and other small, finely made stone and bone tools are the defining elements of technology. Modern humans also made and used tools crafted from organic materials, such as nets and baskets. In many places, they created impressive works of art.

Modern humans, like *Homo erectus* before them, first migrated out of Africa by land to the Middle East, where the oldest modern human fossils outside Africa are found, dated at around 100,000 years ago (Hublin 2000). From there, modern humans probably took a coastal route around the Arabian peninsula, along the coastline of what is now India, and then on to Southeast Asia and the Pacific (Stringer 2000). Modern humans reached Australia around 50,000 years ago. Like the modern humans who later arrived in Europe, modern humans in Australia were prolific artists. Rock paintings in Australia are as old as many of the world-famous Paleolithic cave paintings of Europe.

Other modern humans moved north to Turkey and from there into Eastern and Central Europe. Yet others travelled into Central Asia, Siberia, and eventually the New World.

The arrival of modern humans in Europe marks the beginning of a period of rapidly increasing cultural complexity, often referred to as a cultural revolution or "Golden Age." The first evidence of modern humans in Europe comes from sites in Central Europe, around 40,000 years ago. By around 36,000 years ago, modern humans reached Western Europe. Cultural changes during the European Upper Paleolithic (see Map 2.6) include more complex and specialized tool kits. A major leap forward in symbolic thinking is also indicated by many examples of cave art and portable sculpture.

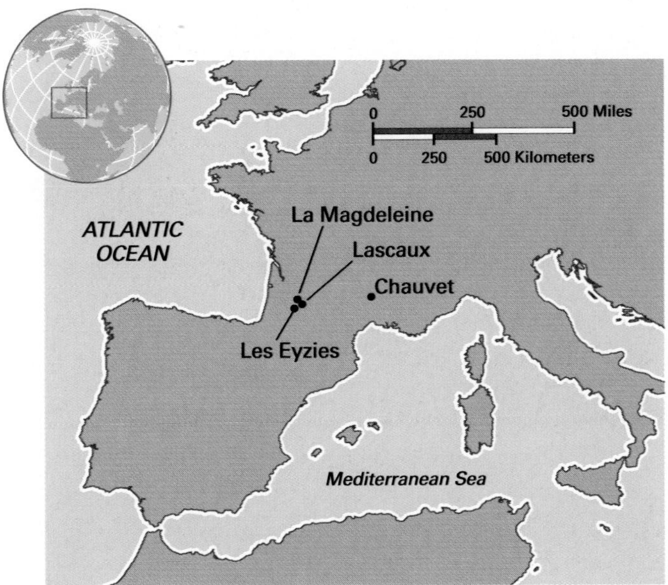

MAP 2.6 Upper Paleolithic Sites in Europe.
This map shows only a small number of the many sites in Europe from the Upper Paleolithic era. Les Eyzies (pronounced lay-zay-zee) is the first site where evidence of Cro Magnons was discovered. Lascaux (pronounced lah-SKOH) and Chauvet (pronounced shoh-VAY) are two of the most important cave art sites in Europe. La Magdeleine (pronounced la-mahd-LEN) is the site for the fourth and last cultural stage of the Upper Paleolithic. At French Magdalenian sites, the main food source of modern humans was reindeer. At Magdalenian sites in Germany and Russia, evidence exists that people had domesticated dogs, perhaps for hunting.

Archaeologists first discovered fossil evidence for modern humans at Cro-Magnon, a rock shelter site in Les Eyzies, France. This site provides the name for the first modern humans in Europe, the **Cro-Magnon** people, who arrived in Europe around 40,000 years ago. Although early Cro-Magnons overlapped in time with Neanderthals, the evidence is unclear as to whether there was interbreeding or cultural exchange.

The Cro-Magnons had a more sophisticated toolkit than the Neanderthals. They also left behind an impressive legacy of art including cave art and portable art. Given their many achievements, some scholars argue that they must have had verbal language. The many cultural accomplishments of the Upper Paleolithic provided the basis for the developments described in the next section of this chapter.

MODERN HUMAN MIGRATIONS INTO THE NEW WORLD By 30,000 years ago, modern humans were migrating from Siberia into present-day Alaska. Two routes are possible: an *ice-free corridor* in Alaska and western Canada, which led them into the rest of North America, and a coastal route. Whichever path they followed, and it may have been both, in just a few thousand years, modern humans had spread throughout most of the unglaciated regions of North America and into Central and South America.

The major body of archaeological evidence about the first modern humans in the New World is that of the **Clovis culture**, a population characterized by the *Clovis point* (Haynes 2002). First discovered in New Mexico (see Map 2.7), a Clovis point is distinct in that it is bifacial and *fluted*, meaning that it has a long, vertical flake chipped from its base. The oldest Clovis sites are dated to slightly before 11,000 years ago, and shortly thereafter Clovis people spread over most of the unglaciated regions of North America (Waters and Stafford 2001, Haynes 2002). Clovis culture, however, lasted only a short while.

For a long time, archaeologists accepted Clovis sites as the earliest human sites in the New World, a position that left a large gap in time between then and when migrants were likely to have begun arriving and settling in the New World, given archaeological data from Siberia. Recently, several claims for pre-Clovis sites have been made. Monte Verde, in Chile, is the most definite of the earliest possible pre-Clovis sites in the New World. It suggests a human presence in South America by 12,500 years ago and raises the possibility of coastal migration and settlements (Dillehay 2000). Recovery of genetic data from *coprolites* (fossilized feces) in a site called Paisley Caves in Oregon proves the existence of modern humans in North America around 12,300 years ago (Gilbert et al. 2008). Such discoveries, with their implications for overthrowing the

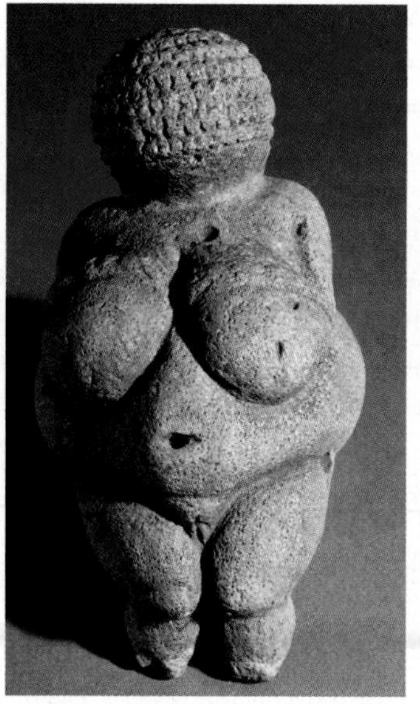

(LEFT) An Upper Paleolithic wall painting at Lascaux, France, depicting a variety of animals. Of the hundreds of figures painted in Lascaux's several galleries, only one depicts a human form, and it has a bird head. (CENTER) A so-called Venus figurine, found at Willendorf, Austria, is carved from fine limestone and is 11 centimeters tall (4 inches). This figurine is 25,000 years old. (RIGHT) A human head carved in mammoth ivory, called the Venus of Brassempouy, is 3.6 centimeters high (an inch and a half). Found in France, it is dated to between 30,000 and 26,000 years ago. Its stratigraphic position was not carefully documented at the time of its discovery. Because of the lack of details about its discovery and its lack of surface corrosion, some archaeologists question its authenticity.

Clovis points are large (11 centimeters long, or about 5 inches), bifacially flaked spear points. So far no evidence of hafting exists, and given the elegant flaking, some archaeologists therefore think that Clovis points were status items. Because many are found near water sources, another theory is that they were made to be used for sacred offerings.

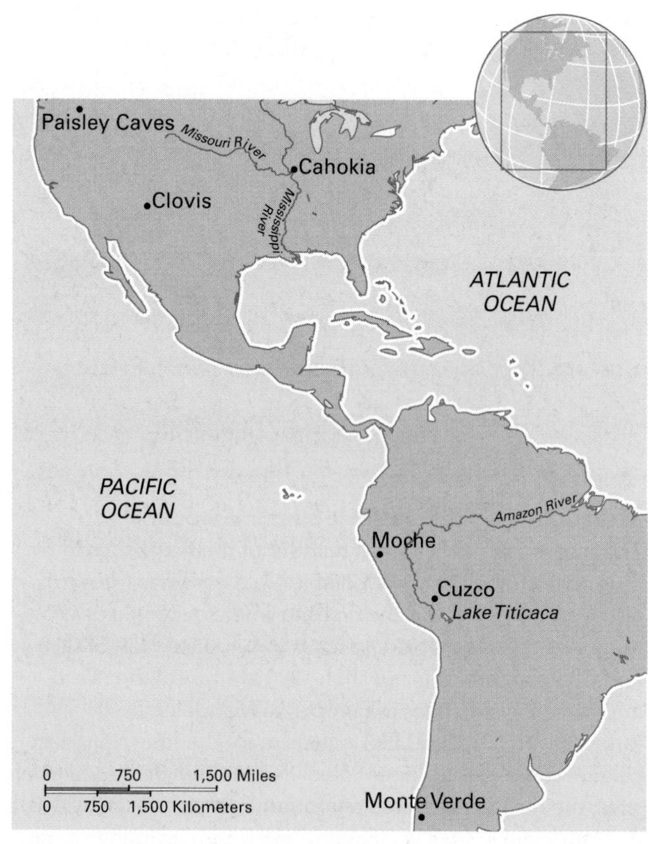

MAP 2.7 New World Sites Mentioned in This Chapter.

Clovis-first theory, create controversy but also open the way for new models of how the New World was occupied.

It is likely there were several migrant streams of modern humans into the New World. Different groups arrived and settled over different periods, and each made its own contribution to the genetic and cultural diversity of New World populations. No matter when, where, and how modern humans arrived in the New World, they spread rapidly over a diverse range of environments and left their enduring mark in settlement sites, artifacts, and fossils.

SUMMARY OF MODERN HUMANS Starting around 300,000 years ago in Africa, modern humans have since then colonized the entire world. Their technological knowledge advanced to include spears and microlithic tools. Plant and animal domestication provided a new degree of control over food sources as well as the ability to follow a more settled life.

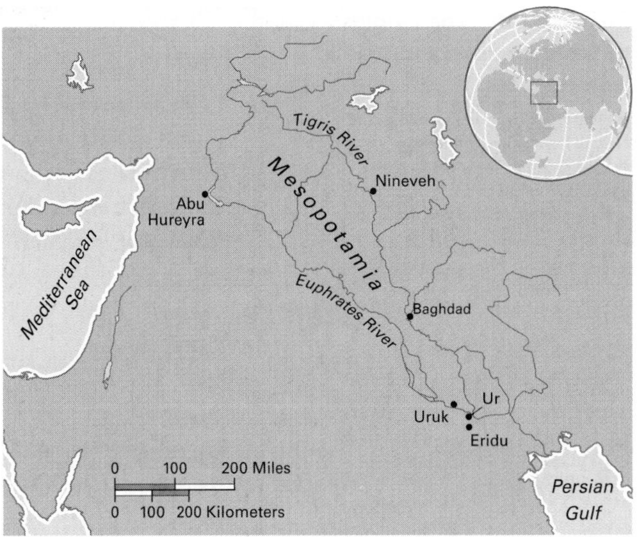

MAP 2.8 Neolithic Sites in the Middle East. Archaeologists have excavated many important Neolithic sites in the Middle East including those mentioned in this chapter, shown here. In Iraq, archaeological sites and artifacts are endangered due to the war and looting.

The Neolithic Revolution and the Emergence of Cities and States

Around 12,000 years ago, people in many places across the world started changing their lives in ways that differed fundamentally from previous times. Many began to live in small, permanent settlements, called **sedentism**. Along with sedentism, people turned to plant and animal domestication instead of relying only on wild foods. Sedentism and plant and animal domestication, along with bipedalism, tool-making, and symbolic communication, are among the most important developments in human evolution (Zeder 2006).

Domestication is the process by which human selection causes changes in the genetic material of plants and animals. Through human selection, new species emerge. The earliest methods of selection could have been as simple as removing undesired plants from around desired plants. Later, more intensive kinds of selection took place, with intentional relocation of desired plants into garden areas. Concerning animal domestication, people may have kept preferred animals and promoted their reproduction while culling less desirable ones. Plant and animal domestication is a major defining feature of humanity's last several thousand years. It supported a new level of food production that promoted the growth of cities and states.

THE NEOLITHIC REVOLUTION

The **Neolithic Revolution** refers to a time of rapid transformation in technology related to plant and animal domestication, including tools such as sickle blades and grinding stones. The story of the Neolithic begins in the Old World in Mesopotamia, especially the region called the *Fertile Crescent* between the Tigris and Euphrates Rivers in present day Iraq (see Map 2.8). Rye, wheat, and barley were first domesticated here, along with animals such as sheep, goats, cattle, and pigs (see Figure 2.6). Domestication of other plants and animals occurred in the Middle East, Africa, North America, Central America, and South America. Some of these events resulted from independent invention, or the creation of a new idea, behavior, or object. In others, diffusion, or the spread of culture through contact, was responsible for the Neolithic transition.

The stages of plant and animal domestication are revealed at several sites in the Middle East. One such site, Abu Hureyra (ah-boo hoo-RYUH-rah) is located near the Euphrates River (Moore et al. 2000). At the time, the region was rich in forest resources and wild grasses, and the climate was warmer and wetter than today. Abu Hureyra, like many Neolithic sites in the region, is a **tell**, a human-made mound resulting from the accumulation of successive generations of

---

sedentism a lifestyle associated with residence in permanent villages, towns, and cities, generally linked with the emergence of farming.

domestication a process by which human selection causes changes in the genetic material of plants and animals.

Neolithic Revolution a time of rapid transformation in technology, related to plant and animal domestication, which includes tools such as sickle blades and grinding stones.

tell a human-made mound resulting from the accumulation of successive generations of house construction, reconstruction, and trash.

FIGURE 2.6 The Origins of Selected Plant and Animal Domesticates.

Source: From *The Human Impact on the Natural Enviroments*, 5th Edition, by Andrew Goudie. Copyright © 2004. Blackwell Publishers Ltd. Reproduced with permission of Blackwell Publishers & Andrew Goudie.

Plants	Region	Approximate Date BCE
Barley, wheat	Middle East	8000–7000
Squash, gourd, maize	Central America	7000–6000
White potato, chile pepper	South America	7000–6000
Rice, millet, water chestnut	East Asia	6000–5000
Pearl millet, sorghum	Africa	3000
African rice	Africa	3000
Animals		
Dog	Russia, Eastern Europe	10,000
Sheep, goat	Middle East	7000
Pig, cattle	Middle East	6000
Chicken	China	6000
Horse	Central Asia	4000
Llama, alpaca	South America	4000
Donkey	Middle East	3500
Bactrian camel	Central Asia	2000
Dromedary camel	Middle East	2000
Turkey	Central America	Unknown

house construction, reconstruction, and trash. Over thousands of years, tells gradually rose above the surrounding plain. The tell at Abu Hureyra is 8 meters high (about 25 feet), and it was occupied from 10,500 to 6000 BCE. The *stratigraphy* (study of the layers over time) of the tell provides the story of change during the Neolithic. The first occupants lived in a village of between 200 and 300 people. They were *sedentary foragers,* whose livelihood depended on hunting and gathering but who lived in a permanent settlement rather than in temporary camps. This residence pattern suggests that the environment could provide adequate food and water, within a fairly narrow region. They hunted gazelle and collected wild plants, including cereals, lentils, fruits, nuts, and berries.

The next levels at the site show the stages in the transition to plant domestication. By 10,000 BCE, the occupants had domesticated rye. After 9000 BCE, they had domesticated wheat and barley. The first domestic grains were probably produced on a small scale through gardening or *horticulture,* defined in Chapter 4 as the growing of domesticated plants by using hand-held tools and relying on natural sources of moisture and soil enrichment. Hunting gazelle was still important, and gazelle constituted 80 percent of the animal food that people ate. Later levels provide evidence of a fully Neolithic lifestyle combining sedentism and domesticated plants and animals, including two herd animals: goats and sheep. Perhaps because of an increasingly arid environment and human over-hunting, the gazelle population had declined, and domesticated animals gradually took their place as sources of animal meat. The scarcity of wild animals may have prompted people to domesticate replacements.

The village grew to 6000 inhabitants by 7000 BCE, when sedentary life was combined with a more intensive form of domesticated grain production called *agriculture* or *farming,* defined in Chapter 4 as the growing of crops on permanent plots of land by using the plow, irrigation, and fertilizer. The series of sequential transitions at Abu Hureyra is typical of those at other sites in the Middle East.

A different pattern of domesticates emerged in Africa's *Sahel,* the grassland regions south of the Sahara desert. For thousands of years, foragers had occupied this region of rich lakesides and abundant wild grasses. Their economy combined

British archaeologists discovered the important Neolithic site of Çatalhöyük (shah-tall-hoy-yuck) in 1958. It is located in south-central Turkey (see Map 14.4, p. 362) and dates to around 7000 BCE. So far, only a small portion of the tell has been excavated.

Stonehenge, in southern England, is the most well-known late Neolithic monumental site. Many similar, though smaller, henge monuments exist in the British Isles and elsewhere in Europe and northern Africa. A henge monument is a construction in the shape of a circular enclosure with an opening at one point in the circle. They are generally interpreted as ceremonial sites. The latest evidence about Stonehenge indicates that it was also a burial ground.

fishing, hunting herd animals, and harvesting wild grasses such as millet, sorghum, and African rice. The domestication of cattle was the first step in the transition to the Neolithic in Africa (Marshall and Hildebrand 2002). The domestication of wild cattle supported the emergence of *pastoralism,* defined in Chapter 4 as an economic strategy in which people depend on domesticated animals for most of their food and which continues to be an important mode of livelihood in the region today.

The transition to the Neolithic in Europe relied on the introduction of plant and animal domesticates from the Middle East. The first plant and animal domesticates appeared in southeastern Europe around 6000 BCE (Richards 2003). By 4000 BCE, the combination of farming and keeping animals had spread across most of Europe. Archaeological evidence for the later Neolithic in Europe documents social status differences, group ceremonies and feasts, and religious sites that drew thousands of pilgrims from wide areas.

PLANT AND ANIMAL DOMESTICATION IN THE NEW WORLD Plant domestication in the New World first began in Middle America (or *Mesoamerica*), the region between North and South America. Later transitions in South America and North America occurred partly through independent invention and partly through the spread of *maize* (corn). Three features distinguish the pattern of plant and animal domestication and sedentism in Middle America:

- The first experiments with domesticated plants took place long before sedentism.
- The first domesticated plants were gourds, squash, beans, and maize, and the first animal domesticates were dogs, turkeys, and honey bees.
- The transition to an entirely agricultural way of life was slower than in the Middle East, extending from 8000 to 2000 BCE.

By 5000 BCE, three domesticated plant species were the most important parts of the diet in Mexico, the so-called *Mesoamerican triad:* maize (corn), squash, and beans. People in the Andes Mountains first domesticated the potato, a member of the tuber family of root crops (Ochoa 1991). Tubers are difficult to find archaeologically because they spread by sending out shoots underground rather than by seeds. Thus the date of 5000 BCE for potato domestication is conjectural, based on the assumption that it occurred around the time of other Andean domesticates, including beans, quinoa (a seed), llamas, alpacas, and guinea pigs. Gourds and squash were domesticated in Ecuador by 10,000 BCE.

By 4000 BCE, people in eastern North America were experimenting with various plants as part of a mixed economic strategy of hunting, collecting wild plants, and cultivating a few domesticated species of seed crops (Smith 1998). The most important indigenous domesticates were seed crops such as goosefoot (similar to spinach, but also grown for its seeds and related to quinoa of South America), sunflowers, and possibly squash. None of these plants, however, could support a sedentary farming population. Between the first and third centuries of the present era, it was the introduction of maize that led to the emergence of farming communities throughout North America.

CITIES AND STATES

The word *civilization* literally means "living in cities." A *city* is distinguished from a village or town by having a larger population (more than 10,000 people as a rough guide) and by having more occupational specialization, more elaborate architecture, and central services such as temples, government agencies, and trade organizations. Along with urbanization came the growth of the political institution of the state. A *state,* as defined in Chapter 10, is a centralized political organization encompassing many communities. States are typically bureaucratic; that is, they have specialized units with authority over limited areas of governance, with trained personnel and usually written records. States have the power to levy taxes, keep the peace through use of legitimate force, and wage war.

Cities and states first emerged in the Old World, once again in what is now Iraq. Mesopotamia, which means "the land between two rivers," referring to the Tigris and the Euphrates, is the home of the world's earliest cities, dated to 3500 BCE. Important early cities in Mesopotamia include Uruk, Ur, Eridu, and Nineveh, all of which were preeminent at different times (see Map 2.8).

Uruk is a well-studied Mesopotamian city. By 3500 BCE, its population was around 10,000 people and it grew to a peak of 50,000 (Adams 1981). People lived in houses, made of dried mud-brick, which were packed tightly together and interspersed with narrow, winding streets (Pollock 1999). Surrounding Uruk was a massive brick wall 7 meters (23 feet) high, its numerous gates and guard towers suggesting the need for defense. Monumental architecture included a prominent feature called a *ziggurat,* a massive stepped platform that supported temples and administrative buildings. Government and religion were closely connected, so temples served both sacred and secular purposes, including storage and redistribution of agricultural surpluses, craft production, and economic management and recordkeeping. Commoner laborers and slaves built and maintained the monumental buildings in which state rule and commerce were managed; they wove the fine linen garments that elite men and women wore; and they pressed the high-quality oils consumed at royal feasts.

Early Mesopotamian cities were centers of regional trade, a feature that some archaeologists view as the primary catalyst for the urban revolution (Algaze 2001). Trade is also probably the catalyst for the development of the world's earliest money and writing. Writing was first invented between 3500 and 3000 BCE in Mesopotamia, for financial recordkeeping (Lawler 2001). Mesopotamian writing, or *cuneiform,* used around 1500 signs, many of which referred to specific goods such as bread and oil. Specially trained scribes worked in administrative roles in what was an early sort of *bureaucracy,* a form of administration that is hierarchical and specialized and relies heavily on recordkeeping. The hundreds of thousands of cuneiform tablets that archaeologists have found in early Mesopotamian cities provide a wealth of information about life at the time.

In the New World, cities and states formed later than in the Old World. Another distinct feature is that some New World states, though powerful and extensive, did not have writing. They did, however, have elaborately constructed capital cities, lavish political feasting, competitive sports, and plentiful gold and other wealth.

The Moche or Mochica civilization emerged around 200 BCE in the deserts of Peru's north coast. Rivers descending from the Andes Mountains fed irrigation works that supported agricultural production to supply dense urban populations (Billman 2002). The Moche civilization is known for distinctive artistic styles and craftwork, especially mold-made portrait vessels and copper, silver, and gold metalwork (Quilter 2002). Warfare was an important component of state formation in the Andes, and Moche ceramics often depict warfare and human sacrifice. Moche civilization reached its

(LEFT) The remains of Uruk in southern Mesopotamia. Occupied starting around 5000 BCE, Uruk had the earliest, grandest, and most numerous monumental buildings in Mesopotamia. The Uruk period saw many innovations including the potter's wheel and the development of writing. (RIGHT) An artist's reconstruction of Anu Ziggurat and the White Temple at Uruk, around 3100 BCE. No written documents exist to indicate the amount of labor involved in constructing such monuments, but it was obviously substantial.

height during the first few centuries of the Common Era. At this time, other civilizations were flourishing throughout the Andes, supported by a successful form of agriculture that was well adapted to high altitudes. It relied on a system of raised fields interspersed by canals. This form of agriculture, over time, fell out of practice, but archaeologists discovered evidence of it. Through their efforts, raised field farming is now reviving in the Andes and helping to provide increased food yields (see the Lessons Applied box).

At the time of the Spanish Conquest in 1532, the Inca had formed the largest empire in the world (MacCormack 2001). The empire was vast, stretching from Colombia in the north to Chile in the south. The city of Cuzco was the empire's capital, and it was linked to distant provinces by a network of roads and bridges. Llamas and alpacas were important domesticated animals, used for their wool and meat and also as pack animals. Hundreds of varieties of potatoes, the most important food crop, were grown on terraced hillsides. The Inca, although a large and powerful empire, had no writing system. Instead, administrators used a system of knotted cords called *khipu* for recordkeeping (see photo on p. 307).

In North America, many complex societies emerged, from the pueblo sites of the southwestern United States to the Iroquois nation of the northeast into Canada. They developed extensive trade networks, engaged in long-distance warfare, and built massive and enduring earthwork monuments. Politically, these societies did not develop state-level institutions but, rather, remained as complex chiefdoms that functioned without urban centers (Earle 1993).

The *Mississippian cultures,* dated to the first century of the Common Era, were located on or near the floodplains of rivers and were based on maize cultivation. Mississippian centers had earthen platform mounds that supported elite residences, ceremonial areas, and burial mounds. Local leaders gained status through the exchange of prestige goods, in which exotic materials and finished goods were traded over large distances (Peregrine 1992). One of the largest Mississippian centers was Cahokia, in present-day Illinois, which gained regional prominence around the year 1000 (Pauketat 2004). Cahokia is located on a vast floodplain where the Mississippi, Ohio, and Missouri Rivers meet. Fish and waterfowl were plentiful, and maize grew in abundance in the fertile and well-watered soil of the floodplain. Terrestrial game was available in the forested uplands. Control over the intersection of several major exchange routes was a key factor in Cahokia's rise to prominence. Enormous for its time and place, Cahokia covered an area of 13 square kilometers, with a peak population of several thousand people. The site contains a large rectangular plaza surrounded by more than 100 earthwork mounds. The largest, Monk's Mound, was 30 meters (over 98 feet) high and is the largest earthwork in North America. Monk's Mound was built in stages between 900 and 1200 CE. The extent of mound construction at Cahokia is a testament to the organizational capacity of the Cahokian political system to harness labor for construction on a grand scale.

Like other powerful chiefdoms, Cahokia had marked social inequality. This inequality is evident in burials, with abundant prestige goods marking high-status burials. Status and gender differences in diet confirm dietary inequalities (Ambrose et al. 2003). High-status people ate more animal protein and less maize, whereas the diet of low-status people was more dependent on maize. Men ate more protein and less maize than women. The diet of low-status women had the highest proportion of maize, about 60 percent.

Moche portrait vessels, considered a brilliant art style, flourished on the northern coast of Peru around the year 500. Many of the pieces depict high-status males with elaborate headdresses and face painting. This piece depicts a woman carrying a load.

▶ *Do research to learn whether the vessels are portraits of actual people or represent generic social categories.*

THINKING OUTSIDE THE BOX

Consider the importance of domesticated guinea pigs as food sources in Central and South America and as family pets in North America. What is the likelihood that guinea pigs will become a popular food source in North America and a popular household pet in Central and South America?

LESSONS applied

Archaeology Findings Increase Food Production in Bolivia

An archaeological research project near the shores of Lake Titicaca in highland Bolivia uncovered prehistoric remains of raised fields separated by an intricate system of canals (Straughan and Schuler 1991). When the Spanish colonialists arrived, they abandoned the raised-field system and replaced it with their own type of cultivation. In the later twentieth century, Bolivian farmers were struggling to produce adequate crops of potatoes from the boggy soil. Frosts also took their toll on the plants before they matured.

Two archaeologists who had been working in the region for several years convinced a local farmer to experiment with the indigenous raised-field system, suggesting that what worked a thousand years ago might succeed again. The other villagers were skeptical but watched with interest as the potato plants on the raised field grew taller than they had ever seen. Then, right before the harvest, 90 percent of the village crop was lost due to a heavy frost. Most of the potatoes in the experimental raised field, however, were fine. They had been protected by a thick mist that had formed over the field. The sun's warmth during the day heats up the canal water, which, in turn, warms the fields at night when the temperature drops.

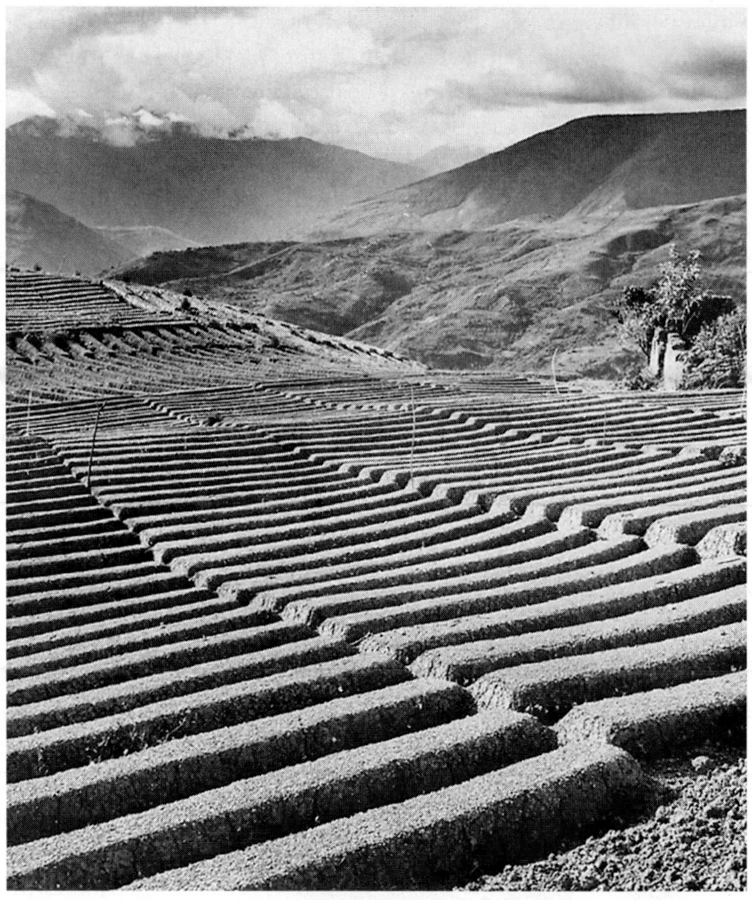

Raised beds in Bolivia. This strategy helps prevent erosion, improves the organic content of the soil, captures moisture, and provides protection for crops from frosts. The main feature of the system, termed *waru waru* in the Quechua language, is a network of embankments and canals.

▶ *To find out more about this system, go to* http://www.loas.usde/publications/Unit/oca59ec/ch27.html.

The community eventually adopted the new–old system, and crop yields rose significantly. Moreover, algae and aquatic plants began to grow in the canals along with nitrogen-fixing bacteria. When the canals are cleaned annually, they yield a rich residue of organic material that can be used to fertilize the fields. The Bolivian government has started a training program to promote the raised-field technique as a way to increase the nation's food supply. Local people now welcome the archaeologists with enthusiasm when they visit. The Lake Titicaca region, once the center of a rich civilization, was reduced to poverty by the effects of European colonialism. Now, through archaeological findings about the past, the agricultural economy is reviving and thriving.

The site of Cahokia suffered substantial damage in the late 1800s and early 1900s as a result of urban development, construction of roads and railways, expansion of farmland, and amateur collecting (Young and Fowler 2000). Many mounds were bulldozed, and their contents, including human bones and artifacts such as copper goods and shell beads, were used as land fill. Concern expressed by a few archaeologists raised public awareness and put a halt to the destruction and neglect. Cahokia is now a World Heritage Site, and Native American groups from across the United States hold regular ceremonies there.

anthropogenic caused by humans.

An artist's reconstruction of Cahokia showing thatch-roofed houses and massive earthworks. The site reached prominence around the year 1000 CE (Common Era) and was largely abandoned by 1400 CE.

▶ *Visit the website* www.cahokiamounds.com/cahokia.html.

CIVILIZATIONS ARE NOT FOREVER Comparative analysis of many early states shows that all past states have gone through cycles of expansion and decline followed by the rise of new states. (Marcus 1998). In fact, periods of decline, rather than the more archaeologically visible episodes of powerful territorial states, are the norm. Why do even the most powerful states always collapse? The answer may lie in the difficulty states have of maintaining territorial integration and extreme social inequality over long periods. Another factor may be the environmental decline that accompanies state building and accumulation. Some archaeologists think that **anthropogenic** (caused by humans) effects on the environment, such as clearing forests and exhausting the soil, contributed to the collapse of many great and powerful civilizations. Changes during the Neolithic and urban revolutions shed light on humanity's prospects in the future and could provide important cautionary notes about the costs and sustainability of "civilization."

2

the BIG questions REVISITED

◆ What do living nonhuman primates tell us about human culture?

Humans belong to the category of primates. Primates vary in size from several ounces to over 400 pounds. All nonhuman primates in the wild provide for their food needs by foraging. Most primates live in a social group.

According to genetic data, modern humans are closely related to the living great apes with which we share a common ancestor between 4 and 8 million years ago. The category of great apes includes the four largest ape species: orangutans, gorillas, chimpanzees, and bonobos. Of these, chimpanzees and bonobos are genetically the most closely related to humans. Although chimpanzees and bonobos are alike in many ways, they also have several differences. Neither the chimpanzee or bonobo model applies neatly to all modern human cultures.

Many nonhuman primate species have behaviors that are learned and shared and are thus cultural. Examples include tool use for procuring food and symbolic forms of greeting and interaction.

◆ What role did culture play during hominin evolution?

Hominins is a category of primates that includes modern humans and extinct species of early human ancestors that are more closely related to humans than to living chimpanzees and bonobos. Hominin evolution can be divided into three stages: the early hominins, archaic *Homo,* and modern humans.

The early hominins span from 8 million years ago to 2 million years ago. The two oldest species, *Sahelanthropus tchadensis* and *Orrorin tugenensis* are important, respectively, for showing that early hominins extended from East Africa into West-Central Africa, and they were bipedal. Australopithecines refers to a category of several extinct species of early hominins found in East and southern Africa. The australopithecine era provides the first stone tools.

Archaic *Homo* includes extinct hominin species that lived from 2.4 million years to 19,000 years ago and had a more modern human-like body shape, larger brains, and smaller jaws and teeth. Stone tools are prominent in the culture of all archaic *Homo* species. One species, *Homo erectus,* is the first hominin species to live widely throughout the Old World. The last archaic *Homo* species, the Neanderthals, are known from many sites in Eurasia. They had some aspects of culture including the beginning of art and music and possibly verbal language.

According to archaeological evidence, modern humans evolved in Africa starting 300,000 years ago, though the earliest fossil evidence is from 160,000 years ago. From Africa, they migrated to the Middle East and Asia, later to Central Asia and Europe, and finally to the New World. The Upper Paleolithic is the period of modern human occupation in Eurasia. The first modern humans in Europe are the Cro-Magnons, who are associated with microlithic tools and cave art.

◆ How has modern human culture changed in the past 12,000 years?

Around 12,000 years ago, some people started changing their lives in ways that differed fundamentally from previous times. The first major change was a trend toward sedentism. With increased sedentism, people turned to plant and animal domestication instead of relying on only wild foods. Plant and animal domestication is a major defining feature of humanity's last several thousand years. It provided new types of foods, such as grains, and an increased level of food production that supported the growth of cities and states.

The Neolithic Revolution was a time of rapid transformation in technology, including tools such as sickle blades and grinding stones. The Neolithic began in Mesopotamia, where plants such as wheat, and barley were first domesticated along with animals such as sheep, goats, cattle, and pigs. Domestication of a different array of plants and animals occurred in the Middle East, Africa, China, and the New World.

Following sedentism and domestication, cities developed and then the state as a new form of political organization. Cities and states first emerged in Mesopotamia. In the New World, cities and states formed later than in the Old World. Some New World states operated without writing. In North America, complex societies emerged with extensive trade networks, long-distance warfare, and massive earthwork monuments, but without a state organization.

KEY CONCEPTS

Acheulian tradition, p. 43
Anatomically Modern Humans (AMH) or ***Homo sapiens,*** p. 47
anthropogenic, p. 57
archaic *Homo*, p. 43
artifact, p. 34
australopithecines, p. 41
bipedalism, p. 40
brachiation, p. 36
Clovis culture, p. 49
Cro-Magnons, p. 49
domestication, p. 51
evolution, p. 34
foraging, p. 35
fossil, p. 34
great apes, p. 36
hominins, p. 40
knuckle-walking, p. 37
Mousterian tradition, p. 46
natural selection, p. 34
Neolithic Revolution, p. 51
Oldowan tradition, p. 43
primates, p. 34
savanna, p. 42
sedentism, p. 51
sociality, p. 35
tell, p. 51
Upper Paleolithic, p. 48

SUGGESTED READINGS

David W. Anthony. *The Horse, the Wheel, and Language*. Princeton, NJ: Princeton University Press, 2007. The author links the domestication of horses around 4800 years ago and then the invention of the wheel to the spread of the Proto-Indo-European language, which at the time existed only in spoken form.

Julian Caldecott and Lera Miles. *World Atlas of Great Apes and Their Conservation.* Berkeley: University of California Press, 2005. This overview describes the current distribution and status of the great apes and information on their ecology and behavior, habitat requirements, conservation efforts, and additional protection needed.

Thomas Dillehay. *The Settlement of the Americas: A New Prehistory.* New York: Basic Books, 2000. This book details efforts to determine who the first modern humans in the Americas were. It reviews dating, paleoenvironments, stone tools, and cultural and linguistic traditions from Paleoindian sites.

Frans de Waal and Frans Lanting. *Bonobo: The Forgotten Ape.* Berkeley: University of California Press, 1998. The book describes the behavior and ecology of bonobos. It covers social relationships, leadership, parent–offspring ties, sexuality, and the relevance of bonobos as the best model for humans.

William C. McGrew. *Chimpanzee Material Culture.* Cambridge: Cambridge University Press, 1992. McGrew discusses chimpanzee behavior as observed at several long-term field sites. Topics include chimpanzee culture and similarities and differences between humans and chimpanzees.

Jeffrey K. McKee. *The Riddled Chain: Chance, Coincidence, and Chaos in Human Evolution.* New Brunswick, NJ: Rutgers University Press, 2000. The author argues that the evidence for linking hominin evolution with changes in the paleoclimates is weak and suggests that paleoanthropologists should pay more attention to the role of chance.

Sarah Milledge Nelson, ed. *Worlds of Gender: The Archaeology of Women's Lives around the Globe.* New York: AltaMira Press, 2007. Chapters in this book provide case studies of gender in archaeology. They show how much a "gendered past" reveals about the variety of ancient social structures.

Sue Savage-Rumbaugh, Stuart G. Shanker, and Talbot J. Taylor. *Apes, Language, and the Human Mind.* Oxford: Oxford University Press, 2001. This book discusses the upbringing of Kanzi, a bonobo who learned to understand spoken English and to communicate using pictorial symbols called lexigrams.

G. J. Sawyer and Viktor Deak, eds. *The Last Human: A Guide to Twenty-Two Species of Extinct Humans.* New York: Yale University Press, 2007. This book provides information on each species in terms of its emergence, chronology, habitat, lifestyle, and cultural capabilities.

Kathy D. Schick and Nicholas Toth. *Making Silent Stones Speak: Human Evolution and the Dawn of Technology.* New York: Simon and Schuster, 1993. The authors trace the prehistory of stone tools from their earliest appearance in the archaeological record up to modern humans.

Eugenie C. Scott. *Evolution vs. Creationism: An Introduction.* Berkeley: University of California Press, 2004. Scott surveys the debate in the United States about teaching evolution in schools. She discusses diverse religious points of view and the scientific evidence for human evolution.

Bruce D. Smith. *The Emergence of Agriculture.* New York: Scientific American Library, 1998. This volume offers an account of the rise of food production in eight world regions, seeking the common processes at work in this transition.

David Whitley, ed. *Handbook of Rock Art Research.* Walnut Creek, CA: AltaMira Press, 2001. An overview of prehistoric rock art worldwide, this volume addresses a wide range of topics from analysis of the meaning of rock art depictions to questions of conservation.

Gregory D. Wilson. *The Archaeology of Everyday Life at Early Moundville.* Tuscaloosa, AL: University of Alabama Press, 2008. This study describes life in a Mississippian polity in west-central Alabama between the twelfth and fifteenth centuries CE.

Cultural anthropologist Robert Bailey and biological anthropologist Nadine Peacock, members of a Harvard University fieldwork team, conversing with some Ituri people who live in the rainforests of the eastern part of the Democratic Republic of Congo.

RESEARCHING CULTURE

the BIG questions

- How do cultural anthropologists conduct research about culture?
- What does fieldwork involve?
- What are some urgent issues in cultural anthropology research today?

This chapter is about how cultural anthropologists do research to learn about people's shared and learned behavior and beliefs, and how they change over time. The first section discusses how methods in cultural anthropology have evolved since the late nineteenth century. The second section covers the steps involved in a research project. The chapter concludes by addressing two urgent topics in cultural anthropology research.

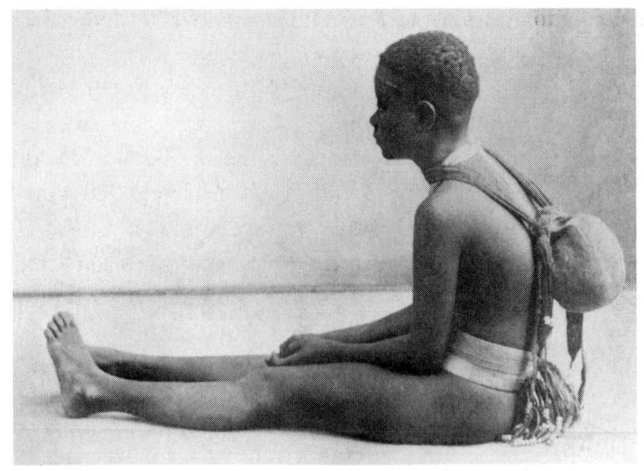

Ethnographic research in the early twentieth century often involved photography. The girl shown here wears the skull of her deceased sister. Indigenous people of the Andaman Islands revere the bones of their dead relatives and would not want them to be taken away, studied, or displayed in a museum.

◆◆◆

Changing Research Methods in Cultural Anthropology

Methods in cultural anthropology today are different in several ways from those used during the nineteenth century. Most cultural anthropologists now gather data by doing **fieldwork**, going to the field, which is wherever people and cultures are, to learn about culture through direct observation. They also use a variety of specialized research techniques.

FROM THE ARMCHAIR TO THE FIELD

The term *armchair anthropology* refers to how early cultural anthropologists conducted research by sitting and reading about other cultures. They read reports written by travelers, missionaries, and explorers but never visited those places or had any kind of direct experience with the people. Sir Edward Tylor, who proposed the first definition of culture in 1871, as noted in Chapter 1, was an armchair anthropologist. Sir James Frazer, another famous founding figure of anthropology, was also an armchair anthropologist. He wrote *The Golden Bough* (1978 [1890]), a multivolume collection of myths, rituals, and symbols that he compiled from his wide reading.

In the late nineteenth and early twentieth centuries, anthropologists hired by European colonial governments moved a step closer to learning directly about the people of other cultures. They traveled to colonized countries in Africa and Asia, where they lived near, but not with, the people they were studying. This approach is called *verandah anthropology* because, typically, the anthropologist would send out for "natives" to come to his verandah for interviewing (verandah anthropologists, like armchair anthropologists, were men). A classic example of verandah anthropology is A. R. Radcliffe-Brown's research on the Andaman Islanders (see Culturama, p. 67). When he went to South Andaman Island at the turn of the twentieth century, the indigenous population had been greatly reduced by diseases brought in by the British colonizers and by the effects of direct colonial violence. Radcliffe-Brown's assignment was to do *salvage anthropology*, to collect what data he could from the remaining people in order to document their language, social life, and religious beliefs.

A bit earlier, in the United States during the mid-nineteenth century, Lewis Henry Morgan had taken steps toward learning about people through direct observation. A lawyer, Morgan lived in Rochester, New York, near the Iroquois territory. He became well acquainted with many of the Iroquois (Tooker 1992). These experiences provided Morgan with important insights into their everyday lives. His writings changed the prevailing Euro-American perception of the Iroquois, and other Native American tribes, as "dangerous savages." Morgan showed that Iroquois behavior and beliefs make sense if an outsider spends time learning about them through direct experience.

PARTICIPANT OBSERVATION

A major turning point in how cultural anthropologists do research occurred in the early twentieth century, during World War I, laying the foundation for the current cornerstone method in cultural anthropology: fieldwork combined with participant observation. **Participant observation** is a research

---

fieldwork research in the field, which is any place where people and culture are found.

participant observation basic fieldwork method in cultural anthropology that involves living in a culture for a long period of time while gathering data.

multisited research fieldwork conducted in more than one location in order to understand the behaviors and ideas of dispersed members of a culture or the relationships among different levels such as state policy and local culture.

method for learning about culture that involves living in a culture for an extended period while gathering data.

The "father" of participant observation is Bronislaw Malinowski. He adopted what was, at the time, an innovative approach to learning about culture while he was in the Trobriand Islands in the South Pacific during World War I (see Culturama, p. 67). For two years, he lived in a tent alongside the local people, participating in their activities and living, as much as possible, as one of them. Through this process adopted by Malinowski, the key elements of participant observation were established:

- Living with the people
- Participating in their everyday life
- Learning the language

By living with the people and participating in their daily round of life, Malinowski learned about their culture in context rather than through secondhand reports. By learning the local language, he could talk with the people without the use of interpreters and thus gain a much more accurate understanding of their culture.

In this early phase of fieldwork and participant observation, a primary goal was to record as much as possible of a people's language, songs, rituals, and social life because many cultures were disappearing. Most early cultural anthropologists did fieldwork in small, relatively isolated cultures. They thought they could study everything about such cultures; those were the days of holism (defined in Chapter 1). Typically, the anthropologist (a White man) would go off with his notebooks to collect data on a standardized list of topics including economics, family life, politics, religion, language, art and crafts, and more.

Today, few if any such seemingly isolated cultures remain. Cultural anthropologists have devised new research methods so that they can study larger-scale cultures, global–local connections, and cultural change. One methodological innovation of the late twentieth century is especially important in addressing these new issues: **multisited research**, which is fieldwork conducted on a topic in more than one location (Marcus 1995). Although especially helpful in studying migrant populations in their place of origin and their new location, multisited research is useful for studying many topics.

Lanita Jacobs-Huey conducted multisited fieldwork in order to learn about the language and culture of hairstyles among African American women (2002). She chose a range of sites throughout the United States and in London, England, in order to explore the many facets of the far-from-simple topic of hair: beauty salons, regional and international hair expos and training seminars, Bible study meetings of a nonprofit group of Christian cosmetologists, standup comedy clubs, a computer-mediated discussion about the politics of Black hair, and a cosmetology school in Charleston, South Carolina.

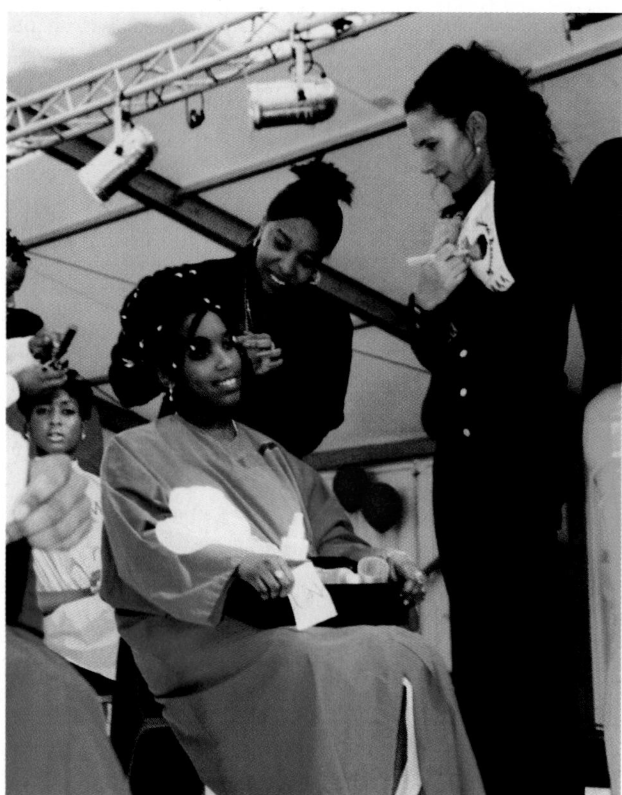

Lanita Jacobs-Huey's fieldsites include hairstyling competitions throughout the United States and in London, England. Here, a judge evaluates the work of a student stylist at the Afro Hair & Beauty Show in London.

Doing Fieldwork in Cultural Anthropology

Fieldwork in cultural anthropology can be exciting, frustrating, scary, boring, and sometimes dangerous. One thing is true: It transforms the lives of everyone involved. This section explores the stages of a fieldwork research project, starting with the initial planning and ending with the analysis and presentation of the findings.

THINKING OUTSIDE THE BOX

As you read this chapter, consider the similarities and differences between research in cultural anthropology and research in other disciplines such as biology, psychology, political science, economics, and history.

In focusing on a single commodity, cultural anthropologists reveal much about local and global cultures. (TOP) Children working on a sugarcane plantation in the Philippines. (CENTER) A model dressed as "Miss Chiquita" stands in front of the Brandenburg Gate in Berlin during Germany's International Green Week and agricultural fair. (BOTTOM) Villagers chewing coca leaves in highland Peru.

informed consent an aspect of fieldwork ethics requiring that the researcher inform the research participants of the intent, scope, and possible effects of the study and seek their consent to be in the study.

BEGINNING THE FIELDWORK PROCESS

Before going to the field, the prospective researcher must select a research topic and prepare for the fieldwork itself. These steps are critical to the success of the project.

PROJECT SELECTION Finding a topic for a research project is a basic first step. The topic should be important and feasible. Cultural anthropologists often find a topic to research by carrying out a *literature review*, or reading what others have already written assessing its adequacy. Conducting a literature review often exposes a gap in previous research. For example, cultural anthropologists realized during the 1970s that anthropological research had bypassed women and girls, and this is how feminist anthropology began (B. Miller 1993).

Notable events sometimes inspire a research topic. The HIV/AIDS epidemic and its rapid spread continue to prompt research. The recent rise in the numbers of international migrants and refugees is another pressing area for study. The fall of state socialism in Russia and Eastern Europe shifted attention to that region. Conflict situations in Afghanistan, Iraq, Sudan, and other places spur cultural anthropologists to ask what causes such conflicts and how post-conflict reconstruction can be most effectively accomplished (Lubkemann 2005).

Some cultural anthropologists choose to study the cultural context of a particular material item, such as sugar (Mintz 1985), cars (D. Miller 2001), beef (Caplan 2000), money (R. Foster 2002), shea butter (Chalfin 2004), wedding dresses (Foster and Johnson 2003), coca (Allen 2002), or cocaine (Taussig 2004). The material item provides a focus for understanding the social relations surrounding its production, use, and trade, and what it means in terms of people's changing identities.

Another idea for a research project is a *restudy*, fieldwork conducted in a previously researched community. Many decades of previous research provide baseline information on which later studies can build. It makes sense to examine changes that have occurred or to look at the culture from a new angle. For her doctoral dissertation research, Annette Weiner (1976) decided to go to the Trobriand Islands, following in the footsteps of Malinowski, to learn what people's lives were like over 50 years after his fieldwork. What she found there prompted her to change her original research plans (see Critical Thinking and Culturama, this chapter).

Even luck can lead to a research topic. Spanish anthropologist María Cátedra (1992) stumbled on an important issue during exploratory fieldwork in rural northern Spain (see Map 3.5). A suicide occurred in a village in the mountains near where she was staying. The local people did not consider the suicide remarkable or strange. In fact, the area had a high rate of suicide. Later she went back and did long-term research on the social dynamics of suicide in this area.

PREPARING FOR THE FIELD After defining the research topic, it is important to secure funding to carry out the research. Academic anthropologists can apply for grants from a variety of sources, governmental and nongovernmental. Several sources of funding are also available for advanced graduate students. Undergraduate students have a more difficult time finding grants to support fieldwork, but many succeed.

Related to the funding question is whether it is appropriate for an anthropologist to conduct research while employed in the research setting. Employment provides financial support for the research, but it raises some problems. A basic dilemma, discussed later in the chapter, is the ethical principle that anthropologists cannot do "undercover" research. If you are working in a factory, for example, while studying what goes on in the factory, you must get people's permission for your study, something that is not always easy. More positively, a work role can help gain people's trust and respect. A British graduate student worked as a bartender in a tourist town in Ireland (Kaul 2004). This position placed him at the center of the village, and people respected him as a hardworking person, thus greatly adding to his ability to learn about the local culture, at least as revealed from a bartender's perspective.

If the project involves international travel, the host government may require a visa and an application for permission to conduct research. These formalities may take a long time and may even be impossible to obtain. The government of India, for example, restricts research by foreigners, especially research related to "sensitive" topics such as tribal people, border areas, and family planning. China's restrictions against foreign anthropologists doing fieldwork have been eased since the 1980s, but it is still not easy to get permission to do fieldwork and participant observation.

Many countries require that researchers follow official guidelines for *protection of human subjects*. In the United States, universities and other institutions that support or conduct research with living people must establish *institutional review boards* (IRBs) to monitor research to make sure it conforms to ethical principles. IRB guidelines follow a medical model related to the need to protect people who participate as "subjects" in medical research. Normally, IRBs require informed consent, in writing, of the research participants. **Informed consent** is an aspect of research ethics requiring that the researcher inform the research participants of the intent, scope, and possible effects of the study and seek their agreement to be in the study. Obtaining written consent of research participants is reasonable and feasible in many anthropological research projects. Written consent, however, is often not reasonable or feasible, especially in oral-based cultures where most people are not literate. Fortunately, IRBs are gaining more experience with the contexts in which most cultural anthropologists do research. Some universities' IRBs will waive the requirement for written informed consent, allowing oral informed consent instead. IRB guidelines do change, so check your institution's website for the latest policy.

Depending on the project location, preparation for the field may involve buying specialized equipment, such as a tent, warm clothing, waterproof clothing, and sturdy boots. Health preparations may require immunization against contagious diseases such as yellow fever. For research in a remote area, a well-stocked medical kit and basic first-aid training are essential. Research equipment and supplies are another important aspect of preparation. Cameras, video recorders, tape recorders, and laptop computers are now basic field equipment. Unlike the traditional paper notebook and pen, though, these machines require batteries and other inputs.

If a researcher is unfamiliar with the local language, intensive language training before going to the field is critical. Even with language training in advance, cultural anthropologists often find that they cannot communicate in the local version of the standardized language they studied in a classroom. Therefore, many fieldworkers rely on help from a local interpreter throughout their study or at least in its early stages.

WORKING IN THE FIELD

A basic first step in establishing a fieldwork project is to decide on the particular location or locations for the research. The second is to find a place to live.

SITE SELECTION A research *site* is the place where the research takes place, and sometimes a project involves more than one site. The researcher often has a basic idea of the area where the fieldwork will occur—for example, a shantytown in Rio de Janeiro, a village in Scotland, or a factory in Malaysia. It is often impossible to know in advance exactly where the project will be located. Selecting a research site depends on many factors. It may be necessary to find a large village if the project involves class differences in work patterns, or a clinic if the study concerns health-care behavior. It may be difficult to

THINKING OUTSIDE THE BOX

At the author's university, the Department of Anthropology has a research fund that supports about a dozen student research projects annually. Visit the website http://www.gwu.edu/~anth/atgw/cotlow_awards.cfm and review the list of student projects. What might you propose to research?

CRITICAL thinking

Shells and Skirts in the Trobriand Islands

A lasting contribution of Bronislaw Malinowski's ethnography *Argonauts of the Western Pacific* (1961 [1922]) is its detailed examination of the **kula**, a trading network linking many islands in the region, in which men have long-standing partnerships for the exchange of everyday goods such as food as well as highly valued necklaces and armlets.

More than half a century later, Annette Weiner (1976) traveled to the Trobriand Islands to study woodcarving. She settled in a village less than a mile from where Malinowski had done his research. She immediately began making startling observations: "On my first day in the village, I saw women performing a mortuary [death] ceremony in which they distributed thousands of bundles of strips of dried banana leaves and hundreds of beautifully decorated fibrous skirts" (1976:xvii).

Bronislaw Malinowski during his fieldwork in the Trobriand Islands, 1915–1918.
▶ *What are some of the differences between what his field research revealed about men's lives in the Trobriand Islands compared to what a "verandah anthropologist" would have learned?*

Nowhere in Malinowski's voluminous writings did he mention the women's activities. Weiner was intrigued and decided to change her research project to investigate women's goods, exchange patterns, and prestige. Men, as Malinowski showed, exchange shells, yams, and pigs. Women, as Weiner learned, exchange bundles of banana leaves and intricately made skirts. Power and prestige derive from both exchange networks.

Reading Malinowski alone informs us about the world of men's status systems and describes them in isolation from half of the islands' population: women. Weiner's book *Women of Value, Men of Renown* (1976) provides an account of women's trading and prestige activities as well as how they are linked to those of men. Building on the work of her predecessor, Weiner shows how a full understanding of one domain requires knowledge of the other.

◆ CRITICAL THINKING QUESTIONS

- Is it possible that Malinowski overlooked women's exchange patterns?
- Do the findings of Annette Weiner simply provide another one-sided view?
- What might a cultural anthropologist discover in the Trobriand Islands now?

find a village, neighborhood, or institution in which the people welcome the researcher and the project. Often, housing shortages mean that even the most welcoming community cannot provide space for an anthropologist.

Here is an example in which a combination of factors came together in a positive way. Jennifer Robertson was seeking a research site in Japan for a study of urban population change. She selected Kodaira, a suburb of Tokyo (see Map 3.2), because of advice from a Japanese colleague. It had available housing and offered a good fit with her research interests. By happy coincidence, she was also familiar with the area:

> I spent my childhood and early teens in Kodaira [but] my personal past did not directly influence my selection of Kodaira as a fieldsite and home. . . . That I wound up living in my old neighborhood in Kodaira was determined more by the availability of a suitable apartment than by a nostalgic curiosity about my childhood haunts. As it turned out, I could not have landed at a better place at a better time. (1991:6)

kula a trading network, linking many of the Trobriand Islands, in which men have long-standing partnerships for the exchange of everyday goods such as food as well as highly valued necklaces and armlets.

CULTURAMA

The Trobriand Islanders of Papua New Guinea

The Trobriand Islands are named after eighteenth-century French explorer Denis de Trobriand. They include 22 flat coral atolls east of the island of New Guinea. The indigenous Trobriand population lives on four main islands. Kiriwina is by far the most populated, with about 28,000 people (digim'Rina, personal communication 2006). The Papua New Guinea (PNG) district office and an airstrip are located on Kiriwina at Losuia.

The islands were first colonized by Great Britain and then ceded to Australia in 1904 (Weiner 1988). The British attempted to stop local warfare and to change many other aspects of Trobriand culture. Christian missionaries introduced the game of cricket as a substitute for warfare (see Chapter 14 for further discussion). In 1943, Allied troops landed as part of their Pacific operations. In 1975, the islands became part of the state of Papua New Guinea.

Island-to-island cultural differences exist. Even within one island, people may speak different dialects, although everyone speaks a version of the language called Kilivila (Weiner 1988). The Trobrianders grow much of their own food, including root crops such as yams, sweet potatoes, and taro; beans and squash; and bananas, breadfruit, coconuts, and betel nuts. Pigs are the main animal raised for food and as prestige items. In the latter part of the twentieth century, Trobrianders were increasingly dependent on money sent to them by relatives working elsewhere in PNG. Current development projects are encouraging people to plant more fruit trees, such as mango (digim'Rina 2005).

Kinship emphasizes the female line, meaning that mothers and daughters form the core of co-residential groups. Fathers, though not co-residential, are nonetheless important family members and spend as much time caring for children as women do (Weiner 1988). Fathers of political status give their babies and children, both boys and girls, highly valued shell earrings and necklaces to wear. Mothers give daughters prized red skirts. Trobriand children attend Western-style schools on the islands, and many go to mainland PNG and beyond for further studies.

Today, elders worry that young people do nothing but dream about "money" and fail to care for the heritage of their ancestors. Another concern is that commercial overfishing is endangering the coral reefs.

Thanks to Linus S. digim'Rina, University of Papua New Guinea, and Robert Foster, University of Rochester, for reviewing this material.

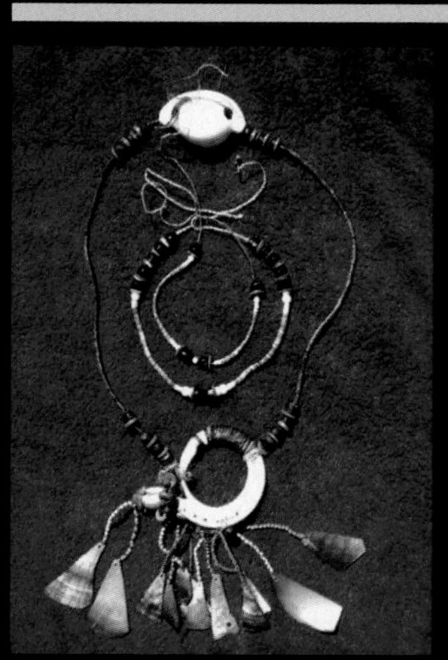

(LEFT) Trobriand men's coveted trade goods include this shell necklace and armlet. (CENTER) A Trobriand girl wears a valued skirt at a dance in honor of the ancestors on Kiriwina Island. She and other female participants coat their skin with coconut oil and herbs and wear decorative flowers.

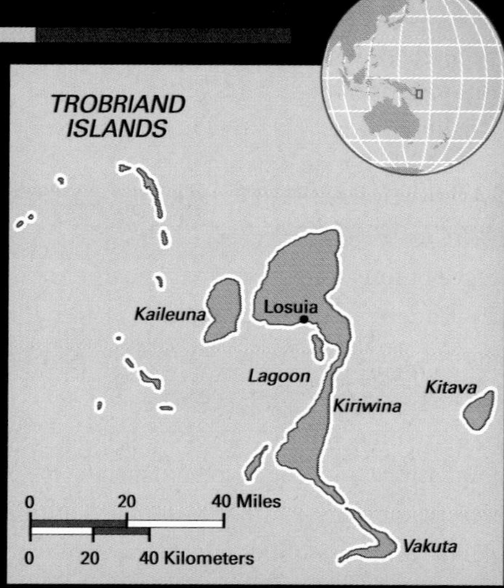

MAP 3.1 Trobriand Islands of Papua New Guinea. Also known as the Kiriwina Islands, these islands are an archipelago of coral atolls lying off the eastern coast of the island of New Guinea.

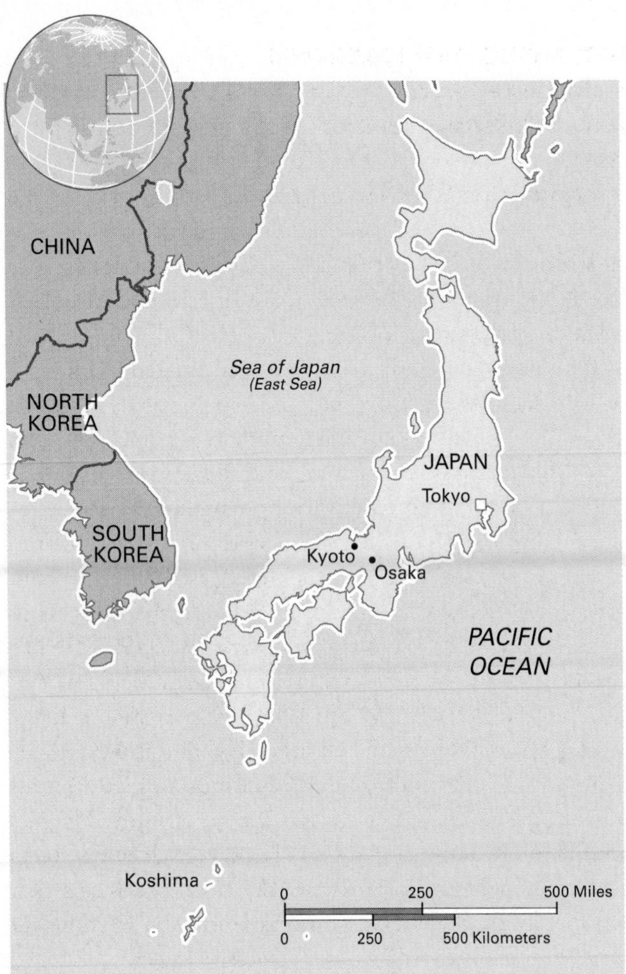

MAP 3.2 Japan.
The State of Japan, or Nihon-koku or Nippon-koku, encompasses over 3000 islands, most of which are mountainous. Its population is nearly 129 million. Greater Tokyo, with over 30 million residents, is the largest metropolitan area in the world. Japan has the world's second largest economy.

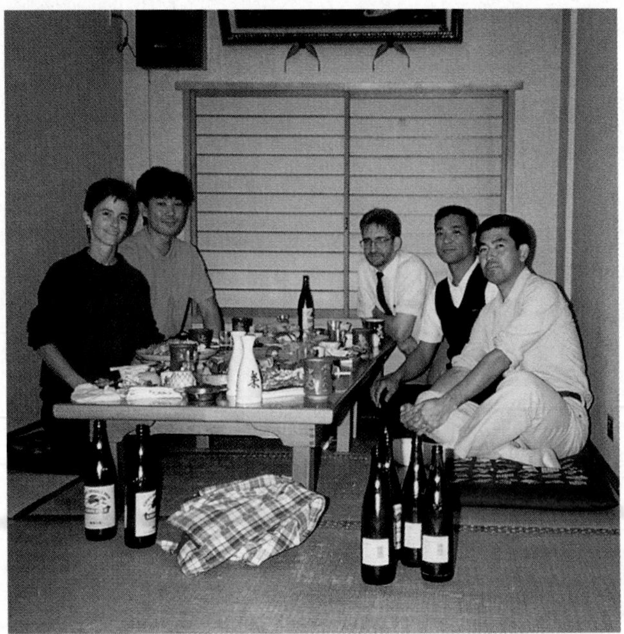

Jennifer Robertson (FAR LEFT) celebrates the publication of her book, *Native and Newcomer* (1991), with several administrators from Kodaira City Hall. This informal gathering at a local restaurant followed a formal ceremony at the City Hall, where Robertson presented her book to the mayor of Kodaira, an event covered by city and regional newspapers.

▶ *What cultural features are noteworthy about this gathering?*

GAINING RAPPORT **Rapport** is a trusting relationship between the researcher and the study population. In the early stages of research, the primary goal is to establish rapport with key leaders or decision makers in the community who may serve as *gatekeepers* (people who formally or informally control access to the group or community).

Gaining rapport involves trust on the part of the study population, and their trust depends on how the researcher presents herself or himself. In many cultures, people have difficulty understanding why a person would come to study them because they do not know about universities and research and cultural anthropology. They may provide their own explanations based on previous experience with outsiders whose goals differed from those of cultural anthropologists, such as tax collectors, family planning promoters, and law-enforcement officials.

Stories about *false role assignments* can be humorous. During his 1970s fieldwork in northwest Pakistan, Richard Kurin reports that in the first stage of his research, the villagers thought he was an international spy from America, Russia, India, or China (1980). Over time, he convinced them that he was not a spy. So what was he? The villagers came up with several roles for Kurin. First, they speculated that he was a teacher of English because he was tutoring one of the village boys. Second, they guessed that he must be a doctor because he gave people aspirin. Third, they thought he might be a lawyer who could help them in local disputes because he could read court orders. Last, they decided he was a descendant of a local clan because of the similarity of his last name and that of an ancestral king. For Richard Kurin, the last of these—being a true "Karan"—was best of all.

Being labeled a spy continues to be a problem for anthropologists. Christa Salamandra, a Western-trained doctoral student in anthropology, went to Damascus, Syria (see Map 3.3) to do research for her dissertation in anthropology (2004). Although Damascus has an ancient history, it is increasingly cosmopolitan. Damascenes, however, have little

---

rapport a trusting relationship between the researcher and the study population.

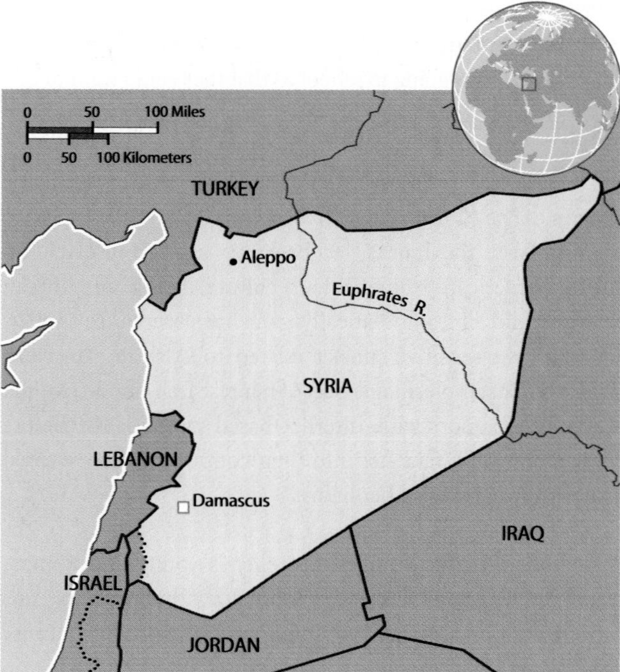

MAP 3.3 Syria.
The Syrian Arabic Republic historically included the present-day territories of Lebanon, Israel, the Palestinian Territories, and parts of Jordan, but not the Jazira region in Syria's northeast. Its population is 19 million people. Syria's capital city, Damascus, with a population of 3 million people, is one of the oldest continually occupied cities in the world.

exposure to anthropology. Syria has no university with a department of anthropology, and there are no Syrian anthropologists. Salamandra's research interests in popular culture (movies, cafés, and fashion) perplexed the local people, who decided she must be a foreign spy. One person said to her, "Your question is CIA, not academic" (2004:5). Nevertheless, she managed to carry out her study and write a book about popular culture in Damascus.

Another situation of an assumed spying role arose in North Carolina, even though the anthropologist, Mary Anglin, shared citizenship with the people (2002). During her fieldwork in a mica-processing factory in the western part of the state, some people thought she was an industrial spy. Anglin came from the northeastern United States, so she was not a "southerner." Moreover, she had no kin connections in the region and no "family" (she was single). The Irish-Scottish residents of the area did not quickly welcome her, but she managed to get the factory owner to let her spend time in the factory as a participant-observer. Several of the women factory workers befriended her, but many of the local people continued to be suspicious. At one point, a rumor circulated that Anglin was an industrial spy, intent on learning about mica processing in order to sell the information to competitors. The rumor died down, but the factory owner later banned her from entering the factory.

GIFT GIVING AND EXCHANGE Giving gifts to people involved in the research can help the project proceed, but gifts should be culturally and ethically appropriate. Learning the local rules of exchange is important (see Figure 3.1).

Matthews Hamabata, a Japanese American who did fieldwork in Japan, learned about the complexities of gift giving among Japanese business families (1990). He developed a close relationship with one family, the Itoos, and helped their daughter apply for admission to universities in the United States. When the applications were completed, Mrs. Itoo invited him to an expensive restaurant to celebrate. After the dinner, she handed him a small, carefully wrapped package, expressing her embarrassment at the inadequacy of her gift in relation to all that he had done for her daughter. When he returned home, he opened the gift. It was a box of chocolates. Upon opening the box, he discovered 50,000 yen (about US$250). Hamabata felt insulted: "Who do the Itoos think they are? They can't buy me or my services!" (1990:21–22). He asked some Japanese friends what he should do. They told him that the gift signaled the Itoos' wish to have a long-standing relationship and that returning the money to the Itoos would be an insult. They advised him to give a return gift later on, in order to maintain the relationship. His gift should leave him ahead by about 25,000 yen, given his status as an anthropologist in relation to the Itoos' status as a rich business family. This strategy worked and the relationship between Hamabata and the Itoos remained intact.

MICROCULTURES AND FIELDWORK Class, race, gender, and age all affect how the local people will perceive and welcome an anthropologist. Some examples illustrate how microcultures influence rapport and affect the research in other ways.

- What an appropriate or an inappropriate gift is
- How to deliver a gift
- How to behave as a gift giver
- How to behave when receiving a gift
- If and how to give a follow-up gift

FIGURE 3.1 Culture and Gift Giving in the Field

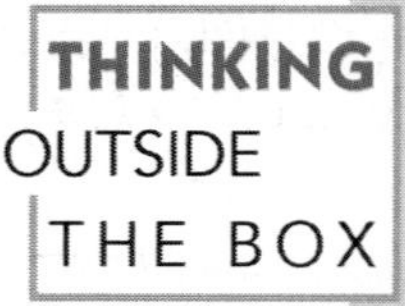

Recall a situation in which either you did not know what would be an appropriate gift to give someone (in terms of quality, cost, or some other factor) or you were faced with some other puzzling situation related to gift exchange. What were the cultural meanings underlying the situation?

CLASS In most fieldwork situations, the anthropologist is more wealthy and powerful than the people studied. This difference is obvious to the people. They know that the anthropologist must have spent hundreds or thousands of dollars to travel to the research site. They see the anthropologist's expensive equipment (camera, tape recorder, video recorder, even a vehicle) and valuable material goods (stainless steel knives, cigarettes, flashlights, canned food, and medicines).

Many years ago, Laura Nader urged that anthropologists should also *study up* by doing research among powerful people such as members of the business elite, political leaders, and government officials (1972). As one example of this approach, research on the high-fashion industry of Japan placed the anthropologist Dorinne Kondo in touch with members of the Japanese elite—influential people capable of taking her to court if they felt she wrote something defamatory about them (1997). Studying up has contributed to awareness of the need, in all fieldwork situations, for recognition of the anthropologist's accountability to the people being studied, whether or not they are able to read what the anthropologist has written about them or wealthy enough to hire a lawyer if they do not like how they and their culture have been presented.

"RACE"/ETHNICITY For most of its history, cultural anthropology has been dominated by Euro-American White researchers who study "other" cultures that are mainly non-White and non-Euro-American. The effects of "Whiteness" on role assignments range from the anthropologist being considered a god or ancestor spirit to being reviled as a representative of a colonialist past or neocolonialist present. While doing research in a village in Jamaica called Haversham, Tony Whitehead learned how "race" and status interact (1986). Whitehead is an African American and from a low-income family. Being of a similar "race" and class as the rural Jamaicans with whom he was doing research, he assumed he would quickly build rapport because of a shared heritage. The people of Haversham, however, have a complex status system that relegated Whitehead to a position that he did not predict, as he explains:

> I was shocked when the people of Haversham began talking to me and referring to me as a "big," "brown," "pretty-talking" man. "Big" was not a reference to my weight but to my higher social status as they perceived it, and "brown" referred not only to my skin color but also to my higher social status. . . . More embarrassing than bothersome were the references to how "pretty" I talked, a comment on my Standard English speech pattern. . . . Frequently mothers told me that their children were going to school so that they could learn to talk as pretty as I did. (1986:214–215)

This experience prompted Whitehead to ponder the complexities of "race" and status cross-culturally.

Similarly, for Lanita Jacobs-Huey, in her research on African American women's hair culture, being an African American did not automatically gain her acceptance (2002). Hairstyle is a sensitive subject related to African American identity. For example, in one part of her research, she attempted to establish rapport with Internet-based participants. Before the women would take her into their confidence, they wanted to know how she styled her hair.

GENDER If a female researcher is young and unmarried, she is likely to face more difficulties than a young unmarried man or an older woman, married or single, because people in most cultures consider a young unmarried female on her own as extremely unusual. Rules of gender segregation may dictate that a young unmarried woman should not move about freely without a male escort, attend certain events, or be

American anthropologist Liza Dalby in formal geisha dress during her fieldwork on geisha culture in Kyoto, Japan.

▶ *Besides learning to dress correctly, what other cultural skills did Liza Dalby probably have to learn?*

---

culture shock persistent feelings of uneasiness, loneliness, and anxiety that often occur when a person has shifted from one culture to a different one.

Tobias Hecht plays a game with some of the street children in his study in Rio de Janeiro, Brazil.

in certain places. A woman researcher who studied a community of gay men in the United States says:

> I was able to do fieldwork in those parts of the setting dedicated to sociability and leisure—bars, parties, family gatherings. I was not, however, able to observe in those parts of the setting dedicated to sexuality—even quasi-public settings such as homosexual bath houses. . . . Thus my portrait of the gay community is only a partial one, bounded by the social roles assigned to females within the male homosexual world. (Warren 1988:18)

Gender segregation may also prevent male researchers from gaining access to a full range of activities. Liza Dalby, a White American, lived with the geishas of Kyoto, Japan, and trained to be a geisha (1998). This research would have been impossible for a man to do.

AGE Typically, anthropologists are adults, and this fact may make it easier for them to gain rapport with people their age than with children or the aged. Although some children and adolescents welcome the participation of a friendly adult in their daily lives and respond to questions openly, others are more reserved.

OTHER FACTORS A researcher's role is affected by even more factors than those just discussed, including religion, dress, and personality. Being the same religion as the residents of a Jewish home for the aged in California helped a Jewish anthropologist establish rapport (Myerhoff 1978). This positive engagement is evident in a conversation between the anthropologist (A) and a woman named Basha (B):

> **B:** "So, what brings you here?"
> **A:** "I'm from the University of Southern California. I'm looking for a place to study how older Jews live in the city." At the word university, Basha moved closer and nodded approvingly. "Are you Jewish?" she asked.
> **A:** "Yes, I am."
> **B:** "Are you married?" she persisted.
> **A:** "Yes."
> **B:** "You got children?"
> **A:** "Yes, two boys, 4 and 8," I answered.
> **B:** "Are you teaching them to be Jews?" (1978:14)

The anthropologist was warmly accepted, and her plan for one year of research grew into a long-standing relationship. In contrast, being Jewish posed a potential problem in another context (Freedman 1986). Diane Freedman conducted research in rural Romania in the 1980s. Given the pervasiveness of anti-Semitism there, she was reluctant to tell the villagers that she was Jewish and also reluctant to lie. Early in her stay, she attended the village church. The priest asked what her religion was. She opted for honesty and found, to her relief, that being Jewish had no negative effects on her research.

CULTURE SHOCK **Culture shock** is the feeling of uneasiness, loneliness, and anxiety that occurs when a person shifts from one culture to a different one. The more different the two cultures are, the more severe the shock is likely to be. Culture shock happens to many cultural anthropologists, no matter how much they have tried to prepare themselves for fieldwork. It also happens to students who study abroad, Peace Corps volunteers, and anyone who spends time living and participating in another culture.

Culture shock can range from problems with food to language barriers and loneliness. Food differences were a major problem in adjustment for a Chinese anthropologist who came to the United States (Shu-Min 1993). American food never gave him a "full" feeling. An American anthropologist who went to Pohnpei, an island in the Federated States of Micronesia (see Map 10.2, p. 247), found that her lack of skills in the local language caused her the most serious adjustment problems (Ward 1989). She says, "Even dogs understood more than I did. . . . [I will never] forget the agony of stepping on a woman's toes. Instead of asking for forgiveness, I blurted out, 'His canoe is blue'" (1989:14).

A frequent psychological aspect of culture shock is the feeling of reduced competence as a cultural actor. At home, the anthropologist is highly competent, carrying out everyday tasks such as shopping, talking with people, and mailing a package without thinking. In a new culture, the simplest tasks are difficult, and one's sense of self-efficacy is undermined. In extreme cases, an anthropologist may have to abandon a project because of an inability to adapt to the fieldwork situation. For most, however, culture shock is a temporary

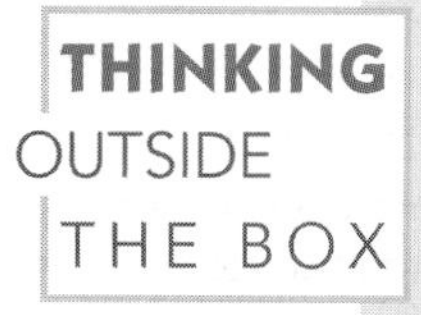

Think of an occasion in which you experienced culture shock, even if as the result of just a brief cross-cultural encounter. How did you feel? How did you cope? What did you learn from the experience?

affliction that subsides as the person becomes more familiar with the new culture.

Reverse culture shock may occur after coming home. An American anthropologist describes his feelings on returning to San Francisco after a year of fieldwork in a village in India:

> We could not understand why people were so distant and hard to reach, or why they talked and moved so quickly. We were a little frightened at the sight of so many white faces and we could not understand why no one stared at us, brushed against us, or admired our baby. (Beals 1980:119)

FIELDWORK TECHNIQUES

The goal of fieldwork is to collect information, or *data,* about the research topic. In cultural anthropology, variations exist about what kinds of data to emphasize and the best ways to collect data.

DEDUCTIVE AND INDUCTIVE RESEARCH AND DATA

A **deductive approach** is a form of research that starts from a research question or hypothesis and then involves collecting data related to the question through observation, interviews, and other methods. An **inductive approach** is a form of research that proceeds without a hypothesis and involves gathering data through unstructured, informal observation, conversation, and other methods. Deductive methods are more likely to collect **quantitative data,** or numeric information, such as the amount of land in relation to the population or numbers of people with particular health problems. The inductive approach in cultural anthropology emphasizes **qualitative data,** or nonnumeric information, such as recordings of myths, conversations, and filming of events. Most anthropologists, however, combine deductive and inductive approaches and quantitative and qualitative data.

Cultural anthropologists have labels for data collected in each approach. **Etic** (pronounced like the last two syllables of "phonetic") refers to data collected according to the researcher's questions and categories, with the goal of being able to test a hypothesis (see Figure 3.2). In contrast, **emic** (pronounced like the last two syllables of "phonemic") refers to data collected that reflect what insiders say and understand about their culture, and insiders' categories of thinking. Cultural materialists (review Chapter 1) are more likely to collect etic data, whereas interpretivists are more likely to collect emic data. Again, however, most cultural anthropologists collect both types of data.

PARTICIPANT OBSERVATION The phrase *participant observation* includes two processes: participating, or being part of the people's lives, while carefully observing. These two activities may sound simple, but they are actually quite complex.

Being a participant means that the researcher adopts the lifestyle of the people being studied, living in the same kind of housing, eating similar food, wearing similar clothing, learning the language, and participating in the daily round of activities and in special events. The rationale is that participation over a long period improves the quality of the data. The more time the researcher spends living among the people, the more likely it is that the people will live their "normal" lives. In this way, the researcher is able to overcome the **Hawthorne effect,** a research bias that occurs when participants change their behavior to conform to the perceived expectations of the researcher. The Hawthorne effect was discovered in the 1930s during a study of an industrial plant in the United States. During the study, research participants altered their behavior in ways they thought would please the researcher.

An anthropologist cannot be everywhere, participate in everything, or observe everyone, so choices are involved in where to be and what to observe. As mentioned earlier, gender, age, and other microcultural factors may limit the anthropologist's participation in certain domains or activities. The sheer need for sleep may mean that the anthropologist misses something important that happens at night, such as a ritual or a moonlight hunting expedition.

Although participant observation is often equated with the casual term "hanging out," in fact, it means constant choices about where to be on a particular day at a particular time, what one observes, with whom, and what, by default, one misses. Depending on the research topic, participant observation may focus on who lives with whom, who interacts with whom

---

deductive approach (to research) a research method that involves posing a research question or hypothesis, gathering data related to the question, and then assessing the findings in relation to the original hypothesis.

inductive approach (to research) a research approach that avoids hypothesis formation in advance of the research and instead takes its lead from the culture being studied.

quantitative data numeric information.

qualitative data non-numeric information.

etic an analytical framework used by outside analysts in studying culture.

emic insiders' perceptions and categories, and their explanations for why they do what they do.

Hawthorne effect research bias due to participants changing their behavior to conform to expectations of the researcher.

interview a research technique that involves gathering of verbal data through questions or guided conversation between at least two people.

questionnaire a formal research instrument containing a pre-set series of questions that the anthropologist asks in a face-to-face setting, by mail, or by email.

Research Approach	Process	Data
Deductive (Etic)	Hypothesis followed by data collection	Quantitative data for hypothesis testing
Inductive (Emic)	No hypothesis, data collection follows from participants' lead	Qualitative data for descriptive insights

FIGURE 3.2 Two Research Approaches in Cultural Anthropology

in public, who are leaders and who are followers, what work people do, how people organize themselves for different activities, rituals, arguments, festivals, funerals, and far more.

TALKING WITH PEOPLE Common sense tells you that participating and observing are important, but what about talking to people and asking questions such as "What is going on here?" "What does that mean?" "Why are you doing that?" The process of talking to people and asking them questions is such an important component of participant observation that the method should actually be called *participant observation and talking*. Cultural anthropologists use a variety of data-collection techniques that rely on talking with people, from informal, casual, and unplanned conversations, to more formal methods.

An **interview** is a technique for gathering verbal data through questions or guided conversation. It is more purposeful than a casual conversation. An interview may involve only two people, the interviewer and the interviewee, or several people in what are called group interviews or focus groups. Cultural anthropologists use different interview styles and formats, depending on the kinds of information they seek, the amount of time they have, and their language skills. The least structured type of interview is an *open-ended interview*, in which the respondent (interviewee) takes the lead in setting the direction of the conversation, topics to be covered, and the amount of time devoted to a particular topic. The interviewer does not interrupt or provide prompting questions. In this way, the researcher discovers what themes are important to the person.

A **questionnaire** is a formal research instrument containing a preset series of questions that the anthropologist asks in a face-to-face setting, or by mail or e-mail. Cultural anthropologists who use questionnaires favor a face-to-face setting. Like interviews, questionnaires vary in the degree to which the questions are *structured* (close-ended) or *unstructured* (open-ended). Structured questions limit the range of possible responses—for example, by asking research participants to rate their positions on a particular issue as "very positive," "positive," "negative," "very negative," or "no opinion." Unstructured interviews generate more emic responses.

When designing a questionnaire, the researcher should have enough familiarity with the study population to be able to design questions that make cultural sense (Fitchen 1990). Researchers who take a ready-made questionnaire to the field with them should ask another researcher who knows the field area to review it in advance to see whether it makes cultural sense. Further revisions may be required in the field to make the questionnaire fit local conditions. A *pilot study* using the questionnaire among a small number of people in the research area can expose areas that need further revision.

COMBINING OBSERVATION AND TALKING A combination of observation of what people actually do with verbal data about what people say they do and think is essential for a well-rounded view of a culture (Sanjek 2000). People may say that they do something or believe something, but their behavior may differ from what they say. For example, people may say that sons and daughters inherit equal shares of family property when the parents die. Research into what really happens may reveal that daughters do not inherit equal shares. Similarly, an anthropologist might learn from people and their laws that discrimination on the basis of skin color is illegal. Research on people's behavior might reveal clear examples of discrimination. It is important for an anthropologist to learn about both what people say and what happens. Both are "true" aspects of culture.

SPECIALIZED METHODS Cultural anthropologists also use many more specific research methods. The choice depends on the anthropologist's research goals.

LIFE HISTORY A life history is a qualitative, in-depth description of an individual's life as narrated to the researcher. Anthropologists differ in their views about the value of the life history as a method in cultural anthropology. Early in the twentieth century, Franz Boas rejected this method as unscientific because research participants might lie or exaggerate (Peacock and Holland 1993). Others disagree, saying that a life history reveals rich information on individuals and how they think, no matter how "distorted" their reports are. For example, some

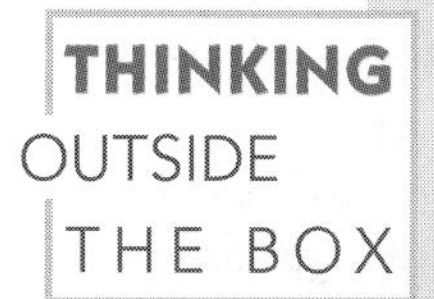

Given the emphasis on observation in fieldwork, is it possible for a blind person to become a cultural anthropologist?

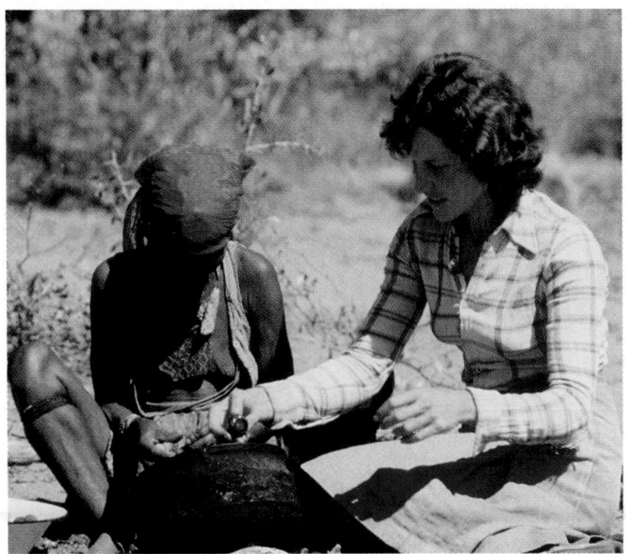

Marjorie Shostak (RIGHT) interviewing Nisa during fieldwork among the Ju/'hoansi in 1975.

▶ *What would you tell an anthropologist about your life?*

anthropologists have questioned the accuracy of parts of *Nisa: The Life and Times of a !Kung Woman* (Shostak 1981), probably the most widely read life history in anthropology. It is a book-length story of a Ju/'hoansi woman of the Kalahari desert of southern Africa (review Culturama, Chapter 1, p. 23). Presented in Nisa's voice, the book offers rich details about her childhood and several marriages. The value of the narrative is not so much whether it is "true" or not; rather, the value is that we learn from Nisa what she wants to tell us, her view of her experiences. That counts as "data" in cultural anthropology, for it is "truly" what she reported to Marjorie Shostak.

In the early days of life history research, anthropologists tried to choose an individual who was somehow typical, average, or representative. It is not possible, however, to find one person who is representative of an entire culture in the scientific sense. Instead, anthropologists now seek individuals who occupy particularly interesting social niches. For example, Gananath Obeyesekere (oh-bay-yuh-SEK-eruh) analyzed the life histories of four Sri Lankan people, three women and one man (1981). Each became a Hindu religious devotee and ascetic, distinguished by their thickly matted hair, twisted into coils like a snake. Their snaky hair is permanently matted and impossible to comb. According to the devotees, a deity is present in their matted hair. Obeyesekere suggests that all four people had suffered deep psychological afflictions during their lives, including sexual anxieties. Their matted hair symbolizes their suffering and provides them with a special status as holy, thus beyond the rules of married life and conjugal sexual relations.

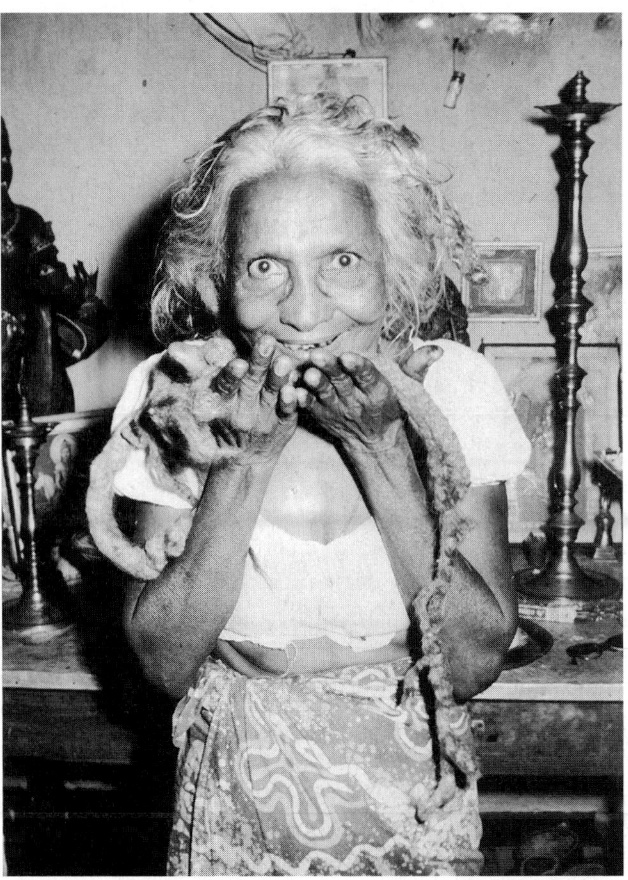

This Sri Lankan woman, whose life story Gananath Obeyesekere analyzed, is a priestess to a deity. She stands in the shrine room of her house, holding her matted, snaky hair.

▶ *How do hairstyles in your culture express a person's religion, marital status, or sexuality?*

TIME ALLOCATION STUDY A *time allocation study* is a quantitative method that collects data on how people spend their time each day on particular activities. This method relies on standard time units as the basic matrix and then labeling or coding the activities that occur within certain time segments (Gross 1984). Activity codes must be adapted to fit local contexts. For example, activity codes for various kinds of work would not be useful in a time allocation study in a retirement home. Data can be collected through observation that may be continuous, at fixed intervals (for instance, every 48 hours), or on a random basis. Continuous observation is extremely time consuming and means that the number of people observed is limited. Spot observations help increase the number of observations but may inadvertently miss important activities. Another option for data collection is to ask people to keep daily time logs or diaries.

TEXTS Many cultural anthropologists collect *textual material,* a category that includes written or oral stories, myths, plays, sayings, speeches, jokes, and transcriptions of people's everyday conversations. In the early twentieth century, Franz Boas collected thousands of pages of texts from Native American groups of the Northwest Coast of Canada,

A multidisciplinary team comprising anthropologists, engineers, and agricultural experts from the United States and Sudan meet to discuss a resettlement project.

including myths, songs, speeches, and accounts of how to perform rituals. These collections provide valuable records of cultures that have changed since the time of his fieldwork. Surviving tribal members have consulted them in order to recover forgotten aspects of their culture.

ARCHIVAL AND HISTORICAL SOURCES Many cultural anthropologists who work in cultures with a written history gain important insights about the present from records of the past preserved in archives maintained in institutions such as libraries, churches, and museums. Ann Stoler pioneered the use of archival resources in understanding the present in her study of Dutch colonialism in Java (1985, 1989) (see Map 1.2, p. 17). Her archival research exposed details about colonial policies, the culture of the colonizers, and relationships with indigenous Javanese people.

National archives in London, Paris, and Amsterdam, to name just a few places, contain records of colonial contact and relations. Regional and local archives contain information about land ownership, agricultural production, religious practices, and political activities. Parish churches throughout Europe keep detailed family histories extending back hundreds of years.

Important information about the past can also come from fieldwork among living people through an approach called the *anthropology of memory*. Anthropologists collect information about what people remember as well as gaps in their memory, revealing how culture shapes memories and how memories shape their culture. Jennifer Robertson's (1991) research about neighborhood people's memories of life in Kodaira, Japan, before the influx of immigrants is an example of this kind of research. She used both interview data and archival data.

MULTIPLE RESEARCH METHODS AND TEAM PROJECTS Most cultural anthropologists use a mix of several different methods. For example, consider what interviews with people in 100 households would provide in breadth of coverage, and then add what you could learn from life histories collected from a subset of five men and five women to provide depth, as well as what long-term participant observation with these people would contribute.

Anthropologists, with their in-depth insights about real people and real people's lives, are increasingly taking part in multidisciplinary research projects, especially projects with an applied focus. Such teamwork strengthens the research by adding more perspectives and methods. Combining data from group interviews, one-on-one interviews, participant observation, and mapping provides rich information on Inuit place names and environmental knowledge (see Eye on the Environment box).

RECORDING CULTURE

How does an anthropologist keep track of all the information collected in the field and record it for future analysis? As with everything else about fieldwork, things have changed since the early times when a notebook and typewriter were the major recording tools. Taking detailed notes, nonetheless, is still a cultural anthropologist's trademark method of recording data.

FIELD NOTES *Field notes* include daily logs, personal journals, descriptions of events, and notes about those notes. Ideally, researchers should write up their field notes each day. Otherwise, a backlog accumulates of daily "scratch notes," or rough jottings made on a small pad or note cards (Sanjek 1990). Trying to capture, in the fullest way possible, the events of even a single day is a monumental task and can result in dozens of pages of handwritten or typed field notes. Laptop computers now enable anthropologists to enter many of their daily observations directly into the computer.

TAPE RECORDING, PHOTOGRAPHY, AND VIDEOS Tape recorders are a major aid to fieldwork. Their use may raise problems, however, such as research participants' suspicions about a machine that can capture their voices, and the ethical issue of protecting the identity of people whose voices are preserved on tape. María Cátedra reports on her use of tape recording during her research in the Asturias region of rural Spain (see Map 3.5):

> At first the existence of the "apparatus," as they called it, was part wonder and part suspect. Many had never seen one before and were fascinated to hear their own voice, but all were worried about what I would do with the tapes. . . . I tried to solve the problem by explaining what I would do with the tapes: I would use them to record correctly what people told me, since my memory was not good enough and I could not take notes quickly enough. . . . One event helped people to accept my integrity in regard to the "apparatus."

eye on the ENVIRONMENT

Researching Inuit Place Names and Landscape Knowledge

The South Baffin Island Place Name Project is dedicated to collecting and recording Inuit place names and landscape knowledge as a means to preserving climatically important information (Henshaw 2006). Inuit is a cluster name for many indigenous peoples who live in the eastern Canadian Arctic. Before contact with Europeans, Inuit life was one of constant mobility. Now, most Inuit are settled in villages and towns. As a result, their detailed knowledge of migration routes, locations along these routes, and how to adapt to changing conditions when on the move are being lost.

Anthropologists and other researchers seek to work with Inuit people to document their traditional knowledge of places and routes. One project looks at **toponymy**, or the naming of places. Inuit toponymy is one aspect of a rich set of **indigenous knowledge**, or local understanding of the environment, climate, plants, and animals.

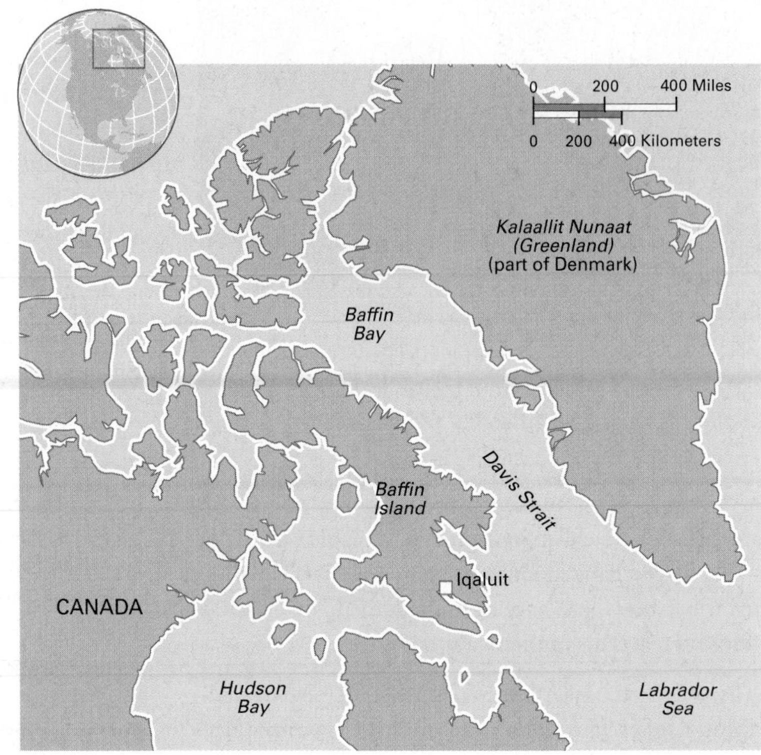

MAP 3.4 Baffin Island in Northeast Canada.
Baffin Island is the largest island in the Canadian Arctic. Iqaluit, a town of about 3,000 people, is the capital of the Nunavut territory. Kalaallit Nunaat, meaning The Human's Land, is the world's largest island and a self-governed Danish territory. Its population of 56,000 people is mainly of mixed descent between the indigenous Kalaallit (Inuit) and Danish people.

The South Baffin Place Names Project used several methods for collecting data. The first step was community-wide workshops, with 10 to 15 people gathered together in a community hall. The researchers laid out large maps, and the Inuit added place names to the map and explained their importance.

The second step was conducting one-on-one interviews with Inuit elders. These elders have lived in particular areas and can provide specialized knowledge about them in terms of use (for shelter, for fishing and hunting, and for storage), routes to and from the site, and likely weather conditions.

The third step was participant observation. The anthropologists, with Inuit collaborators, went to many of the sites. They gained first-hand experience about travel conditions to and from the sites and conditions at the sites themselves. They made video recordings and took photographs.

The fourth step was analytical and archival. The researchers created a computer database, linking the ethnographic data to maps.

This research project has many uses. It will provide a data baseline, starting with the memory of the elders, of important living sites and migration routes. It will show, over time, environmental changes that have occurred and how people are adapting to them. It will create an archive of indigenous knowledge that can be used by future generations of Inuit in protecting their cultural heritage and ways of making a living.

◆ **FOOD FOR THOUGHT**

- Choose an ordinary day in your week and create a map of where you go and how key locations are named (such as dorm room, dining hall, classroom, and other). What names do you use for key sites and what do the place names mean to you? How would you change your daily route depending on differences in the weather or season?

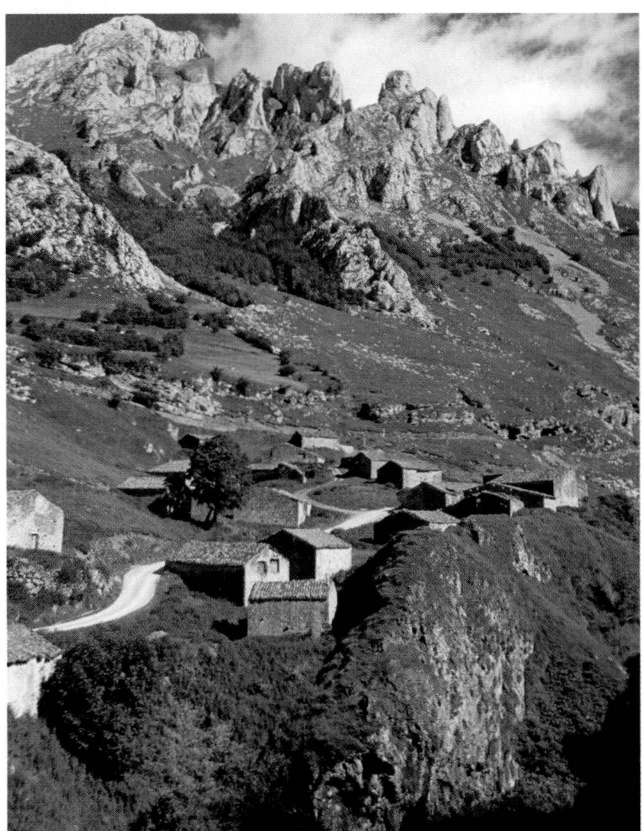

The "autonomous community" of Asturias is located in the far north of Spain. It has extensive coastal beaches but the inland is mainly mountainous. The traditional economy was based in fishing and agriculture. Coal mining and steel production were important in the mid-twentieth century but have declined.

MAP 3.5 Spain.
The Kingdom of Spain is the largest of the three countries occupying the Iberian Peninsula. The geography is dominated by high plateaus and mountain ranges. Spain's population exceeds 40 million. Spain's administrative structure is complex, including autonomous communities, such as Andalucia and Catalonia, and provinces. The central government is granting more autonomy to some of the localities, including the Basque area.

> In the second braña [small settlement] I visited, people asked me to play back what the people of the first braña had told me, especially some songs sung by a group of men. At first I was going to do it, but then I instinctively refused because I did not have the first people's permission. . . . My stand was quickly known in the first braña and commented on with approval. (1992:21–22)

To be useful for analysis, tape recordings have to be transcribed (typed up), either partially or completely. Each hour of recorded talk takes between 5 and 8 hours to transcribe.

Like tape recordings, photographs or videos capture more detail than scratch notes. Any researcher who has watched people performing a ritual, taken scratch notes, and then tried to reconstruct the details of the ritual later on will know how much of the sequencing and related activity is lost to memory within just a few hours. Reviewing photographs or a video recording of the ritual provides a surprising amount of forgotten or missed material. The tradeoff, however, is that if you are using a camera or video recorder, you cannot take notes at the same time.

Kirsten Hastrup describes her use of photography in recording the annual ram exhibition in Iceland (see Map 3.6) that celebrates the successful herding in of the sheep from mountain pastures. This event is exclusively for men, but they allowed her to attend:

> The smell was intense, the light somewhat dim and the room full of indiscernible sounds from some 120 rams and about 40 men. A committee went from one ram to the next noting their impressions of the animal, in terms of its general beauty, the size of the horns and so forth. Measurements were made all over but the decisive measure (made by hand) was the size and weight of the ram's testicles. The air was loaded with sex and I realized that the exhibition was literally and metaphorically a competition of sexual potence. . . . I heard endless sexual jokes and very private remarks. The bursts of laughter followed by side-glances at me conveyed an implicit question of whether I understood what was going on. I did. (1992:9)

Hastrup took many photographs. After they were developed, she was disappointed by how little of the totality of the event they conveyed.

---

toponymy the naming of places.

indigenous knowledge (IK) local understanding of the environment, climate, plants, and animals.

At the National Icelandic Ram Festival in Iceland.

MAP 3.6 Iceland.
The Republic of Iceland has a population of 300,000. A volcanic island, Iceland is the fifth richest country in the world, according to GDP (gross domestic product) per capita. It has a high quality of life and ranked second in the 2005 United Nations Human Development Index. Iceland's economy is based in exporting fish and fish products, technology, and tourism.

DATA ANALYSIS

During the research process, an anthropologist collects a vast amount of data in many forms. How does he or she put the data into a meaningful form? In data analysis, as with data collection, two basic varieties exist: *qualitative* (prose-based description) and *quantitative* (numeric presentation).

ANALYZING QUALITATIVE DATA Qualitative data include descriptive field notes, narratives, myths and stories, songs and sagas, and more. Few guidelines exist for undertaking a qualitative analysis of qualitative data. One procedure is to search for themes, or patterns. This approach involves exploring the data, or "playing" with the data, either "by hand" or with the use of a computer. Jennifer Robertson's analysis of her Kodaira data was inspired by writer Gertrude Stein's (1948) approach to writing "portraits" of individuals, such as Picasso. Robertson says that Stein was a superb ethnographer who was able to illuminate the "bottom nature" of her subjects and their worlds through a process that Stein referred to as "condensation." To do this, "she scrutinized her subjects until, over time, there emerged for her a repeating pattern of their words and actions. Her literary portraits . . . were condensations of her subjects' repeatings" (Robertson 1991:1). Like Stein, Robertson reflected on all that she had experienced and learned in Kodaira, beginning with the years when she lived there as a child. Emerging from all this was the dominant theme, *furusato,* which literally means "old village." References to *furusato* appear frequently in people's accounts of the past, conveying a sense of nostalgia for a more "real" past.

Many qualitative anthropologists use computers to help sort for such *tropes* (key themes). Computer scanning of data offers the ability to search vast quantities of data more quickly and perhaps accurately than with the human eye. The range of software available for such data management is expanding. The quality of the results, though, still depends on careful and complete inputting of the data and an intelligent coding scheme that will tell the computer what it should be scanning for in the data.

The presentation of qualitative data relies on people's own words—their stories, explanations, and conversations. Lila Abu-Lughod followed this approach in conveying Egyptian Bedu women's narratives in her book *Writing Women's Worlds* (1993). Abu-Lughod offers a light authorial framework that organizes the women's stories into thematic clusters such as marriage, production, and honor. Although Abu-Lughod provides an introduction to the narratives, she offers no conclusion, thereby prompting readers to think for themselves about the meanings of the stories and what they say about Egyptian Bedu women's life.

Some anthropologists question the value of such artistic, interpretive approaches because they lack scientific verifiability. Too much depends, they say, on the individual selection process of the anthropologist, and interpretation often depends on a small number of cases. Interpretive anthropologists respond that verifiability, in the scientific sense, is not their goal and is not a worthwhile goal for cultural anthropology. Instead, they seek to provide a plausible interpretation, or a fresh understanding into people's lives that offers detail and richness.

ANALYZING QUANTITATIVE DATA Analysis of quantitative, or numeric, data can proceed in several directions. Some

ethnography a firsthand, detailed description of a living culture, based on personal observation.

	Urban				Rural			
Item	**Group 1**	**Group 2**	**Group 3**	**Total**	**Group 1**	**Group 2**	**Group 3**	**Total**
Number of Households	26	25	16	67	32	30	16	78
Food	60.5	51.6	50.1	54.7	74.1	62.3	55.7	65.8
Alcohol	0.2	0.4	1.5	0.6	0.5	1.1	1.0	0.8
Tobacco	0.8	0.9	0.9	0.9	1.1	1.7	1.2	1.4
Dry Goods	9.7	8.1	8.3	8.7	8.8	10.2	14.3	10.5
Housing	7.3	11.7	10.3	9.7	3.4	5.7	3.9	4.4
Fuel	5.4	6.0	5.0	5.6	3.7	3.9	4.1	3.9
Transportation	7.4	8.2	12.4	8.9	3.0	5.3	7.6	4.9
Health	0.3	0.6	0.7	0.5	1.5	1.4	1.7	1.5
Education	3.5	2.8	3.1	3.2	1.2	2.1	3.0	1.9
Entertainment	0.1	0.9	1.1	0.6	0.0	0.1	0.3	0.2
Other	5.2	8.3	6.9	6.8	2.1	6.0	6.9	4.6
Total*	100.4	99.5	100.3	100.2	99.4	99.8	99.7	99.9

*Totals may not add up to 100 due to rounding.

Source: From "Social Patterns of Food Expenditure Among Low-Income Jamaicans" by Barbara D. Miller in *Papers and Recommendations of the Workshop on Food and Nutrition Security in Jamaica in the 1980s and Beyond*, ed. by Kenneth A. Leslie and Lloyd B. Rankine, 1987.

FIGURE 3.3 Mean Weekly Expenditure Shares (Percentage) in 11 Categories by Urban and Rural Expenditure Groups, Jamaica, 1983–1984

of the more sophisticated methods require knowledge of statistics, and many require the use of a computer and a software package that can perform statistical computations. The author's research on low-income household budgets in Jamaica involved the use of computer analysis: first, to divide the sample households into three income groups (lower, medium, and higher); second, to calculate percentages of expenditures in the three categories of goods and groups of goods, such as food, housing, and transportation (see Figure 3.3). Because the number of households was quite small (120), the analysis could have been done "by hand." But using the computer made the analysis proceed more quickly and more accurately.

REPRESENTING CULTURE **Ethnography**, or a detailed description of a living culture based on personal observation and study, is the main way that cultural anthropologists present their findings about culture. In the early phase of cultural anthropology, in the first half of the twentieth century, ethnographers wrote about "exotic" cultures located far from their homes in Europe and North America. The early ethnographers tended to treat a particular local group or village as a unit unto itself with clear boundaries. Since the 1980s, ethnographies have changed in several ways:

- Ethnographers now treat local cultures as connected with larger regional and global structures and forces. Edward Fischer's book *Cultural Logics and Global Economics: Maya Identity in Thought and Practice* (2001) takes the topic of Maya political activism in Guatemala as its focus and sets it within the context of changing economic systems more widely.
- Ethnographers focus on one topic of interest and avoid a more holistic approach. Laura Miller studied ideas and practices about the body and beauty in Japan. In her book *Body Up: Exploring Contemporary Japanese Body Aesthetics* (2006), she explores beauty salons, beauty products, changing ideas of female and male beauty, and ideas about diet.
- Ethnographers study Western, industrialized cultures as well as other cultures. Philippe Bourgois's research in East Harlem in New York City for his book *In Search of Respect: Selling Crack in El Barrio* (1995) explores how people in one neighborhood cope with poverty and dangerous living conditions. Although this topic sounds like it fits more in sociology than anthropology, a cultural anthropologist will provide rich contextual details about the everyday experiences and perspectives of the people based on participant observation.

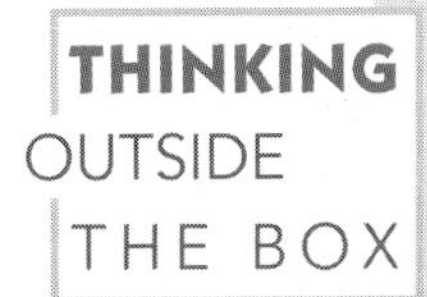

Have you ever had the experience of taking photographs of a place, event, or people and then being terribly disappointed because the results did not capture the essence of your experience? What was missing from the photographs?

◆◆◆

Urgent Issues in Cultural Anthropology Research

This section considers two urgent issues in cultural anthropology research: fieldwork ethics and safety during fieldwork.

ETHICS AND COLLABORATIVE RESEARCH

Anthropology was one of the first disciplines to devise and adopt a code of ethics. Two events in the 1950s and 1960s prompted cultural anthropologists to reconsider their role in research in relation to the sponsors of their research and to the people with whom they were studying. The first was Project Camelot of the 1950s; it was a plan of the U.S. government to influence political leadership in South America in order to strengthen U.S. interests (Horowitz 1967). The U.S. government employed several anthropologists to collect information on political leaders and events, without revealing their purpose.

The second major event was the Vietnam War (or the American War, as people in Vietnam refer to it). It brought to the forefront of anthropology questions about government interests in ethnographic information, the role of anthropologists during wartime, and the protection of the people with whom anthropologists conduct research. Two bitterly opposed positions emerged within anthropology. On one side was the view that all Americans as citizens should support the U.S. military effort in Vietnam. People on this side said that any anthropologist who had information that could help subvert communism should provide it to the U.S. government. The other position stated that an anthropologist's responsibility is first and always to protect the people being studied, a responsibility that takes priority over politics. These anthropologists opposed the war and saw the people of South Vietnam as victims of Western imperialism. They uncovered cases in which anthropologists submitted information about people's political affiliations to the U.S. government, with the result being military actions and death of the people exposed by the research.

This period was the most divisive in the history of U.S. anthropology. It led, in 1971, to the adoption by the American Anthropological Association (AAA) of a code of ethics. The AAA code of ethics states that an anthropologist's primary responsibility is to ensure the safety of the people participating in the research. A related principle is that cultural anthropology does not condone covert or "undercover" research. Further, anthropologists should inform potential research participants about the purposes and scope of the study.

COLLABORATIVE RESEARCH A new direction in methods explicitly seeks to involve members of the study population in collaborative research—from data collection to analysis and presentation. **Collaborative research** is an approach to learning about culture that involves the anthropologist working with members of the study population as partners and teammates rather than as "subjects." This strategy, from the start, forces reconsideration of how anthropologists refer to the people being studied, especially the long-standing term "informant." The term sounds hauntingly and negatively related to espionage or war and implies a passive role on handing over information to someone else. As noted earlier in this chapter, IRBs use the term "human subject," which cultural anthropologists reject for similar reasons. Cultural anthropologists favor the term *research participant*.

Luke Eric Lassiter is a pioneer in collaborative methods. In a recent project, Lassiter involved his undergraduate anthropology students in a collaboration with members of the African American community of Muncie, Indiana. This project resulted in a book with shared authorship between Lassiter, the students, and the community members (2004). The project collected information about African American life that is now housed in a library archive.

Cultural anthropologists are working to find better ways to share the benefits of research with the people and places we study. Research methods in cultural anthropology have come a long way from the armchair to new strategies for nonhierarchical research. More progress lies ahead, however, in democratizing anthropology and making everyone a "barefoot anthropologist."

SAFETY IN THE FIELD

Fieldwork can involve serious physical and psychological risks to the researcher and to members of his or her family. The image of "the anthropologist as hero" has muffled, to a large degree, both the physical dangers and the psychological risks of fieldwork.

The collaborative research team led by Luke Eric Lassiter includes Muncie community members (far left and far right) and students and faculty from Ball State University.

---

collaborative research an approach to learning about culture that involves anthropologists working with members of the study population as partners and participants rather than as "subjects."

The food ration queue at an emergency clinic near Buedu, Sierra Leone in 2001. While conducting his dissertation research in war-torn Sierra Leone, Danny Hoffman combined traditional fieldwork techniques such as participant observation and interviews. He also had to be alert to sudden danger and other risks specific to research during war. Hoffman believes that anthropologists must be willing to take such risks in order to provide essential knowledge about the complex causes and consequences of war that are overlooked by war correspondents writing for the media.

Dangers from the physical environment are often serious and can be fatal. In the 1980s, the slippery paths of the highland Philippines claimed the life of Michelle Zimbalist Rosaldo, a major figure in late twentieth-century cultural anthropology (review Figure 1.2, p. 12). Disease is a frequent problem. Many anthropologists have contracted infectious diseases that have chronic effects or that may be fatal.

Violence figures prominently in some, but not most, fieldwork experiences. During the five years that Philippe Bourgois lived in East Harlem, New York, he witnessed the following: a shooting outside his window, a bombing and machine-gunning of a numbers joint, a shoot-out and police car chase in front of the pizza parlor where he was eating, the aftermath of a fire-bombing of a heroin house, a dozen serious fights, and "almost daily exposure to broken-down human beings, some of them in fits of crack-induced paranoia, some suffering from delirium tremens, and others in unidentifiable pathological fits of screaming and shouting insults to all around them" (1995:32). He was rough-handled by the police several times because they did not believe that he was a professor doing research. He was once mugged for the sum of $8. Although his research placed him in danger, it also enabled him to gain an understanding, from the inside, of everyday violence in the lives of desperately poor and addicted people.

Likewise, some anthropological research involves danger from political violence or even war. A new specialty, ***war zone anthropology***, or research conducted within zones of violent conflict, can provide important insights into topics such as the militarization of civilian lives, civilian protection, the cultural dynamics of military personnel, and postconflict reconstruction (Hoffman and Lubkemann 2005). This kind of research requires skills and judgment that anthropology classes or research methods books do not typically address (Nordstrom 1997, Kovats-Bernat 2002). Previous experience in conflict zones as workers in international aid organizations or the military is helpful.

What about fieldwork danger in supposedly normal situations? After more than 20 years of fieldwork in the Kalahari desert, southern Africa, Nancy Howell (1990) suddenly had to confront the issue of danger in the field when one of her teenage sons was killed and another injured in a truck accident in Botswana, southern Africa, while with their father, Richard Lee, who was doing fieldwork there at the time. In the months following the accident, she heard from many anthropologist friends who shared stories about other fieldwork accidents.

Howell contacted the American Anthropological Association (AAA) to see what advice it provides about fieldwork safety. The answer, she learned, was not much. The AAA responded with financial support for her to undertake a detailed inquiry into fieldwork hazards in anthropology. Howell drew a sample of 311 anthropologists listed as employed in the AAA's *Guide to Departments*. She sent them a questionnaire asking for information on gender, age, work status, health status, and work habits in the field; and she asked for information on health problems and other hazards they had experienced. She received 236 completed questionnaires, a high response rate indicating strong interest in the study.

In her analysis, she found regional variation in risk and danger. The highest rates were in Africa, followed by India, the Asia/Pacific region, and Latin America. Howell offers recommendations about how anthropologists can prepare themselves more effectively for preventing and dealing with fieldwork risks. They include these:

- Increasing risk awareness among fieldworkers
- Training fieldworkers in basic medical care
- Learning about fieldwork safety in anthropology classes

Research methods in cultural anthropology have come a long way from the time of the armchair anthropologists. Topics have changed, as have techniques of data gathering and data analysis. New concerns about ethical research and responsibility and fieldworkers' safety continue to reshape research practices.

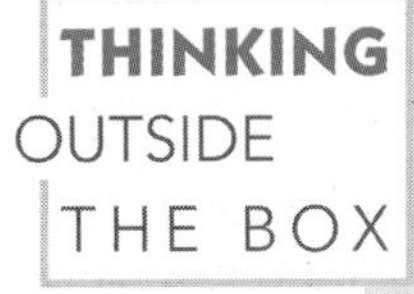

To see the entire AAA Code of Ethics, go to http://www.aaanet.org.

3

the BIG questions REVISITED

◆ How do cultural anthropologists conduct research on culture?

Cultural anthropologists conduct research by doing fieldwork and using participant observation. In the nineteenth century, early cultural anthropologists did armchair anthropology, meaning that they learned about other cultures by reading reports written by explorers and other untrained observers. The next stage was verandah anthropology, in which an anthropologist went to the field but did not live with the people. Instead, the anthropologist would interview a few members of the study population where he (there were no women cultural anthropologists at this time) lived, typically on his verandah.

Fieldwork and participant observation became the cornerstones of cultural anthropology research only after Malinowski's innovations in the Trobriand Islands during World War I. His approach emphasized the value of living for an extended period in the field, participating in the daily activities of the people, and learning the local language. These features are the hallmarks of research in cultural anthropology today.

New techniques continue to develop in response to changing times. One of the most important is multisited research, in which the anthropologist studies a topic at more than one location.

◆ What does fieldwork involve?

Research in cultural anthropology involves several stages. The first is to choose a research topic. A good topic is timely, important, and feasible. Ideas for topics can come from literature review, restudies, current events and pressing issues, and even sheer luck. Once in the field, the first steps include site selection, gaining rapport, and dealing with culture shock. Microcultures affect how the anthropologist will gain rapport and will shape access of the anthropologist to particular cultural domains. Participating appropriately in the culture involves learning local forms of gift giving and other exchanges to express gratitude for people's hospitality, time, and trust.

Specific research techniques may emphasize gathering quantitative or qualitative data. Cultural materialists tend to focus on quantitative data, whereas interpretivists gather qualitative data. When in the field, anthropologists take daily notes, often by hand but now also using a computer. Several other methods of documenting culture include photography, audio recording, and video recording. The anthropologist's theoretical orientation and research goals affect the approach to data analysis and presentation.

Quantitative data may involve statistical analysis and presentation in graphs or tables. The presentation of qualitative data is more likely to be descriptive.

◆ What are some urgent issues in cultural anthropology research today?

Questions of ethics have been paramount to anthropologists since the 1950s. In 1971, U.S. anthropologists adopted a set of ethical guidelines for research to address their concern about what role, if any, anthropologists should play in research that might harm the people being studied. The AAA code of ethics states that an anthropologist's primary responsibility is to maintain the safety of the people involved. Further, cultural anthropologists should never engage in covert research and should always explain their purpose to the people in the study and preserve the anonymity of the location and of individuals. Collaborative research is a recent development that responds to ethical concerns by pursuing research that involves the participants as partners rather than as subjects.

Safety during fieldwork is another important issue. Danger to anthropologists can come from physical sources such as infectious diseases and from social sources such as political violence. A survey of anthropologists in the 1980s produced recommendations about increasing safety during fieldwork.

KEY CONCEPTS

collaborative research, p. 80
culture shock, p. 71
deductive approach (to research), p. 72
emic, p. 72
ethnography, p. 79
etic, p. 72
fieldwork, p. 62
Hawthorne effect, p. 72
indigenous knowledge, p. 76
inductive approach (to research), p. 72
informed consent, p. 65
interview, p. 73
kula, p. 66
multisited research, p. 63
participant observation, p. 62
qualitative data, p. 72
quantitative data, p. 72
questionnaire, p. 73
rapport, p. 68
toponymy, p. 76

SUGGESTED READINGS

Michael V. Angrosino. *Projects in Ethnographic Research.* Long Grove, IL: Waveland Press, 2005. This brief manual provides students with ideas about what conducting research in anthropology is like. It discusses the fundamental stages of three projects, with insights about how students can conduct their own research.

H. Russell Bernard. *Research Methods in Cultural Anthropology: Qualitative and Quantitative Approaches*, 3rd ed. Newbury Park, CA: Sage Publications, 2002. This is a sourcebook of anthropological research methods providing information about how to design a research project, methods of data collection, and data analysis and presentation.

Kathleen M. DeWalt and Billie R. DeWalt. *Participant Observation: A Guide for Fieldworkers.* New York: AltaMira Press, 2002. This book is a comprehensive guide to doing participant observation.

Alexander Ervin. *Applied Anthropology: Tools and Perspectives for Contemporary Practice.* Boston: Allyn and Bacon, 2005. Chapters discuss links between anthropology and policy, the history of applied anthropology, ethics, and specialized methods.

Carolyn Fluehr-Lobban. *Ethics and the Profession of Anthropology: A Dialogue for Ethically Conscious Practice*, 2nd ed. Philadelphia: University of Pennsylvania Press, 2003. The chapters address topics such as covert research, indigenous people's cultural rights, informed consent, and ethics in researching culture in cyberspace.

Peggy Golde, ed. *Women in the Field: Anthropological Experiences*, 2nd ed. Berkeley: University of California Press, 1986. Chapters in this classic collection discuss Margaret Mead's fieldwork in the Pacific, Laura Nader's fieldwork in Mexico and Lebanon, Ernestine Friedl's fieldwork in Greece, and Jean Briggs's fieldwork among the Inuit of the Canadian Arctic.

Joy Hendry. *An Anthropologist in Japan: Glimpses of Life in the Field.* London: Routledge, 1999. This book describes the author's original research design, how her focus changed, and how she reached unanticipated conclusions.

Choong Soon Kim. *One Anthropologist, Two Worlds: Three Decades of Reflexive Fieldwork in North America and Asia.* Knoxville: University of Tennessee Press, 2002. The author reflects on his fieldwork, conducted over 30 years, on Japanese industry in the American South and on Korean families displaced by the Korean war and partition.

Luke Eric Lassiter. *The Chicago Guide to Collaborative Ethnography.* Chicago: University of Chicago Press, 2005. This handbook for doing collaborative anthropology includes historical and theoretical perspectives on collaborative anthropology, exposing its roots in feminist, humanist, and critical anthropology.

Carolyn Nordstrom and Antonius C. G. M. Robben, eds. *Fieldwork under Fire: Contemporary Studies of Violence and Survival.* Berkeley: University of California Press, 1995. The chapters discuss fieldwork experiences in Palestine, China, Sri Lanka, the United States, Croatia, Guatemala, and Ireland.

Tom Ric with Mette Louise Berg, eds. *Future Fields*, special issue of the online journal *Anthropology Matters*, Vol. 6, No. 2, 2004. This issue includes 11 articles that address a range of methodological issues cultural anthropologists face today, including emotional, financial, and ethical challenges as well as how to cope in situations of physical danger. The journal is accessible at no charge at http://www.anthropologymatters.com.

PART II
CULTURAL FOUNDATIONS

ANTHROPOLOGY works

Lara Tabac, medical anthropologist, works at the New York City Department of Health and Mental Hygiene, along with another cultural anthropologist and 6000 other employees. Her responsibilities with the DOHMH's Epidemiology Services require her to collect qualitative information from New Yorkers about how certain health issues affect their lives.

Tabac describes her job as an "unusual joint venture of words and numbers." She explains that the department is traditionally highly quantitative; it uses statistics to determine health-action agendas. The numbers "tell how many, but they do not tell why. In order to be responsive to the health needs of New Yorkers, the DOHMH needs to know why. This is where I come in."

Anthropological training reinforced and shaped Tabac's natural tendency to observe and ask questions. She puts her skills and interests to work through direct interaction with people: "I do a lot of listening on a wide range of topics, and I need only a MetroCard to reach far-flung and eclectic neighborhoods peopled with individuals who share their health dilemmas and life struggles with me, as well as their suggestions for improving the services and programs that will ultimately affect them."

Tabac collects data about the sexual behavior of men who have sex with men. She wants to learn about when individuals in this group use condoms and why they do or do not do so. To gather qualitative information, Tabac has spent many hours conducting interviews. She says, "As a technique, interviewing is crucial for gaining a deep understanding of sensitive issues. . . . People tend to be more honest when they don't feel as though they are going to be judged by their peers." Tabac comments that every interview for this project has been valuable.

Tabac finds her job with the DOHMH challenging and socially relevant. She took the job because she wanted to help improve people's lives. She has not been disappointed.

A family living in a village in the interior Amazon region of Brazil preparing farinha (fuh-reen-yuh), a food staple made from manioc, a root crop. The villagers also eat fruit and vegetables harvested from the rainforest, but these foods are no longer easily available due to extensive clearing of the rainforest by illegal loggers, for cattle ranching, and for industrial farms that grow export crops such as soybeans.

MAKING A LIVING

the BIG questions

- How do cultural anthropologists study economic systems?
- What are the five modes of livelihood?
- How are the five modes of livelihood changing?

OUTLINE

During the many thousands of years of human prehistory, people made their living by collecting food and other necessities from nature. All group members had equal access to life-sustaining resources. Most people throughout the world now live in economies much different from this description.

◆◆◆

Culture and Economic Systems

In anthropology, the term **economic system** includes three components:

- *Livelihood* or production—making goods or money
- *Consumption*—using up goods or money
- *Exchange*—the transfer of goods or money between people or institutions

Economic anthropology is the subfield of cultural anthropology that focuses on economic systems cross-culturally. It differs from the discipline of economics in several ways. First, the subject matter of economic anthropology is much wider. It covers all economics systems, not just modern capitalism. Second, economic anthropologists' methods are different. They tend to collect qualitative data and quantitative data, as discussed in Chapter 3, and they rely on fieldwork and participant observation rather than analyzing "canned" statistical datasets or census information. Third, economic anthropologists believe that it is important to gather emic data in order to understand people's own concepts and categories related to making a living, rather than applying Western concepts and categories.

In spite of these differences between economics and economic anthropology, some shared territory exists. Some economists do learn a foreign language and some try to learn about people's actual economic behavior and thought by conducting fieldwork. In turn, some economic anthropologists analyze large, quantitative datasets. Most fruitfully, some economists and some economic anthropologists work together on research and policy issues.

CATEGORIZING LIVELIHOODS

Many years of ethnographic research on economic systems has produced a rich body of knowledge about livelihoods in diverse settings, the topic of this chapter. Anthropologists organize this information by sorting it into categories, called *modes*. The next section describes five major modes of livelihood. A **mode of livelihood** is the dominant way of making a living in a culture.

---

economic system the linked processes of livelihood, consumption, and exchange.

mode of livelihood the dominant way of making a living in a culture.

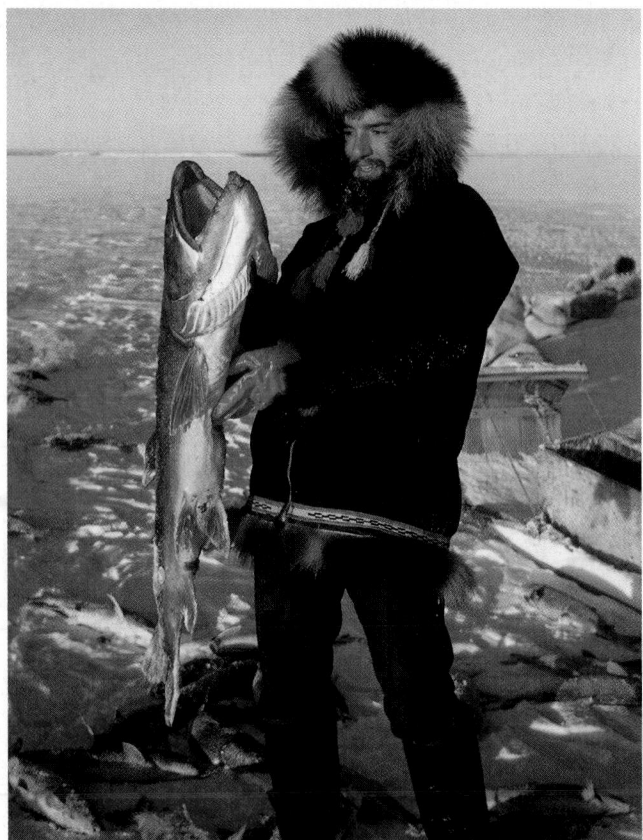

During his fieldwork among the Hare Indians in Northwest Canada, anthropologist Joel Savishinsky holds a 25-pound trout. His dog team is resting behind him.

Categorizing a certain society as having a particular mode of livelihood implies an emphasis on a particular type of livelihood, but it does not mean that only one kind of economic activity exists. In a given society, some people will be involved in the prevailing productive activity, and others will not. A particular individual may be involved in more than one way of making a living. For example, a person could be a farmer and a herder. Another point to keep in mind is that the five modes of livelihood, in reality, blend with and overlap each other. Therefore, some cultures do not fit well within any one mode. Real life is always more complicated than the categories researchers create.

Figure 4.1 presents the five modes of livelihood in order of their historical appearance in the human record. This diagram does not mean that a particular mode evolves into the one following it—for example, foragers do not necessarily transform into horticulturalists, and so on. Nor does this ordering imply a judgment about the sophistication or superiority of more recent modes of livelihood. Figure 4.1 is not a model of "progress" from left to right. The oldest system involves complex and detailed knowledge about the environment that a contemporary city dweller would find difficult to learn quickly enough to ensure survival.

Foraging	Horticulture	Pastoralism	Agriculture	Industrialism/Informatics
Reason for Production				**Reason for Production**
Production for use				Production for profit
Division of Labor				**Division of Labor**
Family-based				Class-based
Overlapping gender roles				High degree of occupational specialization
Property Relations				**Property Relations**
Egalitarian and collective				Stratified and private
Resource Use				**Resource Use**
Extensive and temporary				Intensive and expanding
Sustainability				**Sustainability**
High degree				Low degree

FIGURE 4.1 Modes of Livelihood

MODES OF LIVELIHOOD AND GLOBALIZATION

Although economic anthropologists focus on local economic systems, they are increasingly involved in researching how global and local systems are linked. The spread of Western capitalism in recent centuries has had, and continues to have, marked effects on all other livelihood patterns that it meets.

The intensification of global trade in the past few decades has created a global division of labor, or *world economy,* in which countries compete unequally for a share of the wealth (Wallerstein 1979). In this view, the modern world economy is stratified into three major areas:

- Core
- Periphery
- Semiperiphery

Core areas monopolize the most profitable activities, such as the high-tech service, manufacturing, and financial activities. They have the strongest governments, which play a dominating role in the affairs of other countries. *Peripheral areas* are relegated to the least profitable activities, including livelihood of raw materials, foodstuffs, and labor-intensive goods, and they must import high-tech goods and services from the core. They tend to have weak governments and are dominated, either directly or indirectly, by core states. *Semiperipheral areas* stand in the middle.

In this model, economic benefits are highly unequal across regions, with core areas profiting most. Core states have about 20 percent of the world's population and control 80 percent of the world's wealth (and they create 80 percent of world's pollution). Politically, the core continues to increase its economic power and political influence through international

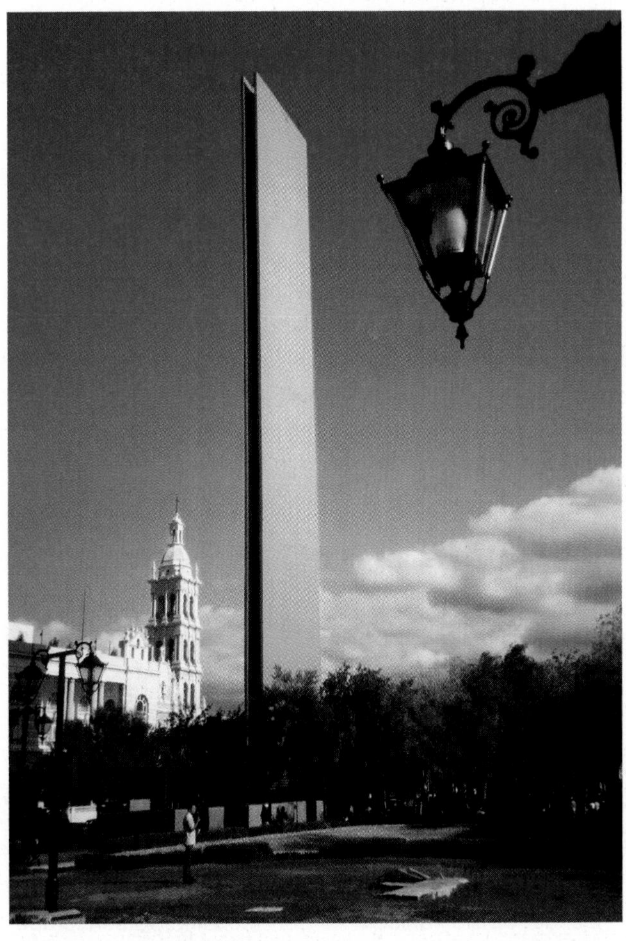

Monterrey, Mexico, is the second most important city in Mexico after the capital. Because of its strong steel industry, it is called "the Pittsburgh of Mexico." It has several major beer breweries and is home to the Mexican Baseball Hall of Fame. The city center has monuments of both Spanish colonialism and cosmopolitan modernity.

organizations such as the World Trade Organization (WTO) and regional arrangements such as the North American Free Trade Agreement (NAFTA). The last section of this chapter returns to the topic of globalization and livelihood change.

◆◆◆

Making a Living: The Five Modes of Livelihood

While reading this section, please bear in mind that most anthropologists are uneasy about typologies because they often do not reflect the complexity of life in any particular context. The purpose of the categories is to help you organize the ethnographic information presented in this book.

FORAGING

Foraging is a mode of livelihood based on resources that are available in nature through gathering, fishing, or hunting. The oldest way of making a living, foraging is a strategy that humans share with our nonhuman primate relatives.

Although foraging supported humanity since our beginnings, it is in danger of extinction. Only around 250,000 people worldwide provide for their livelihood predominantly from foraging now. Most contemporary foragers live in what are considered marginal areas, such as deserts, tropical rainforests, and the circumpolar region. These areas, however, often contain material resources that are in high demand in core areas, such as oil, diamonds, gold, and expensive tourist destinations. Thus, the basis of their survival is threatened by what is called "the resource curse": People in rich countries desire the natural resources in their areas, which leads to conversion of foraging land to mines, plantations, or tourist destinations, in turn leading to the displacement of foragers from their homeland.

Depending on the environmental context, foragers' food sources include nuts, berries and other fruits, and surface-growing vegetables such as melons, roots, honey, insects, and eggs. They trap and hunt a wide variety of birds, fish, and animals. Successful foraging requires sophisticated knowledge of the natural environment and seasonal changes in it. Most critical is knowledge about the location of water sources and of various foods, how to follow animal tracks, how to judge the weather, and how to avoid predators. This unwritten knowledge is passed down over the generations (review Eye on the Environment box, Chapter 3, p. 76).

Foragers rely on a diverse set of tools used for gathering, transporting, and processing wild foods. Tools include digging sticks for removing roots from the ground and for penetrating the holes dug by animals in order to get the animals out, bows and arrows, spears, nets, and knives. Baskets are important for carrying food. For processing raw materials into edible food, foragers use stones to mash, grind, and pound. Meat can be dried in the sun or over fire, and fire is used for cooking either by boiling or by roasting. These activities involve few nonrenewable fuel sources beyond wood or other combustible substances for cooking. Foraging is an **extensive strategy**, a mode of livelihood requiring access to large areas of land and unrestricted population movement. Cultural anthropologists distinguish two major varieties of foraging that are related to different environmental contexts: temperate-climate foraging and circumpolar foraging (see Figure 4.2).

The Ju/'hoansi people of southern Africa, as studied in the early 1960s, moved several times during a year, depending on the seasonal availability of water sources (review Culturama, Chapter 1, p. 23). Each cluster of families regularly returned to "their" territory, reconstructing or completely rebuilding their shelters with sticks for frames, and leaf or thatch coverings. Shelters are sometimes attached to two or three small trees or bushes for support. The amount of time involved in gathering and processing food and constructing shelters is modest.

In contrast to foragers of temperate climates, those living in the circumpolar regions of North America, Europe, and Asia devote more time and energy to obtaining food and providing shelter. The specialized technology of circumpolar peoples includes spears, nets, and knives, as well as sleds and the use of domesticated animals to pull them. Dogs or other

	Temperate-Region Foragers	Circumpolar-Region Foragers
Diet	Wide variety of nuts, tubers, fruits, small animals, and occasional large game	Large marine and terrestrial animals
Gender division of labor in food procurement	Men and women forage; men hunt large game	Men hunt and fish
Shelter	Casual construction, nonpermanent, little maintenance	Time-intensive construction and maintenance, some permanent

FIGURE 4.2 Temperate and Circumpolar Foraging Systems Compared

A Ju/'hoansi traditional shelter.

animals used to pull sleds are an important aspect of circumpolar peoples' technology and social identity (see Everyday Anthropology box). Considerable amounts of labor are needed to construct and maintain igloos or log houses. Protective clothing, including coats, gloves, and boots, is another feature of circumpolar foraging that is time intensive in terms of making and maintaining.

DIVISION OF LABOR Among foraging peoples, the *division of labor,* or occupational specialization (assigning particular tasks to particular individuals), is based on gender and age. Among temperate foraging cultures, a minimal gender-based division of labor exists. Temperate foragers get most of their everyday food by gathering roots, berries, grubs, small birds and animals, and fish, and both men and women collect these basic foods. Hunting large animals, however, tends to involve only men, who go off together in small groups on long-range expeditions. Large game provides a small and irregular part of the diets of temperate-climate foragers. In circumpolar groups, a significant part of people's diet comes from large animals (such as seals, whales, and bears) and fish. Hunting and fishing tend to involve only men. Among circumpolar foragers, therefore, the division of labor is strongly gender-divided.

Age is a basis for task allocation in all modes of livelihood, including foraging. Young boys and girls help collect food. Elderly people tend to stay at the camp area where they are responsible for caring for young children.

PROPERTY RELATIONS The concept of *private property,* in the sense of owning something that can be sold to someone else, does not exist in foraging societies. Instead, the term **use rights** is more appropriate. It means that a person or group has socially recognized priority in access to particular resources such as gathering areas, hunting and fishing areas, and water holes. This access is willingly shared with others by permission. Among the Ju/'hoansi, family groups control access to particular water holes and the territory surrounding them (Lee 1979:58–60). Visiting groups are welcome and will be given food and water. In turn, the host group, at another time, will visit other camps and be offered hospitality there. In India's Andaman Islands (see Culturama), each family group controls a known offshore area for fishing. Sharing access to these resources is expected but only if permission has been requested and granted. Encroaching on someone else's area without permission is a serious misdemeanor and is likely to result in violence.

FORAGING AS A SUSTAINABLE SYSTEM When untouched by outside influences and with abundant land available, foraging systems are *sustainable,* which means that crucial resources are regenerated over time in balance with the demand that the population makes on them. North Sentinel Island, one island in the Andaman Islands, provides a clear case because its inhabitants have long lived in a "closed" system. So far, the few hundred indigenous people live in almost complete isolation from the rest of the world, other than the occasional helicopter flying overhead and the occasional attempt by outsiders to land on their territory.

---

extensive strategy a form of livelihood involving temporary use of large areas of land and a high degree of spatial mobility.

use rights a system of property relations in which a person or group has socially recognized priority in access to particular resources such as gathering, hunting, and fishing areas and water holes.

everyday ANTHROPOLOGY

The Importance of Dogs

Dogs were the first domesticated animal, with evidence of their domestication from sites in eastern Europe and Russia dating to around 18,000 years ago. In spite of dogs' long-standing importance to humans around the world, few cultural anthropologists have focused attention on humans and their dogs. One of the rare ethnographies to do so provides insights about the economic, social, and psychological importance of dogs among a group of circumpolar foragers.

Fewer than 100 Hare Indians constitute the community of Colville Lake in Canada's Northwest Territories (Savishinsky 1974). They live by hunting, trapping, and fishing in one of the harshest environments in the world. Joel Savishinsky went to Colville Lake to study stress, tension, and anxiety among the Hare and how people cope with environmental stress. Environmental stress factors include extremely cold temperatures, long and severe winters, extended periods of isolation, hazardous travel conditions along with the constant need for mobility during the harshest periods of the year, and sometimes food scarcity. Social and psychological stress factors also exist, including contact with White fur traders and missionaries.

Savishinsky discovered the importance of dogs to the Hare people early in his research:

> Later in the year when I obtained my own dogteam, I enjoyed much greater freedom of movement, and was able to camp with many people whom I had previously not been able to keep up with. Altogether I travelled close to 600 miles by dogsled between mid-October and early June. This constant contact with dogs, and the necessity of learning how to drive, train and handle them, led to my recognition of the social and psychological, as well as the ecological, significance of these animals in the lives of the people. (1974:xx)

Among the fourteen households, there are a total of 224 dogs. Some households have as many as four teams, with an average of six dogs per team, corresponding to people's estimation that six dogs are required for travel.

More than being economically useful, dogs play a significant role in people's emotional lives. They are a frequent topic of conversation:

> Members of the community constantly compare and comment on the care, condition, and growth of one another's animals, noting special qualities of size, strength, color, speed, and alertness (1974:169).

Emotional displays, uncommon among the Hare, are significant between people and their dogs:

> The affectionate and concerned treatment of young animals is participated in by people of all ages, and the nature of the relationship bears a striking resemblance to the way in which people treat young children. Pups and infants are, in essence, the only recipients of unreserved positive affect in the band's social life. . . (1974:169–170)

One reason for the sustainability of foraging is that foragers' needs are modest. Anthropologists have typified the foraging lifestyle as the *original affluent society* because needs are satisfied with minimal labor efforts. This term is used metaphorically to remind people living in contemporary consumer cultures that foraging is not a miserable, inadequate way to make a living, contrary to most ethnocentric thinking. In the 1960s, when the Ju/'hoansi people were still foragers, their major food source was mongongo nuts. At that time, these nuts were so abundant that there was never a shortage (Howell 1986). In addition, hundreds of species of edible plants and animals were available, with seasonal variations. The Ju/'hoansi were slender and often complained of hunger throughout the year. Their thinness may be an adaptation to seasonal fluctuations in food supply. Rather than maximizing food intake during times of plenty, they minimize it. Mealtime is not an occasion for stuffing oneself. Ju/'hoansi culture taught that it is good to have a hungry stomach, even when food is plentiful.

Because foragers' needs for goods are limited, minimal labor efforts are required to satisfy them. Foragers typically work fewer hours a week than the average employed North American. In traditional (undisturbed) foraging societies, the people spend as few as five hours a week collecting food and making and repairing tools. They have much time for storytelling, playing games, and resting. Foragers also traditionally enjoyed good health. During the early 1960s, the age structure and health status of the Ju/'hoansi compared well with people in the United States of around 1900 (Lee 1979:47–48). They had few infectious diseases or degenerative diseases (health problems related to aging, such as arthritis).

horticulture a mode of livelihood based on growing domesticated crops in gardens, using simple hand tools.

HORTICULTURE

Both horticulture and pastoralism are recent modes of livelihood, having emerged only as recently as 12,000 years ago in

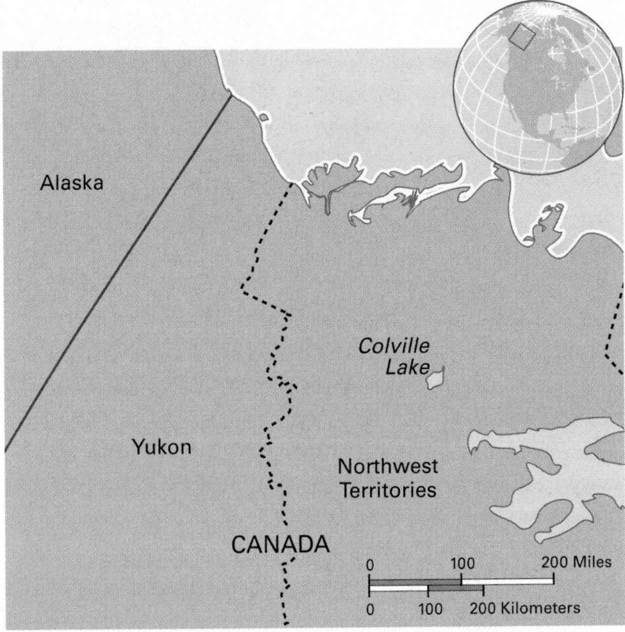

MAP 4.1 **Hare Region near Colville Lake in Northwest Canada.**

Early European colonialists named the local people Hare because of their reliance on snowshoe hares for food and clothing. The Hare people became involved in the wage-labor economy and were afflicted by alcoholism, tuberculosis, and other diseases. Efforts to reestablish claims to ancestral lands began in the 1960s.

Hare Indian children use their family's sled to haul drinking water to their village.

▶ *What tasks are children responsible for in a microculture that you know?*

◆ **FOOD FOR THOUGHT**

- Think of a culture (perhaps yours) in which dogs or some other domesticated animals are a focus of intense human interest. How do people and the animals in question interact? Are there age and gender differences in human relationships with domesticated animals? Hare children use their family's sled to haul drinking water to their village. What tasks are children responsible for in a microculture that you know? (Source: Joel Savishinsky)

the Middle East and then later in Africa, Asia, Europe, and the Western Hemisphere. Both depend on the domestication of plants and animals—that is, the process by which human selection causes genetic changes in plants and animals and leads to their greater control by humans in terms of their location and their reproduction.

Horticulture is a mode of livelihood based on cultivating domesticated plants in gardens using hand tools. Garden crops are often supplemented by foraging and by trading with pastoralists for animal products. Horticulture is still practiced by many thousands of people throughout the world. Prominent horticultural regions are found in sub-Saharan Africa, South Asia, Southeast Asia and the Pacific, Central America, South America, and the Caribbean islands. Major horticultural crops include yams, corn, beans, grains such as millet and sorghum, and several types of roots, all of which are rich in protein, minerals, and vitamins.

Horticulture involves the use of handheld tools, such as digging sticks, hoes, and carrying baskets. Rain is the sole

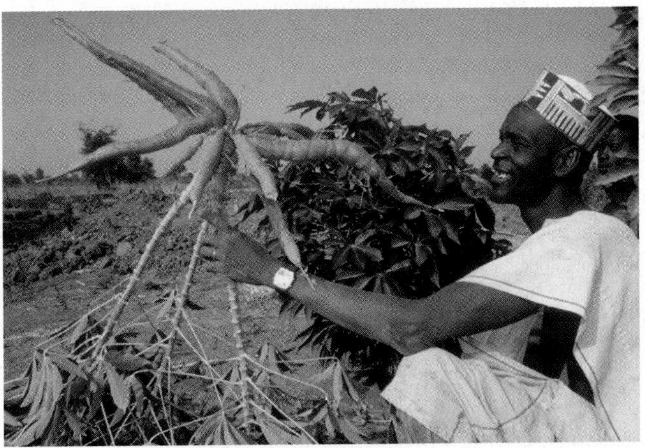

Cassava, also called manioc, is a root crop grown extensively in western Africa. This man displays a cassava plant grown in Niger. Cassava and millet, a grain, are the staple foods for many West Africans.

▶ *Do research to find some West African recipes that include cassava or millet.*

CULTURAMA

The Andaman Islanders of India

The Andaman Islands are a string of islands in the Bay of Bengal that belong to India. For unknown numbers of centuries, many of the islands were inhabited by people who fished, gathered, and hunted for their livelihood. During the eighteenth century, when European countries were expanding trade routes to the Far East, the Andaman Islands were of major strategic importance as a stopping place.

At the time of the first, small settlements of the British in the late eighteenth century, the total indigenous population was estimated at between 6000 and 8000 (B. Miller 1997). Today, over 400,000 people live on the islands, mostly migrants from the Indian mainland. The total number of indigenous people is about 400. British colonialism brought contagious diseases and increased death from violence among disrupted Andaman groups and between the Andaman people and the British.

Only four surviving clusters of indigenous Andamanese now exist. The smallest group, just a few dozen people, consists of the remnants of the so-called Great Andamanese people. They live on a small island near Port Blair, the capital, in what is essentially a reservation area. Several groups of Great Andamanese people formerly lived throughout North and Middle Andaman Islands, but no indigenous people inhabit these islands now. The so-called Jarawa, numbering perhaps 200, live in a reserved area on the southwest portion of South Andaman. Currently, no outsider knows their language or what name they use for themselves. Jarawa is a term that the Great Andamanese people use for them. The Onge, around 100 in number, live in one corner of Little Andaman Island. Another 100 people or so live on North Sentinel Island. Outsiders call them the "Sentinelese." No one has established communication with them, and almost no one from the outside has gotten closer than arrow-range of their shore.

The 2005 tsunami disrupted much of the Andaman Island landscape, particularly areas that had been cleared of mangroves and other trees. As far as anyone knows, none of the indigenous people died as a direct result of the tsunami, though many of the immigrant settlers did (Mukerjee 2005). The future of the indigenous people is more endangered by external culture, in the form of immigration and development, than from nature.

Thanks to Madhusree Mukerjee, independent scholar and activist, and Sita Venkateswar, Massey University, for reviewing this material.

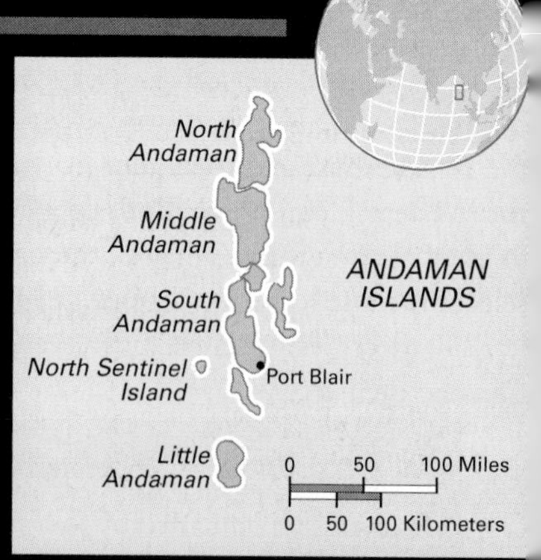

(LEFT) A Jarawa woman receives a handout from a passenger bus driver on the Andaman Trunk Road (ATR). Part of the ATR passes through the Jarawa reservation on South Andaman Island.

(CENTER) Government officials from Pt. Blair make periodic visits by boat to the Jarawa area to attempt to build Jarawa trust. This landmark incident, of getting some Jarawa to board a government boat, occurred in 1998. The Jarawa occupy land that is rich in resources such as ancient hardwood trees. Rumors are that the administration wants to

MAP 4.2 Andaman Islands of India. The 576 islands are geologically part of Myanmar and Southeast Asia. The British Empire controlled them until India's independence in 1947.

Clearing: A section of the forest is cleared, partially or completely, by cutting down trees and brush and then setting the area on fire to burn off other growth. The fire creates a layer of ash that is rich fertilizer. The term *slash and burn cultivation* refers to this stage of clearing.

Planting: People use digging sticks to loosen the soil. They place seeds though the broadcasting method (scattering the seeds by hand) or place slips of plants by hand into the loose soil.

Weeding: Horticulture involves little weeding because the ash cover and shady growing conditions keep weed growth down.

Harvesting: This phase requires substantial labor to cut or dig crops and carry them to the residential area.

Fallowing: Depending on the soil and the crop grown, the land must be left unused for a specified number of years so that it regains its fertility.

FIGURE 4.3 Five Stages in Horticulture

source of moisture. Horticulture requires rotation of garden plots in order for them to regenerate. Thus, another term for horticulture is *shifting cultivation.* Average plot sizes are less than 1 acre, and 2.5 acres can support a family of five to eight members for a year. Yields can support semipermanent villages of 200 to 250 people. Overall population density per square mile is low because horticulture, like foraging, is an extensive strategy. Horticulture is more labor intensive than foraging because of the energy required for plot preparation and food processing. Anthropologists distinguish five phases in the horticultural cycle (see Figure 4.3).

Surpluses in food supply are possible in horticulture. These surpluses enable trade relationships and can lead to greater wealth for some people. Horticulture was the foundation for complex and rich civilizations, such as the Maya civilization of Mexico and Central America, which flourished between 200 and 900 CE.

DIVISION OF LABOR Gender and age are the key factors structuring the division of labor, with men's and women's work roles often being clearly differentiated. Typically, men clear the garden area while both men and women plant and tend the staple food crops. This pattern exists in Papua New Guinea, much of Southeast Asia, and parts of West and East Africa. Food processing involves women often working in small groups, whereas men more typically form small groups for hunting and fishing for supplementary food. Among many horticultural groups, women grow the staple food crops while men grow the "prestige foods" used in ritual feasts. In such contexts, men have higher public status than women.

Two unusual horticultural cases involve extremes in terms of gender roles and status. The first is the precontact Iroquois of central New York State (Brown 1975) (see Map 4.3). Iroquois women cultivated maize, the most important food crop, and they controlled its distribution. This control meant that they were able to decide whether the men would go to war, because a war effort depended on the supply of maize to support it. A contrasting example is that of the Yanomami of the Venezuelan Amazon (see Map 4.4) (Chagnon 1992). Yanomami men clear the fields and tend and harvest the crops. They also do much of the cooking for ritual feasts. Yanomami women, though, are not idle. They play an important role in

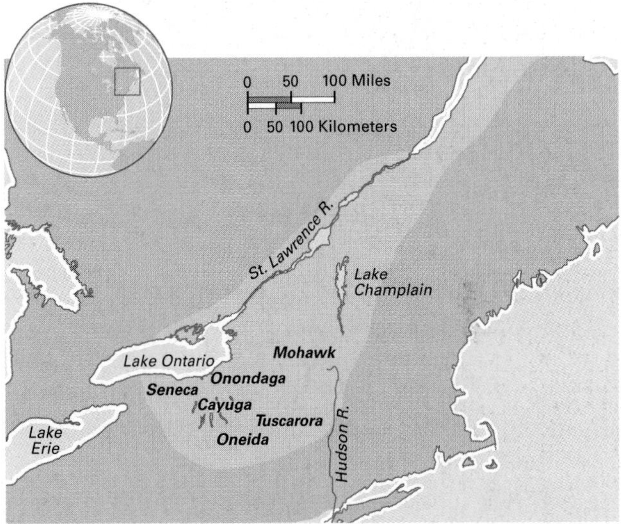

MAP 4.3 Precolonial Iroquois Region.
At the time of the arrival of the European colonialists, the six nations of the Iroquois extended over a wide area. The Mohawk stood guard over the eastern door of the confederacy's symbolic long house, and the Seneca guarded the western door. The six nations worked out a peace treaty among them and established a democracy. A great orator named Hiawatha promoted the plan throughout the tribes, and a Mohawk woman was the first to approve it.

This reconstruction of a pre-colonial Iroquois scene depicts longhouses in which many families lived and shows women in important productive roles.

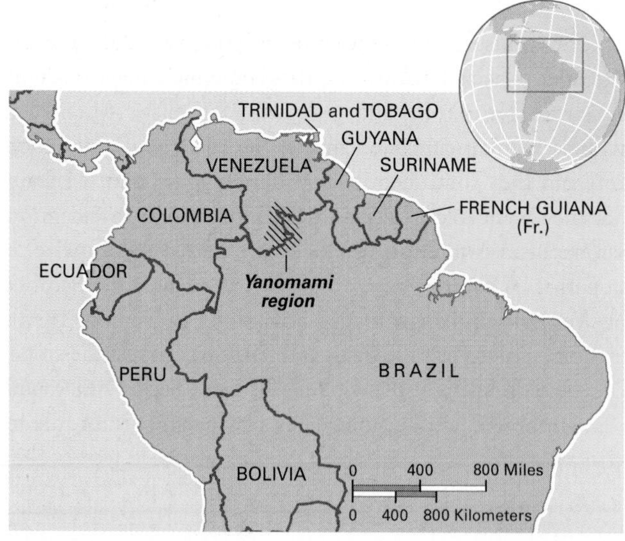

MAP 4.4 Yanomami Region in Brazil and Venezuela. The Yanomami region is supposedly protected from outsiders. But miners, ranchers, loggers, and other commercial developers have encroached on the reserve, extracting natural resources and sexually exploiting women and children.

providing the staple food that comes from manioc, a starchy root crop that requires substantial processing work—it has to be soaked for a long time to remove toxins and then scraped into a mealy consistency. Among the Yanomami, however, men are the dominant decision makers and have more social power than Yanomami women do.

Although anthropologists cannot explain the origins of the different divisions of labor in horticulture, they do know that the differences are related to men's and women's status (Sanday 1973). Analysis of many horticultural societies shows that women's contribution to food production is a necessary but not sufficient basis for women's high status. In other words, if women do not contribute to producing food, their status will be low. If they do contribute, their status may, or may not, be high. The critical factor appears to be control over the distribution of what is produced, especially public distribution beyond the family. Slavery is a clear example of how a major role in production does not bring high status because slaves have no control over the product and its distribution.

Children do more productive work in horticultural societies than in any other mode of livelihood (Whiting and Whiting 1975). The *Six Cultures Study* is a research project that examined children's behavior in horticultural, farming, and industrial settings. Children among a horticultural group, the Gusii (goo-see-eye) of western Kenya, performed the most tasks at the youngest ages. Gusii boys and girls care for siblings, collect fuel, and carry water. Among the Gusii and in other horticultural societies, children do so many tasks because adults, especially women, are busy working in the fields and markets. Children's work in the domestic domain fulfills what are adult roles in other economic systems.

PROPERTY RELATIONS Private property, as something that an individual can own and sell, is not characteristic of horticultural societies. Use rights are typically important, although they are more clearly defined and formalized than among foragers. By clearing and planting an area of land, a family puts a claim on it and its crops. The production of surplus goods allows the possibility of social inequality in access to goods and resources. Rules about sharing within the larger group decline in importance as some people gain higher status.

HORTICULTURE AS A SUSTAINABLE SYSTEM Fallowing is crucial in maintaining the viability of horticulture. Fallowing allows the plot to recover lost nutrients and improves soil quality by allowing the growth of weeds whose root systems keep the soil loose. The benefits of a well-managed system of shifting cultivation are clear, as are the two major constraints involved: the time required for fallowing and the need for access to large amounts of land so that some land is in use while other land is fallowed. Using a given plot for too many seasons or reducing fallowing time quickly results in depletion of soil nutrients, decreased crop production, and soil erosion.

PASTORALISM

Pastoralism is a mode of livelihood based on domesticated animal herds and the use of their products, such as meat and milk, for 50 percent or more of the diet. Pastoralism has long existed in the Middle East, Africa, Europe, and Central Asia, especially where rainfall is limited and unpredictable. In the Western Hemisphere, the only indigenous pastoralist system in existence before the arrival of the Spanish in the fifteenth century was in the Andean region of the New World; it was based on domesticated llamas (Barfield 2001). Sheep, goats, horses, and cattle became prominent after the Spanish conquest. Some Native American groups in the southwestern United States still rely on herding animals.

Worldwide, the six major species are sheep, goats, cattle, horses, donkeys, and camels. Three others have more restricted distribution: yaks at high altitudes in Asia, reindeer in northern sub-Arctic regions, and llamas in highland South America. Many pastoralists keep dogs for protection and for help with herding. Pastoralism can succeed in a variety of environments, depending on the animal involved. For example, reindeer herding is done in the circumpolar regions of Europe and Asia, and cattle and goat herding is common in India and Africa.

In terms of food, pastoralism provides primarily milk and milk products, with occasional slaughtering of animals for meat. Thus, pastoralists typically form trade links with

pastoralism a mode of livelihood based on keeping domesticated animals and using their products, such as meat and milk, for most of the diet.

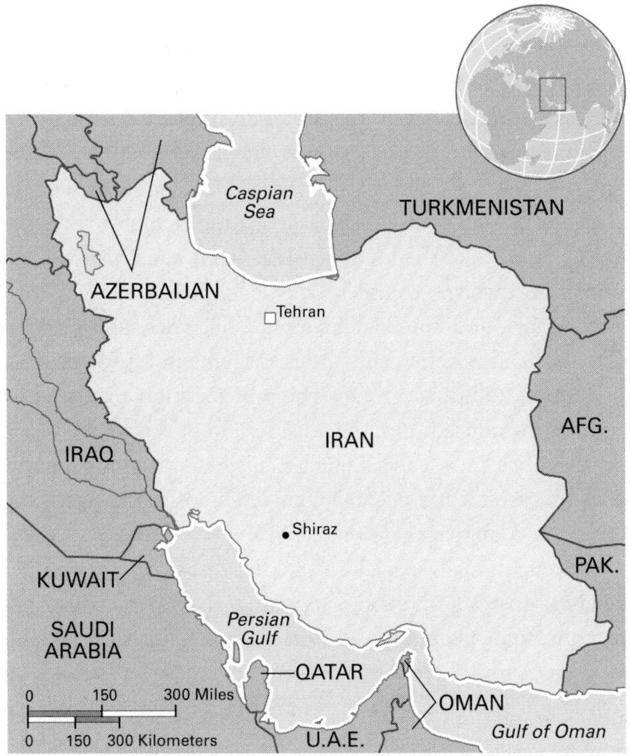

MAP 4.5 Iran.
The Islamic Republic of Iran is one of the world's most mountainous countries. Its economy is based on oil, family farming, and small-scale trading. Iran is OPEC's second-largest oil producer and has the second-largest natural gas reserves in the world after Russia. The population of Iran is over 68 million. The official language is Persian (Farsi) and Shi'a Islam is the official state religion.

foragers, horticulturalists, or farmers in order to obtain food and other goods that they cannot produce themselves. Prominent trade items are food grains and manufactured items, such as cooking pots, for which they offer milk, animals, hides, and other animal products.

Like foraging and horticulture, pastoralism is an extensive strategy. A common problem for all pastoralists is the continued need for fresh pasture and water for their animals. Herds must move or else the grazing area will become depleted. A distinction within the pastoralist category is based on whether the herds move over short or long distances (Fratkin, Galvin, and Roth 1994). The Qashqa'i of Iran are long-distance herders of sheep and camels (Beck 1986). Iran offers a varied and rich natural resource base that supports pastoralism, agriculture, and large urban centers, including the capital city of Shiraz (see Map 4.5). The pastoralism of the Qashqa'i involves seasonal migration to remote pastures separated by about 300 miles. The vast distances make the Qashqa'i vulnerable to raids and create the need for negotiation with village leaders along the route for permission to cross their land. To deal with this vulnerability, the Qashqa'i developed linkages across several tribes that can be mobilized, temporarily, to create a large political unit under one leader. The Qashqa'i are an example of a pastoralist system in which political organization is highly developed.

DIVISION OF LABOR Families and clusters of related families are the basic production unit. Gender and age are, again, key factors in the allocation of work. In many pastoralist cultures, gender roles are clearly divided. Men are in charge of herding—moving the animals from place to place. Women are responsible for processing the herd's products, especially the milk. A cultural emphasis on masculinity characterizes many herding populations. Reindeer herding among the Saami of Finland is closely connected to male identity to the extent that the definition of being a man is to be a reindeer herder (see Lessons Applied, Chapter 16, p. 401). In contrast, women are the herders among the Navajo of the American Southwest. Navajo men's major work role is crafting silver jewelry.

The size of the animal involved is sometimes, but not always, related to the gender division of herding. Girls and women are often herders of smaller animals, perhaps because smaller animals need to graze less widely and can be kept penned near the house. Boys and men tend the animals that

(LEFT) Girls are in charge of herding water buffaloes to the Ganges River, at Varanasi, India, for watering. (RIGHT) Among the Ariaal, herders of northern Kenya, men are in charge of herding camels.

are pastured farther away. Children play important roles in tending herds. Among the cattle-herding groups of Eastern Africa, for example, parents want to have many children to help out with the herds.

PROPERTY RELATIONS The most important forms of property among pastoralists are, by far, animals, followed by housing (such as tents or yurts) and domestic goods (rugs and cooking ware). Depending on the group, ownership of animals is inherited through males, most commonly, or, less frequently, through females, as among the Navajo. A concept of private property exists for animals, which the family head may trade for other goods. A family's housing materials are also their own. Use rights, however, regulate pasture land and migratory routes, and these rights tend to be informally regulated through an oral tradition.

PASTORALISM AS A SUSTAINABLE SYSTEM Pastoralists have developed sustainable cultures in extremely varied environments, from the relative lushness of Iran to the more depleted situation of Mongolia. Pastoralism is a highly successful and sustainable economic system that functions in coexistence with other economic systems. As with foraging and horticulture, however, when outside forces squeeze the space available for migration, overexploitation of the environment soon results. A major external constraint on pastoralism is the goal of many governments to *sedentarize* (settle down) pastoralists. States do not like pastoralists to move across state lines, as they have done long before state boundaries were created. States want pastoralists to stay in one place so that they will be easier to keep track of, tax, and provide with services.

AGRICULTURE

Agriculture is a mode of livelihood that involves growing crops on permanent plots with the use of plowing, irrigation, and fertilizer; it is also called farming. In contrast to foraging, horticulture, and pastoralism, agriculture is an **intensive strategy**. Intensification involves the use of techniques that allow the same plot of land to be used repeatedly without losing its fertility. Crucial inputs include substantial amounts of labor for weeding, use of natural and chemical fertilizers, and control of water supply. The earliest agricultural systems are documented from the Neolithic period, beginning around 12,000 years ago in the Middle East (review Chapter 2). Agricultural systems now exist worldwide, on all continents except Antarctica.

Agriculture relies on the use of domesticated animals for plowing, transportation, and organic fertilizer either in the form of manure or composted materials. It is highly dependent on artificial water sources such as irrigation channels or terracing the land. Like the modes of livelihood already discussed, agriculture involves complex knowledge about the environment, plants, and animals, including soil types, precipitation patterns, plant varieties, and pest management. Long-standing agricultural traditions are now being increasingly displaced by methods introduced from the outside, and so the world's stock of indigenous knowledge about agriculture is declining rapidly. In many cases, it has become completely lost, along with the cultures and languages associated with it.

Occupational specialization increases in agricultural societies. Instead of people repairing their own tools and weapons, some people take on this work as a full-time job and no longer grow their own food, trading their skills for food with farmers. Other specializations that emerge as full-time occupations are political leaders, religious leaders or priests, healers, artisans, potters, musicians, and traders. Two types of agriculture are discussed next.

FAMILY FARMING **Family farming** (formerly termed peasant farming) is a form of agriculture in which production is geared to support the family and to produce goods for sale. Today, more than 1 billion people, or about one-sixth of the world's population, make their living from family farming. Found throughout the world, family farming is more common in countries such as Mexico, India, Poland, and Italy than in more industrialized countries. Family farmers exhibit much cross-cultural variety. They may be full-time or part-time farmers; they may be more or less closely linked to urban markets; and they may be poor and indebted or wealthy and powerful. Major activities in family farming include plowing, planting seeds and cuttings, weeding, caring for irrigation systems and terracing, harvesting crops, and processing and storing crops.

DIVISION OF LABOR The family is the basic labor unit, and gender and age are important in organizing work. Most family farming societies have a marked gender-based division of labor. Cross-cultural analysis of gender roles in 46 cultures reveals that men perform most of the labor in over three-fourths of the societies (Michaelson and Goldschmidt 1971). Anthropologists have proposed various theories to explain why productive work on so many family farms is male dominated (see Figure 4.4). The remaining one-fourth of the sample includes cultures in which men's and women's roles are balanced and cultures in which women play the dominant role.

In farming systems where men play the major role in agriculture, women are likely to work in or near the home, processing food, maintaining the household, and caring for

---

agriculture a mode of livelihood that involves growing crops with the use of plowing, irrigation, and fertilizer.

intensive strategy a form of livelihood that involves continuous use of the same land and resources.

family farming (formerly termed peasant agriculture) a form of agriculture in which farmers produce mainly to support themselves and also produce goods for sale in the market system; formerly called *peasant farming*.

Men and Plowing Hypothesis
This hypothesis is based on the importance of plowing fields in preparation for planting and on the fact that plowing is almost exclusively a male task (Goody 1976). Some anthropologists say that men plow because they are stronger than women and have the advantage of greater aerobic capacity. In southern India, for example, weather patterns require that plowing be accomplished in a very narrow time period (Maclachlan 1983). Assigning the task to the physically stronger gender ensures that the work is done more quickly and is thus an adaptive cultural strategy because it increases the chances for a good crop.

Women and Child Care Hypothesis
This hypothesis says that women are not involved in plowing and other agricultural field labor as much as men because such tasks are incompatible with child care (J. K. Brown 1970).

Women and Food Processing Hypothesis
This hypothesis notes that agriculture increases the demand for labor within and near the house (Ember 1983). Winnowing, husking, grinding, and cooking agricultural products are extremely labor-intensive processes. Linked to women's primary roles in child care and increased fertility in farm families, these labor demands restrict women to the household domain.

FIGURE 4.4 **Three Hypotheses to Explain Male Dominance in the Gender Division of Labor in Family Farming**

children (Ember 1983). This division of labor results in the *public/private dichotomy* in family farm societies, in which men are more involved with the outside, public world and women are more involved in the domestic domain. In this variety of family farming, men work more hours per week than in foraging, horticultural, and pastoralist systems. Women's work hours, in contrast, are as high as they are in horticultural and pastoralist systems.

In family farms in the United States and Canada, men typically have the main responsibility for daily farm operations; women's participation ranges from equal to minimal (Barlett 1989). Women do run farms in the United States and Canada, but generally only when they are divorced or widowed. Women are usually responsible for managing the domestic domain. On average, women's daily work hours are 25 percent more than those of men. A trend is for family farm women to take salaried jobs off the farm to help support the farm.

Balanced work roles between men and women in family farming frequently involve a pattern in which men do the agricultural work and women do marketing. This gender division of labor is common among highland indigenous groups of Central and South America. For example, among the Zapotec Indians of Mexico's southern state of Oaxaca (wuh-HAK-uh), men grow maize, the staple crop, and cash crops such as bananas, mangoes, coconuts, and sesame (Chiñas 1992) (see Map 6.3, p. 144). Women sell produce in the town markets, and they make tortillas, which they sell from their houses. The family thus derives its income from the labor of both men and women working interdependently. Male status and female status are quite equal in such contexts.

Female farming systems, in which women and girls play the major role in livelihood, are found mainly in southern India and Southeast Asia where wet rice agriculture is practiced. This is a highly labor-intensive way of growing rice that involves starting the seedlings in nurseries and transplanting them to flooded fields. Men are responsible for plowing the fields using teams of water buffaloes. Women own land and make decisions about planting and harvesting. Women's labor is the backbone of this type of farming. Standing calf-deep in muddy water, they transplant rice seedlings, weed, and harvest the rice. Why women predominate in wet rice agriculture is an intriguing question but impossible to answer. Its consequences for women's status, however, are clear. In female farming systems, women have relatively high status. They own land, play a central role in household decision making, and have substantial personal autonomy (Stivens et al. 1994).

Children's roles in agricultural societies range from prominent to minor, depending on the context (Whiting and Whiting 1975). *The Six Cultures Study,* mentioned earlier, found low rates of child labor in agricultural villages in North India and Mexico compared to high rates among the horticultural Gusii in Kenya. In many agricultural contexts, however, children's labor participation is high. In villages in Java, Indonesia, and in Nepal, children spend more time caring for

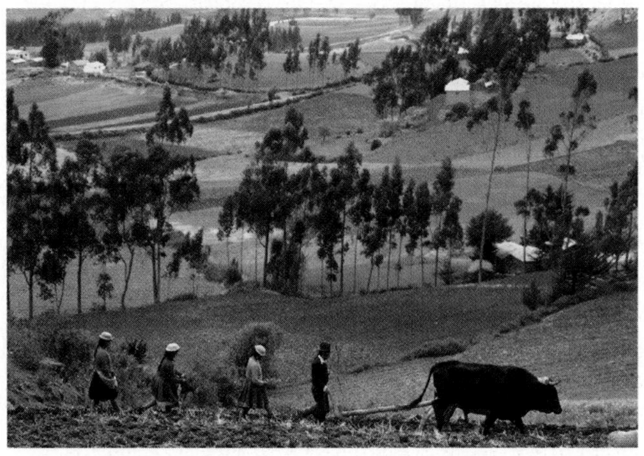

Family farming in highland Ecuador. A man plows while women in the family follow, planting seed potatoes.

farm animals than adults do (Nag, White, and Peet 1978). Girls between 6 and 8 years old spend more time than adults in child care, and girls work more hours each day than boys. Children in the United States are not formally employed in farm work, but many family farms rely on children's contributions on weekends and during summer vacations. Amish farm families rely to a significant extent on contributions from all family members.

PROPERTY RELATIONS Family farmers make substantial investments in land, such as clearing, terracing, and fencing, and these investments are linked to the development of firmly defined and protected property rights. Rights to land can be acquired and sold. Formalized, often written, guidelines exist about inheritance of land and transfer of rights to land through marriage. Social institutions such as law and police exist to protect private property rights.

In family farming systems where male labor and decision making predominate, women and girls are excluded from land rights. Conversely, in female farming systems, inheritance rules regulate the transmission of property rights more often through females.

INDUSTRIAL AGRICULTURE **Industrial capital agriculture** produces crops through capital-intensive means, using machinery and inputs such as processed fertilizers instead of human and animal labor (Barlett 1989). It is commonly practiced in the United States, Canada, Germany, Russia, and Japan and is increasingly being adopted in developing countries such as India, Brazil, Mexico, and China.

Industrial agriculture has brought with it the *corporate farm,* a huge agricultural enterprise that produces goods solely for sale and are owned and operated by companies entirely reliant on hired labor. Industrial agriculture has major social effects (see Figure 4.5).

Much of the labor demand in industrial agriculture is seasonal, creating an ebb and flow of workers, depending on the task and time of year. Large ranches hire seasonal cowboys for roundups and fence mending. Crop harvesting is another high-demand point. Leo Chavez studied the lives of undocumented (illegal) migrant laborers from Central America who work in the huge tomato, strawberry, and avocado fields owned by corporate farms in southern California (1992). Many of the migrants are Maya people from Oaxaca, Mexico (see Map 6.3, p. 144). They cross the border illegally in order to find work to support their families. In the San Diego area of southern California, they live temporarily in shantytowns, or camps. Here is what a men's camp is like on Sunday when they do not go to work in the fields:

> On Sundays, the campsites take on a community-like appearance. Men bathe, and wash their clothes, hanging them on trees and bushes, or on lines strung between the trees. Some men play soccer and basketball, using a hoop someone has rigged up. Others sit on old crates or tree-stumps as they relax, talk, and drink beer. Sometimes the men talk about fights from the night before. With little else to do, nowhere to go, and few outsiders to talk to, the men often drink beer to pass the time on Saturday nights and Sundays. Loneliness and boredom plague them during nonworking hours. (1992:65)

- Increased use of complex technology including machinery, chemicals, and genetic research on new plant and animal varieties.
  Social effects: This feature results in displacement of small landholders and field laborers. For example, replacing mules and horses with tractors for plowing in the U.S. South during the 1930s led to the eviction of small-scale sharecroppers from the land because the landowners could cultivate larger units.
- Increased use of capital (wealth used in the production of more wealth) in the form of money or property.
  Social effects: The high ratio of capital to labor enables farmers to increase production but reduces flexibility. If a farmer invests in an expensive machine to harvest soybeans and then the price of soybeans drops, the farmer cannot simply switch from soybeans to a more profitable crop. Capitalization is most risky for smaller farms, which cannot absorb losses easily.
- Increased use of energy (primarily gasoline to run the machinery and nitrates for fertilizer) to grow crops. This input of energy often exceeds the calories of food energy yielded in the harvest. Calculations of how many calories of energy are used to produce a calorie of food in industrial agricultural systems reveal that some 2.5 calories of fossil fuel are invested to harvest 1 calorie of food—and more than 6 calories are invested when processing, packaging, and transport are taken into account.
  Social effects: This energy-heavy mode of production creates farmers' dependence on the global market of energy supplies.

Source: Adapted from "Industrial Agriculture" by Peggy F. Barlett in *Economic Anthropology,* ed. by Stuart Plattner. Copyright © 1989. Published by Stanford University Press.

FIGURE 4.5 Three Features of Industrial Agriculture and Their Social Effects

Migrant workers picking broccoli in Salinas, California.

THE SUSTAINABILITY OF AGRICULTURE Agriculture requires more in the way of labor inputs, technology, and the use of nonrenewable natural resources than the economic systems discussed earlier. The ever-increasing spread of corporate agriculture worldwide is now displacing other longstanding practices and resulting in the destruction of important habitats and cultural heritage sites in its search for land, water, and energy sources. Intensive agriculture is not a sustainable system. Furthermore, it is undermining the sustainability of foraging, horticulture, and pastoralism. For many years, anthropologists have pointed to the high costs of agriculture to the environment and to humanity (see Critical Thinking).

INDUSTRIALISM AND THE INFORMATION AGE

Industrialism/informatics is the mode of livelihood in which goods and services are produced through mass employment in business and commercial operations and through the creation, manipulation, management, and transfer of information through electronic media. In industrial capitalism, the form of capitalism found in most industrialized nations, most goods are produced not to meet basic needs but to satisfy consumer demands for nonessential goods. Employment in agriculture decreases while jobs in manufacturing and the service sector increase. In some industrialized countries, the number of manufacturing jobs is declining, with more people being employed in service occupations and in the growing area of information processing such as computer programming, data processing, and communications.

An important distinction exists between the **formal sector**, which is salaried or wage-based work registered in official statistics, and the **informal sector**, which includes work that is outside the formal sector, not officially registered, and sometimes illegal. If you have done babysitting and were paid cash that was not formally recorded by your employer (for tax-deduction purposes) or by you (for income tax purposes), then you have participated in the informal sector. Informal sector activities that are illegal are referred to as being part of the underground economy, a huge and uncounted part of global and local economies worldwide.

THE FORMAL SECTOR: FACTORY STUDIES The formal sector includes a wide variety of occupations, ranging from stable and lucrative jobs to unstable or part-time and less lucrative jobs. Cultural anthropologists have done studies of small-scale workplaces, especially factories.

In one factory study, a team of cultural anthropologists and university graduate students studied the role of ethnicity in social relationships in a Miami clothing factory (Grenier et al. 1992). The clothing plant, a subsidiary of the largest U.S. clothing manufacturer, employs about 250 operators,

---

industrial capital agriculture a form of agriculture that is capital-intensive, substituting machinery and purchased inputs for human and animal labor.

industrialism/informatics a mode of livelihood in which goods are produced through mass employment in business and commercial operations and through the creation and movement of information through electronic media.

formal sector salaried or wage-based work registered in official statistics.

informal sector work that is not officially registered and sometimes illegal.

CRITICAL thinking

Was the Invention of Agriculture a Terrible Mistake?

Most Euro-Americans have a "progressivist" view that agriculture is a major advance in cultural evolution because it brought with it so many things that Westerners admire: cities, centers of learning and art, powerful state governments, and monumental architecture:

> Just count our advantages. We enjoy the most abundant and varied foods, the best tools, and material goods, some of the longest and healthiest lives, in history. . . . From the progressivist perspective on which I was brought up, to ask "Why did almost all our hunter–gatherer ancestors adopt agriculture?" is silly. Of course they adopted it because agriculture is an efficient way to get more food for less work. (Diamond 1994 [1987]:106)

Another claim about the advantage of agriculture is that it allows more leisure time, so art could flourish.

On the other hand, many scholars raise serious questions about the advantages of agriculture. These "revisionists" argue that agriculture may be "the worst mistake in the history of the human race," "a catastrophe from which we have never recovered" (Diamond 1994 [1987]: 105–106). Some of the "costs" of agriculture include social inequality; disease; despotism; and destruction of the environment from soil exhaustion and chemical poisoning, water pollution, dams and river diversions, and air pollution from tractors, transportation, and processing plants.

With agriculture, life did improve for many people, but not for all. Elites emerged with distinct advantages, but the gap between the haves and the have-nots increased. Health improved for the elites, but not for the landless poor and laboring classes. With the vast surpluses of food created by agricultural production, elaborate state systems developed with new forms of power exercised over the common people.

◆ **CRITICAL THINKING QUESTIONS**

- What is your definition of "the good life"?
- What are the benefits and costs of achieving the good life among, say, the Ju/'hoansi compared to your vision of the good life in your microculture?
- Who gets to live the good life in each type of economy?

mainly women. The majority of employees are Cuban women who, fleeing from the Castro regime, immigrated to Miami many years ago. As these employees have begun to retire, they are being replaced by new immigrants from Central America as well as Haitians and African Americans.

The workers are organized into a union, but members of the different ethnic groups have more solidarity with each other than with people in the union. Interethnic rivalry exists around the issue of management's treatment of members of different groups. Many non-Cuban workers claim that management favors Cuban employees. Some supervisors and managers expressed ethnic stereotypes, but not always consistent ones: "Depending on whom one listens to, Haitians are either too slow or too fast; Cubans may talk too much or be extraordinarily dedicated workers" (Grenier 1992:75). Managers see ethnic-based competition and lack of cooperation as a key problem that they attempt to deal with in various ways. For example, management banned workers from playing personal radios and installed a system of piped-in music by a radio station that supposedly alternates between "American" and "Latino" songs.

THE INFORMAL SECTOR: STREET VENDORS, DRUGS, AND SEX WORK Uncounted millions of people work in the informal sector. Many are involved in small-scale vending on the street, selling fruits and vegetables, beverages, cigarettes, snacks, books and magazines, ice cream, and souvenirs. Depending on the context, they may or may not have to pay for the location of their stand. Their rights to sell from a particular location are less secure than for someone who owns a shop. Some countries are seeking to remove street vendors in order to create a more modern city look.

A street vendor in Kingston, Jamaica. In many modernizing countries, city planners are taking steps to make street vending illegal on the grounds that such informal stands are unsightly.

▶ *If you were the mayor of Kingston, what position would you take on the street vending issue?*

Informal economies also operate at the global level, including the illegal trafficking of people and goods. The illegal drug industry links informal economies at the global level to the local level. Neither international drug dealers nor street sellers pay income tax on their profits, and their earnings are not part of the official gross national product (GNP) of any country. Currently, the drug traffic from Central and South America into North America is a multibillion-dollar business. Most of the supply moves through Mexico (see Map 6.3, p. 144). Fieldwork in a small, rural town in Mexico's central highlands shows how the legal and illegal economies related to drug trafficking are intertwined (McDonald 2005). This ethnography of the local *narcoeconomy,* or an economy based on the production and sale of addictive drugs, reports, "None of this could happen without deep interconnections between drug traffickers, and networks of well-placed politicians, civil servants, and security forces of various kinds" (McDonald 2005:115).

How does the narcoeconomy affect local life in central Mexico? This ordinary town became a site of extraordinary inequalities: new, opulent houses for some, high-end clothing stores, a cybercafé, and a day spa. New farmers, willing to participate in the narcoeconomy, are moving in and gaining legitimacy in the community. These farmers are typically young men who come from local farm families and have worked in U.S. drug trafficking networks. They are hard working and interested in promoting local economic development. Through their experiences in the United States, they gained business skills and they understand the importance of networking. The positive features of this situation, however, are part of an economic system that is illegal.

In many parts of the world, sex work is illegal. In the United States, it is legal only in the state of Nevada, where income from sex work is taxable. In neighboring Mexico, options for legalized, state-controlled female sex work exist (Kelly 2008). Patty Kelly did fieldwork in a legal brothel in Chiapas, Mexico (see Map 6.3, p. 144), called the Zona Galactica. She uses the term *prostitution* as the exchange of sex for money, and it is therefore one form of *sex work,* which is a broader category that includes services such as erotic dancing, phone sex, and participation in erotic films and other media formats (2008:26). Although the women prostitutes' situation in the legal brothel in Chiapas is not ideal by any means, it has advantages compared to contexts in which prostitution is illegal and prostitutes have absolutely no security or protection.

In Thailand (see Map 6.7, p. 157), laws about sex work are complicated (Jeffrey 2002). It is illegal to sell sex, but not to buy it. Recent legal reforms, however, pertain to the age of the sex seller and involve a prison sentence for anyone having sex with someone 15 years of age or younger. Nevertheless, child sex work in Thailand is an increasingly important part of the economy. The increased fear of HIV/AIDS among men who seek commercial sex leads to the demand for ever-younger sex workers, who are assumed to be less likely to be carriers of the virus. Recruitment of children as young as 6 years old began in the 1990s.

Young sex workers in Thailand. With the advent of HIV/AIDS, men seeking sexual services increasingly want young sex workers, including children, because they are less likely to be contaminated with the disease. International human rights organizations consider sexual transactions with minors to constitute child abuse, and they seek to prevent sex work by minors.

▶ *What is the international definition of a "minor"? Is it universally applicable? If yes, why? If not, why not? Be prepared to support your view.*

How do children become involved in commercial sex work? Family poverty is a major part of the answer in Thailand. Low and declining incomes in rural northern Thailand continue to prompt parents to send children into sex work. Within the context of severe and increasing poverty in northern Thailand, however, a village-based study provides further details about how culture shapes family decisions about sending daughters into sex work (Rende Taylor 2005). In northern Thailand generally, and in the study village, daughters are valued members of the family. Along with their value come obligations to the family. From an early age, the eldest daughter is expected to assume major household responsibilities, including care of her younger siblings. The youngest daughter will inherit the house and, with it, the obligation to care for her aging parents. Middle daughters are the ones most likely to be sent outside to earn an income, often in commercial sex work. Parents are more concerned about the welfare of the family than about a daughter's involvement in commercial sex work. They

THINKING OUTSIDE THE BOX

Some people think that in order to protect child sex workers, they should be unionized. Others argue that unionization conveys a message of acceptance of this role for children. Where do you stand on this issue and why?

say, "The problem here isn't that our daughter sells her body . . . it's that we have no food to eat" (Rende Taylor 2005:416).

Research in a small slum community on the edge of a tourist town, frequented mainly by Europeans, reveals that the children reject the view of child prostitutes as mere victims (Montgomery 2001). They believe the work they do is moral because it is done in support of their family. The child sex workers and their pimps, also children, exercise some choice in deciding which clients to accept and which to reject. These insights do not deny the fact that the child sex workers are exploited and sometimes seriously harmed. They do, however, provide a fuller picture by showing how the children define their work as related to family obligations and how they seek to protect themselves within a context of limited options.

Certainly, the voices of the children should be heard. But scholars and activists must look beyond the children's emic worlds to the global, macroeconomic structures that generate and support the people who pay for sex with children and the poverty in the communities that send children into sex work. So far, the author of this textbook has not seen a study of the people who seek commercial sex.

◆◆◆

Changing Livelihoods

This section looks at recent changes in the five modes of livelihood. Contemporary economic globalization is the latest of many outside forces exerted on local economies. Most notably, European colonialism, starting in the fifteenth century, had dramatic effects on indigenous people's livelihood, mainly through the introduction of cash crops such as tea, coffee, and cotton; co-optation and control of local labor through slavery, indentureship, and hire; and taking over land for colonial plantations and other enterprises.

As noted at the beginning of this chapter, the spread of Western capitalism continues to have far-reaching effects on the local economies with which it comes in contact. In the later part of the twentieth century, surging economic growth in Asia, the demise of socialism in the former Soviet Union, and the increasing economic power of the United States throughout the world combined to spur the growth of a global economy. Social scientists vigorously debate the effects of economic globalization on poverty and inequality. Economists, relying on country-level figures about changing income levels and distribution, often take the view that economic globalization is beneficial, overall, because it increases economic growth. Cultural anthropologists, who work with local-level data and a more "on the ground" view tend to emphasize the negative effects of capitalist expansion into noncapitalist settings (Blim 2000). They point to three major transformations:

- Dispossession of local people of their land and other resource bases and substantial growth in the numbers of unemployed, displaced people. Global capitalism has displaced millions of people from their land and contributed to the growth of the unemployed urban poor.
- Recruitment of former foragers, horticulturalists, pastoralists, and family farmers to work in low levels of the industrialism/informatics sector and their exploitation in that setting. Such people become dependent wage workers as opposed to independent providers.
- Increases in export commodity production in periphery regions in response to the demands of a global market and decreases in food production for family use. This trend may provide higher incomes for people but it also reduces their independent ability to feed themselves. It also contributes to mono-cropping and the decline of biodiversity in food crops.

Examples exist of some foraging-horticultural groups choosing to become involved in the global economy on their own terms (Godoy et al. 2005). Far more often, however, these cultures have been destroyed by the intrusion of Western economic interests, their local knowledge has been lost, and the people have become demoralized, distressed, ill, and suicidal. The following cases illustrate how small-scale cultures react to and deal with Western capitalism and globalization.

FORAGERS: THE TIWI OF NORTHERN AUSTRALIA

The Tiwi (tee-wee) live on two islands off the north coast of Australia (see Map 4.6) (Hart, Pilling, and Goodale 1988). As foragers, the Tiwi gathered food, especially vegetables (such as yams), nuts, grubs, small lizards, and fish. Women provided the bulk of the daily diet with their gathered vegetables and nuts that they ground and cooked into porridge. Men sometimes hunted kangaroos, wild fowl, and other game such as goanna (large lizards). Vegetables, nuts, and fish were abundant year round. The Tiwi lived a more comfortable life than Aboriginal groups of the mainland, where the environment was less hospitable.

The Tiwi have long been in contact with foreign influences, beginning in the 1600s with the arrival of the Portuguese, who were attracted to the islands as a source of iron. Later, in 1897, an Australian buffalo hunter named Joe Cooper came to the islands and kidnapped two native women to train as mainland guides. Cooper and his group greatly changed the Tiwi by introducing a desire for Western goods, especially tobacco. Later, Japanese traders arrived and offered Tiwi men manufactured goods in return for Tiwi women. In the early 1900s, the French established a Catholic mission on one island. The missionaries promoted reading of the Bible and criticized local marriage customs, which allowed a man to have multiple wives. The year 1942 brought World War II to the Tiwi as the Japanese bombed and strafed a U.S. airstrip. Military bases were prominent on the islands, and Tiwi

Aboriginal artist Eymard Tungatalum retouches a traditional Tiwi carving in an art gallery in Australia's Northern Territory. Tungatalum's carvings, along with songs and poems, are an important part of the Aboriginal people's efforts to revive their culture.

dependency on Western manufactured goods increased. In just a few decades, the Tiwi had experienced major culture shocks from contact with outsiders.

In the second half of the twentieth century, Tiwi lifestyle changed substantially. Instead of being regularly on the move in the bush, the Tiwi became settled villagers living in houses built of corrugated iron sheets. Tiwi men now play football (soccer) and water polo and engage in competitive javelin throwing. Tiwi produce art, especially carving and painting, for sale in Australia and internationally. Tiwi are active in public affairs and politics, including the aboriginal rights movement.

Another major factor of change is international tourism, a force that the Tiwi are managing with dignity and awareness. One Tiwi commented that tourism may mean that "white people too will learn to live with and survive in the country" (Hart, Pilling, and Goodale 1988:144–145).

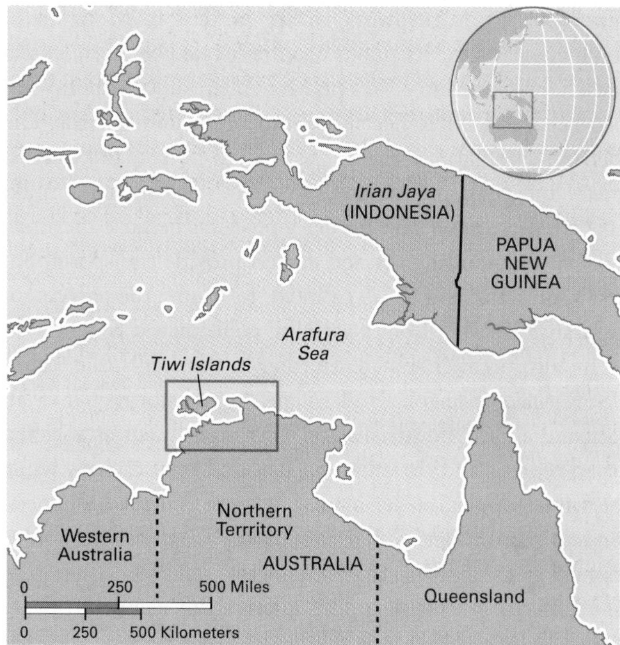

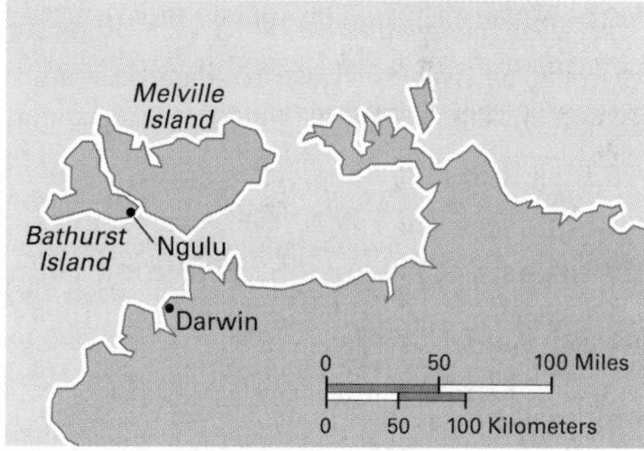

MAP 4.6 Tiwi Region in Northern Australia.
The Tiwi Islands consist of Bathurst and Melville Islands. The total number of Tiwi is about 2500 people. Most Tiwi live on Bathurst Island. In 2001, the Tiwi Islands Local Government Area was established, launching a new era of local government with statutory authority.

HORTICULTURALISTS: THE MUNDURUCU OF THE BRAZILIAN AMAZON

Outside economic and political factors have had major effects on horticultural societies throughout the world. In the Amazon, one force of change is the rubber industry. Its impact on indigenous peoples ranges from their being able to maintain many aspects of traditional life, to the complete loss of traditional lifeways. Like the Tiwi, the Mundurucu have experienced neither cultural preservation nor complete loss (Murphy and Murphy 1985).

After the arrival of Brazilians who were commercial rubber producers in the Amazon in the late nineteenth century, many Indians began to work for the Brazilians as latex tappers. For over a century, Mundurucu men combined their horticultural tasks with seasonal work collecting latex in the rubber area. Marked cultural change occurred when many Mundurucu people opted to leave their traditional villages, migrating to live in the rubber area year-round.

In the traditional villages, men live in a separate structure at one side of the village. Husbands visit wives and children in their houses. In the rubber settlement, husbands and wives live together in their own houses, and there is no separate men's house. In the traditional villages, women's communal work groups share water-carrying tasks. Such groups do not exist in the rubber settlement villages. Husbands in the new villages have taken on the task of carrying the water, so men work harder than they did in the traditional village. Although women in the settlement area work more hours per day than men, they believe that life is better because they like living in the same house with their husbands.

PASTORALISTS: THE HERDERS OF MONGOLIA

In the early 1990s, cultural anthropologist Melvyn Goldstein and biological anthropologist Cynthia Beall (1994) gained permission to do fieldwork among herders in Mongolia, a landlocked and mountainous country located between Russia and China (see Map 4.7). The Mongolian rural economy has long been, and still is, heavily dependent on animal herds. The "big five" animals are sheep, goats, yaks, horses, and camels. Sheep and goats provide meat and clothing and some milk; yaks are most important for dairy products because they give milk all year; and horses and camels provide transportation.

Goldstein and Beall wanted to study the effects of the transformation from a socialist, collectivized economy to a capitalist, market system. Starting in the 1950s, the (then) USSR ruled Mongolia and sought to transform it into an agricultural and industrial state. The government established urban centers, and the urban population began to grow while the rural population declined. The state provided all social services such as health and education. There was no homelessness or unemployment.

Official policy regarding pastoralism banned private ownership and collectivized all herds. The transition was difficult. Collectivization resulted in a 30 percent reduction of livestock, as owners chose to slaughter animals rather than collectivize them (Barfield 1993). Subsequently, state policy was altered to allow herders to control some animals as their own. By the early 1990s, the government's main policy was privatization, a process of transferring collective ownership and provision of goods and services to a system of private ownership. Collective ownership of herds was abandoned, and family-organized livelihood was reinstated.

Goldstein and Beall selected a remote region for their research: the Moost district in the Altai Mountain area in the southeastern part of the country, which is 99.9 percent pasture. At the time, the area contained about 4000 people and 115,000 head of livestock. Goldstein and Beall set up their tent and were immediately welcomed by an invitation to have milk-tea, a hot drink made of tea, water, milk, butter, and salt. During their stay, they spoke with many of the herders, participated in their festivals, and learned about people's perceptions of economic change. First, the people had to adjust to the dramatic restructuring of their economy from private family herding to collectivized herding. Then, in just a few decades, they had to adjust back to private herding.

The transition to privatization created serious problems for the herders. Their standard of living declined markedly in the 1990s. Goods such as flour, sugar, candy, and cooking oil were no longer available. Prices for meat fluctuated widely, making it difficult for them to know how to manage their herd size efficiently. Social services such as health care and schools were less available and of lower quality.

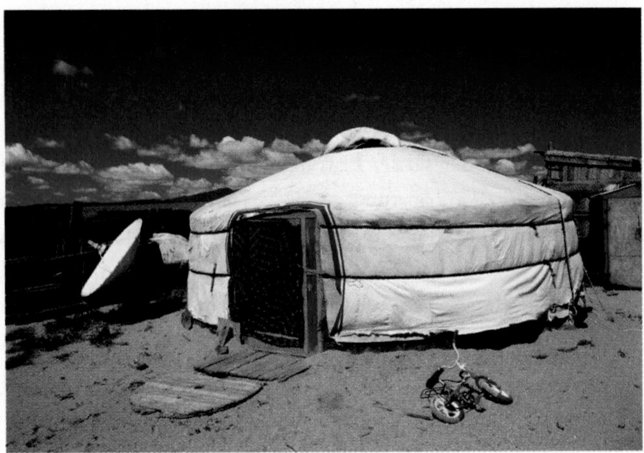

Even the most remote areas of Mongolia are now connected to the wider world through satellite dishes.

FAMILY FARMERS: THE MAYA OF CHIAPAS, MEXICO

Frank Cancian, in 1960, did fieldwork among the Maya of Zinacantán, located in the Chiapas region of Mexico (see Map 6.3, p. 144). He returned in 1983 to conduct a restudy and thus learned of changes that had taken place in the intervening twenty years (1989). At the time of his first research, most Zinacantecos were family farmers, making a living by growing corn and selling some of their crops in a nearby city. They were largely independent of outside forces in terms of their own food supply. The community was closely knit, its social boundaries defined by people's commitment to community roles and ceremonies. Twenty years later, both the local economy and the social system had changed dramatically.

MAP 4.7 Mongolia.
Mongolia, with its population of 2.9 million and its vast territory, is the most sparsely populated country of the world. After Kazakhstan, it is the world's second largest landlocked country. Mountains lie to the north and west and the vast Gobi Desert to the south. The environment is well suited to pastoralism but not to farming. One-third of the population makes a living primarily from pastoralism. Ulan Bator is the capital and largest city, with nearly 40 percent of the population living in and around the city. Many residents are squatters who have migrated to the city in hope of employment and live in a circle of encampments surrounding the capital. Tibetan Buddhism is Mongolia's primary religion.

The main cause of change was a large increase in public spending by the government in the 1970s. This spending supported the construction of roads, dams, schools, and housing throughout the Chiapas region. The government also sponsored outreach programs to promote agricultural change, mainly crop diversification and ways to increase production. Another important factor was the oil boom in northern Chiapas and Tabasco province, which brought unprecedented amounts of cash into the local economy.

By the early 1980s, 40 percent of the households had no land at all and planted no corn. Most people had become involved in wage work, and unemployment, rather than a bad farming season, was the major threat to food security. Wage work included the new opportunities in road construction, government jobs, transportation (of people, food goods, and flowers), and full-time trading in urban markets reachable by the new roads.

This story, in its general outlines, is similar to that of many family farmers throughout the world, especially in developing countries. It involves transformation from production mainly for own use to production mainly for sale within a cash economy geared toward making a profit. Overall, the area became more prosperous, more monetized, and more dependent on the outside economy. A second characteristic is the dislocation of farm owners from their land and their recruitment in the wage labor force. Many self-employed farmers sold their land and entered the wage economy. A third trend is increasing social inequality. Although many Zinacantecos raised their incomes substantially during this period, many others did not. Those who had the ability to buy a truck and take advantage of the new opportunities for urban trade created by the roads were the ones who became rich. Households with the least access to cash were left behind, and these households were characteristically headed by single women.

INDUSTRIALISTS: FACTORY WORKERS IN OHIO

Increased mechanization is a major aspect of change in industry worldwide, and it has marked effects on labor demand and household income of workers. Unemployment and manufacturing declines in America's Rust Belt are well-known trends in industrial lifeways. Gregory Pappas studied unemployment in Barberton, a working-class Ohio town (1989). A tire company that had been the town's major employer closed in 1980, eliminating 1200 jobs. Pappas lived in Barberton for a year, interviewing many people. He also sent a questionnaire to over 600 displaced workers for further information. Pappas learned how unemployed workers cope either by migrating or by finding new ways to spend their time in Barberton. The unemployed factory workers of Barberton are faced with having to construct a new identity for themselves: "For factory workers the place of employment is crucial; their identities are bound up in a particular place, and plant shutdowns compromise their ability to understand themselves" (Pappas 1989:83). As one unemployed man commented, "I don't know who I am anymore." In this context of decline, levels of stress and mental disorder have increased for many people.

GLOBAL CAPITALISM: TAIWANESE INDUSTRIALISTS IN SOUTH AFRICA

In South Africa during the 1990s, after the dismantling of apartheid, political leaders adopted a Western-style, capitalist economic policy (Hart 2002). One step toward expanding production and trade was to forge links with Taiwanese businesses in hopes of transferring to South Africa the Asian economic "miracle." Several Taiwanese industries were established outside major urban areas. Although there is no simple explanation for the so-called Asian economic miracle, one component was family-based production in which power hierarchies based on age and gender ensure compliance among workers.

Taiwanese managers tried to use such a hierarchical family system in South Africa in order to ensure a smoothly functioning labor force. Research in Taiwanese knitwear factories in KwaZulu-Natal province, western South Africa (see Map 9.5, p. 230), reveals substantial worker resentment against the Taiwanese managers. Women workers were especially vocal. Taiwanese patterns of communicating with women workers by using an idiom of family did not work with the South Africans. The women said they felt as though they were being treated like animals. The Taiwanese industrialists were separated from the workers by a wide racial, economic, and social divide. Imposing hierarchical family metaphors failed to create a cooperative workforce in South Africa. Many of the Taiwanese industrialists found themselves a focal point of local political conflict. In one town, a Chinese welcome monument was removed.

Karl Marx predicted that capitalism would wither away, but it has not yet done so. Through contemporary globalization, its effects are ever more powerfully felt in localities worldwide. Marx would be interested to observe how the Tiwi are developing international tourism, how the Maya people in Chiapas took up road construction for cash, and how Taiwanese knitwear manufacturers in KwaZulu-Natal encounter problems in cross-cultural labor management. He would perhaps also be amused to see how, at the same time, cultural anthropologists are trying to document and understand these changes.

4

the BIG questions REVISITED

◆ How do cultural anthropologists study economic systems?

Cultural anthropologists define economic systems as including three interrelated processes: production (making a living), consumption, and exchange. They study economic systems cross-culturally including systems other than modern capitalism. They divide cross-cultural patterns of making a living into five modes: foraging, horticulture, pastoralism, agriculture, and industrialism/informatics.

The current world system economy is increasingly competitive and unequal, placing some countries in the core, where their strong governments protect and expand their economic interests. Some countries are in the semiperiphery, and many are in the periphery. Anthropologists study local economic systems as well as regional and global economic factors that affect local economies.

◆ What are the five modes of livelihood?

Foraging relies on collecting food that is available in nature. In foraging societies, the division of labor is based on gender and age, with temperate foragers having more gender overlap in tasks than circumpolar foragers. All group members have equal rights to resources. Foraging has long-term sustainability when not affected by outside pressure.

Horticulture and pastoralism are extensive strategies that depend on domesticated plants (horticulture) and animals (pastoralism). Horticulture requires fallowing, and pastoralism requires the constant movement of animals to fresh pastures. The division of labor varies, including situations in which men do more productive work, those where women do more work, and those in which workloads are shared between men and women. Use rights are the prominent form of property relations. Both have long-term sustainability when not affected by encroachments.

Family farming systems produce crops for their own use and for sale in the market. Most family farming systems involve more male labor in the fields and more female labor in the domestic domain. Agriculture's sustainability is limited by the need to replenish the land.

In industrialism/informatics, the division of labor is highly differentiated by class, gender, and age. Widespread unemployment is found in many industrial economies. In capitalist societies, private property is the dominant pattern. Industrialism/informatics lacks sustainability, given its high demand for non-renewable energy.

◆ How are the five modes of livelihood changing?

Foragers are being incorporated into settled economies as their access to land is constricted by outside forces and as governments force them to sedentarize. Many former foraging people now work as farm laborers and in other jobs of low status in the mainstream cash economy. Others are advocating for the revitalization of their culture in the new global economy, producing art for sale on the world market, developing cultural tourism opportunities for outsiders, or gaining a share in profits related to commercialization of their indigenous knowledge.

Horticulture and pastoralism are under great pressure from the competing economic forms of agriculture and industrialism. Many former horticulturalists have migrated to plantations or urban areas and become part of the cash economy. States have pressured pastoralists to settle down. Family farms are declining worldwide in number as corporate farms increase. The labor supply has changed from being family based to including a high proportion of migrant laborers. The Information Age has only recently emerged, with its emphasis on economic processes that involve virtual workplaces and the movement of information, creating the new, combined mode of livelihood called industrialism/informatics.

Capitalism increasingly involves international investments and location of production sites in countries where wages are low. Such situations implicate culture in complex ways, including managerial issues and cross-cultural communication.

KEY CONCEPTS

agriculture, p. 98
economic system, p. 88
extensive strategy, p. 90
family farming, p. 98
formal sector, p. 101
horticulture, p. 93
industrial capital agriculture, p. 100
industrialism/informatics, p. 101
informal sector, p. 101
intensive strategy, p. 98
mode of livelihood, p. 88
pastoralism, p. 96
use rights, p. 91

SUGGESTED READINGS

Anne Allison. *Nightwork: Sexuality, Pleasure and Corporate Masculinity in a Tokyo Hostess Club.* Chicago: University of Chicago Press, 1994. Based on the author's participant observation, this book explores what it is like to work as a hostess in a club that caters to corporate male employees and discusses men's corporate work culture.

Mary K. Anglin. *Women, Power and Dissent in the Hills of Carolina.* Urbana: University of Illinois Press, 2002. This book addresses class, gender, and race issues in a mica processing factory in the Blue Ridge Mountains of North Carolina.

Michael Blim. *Equality and Economy: The Global Challenge.* New York: AltaMira Press, 2005. The author examines the relationships between global capitalism and social inequality at three levels: households, states, and international.

Jans Dahl Saqqaq: *An Inuit Hunting Community in the Modern World.* Toronto: University of Toronto Press, 2000. This ethnography of the Saqqaq, people of eastern Greenland, is based on fieldwork carried out at several times since 1980 in order to provide a diachronic perspective.

Daniel Dohan. *The Price of Poverty: Money, Work, and Culture in the Mexican American Barrio.* Berkeley: University of California Press, 2003. This ethnography explores poverty among Mexican Americans in two neighborhoods in California: undocumented immigrants in San Jose who work mainly in the Silicon Valley and urban Chicanos of Los Angeles.

Hallie Eakin. *Weathering Risk in Rural Mexico: Climatic, Institutional, and Economic Change.* Tucson: University of Arizona Press. 2007. Eakin documents the local effects of globalization and climate change through ethnographic studies of three agricultural communities in central Mexico.

J. A. English-Lueck. *Cultures@SiliconValley.* Stanford: Stanford University Press, 2002. A team of professors and anthropology students at San Jose State University conducted research for over a decade in Silicon Valley, and this book is the result of that work. The book describes what life is like for people in a "technology-saturated" environment, from working to shopping to family life.

Nandini Gunewardena and Ann Kingsolver, eds. *The Gender of Globalization: Women Navigating Culture and Economic Marginalization.* Albuquerque, NM: School of American Research Press, 2007. Contributing authors use feminist ethnographic methods to examine how neoliberal capitalist policies affect women in Argentina, Sri Lanka, Mexico, Ghana, the United States, India, Jamaica, and elsewhere.

Patty Kelly. *Lydia's Open Door: Inside Mexico's Most Modern Brothel.* Berkeley: University of California Press, 2008. This ethnography focuses on the personal histories and experiences of the women who work in a state-run brothel in the capital city of Chiapas, Mexico. Kelly shows how the brothel is a social experiment by the state to bring modernity to its poorest region through the business of sex.

Stephen A. Marglin. *The Dismal Science: How Thinking Like an Economist Undermines Community.* Cambridge, MA: Harvard University Press, 2008. Marglin provides an anthropological critique of economics, with attention to how economists' views of autonomous, self-interested individuals and market relationships erode a sense of community.

Heather Montgomery. *Modern Babylon? Prostituting Children in Thailand.* New York: Bergahn Books, 2001. The author conducted fieldwork in a tourist community in Thailand where many parents commit their children to prostitution. She gained a view of this system from the perspective of the children and the parents.

Katherine S. Newman. *Falling from Grace: The Experience of Downward Mobility in the American Middle Class.* New York: The Free Press, 1988. This book provides ethnographic research on downwardly mobile people of New Jersey as a "special tribe," with attention to loss of employment by corporate managers and blue-collar workers and the effects of downward mobility on middle-class family life.

Deborah Sick. *Farmers of the Golden Bean: Costa Rican Households and the Global Coffee Economy.* DeKalb, IL: Northern Illinois University Press, 1999. This book is about coffee-producing households in Costa Rica and the difficulties that coffee farmers face as a consequence of unpredictable global forces.

Michael K. Steinberg, Joseph J. Hobbs, and Kent Mathewson, eds. *Dangerous Harvest: Drug Plants and the Transformation of Indigenous Landscapes.* New York: Oxford University Press, 2004. The chapters in this book address opium and the people of Laos, opium production in Afghanistan and Pakistan, struggles over coca in Bolivia, marijuana growing by the Maya, use of kava in the Pacific, and policy questions.

突破渴望
新新美容城
真老大房食品公司
真老大房
ZHEN LAO
TCL
KFC

Nanjing Road in Shanghai, China. Nanjing Road is the main shopping street in Shanghai and the world's longest shopping street. Attracting over one million visitors a day, it is also one of the world's busiest shopping streets. In terms of status, it ranks with Fifth Avenue in New York City, Oxford Street in London, and the Champs-Elysées in Paris.

CONSUMPTION AND EXCHANGE

the BIG questions

◆ What is consumption in cross-cultural perspective?

◆ What is exchange in cross-cultural perspective?

◆ How are consumption and exchange changing?

OUTLINE

Imagine that it is the late eighteenth century and you are a member of the Kwakwaka'wakw (KWA-kwuh-kayuh-wah-kwah) of British Columbia in Canada's Pacific Northwest region (see Culturama at the end of this chapter, p. 133). You and your tribal group are invited to a **potlatch**, a feast in which the host lavishes the guests with abundant quantities of the best food and many gifts (Suttles 1991). The most honorable foods are fish oil, high-bush cranberries, and seal meat, and they will be served in ceremonial wooden bowls. Gifts include embroidered blankets, household articles such as carved wooden boxes and woven mats, canoes, and items of food. The more the chief gives, the higher his status rises and the more his guests are indebted to him. Later, when it is the guests' turn to hold a potlatch, they will give away as much as, or more than, their host did.

The Pacific Northwest region is rich in fish, game, berries, and nuts, among other foods. Nonetheless, given regional climatic variation, food supplies were often uneven, with some groups each year having surpluses while others faced scarcity. The potlatch system helped to smooth out these variations: Groups with a surplus would sponsor a potlatch and those experiencing a leaner year were guests. In this way, potlatching established a social safety net across a wide area of the Northwest. This brief sketch of potlatching shows the linkages among the three economic processes of making a livelihood, consumption, and exchange. Potlatches are related to food supply, they are opportunities for consumption, and they involve exchange.

Chapter 4 began the discussion of economic systems with the subject of making a living or production. This chapter provides cross-cultural examples of the modes of the other two components of economic systems:

- **Mode of consumption**: the dominant way, in a culture, of using up goods and services.
- **Mode of exchange**: the dominant way, in a culture, of transferring goods, services, and other items between and among people and groups.

The chapter's last section provides examples of contemporary change in consumption and exchange.

◆◆◆

Culture and Consumption

This section examines the concept of consumption, cross-cultural patterns of consumption budgets, and consumption inequalities. It also presents two theoretical positions on food *taboos*, or rules about forbidden food.

WHAT IS CONSUMPTION?

Consumption has two meanings: First, it is a person's "intake" in terms of eating or other ways of using things; second, it is "output" in terms of spending or using resources to obtain those things. Thus, for example, "intake" is eating a sandwich; "output" is spending money at the store to buy a sandwich. Both activities fit within the term "consumption."

People consume many things. Food, beverages, clothing, and shelter are the most basic consumption needs in most cultures. People also may acquire tools, weapons, means of transportation, computers, books and other items of communication, art and other luxury goods, and energy for heating and cooling their residence. In noncash economies, such as that of foragers, people "spend" time or labor in order to provide for their needs. In money-based economies, such as industrialized contexts today, most consumption depends on having cash or some virtual form of money.

MODES OF CONSUMPTION

In categorizing varieties of consumption, it makes sense to consider two contrasting modes, with mixed modes in the middle (see Figure 5.1). They are based on the relationship between demand (what people want) and supply (the resources available to satisfy demand):

- **Minimalism**: a mode of consumption characterized by few and finite consumer demands and an adequate and sustainable means to achieve them. It is most characteristic of free-ranging foragers but is also found to some degree among horticulturalists and pastoralists.
- **Consumerism**: a mode of consumption in which people's demands are many and infinite, and the means of satisfying them are never sufficient, thus driving

---

potlatch a grand feast in which guests are invited to eat and to receive gifts from the hosts.

mode of consumption the dominant pattern, in a culture, of using things up or spending resources in order to satisfy demands.

mode of exchange the dominant pattern, in a culture, of transferring goods, services, and other items between and among people and groups.

minimalism a mode of consumption that emphasizes simplicity, is characterized by few and finite consumer demands, and involves an adequate and sustainable means to achieve them.

consumerism a mode of consumption in which people's demands are many and infinite and the means of satisfying them are insufficient and become depleted in the effort to satisfy these demands.

leveling mechanism an unwritten, culturally embedded rule that prevents an individual from becoming wealthier or more powerful than anyone else.

Foraging	Horticulture	Pastoralism	Agriculture	Industrialism/Informatics
Mode of Consumption Minimalism Finite needs				**Mode of Consumption** Consumerism Infinite needs
Social Organization of Consumption Equality/sharing Personalized products are consumed				**Social Organization of Consumption** Class-based inequality Depersonalized products are consumed
Primary Budgetary Fund Basic needs				**Primary Budgetary Fund** Rent/taxes, luxuries
Mode of Exchange Balanced exchange				**Mode of Exchange** Market exchange
Social Organization of Exchange Small groups, face-to-face				**Social Organization of Exchange** Anonymous market transactions
Primary Category of Exchange The gift				**Primary Category of Exchange** The sale

FIGURE 5.1 Modes of Livelihood, Consumption, and Exchange

colonialism, globalization, and other forms of expansionism. Consumerism is the distinguishing feature of industrial/informatic cultures. Globalization is spreading consumerism throughout the world.

The social organization and meaning of consumption varies cross-culturally. As noted in Chapter 4, foragers are generally egalitarian, whereas social inequality characterizes most agricultural and industrialism/informatics societies. In foraging peoples, sharing within the group is the norm, and everyone has equal access to all resources. Among the Ju/'hoansi (review Culturama in Chapter 1, p. 23): "Even though only a fraction of the able-bodied foragers go out each day, the day's return of meat and gathered foods are divided in such a way that every member of the camp receives an equitable share" (Lee 1979:118).

The distribution of personal goods such as clothing, beads, musical instruments, or smoking pipes is also equal. An important process that operates among small-scale societies and works to keep people equal with each other is called a leveling mechanism. **Leveling mechanisms** are unwritten, culturally embedded rules that prevent an individual from becoming wealthier or more powerful than anyone else. They are maintained through social pressure and gossip. An important leveling mechanism among the Ju/'hoansi requires that any large game animal killed be shared with the group and its killer must be modest, insisting that the meat is meager (Lee 1969). Ju/'hoansi hunters gain no social status or power through their provision of meat. The same applies to other foragers. Leveling mechanisms are important in horticultural and pastoralist societies, too. For example, when someone's herd grows "too large," that person will be subject to social pressure to sponsor a large feast in which many of the herd animals are eaten.

Sharing is also a key value among many contemporary Indian tribes such as the Cheyenne of the Great Plains region of the United States (Moore 1999). Within the family, exchange goes on continuously and includes not just food but also tools, jewelry, and even vehicles. Sharing extends to people beyond the family who are considered part of the group. A Cheyenne woman told anthropologist John Moore about her observations at a child-care center where Anglo people also took their children: "'White people are funny,' she said. 'They spend half their time telling kids which toys are theirs, and the other half trying to get them to share'" (1999:179).

At the other end of the consumption continuum is consumerism, with the United States as the primary example, being the major consumerist country of the world. Since the 1970s, consumption levels in the United States have been the highest of any society in human history, and they show no sign of decline. The mass media send out seductive messages promoting consumerism as the way to happiness. Since China began to adopt aspects of capitalism, it has quickly become a consumerist giant. In the world's poorest countries, too, rising numbers of middle- and upper-class people pursue consumerism.

Well-stocked and brightly lit candy shops are a prominent part of urban nightlife in Valencia, Spain. Sugarcane was introduced into Spain by the Arabs. Later, the Spanish established the first sugarcane plantations on Madeira and the Canary Islands using enslaved laborers from Africa.

▶ *Log your food and drink consumption every day for a week and assess the role that sugar plays in the results.*

Minimalism was sustainable over hundreds of thousands of years, for most of humanity's time on earth. The amount of goods that the world's population consumed in the past 50 years equals what was consumed by all previous generations in human history. The growth of consumerism worldwide has some major costs:

- To the *environment and biological species diversity:* natural features such as rivers and lakes, forests, mountains, and beaches; nonhuman primates and hundreds of other species; and substances such as oil, gold, and diamonds
- To the world's *cultural diversity:* people who live in environments being destroyed by consumerism (these people currently occupy the tropical rainforests, circumpolar regions, deserts, and mountain areas)
- To the *poor* everywhere: people whose real and relative incomes place them in poverty and who experience an ever-widening gap between themselves and the well-off and the super-rich

In the United States, concern about the negative effects of consumerism tends to focus on the natural environment (especially "unspoiled" places for vacations such as national parks and beaches) and endangered nonhuman species rather than on the endangerment and possible extinction of indigenous peoples and other nonindustrialized people—minimalists who "tread lightly on the land." The tragic irony is that more people in North America probably know about an endangered bird species, the spotted owl, than about any single endangered human group.

Some countries have policies that seek to control consumerism and its negative effects. The government of Sweden has invested in public transportation and bicycle paths in cities in order to reduce the use of cars. London recently placed a tax on cars entering the city. San Francisco is working on a plan to recycle dog waste and use it to create energy.

As consumerism spreads throughout the world, changes in the social relations involved in consumption also occur. In small-scale societies—such as those of foragers, horticulturalists, and pastoralists—consumption items are typically produced by the consumers themselves for their own use. If not, they are likely to be produced by people with whom the consumer has a personal, face-to-face relationship—in other words, *personalized consumption*. Everyone knows where products came from and who produced them. This pattern contrasts markedly with consumption in our contemporary globalized world, which is termed *depersonalized consumption* Multinational corporations manage the production of most of the goods that people in industrialized countries consume. These products often are multi-sourced, with parts assembled in diverse parts of the world by hundreds of unknown workers. Depersonalized consumption, by distancing consumers from workers who actually produce goods, makes it more possible for workers to be exploited.

---

consumption fund a category of a personal or household budget used to provide for consumption needs and desires.

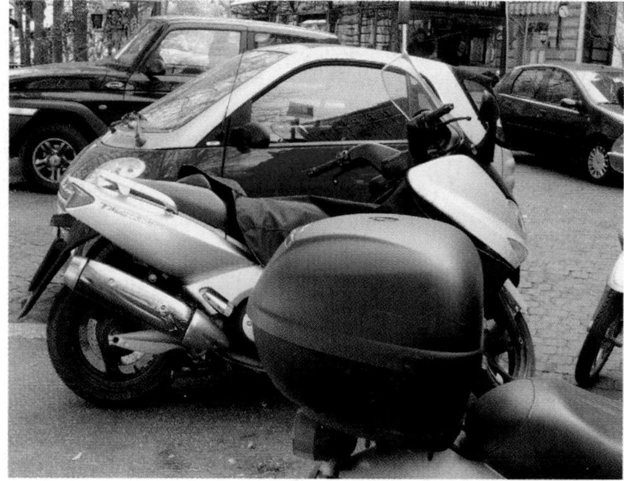

(LEFT) Seoul, capital of the Republic of Korea. The demand for electricity in urban centers worldwide has prompted construction of many large dams to generate power. Food must be shipped to urban markets. In general, cities have high energy costs compared to rural areas. (RIGHT) In Rome, as elsewhere in Europe, mini-cars are popular due to their fuel efficiency and ease of parking.

▶ *Do research to discover the gas mileage of an average new car in the United States or Canada and compare it to that of a mini-car.*

Even in the most industrialized/informatics contexts, though, depersonalized consumption has not completely replaced personalized consumption. The popularity of farmers' markets in urban centers is an example of personalized consumption in which the consumer buys produce from the person who grew it and with whom the consumer may have a friendly conversation, perhaps while sampling one of the farmer's apples.

CONSUMPTION FUNDS

Anthropologists define a **consumption fund** as a category within a person's or household's budget used to provide for his or her needs and desires. Cross-cultural analysis reveals five categories that appear to be relevant universally:

- *Basic needs fund:* for food, beverages, shelter, clothing, fuel, and the tools involved in producing or providing for them
- *Recurrent costs fund:* for maintenance and repair of tools, animals, machinery, and shelter
- *Entertainment fund:* for leisure activities
- *Ceremonial fund:* for social events such as rituals
- *Rent and tax fund:* for payments to landowners or governments for use of land, housing, or services

The categories apply universally, but the proportion of the budget allocated to each category varies widely and in relation to the mode of consumption. Remember: The "spending" involved may be in time, labor, or money, depending on the cultural context.

In the budget of free-ranging foragers, the largest share of expenditures goes into the basic needs fund. Foragers in temperate climates, however, spend far fewer hours per week collecting food than those in circumpolar climates. The next most important consumption fund among foragers is the recurrent costs fund, which supports repair and maintenance

Child labor is prominent in many modes of production. In this photograph, a girl picks coffee beans in Guatemala.

▶ *Should a child have the right to work, or should more international pressure be brought to bear against child labor?*

THINKING OUTSIDE THE BOX

Estimate your monthly expenditures in terms of the five funds. What proportion of your total expenditures goes to each fund? Do your expenditures fit well within the five categories or are different categories needed?

of tools and baskets, weapons, and shelter. Smaller shares are devoted to the entertainment fund and the ceremonial fund. Nothing goes into the rent and tax fund, because access to all land and other resources is free.

Consumption budgets in consumerist cultures differ in several ways from those in foraging, minimalist cultures. First, the absolute size of the budget is larger. People in agricultural and industrial/informatics societies work longer hours (unless they are unemployed), so they "spend" more of their time and labor providing for their consumption than foragers. Depending on their class position, they may have weekly cash budgets that are worth far more than their earnings due to stored wealth. Second, the relative size of the consumption funds varies in household budgets cross-culturally. Take as an example an imagined middle-class person in the United States. His or her consumption funds, compared to those of a forager, might look like this: The basic needs fund is a small portion of the total budget, given the increased overall size of the budget. This finding is in line with the economic principle that budgetary shares for food and housing (basic needs) decline as income rises. For example, someone who earns a total of $1000 a month and spends $800 on food and housing spends 80 percent of his budget in that category. Someone who makes $10,000 a month and spends $2000 a month on food and housing spends only 20 percent of her budget in this category, even though she spends more than twice as much as the first person, in an absolute sense. The largest share of the budget is the rent and tax fund. In some agricultural contexts, tenant farmers have to pay one-third to one-half of their crops to the landlord as rent. Income taxes claim well over 50 percent of personal income in countries such as Japan, Sweden, the Netherlands, and Italy. The entertainment fund receives a larger share than the ceremonial fund.

THEORIZING CONSUMPTION INEQUALITIES

Amartya Sen, an economist and a philosopher, proposed the theory of entitlements in order to explain why some groups suffer more than others during a famine (1981). An **entitlement** is a culturally defined right to provide for one's life needs. According to Sen, everyone has a set, or "bundle," of entitlements. For example, a person might own land, earn cash from a job, be on welfare, or live off an inheritance. Some entitlements are more secure and lucrative than others. *Direct entitlements* are the most secure form. In an agricultural society, for example, owning land that produces food is a direct entitlement. *Indirect entitlements* depend on exchanging something in order to obtain consumer needs: labor, animal hides, money, or food stamps. Because indirect entitlements involve dependency on other people or institutions, they are riskier bases of support than direct entitlements are. When a factory shuts down, animal hides drop in value, or a food stamp program ends, a person depending on those entitlements is in trouble. During times of economic decline, scarcity, or disaster, people with indirect entitlements are the most vulnerable to impoverishment, hunger, and forced displacement.

ENTITLEMENTS CROSS-CULTURALLY Entitlements vary depending on the type of economic system. In foraging societies, everyone has the same entitlement bundle. Entitlements are mainly direct, with the exception of infants and very old people who depend on sharing from group members for food and shelter. In industrial capitalist societies, entitlements are mainly indirect. People who grow all their own food are a small proportion of the total population. Even they depend on indirect entitlements for electricity and inputs required for maintaining their lifestyles. In highly monetized economies, the most powerful entitlements are those that provide a large and steady cash income, such as a good job. Other strong entitlements include home ownership, savings, stocks and bonds, and a retirement fund.

Internationally, entitlement theory exposes contrasts between countries that have secure and direct access to life-supporting resources and those that do not. Countries that produce food surpluses have a more secure entitlement to food than nations that are dependent on imports, for example. Replacing food crops with **cash crops**—plants grown primarily for sale, such as coffee or tobacco, rather than for own use—shifts a country from having mainly direct food entitlements to having mainly indirect entitlements. The same applies to access to energy sources that may be important for transportation to work or for heating homes. Direct access to energy resources is preferable to indirect access. This formula, however, leaves out the important factor of political power as exercised by the core countries of today's global economy. Many core countries lack direct access to critical resources, notably oil, yet they use political force to maintain access to such resources.

At the state (country) level, governments affect people's entitlements through policies related to employment, welfare programs, health care, and tax structures, among others. Political leaders and powerful policy makers decide how many people will live in poverty and how many will be allowed to become rich, or even super-rich. They decide on whether to fund programs that transfer wealth from the rich to the poor or to enact regressive tax structures that tax lower-income people at higher rates than the rich.

The entitlement concept can also be applied to *intra-household* entitlements, or shares of important resources that

---

entitlement a culturally defined right to life-sustaining resources.

cash crop a plant grown primarily for sale rather than for one's own use.

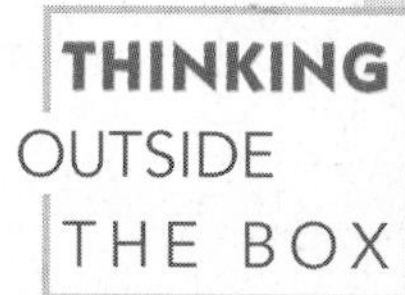

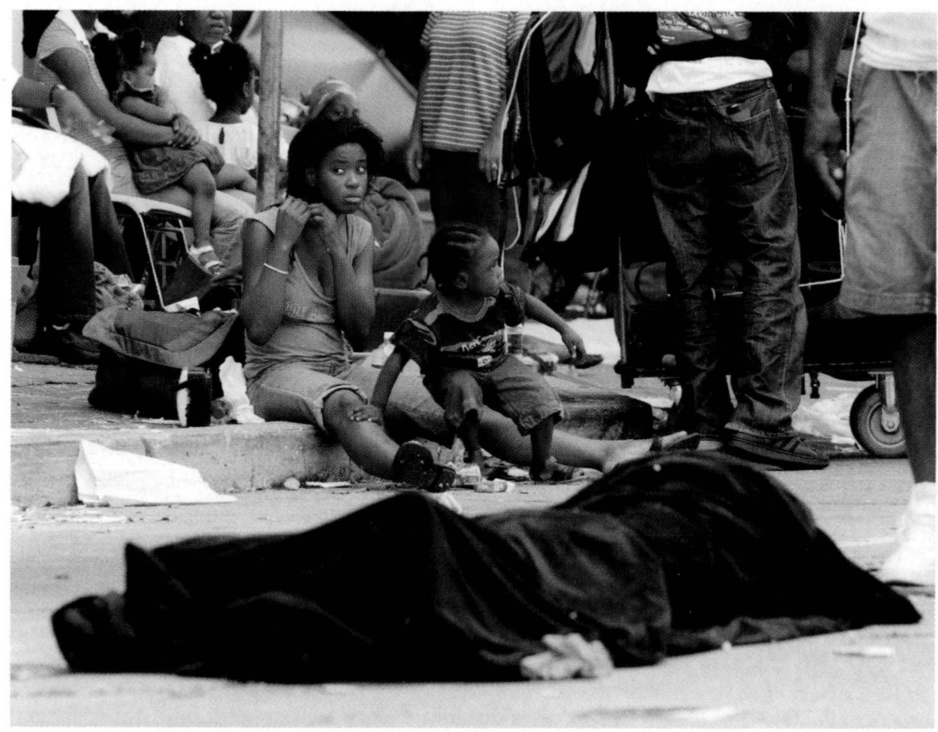

In the aftermath of Hurricane Katrina in 2005, a corpse lies covered as evacuees line the streets outside the convention center in New Orleans, Louisiana. After acknowledging that the initial federal effort to aid victims had failed, President George W. Bush deployed additional U.S. troops to the area.

▶ *Using the Internet, learn what roles cultural anthropologists played in the post-hurricane situation in the Gulf Coast area.*

are allocated to particular household members. Households do not always provide equal entitlements for all members. A household member who is employed and earns wages, for example, may have a more secure position in terms of resources such as preferred food than someone who does not. Commonly, men have more secure intra-household entitlements than women. For example, inheritance practices may ensure that sons receive assets such as land or the family business, whereas daughters are excluded. Intra-household entitlements may also affect expenditures on health care depending on the status and value of particular members.

During crises, entitlement structures often become glaringly clear. Famines are a good example. Famine is defined as massive levels of death resulting from food deprivation in a geographically widespread area. Most people think that famines are caused by overpopulation or by natural disasters such as droughts and floods. Comparative analyses of many famine situations prove, however, that neither overpopulation nor natural disasters are sufficient explanations for famine (Sen 1981). Calculations of world food supply in relation to population prove that there is enough food produced every year to feed the world's population. Furthermore, although natural factors are often catalysts of famine, they do not always cause famine.

Hurricane Andrew of 1992 devastated much of Florida, but state and federal agencies rushed aid to the stricken area. In Louisiana and Mississippi, the hurricanes of 2005 caused many deaths, massive loss of private and commercial property, and displacement of thousands of people. But they did not cause a famine. Anthony Oliver-Smith, an anthropologist who specializes in disasters, has said that there is no such thing as a purely *natural* disaster (2002). His point is that culture always shapes the patterns of human suffering and loss following a "natural" disaster. The social pattern of population displacement as a result of the 2005 hurricanes is testimony to the cultural shaping of disasters.

Entitlement analysis can help improve the effectiveness of humanitarian aid during famines and other crises (Harragin 2004). During the famine in southern Sudan in 1988 (see Map 16.7, p. 412), relief workers failed to understand the local cultural pattern of sharing, which extends to the last cup of rice. As food supplies decreased, local people continued to share whatever food was available. As a result, many people were surviving, but barely. When the food supply declined even more, the social safety net was unable to stretch further. Suddenly hundreds of people were dying. If relief workers had known about the culture of sharing unto death, they might have been able to forecast the breaking point before it happened and to bring in food aid sooner.

THINKING OUTSIDE THE BOX

What is in your personal entitlement bundle? Conduct a self-analysis of your daily consumption needs (food, shelter, entertainment, and other things) and how you provide for them. Then, imagine how you would provide for these needs if, starting today, your usual entitlements no longer had any value.

Homeless children rest by a storefront grate in Ho Chi Minh City, Vietnam.

▶ *Consider how the entitlement system affected children under pure socialism compared to the current transition to a more capitalist system.*

THREE CONSUMPTION MICROCULTURES This section provides examples of three consumption microcultures: class, gender, and "race." Microcultures have distinct entitlement patterns, related levels of health and welfare, and identity associated with consumption. Depending on the cultural context, social inequality may play an important role and have major effects on human welfare.

CLASS AND THE GAME OF DISTINCTION IN ISRAELI BIRTHDAY PARTIES Class differences, defined in terms of levels of income, are reflected in distinctive consumption patterns. Although class differences in consumption may seem too obvious to be worth studying, they constitute an important and growing area in anthropology.

A landmark study about consumer preferences, or "tastes," was conducted by a team of French researchers led by French anthropologist/sociologist Pierre Bourdieu (1984). They sent questionnaires to several thousand people, based on a national sample, and received 1000 responses. Statistical analysis of the responses revealed clear class patterns in, for example, choice of favorite painters or pieces of music. Preferences corresponded with educational level and father's occupation. An overall pattern of *distance from necessity* in tastes and preferences characterized members of the educated upper classes, who were more likely to prefer abstract art. Their goal was to keep "necessity" at a distance. In comparison, the working classes were closer to "necessity," and they preferred realist art. Bourdieu provides the concept of the *game of distinction* in which people of the upper classes continually adjust their preferences to distance themselves from the lower classes, whereas members of the lower classes tend to adopt aspects of upper-class preferences in order to gain status.

Cross-culturally, events such as weddings, funerals, and children's birthday parties are often occasions requiring large expenditures that send messages about the status (real or aspired) of the hosts. Children's birthday parties are a less studied topic but one with much potential, especially because such parties are becoming increasingly popular in cultures around the world. In Israel, children's birthday parties have recently become expensive events among middle-class and upper-class urbanites (Goldstein-Gidoni 2003). Parents hire birthday party professionals to create special themes. "Around the World" themes are popular, especially those drawing on Japanese, Spanish, South American, and Middle Eastern motifs. A current craze for Japanese culture, such as gardens and food, means that the Japanese theme is one of the most

Skiers and snowboarders line up to ride the lift to the top of the Middle East's first indoor ski resort, Ski Dubai, at the Mall of the Emirates in Dubai. Ski Dubai is housed in one of the world's largest malls and features a snow park with a twin track bobsled ride and a ski slope with five runs.

▶ *Plan a fantasy two-week trip to Dubai: How will you get there, where will you stay, where will you eat, what will you do, and how much will the trip cost?*

popular. "Around the World" birthday party themes are ostensibly to help the children learn about other places and people. At the same time, they make a statement about how cosmopolitan, well-off, and stylish the hosts are.

Not everyone, everywhere, buys into the game of distinction. Many individuals and wider social movements actively resist the spread of upper-class consumption patterns and promote alternative cultural practices.

WOMEN'S DEADLY DIET IN PAPUA NEW GUINEA Consumption patterns are often marked by gender and related to discrimination and inequality. Specific foods may be considered "men's food" or "women's food." An example of lethal gender inequalities in food consumption comes from highland Papua New Guinea (see Map 5.1).

The story begins with the eruption of a mysterious disease, with the local name of *kuru*, among the Fore (for-ay), a horticultural people of the highlands (Lindenbaum 1979). Between 1957 and 1977, about 2500 people died of kuru. Most victims, however, were women. The first signs of kuru are shivering tremors, followed by a progressive loss of motor ability along with pain in the head and limbs. Kuru victims could walk unsteadily at first but would later be unable to get up. Death occurred about a year after the first symptoms appeared.

American medical researchers revealed that kuru was a neurological disease. Australian cultural anthropologist Shirley Lindenbaum pinpointed the cultural cause of kuru: cannibalism. Kuru victims had eaten the flesh of deceased people who had died of kuru.

Why were most of the kuru victims women? Lindenbaum learned that among the Fore, it was considered acceptable to cook and eat the meat of a deceased person, although it was not a preferred food. The preferred source of animal protein is meat from pigs, and men receive preferential access to the best food. Fore women had begun to eat human flesh more often because of increased scarcity of pigs. Population density in the region had risen, more land was being cultivated, and forest areas had decreased. Pigs live in forest areas, so as their habitat became more restricted, their numbers declined. The Fore could not move to more pig-abundant areas because they were bounded on the east, west, and north sides by other groups. The south was a harsh and forbidding region. These factors, combined with the Fore's male-biased system of protein consumption, forced women to turn to the less preferred protein source of human flesh. By eating the flesh, including brains, of kuru victims, they contracted the disease.

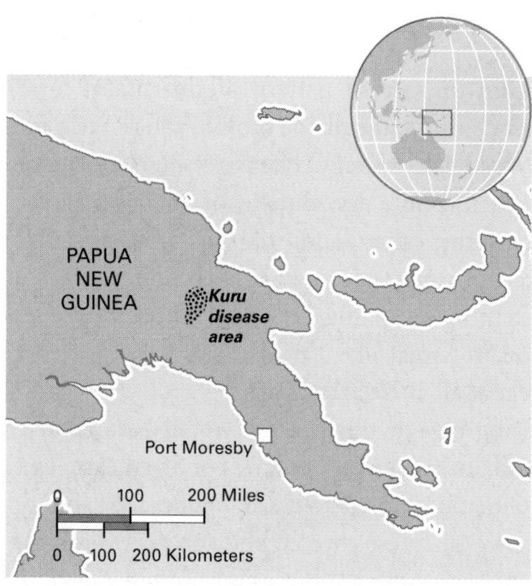

MAP 5.1 Location of the Kuru Epidemic in Papua New Guinea.

"RACE" AND CHILDREN'S SHOPPING IN NEW HAVEN Throughout the world, in countries with "race"-based social categories, inequalities in consumption and quality of life exist, often in spite of anti-discrimination legislation. In the United States, racism and racial discrimination affect many areas of life from access to housing, neighborhood security and services, schooling, health, and whether a person is likely to be ignored by a taxi or stopped by a police officer for speeding. Racial inequality between Black and White Americans has risen steadily since the 1970s in terms of income, wealth, and property ownership, especially house-ownership (Shapiro 2004). Those at the top of the income distribution have increased their share of the wealth most. The share of total income that goes to the top 1 percent of families is nearly the same size as the total income share of the bottom 40 percent.

How is this happening in a country dedicated to equality of opportunity? A large part of the answer lies in the simple fact that, in a capitalist system, inequality leads to more inequality through the transfer of wealth and property across generations. Those who have wealth and property are able to establish their children's wealth through college tuition payments, house down payments, and other financial gifts. The children of poor parents have to provide for their education and housing costs from their wages alone, a fact that makes it far less likely that they will be able to pursue higher education or buy a home.

As a graduate student in anthropology at Yale University, Elizabeth Chin decided to do her dissertation research on consumption patterns among schoolchildren in a poor, African American neighborhood in New Haven, Connecticut (2001) (see Map 5.2). In terms of per capita income, Connecticut is the wealthiest state in the United States. It also harbors some of the most severe poverty and racial inequality in its major cities. Chin describes New Haven as a "patchwork of clearly delineated neighborhoods that can veer quite suddenly from the abjectly poor to the fabulously wealthy" (2001:vii). These zones are largely divided into White and Black groups who are fearful and suspicious of

MAP 5.2 Connecticut, United States.
In terms of per capita income, Connecticut is the wealthiest state in the United States. Its population of about 3.5 million includes a majority of Whites (76 percent), predominantly of Italian, Irish, and English descent. Blacks and Latinos constitute about 10 percent of the population each. Indian tribal peoples are 0.3 percent.

each other. During her research in "Newhallville," Chin found that the Black and White cultural worlds are clearly separate and deeply unequal. In the Black neighborhood, 50 percent of children age 5 and under were living in poverty.

Chin formed a relationship with one fifth-grade class of 22 students. She spent time in the classroom. She explored the neighborhood with some of the children, visited with them and their families in their homes, and accompanied them on shopping trips to the mall. The children are bombarded with media messages about consumption but they have little money to spend. Some receive an allowance for doing household chores; some receive small amounts of pocket money on an ad hoc basis; and some earn money from small-scale ventures such as a cucumber stand. They learn about the basics of household finances and the costs of daily life early on. Seeing their families strain every day to put meals on the table teaches them about the negative effects of overindulgence: "From divvying up the milk to figuring out where to sleep there is an emphasis on sharing and mutual obligation" (2001:5).

These practical lessons shape how the children spend their money when they go to the mall. Practicality and generosity guide their shopping choices. In order to learn about the children's decisions, Chin would give a child $20 and go with him or her to the mall. Most of the girls spent over half their money on gifts for family members, especially their mothers and grandmothers (2001:139). The girls knew their mothers' shoe sizes and clothing sizes. One boy, just before school was to start in the fall, spent $10 on a T-shirt to wear on the first day of school, $6 on a pair of shorts, and the rest on school supplies: pencils, pens, notebook paper, and a binder (2001:135). In her two years of research, Chin never heard a Newhallville child nag a caretaker about buying him or her something or whine about personal consumption desires.

Birthday parties are rare events in Newhallville. The one birthday party Chin observed involved an $18 ice-cream cake. Birthday gifts are few. One girl received three gifts on her tenth birthday: a jump rope and a bingo game from her mother, wrapped in brown paper made from a grocery bag, and an inexpensive plastic toy from her grandmother (2001:72). There was no party, but her mother baked a chocolate cake for her.

FORBIDDEN CONSUMPTION: FOOD TABOOS

Cultural anthropologists have a long-standing interest in trying to explain culturally specific food taboos, or rules about prohibited foods. Cultural materialists and symbolic anthropologists disagree about why food taboos exist.

WHAT CULTURAL MATERIALISM SAYS Cultural materialist Marvin Harris (review Chapter 1) asks why there are Jewish and Muslim taboos on eating pig when pig meat is so enthusiastically consumed in many other parts of the world (1974). He says, "Why should gods so exalted as Jahweh and Allah have bothered to condemn a harmless and even laughable beast whose flesh is relished by the greater part of mankind?" (1974:36). Harris proposes that we consider the role of environmental factors during early Hebrew times and the function of this prohibition in terms of its fit to the local ecology.

Within the overall pattern of this mixed farming and pastoralist complex, the divine prohibition of pork constituted a sound ecological strategy. The pig is thermodynamically ill-adapted to the hot, dry climate of the Negev, the Jordan Valley, and the other lands of the Bible and the Koran. Compared to cattle, goats, and sheep, the pig has an inefficient system for regulating its body temperature. Despite the expression "to sweat like a pig," it has been proved that pigs can't sweat at all (1974:41–42).

Raising pigs in this context would be a luxury. On the other hand, in "pig-loving" cultures of Southeast Asia and the Pacific, climatic factors, including temperature, humidity, and the presence of forest cover (good for pigs) promote raising pigs. There, pigs offer an important protein source that complements the major root crops: yams, sweet potatoes, and taro.

Preparation for a feast in the highlands of Papua New Guinea, where people place much value on consuming roasted pig meat.

▶ *What are the high-status foods in your cultural world(s)?*

Harris acknowledges that not all religiously sanctioned food practices can be explained ecologically and that food practices often serve to communicate and promote social identity. But analysis of food consumption should always consider ecological and material factors of production as basic.

WHAT SYMBOLIC ANTHROPOLOGISTS SAY Symbolic anthropologist Mary Douglas argues, in contrast to Harris, that what people eat has less to do with the material conditions of life (the environment or hunger) than with what food means and how food communicates meaning and identity (1966). For Douglas, people's emic categories about food provide a mental map of the world and people's place in it. *Anomalies*, or things that do not fit into culturally defined categories, become reminders to people of moral problems or things to avoid.

Douglas uses a symbolic approach in examining food categories and anomalies as laid out in the Old Testament book of Leviticus. One rule says that people may eat animals with cloven hoofs and that chew a cud. On the basis of this rule, animals that do not satisfy both criteria are anomalies, and such animals are considered unclean and are taboo as food. These anomalies include camels, pigs, and hares. A pig, for example, has cloven hoofs, but it does not chew a cud. In the interpretation of Douglas, the food rules in Leviticus are a symbolic system defining completeness and purity (the animals one can eat) in contrast to incompleteness and impurity (the animals one cannot eat). By extension, she argues, people who know these rules and follow them are constantly reminded of God's perfection, completeness, and purity. When people follow these rules, they communicate their identity as pure and godly to other people. Thus, according to Douglas, food choices are not about the nutritional content of the food; rather, they have to do with symbols and meaning. She downplays studying the "practical" aspects of food because, she says, that distracts analysts from studying the meaning of food.

Anthropologists, no matter which theoretical perspective they favor about food taboos, recognize that there is more to food than just eating. Douglas emphasizes the importance of food rules as codes, ways of communicating meaning, and this interpretation is clearly valid. Harris says that economic and political aspects of food choices must be considered for a full understanding, and this point is valid, too.

◆◆◆

Culture and Exchange

Exchange is the transfer of something that may be material or immaterial between at least two persons, groups, or institutions. Cultural anthropologists have done much research on gifts and other forms of exchange, starting with Malinowski's work on the kula in the South Pacific (review Culturama, Chapter 3, p. 67) and Boas's research on potlatching among Northwest Coast Indians. In all economic systems, individuals and groups exchange goods and services with others, so. But variation exists in what is exchanged, how goods are exchanged, when exchange takes place, and the meaning of exchange.

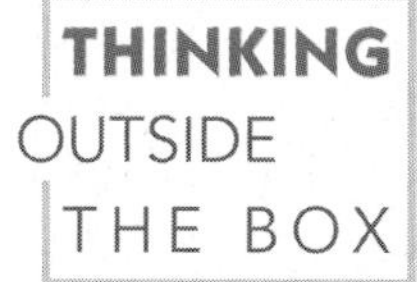

You have invited Jesus, the Buddha, Muhammad, and Moses to dinner. What are you serving?

everyday ANTHROPOLOGY

The Rules of Hospitality

In much of the Middle East, where women spend most of their time in the domestic domain, social visits among women are eagerly anticipated and carefully planned events with complex rules about what foods and drinks should be served (Wikan 1982). In Oman, when women go outside the home, they wear head veils, face masks, and full-length gowns. Their main social activity consists of visits to other women in their homes. A typical visit involves sitting, chatting, and eating snacks.

Social etiquette dictates what should be served and how. Coffee and dates are the traditional entertainment foods offered to close neighbors. Biscuits (cookies), caramel candies, and popcorn are favored snacks. Beyond the particular snack item, the number of dishes offered is important. For neighbors who interact on a daily basis, a single dish is typical. All other visitors should be offered at least two plates with different contents, or else the hostess will be considered stingy. In the case of many guests, the number of plates must be increased, with a minimum of four plates, and the variety of snacks must be greater. Another rule of visitor etiquette requires that guests should leave approximately half of the food served to them; it will be consumed by members of the hostess' household (1982:130–132).

Cooked food, such as meat and sweets, is served when entertaining guests at weddings, seasonal feasts, and burials. In such situations, when cooked food is served, the hosts may never eat with their guests: "Even if the consequence is that the guest must eat all alone, in a separate room, it would be disrespectful to arrange it otherwise" (1982:133).

◆ FOOD FOR THOUGHT

- How do these Omani rules of hospitality resemble or contrast with your rules of hospitality? Think about your choices of items served, numbers of items, and other choices you make about what to serve and how to serve it when entertaining guests.

A Bedu (Bedouin) woman of Muscat, Oman.

▶ *Assume you are going to Oman for a semester abroad. What should you know about the culture before you go?*

WHAT IS EXCHANGED?

The items that people exchange range from seashells to stocks and bonds and may be purely utilitarian (see Figure 5.2). Items of exchange may carry meanings and have a history, or "social life," of their own, as prized kula items do (Appadurai 1986).

Category	Selected Examples
Material Goods	Food to family and group members Gifts for special occasions such as weddings Money
Nonmaterial Goods	Myths, stories, rituals Time, labor
People	Offspring in marriage Slavery

FIGURE 5.2 Items of Exchange

In contemporary industrialized societies, money is the major item of exchange, and such economies are referred to as *monetized.* In nonmarket economies, money plays a less important role, and time, labor, and goods are prominent exchange items. As nonmarket economies are connected, through globalization, they are confronted with the (to them) peculiar and mysterious meaning of Western money. Often, they localize the meanings of money, by treating particular bills as more special than others. In many cultures, money has completely replaced other valued items of exchange, such as shell wealth in Papua New Guinea.

Nonmonetary exchange exists in contemporary industrial societies, too. Hosting dinner parties, exchanging gifts at holiday times, and sharing a bag of potato chips with a friend are examples of common forms of nonmonetary exchange. Some scholars also include kisses, glances, and loyalty (Blau 1964).

MATERIAL GOODS Cross-culturally, food is one of the most common exchange goods both in everyday life and on ritual occasions. Daily meals involve some form of exchange,

Omani biotech scientist, Ms. Wahida al-Amri, at work in her lab in the Omani Marine Science and Fisheries Center.

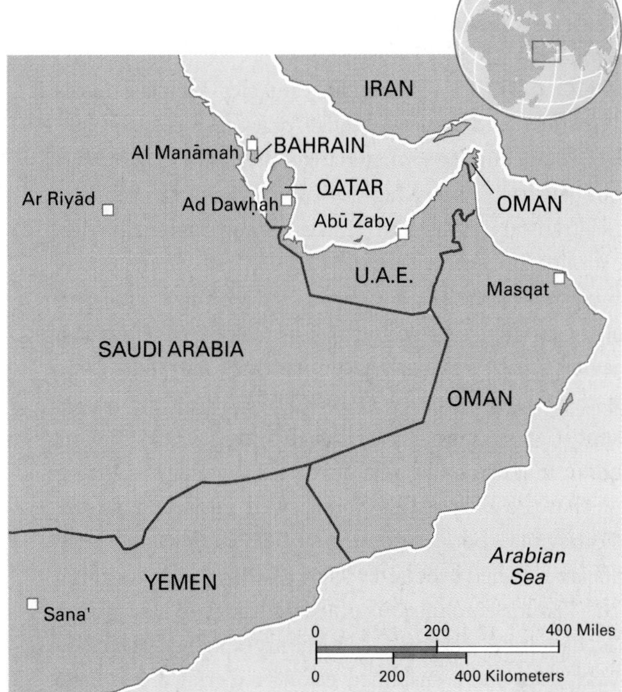

MAP 5.3 Oman.
The Sultanate of Oman is mainly a vast desert plain with a hot, dry climate. The population of nearly 3 million includes over 500,000 immigrant laborers. The economy is based mainly on crude oil. The major religion is Ibādī Islam, a more liberal version of Islam than Sunni or Shi'a Islam. Arabic is the official language, with English a widely spoken second language. Several local dialects are spoken including the Omani dialect of Arabic.

as do most ceremonies and rituals. In many cultures, arranging a marriage involves many stages of food gifts and countergifts exchanged between the families of the couple.

Wedding exchanges among the Nias of northern Sumatra, Indonesia (see Map 8.3, p. 198), provide an illustration of a complex set of exchanges. From the betrothal to the actual marriage, a scheduled sequence of events occurs at which culturally stipulated food and other gifts are exchanged between the families of the bride and groom (Beatty 1992). At the first meeting between the families, when the prospective groom expresses his interest in a betrothal, he and his party visit the bride's house and are fed. The guests receive the lower jaw of a pig (the portion of honor), and they take away with them raw and cooked portions of the pig for the father of the groom-to-be (1992:121). Within the next week or two, the prospective groom brings a gift of 3 to 12 pigs to confirm the engagement. He returns the container used for the pig meat given to him on the previous visit, filled with a certain kind of nut. The groom gives more pigs and gold as the major gift to seal the marriage. For many years following the wedding, the two families continue to exchange gifts.

On an everyday level, exchanges of food and beverages are important in friendships. Among friends, food exchanges involve their own, largely unconscious rules of etiquette (see Everyday Anthropology).

Exchanging alcoholic beverages is an important feature of many community ritual events in Latin America. In a highland village in Ecuador, the San Juan fiesta is the high point of the year (Barlett 1980). The fiesta consists of four or five days during which small groups of celebrants move from house to house, dancing and drinking. The anthropologist reports on the event:

> I joined the groups consisting of the president of the community and the elected *alcaldes* (councilmen and police), who were accompanied by their wives, a few friends, and some children. We met each morning for a hearty breakfast at one house, began drinking there, and then continued eating and drinking in other homes throughout the day and into the evening. . . . Some people drink for only one or two days, others prefer to make visits mainly at night, some people drink day and night for four days. (1980:118–119)

Guests who drink at someone's house will later serve their former hosts alcohol in return.

SYMBOLIC GOODS Intangible valuables such as myths (sacred stories) and rituals (sacred practices) may be exchanged in ways similar to material goods. In the Balgo Hills region of Australia (see Map 5.4), long-standing exchange networks transfer myths and rituals among regionally dispersed groups of women (Poirier 1992). The women may keep important narratives and rituals for a limited time and then must pass them on to other groups. One is the *Tjarada,* a love-magic ritual with an accompanying narrative. The Tjarada came to the women of Balgo Hills from the north. They kept it for about 15 years and then passed it on to another group in a ceremony that lasted for three days. During the time that the Balgo Hills women were custodians of the Tjarada, they incorporated some new elements into it. These elements are retained even after its transfer to the next group. Thus, the Tjarada contains bits of local identity of each group that has had it. A sense of community and responsibility thereby develops and is sustained among the groups that have held the Tjarada.

LABOR In labor-sharing groups, people contribute labor to other people on a regular basis (for seasonal agricultural work such as harvesting) or on an irregular basis (in the event of a crisis such as the need to rebuild a barn damaged by fire). Labor-sharing groups are part of what has been called a "moral economy" because no one keeps formal records on how much any family puts in or takes out. Instead, accounting is socially regulated. The group has a sense of being a moral community based on years of trust and sharing. In Amish communities of North America (see Culturama, Chapter 6, p. 140), sharing labor is a central part of life. When a family needs a new barn that requires group labor, a barn-raising party is called. Many families show up to help. Adult men provide manual labor, and adult women provide food for the event.

MONEY For most of humanity's existence, people did not purchase things. They collected or made things they needed themselves, shared, or exchanged items for other things. The invention of money is recent, only a few thousand years ago. **Money** is a medium of exchange that can be used for a variety of goods (Godelier 1971). Money exists cross-culturally in such diverse forms as shells, salt, cattle, furs, cocoa beans, and iron hoes.

Modern money, in the form of coins and paper bills, has the advantages of being portable, divisible, uniform, and recognizable (Shipton 2001). On the other hand, modern money

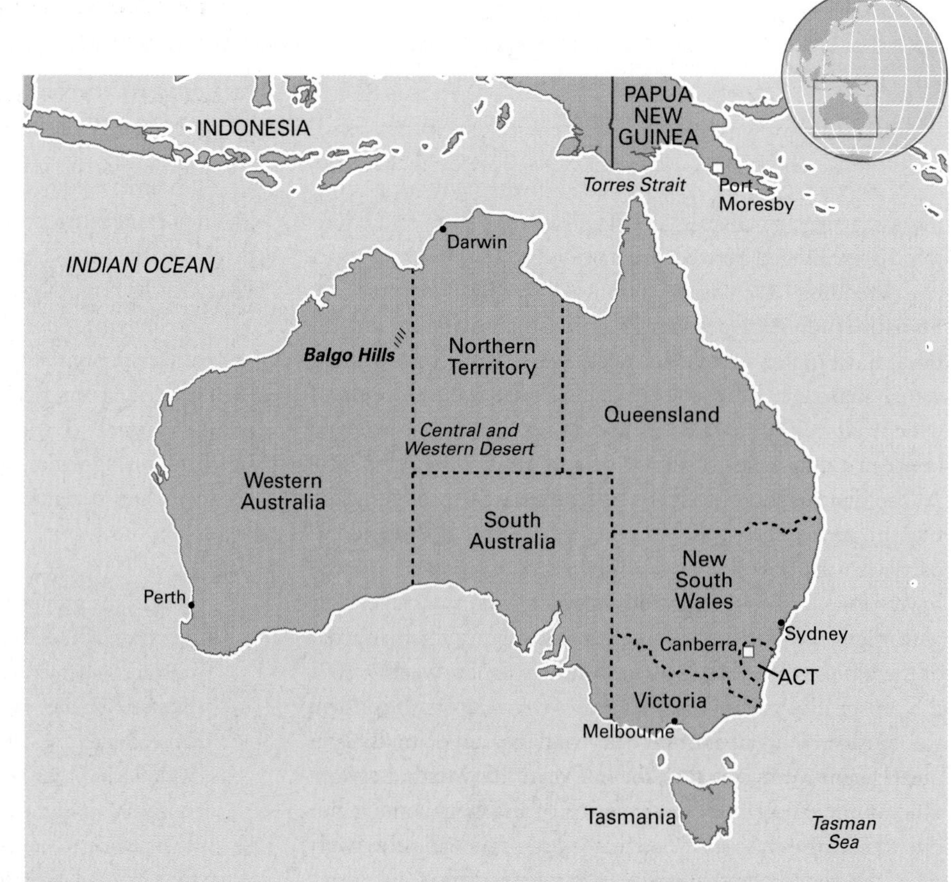

MAP 5.4 The Balgo Hills (Wirrimanu) Region in Western Australia.
The Balgo Hills community is located on the northern edge of the Tanami and Great Sandy Deserts. One of Australia's most isolated indigenous desert settlements, it nevertheless has a flourishing art center. Balgo paintings and glass are highly sought after by collectors. To learn about Balgo art and artists, visit http://www.aboriginalartonline.com/regions/balgo.php.

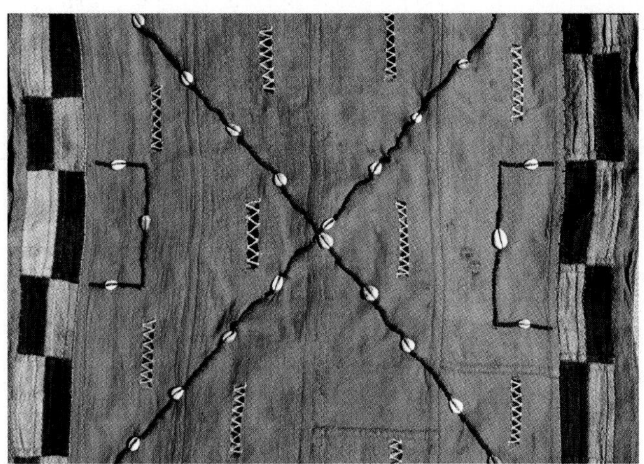

This raffia cloth, from the Democratic Republic of Congo, is woven from palm fibers. Throughout central Africa, raffia cloth functions as limited-purpose money, or money that can be used only for specific purposes, such as marriage or compensation for wrongdoing. It cannot be used for commercial transactions such as buying food, a house, or a car.

is vulnerable to economic changes such as inflation, which reduce its value. The use of modern money is spreading throughout the world. Nonmonetary cultures, however, often adopt modern money in limited ways. They may prohibit its use in religious exchanges or in life-cycle rituals such as marriages. All forms of money, even modern money, are symbolic. They have meaning to the user, and they are associated with the user's identity and sense of self. The color and design of a credit card, for example, may signify status, such as "platinum" for the biggest spenders. As the European Union was forming, lengthy discussion was devoted to what the new currency would look like. As e-money becomes increasingly used, it will be interesting to see what kinds of meaning are attached to it.

PEOPLE Exchange in human beings relegates humans to objects. Throughout history, some people have been able to gain control of other people and treat them as items of exchange, as in slavery and human trafficking. The enslavement of people from many regions of Africa during European colonialism from the fifteenth to nineteenth centuries stands as one of the most heinous processes of treating humans as commodities in the full light of day, with no legal sanctions involved for slave traders or owners. This process cruelly transformed thousands of people into property that could be bought and sold, used and abused, and even murdered.

A long-standing debate in anthropology concerns women as objects of exchange in marriage. Lévi-Strauss proposed many years ago that the exchange of women between men is one of the most basic forms of exchange among humans (1969 [1949]). He based his assertion on the universality of some sort of *incest taboo,* which he defined as a rule preventing a man from marrying or cohabiting with his mother or sister (Chapter 8 provides the current definition). Such a rule, he says, is the logic driving the exchange of women among men: "The fact that I can obtain a wife is, in the final analysis, the consequence of the fact that a brother or father has given her up" (1969:62). Thus, the avoidance of incest forces men to develop exchange networks with other men and, by extension, leads to the emergence of social solidarity more widely. For Lévi-Strauss, the incest taboo provides the foundation for human social organization.

Feminist anthropologists say that this theory overlooks much ethnographic evidence to the contrary. Men do not have rights over women in many foraging societies; instead, women make their own choices about partners (Rubin 1975). In many horticultural and agricultural societies of Southeast Asia, men do not exchange women (Peletz 1987). Instead, women select grooms for their daughters. This pattern turns Lévi-Strauss's theory on its head because it involves women organizing the exchange of men.

MODES OF EXCHANGE

Parallel to the two contrasting modes of consumption described earlier (minimalism and consumerism), two distinct modes of exchange can be delineated (see Figure 5.3):

- **Balanced exchange:** a system of transfers in which the goal is either immediate or eventual balance in value.
- **Unbalanced exchange:** a system of transfers in which one party attempts to make a profit.

BALANCED EXCHANGE The category of balanced exchange contains two subcategories based on the social relationship of the two parties involved in the exchange and the degree to which a "return" is expected. **Generalized reciprocity** is a transaction that involves the least conscious sense of interest in material gain or thought of what might be received in return, and when. Such exchanges often involve goods and services of an everyday nature, such as a cup of coffee. Generalized reciprocity is the main form of exchange between people who know each other well and trust each other. Therefore, it is the main form of exchange in foraging societies. It is also found among close kin and friends cross-culturally.

---

money a medium of exchange that can be used for a variety of goods.

balanced exchange a system of transfers in which the goal is either immediate or eventual equality in value.

unbalanced exchange a system of transfers in which one party seeks to make a profit.

generalized reciprocity exchange involving the least conscious sense of interest in material gain or thought of what might be received in return.

	Balanced Exchange			Unbalanced Exchange	
	Generalized Reciprocity	**Expected Reciprocity**	**Redistribution**	**Market Exchange**	**Theft, Exploitation**
Actors	Kin, friends	Trading partners	Leader and pooling group	Buyers/sellers	Nonkin, nonfriends, unknown
Return	Not calculated or expected	Expected at some time	Feast and give-away	Immediate payment	No return
Example	Buying coffee for a friend	Kula	Moka	Internet shopping	Shoplifting

FIGURE 5.3 Keeping Track of Exchange

A **pure gift** is something given with no expectation or thought of a return. The pure gift is an extreme form of generalized reciprocity. Examples of a pure gift include donating money for a food drive, or making donations to famine relief, blood banks, and religious organizations. Some people say that a truly pure gift does not exist because one always gains something, no matter how difficult to measure, in giving—even if it is just the good feeling of generosity. Parental care of children is said to be a pure gift by some, but others do not agree. Those who say that parental care is a pure gift argue that most parents do not consciously calculate how much they have spent on their children with the intention of "getting it back" later on. Those who do not consider parental care a pure gift say that even if the "costs" are not consciously calculated, parents have unconscious expectations about what their children will "return" to them, whether the return is material (care in old age) or immaterial (making the parent feel proud).

Expected reciprocity is the exchange of approximately equally valued goods or services, usually between people of roughly equal social status. The exchange may occur simultaneously between both parties, or it may involve an understanding about the time period within which the exchange will be completed. This aspect of timing contrasts with generalized reciprocity, in which there is no fixed time limit for the return. In expected reciprocity, if the second party fails to complete the exchange, the relationship will break down. Balanced reciprocity is less personal than generalized reciprocity and, according to Western definitions, more "economic."

The kula is an example of a system of expected reciprocity (review Culturama, Chapter 3, p. 67). Men exchange necklaces and armlets, giving them to their exchange partners after keeping them for a while. Partners include neighbors as well as people on faraway islands who are visited via long canoe voyages on high seas. Trobriand men are distinguished by the particular armlets and necklaces that they exchange, and certain armlets and necklaces are more prestigious than others. One cannot keep one's trade items for long because the kula code dictates that "to possess is great, but to possess is to give." Generosity is the essence of goodness, and stinginess is the most despised vice. Kula exchanges should involve items of equivalent value. If a man trades a very valuable necklace with his partner, he expects to receive in return a very valuable armlet as an equivalent gift). At the time, if one's partner does not possess an equivalent item, he may have to give an intermediary gift, which stands as a token of good faith until a proper return gift can be given. The clinching gift comes later and balances the original gift. The equality of exchange ensures a strong bond between the trading partners and is a statement of trust. When a man arrives in an area where it may be dangerous because of previous raids or warfare, he can count on having a friend to give him hospitality.

Redistribution is a form of exchange in which one person collects goods or money from many members of a group and provides a social return at a later time. At a public event, even several years later, the organizer "returns" the pooled goods to everyone who contributed by sponsoring a generous

---

pure gift something given with no expectation or thought of a return.

expected reciprocity an exchange of approximately equally valued goods or services, usually between people roughly equal in social status.

redistribution a form of exchange that involves one person collecting goods or money from many members of a group, who then, at a later time and at a public event, "returns" the pooled goods to everyone who contributed.

market exchange the buying and selling of commodities under competitive conditions in which the forces of supply and demand determine value.

trade the formalized exchange of one thing for another according to set standards of value.

(LEFT) In China, many marketers are women. These two women display their wares in a permanent food market in a city about an hour's drive from Shanghai. (RIGHT) Workers at Tsukiji, the world's largest fish market in Tokyo, transport frozen tuna on hand carts for the upcoming auction.

▶ *For a research project, learn more about Ted Bestor's research on Tsukiji.*

feast. Compared to the two-way pattern of exchange involved in reciprocity, redistribution involves some "centricity." It contains the possibility of inequality because what is returned may not always equal, in a material sense, what each individual contributed. The pooling group may continue to exist, however, because it benefits from the leadership skills of the person who mobilizes contributions. If a neighboring group threatens a raid, people turn to their redistributive leader for political leadership (discussed further in Chapter 10).

UNBALANCED EXCHANGE **Market exchange**, a prominent form of unbalanced exchange, is the buying and selling of commodities under competitive conditions in which the forces of supply and demand determine value and the seller seeks to make a profit (Dannhaeuser 1989:222). In market transactions, the seller and buyer may or may not have a personal relationship. They may or may not be social equals. Their exchange is not likely to generate social bonding. Many market transactions take place in a marketplace, a physical location in which buying and selling occur. The market system evolved from other, less formal contexts of **trade**, formalized exchange of one thing for another according to set standards of value.

The market system is associated with regional specialization in producing particular goods and trade between regions. Certain products are often identified with a town or region. In Oaxaca, Mexico (see Map 6.3, p. 148), some villages are known for their blankets, pottery, stone grinders, rope, and chili peppers (Plattner 1989). In Morocco, the city of Fez (see Map 5.3, p. 123) is famous for its blue-glazed pottery, whereas the Berber people of the Atlas Mountains are known for their fine wool blankets and rugs. Increasingly, producers of regionally distinct products, such as champagne, are legally copyrighting the regional name to protect it from use by producers of similar products from outside the region. Specialization develops with illegal commodities too. For example, Jamaican marijuana is well known for its high quality, and many tourists travel to Jamaica, especially the Negril area in the west, in order to buy this product in its many forms.

Marketplaces range from informal, small stands that appear in the morning and disappear at night, to huge multistoried shopping centers. One variety found in many parts of the world is a *periodic market,* a site for buying and selling that takes place on a regular basis (for example, monthly) in a particular location but without a permanent physical structure. Sellers appear with their goods and set up a table with perhaps an awning. In contrast, permanent markets are built structures situated in fixed locations. Marketplaces, however, are more than just places for buying and selling. They involve social interactions and even performances. Sellers solicit customers, shoppers meet and chat, government officials drop by, religious organizations may hold services, and traditional healers may treat toothaches. The particularities of how markets are structured, spatially and socially, and how culture shapes market transactions are rich topics for ethnographic research.

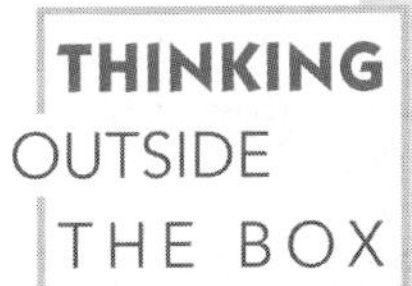

Propose some examples of what might qualify as a "pure gift."

Ted Bestor conducted research over many years in Tsukiji (tsee-kee-jee), the world's largest fish market, located in Tokyo (2004). Tsukiji connects large-scale corporations that supply most of the seafood with small-scale family-run firms that continue to dominate Tokyo's retail food trade. Bestor describes the layout of the huge market, with inner and outer sections as a basic division. The outer market attracts younger, more hip shoppers looking for unusual, trendy gourmet items and a more authentic-seeming shopping experience. It contains sushi bars, noodle stalls, knife shops, and chopstick dealers, as well as temples and graveyards. The inner market contains 11 fresh produce market subdivisions. The seafood section by far overshadows the "veggie" markets in size and transaction level. It is subdivided into several main buildings where auctions occur, activities such as deliveries and dispatches take place, and rows of retail stalls serve 14,000 customers each morning. Bestor gained insight into the verbally coded conversations between experienced buyers and sellers in the stalls that are more likely to yield a better price than what an inexperienced first-time buyer will get. Stalls do not typically post prices, so buyers and sellers have to negotiate them. The verbal codes involve phrases such as "morning mist on a white beach," which, depending on the number of syllables in the phrase, conveys a price offer.

OTHER FORMS OF UNBALANCED EXCHANGE Several forms of unbalanced exchange other than market transactions exist. In extreme instances, no social relationship is involved; in others, sustained unequal relationships are maintained over time between people. These forms include taking something with no expectation of giving any return. They can occur in any mode of livelihood but are most likely to be found in large-scale societies where more options (other than face-to-face) for balanced exchange exist.

GAMBLING *Gambling*, or gaming, is the attempt to make a profit by playing a game of chance in which a certain item of value is staked in hopes of acquiring the much larger return that one receives if one wins the game. If one loses, that which was staked is lost. Gambling is an ancient practice and is common cross-culturally. Ancient forms of gambling include dice throwing and card playing. Investing in the stock market can be considered a form of gambling, as can gambling of many sorts through the Internet. Although gambling may seem an odd category within unbalanced exchange, its goals of making a profit seem to justify its placement here. The fact that gambling within "high" capitalism is on the rise justifies anthropological attention to it. In fact, some scholars have referred to the present stage of Western capitalism as casino capitalism, given the propensity of investors to play risky games in the stock market (Klima 2002).

Indian tribal gambling establishments in the United States have mushroomed in recent years. Throughout the United States, Indian casinos are so financially successful that they are perceived as an economic threat to many state lotteries. The Pequot Indians of Connecticut (see Map 5.2), a small tribe of around 200 people, now operate the most lucrative gaming establishment in the world, Foxwoods Resort and Casino, established in 1992. Through gaming, many Indian tribal groups have become successful capitalists. An important question is what impact casinos will have on Indian tribal people, and anthropologists are involved in trying to answer this question (see Lessons Applied).

THEFT *Theft* is taking something with no expectation or thought of returning anything to the original owner for it. It is the logical opposite of a pure gift. Anthropologists have neglected the study of theft, no doubt a reasonable response because theft is an illegal activity that is difficult to study and might involve danger.

A rare study of theft focused on food stealing by children in West Africa (Bledsoe 1983). During fieldwork among the Mende people of Sierra Leone (see Map 6.6, p. 155), Caroline Bledsoe learned that children in town stole fruits such as mangoes, guavas, and oranges from neighborhood trees. Bledsoe at first dismissed cases of food stealing as rare exceptions, but then she realized that she "rarely walked through town without hearing shouts of anger from an adult and cries of pain from a child being whipped for stealing food" (1983:2). Deciding to look into children's food stealing more closely, she asked several children to keep diaries. Their writings were dominated by themes of *tiefing*, the local term for stealing. Fostered children, who are temporarily placed in the care of friends or relatives, do more food tiefing than children living with their birth families do. Such food stealing can be seen as children's attempts to compensate for their less-than-adequate food shares in their foster homes.

Although much theft worldwide is motivated by skewed entitlements and need, much is also driven by greed. Cultural anthropologists, for obvious reasons, have not done research on high-level theft involving expensive commodities such as drugs, gems, and art, nor have they examined corporate financial malpractice as a form of theft. Given the ethical requirement of informed consent (review Chapter 3), it is unlikely that any anthropologist would be given permission to study such criminal activity.

EXPLOITATION *Exploitation*, or getting something of greater value for less in return, is a form of extreme and persistent unbalanced exchange. Slavery is a form of exploitation in which people's labor power is appropriated without their consent and with no recompense for its value. Slavery is rare among foraging, horticultural, and pastoralist societies. Social relationships that involve sustained unequal exchange do exist between members of different social groups that, unlike pure slavery, involve no overt coercion and entail a certain degree of return by the dominant member to the subdominant member.

LESSONS applied

Evaluating Indian Gaming in California

In 2006, the Center for California Native Nations (CCNN) at the University of California at Riverside released an evaluation of the effects of Indian gaming in California (Spilde Contreras 2006). *Note:* According to current preferences of the people involved, the terms Indian or Indian tribe are used instead of Native American.

Kate Spilde Contreras, applied cultural anthropologist, directed the multidisciplinary team of anthropologists, political scientists, economists, and historians. The research objective was to evaluate the social and economic effects of Indian gaming operations on tribal and local governments in California. The study relies mainly on public data, especially the 1990 and 2000 U.S. Censuses, to supply a "before" and "after" picture during the initial growth phase of Indian gaming in the state. To learn about more recent changes, the research team conducted surveys of tribal and local government officials and in-depth case studies of individual tribal governments.

Casino Sandia, located in the Sandia Pueblo in northern New Mexico, is one of many casinos in the state established in the hope of raising funds to improve the lives of Indian people.

Findings indicate two important factors that shape the effects of Indian gaming in California: gaming establishments are owned by tribal governments, and gaming establishments are located on existing tribal trust lands. Therefore, gaming revenues support community and government activities of the tribal communities, and employment generation is localized within the tribal communities.

Indian reservations in California are more economically heterogeneous than elsewhere in the United States. Since the development of gaming, California also has greater economic inequality between gaming and nongaming reservations than is found in other states. By 2000, the fastest average income growth on California reservations occurred on gaming reservations. A policy response to this situation is a tribal-state gaming contract, the Revenue Sharing Trust Fund (RSTF) that provides for sharing of gaming revenue with nongaming communities.

Spilde Contreras's team considered the effects on gaming beyond the reservation. They found that areas within 10 miles of gaming reservations experienced significant employment increases, greater income growth, and more educational expansion than those farther away. Given the fact that reservations in California are located in the poorest regions, this location effect is progressive; that is, it helps poorer communities in favor of helping better-off communities.

Although the income and other effects of gaming in California are clearly substantial for Indians and their neighbors, Spilde Contreras points to the large gaps that still exist between conditions on Indian reservations and those for most Americans.

◆ **FOOD FOR THOUGHT**

- How does the recent development of Indian casinos connect with the theoretical perspective of structure versus agency? (Review the discussion of these perspectives in Chapter 1.)

Some degree of covert compulsion or dependence is likely to be present, however, in order for relationships of unequal exchange to endure.

Relationships between the Efe (eff-ay), who are "pygmy" foragers, and the Lese (less-ay), who are farmers, in the Democratic Republic of Congo exemplify sustained unequal exchange (Grinker 1994) (see Map 5.5). The Lese live in small villages. The Efe are seminomadic and live in temporary camps near Lese villages. Men of each group maintain long-term, hereditary exchange partnerships with each other. The Lese give cultivated foods and iron to the Efe, and the Efe give meat, honey, and other forest goods to the Lese.

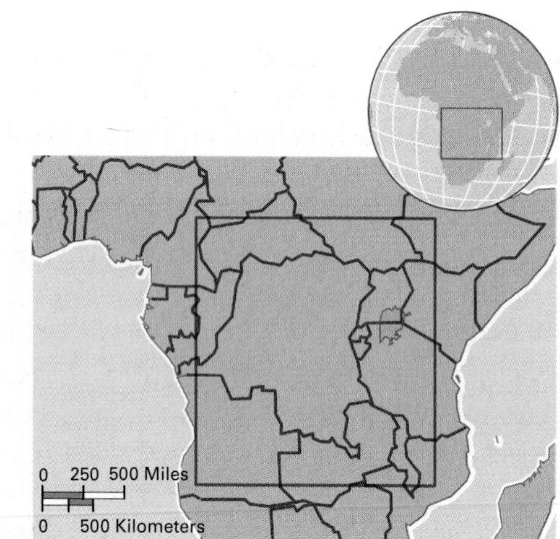

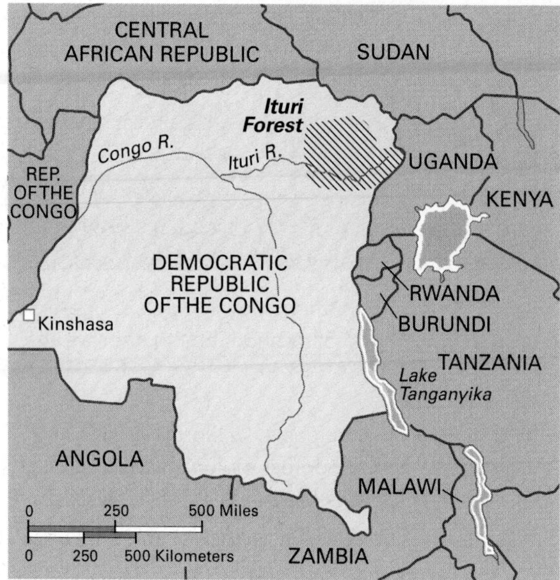

MAP 5.5 Lese and Efe Region in the Democratic Republic of Congo.
The Lese and Efe live in the Ituri Forest, a dense tropical rainforest in the northern part of the Congo River Basin. Cultural Survival supports the Ituri Forest Peoples Fund, which promotes the health and education of Efe foragers and Lese farmers. Go to the Internet to learn about the projects of the Ituri Forest Peoples Fund.

Each Efe partner is considered a member of the "house" of his Lese partner, although he lives separately. Their main link is the exchange of food items, a system conceptualized by the Lese not as trade but as sharing of co-produced goods by partners living in a single unit. Evidence of inequality exists, however, in these relationships, with the Lese having the advantage. The Efe provide much-wanted meat to the Lese, but this role gives them no status. Rather, it is the giving of cultivated foods by the Lese to the Efe that conveys status. Another area of inequality is marital and sexual relationships. Lese men may marry Efe women, and their children are considered Lese. Efe men, however, cannot marry Lese women.

Changing Patterns of Consumption and Exchange

Powerful market forces controlled by the core countries are the main factors affecting changing patterns of consumption and exchange. Local cultures, though, variously adopt and adapt globalizing products and their meanings. Sometimes they resist them outright.

SUGAR, SALT, AND STEEL TOOLS IN THE AMAZON

Katherine Milton, a biological anthropologist, has studied the nutritional effects of Western contact on the consumption patterns and health of indigenous foragers in the Brazilian Amazon. She comments:

> Despite the way their culture traditionally eschews possessions, forest-living people embrace manufactured goods with amazing enthusiasm. They seem to appreciate instantly the efficacy of a steel machete, ax, or cooking pot. It is love at first sight. . . . There are accounts of Indian groups or individuals who have turned their backs on manufactured goods, but such people are the exception. (1992:40)

The attraction to Western goods has its roots in the early decades of the twentieth century, when the Brazilian government sought to "pacify" Amazonian groups by placing cooking pots, machetes, axes, and steel knives along trails. This technique proved so successful that it is still used to "contact" remote groups. According to Milton:

> Once a group has been drawn into the pacification area, all its members are presented with various trade goods—standard gifts include metal cooking pots, salt, matches, machetes, knives, axes, cloth hammocks, T-shirts, and shorts. . . . Once the Indians have grown accustomed to these new items, the next step is to teach them that these gifts will not be repeated. The Indians are now told that they must work to earn money or must manufacture goods for trade so that they can purchase new items.
>
> Unable to contemplate returning to life without steel axes, the Indians begin to produce extra arrows or blowguns or hunt additional game or weave baskets beyond what they normally need so that this new surplus can be traded. Time that might, in the past, have been used for other tasks—subsistence activities, ceremonial events, or whatever—is now devoted to production of barter goods. (1992:40)

Adoption of Western foods has negatively affected the nutrition and health of indigenous Amazonian peoples. They have begun to use table salt and refined sugar. Previously, they consumed small quantities of salt made by burning certain leaves and collecting the ash, and sugar came from wild fruits,

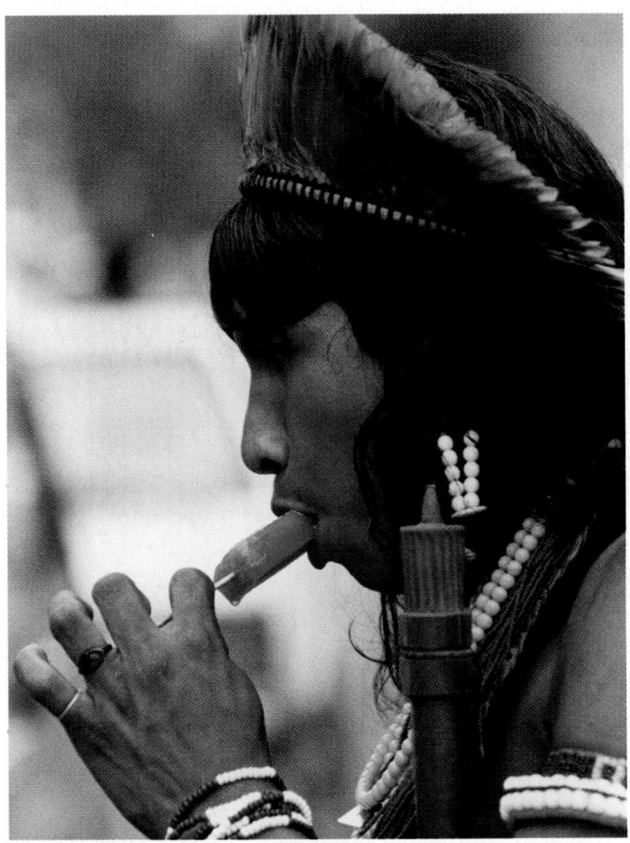

A member of the Kayapo tribe of Brazil eats a popsicle during a break in a meeting of indigenous peoples to protest a dam-building project. Tooth decay, diabetes, and obesity are rising among indigenous peoples worldwide as a result of changing consumption patterns.

in the form of fructose. Sucrose, in contrast, tastes exceptionally sweet, and the Indians get hooked on it. Tooth decay, obesity, and diabetes are new and growing health risks. Milton comments, "The moment manufactured foods begin to intrude on the indigenous diet, health takes a downward turn" (1992:41).

SOCIAL INEQUALITY IN RUSSIA AND EASTERN EUROPE

As the countries of the former Soviet Union entered the global market economy, income inequality within those countries grew dramatically. The new rich own mansions and Mercedes-Benz cars. The influx of Western goods, including sugared soft drinks and junk food, was nicknamed *pepsistroika* by an anthropologist who did fieldwork in Moscow around the time of the transition to capitalism (Lempert 1996). Advertising messages encourage people to adopt new diets that include unhealthy amounts of rich food.

From 1961 to 1988, the consumption of calories, proteins, and fats in what are now Russia and Eastern Europe were above the level recommended by the World Health Organization and exceeded those of most middle-income countries worldwide (Cornia 1994). These countries had full employment and little income inequality, so the high consumption levels were widely shared. This is not to say that diets were perfect. Especially in urban areas and among lower-income groups, people's diets contained less good-quality meat, fruits, vegetables, and vegetable oils. People tended to overconsume cholesterol-heavy products such as eggs and animal fats, sugar, salt, bread, and alcohol.

Income levels and consumption quality have fallen among the newly created poor. Now, there are two categories of poor people: the ultra-poor (those whose incomes are below the subsistence minimum, or between 25 and 35 percent of the average wage) and the poor (those whose incomes are above the subsistence minimum, but below the social minimum, or between 35 and 50 percent of the average wage). The largest increases in the number of ultra-poor occurred in Bulgaria, Poland, Romania, and Russia, where between 20 and 30 percent of the population are ultra-poor and another 20 to 40 percent are poor. Overall calorie and protein intake fell significantly. People in the ultra-poor category substitute less expensive sources of nutrients. They now consume more animal fats and starch, and less milk, animal proteins, vegetable oils, minerals, and vitamins. Rates of low-birthweight babies rose in Bulgaria and Romania, reflecting the deterioration in maternal diets, and the rate of childhood anemia rose dramatically in Russia.

GLOBAL NETWORKS AND ECSTASY IN THE UNITED STATES

In the late 1990s, a sharp increase in the use of ecstasy occurred in the United States (Agar and Reisinger 2003). Ecstasy, or MDMA (an abbreviation for its chemical name), is an illicit drug that produces a high without, apparently, leading to clinical dependence. Fieldwork and interviews in Baltimore, Maryland, revealed that ecstasy use "took off" in the late 1990s as the "up and coming" drug of choice among youth. As one research participant commented, "A lot of people I know like rolling, taking a pill of ecstasy and going to, like, a club or going to a school dance. I mean, alcohol is up and coming among like teenagers, like it's always been, but I think ecstasy's making a pretty powerful fight" (2003:2).

Official statistics confirmed this rise: In 1998, 10 percent of Baltimore County high school seniors reported that they had tried ecstasy; in 2001, the number had increased to nearly 20 percent. Nationwide statistics on reported use, arrests of distributors, and numbers of MDMA-related seizures reveal a similar pattern of increased use during this period. What accounts for this change? Two anthropologists conducted research to assess their hypothesis that there was a major change in the systems that produced and delivered the drug, leading to increased availability.

The standard story of the supply chain goes like this: Ecstasy is produced in the Netherlands and Belgium, distributed to the United States by Israelis, with a fuzzy role for

Russian organized crime along the way. Two anthropologists studied websites and media reports in 2000 and discovered a much more complicated story. They found a network of multiple and shifting production sites all over the world, including the largest illicit drug lab ever reported in Canadian history. Distribution channels are also highly diffuse. Although the simpler story may have been true in 1998, it was no longer true two years later. Perhaps as demand rose in the United States and elsewhere, this rise prompted the development of a wider network of production and distribution.

ALTERNATIVE FOOD MOVEMENTS IN EUROPE AND NORTH AMERICA

Starting in Europe in the 1980s, several alternative food movements have grown in Europe and North America (Pratt 2007). *Alternative food movements* seek to reestablish direct links between food producers, consumers, and marketers by promoting consumption of locally grown food and food that is not mass produced. Such movements exist in direct opposition to the agro-industrial food system, which:

- leads to economic ruin of small-scale producers who promote biodiversity
- shifts diet to fast foods, convenience food, take-away food, and microwave preparation
- transforms meals into eating on the run
- promotes a depersonalized, global market and supply chain, with Wal-Mart as the prime example
- has little regard for the environmental consequences of mass production and global marketing

Many alternative food movements exist. One of the first, Italy's Slow Food Movement, started in the late 1980s and has spread around the world. Naming itself in opposition to Western "fast food," the Slow Food Movement celebrates local agricultural traditions, seeks to protect consumers in terms of food quality, and advocates for social cooking, dining, and conviviality.

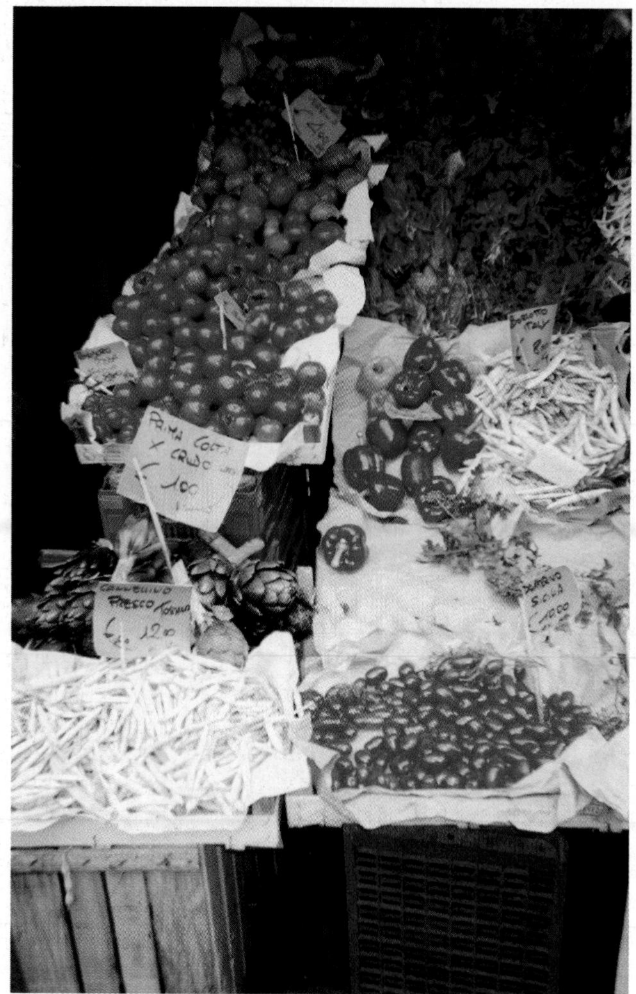

The weekly market in Pistoia, a small town near Firenze (Florence), Italy, is set up each Saturday next to the main church. According to government regulations, all food items are supposed to have labels that identify where they were grown.

CONTINUITIES AND RESISTANCE: THE ENDURING POTLATCH

Potlatching among native peoples of the northwest coast of the United States and Canada was subjected to decades of opposition from Europeans and Euro-Americans (Cole 1991). The missionaries opposed potlatching as an unChristian practice. The government thought it was wasteful and excessive, out of line with their goals for the "economic progress" of the Indians. In 1885, the Canadian government outlawed the potlatch. Of all the Northwest Coast tribes, the Kwakwa̱ka̱'wakw (see Culturama) resisted this prohibition most strongly and for the longest time. In Canada, potlatches are no longer illegal. But it took a long battle to remove restrictions.

Reasons for giving a potlatch today are similar to those in the past: naming children, mourning the dead, transferring rights and privileges, celebrating marriages, and raising totem poles (Webster 1991). The length of time devoted to planning a potlatch, however, has changed. In the past, several years were involved compared to about a year now. Still, it takes much organization and work to accumulate enough goods to ensure that no guest goes away empty-handed, and the guest list may include between 500 and 1000 people. Another change is in the kinds of goods exchanged. Typical potlatch goods now include crocheted items (such as cushion covers, blankets, and potholders), glassware, plastic goods, manufactured blankets, pillows, towels, articles of clothing, and sacks of flour and sugar. The potlatch endures but changes.

CULTURAMA

The Kwakwaka'wakw of Canada

everal Northern First Nations recently adopted the name Kwakwaka'wakw to efer to a cluster of 20 linguistically elated groups of Canada's Pacific Northwest region (Macnair 1995). Kwakwaka'wakw means "the people who speak Kwak'wala." It replaces the earlier term "Kwakiutl," which refers to only one of the several groups, and is therefore insulting to members of the other groups.

Their territory includes many slands as well as the waterways and deep inlets penetrating the Coast Mountains, a region of dense forests and sandy beaches. In earlier times, ravel was mainly by canoe. Families moved seasonally with all their belongings packed in the canoe Macnair 1995).

The Kwakwaka'wakw are famous for aspects of their material culture, including tall, carved wooden totem poles, canoes, masks, and serving bowls, as well as richly decorated capes, skirts, and blankets.

Cedar is vital to the Kwakwaka'wakw. They use its wood for the objects just mentioned and the inner bark for garments. Women pounded the bark strips with a whalebone beater until the fibers separated and became soft. They wove the strips on a loom or handwove them into mats used for sleeping on.

The first contact with Whites occurred in 1792, when explorer Captain George Vancouver arrived (Macnair 1995). At that time, the Kwakwaka'wakw numbered around 8000 people. Franz Boas arrived in 1886 and carried out research with the help of George Hunt, born of an English father and a high-ranking Tlingit (Northwest Coast) mother.

In the late nineteenth century, colonial authorities and missionaries disapproved of matters such as marriage arrangements and the potlatch, and enacted legislation to promote change, including a ban on potlatching from 1884 to 1951. The people continued, however, to potlatch in secret.

The Royal British Columbia Museum (RBCM) in Victoria, British Columbia, Canada, worked closely with Kwakwaka'wakw communities to document their potlatches and promote cultural revitalization (Kramer, personal communication 2006). The first legal potlatch of recent times, hosted by Mungo Martin in 1953, was held outside the RBCM.

Thanks to Jennifer Kramer, University of British Columbia, for reviewing this material.

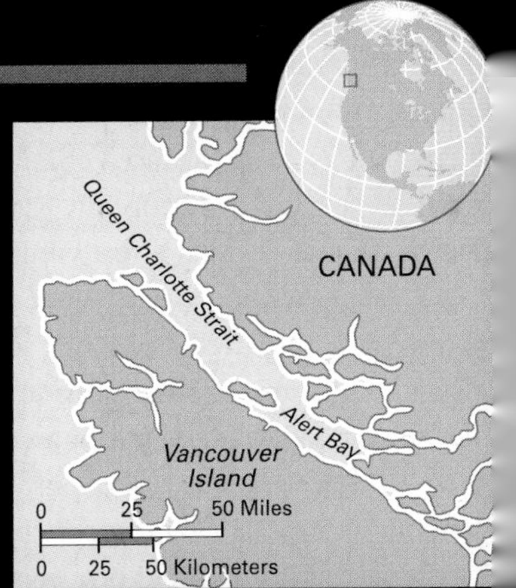

LEFT) Canoes and their crews from other Kwakwaka'wakw villages gather at Alert Bay in 1999 to help celebrate the opening of the newly built Big House.
CENTER) Kwakwaka'wakw students practice the hamat'sa dance at a school in Alert

MAP 5.6 The Kwakwaka' wakw Region in Canada. The total number of Kwakwaka' wakw is over 5000 people.

5 the BIG questions REVISITED

◆ What is consumption in cross-cultural perspective?

Consumption includes a person's "intake" in terms of eating or other ways of using things and "output" in terms of spending or using resources to obtain those things. Anthropologists delineate two major modes of consumption. The first is minimalism, which is characterized by finite needs, the means of satisfying them, and sustainability. The second is consumerism, the mode of consumption with infinite needs, the inability to satisfy all needs, and lack of sustainability. Foraging societies typify the minimalist mode of consumption. Horticulture, pastoralism, and farming are associated with mixed patterns of consumption, with a rising trend toward consumerism. The consumerist mode of consumption is most clearly associated with industrialism/informatics.

In nonmarket economies, most consumers either produce the goods they use themselves or know who produced them. This is called personalized consumption. In market economies, consumption is largely depersonalized through globalized mass production.

Anthropologists define five consumption funds, the proportions of which vary in different economic systems. Microcultures such as "race"/ethnicity, class, and gender are linked to specific consumption patterns. Such patterns may involve inequalities that affect human welfare.

A long-standing area of interest in cultural anthropology is cross-cultural patterns of food taboos and why such taboos exist. Cultural materialists provide interpretations that consider the ecological and environmental contexts of such food taboos and how taboos make sense to people's material lives. Symbolic/interpretive anthropologists interpret food taboos as systems of meaning that give people a sense of identity and communicate that identity to others.

◆ What is exchange in cross-cultural perspective?

Exchange refers to the transfer of goods, both material and intangible, or services between people, groups, or institutions. Cross-culturally, people and groups exchange a wide variety of goods and services. Nonmarket exchange long existed without the use of money. Modern money is now found throughout most of the world, though some groups restrict its use.

Anthropologists define two modes of exchange. In balanced exchange, items of roughly equal value are exchanged over time between people who have a social relationship. In unbalanced exchange, the value of items transferred is unequal and there may or may not be a social relationship between the seller and buyer.

Market exchange, the main form of unbalanced exchange, is a transaction in which the seller's goal of making a profit overrides social relationships. Markets exist in many forms. Some are impermanent and irregular; some are impermanent and regular, as in a weekly farmer's market; and others are permanent. Recent technological developments have led to the creation of virtual marketplaces.

◆ How are consumption and exchange changing?

Globalizing capitalism is leading to many changes in consumption and exchange around the world. Globalization appears to provide benefits to securely entitled people in core countries. In other areas, it affects production, consumption and exchange in complex ways.

Many indigenous peoples are attracted by Western goods, such as steel axes and processed food. In order to obtain these goods, they must have cash, so they are lured into the cash economy and subject to the fluctuations of the world labor market. The nutritional and health status of many such groups has declined with the adoption of Western-style foods, especially large amounts of sugar and salt in food.

Other examples of change include the decline in consumption of nutritious food and increase in alcohol consumption in countries of the post-USSR, the rising popularity of the drug ecstasy among youth in the United States, and the rise of new food movements promoting small farm food production and local food consumption.

In spite of the powerful effects of globalization, some local cultures are standing up and claiming rights to their traditional forms of production, consumption, and exchange. The revitalization of the potlatch in Canada is an example.

KEY CONCEPTS

balanced exchange, p. 125
cash crop, p. 116
consumerism, p. 112
consumption fund, p. 115
entitlement, p. 116
expected reciprocity, p. 126
generalized reciprocity, p. 125
leveling mechanism, p. 113
market exchange, p. 127
minimalism, p. 112
mode of consumption, p. 112
mode of exchange, p. 112
money, p. 124
potlatch, p. 112
pure gift, p. 126
redistribution, p. 126
trade, p. 127
unbalanced exchange, p. 125

SUGGESTED READINGS

Theodore C. Bestor. *Tsukiji: The Fish Market at the Center of the World.* Berkeley: University of California Press, 2004. This ethnography of Tsukiji, the huge fish market in Tokyo, describes how it is a workplace for thousands of people, a central node in the Japanese fishing industry, and part of the global economy.

Denise Brennan. *What's Love Got to Do with It? Transnational Desires and Sex Tourism in the Dominican Republic.* Durham, NC: Duke University Press, 2004. This is an account of global sex tourism in the town of Sosúa, Dominican Republic, where Afro-Dominican and Afro-Haitian women sell sex to foreign, White tourists.

Michael F. Brown. *Who Owns Native Culture?* Cambridge, MA: Harvard University Press, 2003. This book documents the efforts of indigenous peoples to redefine heritage as a resource over which they claim proprietorship. It considers specific cases and proposes strategies for defending the rights of indigenous people within a market system.

Elizabeth Chin. *Purchasing Power: Black Kids and American Consumer Culture.* Minneapolis: University of Minnesota Press, 2001. The author did research with a fifth-grade class in a low-income, African American neighborhood in New Haven, Connecticut. These 10-year-olds, motivated by a strong sense of family responsibility, spend their money mainly on practical items and gifts for family members rather than status symbols.

Maris Boyd Gillette. *Between Mecca and Beijing: Modernization and Consumption among Urban Chinese Muslims.* Stanford, CA: Stanford University Press, 2000. For centuries, the Han majority have labeled Chinese Muslims, or Hui, of northwest China as a "backward" minority. Although the government seeks to "modernize" the Hui, the Hui challenge government policy by maintaining Islamic values.

Dwight B. Heath. *Drinking Occasions: Comparative Perspectives on Alcohol and Culture.* New York: Taylor & Francis, 2000. This book provides an ethnological review of alcohol consumption and looks at questions such as when people drink alcohol, where people drink, who drinks and who does not, what people drink, and why people drink.

Ann Kingsolver. *NAFTA Stories: Fears and Hopes in Mexico and the United States.* Boulder, CO: Lynne Reiner Publishers, 2001. The author collected and followed stories about NAFTA (North American Free Trade Agreement) during the early 1990s as told by everyday people in Mexico City and two cities in Morelos, Mexico. She worked collaboratively with a Mexican anthropologist for both ethical reasons and legal requirements and considers her research, and her book, an example of activist social documentation.

Bill Maurer. *Mutual Life, Limited: Islamic Banking, Alternative Currencies, Lateral Reason.* Princeton, NJ: Princeton University Press, 2005. This comparison of Islamic bankers who seek to avoid interest with local currency proponents who seek to provide an alternative to capitalist financial mechanisms shows how both resist and sometimes replicate Western capitalism.

Lisa Rofel. *Desiring China: Experiments in Neoliberalism, Sexuality, and Public Culture.* Durham, NC: Duke University Press, 2007. Fieldwork in Beijing and Hangzhou informs this study of new material and sexual desires in contemporary China.

Linda J. Seligmann, ed. *Women Traders in Cross-Cultural Perspective: Mediating Identities, Marketing Wares.* Stanford, CA: Stanford University Press, 2001. The chapters include attention to historic patterns of women's participation in Mexico's markets, and case studies of contemporary women marketeers in Java, South India, Ghana, the Philippines, Morocco, and Hungary.

Parker Shipton. *The Nature of Entrustment: Intimacy, Exchange, and the Sacred in Africa.* New Haven, CT: Yale University Press, 2007. This ethnographic study of the Luo people of western Kenya shows how the Luo assess obligations to others, including intimates and strangers.

Two sisters of the Tarahumara people of northern Mexico. The Tarahumara once occupied most of the present-day state of Chihuahua but retreated to the Copper Canyon area in the mountains after the arrival of the Spanish colonialists.

REPRODUCTION AND HUMAN DEVELOPMENT

the BIG questions

- How are modes of reproduction related to modes of livelihood?
- How does culture shape fertility in different contexts?
- How does culture shape personality over the life cycle?

OUTLINE

The process of bearing and raising children into adults and personality and identity formation over the life cycle are the topics of this chapter. The first section provides an overview of reproduction in relation to modes of livelihood. The second section focuses on how culture shapes **fertility**, or the rate of births. The third section provides insights into the cultural shaping of personality and identity over the life cycle.

◆◆◆

Modes of Reproduction

Cultural anthropologists have enough data to support the construction of three **modes of reproduction**, or the predominant pattern of fertility in a culture. They correspond roughly to three of the major modes of production (see Figure 6.1). Reproduction refers to the total number of births and deaths in a population.

THE FORAGING MODE OF REPRODUCTION

Evidence about the foraging mode of reproduction comes from a classic study based on fieldwork conducted with the Ju/'hoansi in the 1970s (Howell 1979) (review Culturama in Chapter 1, p. 23). The study shows that *birth intervals* (the time between a birth and the next birth) among the Ju/'hoansi are often several years in duration. What accounts for these long birth intervals? Two factors are most important: breastfeeding and women's low level of body fat. Frequent and long periods of breastfeeding inhibit progesterone production and suppress ovulation. Also, a certain level of body fat is required for ovulation. Ju/'hoansi women's diets contain little fat, and their regular physical exercise as foragers keeps their body fat level low, further suppressing ovulation. Thus, diet and work are key factors underlying Ju/'hoansi population dynamics.

Ju/'hoansi women, during the time of the study, typically had between two and three live births of which two children survived into adulthood. This mode of reproduction is adaptive to the Ju/'hoansi environment and sustainable over time. Among the Ju/'hoansi who have become farmers or laborers, fertility levels have increased. Their diet contains more grains and dairy products, and they are less physically active.

THE AGRICULTURAL MODE OF REPRODUCTION

Agriculture and sedentism are associated with the highest fertility rates of any mode of production. **Pronatalism**, an ideology promoting many children, emerges as a key value of farm

Foraging	Agriculture	Industrialism/Informatics
Population Growth	**Population Growth**	**Population Growth**
Moderate birth rates Moderate death rates	High birth rates Declining death rates	Industrialized nations—negative population growth Developing nations—high
Value of Children	**Value of Children**	**Value of Children**
Moderate	High	Mixed
Fertility Control	**Fertility Control**	**Fertility Control**
Indirect means Low-fat diet of women Women's work and exercise Prolonged breastfeeding Spontaneous abortion Direct means Induced abortion Infanticide	Increased reliance on direct means Pronatalist techniques Herbs Direct means Induced abortion Infanticide	Direct methods grounded in science and medicine Chemical forms of contraception In vitro fertilization Abortion
Social Aspects	**Social Aspects**	**Social Aspects**
Homogeneous fertility Few specialists	Emerging class differences Increasing specialization Midwifery Herbalists	Stratified fertility Globally, nationally, and locally Highly developed specialization

FIGURE 6.1 Modes of Livelihood and Reproduction

families. It is prompted by the need for a large labor force to work the land, care for animals, process food, and do marketing. In this context, having many children is a rational reproductive strategy related to the mode of production. Thus, people who live in family farming systems cross-culturally have their own "family planning"—which is to have many children.

The groups with the highest fertility rates worldwide are the Mennonites and Hutterites, European-descent Christians of the United States and Canada. Women in these groups typically have between eight and ten children who survive into adulthood. A closely related religious cultural group, the Amish (see Culturama), also have high fertility rates.

Global variation in fertility in farming populations does exist, however, partly because of recent declines due to reduced demands for family labor. High rates of seven or more children per woman exist in several low-income, agricultural countries of Africa, such as Niger (8.0 births per woman), Guinea-Bissau (7.1 births per woman), Mali (7.1 births per woman), and Somalia (7.0 births per woman) (Population Reference Bureau 2005). Lower rates, of two or three children per woman, are found in many agricultural countries in South America, such as Venezuela, Chile, and Argentina.

In rural North India, sons are especially important in farming families (see Everyday Anthropology, this chapter, p. 146). As young boys, they learn to do farm work with their father. As adults, they are responsible for the plowing and for protecting the family land from encroachment by neighboring farmers and animals. When Western family planning experts visited villages in North India in the late 1950s to promote the idea of small families, the farmers expressed dismay (Mamdani 1972). To them, a large family, especially many sons, is a sign of wealth and success, not poverty and failure. Having many children in a family farming system makes sense.

THE INDUSTRIAL/INFORMATICS MODE OF REPRODUCTION

In industrial societies, either capitalist or socialist, reproduction declines to the point of *replacement-level fertility,* in which the number of births equals the number of deaths, leading to maintenance of current population size, or *below-replacement-level fertility,* in which the number of births is less than the number of deaths, leading to population decline. Children in these contexts are less useful in production because of the reduced labor demands of industrialism. Furthermore, children in most industrialized countries must attend school and therefore cannot work for their families much during the school year. Parents respond by having fewer children and by investing more resources in them.

Population changes during the industrial mode of reproduction correspond to what demographers call the **demographic transition,** a process during which the agricultural pattern of high fertility and high mortality becomes the industrial pattern of low fertility and low mortality. There are two phases in the demographic transition model (see Figure 6.2).

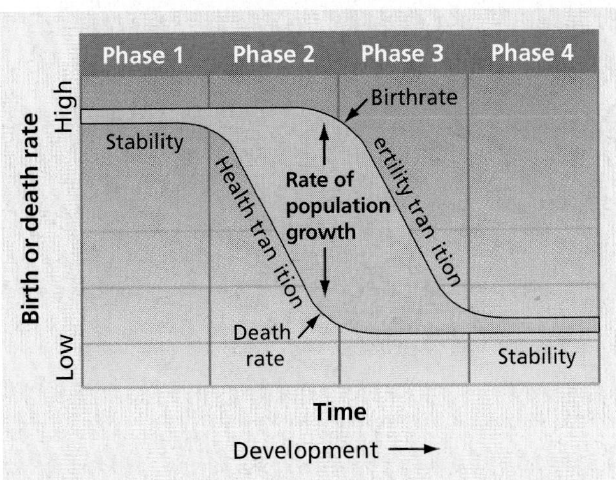

FIGURE 6.2 Model of the Demographic Transition

Source: Nebel, Bernard J.; Wright, Richard T, *Environmental Science: The Way The World Works*, 7th edition. Copyright © 2000. Electronically reproduced by permission of Pearson Education, Inc. Upper Saddle River, New Jersey.

In the first phase, mortality declines because of improved nutrition and health, so population growth rates increase. The second phase occurs when fertility also declines. At this point, low rates of population growth occur.

Cultural anthropologists think the demographic transition model is too narrow because it attributes only one cause to declining population growth: industrialism (Ginsberg and Rapp 1991). They point to examples of other causes. China, for example, began to reduce its population growth rate well before widespread industrialism (Xizhe 1991). Strong government policies and a massive family planning program caused China's demographic transition.

The industrial/informatics mode of reproduction has three distinguishing features. First, social inequality is reflected in population patterns, referred to as *stratified reproduction.* Typically, middle-class and upper-class people tend to have few children, with high survival rates. Among the poor, however, both fertility and mortality rates are high. Brazil, a newly industrializing state, has the world's most extreme income inequality. Parallel to its economic inequality is extremely stratified reproduction.

Increasing international migration adds to the variation of population dynamics within particular countries. In France, the government promotes pronatalism to address its population deficit, but pronatal messages and programs are aimed at the "authentic" French population. In contrast, low-income

---

fertility the rate of births in a population, or the rate of population increase in general.

mode of reproduction the predominant pattern of fertility and mortality in a culture.

pronatalism an ideology promoting many children.

demographic transition the change from the agricultural pattern of high fertility and high mortality to the industrial pattern of low fertility and low mortality.

CULTURAMA

The Old Order Amish of the United States and Canada

The Amish are Christians who live in rural areas of the United States and Canada. In the early twenty-first century, their total population was about 200,000. Their ancestry traces to German-speaking, Swiss Anabaptists in the sixteenth century. To escape religious persecution, they migrated to North America, starting in the early eighteenth century and continuing into the mid-nineteenth century. There are no Amish in Europe today.

The term *Old Order Amish* refers to the main body of the Amish people. A small minority, known as *New Order Amish,* broke off from the Old Order in the late 1960s. Both groups use horse-drawn transportation, but the New Order Amish accept more technology.

The Amish speak a German-derived dialect. They wear modest and conforming clothing. They avoid using electricity from power grids but solar-generated electricity and 12-volt batteries are allowed. Education beyond the eighth grade is seen as unnecessary. A basic theme in Amish life is the need to guard against "worldly" (non-Amish, mainstream U.S.) values, dependencies, and hurriedness, and to maintain the family as a unit that lives and works together. Working with one's own hands is valued, as are humility and modesty. Farming is the traditional means of livelihood among the Amish.

The Amish have high fertility rates, on average six or seven live births per woman. Even though some children leave and join "the English" (non-Amish), their population is doubling every twenty years. In Lancaster County, Pennsylvania, the heartland of the Old Order Amish, a steep rise in population growth starting in the 1970s has exceeded the availability of farmland (Kraybill and Nolt 2004). Now, several hundred Amish businesses exist. Many are small scale and operate from the home, but many others are large scale and earn millions of dollars per year. Amish who enter business try to retain Amish values of family solidarity by working at home and selling products from their home. Many, though, work in businesses away from home, with the English.

Amish youth have the opportunity of deciding whether to be baptized into the faith when they are 16 years old. At this time, called *rumspringa* in Pennsylvania Dutch, or "running around," the young people are allowed to explore the customs of the English world including television. Most stay at home during rumspringa, spending time with Amish friends on the weekends. In rare cases, some experiment with alcohol, drugs, and sex (Shachtman 2006). After rumspringa, around 90 percent of Amish teenagers decide to accept Amish ways and be baptized, choosing a lifestyle that emphasizes humility and community solidarity rather than the "worldly" lifestyle of individualism and competition.

Thanks to Donald B. Kraybill, Elizabethtown College, for reviewing this material.

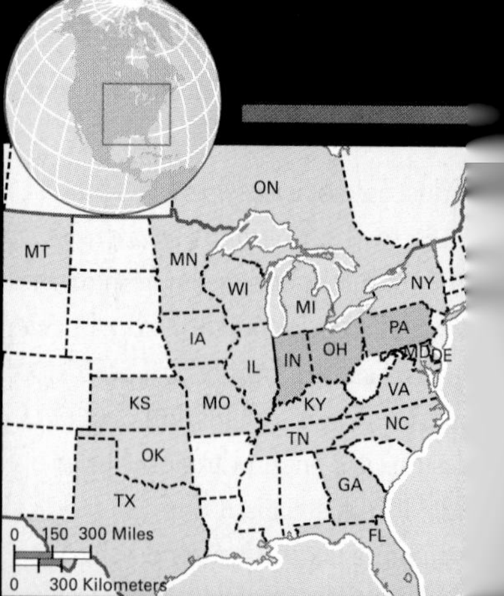

(LEFT) Members of an Amish household sit around their kitchen table. (CENTER) A farmer mows alfalfa with a team of mules and a gasoline engine to power the mower. This mechanism enhances his farm work but does not break

MAP 6.1 Old Order Amish Population of North America. The states of Ohio (55,000), Pennsylvania

Firefighters survey the scene after a fire in a six-story apartment building in Paris, France, in 2005, that was home to low-income African immigrants. The fire killed 17 people, half of whom were children, and injured 30 more.

▶ *What is your opinion on the role of government in ensuring that everyone lives in safe housing?*

immigrants from Mali, West Africa, living in Paris, receive antinatalist messages in clinics (Sargent 2005). Immigrant fertility, rather than being desired by the French government, is a matter of concern, as it strains public resources such as schools and hospitals. The fact that the immigrants are poor, Black, and Muslim, with a culture that values many children, places them in stark contrast to the "authentic" French people who are relatively well-off, White, and have few children.

A second characteristic of industrial/informatics contexts is *population aging,* when the proportion of older people increases relative to younger people. In Japan, the national fertility rate declined to replacement level in the 1950s and later reached the below-replacement level (Hodge and Ogawa 1991). Japan is currently experiencing a decline in population growth of about 15 percent per generation and, simultaneously, rapid aging of the population. As many people enter the senior category, they create a population bulge that is not balanced by the number of younger people (see Figure 6.3). A population projection for the year 2050 suggests that the bulge will increase.

A third distinguishing feature of industrial/informatics demographics is the high level of involvement of scientific (especially medical) technology in all aspects of pregnancy: prevention, termination, and becoming pregnant in the first place (Browner and Press 1995, 1996). This trend is accompanied by increasing levels of specialization in providing the new services.

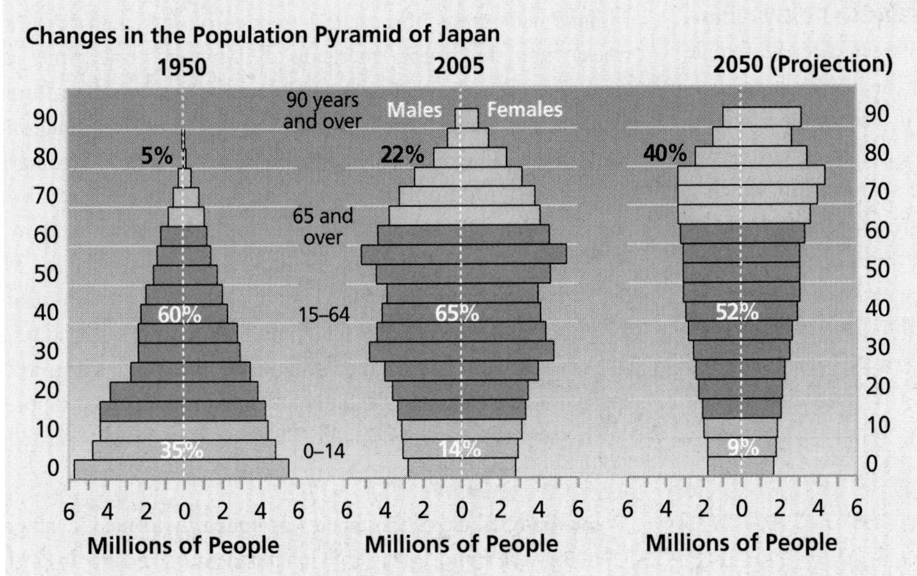

FIGURE 6.3 **Changes in the Population Pyramid of Japan**

Source: Statistics Bureau, MIC, Ministry of Health, Labor and Welfare. Reproduced with permission.

Culture and Fertility

Culture shapes human fertility from its very start, if inception can be taken as sexual intercourse or some other form of fertilization of an ovum. Cultural practices and beliefs about pregnancy and birth affect the viability of the fetus during its gestation as well as the infant's survival and health.

SEXUAL INTERCOURSE

Sexual intercourse usually involves private, sometimes secret, beliefs and behaviors. Anthropological research on sexual practices is thus particularly challenging. The ethics of participant observation prohibit intimate observation or participation, so data can be obtained only indirectly. Biases in people's verbal reports about sexual beliefs and behavior are likely for several reasons. People may be too shy or otherwise unwilling to discuss sex or, conversely, boastful and inflating the truth. Many people may simply be unable to answers questions such as "How many times did you have sexual intercourse last year?" If people do provide detailed information, it might be inappropriate for an anthropologist to publish it because of the need to protect confidentiality.

Bronislaw Malinowski wrote the first anthropological study of sexuality (1929), based on his fieldwork in the Trobriand Islands (review Culturama in Chapter 3, p. 67). He discusses the sexual lives of children, sexual techniques, love magic, erotic dreams, husband–wife jealousy, and other topics. Since the late 1980s, it has become increasingly important to study how culture affects sexuality because of the spread of sexually transmitted diseases (STDs), including HIV/AIDS. Without understanding variations in sexual values and practices, it is impossible to design effective programs for preventing and controlling STDs.

WHEN TO BEGIN HAVING INTERCOURSE? Biologically speaking, sexual intercourse between a fertile female and a fertile male is normally required for human reproduction, although artificial insemination is becoming a widely used option in some contexts. Biology, interacting with environment and culture, defines the time span within which a female is fertile: from **menarche** (men-ar-kee), the onset of menstruation, to **menopause**, the cessation of menstruation. Globally, the beginning of menarche varies from between 12 to 14 years of age (Thomas et al. 2001). Generally, girls in richer countries reach menarche a few years earlier than girls in poorer countries do. For example, the estimated age at menarche in Japan is 12.5 years, but in Haiti it is 15.5 years. Worldwide, a trend is for the age at menarche to become earlier. The reasons for this change are not completely clear. Diet and activity patterns are likely factors involved. The underlying assumption is that today's diets and lifestyles are a sign of "progress" and thus earlier age at menarche is an indicator of social well-being.

Cultures, however, socialize children about the appropriate age to begin sexual intercourse, and cultural rules are more variable than the biological marker of menarche. Cultural guidelines vary by gender, class, race, and ethnicity. In many cultures, sexual activity should begin only with marriage. This rule often applies more strictly to females than to males. In Zawiya, a Muslim town of northern Morocco (see Map 6.2), a bride's virginity is highly valued, whereas that of the groom is ignored (Davis and Davis 1987). Most brides conform to the ideal. Some unmarried young women do engage in premarital sex, however. If they choose to have a traditional wedding, they must somehow meet the requirement of producing blood-stained wedding sheets after the first night. If the bride and the groom have been having premarital sexual relations, the groom may assist in the deception by nicking a finger with a knife and bloodying the sheets himself. Another option is to buy fake blood sold in drugstores.

INTERCOURSE FREQUENCY AND FERTILITY Cross-culturally, the frequency of sexual intercourse varies widely. The relationship between frequency of sexual intercourse and fertility, though, is not simple. A common assumption is that people in cultures with high fertility rates have sexual intercourse frequently. Without modern birth control, such as condoms, the birth control pill, and the intrauterine device (IUD), intercourse frequency would seem, logically, to produce high rates of fertility.

A classic study of reported intercourse frequency among Euro-Americans in the United States and Hindus in India throws this assumption into question (Nag 1972). The Indians had intercourse far less frequently (less than twice a week) than the Euro-Americans did (two to three times a week) in all age groups. Several features of Indian culture limit the frequency of sexual intercourse. The Hindu religion teaches the value of sexual abstinence, thus providing ideological support for limiting sexual intercourse. Hinduism also suggests that one should abstain from intercourse on many sacred days: the first night of the new moon, the first night of the full moon, and the eighth day of each half of the month (the light half and the dark half), and sometimes on Fridays. As many as 100 days each year could be observed as non-sex days. Another factor is Hindu men's belief in what anthropologists term the *lost semen complex.* An anthropologist learned about this complex during his fieldwork in North India:

> Everyone knew that semen was not easily formed; it takes forty days and forty drops of blood to make one drop of semen. . . . Semen of good quality is rich and viscous, like

---

menarche the onset of menstruation.

menopause the cessation of menstruation.

A bride wearing traditional wedding clothing in the city of Meknès, Morocco.

the cream of unadulterated milk. . . . Celibacy was the first requirement of true fitness, because every sexual orgasm meant the loss of a quantity of semen, laboriously formed. (Carstairs 1967:83–86, quoted in Nag 1972:235)

The fact remains, however, that fertility is higher in India than in many other parts of the world where such religiously based restrictions on sexual intercourse do not exist. Obviously, sheer frequency of intercourse is not the explanation because it takes only one act of sexual intercourse at the right time of the month to create a pregnancy. The point of this discussion is to show that *reverse reasoning* (assuming that high fertility means people have nothing better to do than have sex) is wrong. The cultural dynamics of sexuality in India function to restrain sexual activities and thus keep fertility lower than it otherwise would be.

FERTILITY DECISION MAKING

This section explores decision making about fertility at the family, state, and global levels. Within the context of the family unit, decision makers weigh factors influencing why and when to have a child. At the state level, governments plan their overall population goals on the basis of goals that are sometimes pronatalist and sometimes *antinatalist* (opposed to many births). At the global level, powerful economic and political interests influence the reproductive policies of countries and, in turn, of families and individuals.

AT THE FAMILY LEVEL Within the family, parents and other family members consider, consciously or unconsciously, the value and costs of children (Nag 1983). Cross-cultural research indicates that four factors are most important in affecting the desire for children:

- Children's labor value
- Children's value as old-age support for parents
- Infant and child mortality rates
- Economic costs of children

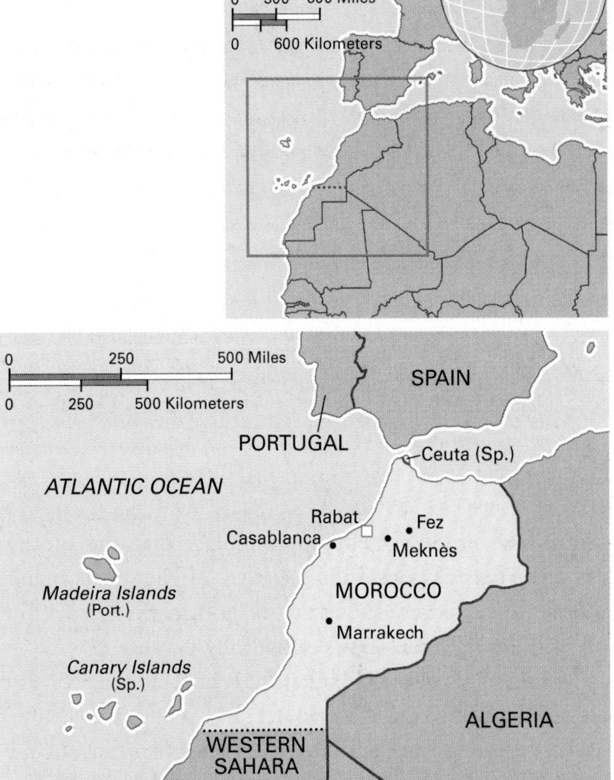

MAP 6.2 Morocco.
The Kingdom of Morocco is the westernmost country of the Arab world. A border dispute continues with the Western Sahara, which Morocco has administered since 1975. Morocco's population is 30 million people. The terrain ranges from coastal lowlands to rugged interior mountains. Morocco's economy is based on mining phosphates, remittances, and tourism. It is one of the world's largest producers and exporters of cannabis and the world's largest per capita consumer of sugar. Most Moroccans are Sunni Muslims. The official language is classical Arabic but, Moroccan Arabic is widely spoken. Over 40 percent of the people speak a variety of Berber.

The first three factors have a positive effect on fertility: When children's value is high in terms of labor or old-age support, fertility is likely to be higher; when infant and child mortality rates are high, fertility rates tend to be high in order to "replace" offspring who do die. In the case of child costs—including direct costs (for food, education, clothing) and

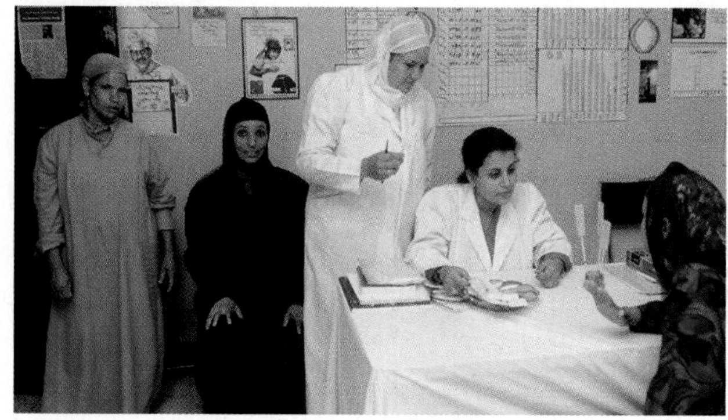

A family planning clinic in Egypt. Throughout much of the world, Western-style family planning advice is controversial because it may conflict with local beliefs and values.

▶ *In your cultural experience, what is the prevailing attitude about family planning?*

indirect costs (employment opportunities that the mother gives up)—the relationship is negative. Higher costs reduce the desire for children. Industrialism/informatics raises child costs and lowers their value dramatically because it tends to avoid using child labor. Mandatory school attendance also pulls children out of the workforce and may involve direct costs for fees, uniforms, and supplies. States that provide old-age security and pension plans reduce the need for children.

Husbands and wives may not always have the same preferences about the number of desired children. In a highland village in the Oaxaca region of Mexico (see Map 6.3), men want more children than women do (Browner 1986). Of women with only one child, 80 percent were content with their present family size. Most men (60 percent) who were satisfied with their present family size had four or more children. One woman said, "My husband sleeps peacefully through the night, but I have to get up when the children need something. I'm the one the baby urinates on; sometimes I have to get out of bed in the cold and change both our clothes" (1986:714).

Depending on the gender division of labor and other social features, families may prefer sons, daughters, or a balance of each. Son preference is widespread, especially in Asia and the Middle East, but it is not universal (see Everyday Anthropology). Throughout much of Southeast Asia, people prefer a balanced number of sons and daughters. Daughter preference is found in some parts of Africa south of the Sahara and some Caribbean populations.

AT THE STATE LEVEL State governments formulate policies that affect rates of population growth within their boundaries. These policies vary from being antinatalist to pronatalist, and they vary in terms of the methods of fertility management promoted. Factors that affect government policies include economic factors such as projected jobs and employment levels, public services, maintaining the tax base, filling the ranks of the military, maintaining ethnic and regional proportions, and dealing with population aging.

AT THE GLOBAL LEVEL The most far-reaching layer that affects fertility decision making occurs at the international level, where global power structures such as pharmaceutical

MAP 6.3 Mexico.
The United Mexican States is the most populous Spanish-speaking country in the world. It was subjected to Spanish rule for three centuries before gaining independence. Its population is 107 million, and the capital has a population of 20 million people. Mexico has a mixed economy of industry, agriculture, and trade, and is the fourth largest oil producer in the world. Ethnically, the population consists of Mestizos (60 percent), Indians (30 percent), and Whites (9 percent). Southern states have the highest proportion of Indians.

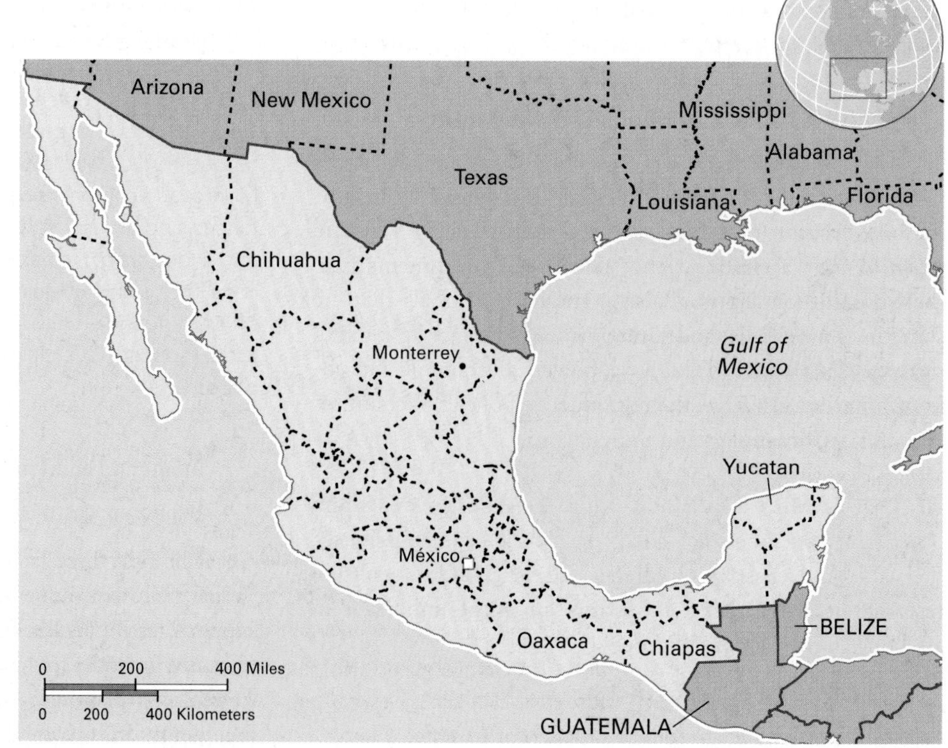

companies and religious leaders influence country-level and individual-level decision making. In the 1950s, there was a wave of enthusiasm among Western nations for promoting family planning programs of many types in so-called developing countries. In the 1990s, the United States adopted a more restricted policy toward family planning, withdrew support for certain features such as abortion, and began to promote abstinence as the foundation of population control.

FERTILITY CONTROL

People in all cultures since prehistory have had ways of influencing fertility, including ways to increase it, reduce it, and regulate its spacing. Some ways are direct, such as using herbs or medicines that induce abortion. Others are indirect, such as long periods of breastfeeding, which reduce the chances of conception.

INDIGENOUS METHODS Hundreds of direct indigenous fertility control methods are available cross-culturally (Newman 1972, 1985).

Research in Afghanistan during the 1980s found over 500 fertility-regulating techniques in just one region (Hunte 1985). In Afghanistan, as in most nonindustrial cultures, it is women who possess this information. Specialists, such as midwives or herbalists, provide further expertise. Of the total number of methods in the Afghanistan study, 72 percent were for increasing fertility, 22 percent were contraceptives, and 6 percent were used to induce abortion. Most methods involve plant and animal substances. Herbs are made into tea and taken orally. Some substances are formed into pills, some steamed and inhaled as vapors, some vaginally inserted, and others rubbed on the woman's stomach.

INDUCED ABORTION A review of 400 societies found that induced abortion was practiced in virtually all of them (Devereaux 1976). Cross-culturally, attitudes toward induced abortion range from absolute acceptability to conditional approval (abortion is acceptable but only under specified conditions), tolerance (abortion is regarded with neither approval nor disapproval), and opposition and punishment for offenders. Methods of inducing abortion include hitting the abdomen, starving oneself, taking drugs, jumping from high places, jumping up and down, lifting heavy objects, and doing hard work. Some methods clearly are dangerous to the pregnant woman. In Afghanistan, a midwife inserts into the pregnant woman an object such as a wooden spoon or stick treated with copper sulphate to cause vaginal bleeding and eventual abortion of the fetus (Hunte 1985).

The reasons women seek to induce abortion are usually related to economic and social factors (Devereaux 1976). Pastoralist women, for example, frequently carry heavy loads, sometimes for long distances. This lifestyle does not allow women to care for many small children at one time. Poverty is another frequent motivation. A woman who is faced with a pregnancy in the context of limited resources may find abortion preferable to bearing a child that cannot be fed. Culturally defined "legitimacy" of a pregnancy and social penalties for bearing an illegitimate child provide long-standing motivations for abortion, especially in Western societies.

Women waiting their turn at the clinic in Bazarak, eastern Afghanistan. The geographical terrain and distance make it difficult to get to a clinic in cases of emergency. Rates of maternal mortality in remote areas of Afghanistan are probably the highest in the world.

▶ *What is the maternal mortality rate in your home country and how does it vary by region, class, or ethnicity?*

Some governments intervene in family decisions to regulate access to abortion, either promoting it or forbidding it. Since the late 1980s, China has pursued a rigorous campaign to limit population growth (Greenhalgh 2008). Its One-Child-per-Couple Policy, announced in 1978, allowed most families to have only one child. It involved strict surveillance of pregnancies, strong group disapproval directed toward women pregnant for the second time or more, and forced abortions and sterilizations. Inadvertently, this policy simultaneously led to an increase in female infanticide, as parents, prompted by son preference, killed or abandoned infant daughters.

Religion and abortion are often related, but there is no simple relationship between what a particular religion teaches about abortion and what people actually do. Catholicism forbids abortion, but thousands of Catholic women have sought abortions throughout the world. Predominantly Catholic countries have laws making induced abortion illegal. This is the case in Brazil where, in spite of the law and Catholic beliefs, many women, especially poor women, resort to abortion. In one impoverished shantytown in the city of Recife,

everyday ANTHROPOLOGY

A Preference for Sons in India

Prospective parents in all cultures may ask themselves questions such as "Will my baby be healthy? Will I have a girl or a boy?" Throughout much of Asia, the baby's gender is often as important as the health of the baby, or more so. The preference for sons is especially strong in northern India.

The population of India has 55 million fewer females than males. Much of this gap is caused by indirect female infanticide and sex-selective abortion (Miller 1997 [1981]). These practices cause the **sex ratio**, or the number of males per 100 females in a population, to become unbalanced. The scarcity of girls is most extreme in northern India. In this region, it is common for mothers to breastfeed infant daughters less often and for a shorter period of time than they do their sons. Hospitals admit twice as many boys as girls, not because more boys are sick than girls but because family decision makers are more willing to allocate time and money to the health of boys than to that of girls.

The regional pattern corresponds with two features of the economy: production and marriage exchanges. The northern plains are dominated by *dry-field wheat cultivation*, which requires intensive labor inputs for plowing and field preparation and then moderate amounts of field labor for sowing, weeding, and harvesting, with women assisting in the latter tasks as unpaid family labor. Production in southern and eastern India relies more on *wet rice cultivation*, in which women form the bulk of the paid agricultural labor force. In much of southern India, women sometimes participate equally with men in agricultural planning and decision making.

Paralleling this regional difference in the gender division of labor is a

A low-income, itinerant vendor in a small town in India's Himalayan region proudly displays her son. Son preference is spreading from the North Indian plains region throughout India.

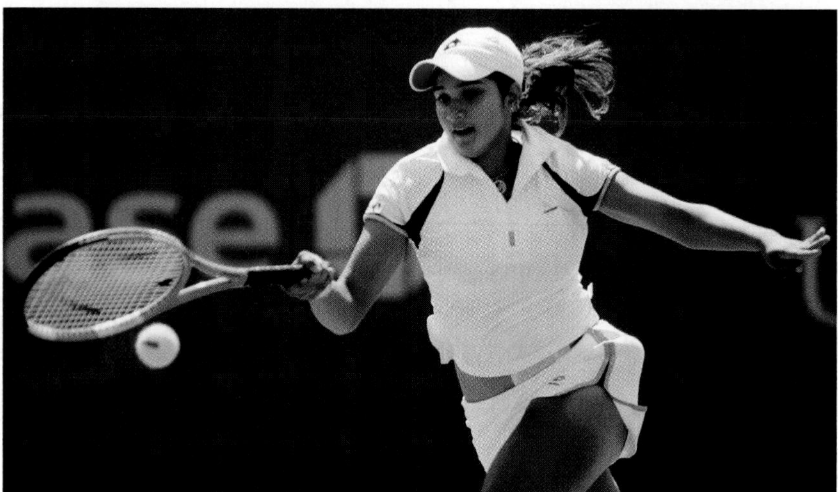

Sania Mirza of India lunges for a return from Marion Bartoli of France during the U.S. Open tennis tournament in Flushing Meadows, New York, in 2005. A Muslim and world-class tennis player, Mirza is the "poster girl" for India's public education campaign to promote awareness of the value of daughters. Slogans urge parents to have daughters and to care for them because their daughter may be the next Sania Mirza. At the same time, some conservative Islamic groups criticize Mirza for wearing immodest clothing.

---

sex ratio the number of males per 100 females in a population.

dowry the transfer of cash and goods from the bride's family to the newly married couple and to the groom's family.

groomprice the transfer of cash and goods, often large amounts, from the bride's family to the groom's family.

brideprice or **bridewealth** the transfer of cash and goods from the groom's family to the bride's family and to the bride.

one-third of the women said that they had aborted at least once (Gregg 2003:71–72). Illegal abortions are more likely to have negative effects on women's health than safe, legal abortion services. Although solid statistics are difficult to obtain, one estimate for Bahia is that at least one-fourth of all maternal deaths were due to complications of abortion (McCallum 2005:222).

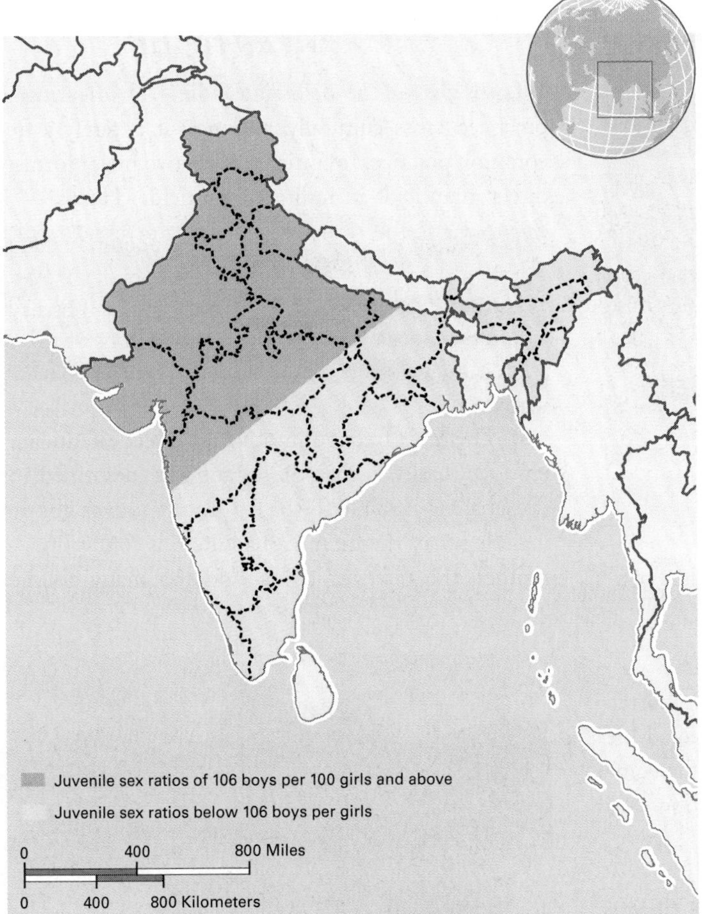

MAP 6.4 India's Regional Pattern of Unbalanced Child Sex Ratios. The number of sons per daughters is distinctly higher in the northwestern region than in the south and east.

contrast in cost related to marriage. In the North, marriage typically requires, especially among the propertied groups, a **dowry**, or **groomprice**—the transfer of money and goods from the bride's family to the groom's family, along with a tradition of passing gold jewelry through the female line from mother to daughter. In recent years, however, dowry has been spreading throughout India.

From a parent's perspective, the birth of several daughters in the northern system is a financial drain. In the North, the more sons per daughter in the household, the better: More dowries coming in will finance a "better" marriage of a daughter. In the South, a daughter is considered a valuable laborer and source of wealth. Importantly, much of northern dowry and southern **brideprice**, or **bridewealth** circulates. In the North, an incoming dowry can be used to finance the marriage of the groom's sister. In the South, cash received at the marriage of a daughter can be used for the marriage of her brother.

The economic costs and benefits to a household of having sons versus daughters in India also vary by class. Middle-class and upper-class families, especially in the North, tend to keep girls and women out of the paid labor force. Thus, daughters are a greater economic liability among them. Among the poor, where girls, as well as boys, may earn money in the informal sector (such as doing piecework at home), daughters are less of a burden. This class difference is mirrored in marriage costs. Among the poor, marriage costs are lower than among the middle and upper classes. They often involve balanced transfers between the bride's and groom's families.

Thus, poverty is not the major cause of some preference and daughter disfavor in India. Instead, the cause is the desire to maximize family status and wealth. If parents have two sons and one daughter in the North Indian marriage system, then two dowries come in with the brides of the sons and only one dowry will be paid out. The incoming dowries can be used to finance an impressive outgoing dowry of one's daughter that will attract a high-status husband. If northern parents have two daughters and one son, the ratio of incoming to outgoing wealth changes dramatically. This situation will impoverish the family.

◆ **FOOD FOR THOUGHT**

- Have you or anyone you know experienced a feeling of being less valued as a child than other children in the family? If you are an "only child," you will need to ponder experiences of your friends.

Islamic teachings forbid abortion. Abortion of female fetuses is nonetheless practiced covertly in Pakistan and by Muslims in India. Hinduism teaches *ahimsa,* or nonviolence toward other living beings, including a fetus whose movements have been felt by the mother. Thousands of Hindus, however, seek abortions every year. In contrast, Buddhism provides no overt rulings against abortion. Japanese

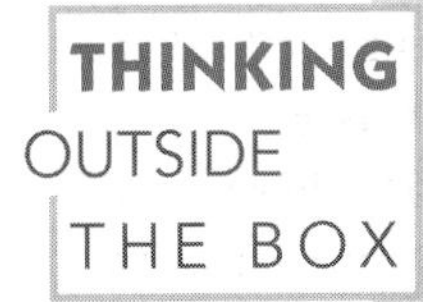

In your microculture, is there a preference about the desired number of sons and daughters? Is there a preference for their birth order?

In Japan, people regularly visit and decorate *mizuko*, small statues in memory of their "returned" fetuses.

▶ *In your cultural world, what is the definition and status of a fetus? Does a fetus have rights? Should it?*

Buddhism teaches that all life is fluid and that an aborted fetus is simply "returned" to a watery world of unshaped life and may later come back (LaFleur 1992). This belief is compatible with people's frequent use of induced abortion as a form of birth control in Japan.

THE NEW REPRODUCTIVE TECHNOLOGIES Since the early 1980s, new forms of reproductive technology have been developed and have been made available in many places around the world.

In vitro fertilization (*IVF*) procedures are an increasingly important part of the new reproductive technologies. This procedure, designed to bypass infertility, is highly sought after by many couples in Western countries, especially middle- and upper-class couples, among whom infertility is inexplicably high. It is also becoming more available in cities worldwide (Inhorn 2003). As IVF spreads globally, people interpret it within their own cultural frameworks. In much of the United States and the United Kingdom, where IVF first became available, people consider its use to be an indication of "reproduction gone awry," of natural inadequacy, and failure (Jenkins and Inhorn 2003). A study of male infertility in two Middle Eastern cities, Cairo in Egypt and Beirut in Lebanon, reveals how closely linked masculine identity is with male fertility (Inhorn 2004). In these cities, infertile men face serious social stigma and feelings of deep inadequacy. In addition, third-party donation of sperm is not acceptable according to Islam.

infanticide the killing of an infant or child.

personality an individual's patterned and characteristic way of behaving, thinking, and feeling.

INFANTICIDE

Infanticide, or the deliberate killing of offspring, is widely practiced cross-culturally, although it is rarely a frequent or common practice. Infanticide takes two major forms: It can be direct infanticide or indirect infanticide (Harris 1977). *Direct infanticide* is the death of an infant or child resulting from actions such as beating, smothering, poisoning, or drowning. *Indirect infanticide,* a more subtle process, may involve prolonged practices such as food deprivation, failure to take a sick infant to a clinic, or failure to provide warm clothing in winter.

The most frequent motive for direct infanticide reported cross-culturally is that the infant was "deformed" or very ill (Scrimshaw 1984:490–491). Other motives for infanticide include sex of the infant, an adulterous conception, an unwed mother, the birth of twins, and too many children in the

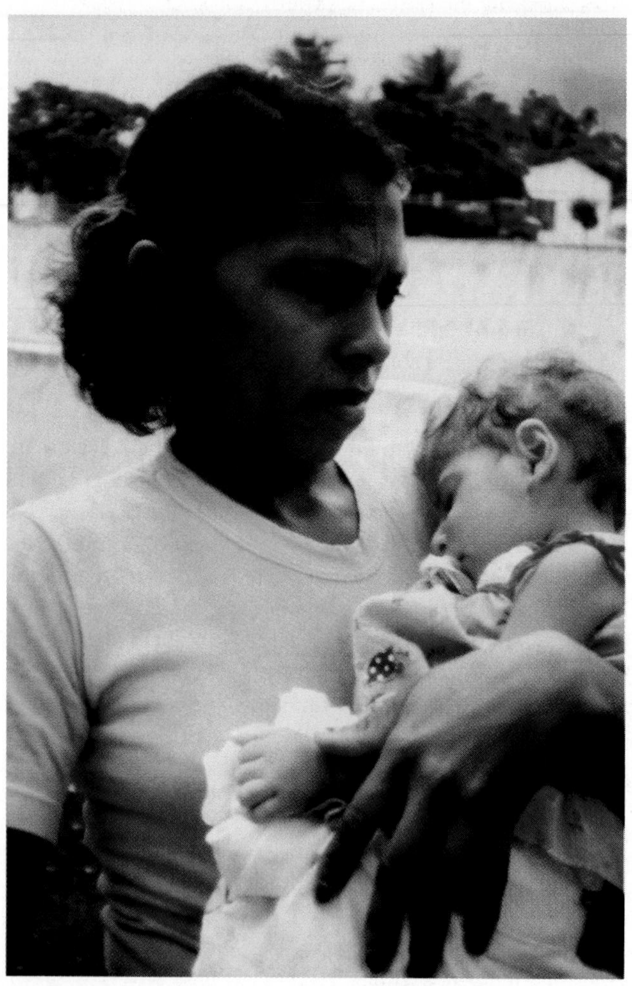

In Bom Jesus, a shantytown in northeastern Brazil, a doctor at the local clinic told this mother that her son was dying of anemia and that she needed to feed him red meat. The mother said, "Now, where am I going to find the money to feed my hopeless son rich food like that?"

▶ *What is your perspective on Western bonding theory, and how did you come to have this view?*

family. A study of 148 cases of infanticide in contemporary Canada found that the mothers convicted of killing their offspring were relatively young and lacked financial and family resources to help them (Daly and Wilson 1984).

Among the poor of northeastern Brazil, indirect infanticide is also related to harsh conditions and poverty (Scheper-Hughes 1992). In a shantytown called Bom Jesus, in the state of Pernambuco, Brazil (see Map 7.1 on p. 165), life expectancy is low. Available data on infant and child mortality in Bom Jesus since the 1960s led anthropologist Nancy Scheper-Hughes to coin the painfully ironic phrase, *the modernization of mortality*. The modernization of mortality in Brazil is class based, mirroring a deep division in entitlements between the rich and the poor. Economic growth in Brazil has brought rising standards of living for many. The *infant mortality rate* (deaths of children under the age of 1 year per 1000 births) declined dramatically in recent decades. This decline, however, is unevenly distributed. High infant death rates are concentrated among the poorest classes of society. Poverty forces mothers to selectively (and unconsciously) neglect babies that seem sickly or weak, sending them to heaven as "angel babies" rather than struggling to keep them alive. People's religious beliefs, a form of Catholicism, provide psychological support for indirect infanticide by allowing mothers to believe that their dead babies are safe in heaven (this ethnographic case is discussed further in the next section).

◆◆◆

Personality and the Life Cycle

Cultural anthropologists think that **personality** is largely formed through *enculturation* (sometimes called socialization), learning of culture through both informal and formal processes. They study how various cultures enculturate their members into having different personalities and identities. Cultural anthropologists also investigate how personalities vary according to cultural context, and some ask why such variations exist. Others study how changing cultural contexts affect personality, identity, and well-being over the life cycle.

BIRTH, INFANCY, AND CHILDHOOD

This section first considers the cultural context of birth itself. It then discusses cultural variations in infant care and how they may shape personality and identity. Last, it deals with the topic of gender identity formation in infancy.

THE BIRTH CONTEXT The cultural context of birth affects an infant's psychological development. Brigitte Jordan (1983), a pioneer in the cross-cultural study of birth, conducted comparative research on birth practices in Mexico, Sweden, Holland, and the United States. She studied the birth setting, including its location and who is present, the types of attendants and their roles, the birth event, and the postpartum period. Among Maya women in Mexico, the midwife is called in during the early stages of labor. One of her tasks is to give a massage to the mother-to-be. She also provides psychological support by telling stories, often about other women's birthing experiences. The husband is expected to be present during the labor so that he can see "how a woman suffers." The woman's mother should be present, along with other female kin, such as her mother-in-law, godmother, sisters, and friends. Thus, a Maya mother is surrounded by a large group of supportive people.

In the United States, hospital births are the norm. The newborn infant is generally taken to the nursery, where it is wrapped in cloth and placed in a plastic crate under bright lights rather than being cared for by a family member. Some critics argue that the hospital-based system of highly regulated birth is extremely technocratic and too managed, alienating the mother—as well as other members of the family and the wider community—from the birthing process and the infant (Davis-Floyd 1992). This critique has led to consideration of how to improve the way birth is conducted.

The Western medical model of birth contrasts sharply with non-Western practices. Sometimes they come into direct conflict. In such situations, anthropological expertise can mediate such conflict by providing what medical specialists now refer to as *cultural sensitivity*, or cultural awareness and respect).

BONDING Many contemporary Western psychological theorists say that parent–infant contact and bonding at the time of birth is crucial for setting in motion parental attachment to the infant. Western specialists say that if this bonding is not established at the time of the infant's birth, it will not develop later. Explanations for juvenile delinquency or other unfavorable child development problems often include reference to lack of proper infant bonding at birth.

Nancy Scheper-Hughes (1992) questions Western bonding theory. She argues that bonding does not necessarily have to occur at birth to be successful. Her observations in Brazil show that many low-income mothers do not exhibit bonding with their infants at birth. Bonding occurs later, if the child survives infancy, when it is several years old. She proposes that this pattern of later bonding is related to the high rate of infant mortality among poor people of northeast Brazil. If women were to develop strong bonds with their newborn infants, they would suffer untold amounts of grief. Western bonding is adaptive in low-mortality/low-fertility societies in which strong maternal attachment is reasonable because infants are likely to survive.

GENDER IN INFANCY Anthropologists distinguish between *sex* and *gender* (review definitions in Chapter 1). Sex is something that everyone is born with. In the view of Western science, it has three biological markers: genitals, hormones, and chromosomes. A male has a penis, more androgens than estrogens, and the XY chromosome. A female has a vagina, more estrogens than androgens, and the XX chromosome. Increasingly, scientists are finding that these two categories are not airtight. In all populations, up to 10 percent of people are born with indeterminate genitals, similar proportions of androgens and estrogens, and chromosomes with more complex distributions than simply XX and XY.

Gender, in contrast, is a cultural construction and is highly variable across cultures (Miller 1993). In the view of most cultural anthropologists, a high degree of human *plasticity* (or personality flexibility) allows for substantial human variation in personality and behavior. More biologically inclined anthropologists, however, continue to insist that many sex-linked personality characteristics are inborn.

Proving the existence of innate (inborn) gender characteristics is made difficult by two factors. First, it is impossible to collect data on infants before they are subject to cultural treatment. Cultural effects may begin to shape infants even in the womb, through exposure to sound and motion, but at this point the scientific data on the cultural effects on the prenatal stage are slim. Second, it is difficult, if not impossible, to remove observer biases when studying and interpreting the behavior of infants. Once birth takes place, culture shapes infants in the way people handle and interact with them. There is no such thing as a "natural" infant—how an infant is held, talked to, and fed is all part of the cultural web.

In spite of the research hazards, scientists still seek to know what is "natural" and what is "cultural" about babies. Studies of infants have focused on assessing the potential innateness of three major Euro-American personality stereotypes (Frieze et al. 1978:73–78):

- Whether infant males are more aggressive than infant females
- Whether infant females are more social than infant males
- Whether infant males are more independent than infant females

What is the evidence? American studies indicate that boy babies cry more than girl babies, and some people accept this difference as evidence of higher levels of inborn aggression in males. An alternative interpretation is that baby boys, on average, tend to weigh more than girls at birth. They therefore are more likely to have a difficult delivery from which it takes time to recover. So they cry more, but not because of aggressiveness. In terms of sociality, baby girls smile more often than boys, and some researchers claim this difference confirms innate personality characteristics. But culture, not nature, may be the explanation as American caretakers smile more at baby girls than they smile at baby boys. Thus, the more frequent smiling of girls is likely to be a learned behavior. In terms of independence or dependence, studies thus far reveal no clear differences in how upset baby boys and girls are when separated from their caretakers. Taken as a whole, studies seeking to document innate differences between girls and boys are not convincing.

Cultural anthropologists who take a constructionist view make two further points. They note that, if gender differences are innate, it is odd that cultures go to so much trouble to enculturate offspring into a particular gender. Also, if gender differences are innate, then they should be the same throughout history and across all cultures, which they clearly are not. The following material explores cross-cultural cases of how culture constructs gender, beginning with childhood.

SOCIALIZATION DURING CHILDHOOD

The Six Cultures Study is a classic cross-cultural research project designed to provide comparative data on how children's activities and tasks shape their personalities (Whiting and Whiting 1975). Researchers used parallel methods at six sites (see Figure 6.4), observing children between the ages of 3 and 11 years. They recorded behavior, such as caring for and being supportive of other children; hitting other children; and performing tasks such as child care, cooking, and errands. The data collected were analyzed in terms of two major personality types: nurturant-responsible and dependent-dominant. A *nurturant-responsible personality* is characterized by caring and sharing acts toward other children. The *dependent-dominant personality* involves fewer acts of caregiving, more acts that assert dominance over other children, and more need for care by adults.

Of the six cultures, the Gusii children of southwestern Kenya had the highest frequency of a nurturant-responsible personality type. Gusii children were responsible for the widest range of tasks and at earlier ages than children in any other culture in the study, often performing tasks that an

Horticultural Groups
Gusii people, Kenya
Maya people, Oaxaca, Mexico
Tarong people, Philippines

Intensive Agriculture or Industrial Groups
Taira village, Okinawa, Japan
Rajput people, village in North India
Middle-class Euro-Americans, Orchard Town, New England, United States

Source: Whiting and Whiting (1975).

FIGURE 6.4 Groups in the Six Cultures Study

puberty a time in the human life cycle that occurs universally and involves a set of biological markers and sexual maturation.

(LEFT) A Yanomami boy acquiring skills necessary for hunting and warfare through play. (RIGHT) An American boy playing a video game.

▶ *Consider examples of children's games that may provide learning and skills related to adult roles in your culture.*

Orchard Town, United States, mother does. Although some children in all six cultures took care of other children, Gusii children (both boys and girls) spent the most time doing so. They began taking on this responsibility at a very young age, between 5 and 8 years old.

In contrast, Orchard Town children had the highest frequency of the dependent-dominant personality type. The differences correlate with the mode of livelihood. The people in Kenya, Mexico, and the Philippines all had more nurturant-responsible children and their economies are reliant on horticulture. The study sites in Japan, India, and the United States were based on either intensive agriculture or industry. How do these different modes of livelihood influence child personality? The key underlying factor is women's work roles. In the horticultural societies, women are an important part of the labor force and spend much time working outside the home. Their children take on many family-supportive tasks and thereby develop personalities that are nurturant-responsible. When women are mainly occupied in the home, as in the second group of cultures, children have fewer tasks and less responsibility. They develop personalities that are more dependent-dominant.

This study has many implications for Western child development experts. For one thing, what happens when the dependent-dominant personality develops to an extreme level—into a *narcissistic personality*? A narcissist is someone who constantly seeks self-attention and self-affirmation, with no concern for other people's needs. Consumerism supports the development of narcissism via its emphasis on identity formation through ownership of self-defining goods (clothing, electronics, cars) and access to self-defining services (vacations, therapists, fitness salons). The Six Cultures Study suggests that involving children more in household responsibilities might result in less self-focused personality formation and more nurturant-responsible people.

ADOLESCENCE AND IDENTITY

The transition from "childhood" to "adulthood" involves certain biological events as well as cultural events that shape the transition to adulthood.

IS ADOLESCENCE A UNIVERSAL LIFE-CYCLE STAGE?

Puberty is a time in the human life cycle that occurs universally and involves a set of biological markers. In males, the voice

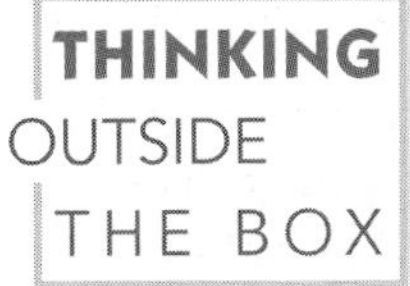

THINKING OUTSIDE THE BOX

Try to recall your daily activities when you were 5 years old, 10 years old, and 15 years old. What tasks did you do? In terms of the Six Cultures Study categories, which type of personality do you have?

deepens and facial and body hair appear; in females, menarche and breast development occur; in both males and females, pubic and underarm hair appear and sexual maturation is achieved. **Adolescence,** in contrast, is a culturally defined period of maturation from around the time of puberty until the attainment of adulthood, usually marked by becoming a parent, getting married, or becoming economically self-sufficient.

Some scholars say that all cultures define a period of adolescence. A comparative study using data on 186 societies argues for the universal existence of a culturally defined phase of adolescence (Schlegel 1995; Schlegel and Barry 1991). The researchers point to supportive evidence in the fact that people in cultures as diverse as the Navajo and the Trobriand Islanders have special terms comparable to the American term "adolescent" to refer to a person between puberty and marriage. Following a biological determinist, Darwinian model, they interpret the supposedly universal phases of adolescence as being adaptive in an evolutionary sense. The logic is that adolescence provides training for parenthood and thus contributes to enhanced reproductive success and survival of parents' genes.

Other anthropologists view adolescence as culturally constructed and as highly variable, and thus impossible to explain on only biological grounds. These researchers point out that people in many cultures recognize no period of adolescence. In some others, identification of an adolescent phase is recent. Moroccan anthropologist Fatima Mernissi (1987), for example, states that adolescence became a recognized life-cycle phase for females in Morocco only in the late twentieth century.

> The idea of an adolescent unmarried woman is a completely new idea in the Muslim world, where previously you had only a female child and a menstruating woman who had to be married off immediately so as to prevent dishonorable engagement in premarital sex (1987:xxiv).

Another line of evidence supporting a constructionist view is that, in different cultures, the length and elaboration of adolescence varies for males and females. In many horticultural and pastoralist societies where men are valued as warriors, as among the Maasai, a long period between childhood and adulthood is devoted to training in warfare and developing solidarity among males. This adolescent period has nothing to do with training for parenthood. Maasai females, on the other hand, move directly from being a girl to being a wife and have no culturally marked adolescent period. They learn adult roles when they are children.

Long periods of male initiation among some highland groups in Papua New Guinea that involve institutionalized homosexual relationships also do not fit within the Darwinian interpretation. Gilbert Herdt conducted research with the Sambia, highland horticulturalists, and learned about their secret male initiation practices (1987). The Sambia believe that, in order for a young boy to mature into a healthy adult, he must join a secret, all-male initiation group. A boy becomes a partner of a senior male who regularly transfers his semen to the youth orally. The Sambia believe that the youth is nourished by ingesting semen. After a period of time in the initiation group, the "grown" youth rejoins society as a man. At that time he will marry a woman and raise children.

In some cultures, females have long adolescent phases during which they live separated from the wider group and gain special knowledge and skills (Brown 1978). After this period of seclusion, they re-emerge as full-fledged women and marry. A cultural explanation exists for why gender affects whether a young person has an adolescent phase of life. Cultural materialism (Chapter 1) offers an explanatory framework that accounts for variation. In this perspective, a prolonged and marked period of adolescence is likely to be preparation for any of several culturally valued adult roles: worker, warrior, or parent. Confirmation comes from the finding that extended adolescence for females in many nonindustrial societies occurs in cultures where adult females are important as food producers (Brown 1978).

COMING OF AGE AND GENDER IDENTITY Margaret Mead made famous the phrase "coming of age" in her book *Coming of Age in Samoa* (1961). It can refer generally to the period of adolescence or specifically to a ceremony or set of ceremonies that marks the boundaries of adolescence. What are the psychological aspects of such special events for the children who go through them? Some ceremonies have a sacrificial element, with symbolic death and rebirth. Most coming of age ceremonies are gender specific, highlighting the importance of adult roles of men and women. These ceremonies often involve marking the body of the initiate in some way. Such marking may include scarification, tattooing, and genital surgery. In many societies, adolescent males undergo genital surgery that involves removal of part of the skin around the tip of the penis; without this operation, the boy would not become a full-fledged male. In others, girls undergo genital cutting of various types, which, similarly, is the only way to become a real woman.

A young Maasai male, in a first-person account of his initiation into manhood, describes the "intolerable pain" he experienced following the circumcision, as well as his feeling of accomplishment two weeks later when his head was shaved and he became a warrior: "As long as I live, I will never forget the day my head was shaved and I emerged a man, a Maasai warrior. I felt a sense of control over my destiny so great that no words can accurately describe it" (Saitoti 1986:71).

---

adolescence a culturally defined period of maturation from the time of puberty until adulthood that occurs in some but not all cultures.

female genital cutting a term used for a range of genital cutting procedures, including the excision of part or all of the clitoris, excision of part or all of the labia, and sometimes infibulation, the stitching together of the vaginal entry.

A Maasai warrior's mother shaves her son's head during part of his initiation ceremony into adulthood. This ritual validates her status as a mother as well as her son's adulthood.

Less common worldwide is **female genital cutting (FGC),** a Western term referring to several forms of genital surgery practiced on females. These practices may involve the excision of part or all of the clitoris, part or all of the labia, and (the least common practice) *infibulation,* the stitching together of the vaginal entry, leaving a small aperture for drainage of menstrual blood. These procedures are performed when the girl is between 7 and 15 years of age. Many people practice some form of female genital cutting in the Sahelian countries extending from Africa's west to east coast. It is also found in Egypt in some groups of the Middle East (particularly among Bedu tribes) and among some Muslim groups in South and Southeast Asia. In terms of religion, FGC is often, but not always, associated with people who are Muslim. In Ethiopia, some Christian groups practice it. Genital cutting occurs in many groups in which female labor participation is high, but also in others where it is not.

Scholars have yet to provide an explanation for the regional and social distribution of female genital cutting. Anthropologists who study this practice ask the people involved for their views. Many young girls say they look forward to the ceremony so that they will be free from childhood tasks and can take on the more respected role of an adult woman. In other cases, anthropologists have reported hearing statements of resistance (Fratkin 1998:60). Fewer issues force the questioning of cultural relativism more clearly than female genital cutting (see Critical Thinking).

Initiation rites often involve themes of death and rebirth as the initiate loses his or her former identity and emerges with a new one. Abigail Adams conducted research during the early 1990s on initiation rituals at what was then a men's military school, the Virginia Military Institute (2002). Freshmen students, called "Rats," are each assigned to an upperclassman, called a "Dyke." The freshman year involves continuous humiliation and other forms of abuse for the Rats. Dykes treat their Rats like infants, telling them how to eat, bathe, and talk and yelling at them in baby talk. Another tradition is called the Rape of the First Sentinel. When the first Rat does guard detail, the seniors attack him, rip off some of his clothes, spray him with shaving cream, and throw rotten food

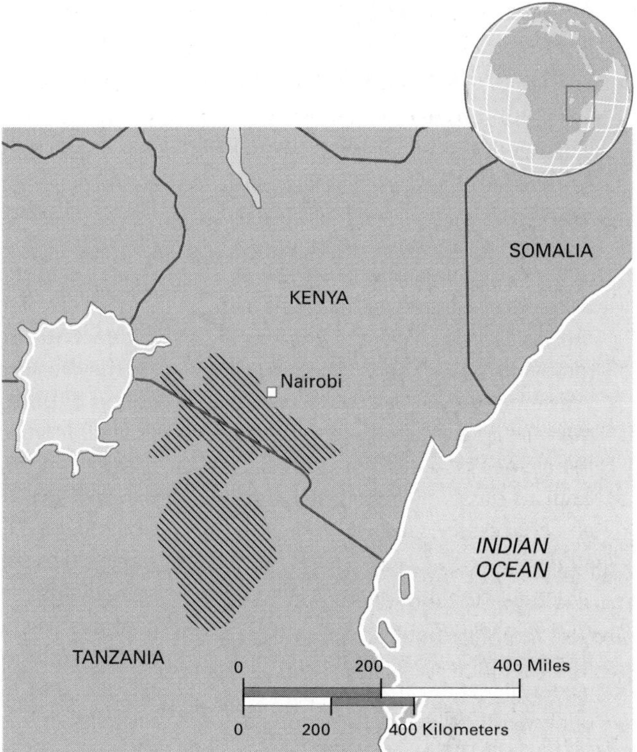

MAP 6.5 Maasai Region of Kenya and Tanzania. An estimated 350,000 Maasai live in Kenya and 150,000 in Tanzania. The climate is semiarid and arid.

Breaking Out, a rite of passage at a military academy in Virginia when it was an all-men's school.

▶ *What rite of passage have you been through and how would you analyze it anthropologically?*

CRITICAL thinking

Cultural Relativism and Female Genital Cutting

In cultures that practice female genital cutting (FGC), it is a necessary step toward full womanhood. Fathers say that an uncircumcised daughter is unmarriageable and will bring no brideprice. Others say that removing the labia makes a woman beautiful by removing "male" parts. The prevailing Western view, increasingly shared by many people who have long practiced female genital cutting, is that FGC is both a sign of low female status and an unnecessary cause of women's suffering.

Female genital cutting is linked with several health risks, including those related to the surgery itself (shock, infection) and future genito-urinary complications (Gruenbaum 2001). Infibulation scars the vaginal canal and may lead to problems during childbirth, sometimes causing the death of the infant and mother.

Having an infibulated bride's husband "open" her, using a stick or knife to loosen the aperture, is both painful and an opportunity for infection. After giving birth, a woman is usually reinfibulated, and the process begins again. Health experts say that repeated trauma to the woman's vaginal area increases the risk of contracting HIV/AIDS.

The Western view argues that the effects of both clitoridectomy and infibulation on a woman's sexual enjoyment are highly negative—for one thing, clitoral orgasm is no longer possible. Some experts also say that FGC is related to the high level of infertility in many African countries, although a comparative study of fertility data from the Central African Republic, Côte d'Ivoire, and Tanzania found no clear relationship between FGC and infertility (Larsen and Yan 2000).

Outsiders often view these practices in oversimplified terms and in the most extreme forms. What are the views of insiders? Is there any evidence for female agency? Or is it all structure and should anthropologists support FGC liberation movements? One voice that transcends insider/outsider divisions is that of Fuambai Ahmadu, who was born and raised in Washington, DC. She is descended from a prominent Kono lineage in Sierra Leone and did research for her doctorate in anthropology on female genital cutting in the Gambia (2000).

In 1991, she traveled to Sierra Leone with her mother and other family members for what she refers to as her "circumcision." Upon her return, she wrote about her initiation experience and what it meant to her. Although the physical pain was excruciating (in spite of the use of anesthetics), "the positive aspects have been much more profound" (2000:306). Through the initiation she became part of a powerful female world. Her analysis addresses the effects of genital cutting on health and sexuality. Ahmadu argues that Westerners exaggerate these issues

---

and used chewing tobacco at him. A "good Rat" takes it "like a man." The Rats who make it through the first year have strong bonds with the Dykes who are their mentors. In turn, the Rats serve them by making their beds and shining their shoes.

The culminating initiation ritual for the Rats takes place during March. The town's firetruck sprays the outskirts of the campus to create a large area of mud. The Rats have to crawl through the mud while sophomores and juniors attack them, shout at them, push them down, sit on them, and fill their eyes, ears, faces, and clothes with mud. The Rats can barely see as they grope their way along, and many lose their pants. The ordeal continues over two banks of earth and a ditch, with continuous harassment from the sophomores and juniors. When the Rats finally reach the top of the second bank, the Dykes rush to greet them, tenderly wash the mud off them, and wrap them in blankets. The moment when the mud is washed away is the transition of the Rat into a cadet.

berdache a blurred gender category, usually referring to a person who is biologically male but who takes on a female gender role.

Adams interprets this ritual as a birthing event with the newborn emerging blinded by and covered with fluids, then cleaned and blanketed. One senior said that being a Dyke "is like having my own child" (2002:39). Many aspects of this ritual, however, are ambiguous, not least of which is the term "Dyke" for male "mothers" (or "fathers"?). The Breaking Out initiation ritual is no longer practiced at VMI. For many years, this all-male school insisted that it could not admit women because the presence of women would destroy the very essence of the school. In the mid-1990s, VMI, as the recipient of public funds, was under pressure to admit women in order to be compliant with the law. After a drawn-out legal battle that ended up in the Supreme Court, VMI admitted its first women students in 1997. Break Out has been replaced with a long weekend series of events involving physical and field challenges.

SEXUAL IDENTITY AND GENDER PLURALISM

Scholars have long debated whether sexual preferences and gender identity are biologically determined (ruled by genetic or hormonal factors) or culturally constructed and learned. Biological anthropologist Melvin Konner (1989) takes a middle position, saying that both factors play a part, but

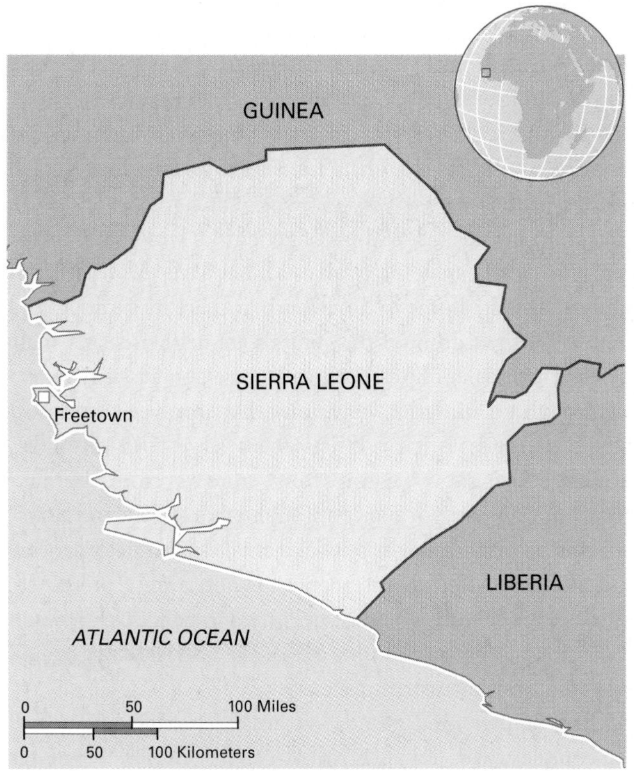

MAP 6.6 Sierra Leone.
The Republic of Sierra Leone was an important center of the transatlantic slave trade. Its capital, Freetown, was established in 1972 as a home for African slaves who fought with the British during the American Revolution. Sierra Leone's coast is covered with mangrove swamps while the interior is plateau, forests, and mountains. The population is 6 million. Sierra Leone suffered a terrible civil war from 1991 to 2002, causing thousands of deaths and the displacement of 2 million people. It has the lowest per capita income in the world. English is the official language, but most people speak local, tribal languages.

by focusing on infibulation rather than on the less extreme forms. She adds, however, that if global pressures against the practice continue, she will go along with that movement and support "ritual without cutting" (2000:308).

◆ **CRITICAL THINKING QUESTIONS**

- Why do you think FGC is a prominent issue in human rights debates in the West, whereas male circumcision and other forms of initiation (such as fraternity and sorority hazing) are not?
- Where do you stand on FGC and why?
- What kinds of cultural remodeling of the female body are practiced in your culture?

simultaneously warning that no one has a simple answer to the question of who is gay.

The cultural constructionist position emphasizes socialization and childhood experiences as more powerful than biology in shaping sexual orientation. These anthropologists find support for their position in the cross-cultural record and its cases in which people change their sexual orientation once, or sometimes more than once, during their lifetimes. The Sambia of Papua New Guinea are one example. In the Gulf state of Oman (see Map 5.3, p. 123), the *xanith* is another example (Wikan 1977). A xanith is a man who, for a time, becomes more like a woman, wears female clothing, and has sex with other men. Later, the xanith returns to a standard male role, marries a woman, and has children. Thus, given the same biological material, some people assume different sexual identities over their lives.

No matter what one's theoretical perspective is, it is clear that homosexuals are discriminated against in many contexts where heterosexuality is the norm. In the United States, homosexuals are disproportionately victims of hate crimes, housing discrimination, and problems in the workplace, including wage and benefits discrimination. They often suffer from being stigmatized by their parents, peers, and the wider society. The psychological damage to their self-esteem by social stigma and discrimination is related to the fact that homosexual youth in the United States have substantially higher suicide rates than heterosexual youth.

Some cultures allow for a *third gender,* which is neither purely "male" nor purely "female," according to a particular culture's definition of those terms. As with the xanith of Oman, these gender categories offer ways for "males" to cross gender lines and assume more "female" behaviors, personality characteristics, and dress. In some Native American groups, a **berdache** (ber-DASH) is a male, in terms of genitals, who opts to wear female clothing, engages in sexual intercourse with a man or a woman, and does female tasks such as basket

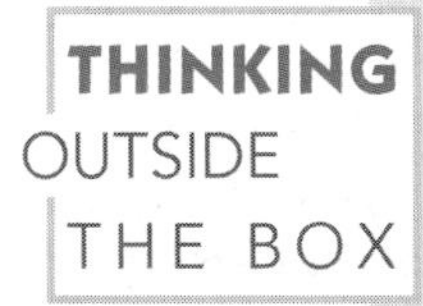

In your cultural world, what economic roles are associated with long periods of seclusion and learning (for example, a college education)? Which are not? Are there gender variations?

A Zuni berdache wearing a traditional woman's ceremonial dress and holding a pottery bowl with sacred corn meal.

weaving and pottery making (Williams 1992). A person may become a berdache in a variety of ways. Sometimes parents, especially if they have several sons, choose one to become a berdache. Sometimes a boy who shows interest in typically female activities or who likes to wear female clothing is allowed to become a berdache. Such a child is a focus of pride for the family, never a source of disappointment or stigma.

During decades of contact with Euro-American colonizers, including Christian missionaries, the outsiders viewed the berdache role with disapproval and ridicule (Roscoe 1991). Native American cultures began to suppress their berdache tradition. Starting in the 1980s, as Native American cultural pride began to grow, the open presence of the berdache and the **amazon** (a woman who takes on male roles and behaviors) has returned. Contemporary Native American cultures, compared to mainstream White culture, are more accepting of gender role fluidity and the contemporary concept of being gay.

In India, the counterpart of the Native American berdache is a **hijra** (hij-ruh). Hijras dress and act like women but are neither truly male nor truly female (Nanda 1990). Many hijras were born with male genitals or with genitals that were not clearly male or female. Hijras have the traditional right to visit the home of a newborn, inspect its genitals, and claim it for their group if the genitals are neither clearly male nor clearly female. Hijras born with male genitals may opt to go through an initiation ceremony that involves cutting off their penis and testicles. Hijras roam large cities of India, earning a living by begging from store to store. Because women do not sing or dance in public, hijras play an important role as performers in public events, especially as dancers or musicians. Mainstream people do not admire or respect hijras, and no family would be delighted to hear that their son has decided to become a hijra. Hijras are a stigmatized group, separated from mainstream society.

In mainland and island Southeast Asia, the situation is also complex, with a wide range of gender options, or **gender pluralism**. Gender pluralism is the existence in a culture of multiple categories of femininity, masculinity, and blurred genders that are tolerated and legitimate (Peletz 2006:310). In Thailand, three gender categories have long existed: *phuuchai* (male), *phuuyung* (female), and *kathoey* (transvestite/transsexual/hermaphrodite) (Morris 1994). A kathoey is "originally" a male who crosses into the body, personality, and dress defined as female. Sexual orientation of kathoeys is flexible, including either male or female partners. In contemporary Thailand, explicit discussion and recognition of homosexuality exists, usually couched in English terms, conveying a sense of its foreignness. The words for lesbian are *thom* (from the word "tomboy") and *thut* (an ironic usage from the U.S. movie *Tootsie* about a heterosexual male transvestite).

ADULTHOOD

Adulthood for most people means entering into some form of marriage, or long-term domestic relationship, and having children. This section considers the psychological aspects of parenthood and the "senior years."

BECOMING A PARENT In Euro-American culture, a woman becomes a mother when she gives birth. **Matrescence** is the cultural process of becoming a mother (Raphael 1975). Like adolescence, matrescence varies cross-culturally in terms of duration and meaning. In some cultures, a woman is transformed into a mother as soon as she thinks she is pregnant. In others, she becomes a mother and is granted full maternal status only when she delivers an infant of the "right" sex, as in much of northern India, where son preference is strong.

In many nonindustrial cultures, matrescence occurs in the context of supportive family members. Some cultures

---

amazon a person who is biologically female but takes on a male gender role.

hijra term used in India to refer to a blurred gender role in which a person, usually biologically male, takes on female dress and behavior.

gender pluralism the existence within a culture of multiple categories of femininity, masculinity, and blurred genders that are tolerated and legitimate.

matrescence motherhood, or the cultural process of becoming a mother.

patrescence fatherhood, or the cultural process of becoming a father.

couvade customs applying to the behavior of fathers during and shortly after the birth of their children.

The South Korean transgender group "Lady" includes four transsexuals.

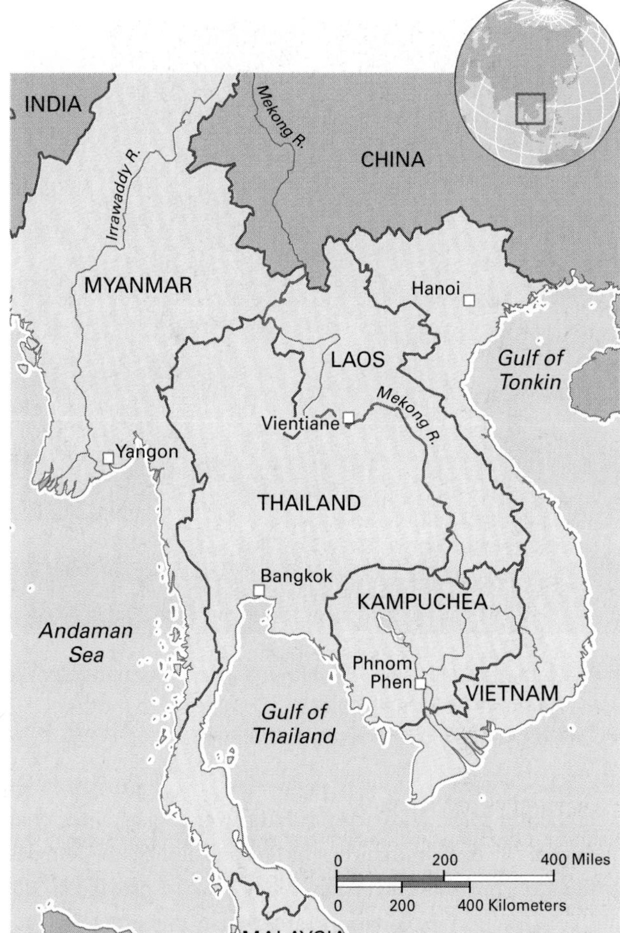

MAP 6.7 Mainland Southeast Asia.
Mainland Southeast Asia comprises Myanmar, Thailand, Laos, Vietnam, Kampuchea, and Malaysia. Although each country has a distinct history, the region shares a tropical monsoon climate, emphasis on wet-rice agriculture, and ethnic contrasts between highlanders and lowlanders. Many national and ethnic languages exist. Languages in the Mon-Khmer language family have the most speakers. Theravada Buddhism, Islam, and Christianity are the major religions. Growth in industry and informatics has created an economic upsurge in many parts of the region.

promote prenatal practices, abiding by particular food taboos, which can be regarded as part of matrescence. Such rules make the pregnant woman feel that she has a role in ensuring that the pregnancy turns out well. In the West, medical experts increasingly define the prenatal period as an important phase of matrescence, and they have issued many scientific and medical rules for potential parents, especially mothers (Browner and Press 1995, 1996). Pregnant women are urged to seek prenatal examinations, be under the regular supervision of a doctor who monitors the growth and development of the fetus, follow particular dietary and exercise guidelines, and undergo a range of tests such as ultrasound scanning. Some anthropologists think that such medical control of pregnancy leads to the greater likelihood of postpartum depression among mothers as a result of their lack of control in matrescence.

Patrescence, or the cultural process of becoming a father, is less marked cross-culturally than matrescence. One exception to this generalization is **couvade**, beliefs and customs applying to a father during his wife's pregnancy and delivery (Broude 1988). In some cases, the father takes to his bed before, during, or after the delivery, and he may experience pain and exhaustion. Couvade often involves rules for the expectant father: He may not hunt a certain animal, eat certain foods, or cut objects. Early theories of why couvade exists relied on Freudian interpretations that men were identifying with the female role in contexts where the father role was weak. Cross-cultural data indicates the opposite because couvade occurs in societies where fathers have prominent roles in child care. In these contexts, couvade is a phase of patrescence: The father's proper behavior helps ensure a safe delivery and a healthy baby. Another interpretation of couvade is that it offers support for the mother.

Once the baby is born, who takes care of it? The widespread pattern of women being the major caretakers of infants and children has led many people to think that something biologically innate about females makes them especially suited

An Aka father and his son. Aka fathers are affectionate caretakers of infants and small children. Compared to mothers, they are more likely to kiss and hug children.

to caretaking roles. Most cultural anthropologists agree that child care is predominantly the responsibility of females worldwide—but not universally. They seek to provide a cultural construction explanation rather than a genetic or hormonal one. As evidence, they point to the cross-cultural variation in child-care roles. For example, throughout the South Pacific, child care is shared across families, and women breastfeed other women's babies. Paternal involvement varies cross-culturally as well. Among Aka foragers of the Central African Republic (see Map 6.8), paternal child care is prominent (Hewlett 1991). Aka fathers are intimate, affectionate, and helpful, spending half their time each day holding or within close reach of their infants. Fathers are more likely to hug and kiss their infants than mothers are. The definition of good fatherhood among the Aka means being affectionate toward children and assisting the mother when her workload is heavy. Among the Aka, gender equality prevails, and violence against women is unknown. This high level of paternal involvement is related to all these patterns and supports a constructionist view of parenting and gender roles rather than a biological determinist view.

MIDDLE AGE In many industrial/informatics societies, a major turning point is the fortieth birthday, especially for men. According to a study of men turning 40 in the United States, the *40 syndrome* involves feelings of restlessness, rebelliousness, and unhappiness that often lead to family breakups (Brandes 1985). A possible reason behind the emphasis on the age 40 as a turning point for males is that it is the current midpoint of a typical life span for a middle-class American man. In cultures with shorter life spans, a so-called midlife crisis would necessarily

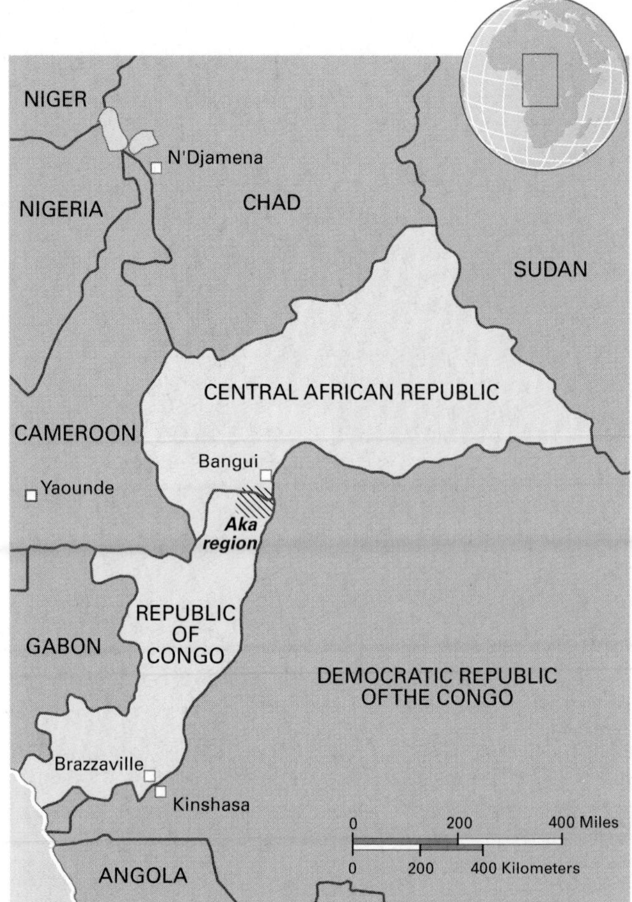

MAP 6.8 Aka Region of the Central African Republic and the Democratic Republic of Congo.
The 30,000 Aka are tropical forest foragers who know hundreds of plants and animals. They eat roots, leaves, nuts, fruits, mushrooms, honey, grubs, caterpillars, and meat from monkeys, rats, mongooses, and porcupines. They trade meat to farmers for manioc and other cultivated foods. They are socially egalitarian, and their religious beliefs are indigenous. Diaka, their main language, is tonal. The Aka territory is critically endangered by commercial loggers.

occur at some point other than the age of 40 years. The midlife crisis in America seems strongly embedded in contemporary culture and its fear and denial of death (Shore 1998).

Menopause, or the cessation of menstruation, is a significant aspect of middle age for women in many, but not all, cultures. A comparative study examined differences in perception and experience of menopause among Maya women of Mexico and rural Greek women (Beyene 1989). Among the Maya women, menopause is not a time of stress or crisis. They consider menstruation an illness and look forward to its end. Menopause among these women is not associated with physical or emotional symptoms. None of the women reported hot flashes or cold sweats. No role changes were associated with menopause. In contrast, the rural Greek women recognized menopause, or *exapi,* as a natural phenomenon that all women experience and one that causes temporary discomfort, which is a phase of hot flashes, especially at night, that may last about a year. The women did not think exapi was serious and did not regard it as worthy of medical attention. Postmenopausal women emphasized the relief and freedom they felt. Postmenopausal women can go into cafes by themselves, something they would never do otherwise, and they can participate more fully in church ceremonies. In Japan, likewise, menopause is minimally stressful and women rarely consider it something that warrants medical attention (Lock 1993).

THE SENIOR YEARS The senior life-cycle stage may be a development of contemporary human society because, like most other mammals, our early ancestors rarely lived beyond their reproductive years (Brooks and Draper 1998). Cross-culturally, the category of the aged is variably recognized, defined, and valued. In many cultures, elders are highly revered and their life experiences are valued as the greatest wisdom. In others, aged people become burdens to their families and to society.

In general, the status and well-being of the elderly is higher when they continue to live with their families (Lee and Kezis 1979). This pattern is more likely to be found in nonindustrial societies than in industrialized ones, where the elderly are increasingly experiencing a shift to "retirement homes." In such age-segregated settings, people have to create new social roles and ties and find new ways of gaining self-esteem and personal satisfaction. Research conducted in a retirement home in a small town in central New York state shows that having a pet promotes a person's sense of well-being (Savishinsky 1991).

THE FINAL PASSAGE: DEATH AND DYING It may be that no one in any culture welcomes death, unless he or she is in very poor health and suffering greatly. The contemporary United States, with its dependence on medical technology, appears to play a leading role in resistance to death, often at high financial and psychological costs. In many other cultures, a greater degree of acceptance prevails.

Virginia Tech students, their relatives, faculty, and others hold a candlelight vigil on the campus in Blacksburg, Virginia, following the murders there in April 2007.

A study of attitudes toward death and dying among Alaskan Inuits revealed a pervasive feeling that people are active participants in their death rather than passive victims (Trelease 1975). The person near death calls friends and neighbors together, is given a Christian sacrament, and then, within a few hours, dies. The author comments, "I do not suggest that everyone waited for the priest to come and then died right away. But the majority who did not die suddenly did some degree of planning, had some kind of formal service or celebration of prayers and hymns and farewells" (1975:35).

Terminally ill people, especially in industrial/informatics societies with a high level of medical technology, are likely to be faced with choices about how and where they should die: at home or in a hospital? Prolong life with "unusual means" or opt for "physician-assisted suicide"? Depending on the cultural context, the options are affected not only by the degree of medical technology and health-care services available but also by matters of kinship and gender role ideals (Long 2005). In urban Japan, terminally ill people have clear ideas of what is a "good death" and multiple "scripts" exist for a "good death." A modern script of dying in a hospital is widely accepted, because it reduces burdens on family members. But a value on dying surrounded by one's family members still prevails; this practice reassures the dying person that he or she will be remembered.

In many cultures, the inability to perform a proper burial and funeral for a deceased person is a cause of serious social suffering. Among refugees from Mozambique living in neighboring Malawi, the greatest cause of stress was being forced to leave behind deceased family members without providing a proper burial for them (Englund 1998). Such improperly treated deaths mean that the unhappy spirit of the deceased will haunt the living. This belief is related to the high rates of mental-health problems among the refugees. A culturally informed recommendation for reducing anxiety among the refugees is to provide them with money to travel home and to perform a proper funeral for their deceased relatives. In that way, the living may carry on in greater peace.

Anthropologists know little about people's grief at the death of a loved one or close community member. It might seem that sadness and grief, and a period of mourning, are only natural. But the outward expression of grief varies from extended, dramatic, public grieving that is overtly emotional to no visible sign of grief at all. The latter pattern is the norm in Bali, Indonesia (see Map 1.2, p. 17), where people's faces remain impassive at funerals and no vocal lamenting occurs (Rosenblatt, Walsh, and Jackson 1976). Do impassive faces and silence mean that the Balinese feel no sadness? Such different modes of expression of loss may be related to the healing process for the survivors by providing socially accepted rules of behavior—in other words, a script for loss. Either highly expressive public mourning or repressed grief may be equally effective, depending on the context.

6

the BIG questions REVISITED

◆ How are modes of reproduction related to modes of livelihood?

Cultural anthropologists define three modes of reproduction that are related to foraging, agriculture, and industrialism/informatics. They differ in terms of desired and actual fertility.

For thousands of years, foragers maintained a balanced level of population through direct and indirect means of fertility regulation. A classic study of the Ju/'hoansi shows how foragers' lifestyles, including a low fat diet and women's physical activity, suppress fertility. As sedentism increased and food surpluses became more available and storable with agriculture, population growth increased. The highest rates of population growth in human prehistory and history are found among settled agriculturalists. Contemporary examples of high-fertility agriculturalists are the Amish and Mennonite people of North America.

◆ How does culture shape fertility in different contexts?

Cross-culturally, many techniques exist for increasing fertility, reducing it, and regulating its timing. From culture to culture, values differ about the right age for people to start having sexual relations and how often. In terms of cultural practices that directly affect fertility, hundreds of different traditional methods exist, including the use of herbs and other natural substances for either preventing or promoting fertilization and for inducing abortion if an undesired pregnancy occurs.

In nonindustrialized societies, the knowledge about and practice of fertility regulation are largely unspecialized and available to all women. In the industrial/informatics mode of reproduction, scientific and medical specialization increases, and most knowledge and expertise are in the hands of professionals rather than of women. Class-stratified access to fertility-regulating methods now exists both globally and within nations.

Population growth is also shaped through the practice of infanticide, which, though of ancient origin, still exists today. It is sometimes performed in response to limited family resources, perceptions of inadequate "fitness" of the child, or preferences about the gender of offspring.

◆ How does culture shape personality over the life cycle?

Cultural anthropologists emphasize the effects of infant care practices on personality formation, including gender identity. Other cross-cultural studies show that children's family and work roles correspond to personality patterns. Adolescence, a culturally defined time beginning around puberty and running until adulthood, varies cross-culturally from being nonexistent to involving detailed training and elaborate ceremonies.

In contrast to the sharp distinction between "male" and "female" in Euro-American culture, many cultures have traditions of third gender identities. Gender pluralism is found in many cultures, especially in some Indian tribal and Asian cultures.

Cross-culturally, adult roles usually involve parenthood. In nonindustrial societies, learning about motherhood is embedded in other aspects of life, and knowledge about birthing and child care is shared among women. In industrialized/informatics cultures, science and medicine play a large part in defining the maternal role.

The senior years are generally shorter in nonindustrialized societies than in industrialized/informatics societies, where life spans tend to be longer. Elder men and women in nonindustrial cultures are treated with respect, are assumed to know the most, and retain a strong sense of their place in the culture. Increasingly in industrialized/informatics societies, elderly people live apart from their families and spend many years in age-segregated institutions or alone.

KEY CONCEPTS

adolescence, p. 152
amazon, p. 156
berdache, p. 155
brideprice or **bridewealth,** p. 147
couvade, p. 157
demographic transition, p. 139
dowry, p. 147
female genital cutting (FGC), p. 153
fertility, p. 138
gender pluralism, p. 156
groomprice, p. 147
hijra, p. 156
infanticide, p. 148
matrescence, p. 156
menarche, p. 142
menopause, p. 142
mode of reproduction, p. 138
patrescence, p. 157
personality, p. 149
pronatalism, p. 138
puberty, p. 151
sex ratio, p. 146

SUGGESTED READINGS

Kamran Asdar Ali. *Planning the Family in Egypt: New Bodies, New Selves.* Austin: University of Texas Press, 2002. The author, a Pakistani doctor and anthropologist, provides a critique of family planning policies and programs in Egypt that pressure women to act in the country's interest by limiting their fertility.

Robbie E. Davis-Floyd. *Birth as an American Rite of Passage,* 2nd ed. Berkeley: University of California Press, 2003. This book provides a cultural critique of the dominant U.S. model of birth as "technocratic" and patriarchal.

Jessica L. Gregg. *Virtually Virgins: Sexual Strategies and Cervical Cancer in Recife, Brazil.* Stanford, CA: Stanford University Press, 2003. Research with women residents of a poor urban area in northeast Brazil and with women cancer victims in a neighborhood maternity clinic shows how the women attempt to deal with racism, sexism, poverty, and violence.

Ellen Gruenbaum. *The Female Circumcision Controversy: An Anthropological Perspective.* Philadelphia: University of Pennsylvania Press, 2001. The author draws on her more than five years of fieldwork in Sudan and discusses how change is occurring through economic development, the role of Islamic activists, health educators, and educated African women.

Marcia C. Inhorn. *Infertility and Patriarchy: The Cultural Politics of Gender and Family Life in Egypt.* Philadelphia: University of Pennsylvania Press, 1996. Based on fieldwork in Alexandria, this book uses narratives from infertile Egyptian women to show how they and their families deal with cultural pressures to bear children.

Shahram Khosravi. *Young and Defiant in Tehran.* Philadelphia: University of Pennsylvania Press, 2008. This ethnographic study documents how youth in the Iranian capital contest official culture and parental domination.

Robert A. LeVine and Rebecca S. New, ed. *Anthropology and Child Development: A Cross-Cultural Reader.* Malden, MA: Blackwell Publishing, 2008. Twenty-four chapters discuss childhood around the world. The collection includes classic essays by Boas, Mead, and Malinowski as well as recent studies. Some chapters present case studies and some are comparative. Topics range from child care in the Kalahari desert to children's play in Italy.

Michael Moffatt. *Coming of Age in New Jersey: College and American Culture.* New Brunswick, NJ: Rutgers University Press, 1991. Based on a year's participant observation in a college dormitory in a university in the eastern United States, this study discusses sexuality, race relations, and individualism.

Leith Mullings and Alaka Wali. *Stress and Resilience: The Social Context of Reproduction in Central Harlem.* New York: Kluwer Academic, 2001. Documenting the daily efforts of African Americans to contend with oppressive conditions, this ethnography focuses on the experiences of women during pregnancy.

Michael G. Peletz. *Gender Pluralism: Southeast Asia since Early Modern Times.* New York: Routledge, 2008. This book provides an understanding of the historical cultural traditions of cross-dressing and the current political climate toward transvestites and homosexuals in Southeast Asia.

Sarah Pinto. *Where There Is No Midwife: Birth and Loss in Rural India.* New York: Bergahn Books, 2008. Pinto examines women's experiences with childbirth and infant death in a poor region in rural northern India with high rates of infant mortality.

Nancy Scheper-Hughes. *Death without Weeping: The Violence of Everyday Life in Brazil.* Berkeley: University of California Press, 1993. This book is a landmark "ethnography of death," based on fieldwork in a shantytown in northeastern Brazil. The author argues that extreme social inequality in Brazil creates a stratified demography.

John W. Traphagan. *Taming Oblivion: Aging Bodies and the Fear of Senility in Japan.* Albany: State University of New York Press, 2000. The author conducted fieldwork in a small town north of Tokyo to investigate people's attitudes and practices related to old age, especially as aging people attempt to prevent the onset of the *boke* condition, or what Westerners call senility.

Andrea S. Wiley. *An Ecology of High-Altitude Infancy: A Biocultural Perspective.* New York: Cambridge University Press, 2004. Ladakh is a district in India's far north, high in the Himalayas. Wiley focuses on the links between biology and culture in birth, infant health and survival, and women's reproductive health.

Steven Benally Jr., an apprentice medicine man, practices for a ceremony in his hogan on the Navajo Reservation near Window Rock, Arizona. An apprentice often studies for a decade or more.

HEALTH, ILLNESS, AND HEALING

the BIG questions

- What is ethnomedicine?
- What are three major theoretical approaches in medical anthropology?
- How are health, illness, and healing changing during globalization?

OUTLINE

Ethnomedicine

Eye on the Environment: Local Botanical Knowledge and Child Health in the Bolivian Amazon

Three Theoretical Approaches in Medical Anthropology

Globalization and Change

Culturama: The Sherpa of Nepal

Lessons Applied: Promoting Vaccination Programs in Developing Countries

Primatologist Jane Goodall once witnessed the consequences of a polio epidemic among the chimpanzees she was studying in Tanzania (Foster and Anderson 1978:33–34). A group of healthy animals watched a stricken member try to reach the feeding area but did not help him. Another badly paralyzed chimpanzee was simply left behind when the group moved on. Humans also sometimes resort to isolation and abandonment of those who are ill and dying. But compared to our nonhuman primate relatives, humans have created more complex ways of interpreting health problems and highly creative methods of preventing and curing them.

Medical anthropology is one of the most rapidly growing areas of research in anthropology. This chapter presents a selection of findings from this subfield. It first describes how people in different cultures think and behave regarding health, illness, and healing. The second section considers three theoretical approaches in medical anthropology. The chapter concludes by discussing how globalization is affecting health.

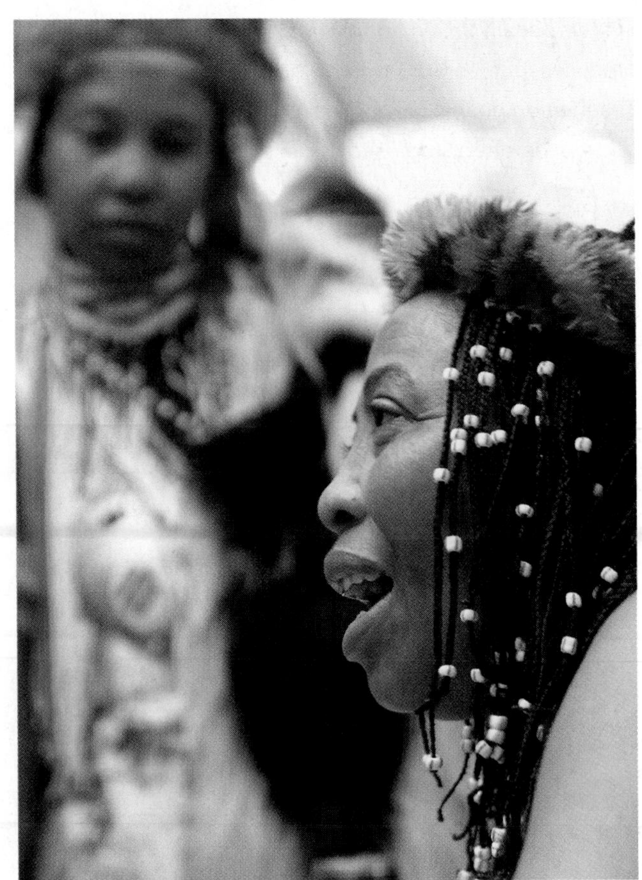

South African healer Magdaline Ramaota speaks to clients in Durban. In South Africa, few people have enough money to pay for AIDS drugs. The role of traditional healers in providing psychological and social support for victims is extremely important.

▶ *Do Internet research to learn about the current and projected rates of HIV/AIDS in African countries.*

◆◆◆

Ethnomedicine

Since the early days of anthropology, the topic of **ethnomedicine**, or the study of cross-cultural health systems, has been a focus of study. A *health system* encompasses many areas: perceptions and classifications of health problems, prevention measures, diagnosis, healing (magical, religious, scientific, healing substances), and healers. Ethnomedicine has expanded its focus to include topics such as perceptions of the body, culture and disability, and change in indigenous or "traditional" healing systems, especially as resulting from globalization.

In the 1960s, when the term ethnomedicine first came into use, it referred only to non-Western health systems and was synonymous with the now abandoned term, *primitive medicine*. The early use of the term was ethnocentric. Contemporary **Western biomedicine (WBM)**, a healing approach based on modern Western science that emphasizes technology in diagnosing and treating health problems related to the human body, is an ethnomedical system, too. Medical anthropologists now study WBM as a cultural system intimately bound to Western values. Thus, the current meaning of the term ethnomedicine encompasses health systems everywhere.

ethnomedicine the study of cross-cultural health systems.

Western biomedicine (WBM) a healing approach based on modern Western science that emphasizes technology for diagnosing and treating health problems related to the human body.

disease in the disease/illness dichotomy, a biological health problem that is objective and universal.

illness in the disease/illness dichotomy, culturally shaped perceptions and experiences of a health problem.

PERCEPTIONS OF THE BODY

In Japan, the concept of *gotai* refers to the ideal of maintaining bodily intactness in life and death, to the extent of not piercing one's ears (Ohnuki-Tierney 1994:235). When Crown Prince Naruhitao was considering whom to marry, one criterion for the bride was that she not have pierced ears. Underlying the value on intactness is the belief that an intact body ensures rebirth. Historically, a warrior's practice of beheading a victim was the ultimate form of killing because it violated the integrity of the body and prevented the enemy's rebirth. Gotai is an important reason for the low rates of surgery in Japan—compared to the United States—and the widespread popular resistance to organ transplantation.

Ideals about the female body are implicated in the high rate of caesarian births in Brazil (McCallum 2005).

MAP 7.1 Federative Republic of Brazil. Brazil, a federation of 26 states, is the largest and most populous country in Latin America and the fifth largest worldwide. Its total population is about 188 million, and São Paulo, its largest city has a population of 11 million. The economy is based on manufacturing, mining, agriculture, and technology. Ethnically, it comprises Europeans, Africans, Indians, and Asians. The official language is Portuguese. Roman Catholicism is the predominant religion, and Brazil has the largest Roman Catholic population in the world. Brazil has the world's most extreme economic and social inequality with many people, especially in the south and east, living in wealth and comfort while others in the urban *favelas* (slums) and in the rural northeast experience extreme poverty, deprivation, and violence.

Ethnographic research in Salvador, a major city of the state of Bahia (bah-EE-yuh) in northeastern Brazil (see Map 7.1), reveals that vaginal childbirth is considered more "primitive," painful, and destructive of a woman's sexuality than caesarian delivery. One doctor said that "more and more, the vulva and the vagina are becoming the organs of sexuality and not parturition" (2005:226). Doctors recommend a caesarian delivery as safe, practical, and causing no "esthetic damage."

Euro-American popular and scientific thinking emphasizes a separation of the mind from the body. Thus, Western medicine has a special category called "mental illness," which treats certain health problems as though they were located only in the mind. In contrast, in the many cultures in which a mind–body distinction does not exist, there is no category of "mental illness" and treatment is more holistic.

Cultures also vary in terms of whether people consider the body to be a bounded physical unit, with healing focused on the body alone, or connected to a wider social context, in which case healing addresses the body within the wider social sphere. Variations in the definition of a living body versus a dead body are also prominent worldwide. Different organs may be seen as critical. In the United States, a person may be declared dead while the heart is still beating, so long as the brain is judged to be "dead." In many other cultures, people do not accept a brain-based definition of life and death (Ohnuki-Tierney 1994).

DEFINING AND CLASSIFYING HEALTH PROBLEMS

Emic diversity in labeling health problems presents a challenge for medical anthropologists and health-care specialists. Western labels, which biomedically trained experts accept as true, accurate, and universal, often do not correspond to the labels in other cultures. One set of concepts that medical anthropologists use to sort out the many cross-cultural labels and perceptions is the *disease/illness dichotomy*. In this model, **disease** refers to a biological health problem that is objective and universal, such as a bacterial or viral infection or a broken arm. **Illness** refers to culturally specific perceptions and experiences of a health problem. Medical anthropologists study both disease and illness, and they show how both must be understood within their cultural contexts.

A first step in ethnomedical research is to learn how people label, categorize, and classify health problems. Depending on the culture, the following may be bases for labeling and classifying health problems: cause, *vector* (the means of transmission, such as mosquitoes), affected body part, symptoms, or combinations of these.

Often, knowledgeable elders are the keepers of ethnomedical knowledge, and they pass it down through oral traditions. Among Native Americans of the Washington–Oregon region, many popular stories refer to health (Thompson and Sloat 2004). The stories convey messages about how to prevent health problems, avoid bodily harm, relieve afflictions, and deal

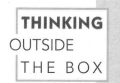

THINKING OUTSIDE THE BOX

In your microculture, what are some prevailing perceptions about the body and how are they related to medical treatment?

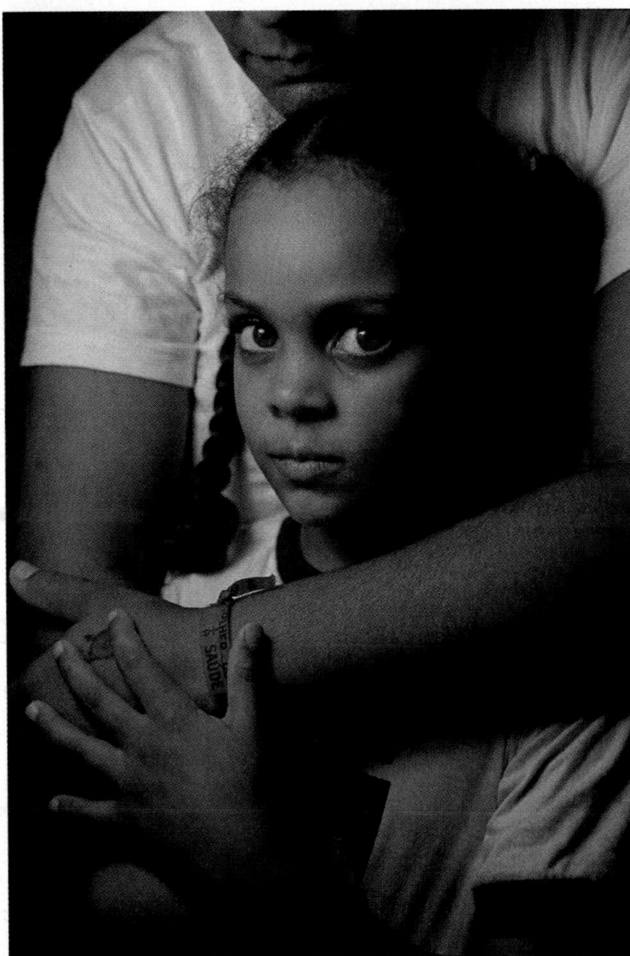

The Brazilian girl, aged 9 years, is HIV positive. Her mother, in the background, contracted HIV from her husband and transmitted it to her child at birth.

with old age. For example, here is the story of Boil, a story for young children:

> Boil was getting bigger.
>
> Her husband told her to bathe.
>
> She got into the water.
>
> She disappeared. (2004:5)

Other, longer stories about Boil add complexities about the location of the boil and how to deal with particular boils, revealing indigenous patterns of classification.

A classic study among the Subanun (soo-BAH-nan) people focused on their categories of health problems (Frake 1961). The Subanun, in the 1950s, were horticulturalists living in the highlands of Mindanao, in the Philippines (see Map 7.2). An egalitarian people, all Subanun, even young children, had substantial knowledge about health problems. Of their 186 labels for health problems, some are a single term, such as "itch," which can be expanded on by using two words such as "splotchy itch." Skin diseases are common afflictions among the Subanun and have several degrees of specificity (see Figure 7.1).

In Western biomedicine, panels of medical experts have to agree about how to label and classify health problems according to scientific criteria. Classifications and descriptions of thousands of afflictions are published in thick manuals that physicians consult before they give a diagnosis. In countries where medical care is privatized, the code selected may determine whether the patient's costs are covered by insurance or not. The International Classification of Diseases

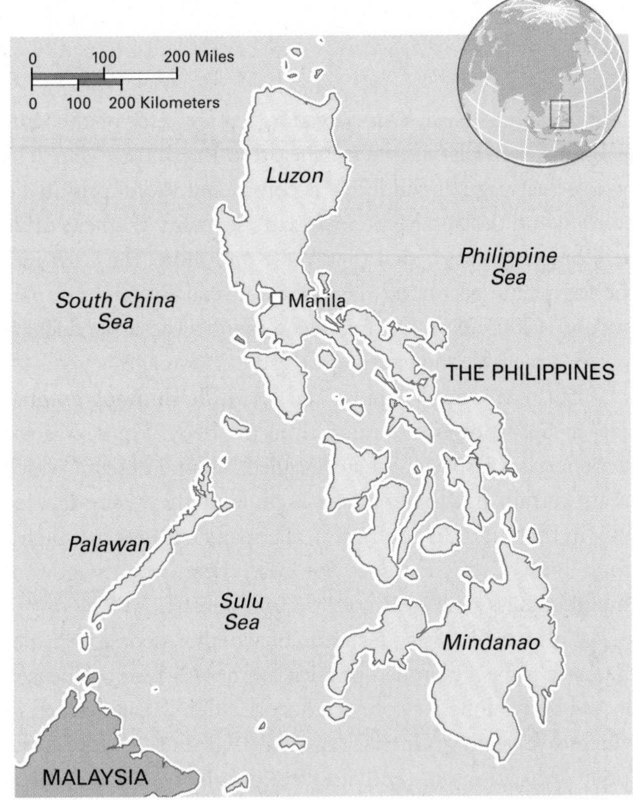

MAP 7.2 The Philippines.
The Republic of the Philippines comprises over 7000 islands, of which around 700 are occupied. The population is 85 million, with two-thirds living on Luzon. The economy is based on agriculture, light industry, and a growing business processing outsourcing (BPO) industry. Over 8 million Filipinos work overseas and remit more than $12 billion a year, a large part of the GDP. Although Filipino and English are the official languages, more than 170 languages are spoken. The Philippines has the world's third largest Christian population, with Roman Catholicism predominant.

---

culture-specific syndrome a collection of signs and symptoms that is restricted to a particular culture or a limited number of cultures.

somatization the process through which the body absorbs social stress and manifests symptoms of suffering; also called embodiment.

- Rash
- Eruption
- Inflammation
  - Eruption
  - Inflamed/Quasi-Bite
  - Ulcerated
- Sore
  - Distal Ulcer
    - Shallow
    - Deep
  - Proximal Ulcer
    - Shallow
    - Deep
  - Simple Sore
  - Spreading Sore
- Ringworm
  - Exposed
  - Hidden
  - Spreading Itch
- Wound

Source: Adapted from Frake 1961:118, Figure 1.

FIGURE 7.1 **Subanun Categories of *Nuka*, Skin-Related Health Problems**

(ICD), now in its tenth edition (1993), is a major source for coding health problems according to Western biomedical standards. Even though it contains abundant details on many health problems and is carefully arranged according to a complex coding system, its categories often prove to be inadequate. For example, following the attacks on the United States of September 11, 2001, medical personnel who had to classify the cause of death of those who perished at the four sites and the health problems of survivors found the ICD-10 codes of little help.

Further, the ICD-10 is biased toward diseases that Western biomedicine recognizes and ignores health problems of many other cultures. Anthropologists have discovered many health problems around the world, often referred to as culture-specific syndromes. A **culture-specific syndrome** is a health problem with a set of symptoms associated with a particular culture (see Figure 7.2). Social factors such as stress, fear, or shock often are the underlying causes of culture-specific syndromes. Biophysical symptoms may be involved, and culture-specific syndromes can be fatal. **Somatization**, or embodiment, refers to the process through which the body absorbs social stress and manifests symptoms of suffering.

Name of Syndrome	Distribution	Attributed Causes	Description and Symptoms
Anorexia nervosa	Middle- and upper-class Euro-American girls; globalizing	Unknown	Body wasting due to food avoidance; feeling of being too fat; in extreme cases, death
Hikikomori	Japan, males from adolescence through adulthood	Social pressure to succeed in school and pursue a position as a salaryman	Acute social withdrawal; refusal to attend school, or leave their room for months, sometimes years
Koro	China and Southeast Asia, men	Unknown	Belief that the penis has retracted into the body
Peito aberto (open chest)	Northeastern Brazil, especially women, perhaps elsewhere among Latino populations	Excessive worry about others	Enlarges the heart and "bursts" through it causing "openings in the heart"
Retired Husband Syndrome (RHS)	Japan, older women whose husbands are retired	Stress	Ulcers, slurred speech, rashes around the eyes, throat polyps
Soufriendo del agua (suffering from water)	Valley of Mexico, low-income people, especially women	Lack of access to secure and clean water	Anxiety
Susto	Spain, Portugal, Central and South America, Latino immigrants in the U.S. and Canada	Shock or fright	Lethargy, poor appetite, problems sleeping, anxiety

Sources: Chowdhury 1996; Ennis-McMillan 2001; Faiola 2005; Gremillion 1992; Kawanishi 2004; Rehbun 1994; Rubel, O'Nell, and Collado-Ardón 1984.

FIGURE 7.2 **Selected Culture-Specific Syndromes**

For example, **susto**, or "fright/shock disease," is found in Spain and Portugal and among Latino people wherever they live. People afflicted with susto attribute it to events such as losing a loved one or having a terrible accident (Rubel, O'Nell, and Collado-Ardón 1984). In Oaxaca, southern Mexico (see Map 6.3, p. 144), a woman said her susto was brought on by an accident in which pottery she had made was broken on its way to market, whereas a man said that his came on after he saw a dangerous snake. Susto symptoms include appetite loss, lack of motivation, breathing problems, generalized pain, and nightmares. The researchers analyzed many cases of susto in three villages. They found that the people most likely to be afflicted were those who were socially marginal or experiencing a sense of role failure. For example, the woman with the broken pots had also suffered two spontaneous abortions and was worried that she would never have children. In Oaxaca, people with susto have higher mortality rates than other people. Thus, social marginality, or a deep sense of social failure, can place a person at a higher risk of dying. It is important to look at the deeper causes of susto.

Medical anthropologists first studied culture-specific syndromes in non-Western cultures. This focus created a bias in thinking that they exist only in "other" cultures. Now, anthropologists recognize that Western cultures also have culture-specific syndromes. Anorexia nervosa and a related condition, bulimia, are culture-bound syndromes found mainly among White middle-class adolescent girls of the United States, although some cases have been documented among African American girls in the United States and among young males (Fabrega and Miller 1995). Since the 1990s, perhaps as a result of Western globalization, cases have been documented in cities in Japan, Hong Kong, and India. Anorexia nervosa's cluster of symptoms includes self-perception of fatness, aversion to food, hyperactivity, and, as the condition progresses, continued wasting of the body and often death. No one has found a clear biological cause for anorexia nervosa, although some researchers claim that it has a genetic basis. Cultural anthropologists say that much evidence suggests a strong role of cultural construction. One logical result of the role of culture is that medical and psychiatric treatments are notably unsuccessful in curing anorexia nervosa (Gremillion 1992). Extreme food deprivation can become addictive and entrapping, and the affliction becomes embodied, intertwined with the body's biological functions. Extended fasting makes the body unable to deal with ingested food. Thus, medical treatment may involve intravenous feeding to override the biological block. Sometimes nothing works, and the affliction is fatal.

Pinpointing the cultural causes of anorexia nervosa, however, is difficult. Some experts cite societal pressures on girls that lead to excessive concern with looks, especially body weight. Others feel that anorexia is related to girls' unconscious resistance to overcontrolling parents. For such girls, food intake may be one thing over which they have power.

ETHNO-ETIOLOGIES

People in all cultures, everywhere, attempt to make sense of health problems and try to understand their cause, or etiology. Following anthropological practice, the term **ethno-etiologies** refers to cross-cultural variations in causal explanations for health problems and suffering.

Among the urban poor of northeastern Brazil, people consider several causal possibilities when they are sick (Ngokwey 1988). In Feira de Santana, the second largest city in the state of Bahia (see Map 7.1, p. 165), ethno-etiologies can be natural, socioeconomic, psychological, or supernatural. Natural causes include exposure to the environment—for example, humidity and rain cause rheumatism, excessive heat causes dehydration, and some types of winds are said to cause migraines. Yet other natural explanations for illness take into account the effects of aging, heredity, personality, and gender. Contagion is another natural explanation, as are the effects of certain foods and eating habits. In the psychosocial domain, emotions such as anger and hostility cause certain health problems. In the supernatural domain, spirits and magic can cause health problems. The African-Brazilian religious systems of the Bahia region encompass many spirits who can inflict illness. They include spirits of the unhappy dead and devil-like spirits. Some spirits cause specific illnesses; others bring general misfortune. In addition, envious people with the evil eye cast spells on people and cause much illness. People also recognize the lack of economic resources, proper sanitation, and health services as structural causes of health problems. In the words of one person, "There are many illnesses because there are many poor" (1988:796).

The people of Feira de Santana also recognize several levels of causality. In the case of stomachache, they might blame a quarrel (*underlying cause*), which prompted the aggrieved party to seek the intervention of a sorcerer (*intermediate cause*), who cast a spell (*immediate cause*), which led to the resulting illness. The multilayered causal understanding opens the way for many possible avenues of treatment.

The multiple understandings of etiology in Bahia contrast with the scientific understandings of causality in Western biomedicine. The most striking difference is the

---

susto fright/shock disease, a culture-specific syndrome found in Spain and Portugal and among Latino people wherever they live; symptoms include back pain, fatigue, weakness, and lack of appetite.

ethno-etiologies culturally specific causal explanations for health problems and suffering.

structural suffering human health problems caused by such economic and political situations as war, famine, terrorism, forced migration, and poverty.

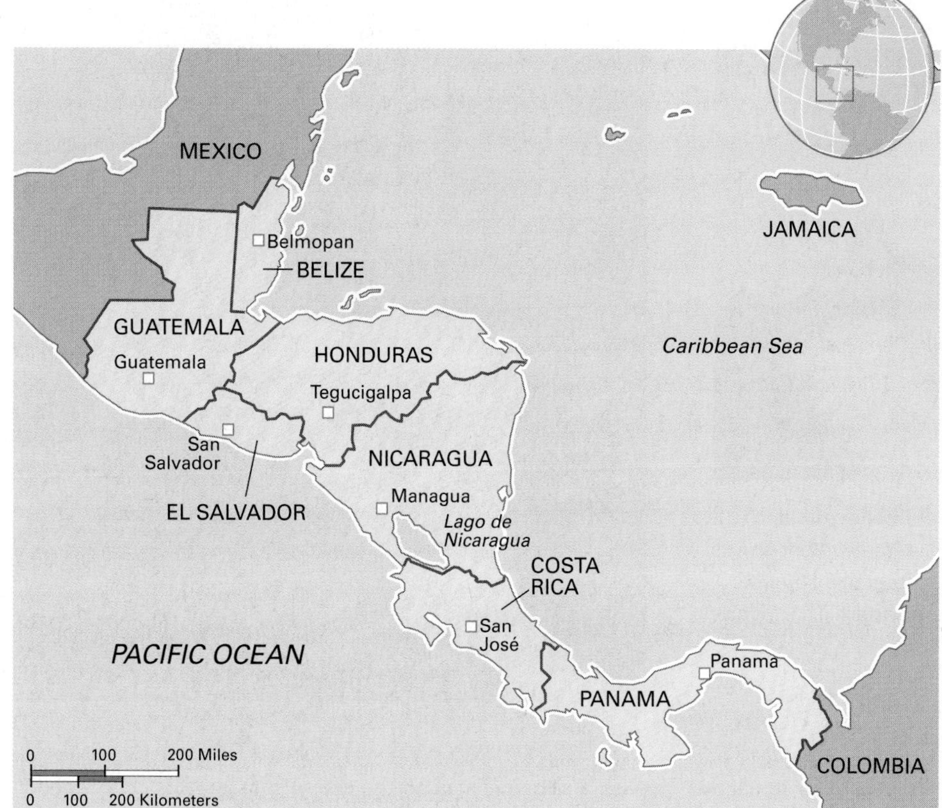

MAP 7.3 Central America. The countries of Central America share a similar geography as part of a long isthmus with a mountainous spine, active volcanoes, and rich soil. A federation that linked much of the region into the United Provinces of Central America existed from 1824 to 1838. The population of the region, around 40 million, includes indigenous peoples and people of mixed indigenous and European ancestry. European colonialism has left a strong mark on the region, which is now heavily influenced by the United States and its interests in hemispheric hegemony. Bananas are the leading export crop of the region.

tendency for biomedical etiologies to exclude as causal structural issues and social inequality. Medical anthropologists use the term **structural suffering**, or social suffering, which refers to health problems that powerful forces such as poverty, war, famine, and forced migration cause (review the definition of the related concept, structurism, in Chapter 1). Structural conditions affect health in many ways, with effects ranging from anxiety and depression to death.

An example of a culture-specific syndrome that clearly implicates structural factors as causal is *sufriendo del agua,* or "suffering from water" (Ennis-McMillan 2001). Research in a poor community in the Valley of Mexico, located in the central part of the country (see Map 6.3, p. 144), reveals that sufriendo del agua is a common health problem, especially among women. The immediate cause is the lack of water for drinking, cooking, and washing. Women, who are responsible for cooking and doing the washing, cannot count on water coming from their taps on a regular basis. This insecurity makes the women feel anxious and constantly in a state of nervous tension. The lack of access to water also means that the people are at higher risk of cholera, skin and eye infections, and other biophysical problems. A deeper structural cause of sufriendo del agua is unequal development. The construction of piped water systems in the Valley of Mexico bypassed low-income communities in favor of servicing wealthier urban neighborhoods and supplying water for irrigation projects and the industrial sector. In Mexico, as a whole, nearly one-third of the population has inadequate access to water, in terms of quantity or quality.

PREVENTION

Many practices, based in either religious or secular beliefs, exist cross-culturally for preventing misfortune, suffering, and illness. Among the Maya of Guatemala (see Map 7.3), *awas* is a common childhood illness (Wilson 1995). Children born with awas have lumps under the skin, marks on the skin, or albinism. People say that events that happen to the mother during her pregnancy cause awas: She may have been denied food she desired or have been pressured to eat food she did not want, or she may have encountered a rude, drunk, or angry person (usually a man). Therefore, to prevent awas in babies, the Maya are extremely considerate of pregnant women. A pregnant woman, like land before planting, is sacred. People make sure to give her the food she wants, and they behave with respect in her presence. The ideal is that a pregnant woman should be content.

Examples of ritual health protection worldwide include charms, spells, and sacred strings tied around parts of the body. An anthropologist working in rural northern Thailand (see Map 6.7, p. 157) learned about a health protection practice that involved the display of carved wooden phalluses

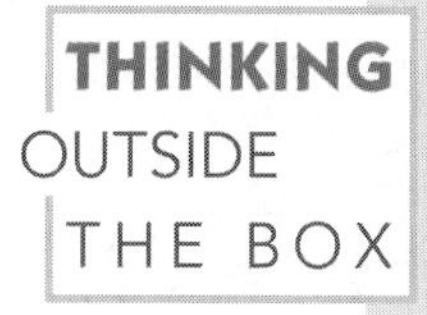

Discuss some examples of culture-specific syndromes in your microculture, or on your campus.

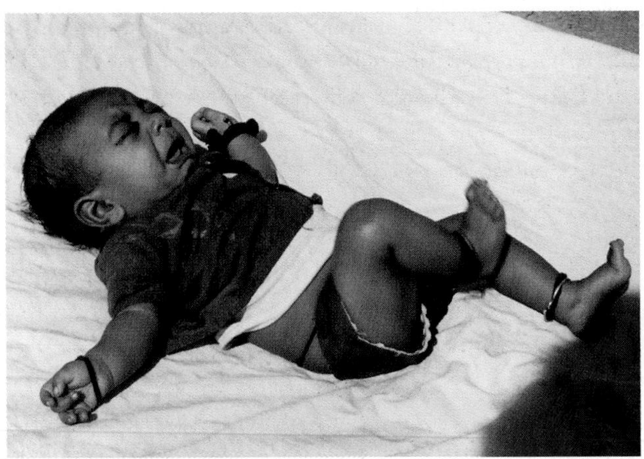

(LEFT) Throughout northern India, people believe that tying on strings provides protection from malevolent spirits and forces. This Muslim baby has five protective strings. (RIGHT) A carved phallus displayed in a northern Thai village to protect men from widow ghost attacks.

throughout a village (Mills 1995). In 1990, fear of an attack by a widow ghost spread throughout the area. It was based on several radio reports of unexplained deaths of Thai migrant men working in Singapore. People interpreted the sudden deaths of men as caused by widow ghosts. People believe that widow ghosts roam about, searching for men whom they take as their "husbands" and with whom they have sexual intercourse. Mary Beth Mills was conducting research in Baan Naa Sakae village at the time of the fear. After being away for a few days, she returned to the village to find all 200 households decorated with wooden phalluses in all shapes and sizes:

> Ranging from the crudest wooden shafts to carefully carved images complete with coconut shell testicles and fishnet pubic hair, they adorned virtually every house and residential compound. The phalluses, I was told, were to protect residents, especially boys and men, from the "nightmare deaths" (*lai tai*) at the hands of malevolent "widow ghosts" (*phii mae maai*). (1995:249)

In the study area, spirits (*phii*) are a recognized source of illness, death, and other misfortunes. One variety of phii, a widow ghost is the sexually voracious spirit of a woman who had an untimely and perhaps violent death. When a seemingly healthy man dies in his sleep, the people blame a widow ghost who arrives in the night and has extreme sex with a sleeping man to the extent that he dies. The wooden phalluses were protection against a possible widow ghost attack. The people said the giant penises are decoys: The sex-starved spirits take their pleasure with the wooden penises and, satisfied, leave the men unharmed. As the radio reports ceased, villagers' concerns about the widow ghosts faded and they removed the phalluses.

HEALING WAYS

The following material describes two approaches to healing, one in southern Africa and the other in Malaysia, Southeast Asia. It also discusses healers and healing substances.

COMMUNITY HEALING SYSTEMS A general distinction can be drawn between private healing and **community healing.** The former addresses bodily ailments in social isolation, whereas the latter encompasses the social context as crucial to healing. Compared to Western biomedicine, many non-Western systems use community healing. An example of community healing comes from the Ju/'hoansi foragers of the Kalahari desert in southern Africa (review Culturama, Chapter 1, p. 23). Ju/'hoansi healing emphasizes the mobilization of community "energy" as a key element in the cure:

> The central event in this tradition is the all-night healing dance. Four times a month on the average, night signals the start of a healing dance. The women sit around the fire, singing and rhythmically clapping. The men, sometimes joined by the women, dance around the singers. As the dance intensifies, *num,* or spiritual energy, is activated by the healers, both men and women, but mostly among the dancing men. As num is activated in them, they begin to *kia,* or

community healing healing that emphasizes the social context as a key component and which is carried out within the public domain.

humoral healing healing that emphasizes balance among natural elements within the body.

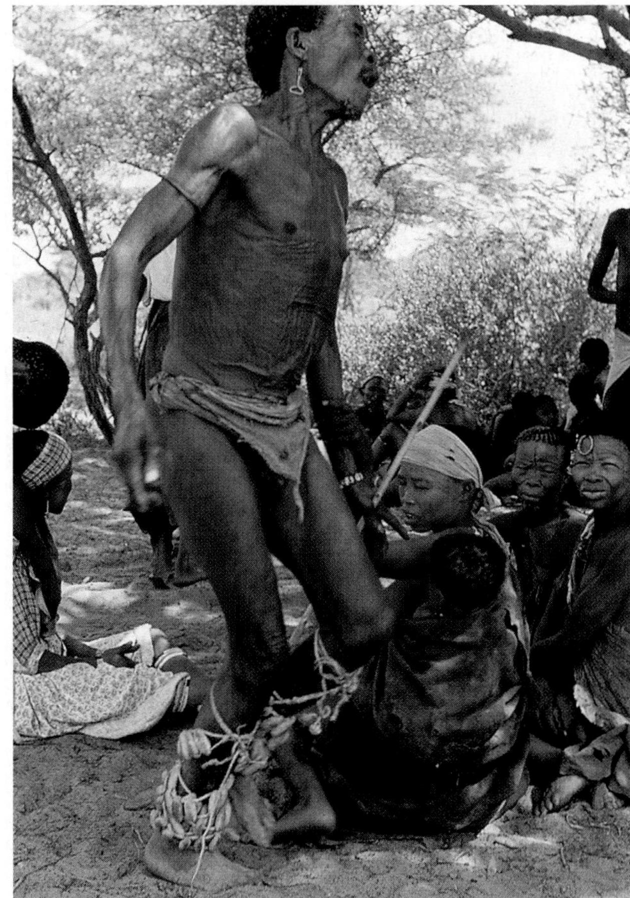

A Ju/'hoansi healer in a trance, in the Kalahari desert, southern Africa. Most Ju/'hoansi healers are men, but some are women.

▶ *In your microculture, what are the patterns of gender, ethnicity, and class among various kinds of healers?*

> experience an enhancement of their consciousness. While experiencing kia, they heal all those at the dance. (Katz 1982:34)

The dance is a community event in which the entire camp participates. The people's belief in the healing power of num brings meaning and efficacy to the dance through kia.

Does community healing "work"? In both ethnic and Western terms, the answer is yes. It "works" on several levels. People's solidarity and group sessions may support mental and physical health, acting as a health protection system. When people fall ill, the drama and energy of the all-night dances may act to strengthen the afflicted in ways that Western science would have difficulty measuring. In a small, close-knit group, the dances support members who may be ill or grieving.

An important aspect of the Ju/'hoansi healing system is its openness. Everyone has access to it. The role of healer is also open. There is no special class of healers with special privileges. More than half of all adult men and about 10 percent of adult women are healers.

HUMORAL HEALING **Humoral healing** is based on a philosophy of balance among certain elements within the body and within the person's environment (McElroy and Townsend 1996). In this system, food and drugs have different effects on the body and are classified as either "heating" or "cooling" (the quotation marks indicate that these properties are not the same as thermal measurements). Diseases are the result of bodily imbalances—too much heat or coolness—that must be counteracted through dietary and behavioral changes or medicines that will restore balance.

Humoral healing systems have been practiced for thousands of years in the Middle East, the Mediterranean, and much of Asia. In the New World, indigenous humoral systems exist and sometimes blend with those that Spanish colonialists brought with them. Humoralism has shown substantial resilience in the face of Western biomedicine, often incorporating into it the Western framework—for example, in the classification of biomedical treatments as either heating or cooling.

In Malaysia (see Map 1.1, p. 10), several different humoral traditions coexist, reflecting the region's history of contact with outside cultures. Malaysia has been influenced by trade and contact between its indigenous culture and that of India, China, and the Arab-Islamic world for around 2000 years. Indian, Chinese, and Arabic health systems all define health as the balance of opposing elements within the body, although each has its own variations (Laderman 1988:272). Indigenous belief systems may have been compatible with these imported models because they also were based on concepts of heat and coolness.

Insights about these indigenous systems before outsiders arrived come from accounts about the Orang Asli, indigenous peoples of the interior who are relatively less affected by contact. A conceptual system of hot–cold opposition dominates Orang Asli cosmological, medical, and social theories. The properties and meanings of heat and coolness differ from those of Islamic, Indian, or Chinese humoralism in several ways. In the Islamic, Indian, and Chinese systems, for example, death is the result of too much coolness. Among the Orang Asli, excessive heat is the primary cause of mortality. In their view, heat emanates from the sun and is associated with excrement, blood, misfortune, disease, and death. Humanity's hot blood makes people mortal, and their consumption of meat speeds the process. Heat causes menstruation, violent emotions, aggression, and drunkenness.

Coolness, in contrast, is vital for health. Health is protected by staying in the forest to avoid the harmful effects of the sun. This belief justifies the rejection of agriculture by some groups because it exposes people to the sun. Treatment of illness is designed to reduce or remove heat. If someone were to fall ill in a clearing, the entire group would relocate to the coolness of the forest. The forest is also a source of cooling leaves and herbs. Healers are cool and retain their coolness by bathing in cold water and sleeping far from the fire.

Umbanda is a popular religion in Brazil and increasingly worldwide. Its ceremonies are often devoted to healing through spiritual means. In this session, tourists at the back of the room watch as Umbanda followers perform a dance related to a particular deity.

▶ *What is your opinion on the role of spirituality in health and healing, and on what do you base your view?*

Extreme cold, however, can be harmful. Dangerous levels of coolness are associated with the time right after birth, because the mother is believed to have lost substantial heat. The new mother should not drink cold water or bathe in cold water. She increases her body heat by tying around her waist sashes that contain warmed leaves or ashes, and she lies near a fire.

HEALERS In an informal sense, everyone is a "healer" because self-treatment is always the first consideration in dealing with a perceived health problem. Yet, in all cultures, some people become recognized as having special abilities to diagnose and treat health problems. Cross-cultural evidence indicates some common criteria of healers (see Figure 7.3).

Specialists include midwives, bonesetters (people who reset broken bones), **shamans** or **shamankas** (male or female healers who mediate between humans and the spirit world), herbalists, general practitioners, psychiatrists, nurses, acupuncturists, chiropractors, dentists, and hospice care providers. Some healing roles may have higher status, more power, and receive higher pay than others.

Midwifery is an important example of a healing role that is endangered in many parts of the world as birth has become increasingly medicalized and brought into the institutional world of the hospital rather than the home. In Costa Rica (see Map 7.3, p. 169), a recent government campaign to promote hospital births with a biomedical doctor in attendance has achieved a rate of 98 percent of all births taking place in hospitals (Jenkins 2003). This achievement means that midwives, especially in rural areas, can no longer support themselves, and they are abandoning their profession. Promotion of hospital births has destroyed the positive elements of community-based midwifery and its provision of social support and techniques such as massage for the mother-to-be.

- *Selection:* Certain individuals may show more ability for entry into healing roles. In Western medical schools, selection for entry rests on apparently objective standards, such as pre-entry exams and college grades. Among the indigenous Ainu of northern Japan, healers were men who had a special ability to go into a sort of seizure called *imu* (Ohnuki-Tierney 1980).
- *Training:* The period of training may involve years of observation and practice and may be arduous and even dangerous. In some non-Western traditions, a shaman must make dangerous journeys, through trance or use of drugs, to the spirit world. In Western biomedicine, medical school involves immense amounts of memorization, separation from family and normal social life, and sleep deprivation.
- *Certification:* Healers earn some form of ritual or legal certification, such as a shaman going through a formal initiation ritual that attests to his or her competence.
- *Professional image:* The healer role is demarcated from that of ordinary people through behavior, dress, and other markers, such as the white coat in the West and the Siberian shaman's tambourine for calling the spirits.
- *Expectation of payment:* Compensation in some form, whether in kind or in cash, is expected for formal healers. Payment level may vary, depending on the status of the healer and other factors. In northern India, strong preference for sons is reflected in payments to the midwife that are twice as high for the birth of a son as for a daughter. In the United States, medical professionals in different specializations receive markedly different salaries.

FIGURE 7.3 Criteria for Becoming a Healer

HEALING SUBSTANCES Around the world, thousands of different natural or manufactured substances are used as medicines for preventing or curing health problems. Anthropologists have spent more time studying the use of medicines in non-Western cultures than in the West, although a more fully cross-cultural approach is emerging

shaman/shamanka a male or female healer.

phytotherapy healing through the use of plants.

eye on the ENVIRONMENT

Local Botanical Knowledge and Child Health in the Bolivian Amazon

The Tsimané are a foraging-horticultural society of Bolivia's northeastern Amazon region, numbering about 8000 people (McDade et al. 2007). Although most people make a living from horticulture, complemented by some gathering and hunting, new opportunities for wage work are increasingly available in logging camps or on cattle ranches, or by selling products from the rainforest. At the time of the study described here, in 2002–2003, the Tsimané were not much affected by outside forces and still relied heavily on local resources for their livelihood.

The study focused on mothers' botanical knowledge and the health of their children. The word *botany* refers to knowledge about plants. Household visits and interviews with mothers provided data on mothers' knowledge of plants. Children's health was assessed with three measures: concentrations of C-reactive protein (or CRP, a measure of both immunity and "infectious burden"); skinfold thickness (which measures body fat); and stature, or height (which indicates overall progress in growth and development).

The results showed a strong relationship between mothers' knowledge of plants and the health of their children. Botanical knowledge promotes healthier children through nutritional inputs, that is, knowledgeable mothers tend to provide healthier plant foods to their children. It also improves children's health by providing herbal ways of treating their illnesses. The overall conclusion is that a mother's knowledge of local plant resources contributes directly to the benefit of her children. In contrast, levels of formal schooling of mothers and household wealth had little, if anything, to do with child health.

Given the positive effects of mothers' botanical knowledge and use of local plants to promote their children's health, it is critical that access to plant resources by indigenous people be protected and sustained and that local botanical knowledge be respected and preserved.

◆ **FOOD FOR THOUGHT**

- What do you know about the effects on your health of particular plants that you eat? When you eat herbs such as oregano or parsley, for example, do you think about their health effects?

MAP 7.4 The Republic of Bolivia.
Situated in the Andes Mountains, Bolivia is the poorest country in South America, although it is rich in natural resources, including the second largest oil field in South America after Venezuela. The population of 10 million includes a majority of indigenous people of nearly 40 different groups. The largest are the Aymara (2 million) and the Quechua-speaking groups (1.5 million). Thirty percent of the population is mestizo and 15 percent are of European descent. Two-thirds of the people are low-income farmers. The official religion is Roman Catholicism, but Protestantism is growing. Religious syncretism is prominent. Most people speak Spanish as their first language, although Aymara and Quechua are also common. Bolivia's popular fiesta known as *El carnival de Oruro* is on UNESCO's list of Intangible Cultural Heritage.

that also examines the use and meaning of Western pharmaceuticals (Petryna, Lakoff, and Kleinman 2007).

Phytotherapy is healing through the use of plants. Cross-culturally, people know about and use many different plants for a wide range of health problems, including gastrointestinal disorders, skin problems, wounds and sores, pain

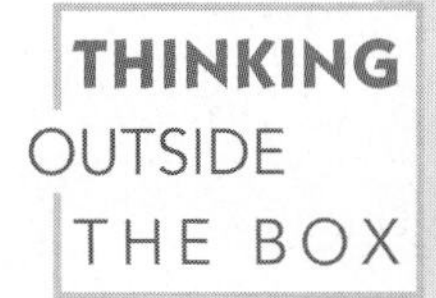

What steps do you take to treat yourself when you have a cold or headache? If you take medicine, do you know what materials are in the medicine?

relief, infertility, fatigue, altitude sickness, and more (see Eye on the Environment). Increasing awareness of the range of potentially useful plants worldwide provides a strong incentive for protecting the world's cultural diversity, because it is people who know about botanical resources (Posey 1990).

Leaves of the coca plant have for centuries been a key part of the health system of the Andean region of South America (Allen 2002). Coca is important in rituals, in masking hunger pains, and in combating the cold. In terms of health, Andean people use coca to treat gastrointestinal problems, sprains, swellings, and colds (Carter, Morales, and Mamani 1981). About 85 percent of 3500 people surveyed in Bolivia reported that they use coca medicinally. The leaf may be chewed or combined with herbs or roots and water to make a *maté,* a medicinal beverage. Trained herbalists have specialized knowledge about preparing matés. One maté, for example, is for treating asthma. Made of a certain root and coca leaves, the patient takes it three or four times a day until cured.

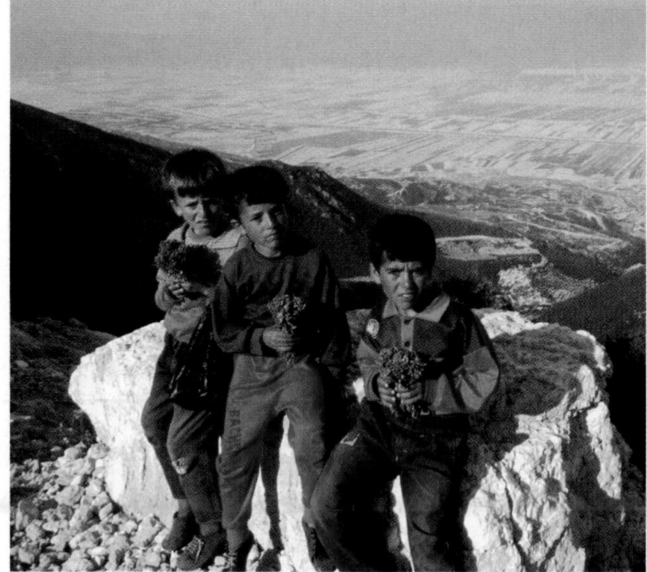

These boys are selling hyssop, a medicinal herb, in Syria. In Unani (Islamic) traditional medicine, hyssop is used to alleviate problems such as asthma.

▶ *Do research to learn more about hyssop and its medicinal uses.*

Minerals are also widely used for prevention and healing. For example, many people worldwide believe that bathing in water that contains high levels of sulfur or other minerals promotes health and cures ailments such as arthritis and rheumatism. Thousands of people every year go to the Dead Sea, which lies beneath sea level between Israel and Jordan, for treating skin diseases. The mud from the shore and the nearby sulfur springs relieves skin ailments such as psoriasis. In Japan, bathing in mineral waters is popular as a health-promotion practice.

In a more unusual practice, thousands of people in the United States and Canada visit "radon spas" every year, seeking the therapeutic effects of low doses of radon gas to alleviate the symptoms of chronic afflictions such as arthritis (Erickson 2007). In the United States, many radon spas are located in mines in the mountains of Montana. At one such spa, the Free Enterprise Mine, the recommended treatment is to go into the mine for 1-hour sessions, two or three times daily, for up to a total of about 30 sessions. The mine contains benches and chairs, and clients read, play cards, chat, or take a

Guests are undergoing radon treatment at the Kyongsong Sand Spa in Haonpho-ri, North Korea. The spa, and its hot spring, has a 500-year history as a healing center. The treatment shown here is a "sand bath" used for chronic diseases such as arthritis, postoperative problems, and some female problems.

nap. Some "regulars" come back every year and plan to meet up with friends from previous visits.

Pharmaceutical medicines are increasingly popular worldwide. Although these medicines have many benefits, some negative effects include frequent use without prescription and overprescription. Sale of patent medicines is often unregulated, and self-treating individuals can buy them in a local pharmacy. The popularity and overuse of capsules and injections has led to a growing health crisis related to the emergence of drug-resistant disease strains.

Three Theoretical Approaches in Medical Anthropology

The first major theoretical approach to understanding health systems emphasizes the importance of the environment in shaping health problems and how they spread. The second highlights symbols and meaning in people's expression of suffering and healing practices. The third points to the need to look at structural factors (political, economic, media) as the underlying causes of health problems and examines Western biomedicine as a cultural institution.

THE ECOLOGICAL/EPIDEMIOLOGICAL APPROACH

The **ecological/epidemiological approach** examines how aspects of the natural environment interact with culture to cause health problems and to influence their spread throughout the population. According to this approach, research should focus on gathering information about the environmental context and social patterns that affect health, such as food distribution within the family, sexual practices, hygiene, and population contact. Research methods and data tend to be quantitative and etic, although a growing tendency is to include qualitative and emic data in order to provide context for understanding the quantitative data (review Chapter 3).

The ecological/epidemiological approach seeks to yield findings relevant to public health programs. It can provide information about groups that are at risk of specific problems. For example, although hookworm is common throughout rural China, epidemiological researchers learned that rice cultivators have the highest rates. The reason is that hookworm can spread through the night soil (human excrement used as fertilizer) applied to the fields in which the cultivators work.

Another significant environmental factor that has important effects on health is urbanization. As archaeologists have documented about the past, settled populations living in dense clusters are more likely than mobile populations to experience a range of health problems, including infectious diseases and malnutrition (Cohen 1989). Such problems are apparent among many recently settled pastoralist groups in

Women working in padi fields in southern China. Agricultural work done in standing water increases the risk of hookworm infection.

▶ *Is hookworm a threat where you live? What is the major infectious disease in your home region?*

East and West Africa. One study compared the health status of two groups of Turkana men in northwest Kenya (see Map 6.5, p. 153): those who were still mobile pastoralists and those who lived in a town (Barkey, Campbell, and Leslie 2001). The two groups differ strikingly in diet, physical activities, and health. Pastoralist Turkana eat mainly animal foods (milk, meat, and blood), spend much time in rigorous physical activity, and live in large family groups. Settled Turkana men eat mainly maize and beans. Their sedentary (settled) life means less physical activity and exercise. In terms of health, the settled men had more eye infections, chest infections, backache, and cough/colds. Pastoralist Turkana men were not, however, free of health problems. One-fourth of the pastoralist men had eye infections, but among the settled men, one-half had eye infections. In terms of nutrition, the settled Turkana were shorter and had greater body mass than the taller and slimmer pastoralists.

Cities present many stressors to human health as well as opportunities for improved health through greater access to health care. Typically, cities comprise diverse social categories, varying by class and ethnicity. These groups have different experiences of health risk. In the United States, the incidence of tuberculosis (TB) has increased in recent years, mainly in urban areas (DeFerdinando 1999). Tuberculosis is spread by infected humans, and its rate of spread is increased by crowding, poverty, poor housing, and lack of access to health care. In the United States, rates of tuberculosis are generally higher in southern than in northern states, with the exceptions of New York and Illinois, given their large urban populations.

---

ecological/epidemiological approach an approach within medical anthropology that considers how aspects of the natural environment and social environment interact to cause illness.

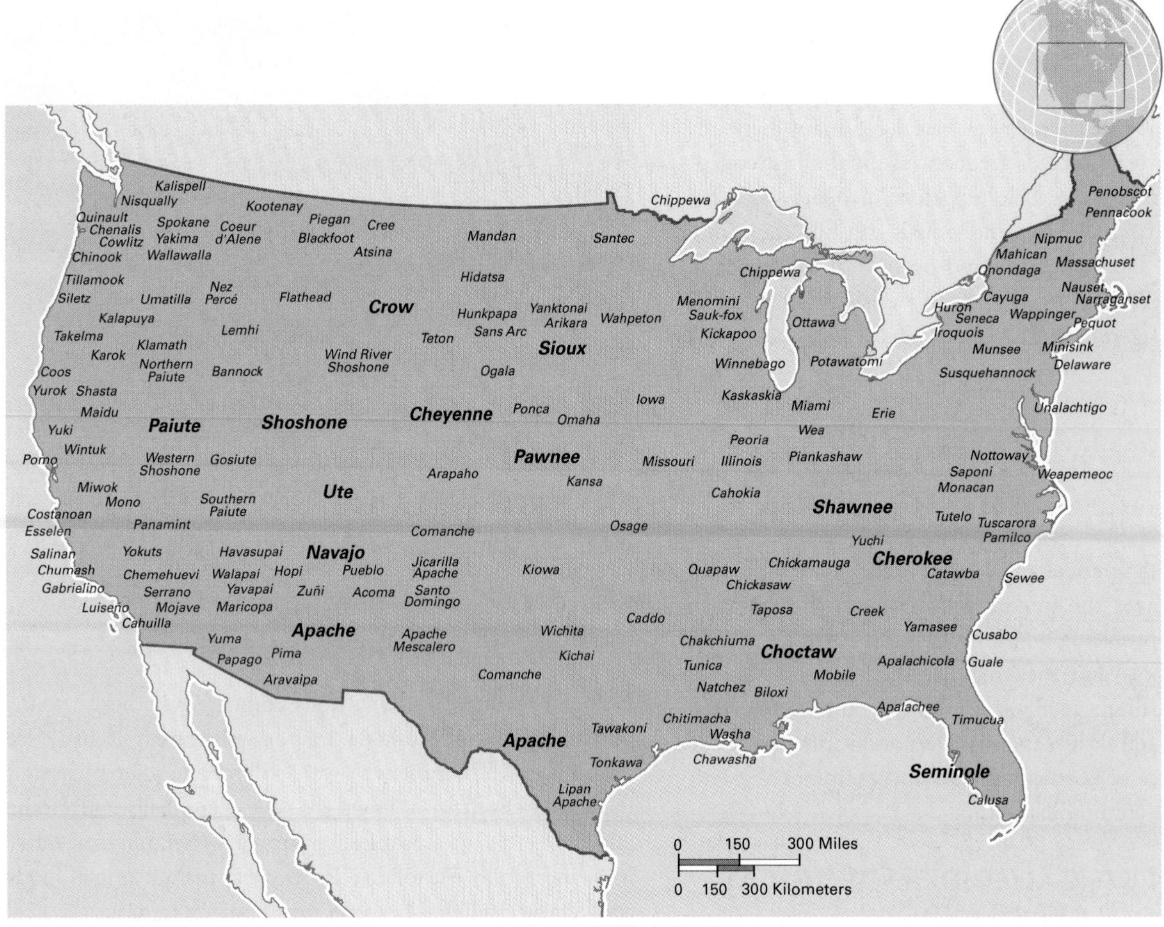

MAP 7.5 Precolonial Distribution of Indian Tribes in the 48 United States. Before the arrival of European colonialists, Indians were the sole occupants of the area. The first English settlers were impressed by their height and robust physical health.

Beginning in the 1990s, outbreaks of *multidrug-resistant tuberculosis* (*MDRTB*), a new strain of TB that is resistant to conventional drugs, led to its being recognized by public health authorities as a major "new" infectious disease. Even more recently, the new threat of *extra- multidrug-resistant tuberculosis* (*XMDRTB*) has emerged. New forms of the disease mutate more rapidly than scientists are able to develop drugs to combat them.

Anthropologists have applied the ecological/epidemiological approach to the study of the impaired health and survival of indigenous peoples resulting from colonial contact. Findings about the effects of colonial contact are negative, ranging from the quick and outright extermination of indigenous peoples to resilient adjustment, among other groups, to drastically changed conditions.

In the Western hemisphere, European colonialism brought a dramatic decline in the indigenous populations, although disagreement exists about the numbers involved (Joralemon 1982). Research indicates that the precontact New World was largely free of the major European infectious diseases such as smallpox, measles, and typhus, and perhaps also of syphilis, leprosy, and malaria. Therefore, the exposure of indigenous peoples to these infectious diseases likely had a massive impact, given the indigenous people's complete lack of resistance. One analyst compared colonial contact to a "biological war":

> Smallpox was the captain of the men of death in that war, typhus fever the first lieutenant, and measles the second lieutenant. More terrible than the conquistadores on horseback, more deadly than sword and gunpowder, they made the conquest by the whites a walkover as compared to what it would have been without their aid. (Ashburn 1947:98, quoted in Joralemon 1982:112)

This quotation emphasizes the importance of the three major diseases in New World colonial history: smallpox, measles, and malaria. A later arrival, cholera, also had severe effects because its transmission through contaminated water and food thrives in areas of poor sanitation.

Besides infectious diseases, indigenous populations were decimated by outright killing, enslavement and harsh labor practices, and the psychological ravages of losing one's livelihood, social ties and support, and access to ancestral burial grounds (see Map 7.5 and Map 7.6).

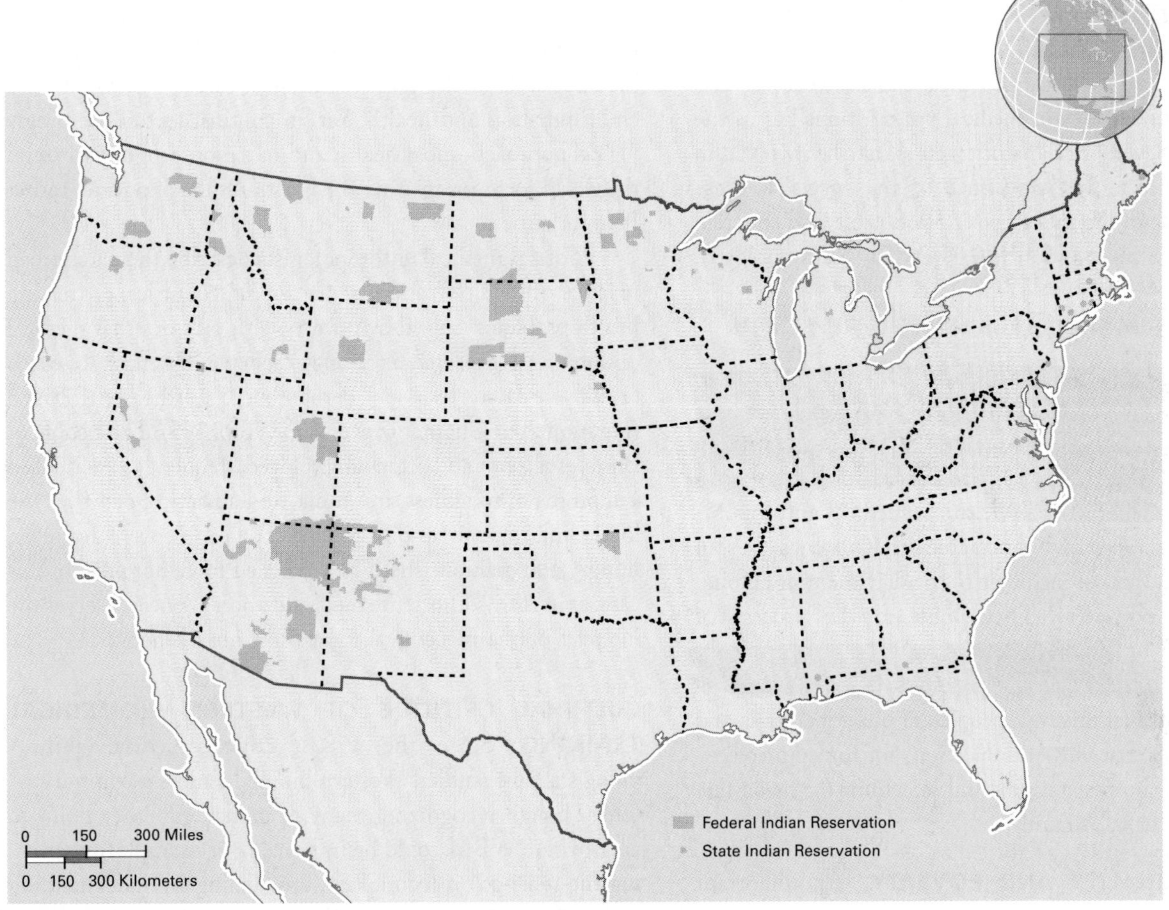

MAP 7.6 Designated Reservations in the 48 United States.
Indian reservations today comprise a small percentage of the U.S. land mass. Reservations are allocated to "recognized tribes." Several states recognize no tribes. Many Indians live off the reservations, often as poorly employed or unemployed urban residents.

Enduring effects of European colonialism among indigenous peoples worldwide include high rates of depression and suicide, low self-esteem, high rates of child and adolescent drug use, and high rates of alcoholism, obesity, and hypertension. **Historical trauma** refers to the intergenerational transfer of the emotional and psychological effects of colonialism from parents to children (Brave Heart 2004). It is closely associated with substance abuse as a vehicle for attempting to cover the continued pain of historical trauma. Troubled parents create a difficult family situation for children, who tend to replicate their parents' negative coping mechanisms. The concept of historical trauma helps to expand the scope of traditional epidemiological studies by drawing on factors from the past to explain the social and spatial distribution of contemporary health problems. Such an approach may prove more effective in devising culturally appropriate ways to alleviate health problems.

THE INTERPRETIVIST APPROACH

Some medical anthropologists examine health systems as systems of meaning. They study how people in different cultures label, describe, and experience illness and how healing systems offer meaningful responses to individual and communal distress. Interpretivist anthropologists have examined aspects of healing, such as ritual trance, as symbolic performances. French anthropologist Claude Lévi-Strauss established this approach in a classic essay called "The Effectiveness of Symbols" (1967). He examined how a song sung by a shaman during childbirth among the Kuna Indians of Panama (see Map 9.4, p. 226) helps women through a difficult delivery. The main point is that healing systems provide meaning to people who are experiencing seemingly meaningless forms of suffering. The provision of meaning offers psychological support to the afflicted and may enhance healing through what Western science calls the **placebo effect**, or **meaning effect**, a

historical trauma the intergenerational transfer of the negative effects of colonialism from parents to children.

placebo effect or **meaning effect** a positive result from a healing method due to a symbolic or otherwise nonmaterial factor.

positive result from a healing method due to a symbolic or otherwise nonmaterial factor (Moerman 2002). In the United States, depending on the health problem, between 10 and 90 percent of the efficacy of medical prescriptions lies in the placebo effect. Several explanatory factors may be involved in the meaning effect: the confidence of the specialist prescribing a treatment, the act of prescription itself, and concrete details about the prescription (see Everyday Anthropology).

CRITICAL MEDICAL ANTHROPOLOGY

Critical medical anthropology focuses on the analysis of how structural factors such as the global political economy, global media, and social inequality affect the prevailing health system, including types of afflictions, people's health status, and their access to health care. Critical medical anthropologists show how Western biomedicine itself often serves to bolster the institution of medicine to the detriment of helping the poor and powerless. They point to the process of **medicalization**, or labeling a particular issue or problem as medical and requiring medical treatment when, in fact, its cause is structural. In this way, people are prescribed pills and injections for poverty, pills and injections for forced displacement from one's home, and pills and injections for being unable to provide for one's family.

SOCIAL INEQUALITY AND POVERTY An important topic to launch this discussion is social inequality and poverty. No matter how you measure these factors, they always have something to say about health. Substantial evidence indicates that poverty is the primary cause of morbidity (sickness) and mortality (death) in both industrialized and developing countries (Farmer 2005). It may be manifested in different ways—for example, in child malnutrition in Chad or Nepal or through street violence among the urban poor of wealthy countries.

At the broadest level, comparing richer countries to poorer countries, distinctions exist between the most common health problems of rich, industrial countries and those of poor, less industrial countries. In the former, major causes of death are circulatory diseases, malignant cancers, HIV/AIDS, excess alcohol consumption, and smoking tobacco. In poor countries, tuberculosis, malaria, and HIV/AIDS are the three leading causes of death. One disease they share is HIV/AIDS.

Within the developing world, rates of childhood malnutrition are inversely related to income. In other words, as income increases, so does calorie intake as a percent of recommended daily allowances (Zaidi 1988). Thus, increasing the income levels of the poor is the most direct way to improve child nutrition and health. Yet, in contrast to this seemingly logical approach, most health and nutrition programs around the world focus on treating the health results of poverty rather than its causes.

Critical medical anthropologists describe the widespread practice of medicalization in developing countries, or treating health problems caused by poverty with pills or other medical options. An example is Nancy Scheper-Hughes's research (1992) in Bom Jesus in Pernambuco, northeastern Brazil (mentioned in Chapter 6; see Map 7.1, p. 165). The people of Bom Jesus, poor and often unemployed, frequently experienced symptoms of weakness, insomnia, and anxiety. Doctors at the local clinic gave them pills to take. The people were, however, hungry and malnourished. They needed food, not pills. In this case, as in many others, the medicalization of poverty serves the interests of pharmaceutical companies, not the poor.

CULTURAL CRITIQUE OF WESTERN BIOMEDICAL TRAINING Since the 1980s, critical medical anthropologists have studied Western biomedicine as a cultural system. Though recognizing many of its benefits, they point to areas where WBM could be improved, for example, by reducing the reliance on technology, broadening an understanding of health problems as they relate to structural conditions and not just biological conditions, and diversifying healing through alternative methods such as massage, acupuncture, and chiropracty.

Some critical medical anthropologists have conducted research on Western medical school training. One study of obstetric training in the United States involved interviews with 12 obstetricians, 10 male and 2 female (Davis-Floyd 1987). As students, they absorbed the *technological model of birth* as a core value of Western obstetrics. This model treats the body as a machine. The physician uses the assembly-line approach to birth in order to promote efficient production and quality control. One of the residents in the study explained, "We shave 'em, we prep 'em, we hook 'em up to the IV and administer sedation. We deliver the baby, it goes to the nursery and the mother goes to her room. There's no room for niceties around here. We just move 'em right on through. It's not hard to see it like an assembly line" (1987:292). The goal is the "production" of a healthy baby. The doctor is a technical expert in charge of achieving this goal, and the mother takes second place. One obstetrician said, "It is what we all were trained to always go after—the perfect baby. That's what we were trained to produce. The quality of the mother's experience—we rarely thought about that. Everything we did was to get that perfect baby" (1987:292).

This goal involves the use of sophisticated monitoring machines. One obstetrician said, "I'm totally dependent

---

critical medical anthropology approach within medical anthropology involving the analysis of how economic and political structures shape people's health status, their access to health care, and the prevailing medical systems that exist in relation to them.

medicalization labeling a particular issue or problem as medical and requiring medical treatment when, in fact, that issue or problem is economic or political.

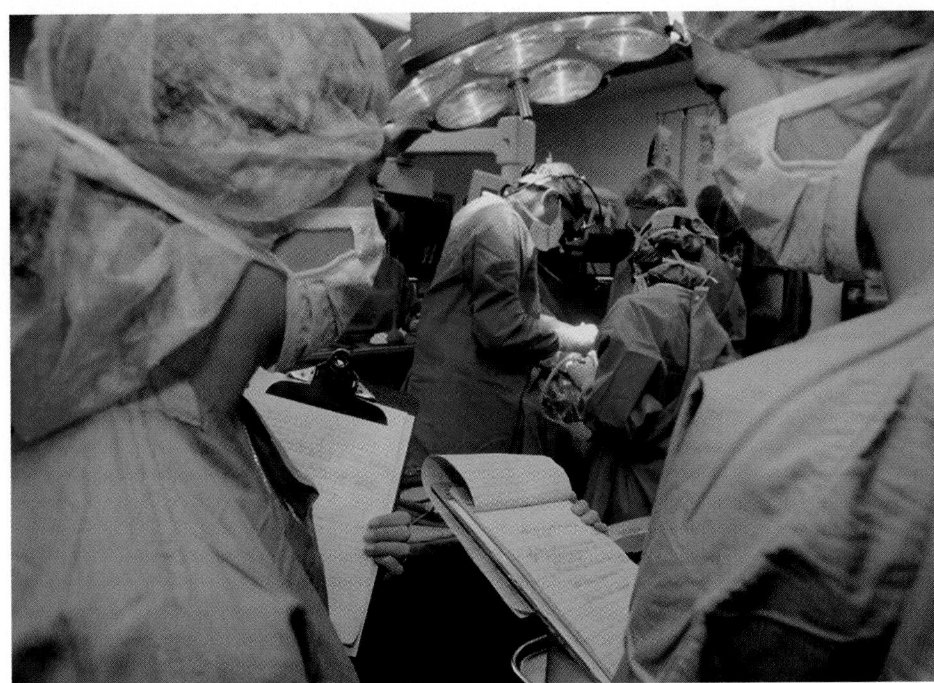

Medical students in training in a Western biomedical setting. These students are observing brain surgery.

▶ *What does this scene convey about values and beliefs of Western medicine?*

on fetal monitors, 'cause they're great! They free you to do a lot of other things. . . . I couldn't sit over there with a woman in labor with my hand on her belly, and be in here seeing 20 to 30 patients a day" (1987:291). Use of technology also conveys status to the physician. One commented, "Anybody in obstetrics who shows a human interest in patients is not respected. What is respected is interest in machines" (1987:291).

How do medical students learn to accept the technological model? Davis-Floyd's research points to three key processes. One way is through physical *hazing,* a harsh rite of passage involving, in this case, stress caused by sleep deprivation. Hazing extends throughout medical school and the residency period.

Second, medical school training in the United States involves a process of *cognitive retrogression* in which students relinquish critical thinking and thoughtful ways of learning. During the first two years of medical school, most courses are basic sciences, and students must memorize vast quantities of material. The sheer bulk of memorization forces students to adopt an uncritical approach. This mental overload socializes students into a uniform pattern, giving them tunnel vision in which the knowledge of medicine assumes supreme importance. As one obstetrician said,

> Medical school is not difficult in terms of what you have to learn—there's just so much of it. You go through, in a six-week course, a thousand-page book. The sheer bulk of information is phenomenal. You have pop quizzes in two or three courses every day the first year. We'd get up around 6, attend classes till 5, go home and eat, then head back to school and be in anatomy lab working with a cadaver, or something, until 1 or 2 in the morning, and then go home and get a couple of hours of sleep and then go out again. And you did that virtually day in and day out for four years, except for vacations. (1987:298–299)

Third, in a process termed *dehumanization,* medical school training works to erase humanitarian ideals through an emphasis on technology and objectification of the patient. One obstetrical student explained, "Most of us went into medical school with pretty humanitarian ideals. I know I did. But the whole process of medical education makes you inhuman . . . by the time you get to residency, you end up not caring about anything beyond the latest techniques you can master and how sophisticated the tests are that you can perform" (1987:299). The last two years of medical school and the four years of residency are devoted primarily to hands-on experience.

◆◆◆

Globalization and Change

With globalization, health problems move around the world and into remote locations and cultures more rapidly than ever before. The HIV/AIDS epidemic is one tragic example. Other new epidemics include SARS (Severe Acute Respiratory Syndrome) and avian (bird) flu. At the same time, Western culture, including biomedicine, is on the move. Perhaps no other aspect of Western culture, except for the capitalist market system and the English language, has so permeated the rest of the world as Western biomedicine. But the cultural flow is not one-way. Many people in North America and Europe are turning to forms of non-Western and nonbiomedical healing, such as acupuncture and massage therapy. This section considers new and emerging health challenges, changes in healing,

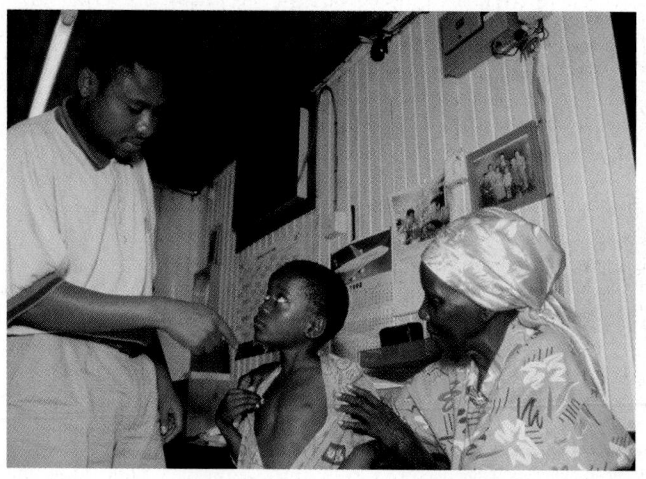

(LEFT) A woman takes her 8-year-old grandson, who has HIV/AIDS, to a clinic in Dar es Salaam, Tanzania. Throughout the world, increasing numbers of children are infected and, at the same time, are orphans because their parents have died of the disease. (RIGHT) Social stigma often adds to the suffering of HIV/AIDS victims. The billboards, near Soweto in South Africa, promote condom use and seek to reduce social rejection and stigma.

and examples of how applied medical anthropology has increasing relevance.

NEW INFECTIOUS DISEASES

In the mid-twentieth century, scientific advances such as antibiotic drugs, vaccines against childhood diseases, and improved technology for sanitation dramatically reduced the threat from infectious disease. The 1980s, however, were the beginning of an era of shaken confidence with the onset and rapid spread of the HIV/AIDS epidemic.

New contexts for exposure and contagion are created through increased international travel and migration, deforestation, and development projects, among others. Increased travel and migration have contributed to the spread of HIV/AIDS and SARS. Deforestation is related to higher rates of malaria, which is spread by mosquitoes; mosquitoes thrive in pools of water in open, sunlit areas as opposed to forest. Development projects such as dam construction and clearing forests often have negative health effects.

DISEASES OF DEVELOPMENT

Diseases of development are health problems (both diseases and illnesses) caused or increased by economic development activities. For example, the construction of dams and irrigation systems throughout the tropical world has brought dramatically increased rates of *schistosomiasis* (shish-to-suh-MY-a-sis), a disease caused by the presence of a parasitic worm in the blood system. Over 200 million people suffer from this debilitating disease, with prevalence rates the highest in sub-Saharan countries in Africa (Michaud, Gordon, and Reich 2004). The larvae hatch from eggs and mature in slow-moving water such as lakes and rivers). When mature, they can penetrate human (or other animal) skin with which they come into contact. Once inside the human body, the adult schistosomes breed in the veins around the human bladder and bowel. They send fertilized eggs through urine and feces into the environment. These eggs then contaminate water in which they hatch into larvae.

Anthropologists' research has documented steep increases in the rates of schistosomiasis at large dam sites in developing countries (Scudder 1973). The increased risk is caused by the dams slowing the rate of water flow. Stagnant water systems offer an ideal environment for development of the larvae. Opponents of the construction of large dams have used this information in support of their position.

New diseases of development continue to appear. One of these is *Kyasanur Forest Disease*, or KFD (Nichter 1992). This viral disease was first identified in 1957 in southern India:

> Resembling influenza, at onset KFD is marked by sudden chills, fever, frontal headaches, stiffness of the neck, and body pain. Diarrhea and vomiting often follow on the third day. High fever is continuous for five to fifteen days, during which time a variety of additional symptoms may manifest themselves, including gastrointestinal bleeding, persistent cough with blood-tinged sputum, and bleeding gums. In more serious cases, the infection progresses to bronchial pneumonia, meningitis, paralysis, encephalitis, and hemorrhage. (1992:224)

In the early 1980s, an epidemic of KFD swept through over 30 villages near the Kyasanur forest in Karnataka state, southern India (see Map 8.5, p. 201). Mortality rates in hospitals ranged between 12 and 18 percent of those admitted.

disease of development a health problem caused or increased by economic development activities that affect the environment and people's relationship with it.

CULTURAMA

The Sherpa of Nepal

The name Sherpa means "person." About 35,000 Sherpa live in Nepal, mainly in the northeastern region. Another 10,000 reside in Bhutan and Sikkim (Fisher 1990), and another 5000 live in cities of Europe and North America.

In Nepal, the Sherpa are most closely associated with the Khumbu region. Khumbu is a valley set high in the Himalayas, completely encircled by mountains and with a clear view of Mount Everest (Karan and Mather 1985). The Sherpa have a mixed economy involving animal herding, trade between Tibet and India, small businesses, and farming, with the main crop being potatoes. Since the 1920s and the coming of Western mountaineers, Sherpa men have become increasingly employed as guides and porters for trekkers and climbers. Many Sherpa men and women now run guest houses or work in guest houses as cooks, food servers, and cleaners.

The Sherpa are organized into 18 separate lineages, or *ru* ("bones"), with marriage taking place outside one's birth lineage. Recently, they have begun marrying into other ethnic groups, thus expanding the definition and meaning of what it is to be Sherpa. Because of increased intermarriage, the number of people who can be considered Sherpa to some degree is 130,000. Status distinctions include "big people," "middle people," and "small people," with the middle group being the largest by far (Ortner 1999:65). The main privilege of those in the top level is not to carry loads. Those in the poorest level are landless and work for others.

The Sherpa practice a localized version of Tibetan Buddhism, which contains non-Buddhist elements having to do with nature spiritualism that connects all beings. The place name Khumbu, for example, refers to the guardian deity of the region.

Tourism has been and still is a major change factor for the Sherpa. In Khumbu, the number of international tourists per year exceeds the Sherpa population.

Global warming is also having significant effects. Glaciers are melting, lakes are rising, and massive flooding is frequent. Some of the swollen lakes are in danger of breaking their banks (United Nations Environment Programme 2002). Many community development projects are aimed at reforestation, planting fruit orchards, and protecting and expanding local knowledge of medicinal herbs.

Thanks to Vincanne Adams, University of California at San Francisco, for reviewing this material.

(LEFT) A Sherpa porter carries a load up a steep mountain path in the Himalayas. Porters earn relatively good wages, especially when they work for international tourists. (CENTER) Nepali children learn writing in a school supported by the Himalayan Trust, an organization founded by Sir Edmund Hillary in 1961, after he climbed Mount Everest and asked the local people he met how he could help them.

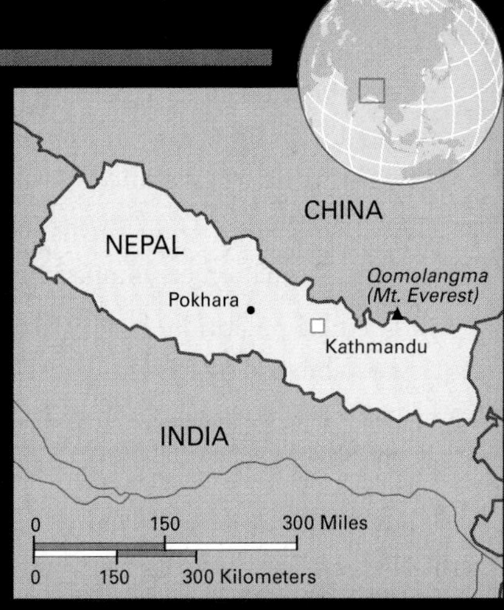

MAP 7.7 Nepal. The Kingdom of Nepal has a population of almost 30 million inhabitants. Most of its territory is in the Himalayas, and Nepal has 8 of the world's 10 highest mountains.

Investigation revealed that KFD especially affected agricultural workers and cattle tenders who were most exposed to newly cleared areas near the forest. In the cleared areas, international companies established plantations and initiated cattle raising. Ticks were the vector transmitting the disease from the cattle to the people. Ticks had long existed in the local ecosystem, but their numbers greatly increased in the cleared area, finding many inviting hosts in the cattle and in the workers. Thus, human modification of the ecosystem through deforestation and introduction of large-scale cattle raising caused the epidemic and shaped its social distribution.

MEDICAL PLURALISM

Contact between cultures may lead to a situation in which aspects of both cultures coexist: two (or more) different languages, religions, systems of law, or health systems, for example. The term **medical pluralism** refers to the presence of multiple health systems within a society. The coexistence of many forms of healing provides clients a range of choices and enhances the quality of health. In other cases, people are confronted by conflicting models of illness and healing, a situation that can result in misunderstandings between healers and clients and in unhappy outcomes.

SELECTIVE PLURALISM: THE CASE OF THE SHERPA The Sherpa of Nepal (see Culturama) are an unusual example of a culture in which preference for traditional healing systems remains strong along with the selective use of Western biomedicine (Adams 1988). Healing therapies available in the Upper Khumbu region in northeastern Nepal fit into three categories:

- Orthodox Buddhist practitioners, which include *lamas,* who Khumbu people consult for prevention and cure through their blessings, and *amchis,* who practice Tibetan medicine, a humoral healing system.
- Unorthodox religious or shamanic practitioners who perform divination ceremonies for diagnosis.
- Biomedical practitioners who work in a clinic that was first established to serve tourists. The clinic was established as a permanent medical facility in 1967, and many Sherpa selectively use it.

Thus, three varieties of health care exist in the region. Traditional healers are thriving, unthreatened by changes brought by the tourist trade, the influx of new wealth, and notions of modernity. The question of why Western biomedicine has not completely taken over other healing practices requires a complicated answer. One part of the answer is that high-mountain tourism does not deeply affect local production and social relations. Although it brings in new wealth, it does not require large-scale capital investment from outside as, for example, mega-hotel tourist developments have elsewhere. So far, the Sherpa maintain control of their productive resources, including trekking knowledge and skills.

CONFLICTING EXPLANATORY MODELS In many other contexts, however, anthropologists have documented conflicts and misunderstandings between Western biomedicine and local health systems. Miscommunication often occurs between biomedical doctors and patients in matters as seemingly simple as a prescription that should be taken with every meal. The Western biomedically trained doctor assumes that this means three times a day. But some people do not eat three meals a day and thus unwittingly fail to follow the doctor's instructions.

One anthropological study of a case in which death resulted from cross-cultural differences shows how complex the issue of communication across medical cultures is. The "F family" are immigrants from American Samoa (see Map 7.8) living in Honolulu, Hawai'i (Krantzler 1987). Neither parent speaks English. Their children are "moderately literate" in English but speak a mixture of English and Samoan at home.

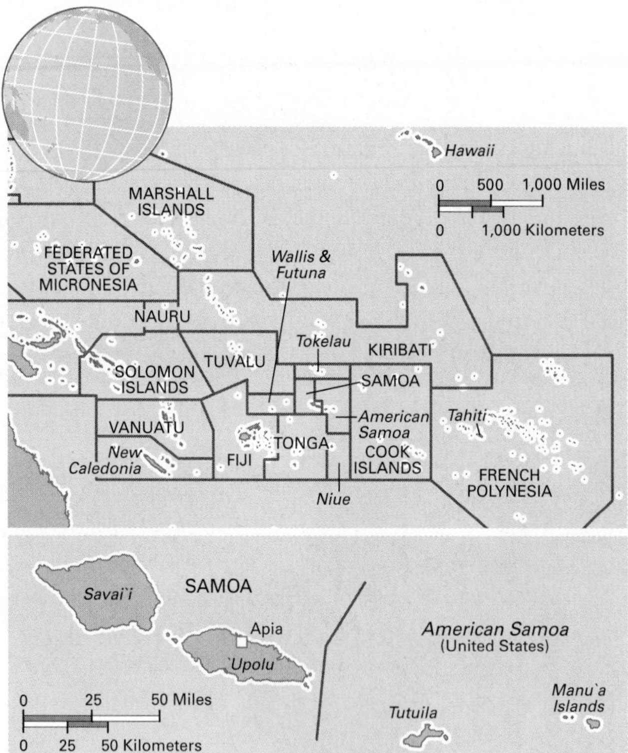

MAP 7.8 Samoa and American Samoa.
Samoa, or the Independent State of Samoa, was known as German Samoa (1900–1919) and Western Samoa (1914–1997) until recognized by the United Nations as a sovereign country. Its population is around 177,000. American Samoa, or Amerika Samoa in Samoan English, is a territory of the United States with a population of about 57,000. During World War II, U.S. Marines in American Samoa outnumbered the local population and had a strong cultural influence. Unemployment rates are now high and the U.S. military is the largest employer.

Mr. F was trained as a traditional Samoan healer. Mary, a daughter, was first stricken with diabetes at age 16. She was taken to the hospital by ambulance after collapsing, half-conscious, on the sidewalk near her home in a Honolulu housing project. After several months of irregular contact with medical staff, she was again brought to the hospital in an ambulance, unconscious, and she died there. Her father was charged with causing Mary's death through medical neglect.

In the biomedical view, her parents failed to give Mary adequate care even though the hospital staff took pains to instruct her family about how to give insulin injections, and Mary was shown how to test her urine for glucose and acetone and counseled about her diet. She was to be followed up with visits to the outpatient clinic and, following the clinic's unofficial policy of linking patients with physicians from their own ethnic group, she was assigned to see the sole Samoan pediatric resident. Over the next few months, Mary was seen once in the clinic by a different resident, she missed her next three appointments, came in once without an appointment, and was readmitted to the hospital on the basis of test results from that visit. At that time, she, her parents, and her older sister were once again advised about the importance of compliance with the medical advice they were receiving. Four months later, she returned to the clinic with blindness in one eye and diminished vision in the other. She was diagnosed with cataracts, and the Samoan physician again advised Mary about the seriousness of her illness and the need for compliance. The medical experts increasingly judged that "cultural differences" were the basic problem and that in spite of all their attempts to communicate with the F family, they were basically incapable of caring for Mary.

The family's perspective, in contrast, was grounded in *fa'a Samoa,* the Samoan way. Their experiences in the hospital were not positive from the start. When Mr. F arrived at the hospital with Mary the first time, he spoke with several different hospital staff, through a daughter as translator. It was a teaching hospital, and so various residents and attending physicians had examined Mary. Mr. F was concerned that there was no single physician caring for Mary, and he was concerned that her care was inconsistent. The family observed a child die while Mary was in the intensive care unit, reinforcing the perception of inadequate care and instilling fear over Mary's chance of surviving in this hospital.

Language differences between Mary's family and the hospital staff added to the problem:

> When they asked what was wrong with her, their perception was that "everyone said 'sugar.'" What this meant was not clear to the family; they were confused about whether she was getting too much sugar or too little. Mary's mother interpreted the explanations to mean she was not getting enough sugar, so she tried to give her more when she was returned home. Over time, confusion gave way to anger, and a basic lack of trust of the hospital and the physicians there developed. The family began to draw on their own resources for explaining and caring for Mary's illness, relying heavily on the father's skills as a healer. (1987:330)

From the Samoan perspective, the F family behaved logically and appropriately. The father, as household head and healer in his own right, felt he had authority. Dr. A, although Samoan, had been resocialized by the Western medical system and alienated from his Samoan background. He did not offer the personal touch that the F family expected. Samoans believe that children above the age of 12 are no longer children and can be expected to behave responsibly. Assigning Mary's 12-year-old sister to assist her with her insulin injections and recording results made sense to them. Also, the hospital in American Samoa does not require appointments. Cultural misunderstanding was the ultimate cause of Mary's death.

APPLIED MEDICAL ANTHROPOLOGY

Applied medical anthropology is the application of anthropological knowledge to further the goals of health-care providers. It may involve improving doctor–patient communication in multicultural settings, making recommendations about culturally appropriate health intervention programs, or providing insights about factors related to disease that medical practitioners do not usually take into account. Applied medical anthropologists draw on ethnomedical knowledge and on any of the three theoretical approaches or a combination of them.

REDUCING LEAD POISONING AMONG MEXICAN AMERICAN CHILDREN An example of the positive impact of applied medical anthropology is in the work of Robert Trotter on lead poisoning among Mexican American children (1987). The three most common sources of lead poisoning of children in the United States are these:

- Eating lead-based paint chips
- Living near a smelter where the dust has high lead content
- Eating or drinking from pottery made with an improperly treated lead glaze

The discovery of an unusual case of lead poisoning by health professionals in Los Angeles in the 1980s prompted investigations that produced understanding of a fourth cause: the use by many Mexican Americans of a traditional healing remedy, *azarcon,* which contains lead to treat a culture-specific

---

medical pluralism the existence of more than one health system in a culture, or a government policy to promote the integration of local healing systems into biomedical practice.

applied medical anthropology the application of anthropological knowledge to furthering the goals of health care providers.

LESSONS applied

Promoting Vaccination Programs in Developing Countries

Vaccination programs in developing countries, especially as promoted by UNICEF, are introduced with much fanfare. But they are sometimes met with little enthusiasm by the target population. In India, many people are suspicious that vaccination programs are clandestine family planning programs (Nichter 1996). In other instances, fear of foreign vaccines prompts people to reject inoculations. Overall, acceptance rates of vaccination are lower than Western public health planners expected.

To understand why people reject inoculations, medical anthropologists conducted surveys in several countries. The results revealed that many parents have a partial or inaccurate understanding of what the vaccines protect against. Some people did not understand the importance of multiple vaccinations. Public health promoters incorporated findings from the survey in two ways:

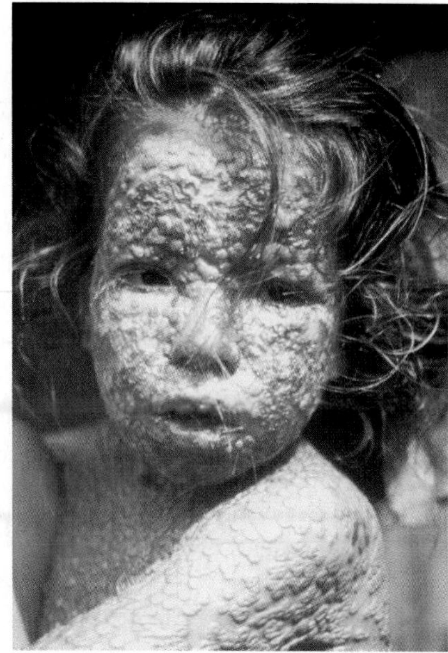

A young girl in Bangladesh, photographed in 1975, has the raised bumps of smallpox. In 1977, the World Health Organization announced that smallpox had been eradicated in Bangladesh.

▶ *Has smallpox been eradicated worldwide?*

- Educational campaigns for the public that addressed their concerns
- Education for the public health specialists about the importance of understanding and paying attention to local cultural practices and beliefs

◆ **FOOD FOR THOUGHT**

- If your job were to promote wider acceptance of vaccinations in your country, what would you want to know before you began an education campaign?

---

syndrome called *empacho*. Empacho is a combination of indigestion and constipation believed to be caused by food sticking to the abdominal wall.

The U.S. Public Health Service asked Trotter to investigate the availability and use of azarcon. He went to Mexico and surveyed the contents of herbal shops. He talked with *curanderos* (traditional healers). His findings convinced the U.S. government to place restrictions on azarcon, and a related remedy called *greta*. Trotter also made recommendations about the need to provide a substitute remedy for the treatment of *empacho* that would not have harmful side effects. He offered ideas about how to advertise the substitute in a culturally effective way. Throughout his involvement, Trotter played several roles—researcher, consultant, and program developer—all of which brought anthropological knowledge to the solution of a public health problem.

PUBLIC HEALTH COMMUNICATION Much work in applied medical anthropology involves health communication (Nichter 1996). Anthropologists can help health educators in the development of more meaningful messages through these methods:

- Addressing local health beliefs and health concerns
- Taking seriously all local illness terms and conventions
- Adopting local styles of communication
- Identifying subgroups within the population that may be responsive to different types of messages and incentives
- Monitoring the response of communities to health messages over time and facilitating corrections in communication when needed
- Exposing and removing possible victim blaming in health messages

These principles helped health-care officials understand local response to public vaccination programs in several countries of Asia and Africa (see Lessons Applied).

WORKING TOGETHER: WESTERN BIOMEDICINE AND NONBIOMEDICAL SYSTEMS Since 1978, the World Health Organization has endorsed the incorporation of local healing practices in national health systems. This policy emerged in response to several factors. First is the increasing appreciation of the value of many non-Western healing traditions. Another is the shortage of trained biomedical personnel. Third is the growing awareness of the deficiencies of Western biomedicine in addressing a person's psychosocial context.

Debates continue about the efficacy of many traditional medical practices as compared to biomedicine. For instance, opponents of the promotion of traditional medicine claim that it has no effect on such infectious diseases as cholera, malaria, tuberculosis, schistosomiasis, leprosy, and others. They insist that it makes no sense to allow for or encourage ritual practices against cholera, for example, when a child has not been inoculated against it. Supporters of traditional medicine as one component of a pluralistic health system point out that biomedicine neglects a person's mind, soul, and social setting. Traditional healing practices fill that gap.

7

the BIG questions REVISITED

◆ What is ethnomedicine?

Ethnomedicine is the study of health systems of specific cultures. Health systems include categories and perceptions of illness and approaches to prevention and healing. Research in ethnomedicine shows how perceptions of the body differ cross-culturally and reveals both differences and similarities across health systems in perceptions of illness and symptoms. Culture-specific syndromes are found in all cultures, not just non-Western societies, and many are now globalizing.

Ethnomedical studies of healing, healing substances, and healers reveal a wide range of approaches. Community healing is more characteristic of small-scale nonindustrial societies. They emphasize group interaction and treating the individual within the social context. Humoral healing seeks to maintain balance in bodily fluids and substances through diet, activity, and behavior. In industrial/ informatics societies, biomedicine emphasizes the body as a discrete unit, and treatment addresses the individual body or mind and frames out the wider social context. Biomedicine is increasingly reliant on technology and is increasingly specialized.

◆ What are three major theoretical approaches in medical anthropology?

Ecological/epidemiological medical anthropology emphasizes links between the environment and health. It reveals how certain categories of people are at risk of contracting particular diseases within various contexts in historical times and the present.

The interpretivist approach focuses on studying illness and healing as a set of symbols and meanings. Cross-culturally, definitions of health problems and healing systems for these problems are embedded in meanings.

Critical medical anthropologists focus on health problems and healing within a structurist framework. They ask what power relations are involved and who benefits from particular forms of healing. They analyze the role of inequality and poverty in health problems. Some critical medical anthropologists have critiqued Western biomedicine as a system of social control.

◆ How are health, illness, and healing changing during globalization?

Health systems everywhere are facing accelerated change in the face of globalization, which includes the spread of Western capitalism as well as new diseases and new medical technologies. The "new infectious diseases" are a challenge to health-care systems in terms of prevention and treatment. Diseases of development are health problems caused by development projects that change the physical and social environments, such as dams and mines.

The spread of Western biomedicine to many non-Western contexts is a major direction of change. As a consequence, medical pluralism exists in all countries. The availability of Western patent medicines has had substantial positive effects, but widespread overuse and self-medication can result in negative health consequences for individuals and the emergence of drug-resistant disease strains.

Applied, or clinical, medical anthropologists play several roles in improving health systems. They may inform medical care providers of more appropriate forms of treatment, guide local people about their increasingly complex medical choices, help prevent health problems through changing detrimental practices, or improve public health communication by making it more culturally informed and effective.

KEY CONCEPTS

applied medical anthropology, p. 183
community healing, p. 170
critical medical anthropology, p. 178
culture-specific syndrome, p. 167
disease, p. 165
disease of development, p. 180
ecological/epidemiological approach, p. 175
ethno-etiologies, p. 168
ethnomedicine, p. 164
historical trauma, p. 177
humoral healing, p. 171
illness, p. 165
medicalization, p. 178
medical pluralism, p. 182
phytotherapy, p. 173
placebo effect, or meaning effect, p. 177
shaman/shamanka, p. 172
somatization, p. 167
structural suffering, p. 169
susto, p. 168
Western biomedicine (WBM) p. 164

SUGGESTED READINGS

Eric J. Bailey. *Medical Anthropology and African American Health*. New York: Greenwood Publishing Group, 2000. This book explores the relationship between cultural anthropology and African American health-care issues. One chapter discusses how to do applied research in medical anthropology.

Ron Barrett. *Aghor Medicine: Pollution, Death, and Healing in Northern India*. Berkeley: University of California Press, 2008. This study of the Aghori, Hindu ascetics of India, shows how they have recently become involved in healing victims of stigmatized diseases.

Bernhard M. Bierlich. *The Problem of Money: African Agency and Western Biomedicine in Northern Ghana*. New York: Bergahn Books, 2008. Fieldwork among the Dagomba people provides the basis for this description of ambivalent attitudes toward Western biomedicine and other aspects of modernity.

Nancy N. Chen. *Breathing Spaces: Qigong, Psychiatry, and Healing in China*. New York: Columbia University Press, 2003. This ethnography explores qigong (chee-gung), a charismatic form of healing popular in China that involves meditative breathing exercises.

Paul Farmer. *Pathologies of Power: Health, Human Rights, and the New War on the Poor*. Berkeley: University of California Press, 2005. Farmer blends interpretive medical anthropology with critical medical anthropology in his study of how poverty kills through diseases such as tuberculosis and HIV/AIDS.

Bonnie Glass-Coffin. *The Gift of Life: Female Spirituality and Healing in Northern Peru*. Albuquerque: University of New Mexico Press, 1998. The author examines women traditional healers in northern Peru. She provides a descriptive account of their practices and an account of how two healers worked to cure her of a spiritual illness.

Richard Katz, Megan Biesele, and Verna St. Davis. *Healing Makes Our Hearts Happy: Spirituality and Cultural Transformation among the Kalahari Ju/'hoansi*. Rochester, VT: Inner Traditions, 1997. This book presents the story of how traditional healing dances help the Ju/'hoansi cope with recent and contemporary social upheaval. Their healing dances help them maintain a sense of community and are important for their cultural survival.

Carol Shepherd McClain, ed. *Women as Healers: A Cross-Cultural Perspective*. New Brunswick, NJ: Rutgers University Press, 1989. Case studies discuss women healers in Ecuador, Sri Lanka, Mexico, Jamaica, the United States, Serbia, Korea, Southern Africa, and Benin.

David McKnight. *From Hunting to Drinking: The Devastating Effects of Alcohol on an Australian Aboriginal Community*. New York: Routledge, 2002. McKnight documents the history of drinking in Australia, causes of excessive alcohol consumption, and vested interests of authorities in the sale of alcohol to Aboriginal people.

Ethan Nebelkopf and Mary Phillips, eds. *Healing and Mental Health for Native Americans: Speaking in Red*. New York: AltaMira Press, 2004. Chapters address mental health and substance abuse among Native North Americans and provide cases of healing that involve Native American culture.

Merrill Singer. *Something Dangerous: Emergent and Changing Illicit Drug Use and Community Health*. Long Grove, IL: Waveland Press, 2005. This ethnography combines theory with research and applied anthropology about drug use and public health responses in the United States.

Paul Stoller. *Stranger in the Village of the Sick: A Memoir of Cancer, Sorcery, and Healing*. Boston: Beacon Press, 2004. After being diagnosed with lymphoma, the author enters the "village of the sick" as he goes through diagnostic testing, chemotherapy, and eventual remission. He describes being a cancer patient in the United States and how he found strength through his earlier association with a West African healer.

Johan Wedel. *Santería Healing*. Gainesville: University of Florida Press, 2004. This book discusses Santería healing in Cuba. The author conducted interviews with priests and others knowledgeable about Santería and observed many Santería consultations.

8 KINSHIP AND DOMESTIC LIFE

9 SOCIAL GROUPS AND SOCIAL STRATIFICATION

10 POLITICS AND LEADERSHIP

11 SOCIAL ORDER AND SOCIAL CONFLICT

PART III
SOCIAL ORGANIZATION

ANTHROPOLOGY works

Fredy Peccerelli, a forensic anthropologist, risks his personal safety working for victims of political violence in Guatemala, his homeland. Peccerelli is founder and executive director of the Guatemalan Forensic Anthropology Foundation (FAFG). FAFG is dedicated to the recovery and identification of the remains of thousands of indigenous Maya whom Guatemalan military forces killed or otherwise "disappeared" during the brutal civil war that raged from the mid-1960s to the mid-1990s.

Peccerelli was born in Guatemala. His family immigrated to the United States when his father, a lawyer, was threatened by death squads. He grew up in New York City and attended Brooklyn College in the 1990s. But he felt a need to reconnect with his heritage and began to study anthropology as a vehicle that would allow him to serve his country.

The FAFG scientists excavate clandestine mass graves, exhume the bodies, and identify them through several means, such as matching dental and/or medical records. In studying skeletons, they try to determine the person's age, gender, ancestry, and lifestyle. DNA studies are few because of the expense. The scientists also collect information from relatives of the victims and from eyewitnesses of the massacres. Since 1992, the FAFG team has discovered and exhumed approximately 200 mass grave sites.

Peccerelli sees the foundation's purpose as applying scientific principles to basic human concerns. Bodies of identified victims are returned to their families to allow them some sense of closure about what happened to their loved ones. Families can honor their dead with appropriate burial ceremonies.

The scientists also give the Guatemalan government clear evidence on the basis of which to prosecute the perpetrators of these atrocities. Members of the longstanding military rulers still hold powerful within the government. Peccerelli, his family, and his colleagues have been harassed and threatened. Bullets have been fired into Peccerelli's home, and it has been burglarized. Eleven FAFG scientists have received written death threats. Nevertheless, the United Nations and other human rights organizations have made it clear to the government that they support FARG's investigations, and exhumations continue with heightened security measures.

The American Association for the Advancement of Science honored Peccerelli and his colleagues in 2004 for their work in promoting human rights at great personal risk. In 1999, *Time* magazine and CNN chose Peccerelli as one of the fifty "Latin American Leaders for the New Millennium." During the same year, the Guatemalan Youth Commission named him an "icon" for the youth of the country.

A Minangkabau bride in Sumatra, Indonesia, wears an elaborate gold headdress. Women play a central role among the Minangkabau, the world's largest matrilineal culture.

KINSHIP AND DOMESTIC LIFE

the BIG questions

- How do cultures create kinship ties through descent, sharing, and marriage?
- What are cross-cultural patterns of households and domestic life?
- How are kinship and households changing?

OUTLINE

Learning how another kinship system works is as challenging as learning another language. Robin Fox became aware of this challenge during his research among the Tory Islanders of Ireland (see Map 8.1) (1995 [1978]). Some Tory Island kinship terms are similar to American English usage; for example, the word *muintir* means "people" in its widest sense, as in English. It can also refer to people of a particular social category, as in "my people," and to close relatives. Another similarity is in *gaolta,* the word for "relatives" or "those of my blood." Its adjectival form refers to kindness, like the English word kin, which is related to "kindness." Tory Islanders have a phrase meaning "children and grandchildren," also like the English term "descendants." One major difference is that the Tory Island word for "friend" is the same as the word for "kin." This usage reflects the cultural context of Tory Island with its small population, all related through kinship. So, logically, a friend is also kin.

All cultures have ways of defining *kinship,* or a sense of being related to another person or persons. Rules about kinship, the combination of rules about who are kin and the expected behavior of kin, are either informal or formalized in law or both. Starting in infancy, people learn about their particular culture's **kinship system,** the predominant form of kin relationships in a culture and the kinds of behavior involved. Like language, one's kinship system is so ingrained that it is taken for granted as something natural rather than cultural.

This chapter first considers cultural variations in three key features of kinship systems. It then focuses on a key unit of domestic life: the household. The last section provides examples of contemporary change in kinship patterns and household organization.

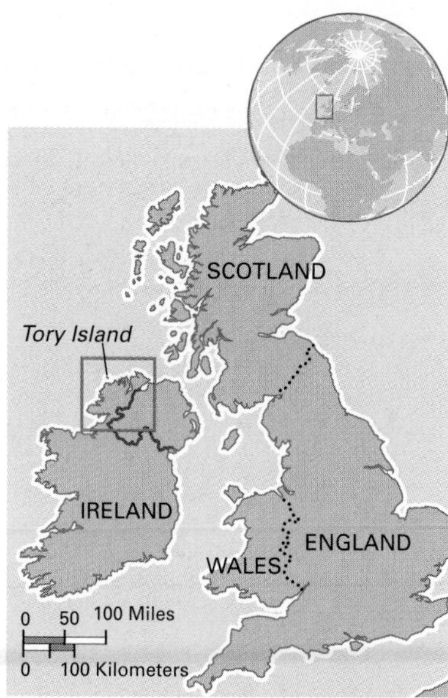

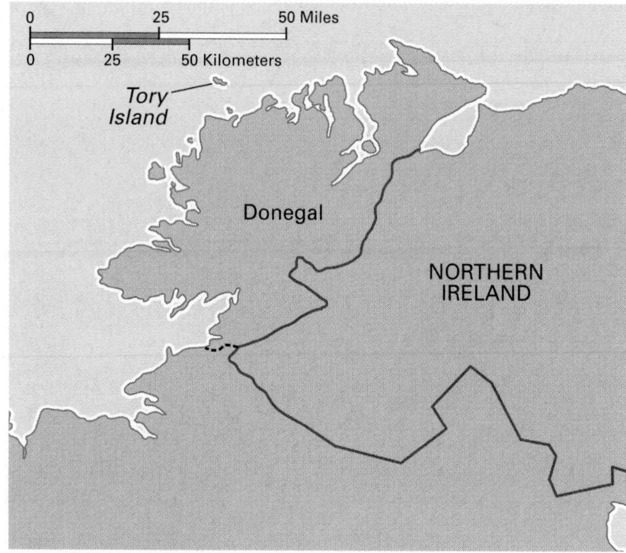

MAP 8.1 Ireland.

Ireland's population is about 4 million. The geography is low central plains surrounded by a ring of mountains. Membership in the European Union (EU) and the rising standard of living earned Ireland the nickname of the Celtic Tiger. Its economic opportunities are attracting immigrants from places as diverse as Romania, China, and Nigeria. Most people are Roman Catholics, followed by the Anglican Church of Ireland.

How Cultures Create Kinship

In all cultures, kinship is linked with modes of livelihood and reproduction (see Figure 8.1). Nineteenth-century anthropologists found that kinship was the most important organizing principle in nonindustrial, nonstate cultures. The kinship group performs the functions of ensuring the continuity of the group by arranging marriages; maintaining social order by setting moral rules and punishing offenders; and providing for the basic needs of members by regulating production, consumption, and distribution. In large-scale industrial/informatics societies, kinship ties exist, but many other kinds of social ties draw people together.

Nineteenth-century anthropologists also discovered that definitions of who counts as kin differed widely from those of Europe and the United States. Western cultures emphasize "blood" relations as primary, or relations through birth from a biological mother and biological father (Sault 1994). "Blood" is not a universal basis for kinship, however. Even in some cultures with a "blood"-based understanding of kinship, variations exist in defining who is a "blood" relative and who is not. For example, in some cultures, male offspring are considered of one "blood," whereas female offspring are not.

Among the Inuit of northern Alaska, behavior is a non-blood basis for determining kinship (Bodenhorn 2000). In this context, people who act like kin are kin. If a person stops acting like kin, then he or she is no longer a kinsperson. So, among the Inuit, someone might say that a certain person "used to be" his or her cousin.

kinship system the predominant form of kin relationships in a culture and the kinds of behavior involved.

Foraging	Horticulture	Pastoralism	Agriculture	Industrialism/Informatics
Descent and Inheritance				**Descent and Inheritance**
Bilineal		Unilineal (matrilineal or patrilineal)		Bilineal
Marital Residence				**Marital Residence**
Neolocal or bilocal		Matrilocal or patrilocal		Neolocal
Household Type				**Household Type**
Nuclear		Extended		Nuclear or single-parent or single-person

FIGURE 8.1 Modes of Livelihood, Kinship, and Household Structure

STUDYING KINSHIP: FROM FORMAL ANALYSIS TO KINSHIP IN ACTION

Anthropologists in the first half of the twentieth century focused on finding out who, in a particular culture, is related to whom and in what way. Typically, the anthropologist would conduct an interview with a few people, asking questions such as "What do you call your brother's daughter? Can you (as a man) marry your father's brother's daughter? What is the term you use to refer to your mother's sister?" The anthropologist would ask an individual to name all his or her relatives, explain how they are related to the interviewee, and provide the terms by which they refer to him or her.

From this information, the anthropologist would construct a *kinship diagram,* a schematic way of presenting the kinship relationships of an individual, called *ego,* using a set of symbols to depict all the kin relations of ego (see Figure 8.2). A kinship diagram depicts ego's relatives, as remembered by ego. In cultures where kinship plays a major role in social relations, ego may be able to provide information on dozens of relatives. When I (the author) took a research methods course as an undergraduate, I interviewed my Hindi language teaching assistant for a class assignment to construct a kinship diagram. He was from an urban, middle-class business family in India. He recalled over 60 relatives on both his father's and mother's sides, providing information for a much more extensive kinship diagram than I would have been able to provide for my middle-class, Euro-American relatives.

In contrast to a kinship diagram, a *genealogy* is a schematic way of presenting a family tree, constructed by beginning with the earliest ancestors that can be traced, then working down to the present. A genealogy, thus, does not begin with ego. When Robin Fox attempted to construct kinship diagrams beginning with ego, the Tory Islanders were uncomfortable with the approach. They preferred to proceed genealogically, so he followed their preference. Tracing a family's complete genealogy may involve archival research

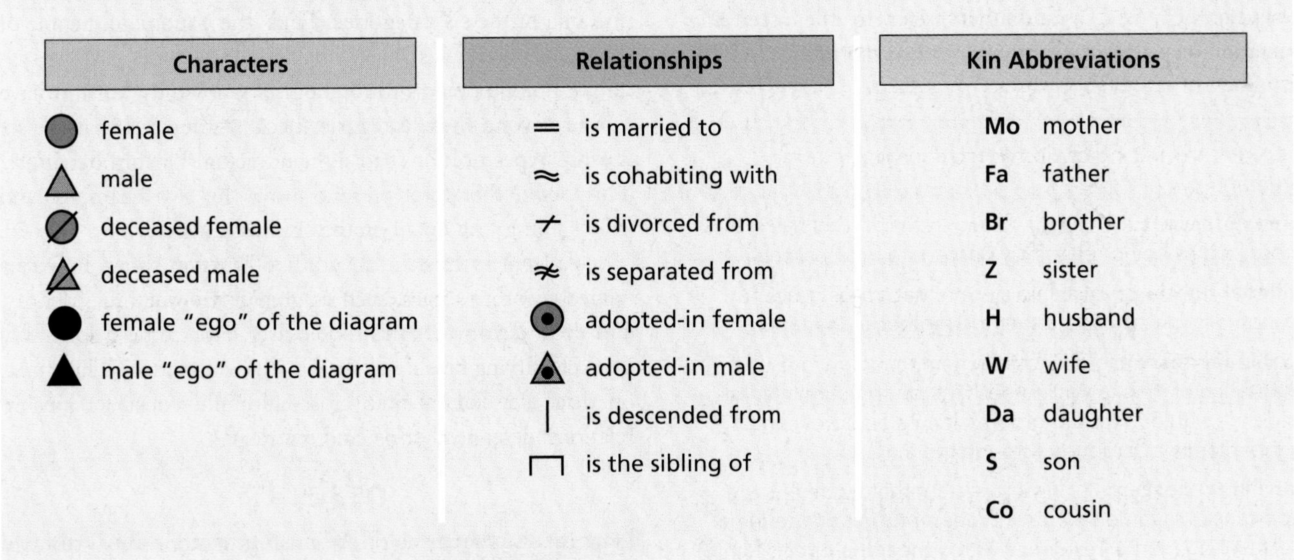

FIGURE 8.2 Symbols Used in Kinship Diagrams

Eskimo Kinship Terms

Uncle Aunt Mo Fa Uncle Aunt

Co Co Co Co Z Br Co Co Co Co

Eskimo kinship terminology, like that of most Euro-Americans, has unique terms for kin within the nuclear family that are not used for any other relatives: mother, father, sister, brother. This fact is related to the importance of the nuclear family. Another feature is that the same terms are used for relatives on both the mother's side and the father's side, a property that is related to bilineal descent.

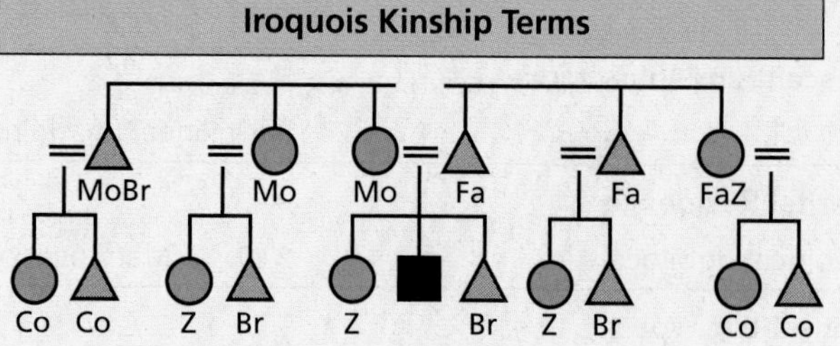

Iroquois kinship terminology operates in unilineal systems. One result is that there are different terms for relatives on the mother's and father's sides and distinctions between cross and parallel cousins. Another feature is the "merging" of one's mother with one's mother's sister (both are referred to as "mother") and of one's father with one's father's brother (both are referred to as "father").

FIGURE 8.3 Two Kinship Naming Systems

in the attempt to construct as complete a history as possible. In Europe and the United States, Christians have long followed a practice of recording their genealogy in the front of the family Bible. Many African Americans and other people are consulting DNA analysts to learn about their ancestry and cultural heritage.

Decades of anthropological research have produced a mass of information on kinship terminology, or the words people use to refer to kin. For example, in Euro-American kinship, a child of one's father's sister or brother or one's mother's sister or brother is referred to by the kinship term "cousin." Likewise, one's father's sister and one's mother's sister are both referred to as "aunt," and one's father's brother and one's mother's brother are both referred to as "uncle." "Grandmother" and "grandfather" refer to the ascending generation on either one's father's or one's mother's side. This *merging pattern* is not universal. In some cultures, different terms apply to kin on one's mother's and father's sides, so a mother's sister has a different kinship term than a father's sister. Another type of kinship system emphasizes solidarity along lines of siblings of the same gender. For example, among the Navajo of the American southwest. one's mother and one's mother's sisters have the same term, which translates as "mother."

Early anthropologists classified the cross-cultural variety in kinship terminology into six basic types, named after groups first discovered to have those systems. Two of the six types, for illustration, are the Iroquois type and the Eskimo type (see Figure 8.3). Anthropologists place various cultures with similar kinship terminology, no matter where they lived, into one of the six categories. Thus, the Yanomami people of the Amazon are classified as having an Iroquois naming system. Contemporary anthropologists who study kinship have moved beyond these categories because they feel that the six kinship types do not shed light on actual kinship dynamics. This book, therefore, presents only the two examples and avoids going into detail on the six classic types.

Current interest in the study of kinship shows how it is related to other topics, such as globalization, ethnic identity, and even terrorism. Anthropologists have come a long way from classifying kinship to showing how it matters. They focus on three key factors that, cross-culturally, construct kinship relations: descent, sharing, and marriage.

DESCENT

Descent is the tracing of kinship relationships through parentage. It is based on the fact that everybody is born from someone else. Descent creates a line of people from whom

descent the tracing of kinship relationships through parentage.

bilineal descent a kinship system in which a child is recognized as being related by descent to both parents.

unilineal descent a kinship system that traces descent through only one parent, either the mother or the father.

patrilineal descent a kinship system that highlights the importance of men in tracing descent, determining marital residence with or near the groom's family, and providing for inheritance of property through the male line.

matrilineal descent a kinship system that highlights the importance of women by tracing descent through the female line, favoring marital residence with or near the bride's family, and providing for property to be inherited through the female line.

someone is descended, stretching through history. But not all cultures reckon descent in the same way. Some cultures have a **bilineal descent** system, in which a child is recognized as being related by descent to both parents. Others have a **unilineal descent** system, which recognizes descent through only one parent, either the father or the mother. The distribution of bilineal and unilineal systems is roughly correlated with different modes of livelihood (see Figure 8.1, p. 193). This correspondence makes sense because economic systems—production, consumption, and exchange—are closely tied to the way people are socially organized.

UNILINEAL DESCENT Unilineal descent is the basis of kinship in about 60 percent of the world's cultures, making it the most common form of descent. This system tends to be found in societies with a fixed resource base. Thus, unilineal descent is most common among pastoralists, horticulturalists, and farmers. Inheritance rules that regulate the transmission of property through only one line help maintain cohesiveness of the resource base.

Unilineal descent has two major forms. One is **patrilineal descent**, in which kinship is traced through the male line. The other is **matrilineal descent**, in which kinship is traced through the female line. In a patrilineal system, only male children are considered members of the kinship lineage. Female children "marry out" and become members of the husband's lineage. In matrilineal descent systems, only daughters are considered to carry on the family line, and sons "marry out."

Patrilineal descent is found among about 45 percent of all cultures. It occurs throughout much of South Asia, East Asia, the Middle East, Papua New Guinea, northern Africa, and among some horticultural groups of sub-Saharan Africa. The world's most strongly patrilineal systems are found in East Asia, South Asia, and the Middle East (see Everyday Anthropology).

Matrilineal descent exists in about 15 percent of all cultures. It traces kinship through the female line exclusively, and the lineage consists of mothers and daughters and their daughters. It is found among many Native North American groups; across a large band of central Africa; among many groups of Southeast Asia and the Pacific, and Australia; in parts of eastern and southern India; in a small pocket of northern Bangladesh; and in parts of the Mediterranean coast of Spain and Portugal. Matrilineal societies are found among foragers and in agricultural societies. Most matrilineal cultures, however, are horticulturalist economies in which women dominate the production and distribution of food and other goods. Often, but not always, matrilineal kinship is associated with recognized public leadership positions for women, as among the Iroquois and Hopi. The Minangkabau (mee-NAN-ka-bow, with the last syllable rhyming with "now") of Indonesia are the largest matrilineal group in the world (see Culturama).

(TOP) Some members of a Bedu household in Yemen. Yemen is the most densely populated country of the Arabian peninsula. The Bedu are a small proportion of the Yemeni population. (BOTTOM) Boys playing in Hababa, Yemen. In this patrilineal culture, public space is segregated by gender.

▶ *If you were a cultural anthropologist working in Yemen, how would you proceed to learn about how Yemeni girls spend their time?*

BILINEAL DESCENT Bilineal descent traces kinship from both parents equally to the child. Bilineal descent is found in about one-third of the world's cultures (Murdock 1965 [1949]:57). The highest frequency of bilineal descent is found at the opposite ends of the modes of livelihood diagram (see Figure 8.1, p. 193). For example, Ju/'hoansi foragers have bilineal descent as do most urban professionals in North America.

Both foraging and industrialism/informatics cultures rely on a flexible gender division of labor in which both males and females contribute, more or less equally, to making a living. Bilineal descent makes sense for foraging and industrial/informatics groups because it fits with small family units that are spatially mobile.

Marital residence rules tend to follow the prevailing direction of descent rules (see Figure 8.1, p. 193). *Patrilocality,*

everyday ANTHROPOLOGY

What's in a Name?

Naming children is always significant. Parents may follow cultural rules that a first-born son receives the name of his father's father or a first-born daughter receives the name of her mother's mother. Some parents believe that a newborn should not be formally named for a year or two, and the child is instead referred to by a nickname. Others think that a name must convey some special hoped-for attribute for the child, or that a name should be unique.

The village of Ha Tsuen is located in the northwest corner of a rural area of Hong Kong (Watson 1986). About 2500 people live in the village. All the males belong to the same patrilineage and all have the same surname of Teng. They are descended from a common male ancestor who settled in the region in the twelfth century. Daughters of Ha Tsuen marry into families outside the village, and marital residence is patrilocal.

Women do not own property, and they have no control of the household economy. Few married women are employed in wage labor. They depend on their husbands for financial support. Local politics is male-dominated, as is all public decision making. A woman's status as a new bride is low, and the transition from daughter to bride can be difficult psychologically. Women's primary role is in reproduction, especially of sons. As a woman bears children, especially sons, her status in the household rises.

The local naming system reflects the power, importance, and autonomy of males. All children are first given a name referred to as their *ming* when they are a few days old. If the baby is a boy, the 30-day ceremony is as elaborate as the family can afford. It may include a banquet for many neighbors and the village elders and the presentation of red eggs to everyone in the community. For a girl, the 30-day ceremony may involve only a special meal for close family members. Paralleling this expenditure bias toward sons is the thinking that goes into selecting the *ming*. A boy's ming is distinctive and flattering. It may have a classical literary connection. A girl's ming often has negative connotations, such as "Last Child," "Too Many," or "Little Mistake." One common ming for a daughter is "Joined to a Brother," which implies the hope that she will be a lucky charm, bringing the birth of a son next. Sometimes, though, people give an uncomplimentary name to a boy such as "Little Slave Girl." The reason behind this naming practice is protection—to trick the spirits into thinking the baby is only a worthless girl so that the spirits will do no harm.

Marriage is the next formal naming occasion. When a male marries, he is given or chooses for himself a *tzu*, or marriage name. Gaining a tzu is a key marker of male adulthood. The tzu is not used in everyday address, but appears mainly on formal documents. A man also has a *wai hao*, "outside name," which is his public nickname. As he enters middle age, he may take a *hao*, or courtesy name, which he chooses and which reflects his aspirations and self-perceptions.

---

or marital residence with or near the husband's family, occurs in patrilineal societies, whereas *matrilocality* or marital residence with or near the wife's family, occurs in matrilineal societies. *Neolocality,* or marital residence in a place different from either the bride's or groom's family, is common in Western industrialized society. Residence patterns have political, economic, and social implications. Patrilineal descent and patrilocal residence, for example, promote the development of cohesive male-focused lineages associated with warfare.

SHARING

Many cultures emphasize kinship ties based on acts of sharing and support. These relationships may be either informal or formally certified. Godparenthood and blood brotherhood are examples of sharing-based kinship that are ritually formalized.

KINSHIP THROUGH FOOD SHARING Sharing-based kinship is common in Southeast Asia, Papua New Guinea, and Australia (Carsten 1995). Among inhabitants of one of Malaysia's many small islands, sharing-based kinship starts in the womb when the mother's blood feeds the fetus. After birth, the mother's breast milk nourishes the infant. This tie is crucial. A child who is not breastfed will not "recognize" its mother. Breastfeeding is also the basis of the incest rule. People who have been fed from the same breast are kin and may not marry. After the baby is weaned, its most important food is cooked rice. Sharing cooked rice, like breast milk, becomes another way that kinship ties are created and maintained, especially between women and children. Men are often away on fishing trips, in coffee shops, or at the mosque and so are not likely to have rice-sharing kinship bonds with children.

ADOPTION AND FOSTERING Another form of sharing-based kinship is the transfer of a child or children from the birth parent(s) to the care of someone else. Adoption is a formal and permanent form of child transfer. Common motivations for adoption include infertility and the desire to

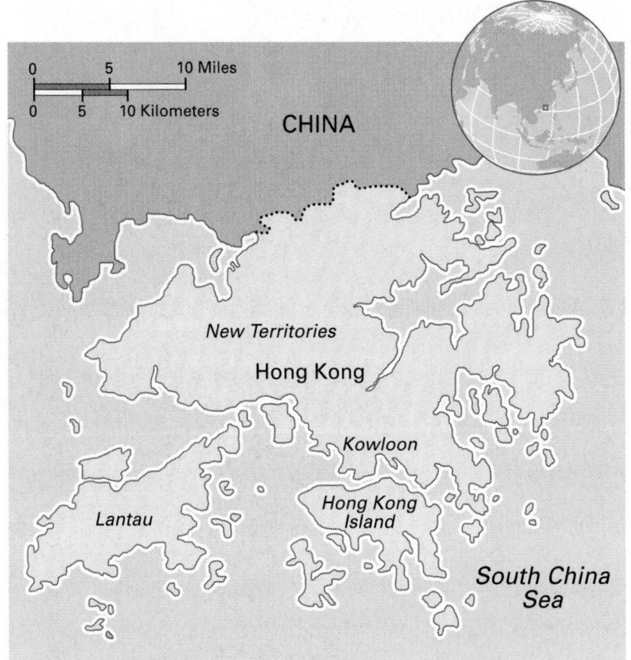

MAP 8.2 Hong Kong.
The formal name of Hong Kong is the Hong Kong Special Administrative Region of the People's Republic of China. A world center of finance and trade, it lacks natural resources and agricultural land, so it imports most of its food and raw materials. With 7 million residents, Hong Kong's population density is high. Most of the population is ethnic Chinese, and many practice ancestor worship. Ten percent of the population is Christian. Religious freedom is protected through its constitution.

In the case of a woman, her ming ceases to exist when she marries. She no longer has a name. Instead, her husband refers to her as *nei jen*, "inner person," because now her life is restricted to the domestic world of household, husband's family, and neighborhood. People may also refer to her by *teknonyms*, or names for someone based on their relationship to someone else, such as "Wife of So and So" or "Mother of So and So." In old age, she becomes *ah po*, "Old Woman".

Throughout their lives, men accumulate more and better names than women. They choose many of the names themselves. Over the course of their lives, women have fewer names than men. Women's names are standardized, not personalized, and women never get to choose any of their names.

◆ **FOOD FOR THOUGHT**

- Go to www.slate.com/id/2116505/ (Trading Up: Where Do Baby Names Come From? by Steven D. Levitt and Stephen J. Dubner) and read about the status game of child naming in the United States. How does your first name fit into this picture?

obtain a particular kind of child (often a son). Motivations for the birth parent to transfer a child to someone else include a premarital pregnancy in a disapproving context, having "too many" children, and having "too many" of a particular gender. Among the Maasai, a woman who has several children might give one to a friend, neighbor, or aged person who has no children to care for her or him (review Culturama, Chapter 6, p. 140).

Since the mid-1800s, adoption has been a legalized form of child transfer in the United States. Judith Modell, cultural anthropologist and adoptive parent, studied people's experiences of adoptees, birth parents, and adoptive parents in the United States (1994). She found that the legal process of adoption constructs the adoptive relationship to be as much like a biological one as possible. In *closed adoption*, the adopted child receives a new birth certificate, and the birth parent ceases to have any relationship to the child. A recent trend is toward *open adoption*, in which adoptees and birth parents have information about each other's identity and are free to interact with one another. Of the 28 adoptees Modell interviewed, most were interested in searching for their birth parents. The search for birth parents involves an attempt to discover "who I really am." For others, such a search is backward-looking instead of being a path toward identity formation. Thus, in the United States, adoption legalizes sharing-based kinship but does not always replace a sense of descent-based kinship for everyone involved.

Fostering a child is sometimes similar to a formal adoption in terms of permanence and a sense of kinship. Or it may be temporary placement of a child with someone else for a specific purpose, with little or no sense of kinship. Child fostering is common throughout sub-Saharan Africa. Parents foster out children to enhance the child's chances for formal education or so that the child will learn a skill such as marketing. Most foster children go from rural to urban areas and from poorer to better-off households. Fieldwork conducted in a neighborhood in Accra, Ghana (see Map 8.4), sheds light on the lives of foster children (Sanjek 1990). Child fostering in the neighborhood is common: About one-fourth of the children were foster children. Twice as many of the foster

CULTURAMA

The Minangkabau of Indonesia

The Minangkabau are the world's largest matrilineal culture, numbering between 4 and 5 million people (Sanday 2002). Most live in West Sumatra, Indonesia, and about 500,000 live in Malaysia. The Minangkabau are primarily farmers, producing substantial amounts of surplus rice. Many Minangkabau, both women and men, take up employment in Indonesian cities for a time and then return home.

In this strongly matrilineal kinship system, Minangkabau women hold power through their control of lineage land, its products, and agricultural employment on their land (Sanday 2002). Many have prominent positions in business, especially having to do with rice. Men are more likely to become scholars, merchants, and politicians. Inheritance of property, including farmland and the family house, passes from mothers to daughters.

Members of each submatrilineage, constituting several generations, live together in a lineage house or several nearby houses. Often, men and older boys live in a separate structure, such as the village mosque. In the household, the senior woman controls the power, and she makes decisions in all economic and ceremonial matters. The senior male of the sublineage has the role of representing its interests to other groups, but he is only a representative, not a powerful person in his own right.

Water buffaloes are important in both the Minangkabau rice economy and symbolically. The roofline of a traditional house has upward curves that echo the shape of water buffalo horns. Minangkabau women's festive headdress has the same shape. The Minangkabau are mostly Muslims, but they mix their Muslim faith with elements of earlier traditions and Hinduism. They have longstanding traditions of music, martial arts, weaving, wood carving, and making fine filigree jewelry of silver and gold.

Many of the traditional wooden houses and palaces in Western Sumatra are falling into a state of disrepair (Vellinga 2004). The matrilineal pattern of only women living in the house is changing, and men and women are more likely to live together in nuclear households.

Thanks to Michael G. Peletz, Emory University, for reviewing this material.

(LEFT) A traditional wooden Minangkabau longhouse with its distinctive upward-pointing roof. The house interiors are divided into separate "bays" for submatrilineal groups. Many are no longer places of residence but are used as meeting halls or are falling into ruin.
(CENTER) The symbolic importance of water buffaloes, apparent in the shape of traditional rooftops, is reiterated in the shape of girls' and women's ceremonial headdress. The headdress represents women's responsibilities for the growth and strength of Minangkabau culture.

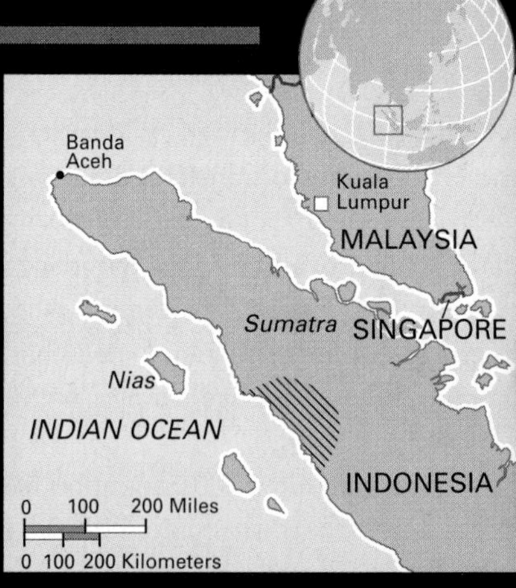

MAP 8.3 Minangkabau Region in Indonesia. The shaded area shows the traditional heartland of Minangkabau culture in western Sumatra. Many Minangkabau people live elsewhere in Sumatra and in neighboring Malaysia.

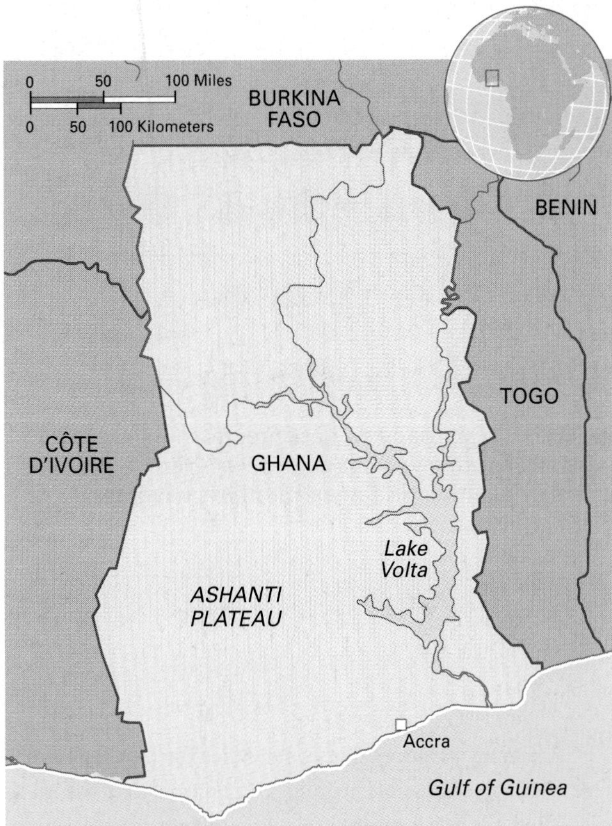

MAP 8.4 **Ghana.**

The Republic of Ghana has over 20 million people. Ghana has rich natural resources and exports gold, timber, and cocoa. Agriculture is the basis of the domestic economy. Several ethnic groups exist, with the Akan people constituting over 40 percent of the population. English is the official language, but another 80 or so languages are also spoken. Over 60 percent of the people are Christian, 20 percent follow traditional religions, and 16 percent are Muslim.

children were girls as boys. School attendance is biased toward boys. All of the boys were attending school, but only 4 of the 31 girls were. An important factor affecting the treatment of the child is whether the fostered child is related to his or her sponsor. Although 80 percent of the foster children as a whole were kin of their sponsors, only 50 percent of the girls were kin. People who sponsor nonkin girls make a cash payment to the girl's parents. These girls cook, do housecleaning, and assist in market work by carrying goods or watching the trading area. Fostered boys, most of whom are kin of their sponsors, do not perform such tasks because they attend school.

RITUALLY ESTABLISHED KINSHIP Ritually defined ties between adults and children born to other people are common among Christians, especially Catholics, worldwide. Relationships between godparents and godchildren often involve strong emotional ties and financial flows from the former to the latter. In Arembepe, a village in Bahia state in northeastern Brazil, children request a blessing from their godparents the first time they see them each day (Kottak 1992:61). Godparents give their godchildren cookies, candy, and money, and larger presents on special occasions.

Among the Maya of Oaxaca, Mexico (see Map 6.3, p. 144), godparenthood is both a sign of the sponsor's status and the means to increased status for the sponsor (Sault 1985). A parent's request that someone sponsor his or her child is a public acknowledgment of the sponsor's standing. The godparent gains influence over the godchild and can call on the godchild for labor. Being a godparent of many children means that the godparent can amass a large labor force when needed and gain further status. Most godparents in Oaxaca are husband–wife couples, but many are women alone, a pattern that reflects the high status of Maya women.

MARRIAGE

The third major basis for forming close interpersonal relationships is through marriage or other forms of "marriage-like" relationships, such as long-term cohabitation. The following material focuses on marriage.

TOWARD A DEFINITION Anthropologists recognize that some concept of *marriage* exists in all cultures, though it may take different forms and serve different functions. What constitutes a cross-culturally valid definition of marriage is, however, open to debate. A standard definition from 1951 is now discredited: "Marriage is a union between a man and a woman such that children born to the woman are the recognized legitimate offspring of both parents" (Barnard and Good 1984:89). This definition says that the partners must be of different genders, and it implies that a child born outside a marriage is not socially recognized as legitimate. Exceptions exist to both these features cross-culturally. Same-gender marriages are legal in Denmark, Norway, and Holland. The legal status of same-gender marriage is a subject of ongoing debate in the United States and Canada. In the United States, as of 2008, the states of Massachusetts and California recognize same-sex marriage.

Jillian Armenante (LEFT), actress on *Judging Amy*, and her bride, Alice Dodd, call friends and family after their marriage ceremony in City Hall, San Francisco, in 2004.

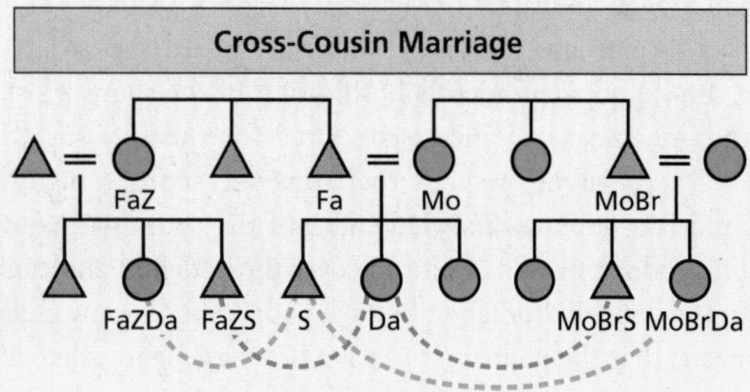
Cross-Cousin Marriage
FaZ
Fa
Mo
MoBr
FaZDa
FaZS
S
Da
MoBrS
MoBrDa
Cross-cousin marriage: A daughter marries either her father's sister's son or her mother's brother's son. A son marries either his father's sister's daughter or his mother's brother's daughter.

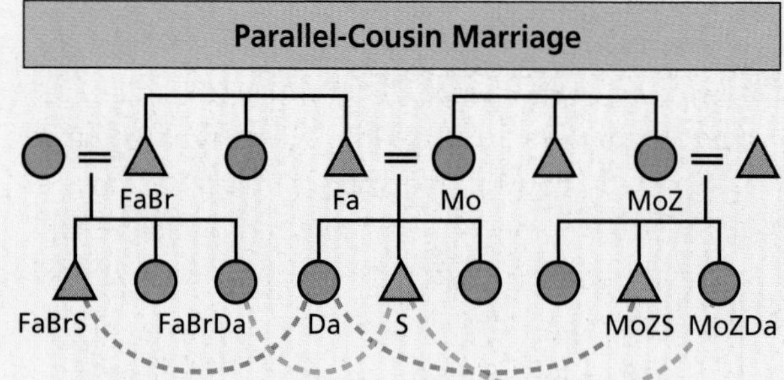
Parallel-Cousin Marriage
FaBr
Fa
Mo
MoZ
FaBrS
FaBrDa
Da
S
MoZS
MoZDa
Parallel-cousin marriage: A daughter marries either her father's brother's son or her mother's sister's son. A son marries either his father's brother's daughter or his mother's sister's daughter.

FIGURE 8.4 Two Forms of Cousin Marriage

In many cultures no distinction is made between legitimate and illegitimate children on the basis of whether they were born within a marriage. Women in the Caribbean region, for example, typically do not marry until later in life. Before that, a woman has sequential male partners with whom she bears children. None of her children is considered more or less "legitimate" than any other.

Other definitions of marriage focus on rights over the spouse's sexuality. But not all forms of marriage involve sexual relations; for example, the practice of *woman–woman marriage* exists among the Nuer of southern Sudan (see Map 16.7, p. 412) and some other African groups (Evans-Pritchard 1951:108–109). In this type of marriage, a woman with economic means gives gifts to obtain a "wife," goes through the marriage rituals with her, and brings her into the residential compound just as a man would who married a woman. This wife contributes her productive labor to the household. The two women do not have a sexual relationship. Instead, the in-married woman will have sexual relations with a man. Her children, though, will belong to the compound into which she married.

marriage a union between two people (usually), who are likely to be, but are not necessarily, coresident, sexually involved with each other, and procreative.

incest taboo a strongly held prohibition against marrying or having sex with particular kin.

endogamy marriage within a particular group or locality.

parallel cousin offspring of either one's father's brother or one's mother's sister.

cross-cousin offspring of either one's father's sister or one's mother's brother.

The many practices that come under the heading of marriage make it impossible to find a definition that will fit all cases. One might accept the following as a working definition of **marriage**: a more or less stable union, usually between two people, who may be, but are not necessarily, coresidential, sexually involved with each other, and procreative with each other.

SELECTING A SPOUSE All cultures have preferences about whom one should and should not marry or with whom one should and should not have sexual intercourse. Sometimes these preferences are informal and implicit, and other times they are formal and explicit. They include both rules of exclusion (who one should not marry) and rules of inclusion (who is a preferred marriage partner).

An **incest taboo**, or rule prohibiting marriage or sexual intercourse between certain kinship relations, is one of the most basic and universal rules of exclusion. In his writings of the 1940s, Claude Lévi-Strauss proposes a reason for the universality of incest taboos by saying that, in premodern societies, incest avoidance motivated men to exchange women between families. In his view, this exchange is the foundation for all social networks and social solidarity beyond the immediate group. Such networks promote trade between areas with different resources and peace through ties established by bride exchange. So, for him, the incest taboo has important social and economic functions: It impels people to create social organization beyond the family.

Contemporary genetic research suggests an alternate theory for universal incest taboos. It says that larger breeding pools reduce the frequency of genetically transmitted conditions. Like the theory of Lévi-Strauss, the genetic theory is functional. Each theory attributes the universal existence of incest taboos to their adaptive contribution to human survival and success, though in two different ways. Anthropological data support both theories, but ethnographic data provide some puzzles to consider.

The most basic and universal form of incest taboo is against marriage or sexual intercourse between fathers and their children, and mothers and their children. Although most cultures forbid brother–sister marriage, exceptions exist. The most well-known example of brother–sister marriage comes from Egypt at the time of the Roman Empire (Barnard and Good 1984:92). Brother–sister marriage was the norm among royalty, but it was common among the general population, with between 15 and 20 percent of marriages between full brothers and sisters.

Further variations in close-relation marriage arise in terms of cousins. Incest taboos do not universally rule out marriage with cousins. In fact, some kinship systems promote cousin marriage, as discussed next.

Many preference rules exist cross-culturally concerning whom one should marry. Rules of **endogamy**, or marriage within a particular group, stipulate that the spouse must be from a defined social category. In kin endogamy, certain relatives are preferred, often cousins. Two major forms of cousin marriage exist. One is marriage between **parallel cousins**, children of either one's father's brother or one's mother's sister—the term *parallel* indicates that the linking siblings are of the same gender (see Figure 8.4). The second is marriage between **cross-cousins**, children of either one's father's sister or one's mother's brother—the term *cross* indicates the different genders of the linking siblings. Parallel-cousin marriage is favored by many Muslim groups in the Middle East and northern Africa, especially the subform called *patrilateral parallel-cousin marriage*, which is cousin marriage into the father's line.

In contrast, Hindus of southern India favor *matrilateral cross-cousin marriage*, which is cousin marriage into the mother's line. Although cousin marriage is preferred, it nonetheless is a minority of all marriages in the region. A survey of several thousand couples in the city of Chennai (formerly called Madras) (see Map 8.5) in southern India showed that three-fourths of all marriages involved unrelated people, whereas one-fourth were between first cross-cousins or between uncle and niece, which is considered to be the same relationship as that of cross-cousins (Ramesh, Srikumari, and Sukumar 1989).

Readers who are unfamiliar with cousin marriage may find it objectionable on the basis of the potential genetic disabilities from close inbreeding. A study of thousands of such marriages in southern India, however, revealed only a small difference in rates of congenital problems compared to cultures in which cousin marriage is not practiced (Sundar Rao 1983). Marriage networks in South India are diffuse, extending over a wide area and offering many options for "cousins." This situation contrasts to the much more closed situation of a single village or town. In cases where cousin marriage exists among a small and circumscribed population, then the possibility of negative genetic effects is high.

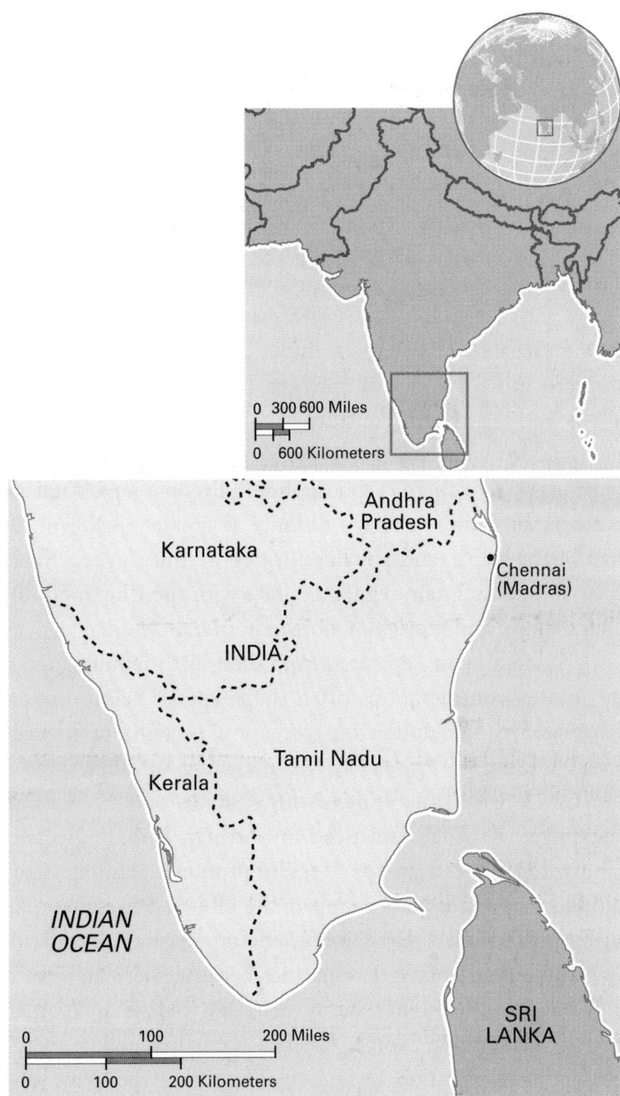

MAP 8.5 South India.
The states of southern India, compared to the northern states, have lower population density, lower fertility rates, higher literacy rates, and less severe gender inequality. Agriculture is the mainstay of the region's economy and the population is predominantly rural. Industry, information technology, and business process outsourcing (BPO) are of increasing importance in cities such as Chennai and Bangalore.

Endogamy may also be based on location. Village endogamy is preferred in the eastern Mediterranean among both Christians and Muslims. It is also the preferred pattern

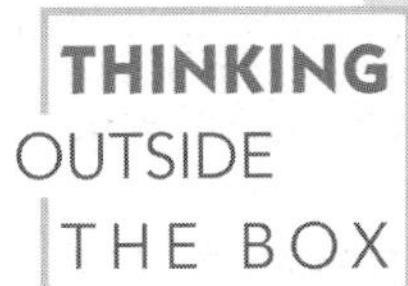

Do some research on www.match.com to learn what cultural preferences people mention in their profiles.

FIGURE 8.5 **Status Considerations in Partner Selection (Heterosexual Pairing)**

Hypergyny	The bride marries a groom of higher status.	The groom may be wealthier, more educated, older, taller.
Hypogyny	The bride marries a groom of lower status.	The bride may be wealthier, more educated, older, taller.
Isogamy	The bride and groom are status equals.	The bride and groom have similar wealth, education, age, height.

among Muslims throughout India and among Hindus of southern India. Hindus of northern India, in contrast, forbid village endogamy and consider it a form of incest. Instead, they practice village **exogamy**, or marriage outside a defined social group. For them, a spouse should live in a far-off village or town. In India, marriage distance is greater in the north than in the south, and northern brides are thus far less likely to be able to maintain regular contact with their birth family. Many songs and stories of northern Indian women convey sadness about being separated from their birth families.

Status considerations often shape spouse selection (see Figure 8.5). (The following discussion pertains to heterosexual marriage.) *Hypergyny*, or "marrying up," refers to a marriage in which the bride has lower status than the groom. Hypergyny is widely practiced in northern India, especially among upper-status groups. It is also prominent among many middle- and upper-class people in the United States. Women in top professions such as medicine and law have a difficult time finding an appropriate partner because there are few, if any, options for higher-status marriage partners. Women medical students in North America are experiencing an increased marriage squeeze because of status hypergyny. The opposite pattern is *hypogyny*, or "marrying down," a marriage in which the bride has higher status than the groom. Hypogyny is rare cross-culturally. *Isogamy*, marriage between partners who are status equals, occurs in cultures where male and female roles and status are equal.

Subtypes of status-based hypergyny and hypogyny occur on the basis of factors such as age and even height. Age hypergyny refers to a marriage in which the bride is younger than the groom, a common practice worldwide. In contrast, age hypogyny is a marriage in which the bride is older than the groom. Age hypogyny is rare cross-culturally but has been increasing in the United States due to the marriage squeeze on women who would otherwise prefer a husband of equal age or somewhat older.

Physical features, such as ability, looks, and appearance, are factors that may be explicitly or implicitly involved in spouse selection. Facial beauty, skin color, hair texture and length, height, and weight are variously defined as important. Height hypergyny (in which the groom is taller than the bride) is more common in male-dominated contexts. Height-isogamous marriages are common in cultures where gender roles are relatively equal and where sexual dimorphism (differences in shape and size of the female body compared to the male body) is not marked, as in much of Southeast Asia.

People with physical disabilities, particularly women, face constraints in marrying nondisabled partners (Sentumbwe 1995). Nayinda Sentumbwe, a blind researcher, conducted fieldwork with participants in education and rehabilitation programs for blind people in Uganda, central Africa. He realized that all of the married blind women in his study had blind spouses. Many of the married blind men had wives who were not blind. In exploring the reason for this pattern, Sentumbwe considered Ugandan gender roles, especially that of the housewife. People said that blindness decreases women's competence as wives and mothers and therefore reduces their desirability as spouses. Ugandan housewives have many roles: mother, hostess, housekeeper, keeper of the homestead, provider of meals, and provider of home-grown food, among others. Because a man wants a "competent" wife, blind women as partners are avoided. Ugandan men, however, often choose blind women as lovers. The relationship between lovers is private and does not involve social competence in the woman.

Men and women in Southeast Asia are similar in height and weight, as is the case with this couple from Bali, Indonesia.

▶ *What are your cultural perceptions of the height of an ideal partner for you?*

exogamy marriage outside a particular group or locality.

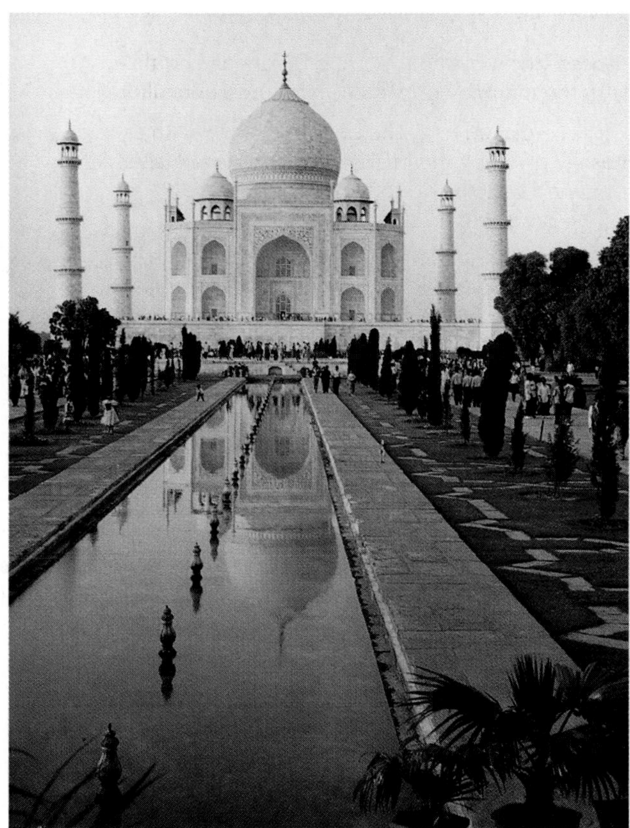

The Taj Mahal, located in Agra, northern India, is a seventeenth-century monument to love. It was built by the Mughal emperor Shah Jahan as a tomb for his wife, Mumtaz Mahal, who died in childbirth in 1631.

The role of romantic love in spouse selection is debated by biological determinists and cultural constructionists. Biological determinists argue that feelings of romantic love are universal among all humans because they play an adaptive role in uniting males and females in care of offspring. Cultural constructionists, in contrast, argue that romantic love is an unusual factor influencing spouse selection (Barnard and Good 1984:94). The cultural constructionists point to variations in male and female economic roles to explain cross-cultural differences in the emphasis on romantic love. Romantic love is more likely to be an important factor in relationships in cultures where men contribute more to subsistence and where women are therefore economically dependent on men. Whatever the cause of romantic love, biological or cultural or both, it is an increasingly common basis for marriage in many cultures (Levine et al. 1995).

Within the United States, microcultural variations exist in the degree to which women value romantic love as a basis for marriage (Holland and Eisenhart 1990). One study interviewed young American women entering college from 1979 to 1981 and again in 1987 after they had graduated and begun their adult lives. The research sites were two southern colleges in the United States, one attended mainly by White Euro-Americans and the other by African Americans. A contrast between the groups of women emerged. The White women were much more influenced by notions of romantic love than the Black women. The White women were also less likely to have strong career goals and more likely to expect to be economically dependent on their spouse. The Black women expressed independence and strong career goals. The theme of romantic love supplies young White women with a model of the heroic male provider as the ideal, with her role being one of attracting him and providing the domestic context for their married life. The Black women were brought up to be more economically independent. This pattern is related to African traditions in which women earn and manage their own earnings and the racially discriminatory job market in the United States that places African American men at a severe disadvantage.

Arranged marriages are formed on the basis of parents' considerations of what constitutes a "good match" between the families of the bride and groom. Arranged marriages are common in many Middle Eastern, African, and Asian countries. Some theorists claim that arranged marriages are "traditional" and love marriages are "modern." They believe arranged marriages will disappear with modernity. Japan presents a case of an industrial/informatics economy with a highly educated population in which arranged unions still constitute a substantial proportion of all marriages, about 25 to 30 percent (Applbaum 1995). In earlier times, marriage partners would be found through personal networks, perhaps with the help of an intermediary who knew both families. Now, in large cities such as Tokyo and Osaka, professional matchmakers play an important role in finding marriage partners. The most important criteria for a spouse are the family's reputation and social standing, the absence of undesirable traits such as a case of divorce or mental illness in the family, education, occupation, and income.

The new billionaires of China (multimillionaires in terms of dollars) are men with wealth and interest in marrying a virgin woman (French 2006). They have turned to advertising to seek applications from prospective brides. In Shanghai, an enterprising lawyer began a business by managing the advertising and applicant screening for over 50 billionaires. On average, the process takes three months.

MARRIAGE GIFTS Most marriages are accompanied by exchanges of goods or services between the partners, members of their families, and friends (see Figure 8.6). The two major forms of marital exchanges cross-culturally are dowry and brideprice.

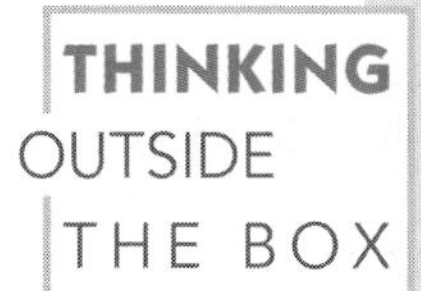

What is your opinion about the relative merits of love marriages versus arranged marriages, and on what do you base your opinion?

FIGURE 8.6 Major Types of Marriage Exchanges

Dowry	Goods and money given by the bride's family to the married couple	European and Asian cultures; agriculturalists and industrialists
Groomprice	Goods and money given by the bride's family to the married couple and to the parents of the groom	South Asia, especially northern India
Brideprice	Goods and money given by the groom's family to the parents of the bride	Asian, African, and Central and South American cultures; horticulturalists and pastoralists
Bride service	Labor given by the groom to the parents of the bride	Southeast Asian, Pacific, and Amazonian cultures; horticulturalists

Dowry, as defined in Chapter 6, is the transfer of goods, and sometimes money, from the bride's side to the new married couple for their use. The dowry includes household goods such as furniture, cooking utensils, and sometimes rights to a house. Dowry is the main form of marriage transfer in farming societies throughout Eurasia, from Western Europe through the northern Mediterranean and into China and India. In much of India, dowry is more accurately termed *groomprice* because the goods and money pass not to the new couple but rather to the groom's family (Billig 1992). In China during the Mao era, the government considered dowry a sign of women's oppression and made it illegal. The practice of giving dowry in China has returned with increased personal wealth and consumerism, especially among the newly rich urban populations (Whyte 1993).

Brideprice, or bridewealth, is the transfer of goods or money from the groom's side to the bride's parents. It is common in horticultural and pastoralist cultures. **Brideservice,** a subtype of brideprice, is a transfer of labor from the groom to his parents-in-law for a designated time period. It is practiced in some horticultural societies, especially in the Amazon.

brideservice a form of marriage exchange in which the groom works for his father-in-law for a certain period of time before returning home with the bride.

monogamy marriage between two people.

polygamy marriage involving multiple spouses.

polygyny marriage of one husband with more than one wife.

polyandry marriage of one wife with more than one husband.

family a group of people who consider themselves related through a form of kinship, such as descent, marriage, or sharing.

household a group of people, who may or may not be related by kinship, who share living space.

nuclear household a domestic unit containing one adult couple (married or partners), with or without children.

extended household a coresidential group that comprises more than one parent–child unit.

The Hausa are an important ethnic group of Ghana. This photograph shows a display of Hausa dowry goods in Accra, the capital city. The most valuable part of a Hausa bride's dowry is the *kayan dak'i* ("things of the room"). It consists of bowls, pots, ornamental glass, and cookware, which are conspicuously displayed in the bride's marital house so that the local women can get a sense of her worth. The bride's parents pay for these status items and for utilitarian items such as everyday cooking utensils.

Many marriages involve gifts from both the bride's and the groom's side. For example, a typical pattern in the United States is that the groom's side is responsible for paying for the rehearsal dinner the night before the wedding, whereas the bride's side bears the costs of everything else.

FORMS OF MARRIAGE Cultural anthropologists distinguish two forms of marriage on the basis of the number of partners involved. **Monogamy** is marriage between two people—a male or female if the pair is heterosexual, or two people of the same gender in the case of a homosexual pair. Heterosexual monogamy is the most common form of marriage cross-culturally, and in many countries it is the only legal form of marriage.

Polygamy is marriage involving multiple spouses, a pattern allowed in many cultures. Two forms of polygamous marriage exist. The more common of the two is **polygyny**, marriage of one man with more than one woman. **Polyandry**, or marriage between one woman and more than one man, is rare. The only place where polyandry is commonly found is in the Himalayan region that includes parts of Tibet, India, and Nepal. Nonpolyandrous people in the area look down on the people who practice polyandrous marriage as backward (Haddix McCay 2001).

The woman on the lower right is part of a polyandrous marriage, which is still practiced among some Tibetan peoples. She is married to several brothers, two of whom stand behind her. The older man with the sash in the front row is her father-in-law.

◆◆◆

Households and Domestic Life

In casual conversation, North Americans might use the words *family* and *household* interchangeably to refer to people who live together. Social scientists, however, propose a distinction between the two terms. A **family** is a group of people who consider themselves related through kinship. In North American English, the term includes both close or immediate relatives and more distant relatives. All members of a family do not necessarily live together or have strong bonds with one another.

A related term is the **household**, a person or persons who occupy a shared living space and who may or may not be related by kinship. Most households consist of members who are related through kinship, but an increasing number do not. An example of a nonkin household is a group of friends who live in the same apartment. A single person living alone also constitutes a household. This section of the chapter looks at household forms and organization cross-culturally and relationships between and among household members.

THE HOUSEHOLD: VARIATIONS ON A THEME

This section considers three forms of households and the concept of household headship. The topic of female-headed households receives detailed attention because this pattern of headship is widely misunderstood.

HOUSEHOLD FORMS Household organization is divided into types according to how many married adults are involved. The **nuclear household** (which many people call the nuclear family) is a domestic group that contains one adult couple (married or "partners"), with or without children. An **extended household** is a domestic group that contains more than one adult married couple. The couples may be related through the father–son line (making a *patrilineal extended household*), through the mother–daughter line (a *matrilineal extended household*), or through sisters or brothers (a *collateral extended household*). Polygynous (multiple wives) and polyandrous (multiple husbands) households are *complex households*, domestic units in which one spouse lives with or near multiple partners and their children.

The precise cross-cultural distribution of these various types is not known, but some broad generalizations can be offered. First, nuclear households are found in all cultures but are the exclusive household type in only about one-fourth of the world's cultures (Murdock 1965 [1949]:2). Extended households are the most important form in about half of all cultures. The distribution of these two household forms corresponds roughly with the modes of livelihood (see Figure 8.1, p. 193). The nuclear form is most characteristic of economies at the two extremes of the continuum: foraging groups and industrialized/informatic societies. This pattern reflects the need for spatial mobility and flexibility in both

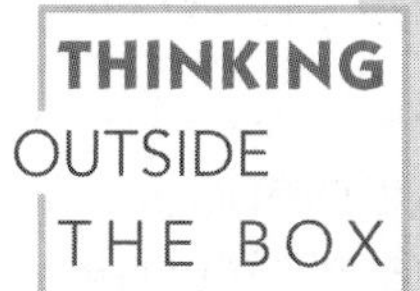

In your microculture, what are the prevailing ideas about wedding expenses and who should pay for them?

In China, the stem household system is changing because many people have one daughter and no son as a result of lowered fertility and the One-Child-Per-Family Policy.

▶ *Speculate about what the next generation of this household might contain.*

modes of production. Extended households constitute a substantial proportion of households in horticultural, pastoralist, and farming economies.

In Japan and other parts of East Asia, a subtype of the extended household structure has endured within the context of an industrial/postindustrial and urban economy. The *ie*, or **stem household**, is a variation of an extended household containing two (and only two) married couples related through the male line. Only one son remains in the household, bringing in his wife, who is expected to perform the important role of caretaker for the husband's parents as they age. Although people throughout East Asia still prefer the ie, it is increasingly difficult to achieve due to changing economic aspirations of children, who do not want to dedicate their lives to caring for their aging parents. Aging parents who find that none of their children is willing to live with them and take responsibility for their care exert considerable pressure on an adult child to come and live with them (Traphagan 2000). A compromise is for an adult child and his or her spouse to live near the parents but not with them.

HOUSEHOLD HEADSHIP The question of who heads a household is often difficult to answer. This section reviews some approaches to this question and provides insights into how cross-cultural perceptions about household headship differ.

The *household head* is the primary person, or persons, responsible for supporting the household financially and making major decisions. This concept of household head is based on a Euro-American view that emphasizes the income contribution of the head, traditionally a man. European colonialism spread the concept of the male, income-earning head of household around the world, along with laws that placed household authority in male headship.

The model of a male household head influences the way official statistics are gathered worldwide. If a household has a coresident man and woman, there is a tendency to report the household as male headed. In Brazil, for example, the official definition of household head considers only a husband to be head of the household, regardless of whether he contributes to the household budget. Single, separated, or widowed women who are responsible for household support are deprived of the title of household head. If they happen to have a man visiting them on the day the census official arrives, he is considered to be the household head (de Athayde Figueiredo and Prado 1989:41). Similarly, according to official reports, 90 percent of households in the Philippines are headed by males (Illo 1985). Filipino women, however, play a prominent role in income generation and budgetary control, and both partners share major decision making. Thus co-headship would be a more appropriate label for many households in the Philippines and elsewhere.

Matrifocality refers to a household pattern in which a woman (or women) is the central, stable domestic figure around whom other members cluster (González 1970). In a matrifocal household, the mother is likely to be the primary or only income provider. The concept of matrifocality does not exclude the possibility that men may be part of the household, but they are not the central income providers or decision makers.

The number of woman-headed households is increasing worldwide, and these households tend to be poorer than other households. In general, a woman-headed household can come

This matrifocal household in rural Jamaica includes two sisters and their children.

stem household a coresidential group that comprises only two married couples related through males, commonly found in East Asian cultures.

matrifocality a household pattern in which a female (or females) is the central, stable figure around whom other members cluster.

about if a partner never existed, if a partner existed at one time, but for some reason—such as separation, divorce, or death—is no longer part of the household, or if a partner exists but is not a coresident because of migration, imprisonment, or some other form of separation.

In terms of the healthy functioning of households, it is not simply the gender of the household head that is critical. What matters are the resources to which the head has access, both material and social, such as property ownership, a decent job, kinship and other supportive social ties, and living in a safe neighborhood.

INTRAHOUSEHOLD DYNAMICS

How do household members interact with each other? What are their emotional attachments, rights, and responsibilities? What are the power relationships between and among members of various categories, such as spouses, siblings, and those of different generations? Kinship systems define what the content of these relationships should be. In everyday life, people may conform more or less to the ideal.

SPOUSE/PARTNER RELATIONSHIPS This section discusses three areas of spousal relationships: marital satisfaction, sexual activity over the life course, and satisfaction within marriage and the "too good" wife in Japan.

A landmark study of marriages in Tokyo in 1959 compared marital satisfaction of husbands and wives in love marriages and arranged marriages (Blood 1967). In all marriages, marital satisfaction declined over time, but differences between the two types emerged. The decline was greatest for wives in arranged marriages and least for husbands in arranged marriages. In love-match marriages, both partners' satisfaction dropped dramatically (a bit earlier for wives and a bit later for husbands), but both husbands and wives reported nearly equal levels of satisfaction after they had been married nine years or more.

Sexual activity of couples can be both an indication of marital satisfaction and a cause of marital satisfaction. Analysis of reports of marital sex from a 1988 survey in the United States shows that frequency per month steadily declines with the duration of marriage, from an average of twelve times per month for people ages 19 to 24 years, to less than once a month for people 75 years of age and older (Call, Sprecher, and Schwartz 1995). Older married people have sex less frequently. Less happy people have sex less frequently. Within each age category, sex is more frequent among three categories of people:

- Those who are cohabiting but not married
- Those who cohabited before marriage
- Those who are in their second or later marriage

In seeking to learn whether such decline is more widespread, an anthropologist and a statistician joined forces to analyze data from a survey conducted with over 90,000 women in 19 developing countries (Brewis and Meyer 2004). One of the survey questions was "When was the last time you had sexual intercourse [with a spouse]?" The *honeymoon effect* (having more frequent sex in the first year of marriage) is significant in only five countries: Brazil, Benin, Ethiopia, Mali, and Kazakhstan. Significant reductions in frequency after the first year of marriage occur in all countries but one: Burkina Faso in West Africa. What is going on here? One factor is that Burkina Faso couples have a significantly lower frequency of reported marital sex during the first year of marriage; in other words, couples do not go through a honeymoon phase of frequent sexual intercourse, and so activity in following years is not that much lower. These intriguing results at the country level need to be followed up by research on local cultural practices and patterns.

Cultures everywhere also define the proper role of a wife or husband. In Japan, a "good wife" should care for her husband's needs and make sure that any problems in the household do not erupt into the public domain (Borovoy 2005). Many Japanese salarymen (corporate workers) consume substantial amounts of alcohol after work. They return home late and drunk. It is the duty of the "good wife" to provide dinner for her husband and get him to go to bed, so he can make it to work the next day. The wives face a profound cultural dilemma: If they continue to perform well the role of the "good wife," they are "codependent" in the husband's alcohol abuse, and contribute to the continuance of the problem. Many middle-class Japanese wives are joining support groups to help them deal with their situation by building new roles for themselves beyond that of the "good wife."

SIBLING RELATIONSHIPS Sibling relationships are an understudied aspect of intrahousehold dynamics. One example comes from research in a working-class neighborhood of Beirut, Lebanon (Joseph 1994). The anthropologist became friendly with several families and was especially close to Hanna, the oldest son in one of them. Hanna was an attractive

Japanese salarymen singing karaoke.

young man, considered a good marriage choice, with friends across religious and ethnic groups. Therefore, the author reports her shock when she once heard Hanna shouting at his 12-year-old sister Flaur and slapping her across the face. Further observation of the relationship between Hanna and Flaur suggested that Hanna was playing a fatherly role to Flaur. He was especially irritated with her if she lingered on the street near their apartment building, gossiping with other girls: "He would forcibly escort her upstairs to their apartment, slap her, and demand that she behave with dignity" (1994:51). Adults in the household thought nothing was wrong. They said that Flaur enjoyed her brother's aggressive attention. Flaur herself commented, "It doesn't even hurt when Hanna hits me." She said that she hoped to have a husband like Hanna.

An interpretation of this kind of brother–sister relationship, common in Arab culture, is that it is part of a socialization process that maintains and perpetuates male domination in the household: "Hanna was teaching Flaur to accept male power in the name of love . . . loving his sister meant taking charge of her and that he could discipline her if his action was understood to be in her interest. Flaur was reinforced in learning that the love of a man could include that male's violent control and that to receive his love involved submission to control" (1994:52).

DOMESTIC VIOLENCE BETWEEN PARTNERS Violence between domestic partners, with males dominating as perpetrators and women as victims, is found in nearly all cultures, although in varying forms and frequencies (Brown 1999). Wife beating is more common and more severe in contexts where men control the wealth. It is less common and less severe where women's work groups and social networks exist (Levinson 1989). The presence of women's work groups is related to a greater importance of women in production and matrifocal residence. These factors provide women with the means to leave an abusive relationship. For example, among the Garifuna, an African-Indian people of Belize, Central America (see Map 7.3, p. 169), incidents of spouse abuse occur, but they are infrequent and not extended (Kerns 1999). Women's solidarity in this matrifocal society limits male violence against women.

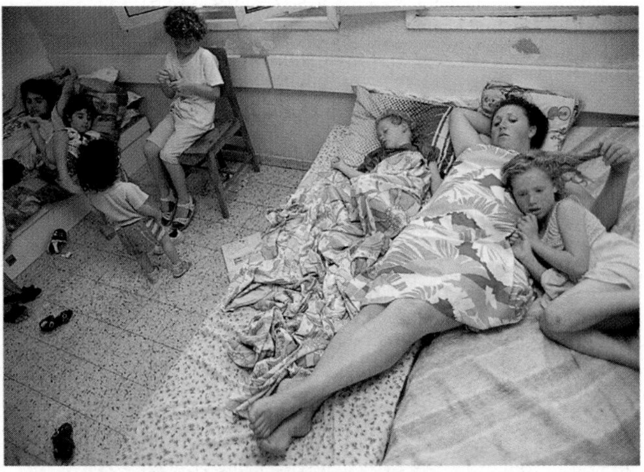

A shared bedroom in a battered woman's shelter, Tel Aviv, Israel. Many people wonder why abused women do not leave their abusers. Part of the answer lies in the unavailability and low quality of shelters throughout much of the world.

Increased domestic violence worldwide throws into question the notion of the house as a refuge or place of security. In the United States, evidence exists of high and increasing rates of intrahousehold abuse of children (including sexual abuse), violence between spouses or partners, and abuse of aged family members. Anthropological research helps policy makers and social workers better understand the factors affecting the safety of individuals within households so they are able to design more effective programs to promote personal safety (see Lessons Applied).

HOUSEHOLD TRANSFORMATIONS The composition and sheer existence of a particular household can change as a consequence of several factors, including divorce, death, and possible remarriage.

Divorce and separation, like marriage and other forms of long-term union, are cultural universals, even though they may be frowned on or forbidden. Important research questions about marital dissolution include the causes for it, the reasons why divorce rates appear to be rising worldwide, and the implications for the welfare of children of divorced parents and other dependents.

Marriages may break up for several reasons: The most common are voluntary separation and death of one of the partners. Globally, variations exist in the legality and propriety of divorce. Some religions, such as Roman Catholicism, prohibit divorce. In Muslim societies, divorce by law is easier for a husband to obtain than for a wife.

One hypothesis for why divorce rates vary cross-culturally says that divorce rates will be lower in cultures with unilineal descent. In such cultures, a large descent group has control over and interests in offspring and control over in-marrying spouses due to their dependence (Barnard and Good 1984:119). Royal lineages, with their strong interests in maintaining the family line, are examples of groups especially unlikely to favor divorce, because divorce generally means losing control of offspring. In bilineal foraging societies, there is more flexibility in both marriage and divorce.

Another question is the effect of multiple spouses on divorce. A study in Nigeria, West Africa, found that two-wife arrangements are the most stable, whereas marriages involving three or more wives have the highest rates of disruption (Gage-Brandon 1992). Similar results come from an analysis of household break-up in a polyandrous group of

LESSONS applied

Ethnography for Preventing Wife Abuse in Rural Kentucky

Domestic violence in the United States is reportedly highest in the state of Kentucky. An ethnographic study of domestic violence in Kentucky reveals several cultural factors related to the high rate of wife abuse (Websdale 1995). The study included interviews with 50 abused wives in eastern Kentucky and with battered women in shelters, police officers, shelter employees, and social workers.

Three categories of isolation exist in rural Kentucky making domestic violence particularly difficult to prevent:

1. *Physical isolation:* The women reported a feeling of physical isolation in their lives. Abusers' tactics were more effective because of geographical isolation. They include disabling motor vehicles so the wife cannot leave the residence; destroying motor vehicles; monitoring the odometer reading on motor vehicles; locking the thermostat in winter; driving recklessly to intimidate the wife; and discharging firearms, for example, at a pet (1995:106–107).

It is difficult or impossible for an abused woman to leave a home located many miles from the nearest paved road, and especially so if the woman has children. No public transportation serves even the paved road. Nearly one-third of households had no phones. Getting to a phone to report abuse results in delay and gives police the impression that the call is less serious and increases a woman's sense of hopelessness. Sheriffs have acquired a very poor reputation among battered women in the region for not attending domestic calls at all.

2. *Social isolation:* Aspects of the rural culture, including gender roles, promote a system of "passive policing." Men are seen as providers and women are tied to domestic work and child rearing. When women do work outside the home, their wages are about 50 percent of men's wages. Marital residence is often in the vicinity of the husband's family. Thus a woman is separated from the potential support of her natal family and limited in seeking help in the immediate vicinity because the husband's family is likely to be nonsupportive of her. Local police officers view the family as a private unit, and so they are not inclined to intervene in family problems. Because the home is the man's world and men are supposed to be dominant in the family, police are unwilling to arrest husbands accused of abuse. In some instances, the police take the batterer's side because they share the belief in a husband's right to control his wife.

3. *Institutional isolation:* Social services for battered women in Kentucky are scarce and especially so in rural areas. The fact that abused women often know the people who run the services ironically inhibits the women from approaching them, given the value of family privacy. Other institutional constraints include low levels of schooling, lack of child-care centers to allow mothers the option to work outside the home, inadequate health services, and religious teaching of fundamentalist Christianity that supports values such as the idea that it is a woman's duty to stay in a marriage and "weather the storm."

These findings suggest some recommendations. First, rural women need more and better employment opportunities to reduce their economic dependency on abusive partners. To address this need, rural outreach programs should be strengthened. Expanded telephone subscriptions would decrease rural women's institutional isolation. Because of the complexity of the social situation in Kentucky, however, no single solution will be sufficient.

◆ **FOOD FOR THOUGHT**

- How do conditions in Kentucky differ from or resemble those in another cultural context where wife beating is frequent.

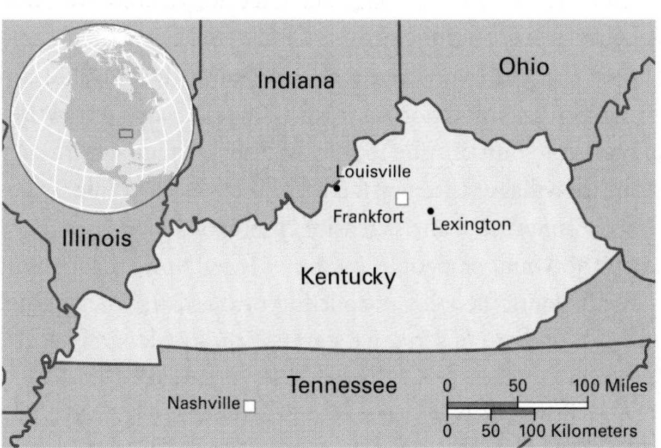

MAP 8.6 Kentucky, United States.
Located in the southeastern United States, in the wider Appalachian region, Kentucky's population is over 4 million. It has more farmers per square mile than any other state. Per capita income is 43rd in the 50 states. Before being occupied by British settlers in the late eighteenth century, Kentucky was the hunting grounds of the Shawnees and Cherokees. The current population is about 91 percent White, 7 percent Black, 0.6 percent American Indian, and 0.9 percent Asian. Kentucky is known for thoroughbred horse breeding and racing, bourbon and whiskey distilling, and bluegrass music.

Tibetan people living in northwestern Nepal (see Map 7.7, p. 181) (Haddix McCay 2001). Wealth of the household is an important factor affecting household stability, but the number of brothers is another strong factor. Polyandrous households comprising two brothers are far less likely to break up than those with four or more brothers. An additional factor, although more difficult to quantify, is the social support and networks that a brother has beyond the polyandrous household. Only with such social support will he be able to build a house and establish a separate household on his own.

The position of a widow or widower carries altered responsibilities and rights. Women's position as widows is often marked symbolically. In Mediterranean cultures, a widow must wear modest, simple, and black-colored clothing, sometimes for the rest of her life. Her sexuality is supposed to be virtually dead. At the same time, her new "asexual" status allows her greater spatial freedom than before. She can go to public coffeehouses and taverns, something not done by women whose husbands are living.

Extreme restrictions on widows are recorded for parts of South Asia where social pressures on a widow enforce self-denial and self-deprivation, especially among the propertied class. A widow should wear a plain white sari, shave her head, eat little food, and live an asexual life. Many widows in India are abandoned, especially if they have no son to support them. They are considered polluting and inauspicious. Widows elsewhere also experience symbolic and life-quality changes much more than do widowers. For example, in South Africa, a widower's body is not marked in any significant way except to have his head shaved. He is required to wear a black button or armband for about six months. A widow's body is marked by shaving her head, smearing a mixture of herbs and ground charcoal on her body, wearing black clothes made from an inexpensive material, and covering her face with a black veil and her shoulders with a black shawl. She may wear her clothes inside out, wear one shoe, eat with her left hand, or eat from a lid instead of a plate (Ramphele 1996).

Changing Kinship and Household Dynamics

This section provides examples of how marriage and household patterns are changing. Many of these changes have roots in colonialism, whereas others are the result of recent changes effected by globalization.

CHANGE IN DESCENT

Matrilineal descent is declining worldwide as a result of both European colonialism and contemporary Western globalization. European colonial rule in Africa and Asia contributed to the decline in matrilineal kinship by registering land and other property in the names of assumed male heads of household, even where females were the heads (Boserup 1970). This process eroded women's previous rights and powers. Western missionaries further contributed to transforming matrilineal cultures into patrilineal systems (Etienne and Leacock 1980). For example, European colonial influences led to the decline of matrilineal kinship among Native North Americans. Before European colonialism, North America had one of the largest distributions of matrilineal descent worldwide. A comparative study of kinship among three reservation-based Navajo groups in Arizona shows that matrilineality is stronger where conditions most resemble the pre-reservation era (Levy, Henderson, and Andrews 1989).

Among the Minangkabau of Indonesia (review Culturama, this chapter, p. 198), three factors explain the decline of matrilineal kinship (Blackwood 1995):

- Dutch colonialism promoted the image of male-headed nuclear families as an ideal.
- Islamic teachings idealize women as wives and men as household heads.
- The modernizing Indonesian state has a policy of naming males as household heads.

CHANGE IN MARRIAGE

Although the institution of marriage in general remains prominent, many of its details are changing including courtship, the marriage ceremony, and marital relationships.

New forms of communication are profoundly affecting courtship. In a village in western Nepal (see Map 7.7, p. 181), people's stories of their marriages reveal that arranged marriages have decreased and elopement has increased since the 1990s (Ahern 2001). In the 1990s, love letters became the most important basis of establishing marital relationships. In this context, dating is not allowed, so sending love letters is how young people court. Of the 200 love letters Ahern collected, 170 were written by men and 30 by women. Typically, the man starts the correspondence. For example, one man's love letter contains the following lines: "I'm helpless and I have to make friends of a notebook and pen in order to place this helplessness before you. . . . I'll let you know by a 'short cut' what I want to say: Love is the union of two souls . . . I'm offering you an invitation to love" (2001:3). Love letters became possible only in the 1990s because of increased literacy rates in the village. Literacy facilitated self-selected marriages and thus supported an increasing sense of personal agency among the younger people of the village. Now, throughout the world, young people are courting through text messaging, even in the most conservative parts of the world such as the Middle East.

Nearly everywhere, the age at first marriage is rising. The later age at marriage is related to increased emphasis on completing a certain number of years of education before marriage

A newly married husband and wife and their relatives in front of a church in Seoul, Republic of Korea.

▶ *How does this wedding group resemble or differ from a wedding you have attended?*

and to higher material aspirations, such as being able to own a house. Marriages between people of different nations and ethnicities are increasing, partly because of growing rates of international migration. Migrants take with them many of their marriage and family practices. They also adapt to rules and practices in their area of destination. Pluralistic practices evolve, such as conducting two marriage ceremonies—one conforming to the "original" culture and the other to the culture in the place of destination.

Marriage crises are situations in which people who want to marry cannot do so for one reason or another. They are more frequent now than in the past, at least as perceived and reported by young people in the so-called marriage market. Two examples illustrate variations in how a marriage crisis comes about and how it plays out for those caught up in it.

In a town of about 38,000 in rural Niger, West Africa, the marriage crisis involves young men's inability to raise the necessary funds for the brideprice and additional gifts to the bride's family (Masquelier 2005). Among these Muslim, Hausa-speaking people, called Mawri, marriage is the crucial ritual that changes a boy into a man. Typically, a prospective groom receives financial assistance from his kin and friends. In Niger, the economy has been declining for some time, and typical farm or other wages are worth less than they were in earlier times. Marriage costs for the groom have not declined, however—quite the opposite. Wealthy young men can afford to give a car to the bride's parents as a wedding gift. But most young Mawri men cannot afford such gifts and are caught in the marriage crisis. They remain sitting at home in their parents' house, something that only females do. The many young, marriage-age women who remain single gain a reputation of being immoral, as they occupy a new and suspect social space between girl and wife.

The marriage crisis for African American women in Syracuse is related to policies promoted by the government of President George W. Bush (Lane et al. 2004). The Bush government earmarked millions of dollars to promote two-parent, heterosexual families. Furthermore, during the George W. Bush era an increasing number of African American men were imprisoned. Besides high rates of imprisonment, African American men die violent deaths at much higher rates than other ethnic populations. In the population of Syracuse, a city in postindustrial decline, there are four African American women for every one African American man, compared to an equal ratio among Whites. Given the strong preference for ethnic endogamous marriages, it is statistically impossible for many African American women to get married.

Weddings are important, culture-revealing events. Style changes in weddings worldwide abound. Factors of changes to consider are the ceremony, costs, appropriate clothing, and the possibility of a honeymoon. Due to globalization, features of the Western-style *white wedding* (a long white gown for the bride, a multitiered wedding cake, and certain kinds of floral arrangements) are spreading around the world, though with fascinating local adaptations. Just considering what the bride and groom wear takes one into the complex connections between weddings and identity of the bride and groom and their families. Clothing choice may reflect adherence to "traditional" values or may reject those in favor of more "modern" values. Throughout much of East and Southeast Asia, advertisements and upscale stores display the Western-style white wedding gown (but less so in India, where white clothing for women signifies widowhood and is inauspicious). Resurgence of local styles is occurring in some contexts, such as in Morocco, where there is a trend for "modern" brides to wear a Berber costume (long robes and silver jewelry characteristic of the rural, mountain pastoralists) at one stage of the wedding ceremony.

CHANGING HOUSEHOLDS

Globalization is creating rapid change in household structure and intrahousehold dynamics. One assumption is that the frequency of extended households will decline with

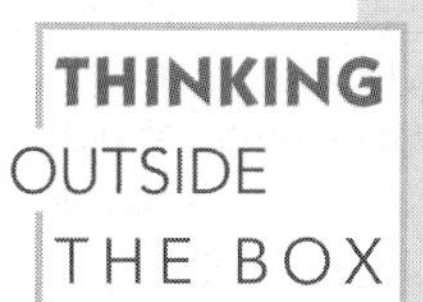

What forms of communication do young people use to court someone in your cultural world? For a class project, interview your parents about courtship communication that they used.

(LEFT) A modern-style Kelabit longhouse built in the 1990s. It is the home of six families who formerly lived in a 20-family longhouse, seen in the background, which is being dismantled. (RIGHT) Since the 1990s, houses built for a nuclear unit have proliferated in the highlands. These houses stand on the site of a former multiunit longhouse.

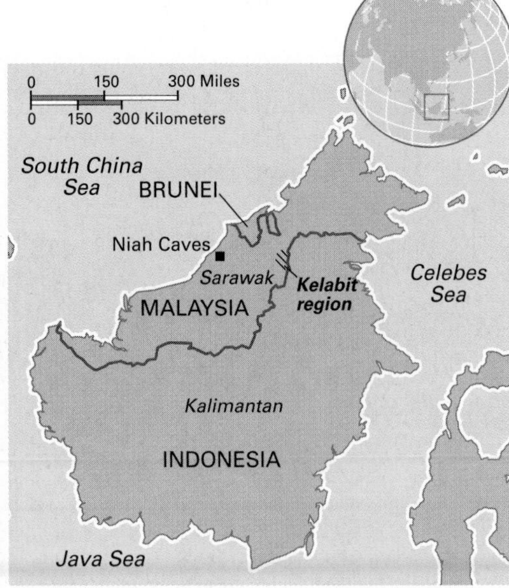

MAP 8.7 Kelabit Region in Malaysia. The Kelabit people's homeland is the Kelabit Highlands in Sarawak, a plateau ringed by mountain peaks that are forest covered. One of Malaysia's smallest indigenous tribes, they number around 6000 people, or 0.4 percent of Sarawak's population of 1.5 million, and 0.03 percent of Malaysia's total population of 22 million. Less than one-third of the Kelabit people live in the highlands.

industrialization and urbanization, and the frequency of nuclear households will rise. Given what this chapter mentioned earlier about the relationship between nuclear households and industrialism/informatics, it is highly possible that with the spread of this mode of production, nuclear households will increase too.

This projection finds strong confirmation in the changes that have occurred in household structure among the Kelabit people of highland Borneo since the early 1990s (Amster 2000) (see Map 8.7). One Kelabit settlement was founded in 1963 near the Indonesian border. At the time, everyone lived in one longhouse with over 20 family units. It was a "modern" longhouse, thanks to roofing provided by the British army and the innovation of private sleeping areas. Like more traditional longhouses, though, it was an essentially egalitarian living space within which individuals could freely move. Today, that longhouse is no more. Most of the young people have migrated to coastal towns and work in jobs related to the offshore oil industry. Most houses are now single-unit homes with an emphasis on privacy. The elders complain of a "bad silence" in the village. No one looks after visitors with the old style of hospitality. There is no longer one common longhouse for communal feasts and rituals.

International migration is another major cause of change in household formation and internal relationships. Dramatic decline in fertility can occur in one generation when members of a farming household in, for example, Taiwan or Egypt, migrate to England, France, Canada, or the United States. Having many children makes economic sense in their homeland, but not in the new destination. Many such migrants decide to have only one or two children. They tend to live in small, isolated nuclear households. International migration creates new challenges for relationships between parents and children. The children often become strongly identified with the new culture and have little connection with their ancestral culture. This rupture creates anxiety for the parents and conflict between children and parents over issues such as dating, dress, and career goals.

In 1997, the people of Norway were confronted with a case of kidnapping of an 18-year-old Norwegian citizen named "Nadia". Her parents took her to Morocco and held her captive there. The full story is complicated, but the core issues revolve around conflict between Moroccan and Norwegian family values. Nadia's parents felt that she should be under their control and that they had the right to arrange her marriage in Morocco. Nadia had a Norwegian concept of personal autonomy. In the end, Nadia and her parents returned to Norway, where the courts ruled that, for the sake of the family, the parents would not be jailed for kidnapping their daughter. The case brought stigma to Nadia among the Muslim community of Norway, who viewed her as a traitor to her culture. She now lives at a secret address and avoids publicity. An anthropologist close to this case who served as an expert cultural witness during the trial of her parents reports that, in spite of her seclusion, Nadia has offered help to other young women.

At the beginning of the twenty-first century, three kinds of households are most common in the United States: households composed of couples living in their first marriage, single-parent households, and households formed through remarriage. A new fourth category is the multigenerational household, in which an *adult child,* or *boomerang kid,* lives with his or her parents. About one in three unmarried adults between the ages of 25 and 55 share a home with their mother or father or both (*Psychology Today* 1995 [28]:16). In the United States, adult offspring spend over 2 hours a day doing household chores, with adult daughters contributing about 17 hours a week and adult sons 14.4 hours. Daughters spend most of their time doing laundry, cooking, cleaning, and washing dishes. Sons are more involved in yard work and car care. Parents in multigenerational households still do three-quarters of the housework.

Kinship and household formation are certainly not dull or static topics. Just trying to keep up with changing patterns in North America is a daunting task, to say nothing of tracking changes worldwide.

8

the BIG questions REVISITED

◆ How do cultures create kinship?

Key differences exist between unilineal and bilineal descent systems. Within unilineal systems, further important variations exist between patrilineal and matrilineal systems in terms of property inheritance, residence rules for married couples, and the relative status of males and females. Worldwide, unilineal systems are more common than bilineal systems. Within unilineal kinship systems, patrilineal kinship is more common than matrilineal kinship.

A second important basis for kinship is sharing. Sharing one's child with someone else through either informal or formal processes is probably a cultural universal. Sharing-based kinship is created through food transfers, including breastfeeding (in some cultures, children breastfed by the same woman are considered kin and cannot marry). Ritualized sharing creates kinship, as in the case of godparenthood.

The third basis for kinship is marriage, another universal factor, even though definitions of marriage may differ substantially. All cultures have rules of exclusion and preference rules for spouses.

◆ What are cross-cultural patterns of households and domestic life?

A household may consist of a single person living alone or may be a group comprising more than one person who may or may not be related by kinship; these individuals share a living space and, often, financial responsibilities for the household.

Nuclear households consist of a mother and father and their children, but they also can be just a husband and wife without children. Nuclear households are found in all cultures but are most common in foraging and industrial societies. Extended households include more than one nuclear household. They are most commonly found in cultures with a unilineal kinship system. Stem households, which are most common in East Asia, are a variant of an extended household in which only one child, usually the first born, retains residence with the parents.

Household headship can be shared between two partners or can be borne by a single person, as in a woman-headed household. Study of intrahousehold dynamics between parents and children and among siblings reveals complex power relationships as well as security, sharing, and sometimes violence. Household break-up comes about through divorce, separation of cohabiting partners, or death of a spouse or partner.

◆ How are kinship and households changing?

The increasingly connected world in which we live is having marked effects on kinship formation and household patterns and dynamics. Matrilineal systems have been declining in distribution since European colonialist expansion beginning in the 1500s.

Many aspects of marriage are changing, including a trend toward later age at marriage in many developing countries. Although marriage continues to be an important basis for the formation of nuclear and extended households, other options (such as cohabitation) are increasing in importance in many contexts, including urban areas in developed countries.

Contemporary changes in kinship and in household formation raise several serious questions for the future, perhaps most importantly about the care of dependent members such as children, the aged, and disabled people. As fertility rates decline and average household size shrinks, kinship-based entitlements to basic needs and emotional support disappear.

KEY CONCEPTS

bilineal descent, p. 195
brideservice, p. 204
cross-cousin, p. 201
descent, p. 194
endogamy, p. 201
exogamy, p. 202
extended household, p. 205
family, p. 205
household, p. 205
incest taboo, p. 200
kinship system, p. 192
marriage, p. 200
matrilineal descent, p. 195
matrifocality, p. 206
monogamy, p. 205
nuclear household, p. 205
parallel cousin, p. 201
patrilineal descent, p. 195
polyandry, p. 205
polygamy, p. 205
polygyny, p. 205
stem household, p. 206
unilineal descent, p. 195

SUGGESTED READINGS

Irwin Altman and Joseph Ginat, eds. *Polygynous Families in Contemporary Society.* Cambridge: Cambridge University Press, 1996. This book provides a detailed account of polygyny as practiced in two fundamentalist Mormon communities of Utah, one rural and the other urban.

Dorothy Ayers Counts, Judith K. Brown, and Jacquelyn C. Campbell, eds. *To Have and to Hit: Cultural Perspectives on Wife Beating.* Champaign/Urbana: University of Illinois Press, 1999. Chapters include an introductory overview and cases from Australia, southern Africa, Papua New Guinea, India, Central America, the Middle East, and the Pacific.

Amy Borovoy. *The Too-Good Wife: Alcohol, Codependency, and the Politics of Nurturance in Postwar Japan.* Berkeley: University of California Press, 2005. This book explores the experiences of middle-class women in Tokyo who participated in a weekly support meeting for families of substance abusers. The women attempt to cope with their husbands' alcoholism while facing the dilemma that being a good wife may be part of the problem.

Deborah R. Connolly. *Homeless Mothers: Face to Face with Women and Poverty.* Minneapolis: University of Minnesota Press, 2000. Poor, White women on the margin of mainstream society in Portland, Oregon, describe how they attempt to be good mothers with no money, no home, and no help.

Charles N. Durran, James M. Freeman, and J.A. English-Lueck. *Busier Than Ever! Why American Families Can't Slow Down.* Stanford, CA: Stanford University Press, 2007. The authors followed the daily activities of 14 American families in California. Their findings show how people try to balance the demands of work and family in a cultural context in which "busyness," or always being busy, is an indication of success and the good life.

Helen Bradley Foster and Donald Clay Johnson, eds. *Wedding Dress across Cultures.* New York: Berg, 2003. Chapters examine the evolution and ritual functions of wedding attire in cultures such as urban Japan, Alaskan Indians, Swaziland, Morocco, Greece, and the Andes.

Jennifer Hirsch. *A Courtship after Marriage: Sexuality and Love in Mexican Transnational Marriages.* Berkeley: University of California Press, 2003. This study uses an innovative method of pairing 13 migrant women living in Atlanta, Georgia, with 13 nonmigrant counterparts in two rural towns in Mexico to learn about marriage and married life.

Suad Joseph, ed. *Intimate Selving in Arab Families: Gender, Self, and Identity.* Syracuse, NY: Syracuse University Press, 1999. Chapters discuss family life and relationships in Arab culture with attention to connectivity, gender inequality, and the self. Case studies are from Lebanon and Egypt.

Laurel Kendall. *Getting Married in Korea: Of Gender, Morality, and Modernity.* Berkeley: University of California, 1996. This book examines preferences about desirable spouses, matchmaking, marriage ceremonies and their financing, and the effect of women's changing work roles on their marital aspirations.

Sulamith Heins Potter. *Family Life in a Northern Thai Village: A Structural Study in the Significance of Women.* Berkeley: University of California Press, 1977. This ethnography of matrifocal family life in rural Thailand focuses on work roles, rituals, and intrafamily relationships.

Kanchana Ruwanpura. *Matrilineal Communities, Patriarchal Realities: A Feminist Nirvana Uncovered.* Ann Arbor: University of Michigan Press, 2007. This book describes Muslim, Sinhala, and Tamil households headed by women in Sri Lanka.

Margaret Trawick. *Notes on Love in a Tamil Family.* Berkeley: University of California Press, 1992. This reflexive ethnography takes a close look at the daily dynamics of kinship in one Tamil (South Indian) family. Attention is given to sibling relationships, the role of older people, children's lives, and love and affection.

Toby Alice Volkman, ed. *Cultures of Transnational Adoption.* Durham, NC: Duke University Press, 2005. Chapters discuss Korean adoptees as a global family, transnational adoption in North America, shared parenthood among low-income people in Brazil, and representations of "waiting children."

A young woman of the Kabylie people, a Berber group of Algeria, wears a headband that signifies mourning during a public march to protest the government's denial of human rights to the Kabylie people.

SOCIAL GROUPS AND SOCIAL STRATIFICATION

the BIG questions

- What are social groups and how do they vary cross-culturally?
- What is social stratification?
- What is civil society?

OUTLINE

In the early 1800s, when French political philosopher Alexis de Tocqueville visited the United States and characterized it as a "nation of joiners," he implied that people in some cultures are more likely to join groups than others. The questions of what motivates people to join groups, what holds people together in groups, and how groups deal with leadership and participation have intrigued scholars in many fields for centuries.

This chapter focuses on nonkin groups and microculture formation. Chapter 1 defined several factors related to microcultures: class, "race," ethnicity, indigeneity, gender, age, and institutions such as prisons and retirement homes. So far, chapters in this book have discussed how microcultures affect fieldwork and how they vary in different economies and reproductive and kinship systems. This chapter looks at how microcultures shape group identity and organization and the relationships among different groups in terms of hierarchy and power. It first examines a variety of social groups ranging from small scale to large scale and then considers inequalities among social groups. The last section considers the concept of civil society and provides examples.

◆◆◆

Social Groups

A **social group** is a cluster of people beyond the domestic unit who are usually related on grounds other than kinship, although kinship relationships may exist between people in the group. Two basic categories exist: the **primary group**, consisting of people who interact with each other and know each other personally, and the **secondary group**, consisting of people who identify with each other on some common ground but who may never meet with one another or interact with each other personally.

Members of all social groups have a sense of rights and responsibilities in relation to the group. Membership in a primary group, because of face-to-face interaction, involves more direct accountability about rights and responsibilities than secondary group membership. When discussing different kinds of groups, cultural anthropologists also draw a distinction between *informal groups* and *formal groups* (March and Taqqu 1986:5):

- Informal groups are smaller and less visible.
- Members of informal groups have close, face-to-face relationships with one another; members of formal groups may or may not know each other.
- Organizational structure is less hierarchical in informal groups.
- Informal groups do not have legal recognition.

Modes of livelihood affect the formation of social groups, with the greatest variety of groups found in agricultural and industrial/informatics societies (see Figure 9.1). One theory for this pattern is that mobile populations, such as foragers and pastoralists, are less likely to develop enduring social groups beyond kin relationships simply because they have less social density and continuous interaction than more settled populations. Although foragers and pastoralists do have less variety of social groups, they do not completely lack social groupings. A prominent form of social group among foragers and pastoralists is an **age set**, a group of people close in age who go through certain rituals, such as circumcision, at the same time.

Although it is generally true that settled populations have more social groups as a way to organize society, some important exceptions exist. In accordance with this generalization, many informal and formal groups are active throughout Africa, Latin America, and Southeast Asia. In northern Thailand's Chiangmai region (see Map 6.7, p. 157), for example, many social groups exist (Potter 1976). Villagers support the Buddhist temple, irrigation canals, the cremation grounds, and village roads through donations of food, cash, and labor. Several more formal and focused groups exist: the temple committee that arranges festivals, the school committee, the Young People's Club (youth from about the age of 15 until marriage who assist at village ceremonial functions), the village dancers (about a dozen young, unmarried women who host intervillage events), and the funeral society (which provides financial aid for funeral services).

Social groups, however, are typically less prominent in South Asia, a region that includes Pakistan, India, Nepal, Bhutan, Bangladesh, and Sri Lanka. In Bangladesh (see Map 9.1), for example, a densely populated and agrarian country of South Asia, indigenous social groups are rare. The most prominent ties beyond the immediate household are kinship based (Miller and Khan 1986). In spite of the lack of indigenous social groups, however, Bangladesh has gained world renown since the later twentieth century for its success in forming local microcredit (small loans) groups through an organization called the Grameen Bank, which gives loans to poor people to help them start small businesses. Likewise,

---

social group a cluster of people beyond the domestic unit who are usually related on grounds other than kinship.

primary group a social group in which members meet on a face-to-face basis.

secondary group people who identify with each other on some basis but may never meet with one another personally.

age set a group of people close in age who go through certain rituals, such as circumcision, at the same time.

Foraging	Horticulture	Pastoralism	Agriculture	Industrialism/Informatics
Characteristics				**Characteristics**
Informal and primary Egalitarian structure Ties based on balanced exchange		Ritual ties	Formal and secondary Recognized leadership Dues and fees	
Functions				**Functions**
Companionship		Special purposes Work, war, lobbying government		
Types				**Types**
Friendship	Friendship Age-based work groups Gender-based work groups		Status Groups: Class, race, ethnicity, caste, age, gender Institutional Groups: Prisons, retirement homes Quasi-Political Groups: Human rights, environmental groups	Friendship Urban youth gangs Clubs, associations

FIGURE 9.1 **Modes of Livelihood and Social Groups**

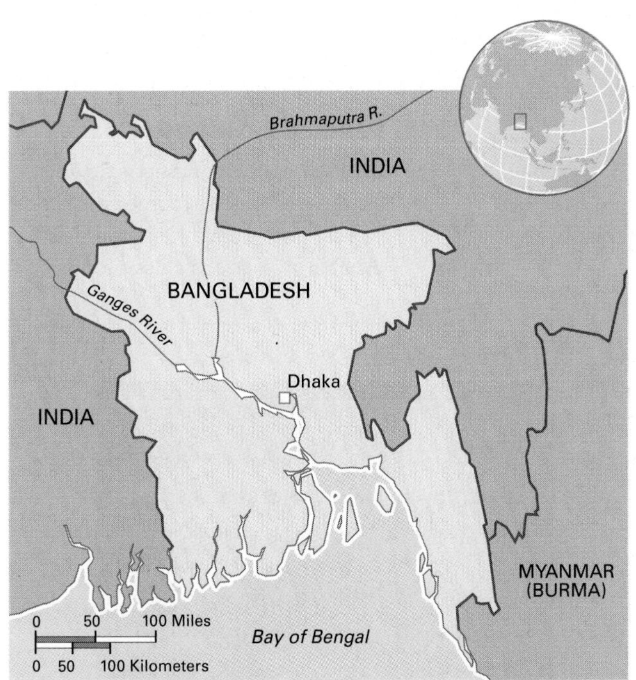

MAP 9.1 **Bangladesh.**

The People's Republic of Bangladesh is located on a deltaic floodplain with rich soil and risk of flooding. One of the world's most densely populated countries, its nearly 150 million people live in an area about the size of the state of Wisconsin. Bangladesh is the world's third-largest Muslim majority country.

throughout the rest of South Asia, the modern era has seen the rise of many active social groups including those dedicated to preserving traditional environmental knowledge, promoting women and children's health and survival, and advocating for lesbian/gay rights.

This section describes a variety of social groups, starting with the most face-to-face, primary groups of two or three people based on friendship. It then moves to larger and more formal groups such as countercultural groups and activist groups.

FRIENDSHIP

Friendship refers to close social ties between at least two people that are informal, voluntary, and involve personal, face-to-face interaction. Generally, friendship involves people who are nonkin, but in some cases kin are also friends (recall the Tory Islanders discussed in Chapter 8). Friendship fits in the category of a primary social group. One question that cultural anthropologists ask is whether friendship is a cultural universal. Two factors make it difficult to answer this question. First, insufficient cross-cultural research exists to answer the question definitively. Second, defining friendship cross-culturally is problematic. It is likely, however, that something like "friendship" is a cultural universal but shaped in different degrees from culture to culture (see Everyday Anthropology).

everyday ANTHROPOLOGY

Making Friends

People's daily activities are often the basis of friendship ties. In Andalucia, southern Spain (see Map 3.5, p. 77), men and women pursue separate kinds of work and, relatedly, have differing friendship patterns (Uhl 1991). Men's work takes place outside the house and neighborhood, either in the fields or in manufacturing jobs. Women devote most of their time to unpaid household work within the domestic domain. This dichotomy is somewhat fluid, however, as women's domestic roles sometimes take them to the market or the town hall.

For men, an important category of friend is an *amigo,* a friend with whom one casually interacts. This kind of friendship is acted out and maintained in the context in bars, as men drink together night after night. Bars are a man's world. Amigos share common experiences of school, sports and hobbies, and working together. In contrast, women refer to their friends either with kin terms or as *vecina,* "neighbor," reflecting women's primary orientation to family and neighborhood.

Differences also emerge in the category of *amigos(as) del verdad,* or "true friends." True friends are those with whom one shares secrets without fear of betrayal. Men have more true friends than women do, a pattern that reflects their wider social networks.

A shepherd in Andalucia, southern Spain. In rural areas of Andalucia, as in much of the Mediterranean region, the gender of division of labor is distinct, with men working outside the home and women working inside or near the home. Friendship formation follows this pattern. Men form ties with men in cafes and bars after work, and women establish ties with other women in the neighborhood.

◆ FOOD FOR THOUGHT

- What categories of friends do you have? Are friends in some categories "closer" or "truer" than others? What is the basis of close friendship?

SOCIAL CHARACTERISTICS OF FRIENDSHIP People choose their friends, and friends remain so on a voluntary basis. Even so, the criteria for who qualifies as a friend may be culturally structured. For instance, gender segregation may prevent cross-gender friendships and promote same-gender friendships, and racial segregation limits cross–"race" friendships. Another characteristic of friendship is that friends are supportive of each other, psychologically and sometimes materially. Support is mutual, shared back and forth in an expectable way (as in balanced exchange, see Chapter 5). Friendship generally occurs between social equals, although there are exceptions, such as friendships between older and younger people, a supervisor and a staff worker, or a teacher and a student.

In a low-income neighborhood in Rio de Janeiro, Brazil, men play dominoes and drink beer while others observe.

▶ *Discuss a comparable scene of female leisure activities in your microcultural experience.*

Sharing stories is often a basis of friendship groups. According to a study of men's friendship groups that focused on interactions in rumshops in Guyana (gai-ANN-uh)

MAP 9.2 Caribbean Countries of South America. The ethnically and linguistically diverse countries of the Caribbean region of South America include Guyana, Suriname, and French Guiana. Guyana, or the Co-operative Republic of Guyana, is the only South American country whose official language is English. Other languages are Hindi, Wai Wai, and Arawak. Its population is 800,000. The Republiek Suriname, or Surinam, was formerly a colony of the Netherlands and is the smallest independent state in South America. Its population is 440,000. Dutch is the official language but most Surinamese also speak Sranang Tongo, or Surinaams, a mixture of Dutch, English Portuguese, French, and local languages. French Guiana is an overseas department of France and is thus part of the European Union. The smallest political unit in South America, its population is 200,000. Its official language is French, but several other languages are spoken, including indigenous Arawak and Carib.

(see Map 9.2), Indo-Guyanese men who have known each other since childhood spend time every day at the rumshop, eating, drinking, and regaling each other with stories (Sidnell 2000). Through shared storytelling about village history and other aspects of local knowledge, men display their equality with each other. The pattern of storytelling, referred to as "turn-at-talk," in which efforts are made to include everyone as a storyteller in turn, also serves to maintain equality and solidarity. These friendship groups are tightly knit, and the members can call on one another for economic, social, political, and ritual help.

Participant observation and interviews with a sample of rural and urban, low-income Jamaicans reveals that cell phone use is frequent (Horst and Miller 2005). Jamaicans are keenly aware of their call lists and how often they have kept in touch with the many individuals on their lists. Cell phones allow for "linking up," or creating extensive networks that include close friends, possible future sexual partners, and members of one's church. Phone numbers of kin are also prominent on people's cell phone number lists. By linking up periodically with people on their lists, low-income Jamaicans maintain friendship and other ties with people who they can call on when they need support. Cell phones allow a more extensive network of friends and other contacts than was previously possible.

FRIENDSHIP AMONG THE URBAN POOR Carol Stack's study of how friendship networks promote economic survival among low-income, urban African Americans is a landmark contribution (1974). She conducted fieldwork in the late 1960s in "The Flats," the poorest section of a Black community in a large, midwestern city. She found extensive networks of friends "supporting, reinforcing each other—devising schemes for self help, strategies for survival in a community of severe economic deprivation" (1974:28). Close friends, are referred to by kin terms.

People in the Flats, especially women, maintain a set of friends through exchange: "swapping" goods (food, clothing) needed by someone at a particular time, sharing "child keeping," and giving or lending food stamps and money. Such exchanges are part of a clearly understood pattern—gifts and favors go back and forth over time. Friends thus bound together are obligated to each another and can call on each other in time of need. In opposition to theories that suggest the breakdown of social relationships among the very poor, this research documents how poor people strategize and cope through social ties.

CLUBS AND FRATERNITIES

Clubs and fraternities are social groups that define membership in terms of a sense of shared identity and objectives. They may comprise people of the same ethnic heritage (such as the Daughters of the American Revolution in the United States), occupation or business, religion, or gender. Although many clubs appear to exist primarily to serve functions of sociability and psychological support, deeper analysis often shows that these groups have economic and political roles as well.

Women's clubs in a lower-class neighborhood in Paramaribo, Suriname (see Map 9.2), have multiple functions (Brana-Shute 1976). Here, as is common elsewhere in Latin America, clubs raise funds to sponsor special events and support individual celebrations, meet personal financial needs, and send cards and flowers for funerals. Members attend each other's birthday parties and death rites as a group. The clubs thus offer the women psychological support, entertainment, and financial help. A political aspect exists, too. Club members often belong to the same political party and attend political rallies and events together. The clubs therefore constitute political interest groups that can influence political outcomes. Politicians and party workers confirmed that real pressure is exerted on them by women individually and in groups.

College fraternities and sororities are highly selective groups that serve a variety of explicit functions, such as entertainment and social service. They also form bonds between

(LEFT) Students gather outside a fraternity house near the University of San Francisco campus for a weekend party.
(RIGHT) Members of a fraternity at the University of Texas at Austin engage in public service by planting trees at an elementary school.
▶ *What knowledge do you have of the positive and negative social aspects of college fraternities and sororities? How could anthropological research provide a clearer picture?*

members that may help in securing jobs after graduation. Few anthropologists have studied the "Greek system" on U.S. campuses. An exception is Peggy Sanday, who was inspired to study college fraternities after the gang rape of a woman student by several fraternity brothers at the campus where she teaches. In her book *Fraternity Gang Rape: Sex, Brotherhood, and Privilege on Campus* (1990), she explores initiation rituals and how they are related to male bonding solidified by victimization and ridicule of women. Gang rape, or a "train," is a prevalent practice in some, not all, fraternities. Fraternity party invitations may hint at the possibility of a "train." Typically, the brothers seek out a "party girl"—a somewhat vulnerable young woman who may be especially needy of acceptance or especially high on alcohol or other substances (her drinks may have been "spiked"). They take her to one of the brothers' rooms, where she may or may not agree to have sex with one of the brothers, and she often passes out. Then a "train" of men have sex with her. Rarely prosecuted, the male participants reinforce their sense of privilege, power, and unity with one another through a group ritual involving abuse of a female outsider.

In many indigenous Amazonian groups, the men's house is fiercely guarded from being entered by women. If a woman trespasses on male territory, men punish her by gang rape. One interpretation of this cultural practice is that men have a high degree of anxiety about their identity as fierce warriors and as sexually potent males (Gregor 1982). Maintaining their identity as fierce and forbidding toward outsiders involves taking an aggressive position in relation to women of their own group.

Cross-culturally, women do not tend to form *androphobic* ("man-hating" or otherwise anti-male) clubs, the logical parallel of *gynophobic* ("woman-hating" or otherwise anti-female) men's clubs. College sororities, for example, are not mirror images of college fraternities. Although some sororities' initiation rituals are psychologically brutal to the pledges, bonding among the members does not involve abusive behavior toward men.

COUNTERCULTURAL GROUPS

Several kinds of groups comprise people who, for one reason or another, are outside the "mainstream" of society and resist conforming to the dominant cultural pattern, as in the so-called hippie movement of the 1960s. One similarity among these groups, as with clubs and fraternities, is the importance of bonding through shared initiation and other rituals.

YOUTH GANGS The term **youth gang** refers to a group of young people, found mainly in urban areas, who are often considered a social problem by adults and law enforcement officials (Sanders 1994).

Youth gangs vary in terms of how formally they are organized. Like clubs and fraternities, gangs often have a recognized leader, formalized rituals of initiation for new members, and symbolic markers of identity such as tattoos or special clothing. An example of an informal youth gang with no formal leadership hierarchy or initiation rituals is that of the "Masta Liu" in Honiara, the capital city of the Solomon Islands in the South Pacific (Jourdan 1995) (see Map 9.3). The primary unifying feature of the male youth who become Masta Liu is the fact that they are unemployed. Most have

youth gang a group of young people, found mainly in urban areas, who are often considered a social problem by adults and law enforcement officials.

migrated to the city from the countryside to escape what they consider an undesirable lifestyle there: working in the fields under control of their elders. Some Liu live with extended kin in the city; others organize Liu-only households. They spend their time wandering around town (*wakabaot*) in groups of up to ten: "They stop at every shop on their way, eager to look at the merchandise but afraid to be kicked out by the security guards; they check out all the cinemas only to dream in front of the preview posters . . . not even having the $2 bill that will allow them to get in; they gaze for hours on end, and without moving, at the electronic equipment displayed in the Chinese shops, without saying a word: One can read in their gaze the silent dreams they create" (1995:210).

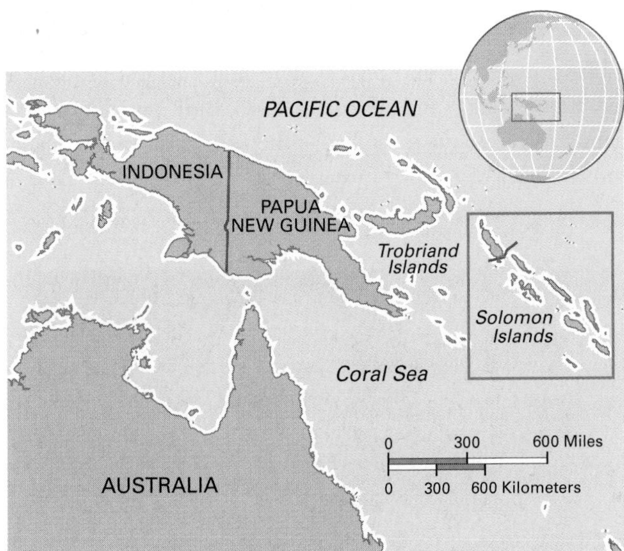

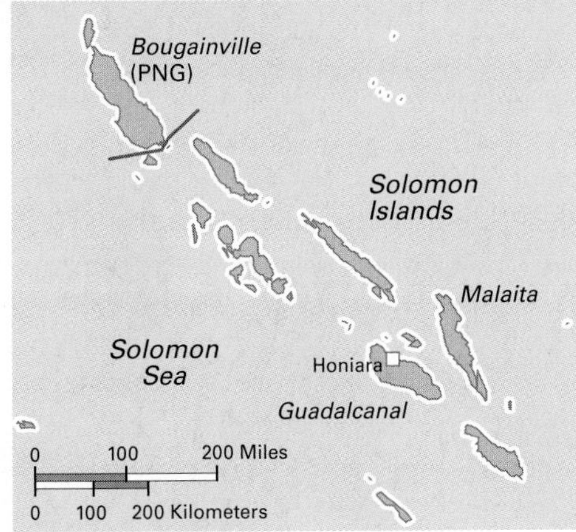

MAP 9.3 The Solomon Islands.
This country consists of nearly 1000 islands. Its capital, Honiara, is located on the island of Guadalcanal. The population is 540,000. Most of the people earn a living through small-scale farming and fishing. Commercial exploitation of local timber has led to severe deforestation. Over 70 languages are spoken, and 4 have recently gone extinct. The majority of the people are Christian, mainly Anglican. The Solomons were the site of some of the bitterest fighting during World War II.

Street gangs are a more formal variety of youth gang. They generally have leaders and a hierarchy of membership roles and responsibilities. They are named, and their members mark their identity with tattoos or "colors." Much popular thinking associates street gangs with violence, but not all are involved in violence. An anthropologist who did research among nearly 40 street gangs in New York, Los Angeles, and Boston learned much about why individuals join gangs, providing insights that also contradict popular thinking (Jankowski 1991). One common perception is that young boys join gangs because they are from homes with no male authority figure with whom they could identify. In the gangs studied, about half of the gang members were from intact nuclear households. Another common perception is that the gang replaces a missing feeling of family. This study showed that the same number of gang members reported having close family ties as those who did not.

Why, then, did young men join an urban gang? The research revealed that many gang members had a particular personality type called a *defiant individualist*. The defiant individualist type has five characteristics:

- Intense competitiveness
- Mistrust of others
- Self-reliance
- Social isolation
- Strong survival instinct

A structurist view suggests that poverty, especially urban poverty, leads to the development of this kind of personality, which is a reasonable response to the prevailing economic obstacles and uncertainty. In terms of explaining the global spread of urban youth gangs, structurists point to global economic changes in urban employment opportunities. In many countries, the declining urban industrial base has created persistent poverty in inner-city communities (Short 1996). At the same time, schooling and the popular media promote aspirations for a better life. Urban gang members, in this view, are the victims of large structural forces beyond their control that both inspire them to want aspects of a successful lifestyle while preventing them the legal means to obtain their aspirations. Many of these youth want to be economically successful, but social conditions channel their interests and skills into illegal pursuits rather than into legal pathways to achievement.

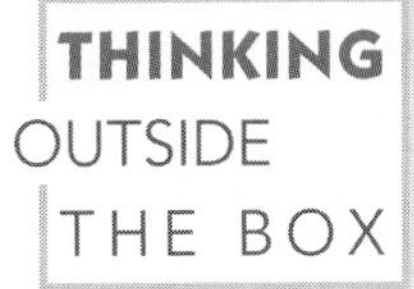

Think of some examples in which socially excluded groups have contributed to changing styles of music, dress, and other forms of expressive culture of so-called mainstream groups.

Members of the gang "18" in San Salvador, El Salvador, passing time on the street. The group's leader prohibits the use of alcohol and drugs except on Saturdays and Sundays.

▶ *Consider how the social life of gangs worldwide is affected by contemporary globalization.*

BODY MODIFICATION GROUPS One of the many countercultural movements in the United States includes people who have a sense of community strengthened through forms of body alteration. James Myers (1992) did research in California among people who feel they are a special group because of their interest in permanent body modification, especially genital piercing, branding, and cutting. Fieldwork involved participant observation and interviews: Myers was involved in workshops organized for the San Francisco SM (sadomasochist) community; he attended the Fifth Annual Living in Leather Convention held in Portland, Oregon, in 1990; he spent time in tattoo and piercing studios; and he talked with students and others in his hometown who were involved in these forms of body modification. The study population included males and females, heterosexuals, gays, lesbians, bisexuals, and SMers. The single largest group was SM homosexuals and bisexuals. The study population was mainly White, and most had either attended or graduated from college.

(LEFT) A Tahitian chief wears tattoos that indicate his high status. (RIGHT) A woman with tattooed arms and pierced nose in the United States.

▶ *In your microcultural experience, what do tattoos mean to you when you see someone with them?*

Myers witnessed many modification sessions at workshops: Those seeking modification go up on stage and have their chosen procedure done by a well-known expert. Whatever the procedure, the volunteers exhibit little pain—usually just a sharp intake of breath at the moment the needle passes through or the brand touches skin. After that critical moment, the audience breathes an audible sigh of relief. The volunteer stands up and adjusts his or her clothing, and members of the audience applaud. This public event is a kind of initiation ritual that binds the expert, the volunteer, and the group together. Pain is an important part of many rites of passage. In this case, the audience witnesses and validates the experience and becomes joined to the initiate through witnessing.

The study revealed that a prominent motivation for seeking permanent body modification was a desire to identify with a specific group of people. As one participant said,

> It's not that we're sheep, getting pierced or cut just because everyone else is. I like to think it's because we're a very special group and we like doing something that sets us off from others. . . . Happiness is standing in line at a cafeteria and detecting that the straight-looking babe in front of you has her nipples pierced. I don't really care what her sexual orientation is, I can relate to her. (1992:292)

COOPERATIVES

Cooperatives are a form of economic group in which surpluses are shared among the members and decision making follows the democratic principle of one person/one vote (Estrin 1996). Agricultural and credit cooperatives are the most common forms of cooperatives worldwide, followed by consumer cooperatives. Two examples of cooperatives show how human agency, within different structures, can bring about positive results. In the first case, the cooperative gives its members economic strength and checks the power of the richest farmers in one region of India. In the second case, women craft producers in Panama achieve economic position within the world market and also build social ties and political leadership skills.

FARMERS' COOPERATIVES IN WESTERN INDIA In India's western state of Maharashtra, the sugar industry is largely owned and operated through farmer cooperatives (Attwood 1992). Most shareholders are small farmers, producing just one or two acres of sugar cane. Yet the sugar industry, owned and managed cooperatively, is huge, almost as large as the state's iron and steel industry. In contrast, in the northern states where sugarcane is grown, cooperatives are not prominent.

How and why are sugar cooperatives so successful in this region? The answer lies in the different pattern of social stratification. The rural social stratification system in Maharashtra is simpler than in northern India. In most villages, the Marathas are the dominant caste, but here they constitute even more of a majority and control even more village land than is typical of dominant castes. They also have stronger local ties with each other because their marital arrangements are locally centralized. Thus, they have a better basis for cooperating with each other in spite of class differences among themselves. Large farmers dominate the elected board of directors of the cooperatives. These "sugar barons" use their position to gain power in state politics. However, within the cooperatives their power is held in check. They do not form cliques that exploit the cooperatives to the detriment of the less wealthy. In fact, large farmers cannot afford to alienate the small and midsize farmers, for that would mean economic ruin for the cooperative and the loss of their own profits.

The technology of sugarcane processing requires wide participation of the farmers. Mechanization involves investing in expensive heavy equipment. The machinery cannot be run at a profit unless it is used at full capacity during the crushing season. If small and midsize farmers were displeased with their treatment, they might decide to pull out of the cooperative and put their cane into other uses. Then capacity would be underused and profits would fall.

CRAFT COOPERATIVES IN PANAMA In Panama's east coastal region, indigenous Kuna women have long sewn beautiful *molas,* or cloth with appliquéd designs (see Map 9.4). Kuna make this cloth for their own use as clothing, but since the 1960s, molas have been important items for sale both on the world market and to tourists who come to Panama (Tice 1995). Revenue from selling molas to tourists as well as internationally is now an important part of the household income of the Kuna. Some women continue to operate independently, buying their own cloth and thread and selling their molas either to an intermediary who exports them or in the local tourist market. But many women have joined cooperatives that offer them greater economic security. The cooperative buys cloth and thread in bulk and distributes it to the women. The women are paid almost the entire sale price for each mola, with only a small amount of the eventual sale prices being taken out for cooperative dues and administrative costs. Their earnings are steadier than what the fluctuating tourist season offers. Other benefits from being a member of the cooperative include the use of the cooperative as a consumer's cooperative (buying rice and sugar in bulk for members), a source of mutual strength and support, and a place for women

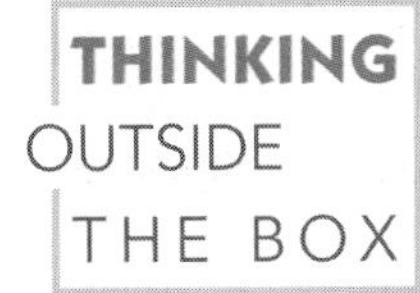

Do research on the current global distribution of Alcoholics Anonymous.

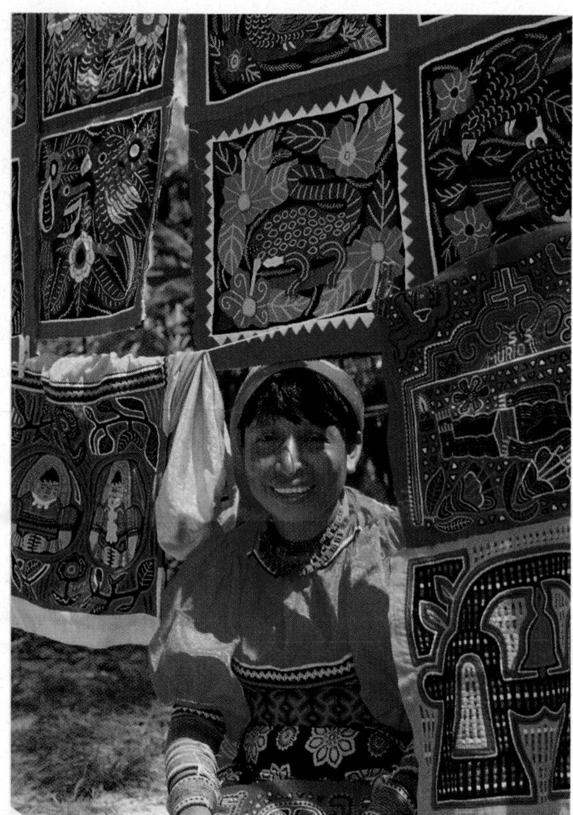

Kuna Indian woman selling molas, San Blas Islands, Panama.
▶ *Learn more about molas from the Web.*

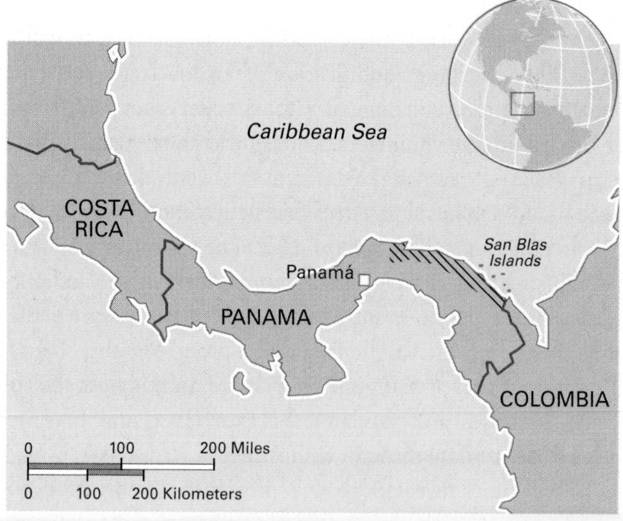

MAP 9.4 Kuna Region in Panama.
The Kuna are an indigenous people who live mainly in the eastern coastal region of Panama, including its offshore islands. Some live in cities and a few live in villages in neighboring Colombia. The Kuna population is around 150,000. Farming, fishing, and tourism are important parts of the economy. Each community has its own political organization, and the Kuna as a whole are organized into the Kuna General Congress. Most speak Kuna, or Dulegaya ("People's Language") and Spanish. They follow traditional religious practices, often with a mixture of Christian elements.

to develop greater leadership skills and to take advantage of opportunities for political participation in the wider society.

SELF-HELP GROUPS

Recent years have seen a worldwide proliferation of *self-help groups,* or groups formed to achieve specific personal goals, such as coping with illness or bereavement, or lifestyle change, such as trying to exercise more or lose weight. Self-help groups also increasingly use the Internet to form virtual support communities. Anthropologists who study these groups focus on why members join, on rituals of solidarity, and on leadership and organization patterns.

An ethnography of Alcoholics Anonymous groups in Mexico City (see Map 6.3, p. 144) reports that most members are low-income, working-class males (Brandes 2002). They migrated to Mexico City from rural areas several decades earlier to find work and improve their standard of living. Their drinking problems are related both to their poverty and to the close links between alcohol consumption and male gender identity in Mexico: A "real man" consumes a lot of alcohol. Through a dynamic of shared stories and regular meetings, AA members in Mexico City achieve a high rate of sobriety.

The success of AA in Mexico is leading to a rapid proliferation of groups. Membership is growing at about 10 percent a year, a remarkably high rate of growth for a self-help organization. At the end of the twentieth century, Latin America accounted for almost one-third of the world AA membership. Thus, a model of a middle-class self-help organization that originated in the United States has been adopted and culturally localized by low-income men throughout Latin America.

◆◆◆

Social Stratification

Social stratification consists of hierarchical relationships between different groups, as though they were arranged in layers or *strata.* Stratified groups may be unequal on a variety of measures, including material resources, power, human welfare, education, and symbolic attributes. People in groups in higher positions have privileges not experienced by those in lower-echelon groups, and they are likely to be interested in maintaining their privileged position. Social stratification appeared late in human history, most clearly with the emergence of agriculture. Now some form of social stratification is nearly universal.

Analysis of the categories—such as class, "race," gender, age, and indigeneity—that form stratification systems reveals a crucial difference among them in the degree to which membership in a given category is an **ascribed position,** based on qualities of a person gained through birth, or an **achieved position,** based on qualities of a person gained through action.

Ascribed positions may be based on one's "race," ethnicity, gender, age, and physical ability. These factors are generally out of the control of the individual, although some flexibility exists for gender (through surgery and hormonal treatments) and for certain kinds of physical conditions. Also, one can sometimes "pass" as a member of another "race" or ethnic group. Age is an interesting ascribed category because an individual goes through several different status levels associated with age. Achievement as a basis for group membership means that a person belongs on the premise of some valued attainment. Ascribed systems are thus more "closed" and achievement-based systems more "open" in terms of mobility within the system (either upward or downward). Some scholars of social status believe that increasing social complexity and modernization led to an increase in achievement-based positions and a decline in ascription-based positions. The following material explores how social categories define group membership and relations of inequality among groups.

Societies place people into categories—student, husband, child, retired person, political leader, or member of Phi Beta Kappa—referred to as a person's **status**, or position or standing in society (C. Wolf 1996). Each status has an accompanying role, which is expected behavior for someone of a particular status, and a "script" for how to behave, look, and talk. Some statuses have more prestige attached to them than others. Within societies that have marked status positions, different status groups are marked by a particular lifestyle, including goods owned, leisure activities, and linguistic styles. The maintenance of group position by higher-status categories is sometimes accomplished by exclusionary practices in relation to lower-status groups through a tendency toward group in-marriage and socializing only within the group. Groups, like individuals, have status, or standing in society.

ACHIEVED STATUS: CLASS

Social class (defined in Chapter 1) refers to a person's or group's position in society defined primarily in economic terms. In many cultures, class is a key factor in determining a person's status, whereas in others, it is less important than, for example, birth into a certain family. Class and status, however, do not always match. A rich person may have become wealthy in disreputable ways and never gain high status. Both status and class groups are secondary groups, because a person is unlikely to know every other member of the group, especially in large-scale societies. In most instances, they are also informal groups; there are no recognized leaders or elected officials of the "urban elite" or the "working class." Subsegments of these large categories do organize themselves into formal groups, such as labor unions or exclusive clubs for the rich and famous. Class can be both ascribed and achieved because a person who is born rich has a greater than average chance of living an upper-class lifestyle.

In capitalist societies, the prevailing ideology is that the system allows for upward mobility and that every individual has the option of moving up. Some anthropologists refer to this ideology as *meritocratic individualism,* the belief that rewards go to those who deserve them (Durrenberger 2001). This ideology would seem to be most valid for people with decent jobs rather than menial workers or the unemployed, but in fact the ideology is widely held outside the middle class. In the United States, the pervasive popular belief in rewards for equal opportunity and merit is upheld and promoted in schools and universities, even in the face of substantial evidence to the contrary.

Conservative governments have long sought to weaken labor unions, and they continue to promote the fantasy of a classless society based on meritocratic individualism to support their antiunion policies. Anthropologists who take a structurist perspective point to the power of economic class position in shaping a person's lifestyle and his or her ability to choose a different one. Obviously, a person who was born rich can, through individual agency, become poor, and a poor person can become rich. In spite of exceptions to the rule, a person born rich is more likely to lead a lifestyle typical of that class, just as a person born poor is more likely lead a lifestyle typical of that class.

The concept of class is central to the theories of Karl Marx. Situated within the context of Europe's Industrial Revolution and the growth of capitalism, Marx wrote that class differences, exploitation of the working class by the owners of capital, class consciousness among workers, and class conflict are forces of change that would eventually spell the downfall of capitalism. In contrast to Marx's approach, French sociologist Emile Durkheim viewed social differences (including class) as the basis for social solidarity (1966 [1895]). He distinguished two major forms of societal cohesion: **mechanical solidarity**, social cohesion among similar groups, and **organic solidarity**, social cohesion among groups with different abilities and resources. Mechanical solidarity creates less enduring relationships because it involves little mutual need. Organic solidarity builds on need and provides

---

social stratification hierarchical relationships between different groups as though they were arranged in layers, or "strata."

ascribed position a person's standing in society based on qualities that the person has gained through birth.

achieved position a person's standing in society based on qualities that the person has gained through action.

status a person's position, or standing, in society.

mechanical solidarity social bonding among groups that are similar.

organic solidarity social bonding among groups with different abilities and resources.

(TOP) Salvatore Ferragamo headquarters in Firence (Florence), Italy. Top brand names such as Ferragamo are highly sought after by consumers internationally who can afford to buy these luxury goods. (BOTTOM) Warren Buffett, the world's richest man as of 2009. American businessman, investor, and philanthropist, Buffett is worth around US $62 billion. He is, however, known for his frugal life style.

▶ *For a class project, do research for a report on Buffett's biography with attention to cultural context.*

complementary resources to different groups, thus creating stronger bonds than mechanical solidarity does. Durkheim placed these two concepts in an evolutionary framework, saying that in nonindustrial times, the division of labor was only minimally specialized: Everyone did what everyone else did. With increasing social complexity and economic specialization, organic solidarity emerged as increasingly important.

ASCRIBED STATUS: "RACE," ETHNICITY, AND CASTE

Three major ascribed systems of social stratification are based on divisions of people into unequally ranked groups on the basis of "race," ethnicity (defined in Chapter 1), and caste, a ranked group, determined by birth, often linked to a particular occupation and to South Asian cultures. Like status and class groups, these three categories are secondary social groups, because no one can have a personal relationship with all other members of the entire group. Each system takes on local specificities depending on the context. For example, "race" and ethnicity are interrelated and overlap with conceptions of culture in much of Latin America, although differences in what they mean in terms of identity and status occur in different countries in the region (de la Cadena 2001). For some, the concept of **mestizaje** (mes-tee-ZAH-jay), mestizo, literally means "racial" mixture. In Central and South America, it refers to people who are cut off from their Indian roots, or literate and successful people who retain some indigenous cultural practices. One has to know the local system of categories and meanings attached to them to understand the dynamics of inequality that go with them.

Systems based in difference defined in terms of "race," ethnicity, and caste share with each other, and with class-based systems, some important features. First, they relegate large numbers of people to particular levels of entitlement to livelihood, power, security, esteem, and freedom (Berreman 1979 [1975]:213). This simple fact should not be overlooked. Second, those with greater entitlements dominate those with lesser entitlements. Third, members of the dominant groups tend to seek to maintain their position, consciously or unconsciously. They do this through institutions that control ideology among the dominated and through institutions that physically suppress potential rebellion or subversion by the dominated (Harris 1971, quoted in Mencher 1974:469). Fourth, in spite of efforts to maintain systems of dominance, instances of subversion and rebellion do occur, indicating the potential for agency among the oppressed.

"RACE" Racial stratification is a relatively recent form of social inequality. It results from the unequal meeting of two formerly separate groups through colonization, slavery, and other large-group movements (Sanjek 1994). Europe's "age of discovery," beginning in the 1500s, ushered in a new era of

Boys in a small town of Brazil exhibit some of the skin-color diversity in the Brazilian population.

global contact. In contrast, in relatively homogeneous cultures, ethnicity is a more important distinction than "race." In contemporary Nigeria, for example, the population is largely homogeneous, and ethnicity is the more salient term (Jinadu 1994). A similar situation prevails in other African states as well as in the Middle East, Central Europe and Eurasia, and China.

A key feature of racial thinking is its insistence that behavioral differences among peoples are "natural," inborn, or biologically caused (in this, it resembles sexism, ageism, and casteism). Throughout the history of racial categorizations in the West, such features as head size, head shape, and brain size have been accepted as the reasons for behavioral differences. Writing early in the twentieth century, Franz Boas contributed to de-linking supposed inborn, racial attributes from behavior (review Chapter 1). He showed that people with the same head size but from different cultures behaved differently and that people with various head sizes within the same cultures behaved similarly. For Boas and his followers, culture, not biology, is the key explanation for behavior. Thus "race" is not a biological reality; there is no way to divide the human population into "races" based on certain biological features. Yet social race and racism exist. In other words, the concept of "race" in many contexts has a social reality in terms of people's entitlements, status, and treatment. In spite of some progress in reducing racism in the United States in the twentieth century, racial discrimination persists. One way of understanding this persistence is to see racial discrimination as linked to class formation rather than separate from it (Brodkin 2000). In this view, racial stereotyping and discrimination function to keep people in less desirable jobs or unemployed, as necessary aspects of advanced industrial capitalism, which depends on there being a certain number of low-paid workers and even a certain amount of unemployment.

Racial classifications in the Caribbean and in Latin America involve complicated systems of status classification. This complexity results from the variety of contact over the centuries between peoples from Europe, Africa, Asia, and indigenous populations. Skin tone is one basis of racial classification, but it is mixed with other physical features and economic status as well. In Haiti, for example, racial categories take into account physical factors such as skin texture, depth of skin tone, hair color and appearance, and facial features (Trouillot 1994). Racial categories also include a person's income, social origin, level of formal education, personality or behavior, and kinship ties. Depending on how these variables are combined, a person occupies one category or another—and may even move between categories. Thus, a person with certain physical features who is poor will be considered to be a different "color" than a person with the same physical features who is well-off.

An extreme example of racial stratification was the South African policy of apartheid, legally sanctioned segregation of dominant Whites from non-Whites. White dominance in South Africa (see Map 9.5) began in the early 1800s with White migration and settlement. In the 1830s, slavery was abolished. At the same time, increasingly racist thinking developed among Whites (Johnson 1994:25). Racist images, including visions of Africans as lazy, out of control, and sex driven, served as the rationale for colonialist domination in place of outright slavery. In spite of years of African resistance to White domination, the Whites succeeded in maintaining and increasing their control for nearly two centuries. In South Africa, Blacks constitute 90 percent of the population, a numerical majority dominated, through strict apartheid, by the White minority until only recently. Every aspect of life for the majority of Africans was far worse than for the Whites. Every measure of life quality—infant mortality, longevity, education—showed great disparity between the Whites and the Africans. In addition to physical deprivation, the Africans experienced psychological suffering through constant insecurity about raids from the police and other forms of violence. Now, they face the scourge of continuing poverty and disentitlement as well as excess death and suffering from HIV/AIDS.

In contrast to the explicitly racist discrimination of South African apartheid, racism exists even where it is against the law to discriminate against people on the basis of race. In such contexts, racism is often denied and therefore a challenge

---

mestizaje literally, racial mixture; in Central and South America, indigenous people who are cut off from their Indian roots, or literate and successful indigenous people who retain some traditional cultural practices.

In 2003, the Treatment Action Campaign (TAC) began a program of civil disobedience to prompt the government of South Africa to sign and implement a National Prevention and Treatment Plan for HIV/AIDS. The TAC uses images of Hector Peterson, the first youth killed in the Soweto uprising against apartheid, and slogans such as "The Struggle Continues: Support HIV/AIDS Treatment Now."

▶ *Take a position, and be prepared to defend it, on whether or not a country's government should take responsibility for preventing and treating HIV/AIDS.*

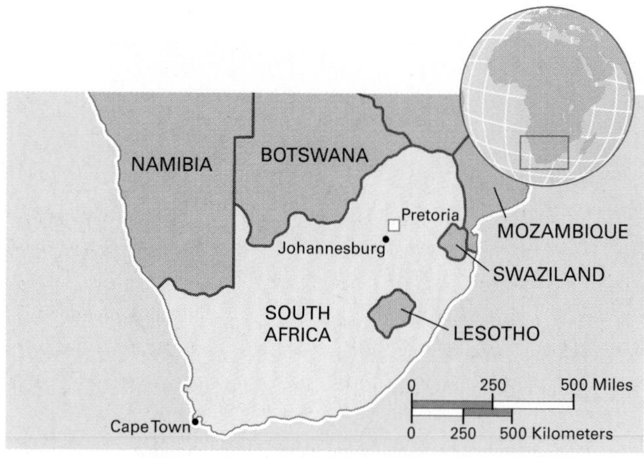

MAP 9.5 South Africa.
The Republic of South Africa experienced the highest level of colonial immigration of any African country. Its rich mineral wealth attracted interest from global powers through the Cold War era. Of its population of over 46 million, 80 percent are Black South Africans. The rest are of mixed ethnic backgrounds (referred to as "Coloureds"), Indian (from India), or White descendants of colonial immigrants. South Africa has 11 official languages, and it recognizes 8 nonofficial languages. Afrikaans and English are the major languages of the administration. Nonofficial languages include those of the San and other indigenous peoples.

to fight. In the United States, racism plays out in many areas of life including environmental pollution (see Eye on the Environment).

ETHNICITY Ethnicity is a sense of group membership based on a shared sense of identity (Comaroff 1987). Identity may be based on the perception of shared history, territory, language, religion, or a combination of these. Ethnicity can be a basis for claiming entitlements to resources (such as land, buildings, or artifacts) and for defending or regaining those resources.

States are interested in managing ethnicity to the extent that it does not threaten security. China has one of the most formalized systems for monitoring its many ethnic groups, and it has an official policy on ethnic minorities, meaning the non-Han groups (Wu 1990). The government lists a total of 54 groups other than the Han majority, which constitutes about 94 percent of the total. The other 6 percent of the population is made up of these 54 groups, about 67 million people. The non-Han minorities occupy about 60 percent of China's land mass and are located in border or "frontier" areas such as Tibet, Yunnan, Xinjiang, and Inner Mongolia. Basic criteria for defining an ethnic group include language, territory, economy, and "psychological disposition." The Chinese government establishes strict definitions of group membership and group characteristics; it even sets standards for ethnic costumes and dances.

The Chinese treatment of the Tibetan people is especially severe and can be considered *ethnocide,* or annihilation of the culture of an ethnic group by a dominant group.

The Chinese government's treatment of Tibetan traditional medicine over the past several decades illustrates how the Han majority exploits aspects of minority cultures. In 1951, China forcibly incorporated Tibet, and the Chinese government undertook measures to bring about the social and economic transformation of what was formerly a decentralized, Buddhist feudal regime. This transformation has caused increasing ethnic conflict between Tibetans and Han Chinese, including demonstrations by Tibetans and crackdowns from the Chinese. Traditional Tibetan medicine has become part of the Chinese–Tibetan conflicts because of its cultural significance and importance to religion in Tibetan society (Janes 1995:7). Previously based on a model of apprenticeship training, it is now westernized and involves several years of classroom-based, lecture-oriented learning followed by an internship. At Tibet University, only half of all formal lecture-based instruction is concerned with traditional Tibetan medicine. Curriculum changes have reduced the integrity of Tibetan medicine: It has been separated from its Buddhist content, and parts of it have been merged with a biomedical approach. Some might say that overall, traditional Tibetan medicine has been "revived" in China, but stronger evidence supports the argument that the state has co-opted it and transformed it for its own purposes.

---

diaspora population a dispersed group of people living outside their original homeland.

eye on the ENVIRONMENT

Industrial Pollution and Activism in an African American Community in Georgia, the United States

"But I know it's true" is an often repeated phrase among African American residents of the Hyde Park area of Augusta, Georgia (Checker 2005, 2007). Following World War II, many rural African American families in Georgia bought land in Hyde Park, a swampy area, but nonetheless one that allowed them access to nearby jobs in factories or as domestic workers. The neighborhood was vibrant with shops and churches. It was, however, poorly serviced by the government and surrounded by several industrial enterprises including Southern Wood Piedmont (SWP), a wood-preserving factory.

In the 1980s, several residents fell ill with uncommon and mysterious forms of cancer and skin diseases. SWP was found to be polluting the ground water in the neighborhood with dioxins, chlorophenols, and other chemicals. The factory closed in 1988 and began efforts to remediate the contamination. A nearby low-income neighborhood that was predominantly White settled a class-action lawsuit against SWP and received compensation. The residents of Hyde Park were not told of the lawsuit or asked to join it, and they therefore received no compensation.

Hyde Park residents began to learn of other sources of industrial pollution including PCBs. More cases emerged, especially among children, of rashes, lupus, respiratory and circulatory problems, and rare forms of cancer. People stopped letting their children play in the backyard, in order to avoid contact with contaminated ditch water and soil. They stopped growing vegetables in their home gardens. The value of their homes fell dramatically. In sum, they lost their health, their freedom to use their own property for play, and their economic security.

Over time, more studies showed high levels of chemicals and heavy metals in the groundwater and soil in Hyde Park. Georgia's Environmental Protection Division (EPD) continued to argue that levels were within normal ranges. Hyde Park residents, however, were convinced that the pollution was causing their health and other problems. They organized in order to make their claims heard.

Environmental justice activism refers to social movements dedicated to documenting the structural violence and inequality that place certain groups at risk of losing their entitlements to live in a safe and healthy environment and in helping such groups gain compensation or other forms of redress. Hyde Park residents, along with a nearby African American neighborhood, formed HAPIC, the Hyde and Aragon Park Improvement Committee. HAPIC activists use a unique blend of Black solidarity, church-based organizing principles, computers to bridge the digital divide (see Chapter 12), and connections with wider environmental groups such as the Sierra Club to make its voice heard in the state political arena.

◆ FOOD FOR THOUGHT

- Do Internet research to learn about the current status of the Hyde Park residents' efforts to make their neighborhood livable and gain compensation for damages to their health and household security.

People of one ethnic group who move from one niche to another are at risk of exclusionary treatment by the local residents. Roma (formerly called gypsies by outsiders but considered a derogatory term by the Roma), are a **diaspora population**, a dispersed group living outside their original homeland, and are scattered throughout Europe and the United States (see Culturama). A less difficult but still not easy adjustment is being experienced by Indo-Canadians (immigrants from India to Canada). In research among a sample of nearly 300 Indo-Canadians in Vancouver, British Columbia, about half of all the respondents reported experiencing some form of discrimination in the recent past (Nodwell and Guppy 1992). The percentage was higher among men (54 percent) than among women (45 percent). The higher level for men was consistent across the four categories: verbal abuse, property damage, workplace discrimination, and physical harm. Verbal abuse was the most frequent form of discrimination, reported by 40 percent of both men and women. Indo-Canadians of the Sikh faith who were born in India say that they experience the highest levels of discrimination in Canada. Apparently, however, their actual experience of discrimination is not greater than for other Indo-Canadians. The difference is that Sikhs who were born in India are more sensitive to discrimination than others. Sikhism, as taught and practiced in India, supports a strong sense of honor, which should be protected and, if wronged, avenged. This study helps explain differences in perception of discrimination among ethnic migrants. It does not, however, explain why such high levels of discriminatory treatment exist in a nation committed to ethnic tolerance.

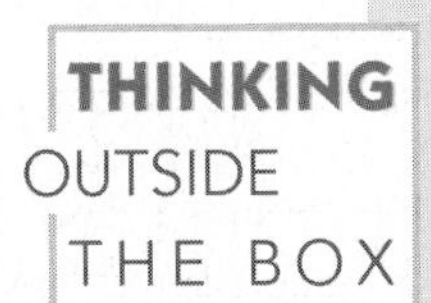

With which ethnic or other kind of social group do you identify? What are the bases of this identification? Is your social group relatively high or low in terms of social status?

The Roma of Eastern Europe

The Roma, better known by the derogatory term "Gypsies," are Europe's largest minority population. They live in nearly all the countries of Europe and Central Asia. In Europe, their total is between 7 and 9 million people (World Bank 2003). They are most concentrated in the countries of Eastern Europe, where they constitute around 10 percent of the population.

Roma history is one of mobility and marginality ever since several waves of migrants left their original homeland in northern India between the ninth and fourteenth centuries CE (Crowe 1996). For many Roma in Europe, their lifestyle continues to involve movement. Temporary camps of their wagons often appear overnight on the outskirts of a town. Settled Roma typically live in marginalized areas that lack decent housing, clean water, and good schools. Most members of mainstream society look down on, and even despise, the Roma.

In Budapest, Hungary, the Roma minority is the most disadvantaged ethnic group (Ladányi 1993). Not all Roma in Budapest, however, are poor. About 1 percent have gained wealth. The other 99 percent live in substandard housing in the slums of inner Pest. Since the fall of state socialism in Hungary, discrimination against the Roma has increased. The government of Hungary has a policy that allows the Roma a degree of local minority self-government (Schaft and Brown 2000). Some Roma communities are mobilizing to improve their living conditions.

In Slovakia, one-third of the Roma live in ghetto-like enclaves called *osada* (Scheffel 2004). The heaviest concentration of osadas is in the eastern province. These settlements lack clean water, sewage treatment, reliable electricity, access to decent housing, good schools, and passable roads. They exist in close proximity to affluent neighborhoods of ethnic Slovaks, or "Whites." In one village, Svinia (SVEEH-nee-yuh), roughly 700 Roma are crowded together on a hectare of swampy land while their 670 ethnic Slovak neighbors own over 1400 hectares of land (2004:8).

As more Eastern European countries seek to enter the European Union, they are initiating programs to improve Roma living conditions and enacting laws to prevent discrimination. Fieldwork in Slovakia indicates that the government there is doing little to improve the lives of the Roma. The situation in Hungary is better. After Hungary joined the European Union in 2004, it elected two Roma to the EU Parliament. In Bulgaria, the Roma won a court case in 2005 declaring that segregated schools were unconstitutional.

Thanks to David Z. Scheffel, Thompson Rivers University, for reviewing this material.

(LEFT) The Roma settlement of Svinia in 1993. The standard of living has not improved since the 1990s, but the population has increased by nearly 50 percent, resulting in overcrowding and high levels of stress.
(CENTER) Roma children's access to school facilities is severely restricted. A few Romani schoolchildren participate in the school lunch program but in a separate room next to the cafeteria.

MAP 9.6 Roma Population in Eastern Europe. Romania has the highest number of Roma of any country in the world, between 1 and 2 million. Macedonia has the highest percentage of Roma in its population.

CASTE The **caste system** is a social stratification system linked with Hinduism and based on a person's birth into a particular group. It exists in its clearest form in India, among its Hindu population, and in other areas of Hindu culture such as Nepal, Sri Lanka, and Fiji. The caste system is particularly associated with Hindu peoples because ancient Hindu scriptures are taken as the foundational sources for defining the major social categories called *varnas* (a Sanskrit word meaning "color") (see Figure 9.2). The four varnas are the *brahmans,* priests; the *kshatriya,* warriors; the *vaishya,* merchants; and the *shudras,* laborers. Men of the first three varnas go through a ritual ceremony of initiation and "rebirth," after which they may wear a sacred thread across their chest, indicating their purity and high status as "twice-born." Beneath the four varna groups are people considered so low that they are outside the caste system itself, hence the English term "outcast." Another English term for them is "untouchables," because people of the upper varnas avoided any kind of contact with them in order to maintain their purity. Mahatma Gandhi, himself a member of an upper caste, renamed them *harijans* ("children of god") in his attempt to raise their status into that of the shudras. Currently, members of this category have adopted the term **dalit** (dah-lit), which means "oppressed" or "ground down."

The four traditional varnas and the dalit category contain many hundreds of locally named groups called castes, or, more appropriately, *jatis* (birth group). The term "caste" is a Portuguese word meaning "breed" or "type." Portuguese colonialists first used it in the fifteenth century to refer to the closed social groups they encountered (Cohn 1971:125). Jati, a more emic term, conveys the meaning that a Hindu is born into his or her group. Jatis are ascribed status groups. Just as the four varnas are ranked relative to each other, so are all the jatis within them. For example, the jati of brahmans is divided into priestly and nonpriestly subgroups; the priestly brahmans are separated into household priests, temple priests, and funeral priests; the household priests are broken down into two or more categories; and each of those are divided into subgroups based on lineage ties (Parry 1966:77). Within all these categories exist well-defined status hierarchies.

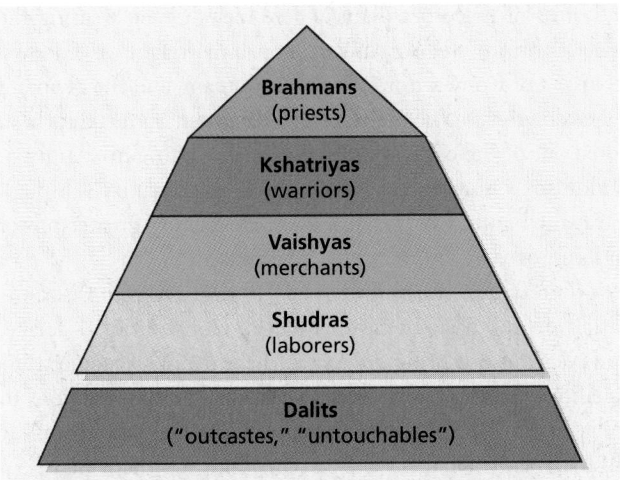

FIGURE 9.2 Model of India's Varna Categories

Status levels also exist among dalits. In western Nepal, which, like India, has a caste system, dalit artisans such as basket weavers and ironsmiths are the highest tier (Cameron 1995). They do not touch any of the people beneath them. The second tier includes leatherworkers and tailors. The bottom tier comprises people who are "untouchable" to all groups, including other dalits, because their work is extremely polluting according to Hindu rules. This category includes musicians (because some of their instruments are made of leather and they perform in public) and sex workers.

Indian anthropologist M. N. Srinivas (1959) contributed the concept of the *dominant caste* to refer to the tendency for one caste in any particular village to control most of the land and, often, to be numerically preponderant as well. Brahmans are at the top of the social hierarchy in terms of ritual purity, and they are often, but not always, the dominant caste. Throughout northern India, it is common for jatis of the kshatriya varna to be the dominant village group. This is the case in Pahansu village, where a group called the Gujars is dominant (Raheja 1988). The Gujars constitute the numerical majority, and they control most of the land. Moreover, they dominate in the *jajmani system,* a patron-provider system in which landholding patrons (*jajmans*) are linked, through exchanges of food for services, with brahman priests, artisans (blacksmiths, potters), agricultural laborers, and other workers such as sweepers. In Pahansu, Gujars have power and status as the major patrons, supporting many different service providers who are beholden to them.

Some anthropologists have described the jajmani service system as one of mutual interdependence (organic solidarity, to use Durkheim's term) that provides security for the less well-off. Others argue that the system benefits those at the top to the detriment of those at the bottom. This perspective, from "the bottom up," views the patron-service system and the entire caste system as one of exploitation by those at the top (Mencher 1974). The benign interpretation is based on research conducted among the upper castes who present this view. From low-caste people's perspective, it is the patrons who have the power. Dissatisfied patrons can dismiss service providers, refuse them loans, or not pay them. Service providers who are dissatisfied with the treatment they receive

---

caste system a form of social stratification linked with Hinduism and based on a person's birth into a particular group.

dalit the preferred name for the socially defined lowest groups in the Indian caste system, meaning "oppressed" or "ground down."

(LEFT) Only a special category of brahman priests can officiate at the Chidambaram temple in Tamil Nadu, southern India. Here, members of a mixed-age group sit for a moment's relaxation. (RIGHT) A village carpenter in front of his house in a north Indian village. The status of carpenters is midlevel, between the landholding elites or brahman priests and those who deal with polluting materials such as animal hides or refuse.

▶ *In your culture, what social status do carpenters, toolmakers, or other skilled manual laborers have?*

from their patrons have little recourse. In addition, male patrons often demand sexual access to females of service-providing households.

Throughout South Asia, the growth of industrial manufacturing has reduced the need for some service providers, especially tailors, potters, and weavers. Many of these people have left their villages to work in urban areas. The tie that remains the strongest is between patrons and their brahman priests, whose ritual services cannot be replaced by machines.

The caste system involves several mechanisms that maintain it: marriage rules, spatial segregation, and ritual. Marriage rules strictly enforce jati endogamy (in-group marriage). Marriage outside one's jati, especially in rural areas and particularly between a higher-caste female and lower-caste male, is cause for serious, even lethal, punishment by caste elders and other local power-holders. Among urban educated elites, a trend toward inter-jati marriages is emerging.

Spatial segregation functions to maintain the privileged preserve of the upper castes and to remind the lower castes continually of their marginal status. In many rural contexts, the dalits live in a completely separate cluster; in other cases, they have their own neighborhood sections into which no upper-caste person will venture. Ritual rules and practices also serve to maintain dominance. The rich upper-caste leaders sponsor important annual festivals, thereby regularly restating their claim to public prominence (Mines 1994).

Social mobility within the caste system has traditionally been limited, but instances have been documented of group "up-casting." Several strategies exist, including gaining wealth, affiliation or merger with a somewhat higher jati, education, migration, and political activism (Kolenda 1978). A group that attempts to gain higher jati status takes on the behavior and dress of twice-born jatis. These include men wearing the sacred thread, vegetarianism, non-remarriage of widows, seclusion of women from the public domain, and the giving of larger dowries for the marriage of a daughter. Some dalits have opted out of the caste system by converting to Christianity or Buddhism. Others are becoming politically organized through the Dalit Panthers, a social movement seeking greater power and improved economic status for dalits.

The Indian constitution of 1949 declared that discrimination on the basis of caste is illegal. Constitutional decree, however, did not bring an end to these deeply structured inequalities. In the late twentieth century, the government of India instituted policies to promote the social and economic advancement of dalits, such as reserving for them places in medical schools, seats in the government, and public-sector jobs. This "affirmative action" plan has infuriated many of the upper castes, especially brahmans, who feel most threatened. Is the caste system on the decline? Surely aspects of it are changing. Especially in large cities, people of different jatis can "pass" and participate on a more nearly equal basis in public life—if they have the economic means to do so.

◆◆◆

Civil Society

Civil society consists of the social domain of diverse interest groups that function outside the government to organize economic, political, and other aspects of life. It has a long history in Western philosophy, and many different definitions have been proposed by thinkers such as John Locke, Thomas Paine, Adam Smith, and Karl Marx (Kumar 1996:89). According to the German philosopher Hegel, civil society encompasses the social groups and institutions between the individual and the state. Italian social theorist Gramsci wrote that there are two basic types of civic institutions: those that support the state, such as the church and schools, and those that oppose state power, such as trade unions, social protest groups, and citizens' rights groups.

CIVIL SOCIETY FOR THE STATE: THE CHINESE WOMEN'S MOVEMENT

In some instances, governments seek to build civil society to further their goals. The women's movement in China is an example of such a state-created organization. Canadian anthropologist Ellen Judd (2002) conducted a study of the women's movement in China, within the constraints that the government imposes on anthropological fieldwork by foreigners. Under the Mao leadership, foreign anthropologists were not allowed to do research of any sort in China. The situation began to change in the 1980s when some field research, within strict limitations, became possible.

Judd developed a long-term relationship with China over several decades, having lived there as a student from 1974 to 1977, undertaking long-term fieldwork there in 1986, and returning almost every year since for research or some other activity, such as being involved in a development project for women or attending the Beijing Fourth World Conference on Women. According to Judd, "These various ways of being in China all allowed me some interaction with Chinese women and some knowledge of their lives" (2002:14). In her latest project to study the Chinese women's movement, she wanted to conduct research as a cultural anthropologist would normally do, through intensive participant observation over a long period of time.

Even now, the Chinese government limits such research, keeping foreigners at a distance from everyday life. Judd was not allowed to join the local women's organization or to speak privately with any of the women. Officials accompanied her on all household visits and interviews. She was allowed to attend meetings, however, and she had access to all the public information about the goals of the women's movement, which is called the Women's Federations. A policy goal of the Chinese government is to improve the quality of women's lives, and the Women's Federations were formed to address that goal. The government oversees the operation at all levels, from the national level to the township and village. The primary objective is to mobilize women, especially rural women, to participate in literacy training and market activities.

Judd's fieldwork, constrained as it was by government regulations, nevertheless yielded insights. She learned, through interviews with women members, about some women who have benefited from the programs, and she discovered how important education for women is in terms of their ability to enter into market activities. The book she wrote is largely descriptive, focusing on the "public face" of the Women's Federations in one locale. Such a descriptive account is the most that can emerge from research in China at this time. Given that the women's organizations are formed by and for the government, this example stretches the concept of civil society.

ACTIVIST GROUPS

Activist groups are groups formed with the goal of changing certain conditions, such as political repression, violence, and human rights violations. In studying activist groups, cultural anthropologists are interested in learning what motivates the formation of such groups, what their goals and strategies are, and what leadership patterns they exhibit. Sometimes anthropologists join the efforts of activist groups and use their knowledge to support these groups' goals (see Lessons Applied).

Many activist groups are initiated and organized by women. CO-MADRES of El Salvador (see Map 15.5, p. 383) is an important, women-led social movement in Latin America (Stephen 1995). CO-MADRES is a Spanish abbreviation for an organization called, in English, the Committee of Mothers and Relatives of Political Prisoners, Disappeared and Assassinated of El Salvador. It was founded in 1977 by a group of mothers protesting the atrocities committed by the Salvadoran government and military. During the civil war that lasted from 1979 until 1992, a total of 80,000 people died and 7000 more disappeared, or one in every 100 El Salvadorans.

The initial group comprised nine mothers. A year later, it had grown to nearly 30 members, including some men. In 1979, the group made its first international trip to secure wider recognition. This developed into a full-fledged and successful campaign for international solidarity in the 1980s,

---

civil society the collection of interest groups that function outside the government to organize economic and other aspects of life.

LESSONS applied

Advocacy Anthropology and Environmental Activism in Papua New Guinea

A controversial issue in applied anthropology is whether an anthropologist should take on the role of community activist, acting as an advocate on behalf of the people among whom he or she has conducted research (Kirsch 2002). Some say that anthropologists should maintain a neutral position in a conflict situation and simply offer information on issues that may be used by either side. Others say that it is appropriate and right for anthropologists to take sides and help support less powerful groups against more powerful groups. Those who endorse anthropologists taking an activist or advocacy role argue that neutrality is never truly neutral: By seemingly taking no position, one indirectly supports the status quo, and information provided to both sides will generally serve the interests of the more powerful side in any case.

Yonggom people gather at a meeting in Atkamba village on the Ok Tedi River, Papua New Guinea, to discuss legal proceedings in 1996. At the end of the meeting, leaders signed an agreement to an out-of-court settlement, which was presented to the Victorian Supreme Court in Melbourne, Australia. The current lawsuit concerns the Yonggom people's claim that the 1996 settlement agreement has been breached.

Stuart Kirsch took an activist role after conducting field research for over 15 years in a region of Papua New Guinea that has been negatively affected by a large copper and gold mine called the Ok Tedi mine (see Map 1.3, p. 19). The mine releases 80,000 tons of mining wastes into the local river system daily, causing extensive environmental damage that in turn affects people's food and water sources. Kirsch has joined with the local community in its extended legal and political campaign to limit further pollution and to gain compensation for damages suffered. He explains his involvement with the community as a form of reciprocal exchange. The community members have provided him with information about their culture for over 15 years. He believes that his knowledge is part of the people's cultural property and that they have a rightful claim to its use.

Kirsch's support of the community's goals took several forms. First, his scholarly research provided documentation of the problems of the people living downstream from the mine. Community activists incorporated his findings in their speeches when traveling in Australia, Europe, and the Americas to spread awareness of their case and gather international support. During the 1992 Earth Summit, one leader presented the media with excerpts from an article by Kirsch during a press conference held aboard the Greenpeace ship, *Rainbow Warrior II,* in the Rio de Janeiro harbor. Second, he worked closely with local leaders, helping them decide how best to convey their views to the public and in the court. Third, Kirsch served as a cultural broker in discussions among community members, politicians, mining executives, lawyers, and representatives of nongovernmental organizations (NGOs) in order to promote solutions for the problems faced by people living downstream from the mine. Fourth, he convened an international meeting of environmental NGOs in Washington, DC, in 1999 and secured funding to bring a representative from the community to the meeting.

In spite of official reports recommending that the mine be closed in 2001, its future remains uncertain. No assessment of past damages to the community has been prepared. As the case goes on, Kirsch will continue to support the community's efforts by sharing with them the results of his research, just as they have for so long shared their culture with him. Indigenous people worldwide are increasingly invoking their rights to anthropological knowledge about themselves. According to Kirsch, these claims require anthropologists to rethink their roles and relationships with the people they study. It can no longer be a relationship in which the community provides knowledge and the anthropologist keeps and controls that knowledge for his or her intellectual development alone. Although the details are still being worked out, the overall goal must be one of collaboration and cooperation.

◆ FOOD FOR THOUGHT

- Consider the pros and cons of anthropological advocacy and decide what position you would take on the Ok Tedi case. Be prepared to defend your position.

with support in other Latin American countries, Europe, Australia, the United States, and Canada. The group's increased visibility earned it repression from the government. Its office was bombed in 1980 and then four more times after that. Forty-eight members of CO-MADRES have been detained since 1977; five have been assassinated. Harassment and disappearances continued even after the signing of the Peace Accords in January 1992: "In February 1993, the son and the nephew of one of the founders of CO-MADRES were assassinated in Usulutan. This woman had already lived through the experience of her own detention, the detention and gang rape of her daughter, and the disappearance and assassination of other family members" (1995:814).

In the 1990s, CO-MADRES focused on holding the state accountable for human rights violations during the civil war, providing protection for political prisoners, seeking assurances of human rights protection in the future, working against domestic violence, educating women about political participation, and initiating economic projects for women. The work of CO-MADRES, throughout its history, has incorporated elements of both the "personal" and the "political," concerns of mothers and other family members for lost kin and for exposing and halting abuses of the state and military. The lesson learned from the case of CO-MADRES is that activist groups formed by women can be based on issues related to the domestic domain (murdered sons and other kin), but their activities can extend to the top of the public political hierarchy.

Another example of activist group formation under difficult conditions comes from urban Egypt (Hopkins and Mehanna 2000). The Egyptian government frowns on overt political action outside the realm of the government. Although Egyptian citizens are deeply concerned about environmental issues such as waste disposal, clean air and water, and noise, group formation for environmental causes is not easily accomplished. People interviewed in Cairo reported that they rarely discuss environmental issues with one another. One case of environmental concern, however, did result in the closing of a highly polluting lead smelter. People in the affected neighborhood banded together around this particular issue and called attention to the situation in the public media, prompting high-level officials to take up their case. They were successful because their target was localized on one relatively small industry and because the industry was so clearly guilty of polluting the environment.

A march of the "Mothers of the Disappeared" in Argentina. This organization of women combines activism motivated by personal causes (the loss of one's child or children to political torture and death) and the public issue of state repression.

▶ *How many activist groups in your culture can you name, and what are their goals?*

NEW SOCIAL MOVEMENTS AND CYBERPOWER

Social scientists have begun to use the term *new social movements* to refer to the many social activist groups that emerged in the late twentieth century around the world (Chapter 16 presents some examples in the context of international development). These groups are often formed by oppressed minorities such as indigenous peoples, ethnic groups, women, and the poor.

New social movements are taking advantage of cybertechnology to broaden their membership, exchange ideas, and raise funds (Escobar 2002). Cyber-enhanced social movements are important new political institutions that offer new ways to question, resist, and transform current structures. The importance of cybernetworking has not gone unnoticed by formal political leaders, who are paying increased attention to enhancing their personal websites and those of their parties.

9

the BIG questions REVISITED

◆ What are social groups and how do they vary cross-culturally?

Social groups can be classified in terms of whether all members have face-to-face interaction with one another, whether membership is based on ascription or achievement, and how formal the group's organization and leadership structure are. They extend from the most informal, face-to-face groups, such as those based on friendship, to groups that have formal membership requirements and whose members are widely dispersed and never meet each other. All groups have criteria for membership, often based on a perceived notion of similarity in terms of gender or class identity, work roles, opposition to mainstream culture, economic goals, or self-improvement.

Many groups require a formal ritual of initiation of new members. In some cases, initiation into the group involves dangerous or frightening activities that serve to bond members to one another through a shared experience of helplessness.

◆ What is social stratification?

Social stratification consists of hierarchical relationships between and among different groups, usually based on some culturally defined concept of status. Depending on the context, categories such as class, "race," ethnicity, gender, sexual preference, age, and ability may determine group and individual status.

The degree of social inequality among different status groups is highly marked in agricultural and industrial/informatics societies. Marked status inequalities are not characteristic of most foraging societies. Status inequalities are variable in pastoralist and horticultural societies, with leveling mechanisms typically at play to prevent the formation of severe inequalities.

India's caste-based system is an important example of a rigid structure of severe social inequality based on a person's birth group. According to ancient Hindu scriptures, the population is divided into mutually exclusive groups with different rights and privileges. Discrimination on the basis of caste is banned by the Indian constitution, yet it still exists, as does racism in other contexts even though formally illegal.

◆ What is civil society?

Civil society consists of groups and organizations that, although they are not part of the formal government, perform similar or complementary economic, political, or social functions. Civil society groups can be divided into those that support government policies and initiatives, and thus further the interests of government, and those that oppose government policies and actions.

Some anthropologists who study activist groups decide to take an advocacy role and apply their knowledge to further the goals of the community. This direction in applied anthropology is related to the view that anthropological knowledge is partly the cultural property of the people who have shared their lives and insights with the anthropologist.

New forms of information and communication technology help civil society groups gain visibility and stay in touch with their supporters.

KEY CONCEPTS

achieved position, p. 226
age set, p. 218
ascribed position, p. 226
caste system, p. 233
civil society, p. 235
dalit, p. 233
diaspora population, p. 231
mechanical solidarity, p. 227
mestizaje, p. 228
organic solidarity, p. 227
primary group, p. 218
secondary group, p. 218
social group, p. 218
social stratification, p. 226
status, p. 227
youth gang, p. 222

SUGGESTED READINGS

Sandra Bell and Simon Coleman, eds. *The Anthropology of Friendship*. New York: Berg, 1999. Following an introductory chapter by the editors on the anthropology of friendship, case studies discuss friendship in contemporary Melanesia, friendship as portrayed in Icelandic sagas, friendship in the context of a game of dominoes in a London pub, how friendship creates support networks in northern Europe, and the globalization of friendship ties in East Africa.

Gerald Berreman. *Caste and Other Inequities: Essays on Inequality*. Delhi, India: Folklore Institute, 1979. Berreman wrote these essays on caste and social inequality in India over a period of 20 years. Topics include caste and economy, caste ranking, caste and social interaction, and a comparison of caste with "race" in the United States.

Rosabelle Boswell. *Le Malaise Créole: Ethnic Identity in Mauritius*. New York: Bergahn Books, 2007. This book examines the marginalization of the Creole population in Mauritius. Most Creoles are descendants of slaves brought to the island from mainland Africa between the seventeenth and nineteenth centuries.

Stanley Brandes. *Staying Sober in Mexico City*. Austin: University of Texas Press, 2002. This ethnography of Alcoholics Anonymous groups in Mexico City focuses on how these groups help low-income men remain sober through social support. Although emphasizing the role of human agency in the men's attempts to remain sober, the author argues that the high rate of alcoholism among poor Mexican men must be viewed in the context of structural conditions.

Kia Lilly Caldwell. *Negras in Brazil: Re-Envisioning Black Women, Citizenship, and the Politics of Identity*. New Brunswick, NJ: Rutgers University Press, 2007. Fieldwork over more than a decade in several cities of Brazil informs this study of how Afro-Brazilian women see themselves as women, as Black, and as Brazilian. Narratives of 35 women show the connections between "race," gender, and social activism.

Liliana Goldin, ed. *Identities on the Move: Transnational Processes in North America and the Caribbean Basin*. Austin: University of Texas Press, 2000. This collection offers chapters on identity formation and change in the process of voluntary migration or displacement and on how states label and exclude transnationals, often in racialized ways.

Thomas A. Gregor and Donald Tuzin, eds. *Gender in Amazonia and Melanesia: An Exploration of the Comparative Method*. Berkeley: University of California Press, 2001. Two anthropologists, one a specialist on indigenous peoples of Amazonia and the other on Papua New Guinea, edited this volume, which includes a theoretical overview chapter and several chapters addressing similarities and differences between the two regions in fertility cults, rituals of masculinity, gender politics, and age-based gender roles.

Steven Gregory and Roger Sanjek, eds. *Race*. New Brunswick: Rutgers University Press, 1994. Following an introductory chapter by each editor, chapters discuss topics including racism in the United States and the Caribbean, how "race" articulates with other inequalities, and racism in higher education and anthropology.

Jake Kosek. *Understories: The Political Life of Forests in Northern New Mexico*. Durham: Duke University Press, 2007. This book is based on fieldwork in New Mexico and archival research. It exposes the racial, class, and other factors that shape the political disputes over forest resources in the Española Valley.

Cris Shore and Stephen Nugent, eds. *Elite Cultures: Anthropological Perspectives*. New York: Routledge, 2002. This volume contains two introductory chapters and a concluding chapter framing 12 ethnographic cases from around the world. Issues addressed are how elites in different societies maintain their positions, how elites represent themselves to others, and how anthropologists study elites.

Karin Tice. *Kuna Crafts, Gender and the Global Economy*. Austin: University of Texas Press, 1995. This ethnography looks at how the tourist market has affected women's production of molas in Panama and how women have organized into cooperatives to improve their situation.

Kevin A. Yelvington. *Producing Power: Ethnicity, Gender, and Class in a Caribbean Workplace*. Philadelphia, PA: Temple University Press, 1995. This ethnography examines class, "race," and gender inequalities as linked processes of social stratification within the context of a factory in Trinidad and in the wider social sites of households, neighborhoods, and global interconnections.

A political leader of the Ashanti people, Ghana. British colonialists referred to such leaders with the English term "chief" although the English word "king" might have been more appropriate.

POLITICS AND LEADERSHIP

the BIG questions

- What does political anthropology cover?
- What are the major cross-cultural forms of political organization and leadership?
- How are politics and political organization changing?

Anthropologists in all four fields address political and legal topics. Archaeologists study the evolution of centralized forms of political organization and the physical manifestations of power in monumental architecture, housing, and material possessions. Primatologists do research on dominant relationships, coalitions, and aggression among nonhuman primates. Linguistic anthropologists analyze power differences in interpersonal speech, the media, political propaganda, and more.

Political anthropology is the subfield of cultural anthropology that focuses on human behavior and thought related to power: who has it and who does not, degrees of power, bases of power, abuses of power, political organization and government, and relationships between political and religious power.

Politics and Culture

Is politics a human universal? Some anthropologists would say no. They point to instances of cultures with scarcely any institutions that can be called political, with no durable ranking systems, and with very little aggression. Foraging lifestyles, as a model for early human evolution, suggest that nonhierarchical social systems characterized human life for 90 percent of its existence. They point out that only with the emergence of private property, surpluses, and other changes did formal government emerge.

Many studies show how dominance seeking is a learned behavior, emphasized in some cultures and among some segments of the population, such as the military, and deemphasized among others, such as religious leaders, healers, and child-care providers. Being a good politician or a five-star general, therefore, is a matter of socialization rather than reflecting some innate drive (see Everyday Anthropology). Other anthropologists would argue that all societies, no matter how small and egalitarian, require some way to organize decision making and maintain social control. Thus in such societies, something like "politics" exists.

Compared to political scientists, cultural anthropologists take a broader view of politics that includes many kinds of behavior and thought beyond formal party politics, voting, and state governments. Cultural anthropologists offer examples of political systems and behavior that might not look "political" to people who have grown up in modern states. This section explores basic political concepts from an anthropological perspective.

British anthropologists, especially Bronislaw Malinowski and A. R. Radcliffe-Brown, long dominated theory making in political anthropology. Their approach, referred to as functionalism (review the discussion of this concept in Chapter 1), emphasized how institutions such as political organization and law promote social cohesion. Later, the students of these two teachers moved in new directions and began to look at aspects of political organization that pull societies apart. More recently, anthropologists have studied topics such as the politics of resistance of oppressed groups and how globalization and new media are changing power and politics everywhere. The history of political anthropology in the twentieth century and into the twenty-first century illustrates the theoretical tensions between the individual-as-agent approach and the structurist perspective that sees people as constrained in their choices by larger forces. Examples in this chapter show that power and politics are a double-edged sword: They can be both individually liberating and controlling.

POLITICS: THE USE OF POWER, AUTHORITY, AND INFLUENCE

This book uses the term *politics* to refer to the organized use of public power, not the more private micropolitics of family and domestic groups. **Power** is the ability to bring about results, often through the possession or use of forceful means. Closely related to power are authority and influence. **Authority** is the right to take certain forms of action. It is based on a person's achieved or ascribed status or moral reputation. Authority differs from power in that power is backed up by the potential use of force, and power can be wielded by individuals without their having authority in the moral sense. **Influence** is the ability to achieve a desired end by exerting social or moral pressure on someone or some group. Unlike authority, influence may be exerted from a low-status and marginal position.

All three terms are relational. A person's power, authority, or influence exists in relation to other people. Power implies the greatest likelihood of a coercive and hierarchical relationship, and authority and influence offer the most scope for consensual, cooperative decision making. Power, authority, and influence are all related to politics, power being the strongest basis for action and decision making—and potentially the least moral.

power the capacity to take action in the face of resistance, through force if necessary.

authority the ability to take action based on a person's achieved or ascribed status or moral reputation.

influence the ability to achieve a desired end by exerting social or moral pressure on someone or some group.

political organization the existence of groups for purposes of public decision making and leadership, maintaining social cohesion and order, protecting group rights, and ensuring safety from external threats.

everyday ANTHROPOLOGY

Socialization and Women Politicians in Korea

Parental attitudes and child-rearing practices affect children's involvement as adults in public political roles. Chunghee Sarah Soh's (1993) research in the Republic of Korea reveals how variation in paternal roles affects daughters' political leadership roles. Korean female members of the National Assembly can be divided into two categories: elected members (active seekers) and appointed members (passive recipients). Korea is a strongly patrilineal and male-dominated society, so female political leaders represent "a notable deviance from the usual gender-role expectations" (1993:54). This "deviance" is not stigmatized in Korean culture; rather, it is admired within the category of *yŏgŏl*. A yŏgŏl is a woman with "manly" accomplishments. Her personality traits include extraordinary bravery, strength, integrity, generosity, and charisma. Physically, a yŏgŏl is likely to be taller, larger, and stronger than most women and to have a stronger voice than other women. Why do some girls grow up to be yŏgŏls?

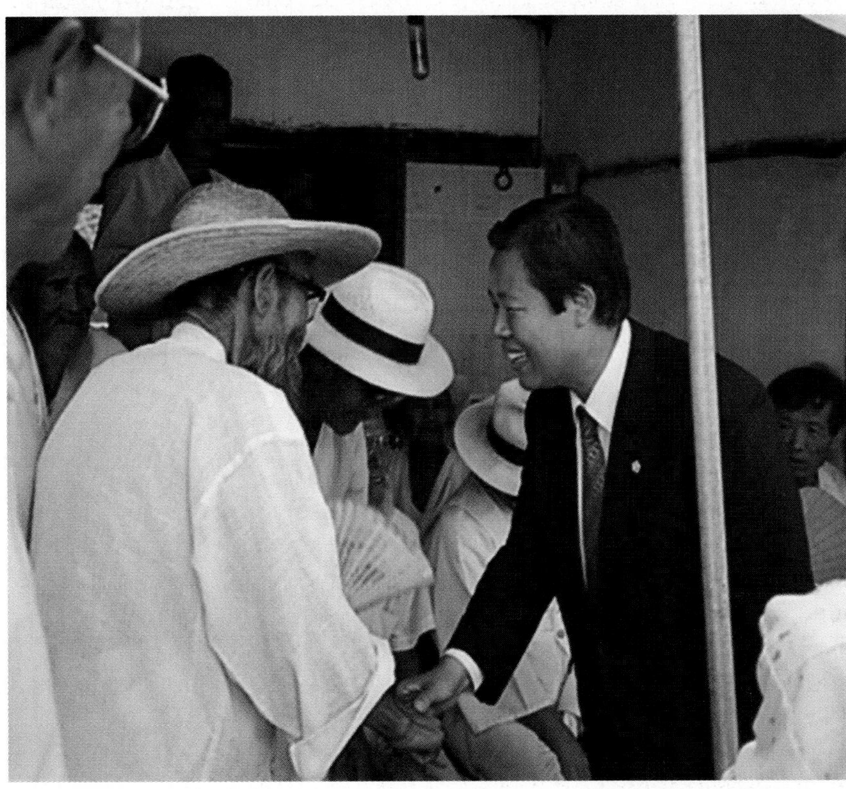

Representative Kim Ok-son greets some of her constituents who are members of alocal Confucian club in Seoul, Republic of Korea. She is wearing a men's-style suit and has a masculine haircut.

Analysis of the life histories of elected and appointed female legislators offers clues about differences in their socialization. Elected female legislators were likely to have had atypical paternal experiences of two types: either an absent father or an atypically nurturant father. Both of these experiences facilitated a girl's socialization into yŏgŏl qualities, or, in the words of Soh, into developing an androgynous personality that combines both masculine and feminine traits. In contrast, the presence of a "typical" father results in a girl developing a more "traditional" female personality that is submissive and passive.

An intriguing question follows from Soh's findings: What explains the socialization of different types of fathers—those who help daughters develop leadership qualities and those who socialize daughters for passivity?

◆ **FOOD FOR THOUGHT**

- Given your microcultural experience, what socialization factors do you think might influence boys or girls to become politicians?

Political Organization and Leadership

Political organization is the existence of groups for purposes such as public decision making and leadership, maintaining social cohesion and order, protecting group rights, and ensuring safety from external threats. Power relationships situated in the private domain—within the household, for example—may be considered "political" and may be related to wider political realities, but they are not forms of political organization. Political organizations have several features, some of which

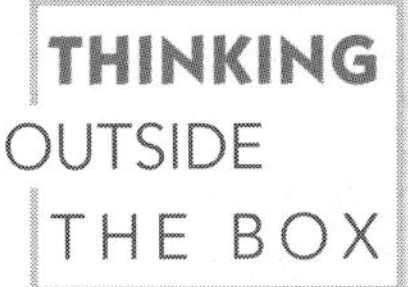

Consider the concepts of power, authority, and influence as defined here in the context of campus politics or in some other context with which you are familiar.

overlap with some groups and organizations discussed in Chapter 9 (Tiffany 1979:71–72):

- Recruitment principles: criteria for determining admission.
- Perpetuity: assumption that the group will continue to exist indefinitely.
- Identity markers: characteristics that distinguish it from others, such as costume, membership card, or title.
- Internal organization: orderly arrangement of members in relation to each other.
- Procedures: rules for behavior of group members.
- Cultural anthropologists cluster the many forms of political organization that occur cross-culturally into four major types (see Figure 10.1). These four types correspond, roughly, to the major livelihood modes. As with livelihood categories, overlap also exists between types of political organization.

BANDS

A **band**, the form of political organization associated with foraging groups, involves flexible membership and the lack of formal leaders. Because foraging has been the predominant mode of production for almost all of human history, the band has been the most long-standing form of political organization. A band comprises between 20 people and a few hundred people at most, all related through kinship. These units come together at certain times of the year, depending on their foraging patterns and ritual schedule.

Band membership is flexible: If a person has a serious disagreement with another person or a spouse, one option is to leave that band and join another. Leadership is informal, with no one person named as a permanent leader. Depending on events, such as organizing the group to relocate or to send people out to hunt, a particular person may come to the fore as a leader for that time. This is usually someone whose advice and knowledge about the task are especially respected.

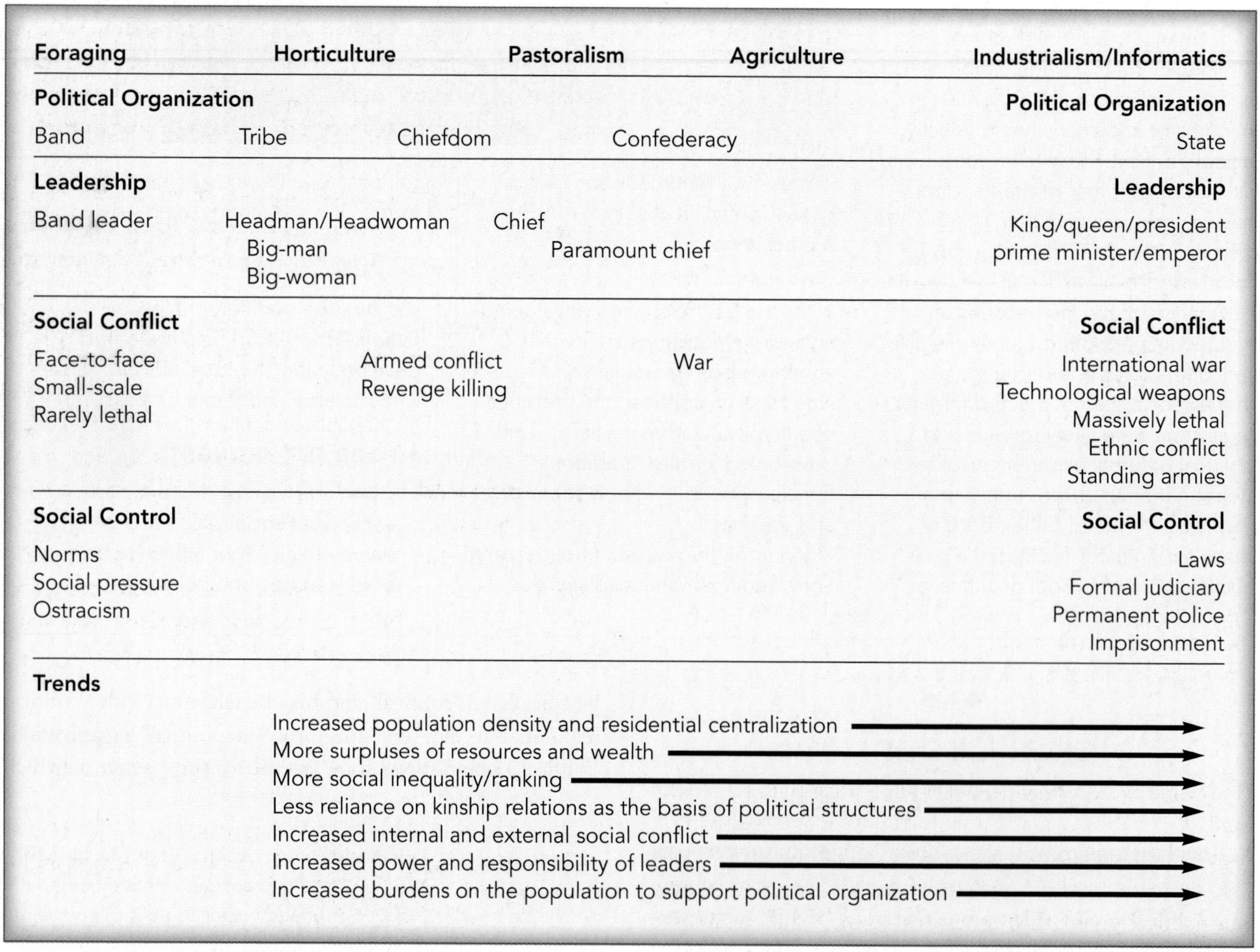

Foraging	Horticulture	Pastoralism	Agriculture	Industrialism/Informatics
Political Organization				**Political Organization**
Band	Tribe; Chiefdom		Confederacy	State
Leadership				**Leadership**
Band leader	Headman/Headwoman; Big-man; Big-woman	Chief; Paramount chief		King/queen/president; prime minister/emperor
Social Conflict				**Social Conflict**
Face-to-face; Small-scale; Rarely lethal	Armed conflict; Revenge killing		War	International war; Technological weapons; Massively lethal; Ethnic conflict; Standing armies
Social Control				**Social Control**
Norms; Social pressure; Ostracism				Laws; Formal judiciary; Permanent police; Imprisonment

Trends

- Increased population density and residential centralization →
- More surpluses of resources and wealth →
- More social inequality/ranking →
- Less reliance on kinship relations as the basis of political structures →
- Increased internal and external social conflict →
- Increased power and responsibility of leaders →
- Increased burdens on the population to support political organization →

FIGURE 10.1 Modes of Political Organization, Conflict, and Social Control

San hunters examining animal tracks near Kalahari Gemsbok National Park, a transnational park spanning Botswana and Namibia that is advertised as a natural area free from human influence. The San, like many indigenous peoples worldwide, are excluded from living and foraging in their traditional territories which are protected by law for the use of tourists as "natural" places.

▶ *Go to the Web and learn about tourist accommodations in the park and transportation access to the park for tourists. How might the presence of tourists affect the "natural" aspects of the park?*

All members of the group are social equals, and a band leader has no special status. He has a certain degree of authority or influence, as perhaps a respected hunter or storyteller, but he does not have power, nor can he enforce his opinions on others. Social leveling mechanisms prevent anyone from accumulating much authority or influence. Political activity in bands involves mainly decision making about migration, food distribution, and resolution of interpersonal conflicts. External conflict between groups is rare because territories of different bands are widely separated and the population density is low.

The band level of organization barely qualifies as a form of political organization because groups are flexible, leadership is ephemeral, and there are no signs or emblems of political affiliation. Some anthropologists argue that true "politics" did not exist in undisturbed band societies because political organization, as defined above, did not exist.

TRIBES

A **tribe** is a more formal type of political organization than the band. Typically associated with horticulture and pastoralism, tribal organization emerged between 10,000 to 12,000 years ago, with the emergence of these modes of production. A tribe is a political group that comprises several bands or lineage groups, each with similar language and lifestyle and each occupying a distinct territory. Tribal groups may be connected through a *clan* structure in which most people claim descent from a common ancestor, although they may be unable to trace the exact relationship. Kinship is the primary basis of membership. Tribal groupings contain from 100 to several thousand people. Tribes are found in the Middle East, South Asia, Southeast Asia, the Pacific, and Africa, as well as among Native Americans.

A tribal headman (most tribal leaders are male) is a more formal leader than a band leader. Key qualifications for this position are being hardworking and generous and possessing good personal skills. A headman is a political leader on a part-time basis only, yet this role is more demanding than that of a band leader. Depending on the mode of production, a headman will be in charge of determining the times for moving herds, planting and harvesting, and setting the time for seasonal feasts and celebrations. Internal and external conflict resolution is also his responsibility. A headman relies mainly on authority and persuasion rather than on power. These strategies are effective because tribal members are all kin and have loyalty to each other.

Among many horticultural groups of the Amazonian rainforest, such as the Kayapo (see Map 10.1), tribal organization is the dominant political pattern. Each local tribal unit, which is itself a lineage, has a headman (or perhaps two or three). Each tribal group is autonomous, but recently many have united temporarily into larger groups, in reaction to threats to their environment and lifestyle from outside forces.

Pastoralist tribal formations are often linked into a *confederacy,* a loose umbrella organization linking several local tribal units or segments that maintain substantial autonomy. Normally, the local segments meet together rarely, perhaps only at an annual festival. In case of an external threat, however, the confederacy gathers together under one leader to deal with the problem. Once the threat is removed, local units resume their autonomy. This equality and autonomy of tribal units having the ability to unite and then disunite, is referred to as a **segmentary model** of political organization. It exists among pastoralists worldwide (Eickelman 1981). For example, the Qashqa'i (kash-kai), pastoralists of Iran (see Map 4.5, p. 97) have three levels of political organization: subtribe, tribe, and confederacy (Beck 1986). Leaders at each level deal with higher-level authorities and external forces on behalf of the

---

band the political organization of foraging groups, with minimal leadership and flexible membership.

tribe a political group that comprises several bands or lineage groups, each with similar language and lifestyle and occupying a distinct territory.

segmentary model type of political organization in which smaller units unite in the face of external threats and then disunite when the external threat is absent.

MAP 10.1 Kayapo Region in Brazil.
The Kayapo live in several rainforest villages in the Matto Grosso plains region. Their population is around 7000. The Kayapo use their traditional political organizing skills to help them deal with outsiders who seek to pursue commercial logging, mining, and hydroelectric development in the area.

tribespeople. They also help group members who are in economic need.

Leadership among the Qashqa'i combines both ascribed and achieved features (review Chapter 9). Subtribe headmen's positions are based mainly on achievement. Both *khans* (tribe leaders) and *ilkhanis* (confederacy leaders) are members of noble lineages. They gain their positions through patrilineal descent, with the eldest son favored. The role of the Qashqa'i ilkhani is similar in many ways to that of a chief (described in the next section). The increased power of the Iranian state in recent decades has undermined the role of tribal leaders (Beck 1991). The state government formulated new policies regulating migratory schedules, pasture use, and prices of animal products. These rules constrain the power of tribal leaders who then lose significance to their followers who in turn withdraw their support from them and turn increasingly to state-level leaders.

BIG-MAN AND BIG-WOMAN LEADERSHIP In between tribal and chiefdom organizations is the **big-man system** or **big-woman system,** a form of political organization in which individuals build a political base and gain prestige, influence, and authority through a system of redistribution based on personal ties and grand feasts (mentioned in Chapter 5). Anthropological research in Melanesia (see Map 10.2), a large region in the South Pacific, established the existence of big-man politics (Sahlins 1963). Personalistic, favor-based political systems are, however, found elsewhere.

Political ties of a successful big-man or big-woman include people in several villages. A big-man tends to have greater wealth than his followers, although people continue to expect him to be generous. The core supporters of a big-man tend to be kin, with extended networks including nonkin. A big-man has heavy responsibilities. He is responsible for regulating internal affairs, such as the timing of crop planting, and external affairs, such as intergroup feasts, trade, and war. In some instances, a big-man is assisted in carrying out his responsibilities by a group of other respected men. These councils include people from the big-man's different constituencies.

In several tribes in the Mount Hagen area of the Papua New Guinea highlands (see Map 1.3, p. 19), an aspiring big-man develops a leadership position through a process called *moka* (Strathern 1971). **Moka** is a strategy for developing political leadership that involves exchanging favors and gifts, such as pigs, and sponsoring large feasts where further gift giving occurs. A crucial factor in big-manship in the Mount

Chief Paul Payakan, leader of the Kayapo. Payakan was instrumental in mobilizing widespread resistance among the Kayapo and several other tribes to the construction of a large hydroelectric dam at Altamira on the Xingu River.

▶ *Find updated information on the Kayapo and the proposed Altamira dam project on the Web.*

big-man or **big-woman system** a form of political organization midway between tribe and chiefdom involving reliance on the leadership of key individuals who develop a political following through personal ties and redistributive feasts.

moka a strategy for developing political leadership in highland Papua New Guinea that involves exchanging gifts and favors with individuals and sponsoring large feasts where further gift giving occurs.

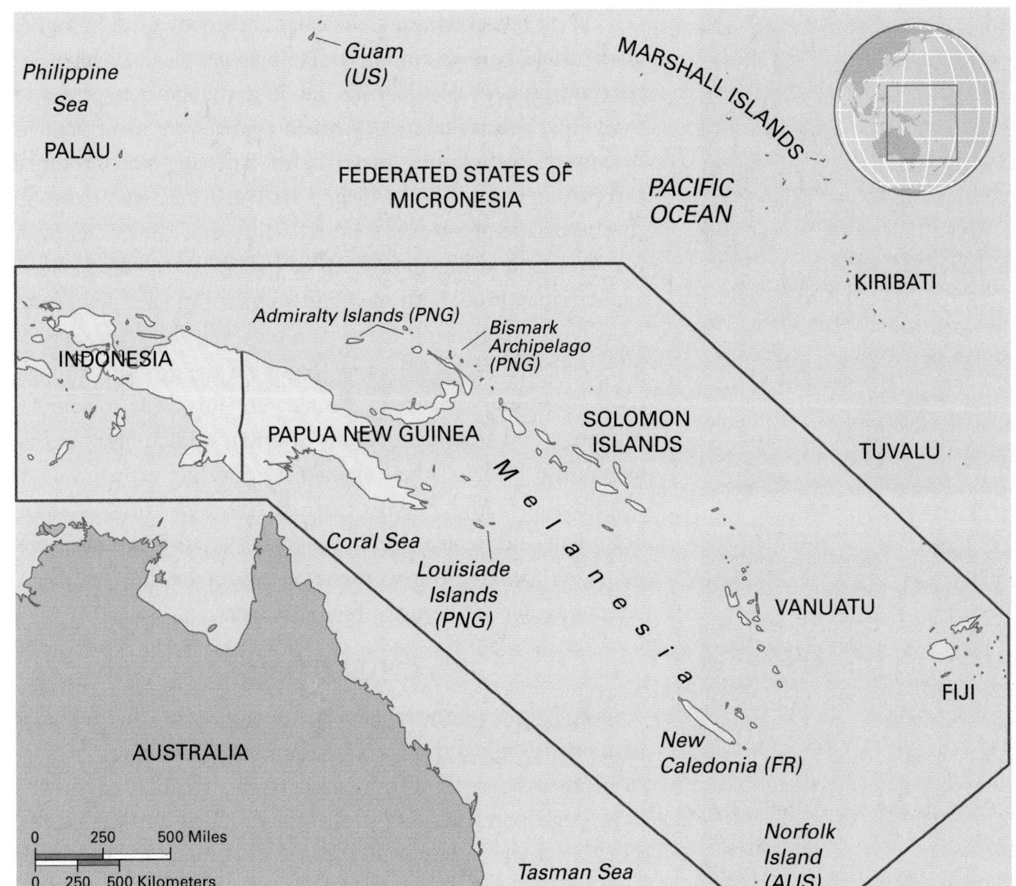

MAP 10.2 Melanesia. Melanesia is a region in the South Pacific that includes the independent states of Papua New Guinea, the Republic of Vanuatu, the Solomon Islands, and Fiji as well as many islands that are controlled by other countries. It also encompasses the western part of the island of New Guinea, which is controlled by Indonesia, and islands to the west of it, though the people there do not self-identify as Melanesians.

Hagen area is having at least one wife. An aspiring big-man urges his wife or wives to work harder than ordinary women in order to grow more food to feed more pigs. The number of pigs a man has is an important measure of his status and worth. Given the importance of a wife or wives in maintaining a large collection of pigs, a man whose parents die when he is young is at an extreme disadvantage because he lacks financial support for the bridewealth required for marriage. Without parents, he has no bridewealth, no wife, no one to feed and care for pigs, no resource base for moka, and no chance of becoming a big-man.

A married man uses his wife's or wives' production as a basis for developing and expanding exchange ties with contacts throughout the region. An aspiring big-man builds moka relationships first with kin and then beyond. By giving goods to people, he gains prestige over them. The recipient is under pressure to make a return gift of equal or greater value. The exchanges go back and forth, over the years. The more the aspiring big-man gives, and the more people he can maintain in his exchange network, the greater prestige he develops.

Although big-manship is an achieved position, most big-men in the Mt. Hagen area are the sons of big-men, meaning that ascription is also involved (see Figure 10.2). Ascription plays a role especially for major big-men, of whom over three-quarters were sons of former big-men. It is unclear whether this pattern results from the greater wealth and prestige of big-man families, from socialization into big-manship through paternal example, or from both.

	Father Was a Big-Man	Father Was Not a Big-Man	Totals
Major Big-Men	27	9	36
Minor Big-Men	31	30	61
Total	58	39	97

Source: *The Rope of Moka: Big Men and Ceremonial Exchange of Big-Men in Mount Hagen, Papua New Guinea* by Andrew Starthern. Copyright © Cambridge University Press 1971. Reprinted with permission of Cambridge University Press.

FIGURE 10.2 Family Background of Big-Men in Mt. Hagen, Papua New Guinea

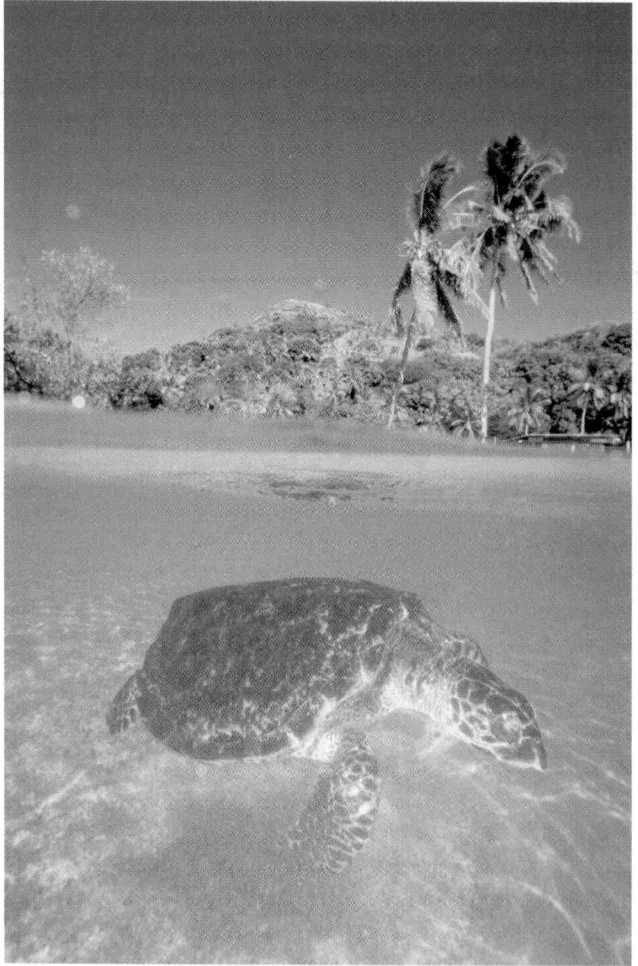

(TOP) Throughout much of the South Pacific, big-man and big-woman politics has long involved the demonstration of political leaders' generosity. Leaders are expected to be able to mobilize resources for impressive feasts such as this one on Tanna Island, one of the many islands of the Republic of Vanuatu in the region of Melanesia. (BOTTOM) A sea turtle off the coast of Fiji, where local people consider them sacred and important as a feasting item.

▶ *How does public feasting play a role in politics in a context with which you are familiar?*

With few exceptions, the early anthropological literature about tribal politics among indigenous peoples of Melanesia portrays men as dominating public exchange networks and the public political arenas. Women as wives are mentioned as important in providing the material basis for men's political careers. A study on the island of Vanatinai, an island in the Louisiade group (see Map 10.2), reveals the existence of big-women and big-men (Lepowsky 1990). In this gender-egalitarian culture, both men and women can gain power and prestige by sponsoring feasts at which valuables are distributed, especially *mortuary feasts* (feasts for the dead). Although more Vanatinai men than women are involved in political exchange and leadership, some women are extremely active as political leaders. These women lead sailing expeditions to neighboring islands to visit their exchange partners, who are both male and female, and they sponsor lavish feasts attended by many people. Big-women are also powerful sorcerers, famous healers, and successful gardeners.

CHIEFDOMS

A **chiefdom** is a form of political organization that includes permanently allied tribes and villages under one chief, a leader who possesses power. Compared to most tribes, chiefdoms have large populations, often numbering in the thousands. They are more centralized and socially complex. Hereditary systems of social ranking and economic stratification emerge in chiefdoms. Social divisions exist between the chiefly lineage(s) and nonchiefly groups. Chiefs and their descendants have higher status than commoners, and intermarriage between the two strata is forbidden. Chiefs are expected to be generous, but they may have a more luxurious lifestyle than the rest of the people.

The chiefship is an "office" that must be filled at all times. When a chief dies or retires, he or she must be replaced. In contrast, the death of a band leader or big-man or big-woman does not require that someone else be chosen as a replacement. A chief has more responsibilities than a band or tribal leader. He or she regulates production and redistribution, solves internal conflicts, and plans and leads raids and warring expeditions. Criteria for becoming a chief are clearly defined. Besides ascribed criteria (birth in a chiefly lineage or being the first son or daughter of the chief), achievement is also important. Achievement is measured in terms of personal leadership skills, charisma, and accumulated wealth. Chiefdoms have existed throughout the world.

Anthropologists and archaeologists are interested in how and why chiefdom systems evolved as an intermediary unit between tribes and states and in what the political implications of this evolution are (Earle 1993). Several political strategies support the expansion of power in chiefdoms: improving local production systems and increasing wealth, distributive feasting and gift exchanges, controlling ideological legitimacy applying force internally, and forging stronger and wider external ties. Depending on local conditions, different strategies were employed. For example, internal control of irrigation systems was the most important factor in the emergence of chiefdoms in prehistoric southeastern Spain, whereas control of external trade was more important in the prehistoric Aegean region (Gilman 1991).

GENDER AND LEADERSHIP IN CHIEFDOMS Much evidence about leadership patterns in chiefdoms comes from historical examples. Prominent chiefs—men and women—are documented in colonial archives and missionary records. Many historical examples of women chiefs and women rulers come from West Africa, including the Queen Mother of the Ashanti of Ghana and of the Edo of Nigeria (Awe 1977).

Oral histories and archival records show that Yoruba women had the institution of the *iyalode,* chief of the women.

The last queen of Hawai'i, Queen Lili'uokalani. Inheriting the throne from her brother, Queen Lili'uokalani reigned for only two years, from 1891 to 1893. She attempted to establish constitutional rights for Hawai'ans and Asians living in the islands. In 1893 she was deposed by a group of European and American businessmen who took political control of the islands. The status of Hawai'i is still contested today by local groups who seek autonomy from the United States.

▶ *What did you learn about Hawai'i in your high school history or government classes? Did you learn about Queen Lili'uokalani and her attempt to assert native rights?*

Chief Joseph, or Hin-mah-too-yah-lat-kekt (Thunder Rolling Down the Mountain), of the Nez Perce, was born in northern Oregon in 1840. His father, Joseph the Elder, had been an active supporter of peace with the Whites and signed an agreement establishing the Nez Perce Reservation. In 1863, following the discovery of gold, the government took back 6 million acres of land. After Joseph the Elder died, Joseph the Younger was elected Chief. He favored peace, but continued White encroachments on Nez Perce land and government attempts to forcibly relocate his people prompted him to lead a war of resistance.

▶ *Go the Internet and read Chief Joseph's famous speech of surrender delivered in 1877.*

The *iyalode* was the women's political spokes person in the "council of king makers," the highest level of government. She was a chief in her own right, with chiefly insignia, including the necklace of special beads, a wide-brimmed straw hat, a shawl, personal servants, special drummers, and bell ringers.

---

chiefdom a political unit of permanently allied tribes and villages under one recognized leader.

(LEFT) A Ugandan soldier guarding the President's car. (CENTER) President George W. Bush arrives in Airforce One at the Daytona Beach International Airport, Florida, to watch the NASCAR races in 2004. (RIGHT) Queen Elizabeth in her royal carriage in London following her coronation in 1953.

▶ *Think of other political contexts in which a leader would avoid signaling his or her high status through a special mode of transportation.*

She also had her own council of subordinate chiefs. The position of iyalode was based on achievement. The most important qualifications were her proven ability as a leader, economic resources to maintain her new status as chief, and popularity. Tasks included settling disputes via her court and meeting with women to formulate women's stand on such policy issues as the declaration of war and the opening of new markets. Although she represented all women in the group and had widespread support among women, she was outnumbered at the council of king makers because she was the only female and the only representative of all women.

The Iroquois provide a case of women's indirect political importance (J. K. Brown 1975) (see Map 4.3, p. 95). Men were chiefs, but women and men councilors were the appointing body. Most men were gone for extended periods, waging war as far away as Delaware and Virginia. Women controlled production and distribution of the staple crop, maize. If the women did not want warriors to leave for a particular campaign, they would refuse to provide them with maize, thereby vetoing the plan. Some anthropologists and others argue that the prehistoric Iroquois are an example of a **matriarchy**, or a society in which women are dominant in terms of economics, politics, and ideology. Most anthropologists, however, characterize the Iroquois as an egalitarian society, because women did not control the society to the exclusion of men nor did they oppress men as a group. Men and women participated equally on the councils.

Why do women play greater political roles in some chiefdoms than in others? The most satisfactory answers point to women's economic roles as the basis for their political power, as among the Iroquois and in many African horticultural societies. In societies where women's economic entitlements are limited, women are unlikely to have public political roles.

The effects of European and North American colonial and missionary influences on nonstate societies have resulted in the decline of women's political status (Etienne and Leacock 1980). For example, British colonialists redefined the institution of iyalode in Nigeria. Now "she is no longer a member of any of the important councils of government. Even the market, and therefore the market women, have been removed from her jurisdiction, and have been placed under the control of the new local government councils in each town" (1980:146). Ethnohistorical research on chiefdoms in Hawai'i documents the existence of powerful women chiefs in precolonial times (Linnekan 1990). Following Captain Cook's arrival in 1778, the colonialists established a Western-model monarchy. By the time the United States annexed the islands in 1898, foreign men had completely displaced indigenous Hawai'ian leaders.

CONFEDERACIES Parallel to the situation discussed in the section on tribes, an expanded version of the chiefdom occurs when several chiefdoms are joined in a confederacy. Such a group is headed by a chief of chiefs, "big chief," or paramount chief. Many prominent confederacies existed, for example, in Hawai'i in the late 1700s, the Iroquois league of five nations, the Cherokee of Tennessee, and the Algonquins of the Chesapeake region in present-day Virginia and Maryland. In the Algonquin confederacy, each village had a chief, and the regional council was composed of local chiefs and headed by the paramount chief. Powhatan, father of Pocahontas, was paramount chief of the Algonquins when the British arrived in the early 1600s.

Chiefdom confederacies of the New World were supported financially by contributions of grain from each local unit. Kept in a central storage area where the paramount

matriarchy a society in which women are dominant in terms of economics, politics, and ideology.

eye on the ENVIRONMENT

Water, Pollution, and International Politics

Like air, water can move across state boundaries, carrying environmental pollution. Such movements can cause serious international political conflict and extended negotiations about reparations and planning to prevent future damages. One case is that of mining-related pollution of the Tisza (TEET-zuh) River that flows from Romania to Hungary and beyond, within the Danube River basin.

In January 2000, a dam in Romania holding *tailings* (metal-processing byproducts) from a gold mine breached and released water containing high levels of cyanide, copper, zinc, and other heavy metals into nearby streams (Harper 2005). Three days later, the *plume*, or water carrying the byproducts, had reached Hungary's Tisza River. Within the month, it moved on to Serbia and Bulgaria and eventually reached the Black Sea.

In Hungary, the cyanide killed thousands of tons of fish and waterfowl and raised alarms about people's drinking water. Farmers in the affected region reported the death of cows, and they were unable to sell their farm produce due to negative public perceptions about polluted products. Although cyanide is lethal in the short run, it soon dissipates from the environment as opposed to the heavy metals, which remain in the river's sediments and continue to affect riverine life for a long time.

In spite of the severity of the disaster, the Hungarian state was slow to file claims against the offending corporation or for compensation from Romania. Although postsocialist Hungarian political leaders took up the cause of environmental activism in their rhetoric, they did not follow through with action. This lack of action may be related to the heritage of state socialism, which did not take environmental problems seriously. Another explanatory factor is that a large number of Hungarians live in Romania, and Hungary's leaders may have wished to avoid an international confrontation that would put Hungarians in Romania at risk.

MAP 10.3 The Danube and Tisza Rivers in Eastern Europe.
The Danube River and its major tributary, the Tisza. Europe's largest remaining natural wetland is in the Danube delta. The core of the Danube delta, which lies mainly in Romania but crosses into Ukraine, was declared a UNESCO World Natural Heritage Site in 1991.

One positive development is that the European Union offered a wider political framework in which to address the issue of the Tisza River pollution. The Tisza disaster was the first environmental disaster in which the EU took a prominent role. In the end, Hungary decided to sue the mining company for damages in a civil lawsuit rather than taking on an international lawsuit with its neighbor.

◆ **FOOD FOR THOUGHT**

- The exact reasons for the Hungarian government's inaction are not clear. How can one learn the true reasons behind politicians' actions or inactions?

Rescue workers remove dead fish from the Tisza River in the year 2000 following an accident at a gold mine in northwestern Romania that deposited cyanide and other toxic substances into the Tisza that also flowed into the Danube River and the Black Sea. The accident caused environmental damage in a vast area involving several countries.

(LEFT) Afghanistan President Hamed Karzai wears a carefully assembled collection of regional political symbols. The striped cape is associated with northern tribes. The Persian-lamb hat is an Uzbek style popular in the capital city, Kabul. He also wears a tunic and loose trousers, which are associated with villagers, and sometimes adds a Western-style jacket as well. His clothing implies a statement of unity and diversity about his country. (RIGHT) Secretary of State Condoleeza Rice arrived at the Weisbaden Army Airfield in February 2005 to introduce U.S. President George W. Bush and First Lady Laura Bush to American troops based in Germany.

▶ *Study clothing styles of other state leaders and see if you can "read" their symbolic messages.*

chief lived, the grain was used to feed warriors during external warfare that maintained and expanded the confederacy's borders. A council building existed in the central location, where local chiefs came together to meet with the paramount chief to deliberate on questions of internal and external policy.

STATES

A *state,* defined in Chapter 2, is a centralized political unit encompassing many communities, a bureaucratic structure, and leaders who possess coercive power.

THE POWERS AND ROLES OF THE STATE States have much more power over their members compared to bands, tribes, and chiefdoms. and state leaders have more responsibilities:

- States engage in international relations in order to deal with other states about mutual concerns (see Eye on the Environment). The state may use force defensively to maintain its borders and offensively to extend its territory.
- States monopolize the use of force and the maintenance of law and order internally through laws, courts, and the police.
- States maintain standing armies and police (as opposed to part-time forces).
- States define citizenship and its rights and responsibilities. In complex societies, since early times, not all residents were granted equal rights as citizens.
- States keep track of the number, age, gender, location, and wealth of their citizens through census systems that are regularly updated.
- States have the power to extract resources from citizens through taxation. Public finance in states is based on formal taxation that takes many forms. **In-kind taxation** is a system of mandatory, noncash contributions to the state. Cash taxes, such as the income tax that takes a percentage of wages, emerged only in the past few hundred years.
- States manipulate information. Control of information to protect the state and its leaders can be done directly

in-kind taxation a system of mandatory noncash contributions to the state.

(through censorship, restricting access to certain information by the public, and promotion of favorable images via propaganda) and indirectly (through pressure on journalists, television networks, and other media to selectively present information or to present information in certain ways).

SYMBOLS AND STATE POWER Religious beliefs and symbols are often closely tied to the power of state leadership: The ruler may be considered to be a deity or part deity, or may be a high priest of the state religion, or perhaps be closely linked with the high priest, who serves as advisor. Architecture and urban planning remind the populace of the greatness of the state. In pre-Columbian Mexico, the central plaza of city-states, such as Tenochtitlan (founded in 1345), was symbolically equivalent to the center of the cosmos and was thus the locale of greatest significance (Low 1995). The most important temples and the residence of the head of state were located around the plaza. Other houses and structures, in decreasing order of status, were located on avenues in decreasing proximity to the center. The grandness and individual character of the leader's residence indicate power, as do monuments—especially tombs to past leaders or heroes or heroines. Egypt's pyramids, China's Great Wall, and India's Taj Mahal are a few of the world's great architectural monuments of state power.

In democratic states where leaders are elected by popular vote and in socialist states where political rhetoric emphasizes social equality, expense and elegance are muted by the adoption of more egalitarian ways of dress (even though in private, these leaders may live relatively opulent lives in terms of housing, food, and entertainment). The earlier practice of all Chinese leaders wearing a "Mao jacket," regardless of their rank, was a symbolic statement of their antihierarchical philosophy. A quick glance at a crowd of people, including the Prime Minister of Canada or Britain or the President of the United States, would not reveal who was the leader because dress differences are avoided. Even members of British royalty wear "street clothes" on public occasions where regalia are not required.

Beyond clothing, other commodities associated with top leadership position include housing quality, food, and modes of transportation. State leaders live in grand mansions and often have more than one residence. The King of Morocco, for example, has several official palaces around the country, and he regularly travels from one to another. President George W. Bush was considered "one of the people" because he liked to eat hamburgers. State leaders do not travel the way ordinary citizens do. For security reasons, their ground vehicles may have bulletproof windows, and a cavalcade of security vehicles protects the leader's vehicle. In many African countries, the most important new symbol of political power is an expensive imported car (Chalfin 2008).

LOCAL POWER AND POLITICS IN DEMOCRATIC STATES The degree to which states influence the lives of their citizens varies, as does the ability of citizens to influence the political policies and actions of their governments. Some anthropologists, as citizens, use their knowledge of culture at home or abroad to influence politics in their own countries.

In highly centralized states, the central government controls public finance and legal institutions, leaving little power or autonomy in these matters to local governments. In decentralized systems, local governments are granted some forms of revenue generation (taxation) and the responsibility of providing certain services.

Local politics in Japan, Belize, and France illustrate three patterns of local political dynamics. The Japanese case illustrates a community-focused system. The Belize case shows how local politics vary even within the same region. Local politics in both Japan and Belize involve the exchange of gifts and favors. The case of rural France demonstrates the importance of ascription in achieving a leadership position.

In Japan, egalitarian systems of local power structures exist in villages and hamlets. Families subtly vie for status and leadership roles through gift giving, as is common in local politics worldwide (Marshall 1985). Egalitarianism prevails as a community value, but people strive to be "more than equal" by making public donations to the *buraku,* or hamlet. The custom of giving a gift to the community is a way that hamlet families can improve their positions in the local ranking system. In one hamlet, all 35 households recently gave gifts to the community on specified occasions: the 42nd birthday of male family members, the 61st birthday of male family members, the 77th birthday of male family members, the marriage of male family members, the marriage of a female family member whose husband will be the household successor, the birth of the household head or successor couple's first child, and the construction of a new house. These occasions for public gift giving always include a meal to which members of all hamlet households are invited. Since the 1960s, it has also become common to give an item that is useful for the hamlet, such as a set of fluorescent light fixtures for the hamlet hall, folding tables, space heaters, and vacuum cleaners.

Local politics within a democratic framework may involve another type of gift giving and exchange in the interest of maintaining or gaining power. People in elected positions of power give favors in expectation of political loyalty in return. In these cases, various factions vie with each other.

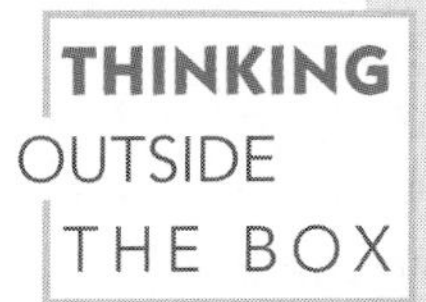

What are some key symbols of state power in your home country?

A **faction** is a politically oriented group whose members are mobilized and maintained by a leader to whom the ties of loyalty are lateral—from leader to follower (Brumfiel 1994). Factions tend to lack formal rules and formal succession in their leadership.

Two villages in Belize show a contrast in the development and role of factional politics (Moberg 1991) (see Map 10.4). One village, Mt. Hope, is faction free; the other village, Charleston, has divisive factionalism. Economic differences between the two villages are important. In Mt. Hope, the government provided residents with land and established a marketing board to purchase villagers' crops. Farmers grow rice for the domestic market and citrus crops for export. Citrus growers account for about half of Mt. Hope's households, receive more than three-fourths of its total income, and control about 87 percent of the land. In Charleston, most men work in small-scale fishing augmented by part-time farming. Lack of a road that would allow export of agricultural crops has inhibited the development of commercial agriculture. Start-up costs for citrus cultivation (fertilizer, insecticide, tractors) are prohibitive for most Charleston households. Charleston is "racked by intense intergroup conflict," and that includes factional conflict that divides kin groups: "One of the village's most acrimonious political conflicts exists between two brothers whose relationship deteriorated when the allies of one brother were excluded from a cooperative that the other had organized" (1991:221). Intense factionalism in Charleston is sustained by outside political party patronage and favor giving. Local faction leaders vie with one another to obtain grants and other benefits from the state. In return, national political parties look to Charleston as a base for developing political loyalties. The national parties have bypassed Mt. Hope because economic development created less dependence on state favors for projects such as a cooperative or a road. Charleston was ripe for political manipulation; Mt. Hope was not.

In rural France, family ties and family reputation influence who becomes an elected local leader (Abélès 1991). The department of Yonne, located in the Burgundy region (see Map 10.5) southeast of Paris, is the provincial heartland of France. Fieldwork sought to understand how individuals gained access to local political office; it involved interviewing local politicians, attending town council meetings, and following local elections.

France is divided into 36,000 communes that are grouped in 96 departments. Communes and departments are the major arenas for local politics. At the commune level, elected officials are the mayor and town councilors. Several political parties contest the elections—the Socialist party, the Union for French Democracy, and others, including scattered support for the Communist party. In France, the only legal requirements for office are French citizenship and age. Other than that, elected positions are, in principle, open to anyone interested in contesting them. According to the perspective that emphasizes human agency in shaping behavior and events, one would hypothesize nearly complete openness in elections and low predictive value of "name" or "family" in determining electoral success. But such "openness" does not seem to be the case in rural Burgundy (Bourgogne) and may not exist elsewhere.

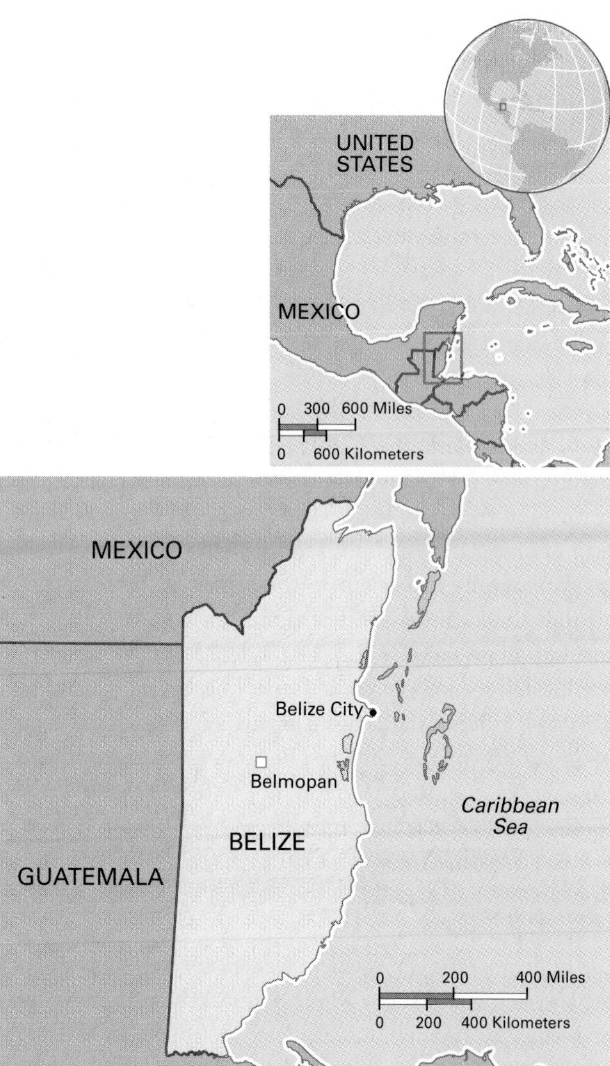

MAP 10.4 Belize.
The only English-speaking country in Central America, Belize was a British colony known as British Honduras until 1973. Agriculture and international tourism are the most important parts of the economy. The population is 300,000 and growing rapidly. Belize's fertility rate is among the highest in the world. The dominant religion is Christianity in various forms, especially Roman Catholicism. English is the official language, but the most commonly used language is Belizean Kriol, spoken by 70 percent of the population as a first language. Mayan languages are spoken in the west and north.

faction a politically oriented group with strong lateral ties to a leader.

MAP 10.5 **France.**
The French Republic comprises a wide variety of landscapes throughout its many departments, both on the mainland (Metropolitan France) and in its overseas departments and territories. France possesses the second largest Exclusive Economic Zone (EEZ) in the world, after the United States. The population of metropolitan France is 61 million people. France is one of the most ethnically diverse countries of the world, with over half of its population claiming a foreign background. The official language is French, although several regional languages are spoken throughout metropolitan France, along with immigrant communities' languages that include many African languages, several varieties of Chinese, Khmer, and Turkish.

In terms of local culture in France, a successful candidate for either commune or department positions should have local roots and come from a distinguished family. Typically, the same family names recur again and again. In one town, the Truchots and the Rostains dominated public life for over a half century. Both families were grain and wine merchants. Another factor influencing electoral choice is a bias toward incumbents. The monopoly of political office by a certain family is perceived by local people to contribute to order and peace. Thus, local roots, reputation, and networks combine with a value placed on continuity as the ingredients for electoral success in rural France. This combination is summed up in the concept of legitimacy. "To enjoy legitimacy is to belong to a world of eligible individuals, those to whom responsibilities can be entrusted. Legitimacy is an elusive quality at first glance: certain individuals canvassing the votes of their fellow-citizens are immediately recognized as legitimate, while others, despite repeated efforts, are doomed to failure. . . . It is as though a candidate's legitimacy is something people instinctively recognize" (1991:265).

GENDER AND LEADERSHIP IN STATES Most contemporary states are hierarchical and patriarchal, excluding members of lower classes and women from equal participation. Some states are less male dominated than others, but none is female dominated. One view of gender inequality in states suggests that increasing male dominance with the evolution of the state is based on men's control of the technology of production and warfare (Harris 1993). Women in most cultures have limited access to these areas of power. In more peaceful states, such as Finland, Norway, Sweden, and Denmark, women's political roles are more prominent.

Strongly patriarchal contemporary states preserve male dominance through ideologies that restrict women's political power. In much of the Muslim Middle East, Central Asia, Pakistan, and northern India, the practice of *purdah,* female seclusion and segregation from the public world, limits women's public roles. In China, scientific beliefs that categorize women as less strong and dependable than men have long been used to rationalize the exclusion of women from politics (Dikötter 1998). Socialist states typically attempt to increase women's political roles, and the proportion of female members of legislative bodies is higher in socialist states than in capitalist democracies. But it is still not equal to that of men. Although women account for roughly half of the world's population, they form only, on average, 16 percent of the world's parliamentary members (Lederer 2006). Regional differences range from an average of 40 percent female parliamentarians in the Nordic states to 8 percent in Arab states.

A few contemporary states have or have recently had women as prime ministers or presidents. Powerful women heads of state in recent times include Indira Gandhi in India, Golda Meir in Israel, Margaret Thatcher in the United Kingdom, Benazir Bhutto in Pakistan, Michele Bachelet in Chile, Angela Merkel in Germany, Ellen Johnson-Sirleaf in Liberia, and Tarja Halonen in Finland. Some female heads of state are related by kinship, as wife or daughter, to male heads of state. Indira Gandhi, for example, was the daughter of the popular first prime minister of independent India, Jawaharlal Nehru (she was not related to Mahatma Gandhi). It is unclear whether these women inherited the role or achieved it indirectly through their socialization as a result of being born into political families.

Women's political roles can also be indirect, as mothers or wives of male rulers, such as Eva Peron in Argentina as wife of the president and Hillary Clinton in the United States when she was First Lady. Women may wield indirect political power through their children, especially sons. In Turkey, most parents consider politics an undesirable career for their children but more women than men are favorable toward their sons' political ambitions (Günes-Ayata 1995:238–239).

Mothers of male political leaders use their maternal position to influence politics in a context in which direct political roles are largely closed to them.

◆◆◆

Changing Politics

In the early days of political anthropology, researchers examined the varieties of political organization and leadership and created the categories of bands, tribes, chiefdoms, and states. Political anthropologists are now more interested in political dynamics and change, especially in how the state affects local people's lives.

EMERGING NATIONS AND TRANSNATIONAL NATIONS

Many different definitions exist for a nation, and some of them overlap with definitions given for a state (Maybury-Lewis 1997b:125–132). One definition says that a **nation** is a group of people who share a language, culture, territorial base, political organization, and history (Clay 1990). In this sense, a nation is culturally homogeneous, and the United States would be considered not a nation but rather a political unit composed of many nations. According to this definition, groups that lack a territorial base cannot be termed nations. A related term is the *nation-state*, which some say refers to a state that comprises only one nation, whereas others think it refers to a state that comprises many nations. An example is the Iroquois nation (see Map 4.3, p. 95).

Depending on their resources and power, nations and other groups may constitute a political threat to state stability and control. Examples include the Kurds in the Middle East (see Culturama, this chapter), the Maya of Mexico and Central America (see Culturama, Chapter 11, p. 273), Tamils in Sri Lanka, Tibetans in China, and Palestinians in the Middle East. In response to this real or perceived threat, states seek to create and maintain a sense of unified identity. Political scientist Benedict Anderson, in his book *Imagined Communities* (1991 [1983]) writes about the symbolic efforts that state builders employ to create a sense of belonging—"imagined community"—among diverse peoples. State symbolic strategies include:

- The imposition of one language as the national language.
- The construction of monuments and museums that emphasize unity.
- The use of songs, dress, poetry, and media messages.

Some states, such as China, control religious expression in the interest of promoting loyalty to and identity with the state. Another strategy is to draw on symbols of minority or ancestral groups and bring them into the center, thus creating a sense of belonging through recognition. Such recognition may also be interpreted as a form of co-optation, depending on the context. When South Africa launched its new Coat of Arms in 2000, (then) President Mbeke pointed out that the inclusion of a rock art drawing and a slogan in an extinct San language were intended to evoke both South Africa's distant past and its emerging identity as a socially complex and peaceful country (Barnard 2004).

The Coat of Arms of South Africa, adopted in 2000, is meant to highlight democratic change and multicultural unity.

▶ *For a research project, study the coat of arms of several countries and analyze the meaning of their symbols and slogans in terms of Benedict Anderson's concept of "imagined community."*

Inspired by Anderson's writings, many anthropologists study state laws, policies, and other practices that seek to create a sense of unity out of diversity. Their work shows that attempts by states to force homogenization of nations and ethnic groups will inevitably prompt resistance of varying degrees from those groups that wish to retain or regain autonomy. Mexico, for example, is promoting a unified identity centered in mestizaje, defined in Chapter 9 as people of mixed Spanish and Indian ancestry, culture, and heritage in Central and South America (Alonso 2004). Monuments and museums in Mexico City, for example, give prominence to mestizaje symbols and emphasize links to Aztec ancestors while muting connections with highland Indians and the Spanish colonialists. The goal is to forge a new sense of political nationalism and consciousness that values hybridity and mixture. Emphasizing the Aztecs as the cultural roots of Mexican heritage frames out living indigenous groups, further marginalizing their position in the imagined nation-state of Mexico.

For the past few centuries, leading global powers have promoted the notion of the strong state as the best option for

---

nation a group of people who share a language, culture, territorial base, political organization, and history.

CULTURAMA

The Kurds of the Middle East

The Kurds are an ethnic group of between 20 to 30 million people, most of whom speak some dialect of the Kurdish language, which is related to Persian (Major 1996). The majority are Sunni Muslims. Kurdish kinship is strongly patrilineal, and Kurdish family and social relations are male dominated.

Their home region, called Kurdistan ("Place of the Kurds"), extends from Turkey into Iran, Iraq, and Syria. This area is grasslands, interspersed with mountains, with no coastline. Before World War I, many Kurds were full-time pastoralists, herding sheep and goats. Following the war and the creation of Iraq, Syria, and Kuwait, many Kurdish herders were unable to follow their traditional grazing because they crossed the new country borders. Herders no longer live in tents year-round, though some do for part of the year. Others are farmers. In towns and cities, Kurds own shops, are professionals, and are employed in many different occupations.

Reliable population data for the Kurds in the Middle East do not exist, and estimates vary widely. About half of all Kurds, numbering between 10 and 15 million, live in Turkey, where they constitute 20 percent or perhaps more of the total population. Approximately 6 million live in Iran, 4 to 5 million in Iraq, and 1.5 million in Syria. Others live in Armenia, Germany, France, and the United States.

The Kurds have attempted to establish an independent state for decades, with no success and often facing harsh treatment from government forces. In Turkey, the state used to refer to them as "Mountain Turks," and in many ways still refuses to recognize them as a legitimate minority group. Use of the Kurdish language is restricted in Turkey. The Kurds have faced similar repression in Iraq, especially following their support of Iran in the 1980–1988 Iran–Iraq war. Saddam Hussein razed villages and used chemical weapons against the Kurds. After the Persian Gulf War, 2 million Kurds fled to Iran. Many others have emigrated to Europe and the United States. Iraqi Kurds gained political autonomy from Baghdad in 1991 following a successful uprising aided by Western forces.

Many Kurds feel united by the shared goal of statehood, but several strong internal political factions and a guerrilla movement in Turkey also exist among the Kurds. Kurds in Turkey seek the right to have Kurdish-language schooling and television and radio broadcasts, and they would like to have their folklore recognized as well. The Kurds are fond of music and dancing, and Kurdish villages are known for their distinct performance styles.

Thanks to Diane E. King, University of Kentucky, for reviewing this material.

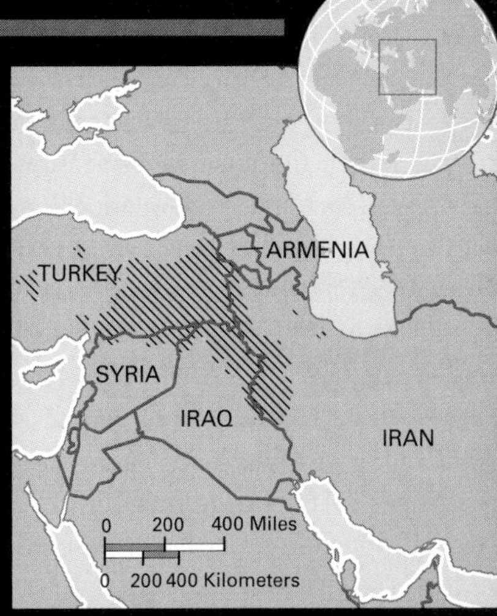

(LEFT) Herding goats and sheep is a major part of the economy throughout Kurdistan.

(CENTER) In Dohuk, Iraq, the Mazi Supermarket and Dream City are a combination shopping center and amusement park. The goods in the market come mainly from Dubai and Turkey.

MAP 10.6 Kurdish Region in the Middle East. Kurdistan includes parts of Iran, Iraq, Syria, Turkey, and Armenia. About half of all Kurds live in Turkey.

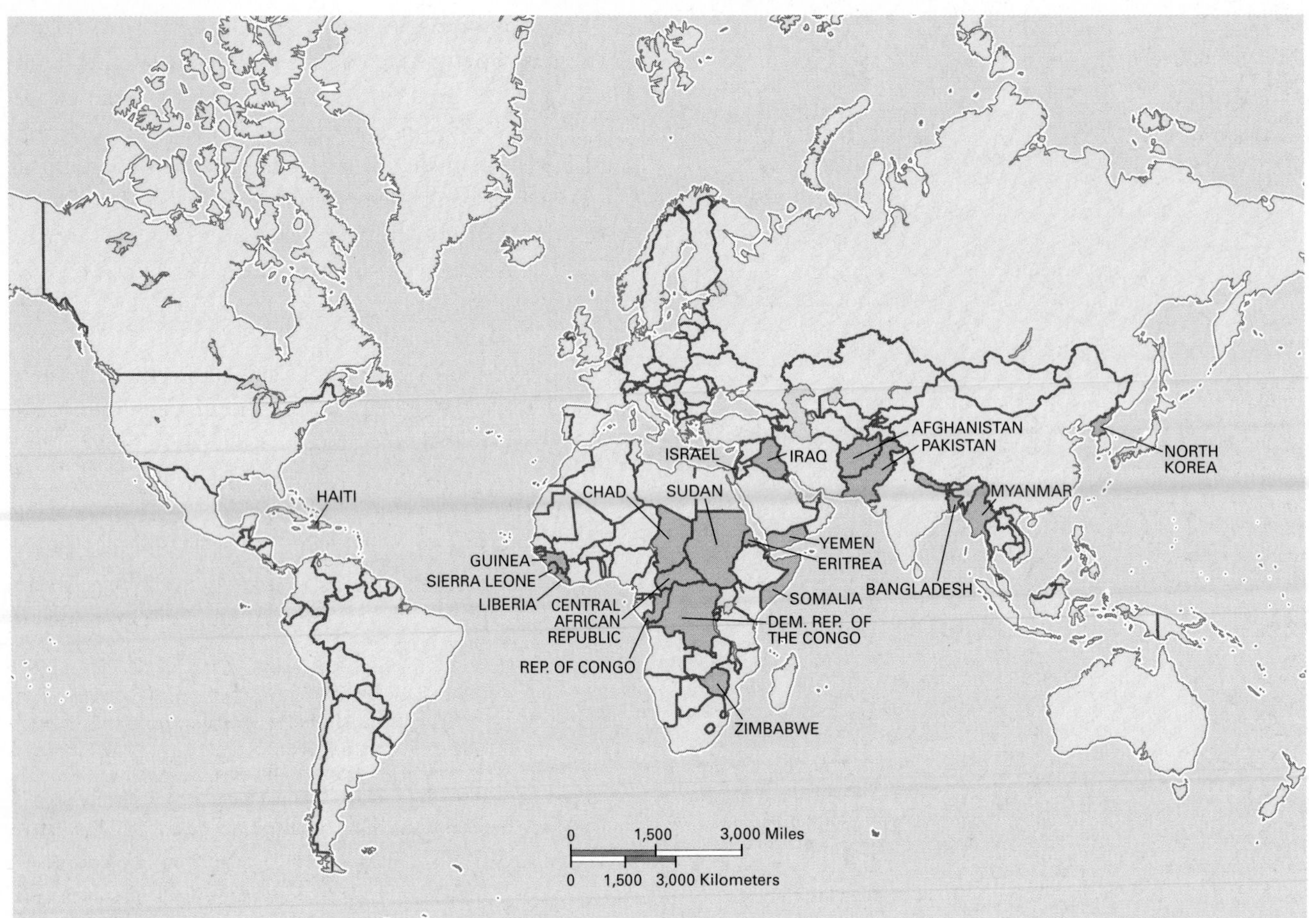

MAP 10.7 **Least Stable States of the World, 2008.**
The index for unstable and failed states includes criteria such as these: the government does not have effective control over its territory, is not seen as legitimate by a significant proportion of its population, does not provide services and domestic security to its citizens, and lacks a monopoly on the use of force.

promoting world peace. To that end, minority group movements for autonomy have been suppressed, sometimes brutally, or they lead to long-term internal conflicts. Political theorists and world leaders fear that weak and unstable states are easy targets for outside intervention and provide havens for terrorists. Thus, much international aid and military support goes to programs that aim at strengthening weak states. *Failed states* share features of a breakdown in law and order, economic deterioration, the collapse of service delivery such as education and health, a sharp decline in living standards, and loss of people's loyalty to the government (Foreign Policy 2008). The 2008 index of failed and least stable states included many countries of Africa (see Map 10.7). Between 2007 and 2008, Nepal dropped from the list of least stable states, but Israel was added.

With so many examples of failed and unstable states, some anthropologists ask if perhaps the idea of the state should be reconsidered (Graeber 2004). Options include the development of more, smaller states that correspond more closely to national/ethnic identities, or, on the other hand, the abandoning of country borders and creation of a global state within which all people could move freely. If the point of a state is to prevent human suffering by providing a benevolent structure that provides for people's welfare and human rights, and given the evidence that many states are unable to accomplish this goal, then perhaps other options for governance should be explored.

Globalization and increased international migration also prompt anthropologists to rethink the concept of the state (Trouillot 2001). The case of Puerto Rico (see Map 10.8) is illuminating because of its continuing status as a quasi-colony of the United States (Duany 2000). Puerto Rico is neither fully a state of the United States nor an autonomous political unit with its own national identity. Furthermore, Puerto Rican people do not coexist in a bounded spatial territory. By the late 1990s, nearly as many Puerto Ricans lived in the United States mainland as on the island of Puerto Rico. Migration to Puerto Rico also occurs, creating cultural diversity there. Migrants include returning Puerto Ricans and others from the United States, such as Dominicans and Cubans.

These migration streams—outgoing and incoming—complicate in two ways the sense of Puerto Rico as constituting

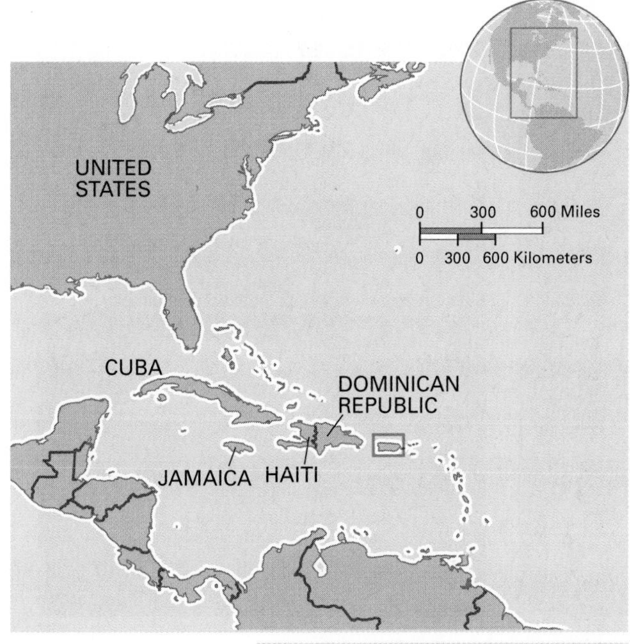

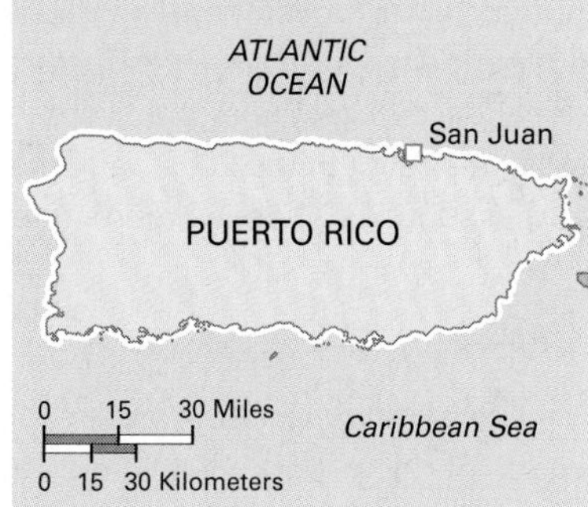

MAP 10.8 **Puerto Rico.**
The Commonwealth of Puerto Rico is a U.S. territory with commonwealth status. The indigenous population of the island, the Tainos, is extinct. Analysis of DNA of current inhabitants of Puerto Rico reveals a mixed ancestry, including the Taino, Spanish colonialists, and Africans who came to the island as slaves. The economy is based on agriculture, and sugarcane is the main crop. Tourism is also important, as are remittances. Official languages are Spanish and English. Roman Catholicism is the dominant religion, although Protestantism is increasing.

a nation. First, half of the "nation" lives outside the home territory. Second, within the home territory, ethnic homogeneity does not exist because of the diversity of people who migrate there. The Puerto Ricans who are return migrants are different from the islanders because many have adopted English as their primary language. All of these processes foster the emergence of a transnational identity, which differs from a national identity centered in either the United States or Puerto Rico.

DEMOCRATIZATION

Democratization is the process of transformation from an authoritarian regime to a democratic regime. This process includes several features: the end of torture, the liberation of political prisoners, the lifting of censorship, and the toleration of some opposition (Pasquino 1996). In some cases, what is achieved is more a relaxation of authoritarianism than a true transition to democracy, which would occur when the authoritarian regime is no longer in control. Political parties emerge, some presenting traditional interests and others oppositional.

The transition to democracy appears to be most difficult when the change is from highly authoritarian socialist regimes. This pattern is partly explained by the fact that democratization implies a transition from a planned economy to one based on market capitalism (Lempert 1996). The spotty record of democratization efforts also has to do with the nonfit of many principles of democracy with local political traditions that are based solely on kinship and patronage.

WOMEN IN POLITICS: NEW DIRECTIONS?

Two questions arise in the area of changing patterns of women in contemporary politics: Is the overall participation of women at varying political levels increasing? Do women in politics bring more attention to women's issues such as the division of labor and wages, access to health care, and violence? The answer to the first question is yes, as noted earlier, although the increase is modest. In terms of the second question, the answer is mainly no, perhaps because women political leaders become "like men" or have to avoid "feminist issues" in order to maintain their position. In all countries, women lack political status equal to that of men. In general, women are marginalized from formal politics and must seek to achieve their goals either indirectly, as wives or mothers of male politicians, or through channels other than formal politics, such as grassroots movements. Nonetheless, some signs of progress exist.

In contrast, in some Native American groups, recovery of women's former political power is occurring (B. G. Miller 1994). In several communities, female participation in formal politics is increasing dramatically, and it is bringing more attention to issues that face women. This change is taking place within the context of colonialism's effects, which resulted in women's greatly decreased political roles compared to the pre-colonial era. One explanation for the recent improvement is that women are obtaining newly available managerial positions on reservations. These positions give women experience in dealing with the outside world and authority for assuming public office. In addition, they face less resistance from men than women in more patriarchal contexts do. Most Native Americans do not view women's roles as contradictory to public authority roles.

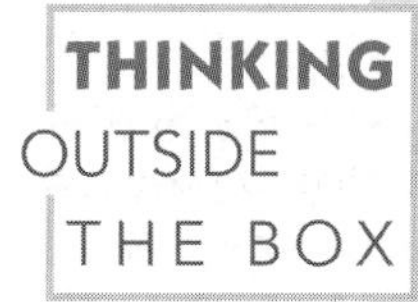

What is your position on states: Are they the best option for a peaceful world and for providing internal security and services for citizens? What are some examples of successful states?

(LEFT) Aung San Suu Kyi is the leader of the Burmese democracy and human rights movement. The daughter of Burma's national hero, Aung San, who was assassinated just before Burma gained its independence from the British, has frequently been placed under house arrest since 1989. Aung San Suu Kyi was awarded the Nobel Peace Prize, the eighth woman to receive the award. (RIGHT) An Iraqi Shi'ite woman in the city of Najaf, south of Baghdad, casts her ballot in the 2005 parliamentary elections. Promoting women's participation in democratic processes is challenging in contexts where women's role in the public domain is constrained.

Barack Obama, an African American, was elected the 44th President of the United States in November, 2008.

▶ *Should the proportion of various ethnic groups in a country be accurately reflected in state-level political bodies such as the United States Senate and House of Representatives? If no, why not. If yes, why, and how could it be achieved?*

The resurgence in women's political roles among the Seneca of New York State and Pennsylvania echoes these themes (Bilharz 1995). From women's precolonial position of at least equal political power with men, Seneca women's political status had declined in many ways. Notably, when the constitution of the Seneca Nation was drawn up on a European model in 1848, only men were granted the right to vote. In 1964, Seneca women finally gained the right to vote. Even before enfranchisement, women were politically active and worked on committees formed to stop the building of Kinzua Dam in Pennsylvania. For Seneca women, job creation through the Seneca Nation of Indians (SNI) brought new employment opportunities. Although no woman has run for president of the Seneca Nation as yet and only a few women have been head of a reservation, many women hold elective offices of clerk and judge, and many women head important service departments of the SNI, such as in the areas of education and health. Women of the Seneca Nation still retain complete control over the "clearing" (the cropland), and "their primacy in the home has never been challenged" (1995:112). According to Bilharz, Seneca women have regained a position of equality.

POLITICAL LEADERSHIP IN NEW SOCIAL MOVEMENTS

The Rural Landless Workers' Movement (NSM) in Brazil is one of the most dynamic social movements in Central and South America today (Veltmeyer and Petras 2002). The NSM is a movement of small farmers united in a political struggle for social change through pro-poor programs of land redistribution and limitations on state power. Brazil's NSM is characterized by especially successful leaders who are able to mobilize and sustain popular support. Analysis of NSM leaders' characteristics finds the following features of successful leaders:

- Deep and continuing roots in the countryside
- Relatively more education and strong commitment to education
- Ability to solve problems and take practical action
- Shared vision of alternative social system
- Personality with style and mystique to sustain popular loyalty in difficult times
- Optimism

The opposite of these characteristics define an unsuccessful political leader: origin in a distant social class from the constituency, from the same class but poorly educated, inspired by theory and ideology rather than being pragmatic, lacking in style and charisma, and with little sense of positive alternatives for the future.

GLOBALIZATION AND POLITICS

Since the seventeenth century, the world's nations have been increasingly linked in a hierarchical structure that is largely regulated through international trade. In the seventeenth century, Holland was the one core nation dominating world trade. It was then surpassed by England and France, which remained the two most powerful nations up to around 1900. In the early part of the twentieth century, challenges for world dominance were made by the United States and later Germany and Japan. The outcome of World War II placed the United States as leader of the "core" (see Chapter 4). Recently, Japan, the European Union, and China have been playing larger roles.

A flight operation specialist of the European Space Agency (ESA) waits for the launch of Cryosat satellite in Darmstadt, near Frankfurt, Germany, in 2005. Cryosat will circuit on a polar orbit with the primary mission of testing the prediction that polar ice is thinning due to global warming.

Cultural anthropology's traditional strength has been the study of small, bounded local groups, so anthropologists have come late to the study of international affairs (Wilson 2000). Now, more anthropologists have enlarged their focus to the international level, studying both how global changes affect local politics and how local politics affect international affairs. Worldwide communication networks facilitate global politics. Ethnic politics, although locally initiated, increasingly has international repercussions. Migrant populations promote interconnected interests across state boundaries.

A pioneering study in the anthropology of international affairs is Stacia Zabusky's (1995) research on patterns of cooperation among international scientists at the European Space Agency (ESA). The ESA involves people from different European nations seeking to cooperate in joint ventures in space and, more indirectly, to promote peaceful relations in Europe. Zabusky attended meetings and interviewed people at the European Space Research and Technology Centre, ESA's primary production site, in the Netherlands. Focusing on people's work roles, their styles of reaching consensus at meetings, and the role of national differences in this cooperative effort, she found that language plays a key part in affecting cooperation. The official languages of the ESA are English and French, but most interactions take place in English. Some nonnative English speakers felt that this gave the British an automatic advantage, especially in meetings where skill in speech can win an argument. A major divisive factor is the sheer geographic dispersal of the participants throughout Europe. This means that travel is a constant, as scientists and engineers convene for important meetings. Despite logistical problems, meetings are an important part of the "glue" that promotes cooperation above and beyond just "working together." Conversations and discussions at meetings allow people to air their differences and work toward agreement.

Zabusky concludes that the ESA represents an ongoing struggle for cooperation that is motivated by more than just the urge to do "big" science. "In working together, participants were dreaming about finding something other than space satellites, other than a unified Europe, or even a functioning organization at the end of their travails. Cooperation indeed appeared to participants not only as an achievement but as an aspiration" (1995:197).

Culture exists at all levels of human interaction—local, national, international, and transnational, and even in cyberspace—and power relations are embedded in culture at all these levels. Anthropologists must "study up," as Laura Nader urged them to do several decades ago (1972), because people, power, and culture are "up" there just as much as they are out in remote villages. As one anthropologist urges, anthropologists should move into research on institutions with lethal powers (Feldman 2003).

10

the BIG questions REVISITED

◆ What does political anthropology cover?

Political anthropology is the study of power relationships in the public domain and how they vary and change cross-culturally. Political anthropology has moved from a mainly functional perspective about local political systems, characteristic of the first half of the twentieth century, to looking at more macro and global issues related to inequality and conflict and to the role of individual agency in contesting political structures.

Political anthropologists study the concept of power, as well as related concepts such as authority and influence. They have discovered differences between politics and political organization in small-scale societies and large-scale societies by examining issues such as leadership roles and responsibilities, the social distribution of power, and the emergence of the state. Although politics in some form or another is a cultural universal, cross-cultural studies show wide variation in the bases and extent of political leadership and the informality or formality of political organization.

◆ What are the major cross-cultural forms of political organization and leadership?

Patterns of political organization and leadership vary according to mode of production and global economic relationships. Foragers have a minimal form of leadership and political organization in the band. Band membership is flexible. If a band member has a serious disagreement with another person or a spouse, one option is to leave that band and join another. Leadership in bands is informal. A tribe is a more formal type of political organization than the band. A tribe comprises several bands or lineage groups, with a headman or headwoman as leader. Big-man and big-woman political systems are an expanded form of tribe, with leaders having influence over people in several different villages. Chiefdoms may include several thousand people. Rank is inherited, and social divisions exist between the chiefly lineage(s) and nonchiefly groups.

A state is a form of political organization with a bureaucracy and diversified governmental institutions designed to administer large and complex societies. States conduct international relations in their dealings with other states. They control power within state borders and define citizenship and citizens' rights. They maintain records of citizens and have the power to levy indirect and direct taxes. State leaders employ a variety of symbols to bolster their image, including dress, housing, food, and modes of transportation. Strategies for building a sense of unity in culturally plural states may include imposition of one language as the national language; construction of monuments and museums; and promotion of songs, poetry, and other media-relayed messages about the homeland. Ethnic/national politics has emerged within and across states as groups compete for either increased rights within the state or autonomy from it.

States are differentiated in terms of their strength and ability to carry out their responsibilities to their citizens. The concept of a failed or unstable state refers to a government that is unable to maintain order and provide services. In recent decades, several states, especially in Africa, are considered to be failed states. Globalization, increased transnational migration, and the development of international organizations such as the United Nations and the World Trade Organization are major contemporary forces that have certain powers that transcend states.

◆ How are politics and political organization changing?

The anthropological study of change in leadership and political organization has documented several trends, most of which are related to the influences of European colonialism or contemporary capitalist globalization. Postcolonial nations struggle with internal ethnic divisions and pressures to democratize. Women as leaders of states are still a tiny minority. In some groups, however, women leaders are gaining ground, as among the Seneca. Globalized communication networks promote the growth of global politics.

Cultural anthropologists have rarely addressed the topic of international political affairs and the role of international organizations such as the United Nations. They are, however, increasingly interested in demonstrating the usefulness of cultural anthropology in global peacekeeping and conflict resolution.

KEY CONCEPTS

authority, p. 242
band, p. 244
big-man or **big-woman system,** p. 246
chiefdom, p. 248
faction, p. 254
influence, p. 242
in-kind taxation, p. 252
matriarchy, p. 250
moka, p. 246
nation, p. 256
political organization, p. 243
power, p. 242
segmentary model, p. 245
tribe, p. 245

SUGGESTED READINGS

Stanley R. Barrett. *Culture Meets Power*. Westport, CT: Praeger, 2002. The author argues that the two concepts, culture and power, should be considered in understanding contemporary affairs, including events such as the September 11, 2001, attacks on the United States.

Kimberley Coles. *Democratic Designs: International Intervention and Electoral Practices in Postwar Bosnia-Herzegovina*. Ann Arbor: University of Michigan Press, 2008. This book provides an ethnographic analysis of the interaction between international humanitarian aid workers and the postwar political process.

Elizabeth F. Drexler. *Aceh, Indonesia: Securing the Insecure State*. Philadelphia: University of Pennsylvania Press, 2008. The author examines corruption, political violence, and the failure of international humanitarian interventions in the Indonesian province of Aceh.

Mona Etienne and Eleanor Leacock, eds. *Women and Colonization: Anthropological Perspectives*. New York: Praeger, 1980. This classic collection examines the impact of Western colonialism and missionary intervention on women of several indigenous groups of North America and South America, Africa, and the Pacific.

Magnus Fiskesjö. *The Thanksgiving Turkey Pardon, The Death of Teddy's Bear, and the Sovereign Exception of Guantáno*. Chicago: Prickly Paradigm Press, 2003. This interpretation of the U.S. presidential ritual of "pardoning" a turkey every Thanksgiving sheds light on notions of the presidency and its power in the United States.

David Graeber. *Fragments of an Anarchist Anthropology*. Chicago: Prickly Paradigm Press, 2004. The author presents examples of nonstate societies as evidence that alternatives to the state exist and can function. He discusses the tendency of cultural anthropologists to favor small-scale, nonstate political organization as more peaceful and egalitarian than contemporary mega-states.

David H. Lempert. *Daily Life in a Crumbling Empire*. New York: Columbia University Press, 1996. This two-volume ethnography is based on fieldwork conducted in Moscow before perestroika. It is the first comprehensive ethnography of urban Russia and its economic, political, and legal systems and reforms.

Mark Moberg. *Citrus, Strategy, and Class: The Politics of Development in Southern Belize*. Iowa City: University of Iowa Press, 1992. The theoretical debate of structure versus agency frames this ethnography of household and village economies within the world economy and the transformation from factional politics to class formation. The author provides quantitative data and insights from five individuals' lives.

Dan Rabinowitz. *Overlooking Nazareth: The Politics of Exclusion in Galilee*. New York: Cambridge University Press, 1997. This study of Palestinian citizens in an Israeli new town examines conflict and cooperation and provides theoretical insights into nationalism and ethnicity. Biographical accounts of three Palestinians—a medical doctor, a basketball coach, and a local politician—are included.

David Sneath. *The Headless State: Aristocratic Orders, Kinship Society, and Misrepresentations of Inner Asia*. New York: Columbia University Press, 2008. The author describes how anthropologists, since the nineteenth century, have misrepresented Inner Asian nomadic political culture. His analysis continues through to the Soviet and post-Soviet periods and then offers a less essentialized interpretation.

Joan Vincent, ed. *The Anthropology of Politics: A Reader in Ethnography, Theory, and Critique*. Malden, MA: Blackwell Publishers, 2002. Over 40 essays are arranged in four sections: classics of the Enlightenment through the nineteenth century, early ethnographies paired with contemporary updates on the same culture, colonialism and imperialism, and political cosmopolitanism.

Jack M. Weatherford. *Tribes on the Hill*. New York: Rawson, Wade Publishers, 1981. This analysis of politics and political culture within the United States Congress examines the effects of male privilege and seniority on ranking, lobbying tactics, and ritual aspects of the legislation process.

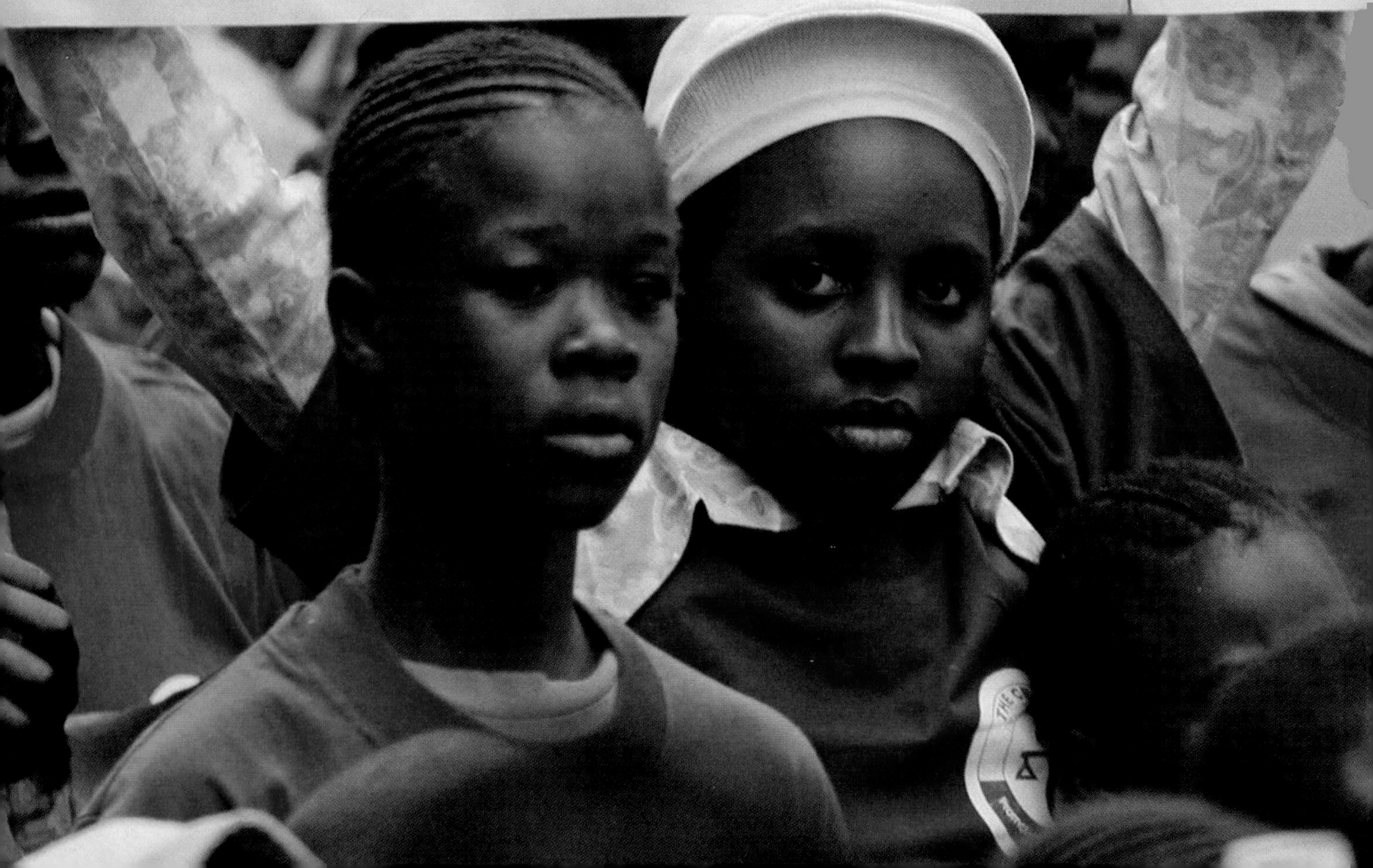
PROTECT
ME
I'AM A CHILD

School children hold banners and posters calling for protection of children's interests while marching in Nairobi, Kenya. The "Day of the African Child" falls on June 16. In 2007, its theme was "Stop the Trafficking of Children."

SOCIAL CONTROL AND SOCIAL CONFLICT

the BIG questions

- How do different cultures maintain social control?
- What are cross-cultural patterns of social conflict and violence?
- How does cultural anthropology contribute to world peace and order?

OUTLINE

(LEFT) Wreaths of red roses and an eternal flame decorate the Tomb of the Unknown Soldier beneath the Arc de Triomphe in Paris. (CENTER) A woman presses a rose against the monument to "Memory and Truth" in San Salvador, El Salvador. The monument has the names etched in stone of some 25,000 people who were assassinated or disappeared during the country's civil war of 1970 to 1991. (RIGHT) A young woman in the Philippines holds a black paper rose during an antiwar rally in Manila, in 2003, protesting a possible U.S.-led strike on Iraq.

▶ *Why do you think roses are associated with death and war in these three disparate contexts?*

Many Maasai people of Tanzania and Kenya work in cities and interact with international tourists, and some attend universities. But most rural Maasai, traditionally pastoralists who value their freedom to roam over vast areas, have limited knowledge of global events. Some rural villages lack electricity, so not everyone has access to a television. In 2002, when Kimeli Naiyomeh returned to his village in a remote area of Kenya following his medical studies at Stanford University in California, he told stories that stunned the villagers (Lacey 2002). They had not heard about the attacks on the United States on September 11, 2001. He described how massive fires destroyed buildings so high that they stretched into the clouds. The villagers could not believe that a building could be so tall that people jumping from it would die.

The stories about 9/11 saddened the villagers. They decided they should do something to help the victims. Cows are the most precious objects among the Maasai. As Kimeli Naiyomeh comments, "The cow is almost the center of life for us. . . . It's sacred. It's more than property. You give it a name. You talk to it. You perform rituals with it" (2002:A7). In June 2002, in a solemn ceremony, the villagers gave 14 cows to the United States. After the cows were blessed, they were transferred to the deputy chief of the U.S. Embassy in Kenya. He expressed his country's gratitude and explained that transporting the cows to the United States would be difficult. The cows were sold and the money went to support Maasai schools. Violence now has global implications more than ever before.

This chapter begins with the cross-cultural study of social order, then moves to a discussion of conflict and violence, and concludes with a section on how cultural anthropology is relevant to world peace and order. Anthropologists in all four fields study these issues. Archaeologists examine artifacts such as weapons, remains of forts, and the growth and decline of political centers in order to understand group conflict in the past. Primatologists study nonhuman primate patterns of cooperation, coalitions, and conflict. Linguistic anthropologists do research on social conflict related to state language policies and on how communication patterns in the courtroom and in international relations influence outcomes.

This chapter's subject matter is the subfield of *legal anthropology*. Legal anthropology, like political anthropology (Chapter 10), has its theoretical foundations in functionalism (the way a particular practice or belief contributes to social cohesion). Launching the subfield through his classic book *Crime and Custom in Savage Society* (1962 [1926]), Bronislaw Malinowski wrote that in the Trobriand Islands, social ties themselves promoted social obligation and social harmony. No separate legal institutions existed; instead, law was embedded in social life. The discovery that social relationships can perform the same functions as laws and courts was one of Malinowski's major contributions.

critical legal anthropology an approach within legal anthropology that examines how law and judicial systems serve to maintain and expand dominant power interests rather than protecting marginal and less powerful people.

social control processes that maintain orderly social life, including informal and formal mechanisms.

norm a generally agreed-upon standard for how people should behave, usually unwritten and learned unconsciously.

law a binding rule created through enactment or custom that defines right and reasonable behavior and is enforceable by threat of punishment.

Like political anthropology, legal anthropology has moved toward studying conflict and inequality. In the late twentieth century, **critical legal anthropology** emerged. It is the study of how law and judicial institutions serve to maintain and expand dominant power interests rather than protecting marginal and less powerful people. Critical legal anthropology focuses on state-level societies in which social inequalities are pronounced. Many cultural anthropologists now study violence and what triggers it; how violence victimizes particular groups in terms of ethnicity, indigeneity, class, gender, and age; and how post-conflict recovery can be achieved more effectively by taking culture into account.

◆◆◆

Systems of Social Control

Social control is the process by which people maintain orderly life in groups (Garland 1996:781). Social control systems define agreed-upon rules and ways to ensure conformity to those rules. Because some people may violate the rules (what sociologists refer to as *deviant behavior*), social control systems include ways to deal with such breaches.

Social control systems include internalized social controls that exist through socialization for proper behavior, education, and peer pressure. They may also include formal systems of codified rules about proper behavior and punishments for deviation. In the United States and Canada, the Amish (review Culturama in Chapter 6, p. 140) and Mennonites rely on internalized social controls far more than most microcultural groups. These groups have no police force or legal system; the way social order is maintained is through religious teaching and group pressure. If a member veers from correct behavior, punishment such as ostracism ("shunning") may be applied.

Cultural anthropologists distinguish two major instruments of social control: norms and laws. A **norm** is an accepted standard for how people should behave that is usually unwritten and learned unconsciously through socialization. All societies have norms. Norms include, for example, the expectation that children should follow their parents' advice, that people standing in line should be orderly, and that an individual should accept an offer of a handshake (in cultures where handshakes are the usual greeting) when meeting someone for the first time. In rural Bali, Indonesia, etiquette dictates certain greeting forms between people of different status: "Persons of higher status and power are shown very marked respect. . . . If [they are] seated, then others moving past them crouch" (Barth 1993:114). Enforcement of norms tends to be informal; for example, a violation may simply be considered rude and the violator would be avoided in the future. In others, direct action may be taken, such as asking someone who disrupts a meeting to leave.

A **law** is a binding rule created through custom or official enactment that defines correct behavior and the punishment for misbehavior. Systems of law are more common and more elaborate in state-level societies, but many nonstate societies have formalized laws. Religion often provides legitimacy for law. Australian Aborigines believe that law came to humans during the "dreamtime," a period in the mythological past when the ancestors created the world. Law and religion are synonymous in contemporary Islamic states. Secular Western states consider their laws to be religiously neutral. In fact, much Western law is based in Judeo-Christian beliefs.

The following material considers forms of social control in small-scale societies and in large-scale societies, namely states (see Figure 10.1, p. 244). Small-scale societies are characterized more by the use of norms. States rely more on legal sanctions, although local-level groups, such as neighbors, practice social sanctions among themselves. This section also provides an example of critical legal anthropology and discussion of change in legal systems.

SOCIAL CONTROL IN SMALL-SCALE SOCIETIES

Among small-scale groups such as foragers, formal laws are rare. Because bands are small, close-knit groups, disputes are usually handled at the interpersonal level through discussion or one-on-one fights. An observer's notes on his conversation with some Kalahari foragers (see Map 1.4, p. 23) lend insight into social order in small groups (Ury 1990): Kalahari foragers say that, if a man takes your bow and arrows, go to the man and tell him not to do it again. If your daughter wants to go off with a man you dislike, try to convince her not to go. If she does not agree, let her go. She will learn her lesson and eventually come back. In the most serious disputes, when a man runs off with another man's wife, the husband should go and get her and then move far away so the other man cannot come to get her. If his wife goes off with another man, the husband should go and fetch her again. If she refuses to come back, he should take the children and move far away, leaving her with the new man.

Group members may act together to punish an offender through shaming and ridicule. Emphasis is on maintaining social order and restoring social equilibrium, not hurtfully punishing an offender. *Ostracizing* an offending member (forcing the person to leave the group) is a common means of punishment. Capital punishment (execution) is rare.

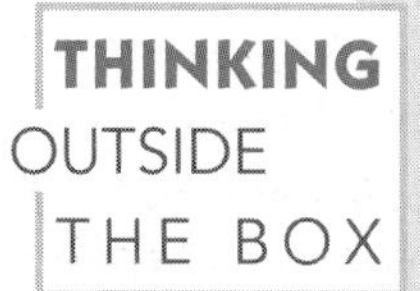

What are some forms of conflict prevention and conflict resolution used among small-scale political groups in your cultural world? Which are more effective and why?

Amish men in a communal barn-raising in Pennsylvania. Amish norms support sharing labor and other transfers of goods and services within the group.

▶ *Think of an example of shared work from your microcultural experience.*

In some Australian Aboriginal societies, laws restrict access to religious rituals and paraphernalia to men who have gone through a ritual initiation. If an initiated man shared secrets with an uninitiated person, the elders would delegate one of their group to kill the offender. In such instances, the elders act like a court.

The overall goal in dealing with conflict in small-scale societies is to return the group to harmony. Village fission (breaking up) and ostracism are mechanisms for dealing with more serious conflict.

SOCIAL CONTROL IN STATES

In densely populated societies with more social stratification and more wealth, increased social stress occurs in relation to the distribution of surplus, inheritance, and rights to land. In addition, increased social scale means that not everyone knows everyone else. Face-to-face accountability exists only in localized groups. Three important factors of state systems of social control are:

- Increased specialization of roles involved in social control
- Formal trials and courts
- Power-enforced forms of punishment, such as prisons and the death penalty

Informal mechanisms of social control, however, exist alongside these formal systems at the local level. In Lessons Applied, an activist anthropologist provides a cultural critique of one example of informal social control in states.

SPECIALIZATION The specialization of tasks related to law and order, such as police, judges and lawyers, increases with the emergence of state organization. In nonstate societies, society at large determines right from wrong and punishes offenders, or the elders may have special authority and be called on for advice. In chiefdoms, special advisors, such as the "leopard-skin chief" of the Nuer of southern Sudan, traditionally played a key role in decision making about crime and punishment. The leopard-skin chief was distinguished by his knowledge and authority as well as the privilege of wearing a leopard-skin upper garment. Full-time professionals, such as judges and lawyers, emerged with the state. These professionals are often members of powerful social groups, a fact that perpetuates elite biases in the justice process itself. In the United States, the legal profession is committed to opposing discrimination on the basis of gender and ethnicity. Nonetheless, women and minority lawyers are severely underrepresented, and minority women face a double bind and are especially underrepresented (Chanen 1995).

Policing is a form of social control that includes processes of surveillance and the threat of punishment related to maintaining social order (Reiner 1996). Police are the specific organization and personnel who discover, report, and investigate crimes. As a specialized group, police are associated with states.

Japan's low crime rate has attracted the attention of Western law-and-order specialists, who think that it may be the result of the police system there. They ask whether solutions to U.S. crime problems can be found in such Japanese policing practices as neighborhood police boxes staffed by foot patrolmen and volunteer crime prevention groups organized on a neighborhood basis. Fieldwork among police detectives in the city of Sapporo (see Map 3.2, p. 68) reveals aspects of Japanese culture and policing that promote low crime rates (Miyazawa 1992). In Japan, the police operate under high expectations that no false arrests will be made and that all arrests should lead to confession. And, in fact, the rate of confession is high. The high rate of confession may be due to the fact that the police do an excellent job of targeting the guilty party, or it may result from the nearly complete control of interrogation by the police. The police are allowed to keep suspects isolated for long periods of time, which can wear down resistance and potentially distort the process of justice. The suspect's statements are not recorded verbatim or taped; instead, the detectives write them down and the suspect is asked to sign them. Overall, policing culture in Japan gives more power to the police and less to the defendant than in the United States.

TRIALS AND COURTS In societies where spirits and ancestors define wrongdoing and punishment, a person's guilt is proved simply by the fact that misfortune has befallen him

---

policing the exercise of social control through processes of surveillance and the threat of punishment related to maintaining social order.

trial by ordeal a way of determining innocence or guilt in which the accused person is put to a test that may be painful, stressful, or fatal.

LESSONS applied

Legal Anthropologist Advises Resistance to "Coercive Harmony"

This box shows how an anthropologist uses cross-cultural insights to provide a critique of her own culture, with an eye to producing improved social relations (Nader 2001). Laura Nader has conducted extensive fieldwork in Latin America, as well as in the World Court in Europe. Her main interest lies in cross-cultural aspects of conflict and conflict resolution.

In terms of her observations of her home country, the United States, she points out that leading politicians of the early twenty-first century emphasized the need for unity, consensus, and harmony among the American people. But the United States, she points out, was founded by dissenters, and democracy depends on people speaking out. Democracy, in her view, supports the right to be indignant and the idea that "indignation can make Americans more engaged citizens" (2001:B13).

A professor of anthropology at the University of California at Berkeley, Nader fosters the expression of critique, opinion, and even indignation when she teaches. One of her students commented that "Dr. Nader is a pretty good professor, except she has opinions" (2001:B13). She took that as a compliment.

Nader feels that Europeans are generally less concerned about social harmony than are people in the United States. Americans consider it bad manners to be contentious, whereas in Europe, debate—even bitterly contentious debate—is valued. She uses the term "coercive harmony" to refer to the informal but strong pressure in the United States to agree, to be nice, to avoid digging beneath the surface, to stifle indignation at the lack of universal health care or the low voter turnout in presidential elections. The unstated, informally enforced policy of coercive harmony labels cultural critique as negative rather than positive. Nader finds it alarming that in a country that proclaims freedom as its primary feature, coercive harmony in fact suppresses contrary views and voices through the idiom of politeness, niceness, and friendliness.

How can this insight be used to improve the situation in the United States? Nader suggests one step: Make sure that critique, dissent, and indignation are supported in schools. Teachers should avoid contributing to the informal enforcement of social harmony and consensus and should instead encourage critique.

◆ **FOOD FOR THOUGHT**

- Watch several television interview shows with politicians on mainstream North American channels and then watch several similar shows on BBC (try to see Jeremy Paxman, one of Britain's most infamous political interviewers). Compare the interview styles between the North American and British shows. How do they compare and what do the possible differences have to do with Nader's position?

---

or her. If a person's crops were damaged by lightning, for instance, then that person must have done something wrong. In other cases, guilt may be determined through **trial by ordeal**, a way of judging guilt or innocence in which the accused person is put through a test that is often painful. An accused person may be required to place his or her hand in boiling oil, for example, or to have a part of his or her body touched by a red-hot knife. Being burned is a sign of guilt, whereas not being burned means the suspect is innocent.

The *court system,* with lawyers, judge, and jury, is used in many contemporary societies, although variation exists in how cases are presented and juries constituted. The goal of contemporary court trials is to ensure both justice and fairness. Analysis of courtroom dynamics and patterns of decision making in the United States and elsewhere, however, reveals serious problems in achieving these goals.

PRISONS AND THE DEATH PENALTY Administering punishment involves doing something unpleasant to someone who has committed an offense. As noted earlier, the most extreme form of punishment in small-scale societies is ostracism and only rarely death. A common form of punishment in the case of theft or murder in pastoralist societies, especially in Islamic cultures of the Middle East, is that the guilty party must pay compensation to members of the harmed family.

The *prison,* as a place where people are forcibly detained as a form of punishment, has a long history but probably emerged only with the state. The dungeons of historic forts and castles are vivid evidence of the power of some people to detain and inflict suffering on others. In Europe, long-term detention of prisoners did not become common until the 1600s (Foucault 1977). The first prison in the United States was built in Philadelphia in the late 1700s (Sharff 1995).

Percentages of imprisoned people vary widely around the world. The United States imprisons more people than any other country in the world, followed by China (Pew Center

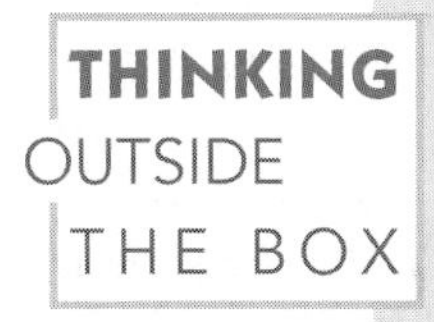

What is your position on the death penalty? How does your microculture shape your views?

Interior scene of the Cellular Jail in India's Andaman Islands, which was so named because all prisoners had single cells, arranged in rows, to prevent them from engaging in social interaction and possible collusion to escape or rebel.

2008). In the United States, the prison population of 1.6 million has more than doubled since 1985 (Walmsley 2007). Prison populations have also doubled in that time period in Brazil and Mexico.

It is important to look at the rate of imprisonment as well as sheer numbers. The national *incarceration rate* is calculated as the number of people in prison per 100,000 people in a country. Countries vary widely in their incarceration rate. The United States has the highest incarceration rate of 737 per 100,000 people followed by Russia at 611, Turkmenistan at 489, Cuba at 487, Belarus at 426, South Africa at 335, Iran at 214, and Spain at 145 (Walmsley 2007).

It is also important to look inside national rates. In England and France, a disproportionate number of prisoners are Muslims (Moore 2008). Ethnic and gender differences in incarceration exist in the United States. One in 15 adult black men is in prison, and among black men ages 20 to 34 years, 1 in 9 men is in prison. One in 355 white women ages 35 to 39 years is in prison, whereas 1 in 100 black women is behind bars. Among Hispanics, 1 in 36 adult Hispanic men is in prison. The state with the highest incarceration rate is Louisiana, and southern states in general have higher rates than northern states.

Inefficient justice systems may mean that many prisoners are in jail for many years awaiting trial; they have not been convicted of a crime but they are imprisoned. In Haiti, 9 of every 10 prisoners are awaiting trial (Walmsley 2007).

The death penalty (capital punishment) is rare in non-state societies because condemning someone to death requires a great deal of power. A comparison of capital punishment in the contemporary United States with human sacrifice among the Aztecs of Mexico of the sixteenth century reveals striking similarities (Purdum and Paredes 1989). Both systems involve the death of mainly able-bodied males who are in one way or another socially marginal. In the United States, most people who are executed are non-White, have killed Whites, are poor, and have few social ties. Aztec sacrificial victims were mainly male war captives from neighboring states, but Aztec children were also sometimes sacrificed. The deaths in both contexts communicate a political message to the general populace about the state's power and strength, which is why they are highly ritualized and widely publicized events.

SOCIAL INEQUALITY AND THE LAW

Critical legal anthropologists examine the role of law in maintaining power relationships through discrimination against such social categories as indigenous people, women, and minorities. Systematic discrimination has been documented in judicial systems around the world, including long-standing democracies. This section presents an example from Australia.

At the invitation of Aboriginal leaders in Australia, Fay Gale and her colleagues conducted research comparing the treatment of Aboriginal youth and White youth in the judicial system (1990). The question posed by the Aboriginal leaders was: Why are our kids always in trouble? Two directions can be pursued to find the answer. First, structural factors—such as

This man, in a military prison in Chechnya, is accused by the Russian government of participating with Chechen rebel forces. Human rights activists have been concerned about the mistreatment of prisoners in Chechnya for several years.

▶ *What human rights do prisoners have in your country?*

	Aboriginal Youth (percent)	White Youth (percent)
Brought into system via arrest rather than police report	43.4	19.7
Referred to Children's Court rather than diverted to Children's Aid Panels	71.3	37.4
Proportion of court appearances resulting in detention	10.2	4.2

Note: Most of these youths are male; data are from 1979 to 1984.

Source: *Aboriginal Youth and The Criminal Justice System: The Injustice of Justice,* by Fay Gale, Rebecca Bailey-Harris, Joy Wundersitz, Copyright © Cambridge University Press 1990. Reprinted by permission of Cambridge University Press.

FIGURE 11.1
Comparison of Outcomes for Aboriginal and White Youth in the Australian Judicial System

Aboriginal displacement from their homeland, poverty, poor living conditions, and bleak future prospects—can be investigated. These factors might make it more likely for Aboriginal youth to commit crimes than the relatively advantaged White youth. Second, the criminal justice system can be examined to see whether it treats Aboriginal and White youth equally. The researchers decided to direct their attention to the judicial system because little work had been done on that area by social scientists. Australia, a former colony of England, adopted the British legal system, which claims to administer the law equitably. The research assessed this claim in one state, South Australia (see Map 5.4, p. 124).

Findings show that Aboriginal youth are overrepresented at every level of the juvenile justice system, from apprehension (being caught by the police) through pretrial processes, to the ultimate stage of adjudication (the judge's decision) and disposition (the punishment): "A far greater proportion of Aboriginal than other young people follow the harshest route. . . . At each point in the system where discretion operates, young Aborigines are significantly more likely than other young persons to receive the most severe outcomes of those available to the decision-makers" (1990:3). At the time of apprehension (being caught by the police), the suspect can be either formally arrested or informally reported. A formal arrest is made to ensure that the offender will appear in court. Officers ask the suspects for a home address and whether they have a job. Aboriginal youth are more likely than White youth to live in a poor neighborhood in an extended family, and they are more likely to be unemployed. Thus, they tend to be placed in a category of "undependable," and they are formally arrested more than White youth for the same crime (see Figure 11.1). The next step determines whether the suspect will be tried in Children's Court or referred to Children's Aid Panels. The Children's Aid Panels in South Australia have gained acclaim worldwide for the opportunities they give to individuals to avoid becoming repeat offenders and take their proper place in society. But most Aboriginal youth offenders are denied access to them and instead have to appear in court, where the vast majority of youthful offenders end up pleading guilty. The clear and disturbing finding from this study is that the mode of arrest tends to determine each subsequent stage in the system.

CHANGE IN LEGAL SYSTEMS

Law-and-order systems, like other cultural domains, change over time. European colonialism since the seventeenth century has had major effects on indigenous systems. Legal systems of contemporary countries have to deal with social complexity that has its roots in colonialism and new patterns of migration.

EUROPEAN COLONIALISM AND INDIGENOUS SYSTEMS

Colonial governments, to varying degrees, attempted to learn about and rule their subject populations through what they termed "customary law" (Merry 1992). By seeking to codify customary law, colonial governments created fixed rules where flexibility and local variation had formerly existed. Often the colonialists totally ignored local customary law and imposed their own laws. Homicide, marriage, land rights, and indigenous religion were frequent areas of European imposition. Among the Nuer of southern Sudan, for example, British legal interventions resulted in confusion concerning blood feuds (Hutchinson 1996). In a case of homicide, Nuer practice requires either the taking of a life in repayment or the payment in cattle, depending on the relationship between the victim and the assailant, the type of weapon used, and the current rate of bridewealth as an index of value. In contrast, the British determined a fixed amount of indemnity, and they imprisoned people for committing murder. The Nuer interpreted being put in prison as a way of protecting the person from a reprisal attack.

Colonial imposition of European legal systems onto indigenous systems added another layer, and one that had

This scene occurred in Mantes-la-Jolie, France, in 1994. Female Muslim students who wish to wear a head scarf while attending public schools in France have been banned from doing so by the government. This ban has led to protests and court disputes for two decades.

▶ *What is the current position of the French government on headscarves?*

preeminent power over others. **Legal pluralism** is a situation in which more than one way exists of defining acceptable and unacceptable behavior and ways to deal with the latter. It raises questions such as whether a case of murder in the Sudan should be tried according to indigenous Sudanese principles or European principles. Several postcolonial countries are now in the process of attempting to reform their legal systems and develop more unified codes (Merry 1992:363). In some contexts, indigenous minority groups seek to have their customary law and practices gain greater recognition (see Culturama).

LAW AND COMPLEXITY In situations where several cultural groups are subject to a single legal code, misunderstandings between the perspectives of both legal specialists and the affected people are likely and may result in conflict. For example, in the United States and Canada, female genital cutting (recall Chapter 6) is against the law. Members of some immigrant groups, however, wish to have their daughters go through this procedure. Cultural relativists (Ahmadu 2000, Shweder 2003) support people's freedom to pursue their traditional cultural practices.

The issue of whether Muslim girls can wear head scarves in school in non-Muslim countries is another example of cultural rights versus state laws (Ewing 2000). For many Muslims, the head scarf is a sign of proper Muslim society, a rejection of Western secularism, and an aspect of religious freedom. Westerners typically view the head scarf as a sign of women's oppression and as a symbol of resistance to the goals of schooling and values of modernity. In France, beginning in 1989, disputes have erupted over girls wearing head scarves in school. In 1994, the French education director stated that head scarves would not be permitted in school, yet Jewish boys were allowed to wear yarmulkes (head caps). Muslim leaders responded by taking the issue to court. As of 2008, the issue has not been settled.

legal pluralism a situation in which more than one way exists of defining acceptable and unacceptable behavior and ways to deal with the latter.

◆◆◆

Social Conflict and Violence

All systems of social control have to deal with the fact that conflict and violence may occur. This section considers the varieties of social conflict studied by cultural anthropologists. Conflict can occur at any social level, from the private microlevel of the household to the public situation of international warfare.

INTERPERSONAL CONFLICT

Interpersonal conflict encompasses a wide range of behavior, from arguments to murder. At the most micro level, the household, interpersonal disputes are common (review Chapter 8's section on domestic violence). Some might say that it is easier to kill or be cruel to an anonymous enemy. But abusive and lethal conflict between people who are intimately related as lovers or family members is frequent cross-culturally. Dating violence among high school and college students is an increasing problem (Makepeace 1997, Sanday 1996).

Beyond the household, interpersonal conflict occurs between neighbors and residents of the same town or village, often over resources or territory. Since the 1970s, villagers of the Gwembe Valley in southern Zambia (see Map 11.2) have kept diaries documenting economic and demographic information and reports of disputes (Colson 1995). Over the years, the number of disputes has increased. There are two possible reasons for this change: Disputing may actually be on the rise because of the increased availability of beer and guns, or the people have become more willing to discuss negative features of their communities, or both. One thing is clear: Disputes still occur over the same issues—cattle damage to growing crops, land encroachment, inheritance, elopement and impregnation damages, marriage payments and marriage difficulties, slander, accusations of sorcery, theft, physical violence, and the rights of senior people over the labor of younger men and women. Financial debts are a major new cause for disputes.

A different pattern of interpersonal conflict emerges from interviews with 100 middle-class, U.S. suburbanites: "In the first five minutes of listening to suburbanites discuss neighbors, it became clear that dogs are the most worrisome population" (Perin 1988:108). Problems include dogs roaming

CULTURAMA

The Māori of New Zealand

The term "Māori" (mao-ree) refers to all indigenous people of New Zealand or Aotearoa. Their claim to specific territories is a matter of oral tradition, not law. About 530,000 Māori people live in New Zealand, representing 15 percent of the country's total population.

Traditionally, Māori livelihood was based on foraging, especially fishing, and horticulture. Now they are increasingly involved as wage workers in the industrial sector. Compared to the Paheka (European descent people), Māori have lower incomes and lower life expectancies, and higher rates of unemployment, infant mortality, and imprisonment (Olsen, Maxwell, and Morris 1995).

Māori consider themselves descended from the natural elements (Solomon and Watson 2001). Reciprocity with nature and care for nature are essential. Before cutting down a tree or taking fish from the sea, the Māori give a blessing. Of key importance is the protection of native places, plants, and animals, and the traditional knowledge about them.

Several tribes claim that their rights have been violated repeatedly since the Treaty of Waitungi was signed with the British in 1840 (Solomon and Watson 2001). The Treaty guarantees the Māori full and exclusive ownership of their lands, forests, fisheries, and other "treasured possessions." The tribes advocated for the establishment of a new organization, called the Waitungi Tribunal, to hear claims from any person of Māori descent about acts inconsistent with the Waitungi Treaty. Established in 1975, the Tribunal began meeting in the mid-1980s. Of 16 members, 8 are Māori and 8 are Paheka.

Tribunal hearings take place in the traditional community meeting area of the Māori (Solomon and Watson 2001). Witnesses are surrounded by extended family members with whom cultural knowledge is shared. The ancestors, represented in carvings around the meeting house, lend further support. The Māori language is used for testimony, with interpreters providing English translation.

In spite of the attempt to bring Māori culture to the fore in the Tribunal hearings, British legal procedure and government interests dominate. Māori input is often more of a token gesture. Government restrictions on funding for the Tribunal process result in long delays in scheduling a hearing, and over 1000 cases are pending (Te Pareake Mead et al. 2004). Furthermore, the current political environment is not sympathetic to Māori issues (Charters 2006).

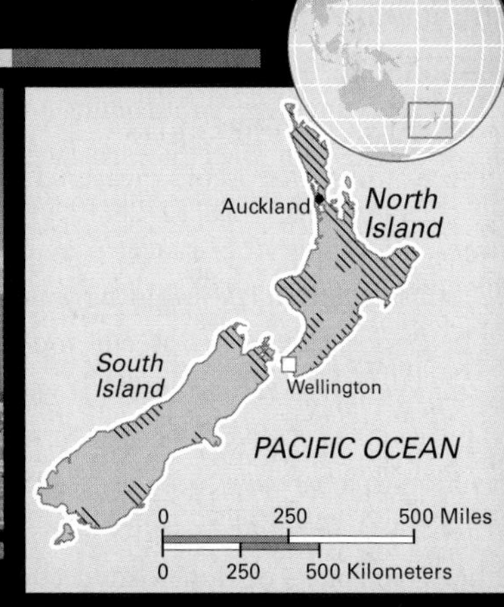

(LEFT) Dr. Pita Sharples, or Ko Tākuta Pita Russell Sharples, leads a procession to Parliament in Wellington in 2004. Sharples, an academic and politician, is head of the Māori Party.
(CENTER) Most Māori are Christian. Many denominations exist, and all are localized to some degree. This Māori religious center is located on North Island.

MAP 11.1 Māori Regions in New Zealand. The Māori name for New Zealand is Aotearoa. It is widely used but unofficial.

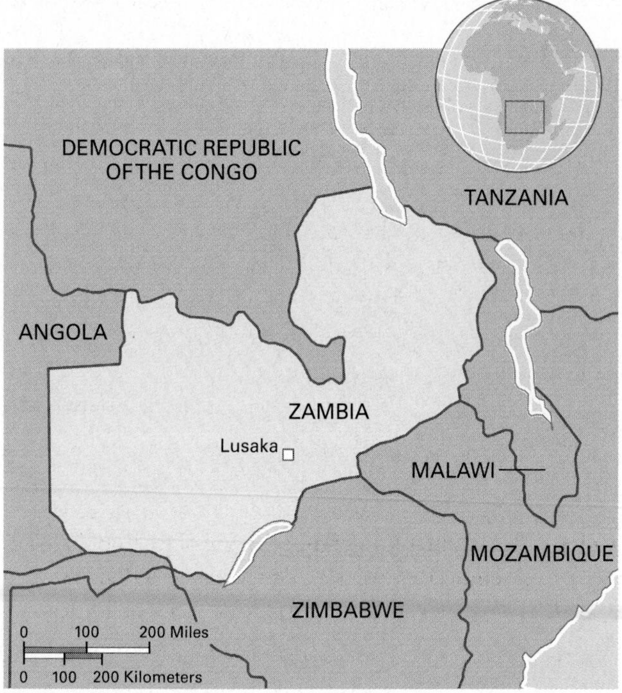

MAP 11.2 Zambia.
The Republic of Zambia consists of high plateaus and mountains. Heavily mined by the British for its copper, Zambia has one of the highest poverty rates in the world. The prevalence of HIV/AIDS is high. Zambia's population of about 11 million consists of over 70 Bantu-speaking ethnic groups. Zambia has a highly urbanized population with more than 2 million people living in the capital city of Lusaka. Small-scale farming is the basis of the rural economy. Christianity is the official religion, and several denominations exist as well as localized versions.

off the leash; barking; relieving themselves; chewing garbage bags; biting; and threatening children, joggers, and bicyclists.

How do U.S. suburbanites deal with conflicts about dogs? Some opt for a face-to-face solution; others resort to the dog warden after trying to talk to the neighbor several times. In taking the issue to court, every complaint has to be substantiated. A building inspector in Houston said, "The barking dog isn't as cut and dried a thing as it might seem. We watch it for a week. If we're going to court, we have to prove it's excessive. We have to keep numbers. People's first reaction to a barking complaint is that they're not in violation" (1988:113). Mutual hostility may continue for a long time. The seriousness of dog-related conflicts led to an expanded role of the courts. In Middlesex District Court in Massachusetts, one day each month is devoted to dog cases, and two days a month are needed in Portland, Oregon. In Santa Barbara, California, the city attorney's office provides professional mediation for dog-related disputes.

BANDITRY

Banditry is a form of aggressive conflict that involves socially patterned theft. It is usually practiced by a person, or group of persons, who is socially marginal and who gains a special social status from illegal activity. Political scientists, sociologists, historians, and anthropologists have proposed various theories to explain why banditry appears at particular times and places more than others, why it is persistent in some contexts, and what sentiments inspire bandits. One theory is that bandits flourish in the context of weak states and decline as states grow stronger and increase their control of violence (Blok 1972). Another view is that banditry is a form of protest, expressing a yearning for a just world (Hobsbawm 1969). Neither theory can explain, however, the surge of banditry in late-nineteenth-century Egypt during the time of British colonialism (Brown 1990). British control was not weak, nor was this banditry an expression of anti-British sentiment (banditry existed in Egypt long before the British arrived). Instead, the answer appears to be that the British chose to highlight the presence of banditry as a social problem so that they could justify their presence and role in imposing law and order.

One anthropologist has, somewhat humorously, termed banditry "adventurist capital accumulation" (Sant Cassia 1993), but it is usually about more than just money. For example, banditry, male identity and status, and the creation of social alliances are closely associated on the Greek island

Anthropologist Michael Herzfeld (far right) observes and interacts with men at a coffeehouse while doing fieldwork on banditry and male identity in Crete.

▶ *Could a woman anthropologist conduct fieldwork on the same topics in Crete?*

banditry a form of aggressive conflict that involves socially patterned theft, usually practiced by a person or group of persons who are socially marginal and who may gain a mythic status.

feuding long-term, retributive violence that may be lethal between families, groups of families, or tribes.

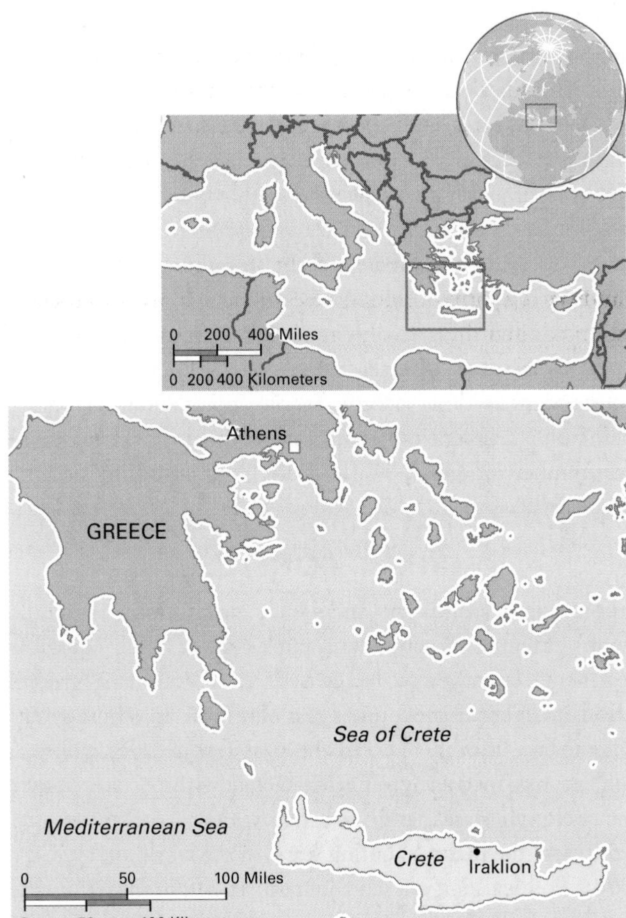

MAP 11.3 Crete.
Crete is the largest of the Greek islands and, after Cyprus, the second largest in the eastern Mediterranean. Its terrain is mountainous interspersed with fertile plateaus. Farming is the traditional basis of the economy with tourism growing in importance.

of Crete (Herzfeld 1985) (see Map 11.3). In this sheepherding economy, manhood and male identity depend on a local form of banditry: stealing sheep. "Coming out on the branch" is a metaphor for the attainment of manhood following a young man's first theft. This phrase implies that he is now a person with whom to be reckoned. To not participate in sheep raids is to be effeminate. Each theft, however, requires a countertheft in revenge, and so the cycle goes on. For protection of his flock from theft and to be able to avenge any theft that occurs, a shepherd relies heavily on male kin through his patrilineage and through marriage. Another important basis for social ties is sheep stealing itself. After a series of thefts and counterthefts and rising hostility between the two groups, a mediator is brought in to resolve the tension, the result being that the enemies swear to be loyal friends from then on. Male identity formation through sheep stealing in highland Crete is still strong, although it is declining as some shepherds take up farming. The government seeks, mainly unsuccessfully, to suppress the raiding and to define sheep stealing as a crime.

Analysis of many instances of banditry reveals that they often involve *mythification* of bandits (Sant Cassia 1993). In this process, the imagined character of the bandit becomes more significant than what the bandit actually did. The story of Phulan Devi, India's "Bandit Queen," contains many aspects of banditry mythification: her low socioeconomic status, traditions of pastoralism, and raiding as honorable. Villagers have composed songs praising her, and a movie appeared in 1995 depicting her as a heroine who suffered, resisted, and ultimately triumphed.

FEUDING

Feuding is a form of intergroup aggression that involves long-term, retributive violence that may be lethal between families, groups of families, or tribes. A concept of revenge motivates such back-and-forth violence between two groups. It is widely distributed cross-culturally.

Feuding long had an important role among the horticultural Ilongot people of the highlands of Luzon, the Philippines (Rosaldo 1980) (see Map 7.2, p. 166). From 1883 to 1974, Ilongot feuds were structured around head-hunting as redress for an insult or offense. Manhood was defined by the taking of a first head, and fathers were responsible for transferring the elaborate knowledge of head-hunting to their sons. In 1972, the government banned head-hunting and attempted to stop the Ilongot from practicing horticulture. The repercussions were devastating for the Ilongot. The end of head-hunting weakened father–son ties that had been solidified across the generations by the handing down of the elaborate techniques of head-hunting. More than that, the people said they were no longer Ilongots.

Sometimes economic development and change leads to increased feuding, as in Thull, a village in northern Pakistan of about 6000 people (Keiser 1986). Blood feuds, which involve the death of someone in the enemy group, increased in frequency and intensity over a 15-year period in the 1960s and 1970s. Previously, there had been fights, usually expressing hostility between members of three patrilineal clans, but they rarely involved deadly weapons. According to the traditional honor code in this region, an act of avenging should not exceed the original act: A blow should answer a blow; a death, a death. For a murder, a man prefers to kill the actual murderer, but a father, adult brother, or adult son is a permissible substitute; killing women and children is unknown. Wrongs committed against a man through his wife, sister, or daughter are special, and whatever the transgression, the most appropriate response is to kill the offender. For example, staring at a man's wife or his daughter or sister (if she is of marriageable age) demands a deadly retaliation. Thus, according to some people in Thull, one man killed another man because he had apparently come to his house to catch a glimpse of his attractive young wife.

Why did the incidence of blood feuds increase in Thull? The answer lies in the effects of economic change on the area. The government built a new road so that commercial logging could begin in the region. The logging involved local men in wage work and greatly increased the amount of cash available. The new road transformed local production from a blend of herding and farming to an emphasis on growing cash crops, especially potatoes. These changes led to increased tension among men, and they became more vigilant about defending their honor. Along with more cash came a dramatic rise in the number of guns. With more guns, feuding became more deadly.

(TOP) Phulan Devi, India's "Bandit Queen" and heroine of the poor, became an elected member of Parliament after 11 years in prison. Here, she participates in Parliament in New Delhi in 2000. She was assassinated in 2001. (BOTTOM) The Hatfield clan in West Virginia in 1899. The long-standing feud between the Hatfields and the McCoys is part of American legend.

▶ *For a research project, read a biography of her, watch the video called "The Bandit Queen," read commentary on the Internet, and be prepared to comment on the "mythic" aspects of her life story.*

ETHNIC CONFLICT

Ethnic conflict and grievances may result from an ethnic group's attempt to gain more autonomy or more equitable treatment. It may also be caused by a dominant group's actions to subordinate, oppress, or eliminate an ethnic group by genocide or ethnocide. In the past few decades, political violence has increasingly been enacted within states rather than between states, and intrastate violence constitutes the majority of the many "shooting wars" in the world today (Clay 1990). Political analysts and journalists often cite ethnicity, language, and religion as the causes of certain conflicts. It is true that ethnic identities give people an ideological commitment to a cause, but one must look beneath the labels to see whether deeper issues exist, such as claims to land, water, ports, and other material resources.

Consider Central Asia (see Map 11.4), a vast region populated by many ethnic groups, none of which has a pristine indigenous claim to the land. Yet, in Central Asia, every dispute appears on the surface to have an ethnic basis: "Russians and Ukrainians versus Kazakhs over land rights and jobs in Kazakhstan, Uzbeks versus Tajiks over the status of Samarkhand and Bukhara, conflict between Kirghiz and Uzbeks in Kyrgyzstan, and riots between Caucasian Turks and Uzbeks in the Fergana Valley of Uzbekistan" (Clay 1990:48).

Attributing the causes of all such problems to ethnic differences overlooks resource competition based on regional, not ethnic, differences. Uzbekistan has most of the cities and irrigated farmland, whereas Kyrgyzstan and Tajikistan control most of the water, and Turkmenistan has vast oil and gas riches. Competition among groups in these different regions appears to be "ethnic," when in fact it is rooted in the local and global political economy.

So-called ethnic conflicts are waged in many different ways, from the cruelest and most gruesome killings and rapes to more subtle forms. Throughout the history of the state, and seemingly at increasing rates in recent decades, violence linked to ethnicity has led to the break-up of states and the

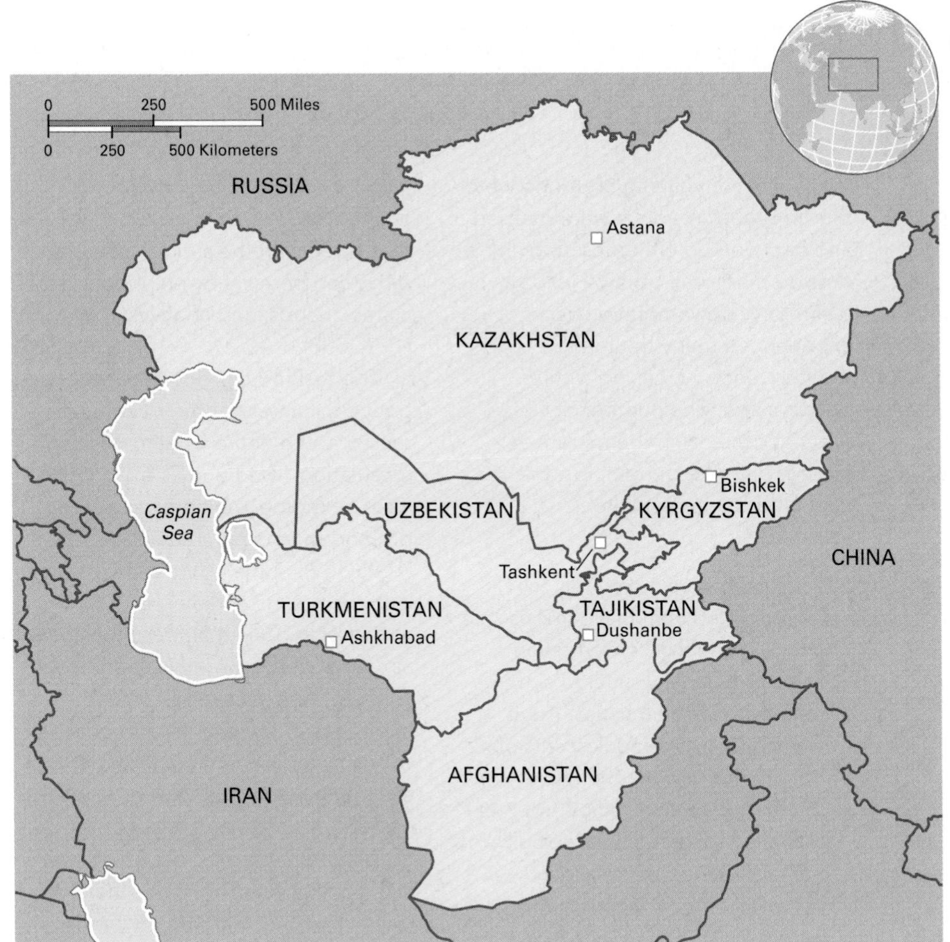

MAP 11.4 Central Asian States. The five states of Central Asia are Kazakhstan, Turkmenistan, Uzbekistan, Kyrgyzstan, and Tajikistan. It is a large, landlocked region that is historically linked with pastoralism and the famous Silk Road, a trade route linking the Middle East with China. The region's terrain encompasses desert, plateaus, and mountains. Given its strategic location near several major world powers, it has often been a battleground of other states' interests. The predominant religion is Islam, and most Central Asians are Sunnis. Languages are of the Turkic language group. Central Asia has an indigenous form of rap-style music in which lyrical improvisers engage in battles, usually accompanied by a stringed instrument. These musical artists, or *akyns*, are now using their art to campaign for political candidates.

forced displacement of millions of people (see Everyday Anthropology).

REVOLUTION

A **revolution** is a form of conflict involving illegal and usually violent actions by subordinate groups that seek to change the status quo (Goldstone 1996:740). Revolutions have occurred in a range of societies, including monarchies, postcolonial developing countries, and totalitarian states. Comparison of revolutions in recent times—England, 1640; France, 1789; Mexico, 1910; China, 1911; Russia, 1917; and Iran, 1979—reveal that their causes involve interrelated factors, such as a military crisis, a fiscal crisis, and a weak state. The process of revolution varies in terms of the degree of popular participation, the roles of radicals and moderates, and leadership.

Theorists argue about the different roles of rural and urban sectors in fostering revolution. Many revolutions occurred in agrarian countries and were propelled by rural participants, not by urban radicalism (Skocpol 1979, Wolf 1969). Agrarian-based revolutions include the French, Russian, and Chinese revolutions. A rural-based movement also characterized many national liberation movements against colonial powers such as French Indo-China, Guinea-Bissau, Mozambique, and Angola (Gugler 1988). Algeria was a somewhat more urbanized country, but it was still about two-thirds rural in 1962 when the French finally made peace there. In these cases, the colonial power was challenged by a rural-based guerrilla movement that controlled crop production, processing, and transport and thus could strike at the heart of the colonial political economy.

In contrast, some revolutions have been essentially urban in character, as in Bolivia, Iran, and Nicaragua. The importance of cities in these revolutions is related to the fact that the countries were highly urbanized. Thus, revolutionary potential exists where resources are controlled and where the bulk of the population is located. Given the rapid urban growth in most developing countries, it is possible that the world has entered "the age of urban revolutions" (Gugler 1988).

The case of the Cuban revolution is mixed. Rural-based guerrillas played a prominent role in the revolution that placed Fidel Castro in power. Cities, however, provided crucial support for the guerrillas.

WARFARE

Several definitions of war exist (Reyna 1994), including the view that it is an open and declared conflict between two political units. This definition would rule out many war-like

---

revolution a political crisis prompted by illegal and often violent actions of subordinate groups that seek to change the political institutions or social structure of a society.

everyday ANTHROPOLOGY

Narrating Troubles

Refugee survivors of violence are especially at risk of various mental health problems, including what Western psychiatrists call post-traumatic stress disorder, or PTSD. It includes symptoms such as depression, anxiety, sleep disorders, and changes in personality. In treating refugee survivors in North America, several approaches have been used, including *narrative therapy* in which the sufferer tells about his or her experiences as a way of unloading the pent-up memories. Narrative therapy, also called the testimony method, is usually combined with other forms of therapy, such as support groups. The method involves asking the individual to tell in detail, in a safe and caring interpersonal setting, the story of what happened to him or her.

A study of 20 Bosnian refugees who now live in the United States sheds light on the positive effects of having survivors narrate their experiences of terror and suffering (Weine et al. 1995). Ten of the refugees in the study were male and 10 were female. They belonged to six families and ranged in age from 13 to 62 years. All but one were Muslims, and all adults were married and had worked either inside or outside the home. Analysis of the testimony showed that all had experienced many traumatic events, the frequency increasing with a person's age. The number of traumatic events in the narratives did not differ by gender, but the qualitative aspects of the trauma did:

> Adult men were more likely to be separated from their families and to be held in concentration camps where they suffered extreme deprivation and atrocities. Adult women (as well as adolescents of both genders) were often held briefly in detention camps and then they spent months fleeing from capture or being held in occupied territory where they were subjected to violence. (1995:537)

Almost all the refugees experienced the destruction of their homes, forced evacuation, food and water deprivation, disappearance of family members, exposure to acts of violence or death, detainment in a refugee camp, and forced emigration: "Nearly all the refugees emphasized the shock that came with the sudden occurrence of human betrayal by neighbors, associates, friends, and relatives" (1995:538).

The testimonies document the genocidal nature of the traumas directed at the entire Muslim Bosnian population. The traumas experienced were "extreme, multiple, repeated, prolonged, and communal" (1995:539). Some of the survivors carry with them constant images of death and atrocity. One man describes them as "films" that play in his head. In contrast, others have lost their memories of the events, and one woman was later unable to remember the trauma story she told three weeks earlier: "All kinds of things come together. Being expelled. Things we lost. Twenty years of work—then suddenly being without anything. . . . All the memories come at the same moment and it's too much" (1995:541).

The massiveness of their suffering, the psychiatrists report, extends beyond the bounds of the current diagnostic category of PTSD. Yet, in spite of their deep and extensive

---

conflicts, including the American–Vietnam War because it was undeclared. Or, war may be defined simply as organized aggression. This definition is too broad because not all organized violence can be considered warfare. Perhaps the best definition is that **war** is organized conflict involving group action directed against another group and involving lethal force. Lethal force during war is legal if it is conducted according to the rules of battle.

Cultural variation exists in the frequency and seriousness of wars. Intergroup conflicts among free-ranging foragers that would fit the definition of war do not exist in the ethnographic record. The informal, nonhierarchical political organization among bands is not conducive to waging armed conflict. Bands do not have specialized military forces or leaders.

Archaeological evidence indicates that warfare emerged during the Neolithic era (review Chapter 2). Plant and animal domestication required extensive land use, and they were accompanied by increased population density. The resulting economic and demographic pressures put more and larger groups in more direct and intense competition with each other. Tribal leadership patterns facilitate mobilization of warrior groups for raids (recall the discussion of the segmentary model in Chapter 10). Tribal groups everywhere, though, do not all have the same levels of warfare. At one extreme, with reported high levels of warfare, are the Yanomami of the Amazon (see Map 4.4, p. 96, and Critical Thinking, p. 280).

Many chiefdoms have high rates of warfare and high casualty rates. They have increased capacity for war in terms of personnel and surplus foods to support long-range

---

war organized and purposeful group action directed against another group and involving lethal force.

A forensic expert clears the soil from a skull found in a mass grave in Bosnia. The grave is believed to contain bodies of perhaps 500 Muslim civilians killed by the Bosnian Serb forces during the 1992–1995 war.

MAP 11.5 Bosnia and Herzegovina.
Formerly part of the Socialist Federal Republic, Bosnia and Herzogovina have a population of around 4 million. Bosnia occupies the northern areas of the country, about four-fifths of the total area, whereas Herzegovina occupies the southern part. The country still faces the challenges of reconstruction following the war of 1992–1995. On a brighter note, it has one of the best income equality rankings in the world, placing eighth among 193 countries. Bosnia and Herzegovina are world champions in Paralympics volleyball, with a team consisting of players who lost their legs in the Yugoslav War.

suffering, many Bosnian refugees in the United States are recovering and rebuilding their lives, perhaps in part due to the success of narrative therapy. Studies of this therapeutic approach among refugees of other cultures, however, reveal that some people are extremely reluctant to discuss their experiences, even in a supportive setting. Thus, narrative therapy may not be effective in all cultures.

◆ FOOD FOR THOUGHT

- How would you react to narrative therapy, assuming you had gone through traumatic experiences? Is your culture one in which narrative therapy might be effective or not?

expeditions. The chief could call on his or her retainers as a specialized fighting force as well as the general members of society. Chiefs and paramount chiefs could be organized into effective command structures (Reyna 1994:44–45).

In states, standing (permanent) armies and complex military hierarchies are supported by increased material resources through taxation and other forms of revenue generation. Greater state power allows for more powerful and effective military structures, which in turn increase the state's power. Thus, a mutually reinforcing relationship emerges between the military and the state. Although most states are generally highly militarized, not all are, nor are all states equally militarized. Costa Rica (see Map 14.2, p. 358) does not maintain an army, whereas Turkey has one of the world's largest.

Examining the causes of war between states has occupied scholars in many fields for centuries. Some experts have pointed to common, underlying causes, such as attempts to extend boundaries, secure more resources, ensure markets, support political and economic allies, and resist aggression from other states. Others point to humanitarian concerns that prompt participation in "just wars," to defend values such as freedom or to protect human rights that are defined as such by one country and are being violated in another.

Causes of war in Afghanistan have changed over time (Barfield 1994). Since the seventeenth century, warfare increasingly became a way in which kings justified their power in terms of the necessity to maintain independence from

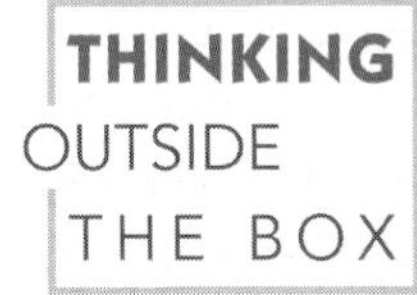

How do you define war? Given your definition, how many wars are currently ongoing and where are they?

CRITICAL thinking

Yanomami: The "Fierce People"?

The Yanomami are a horticultural people who live in dispersed villages of between 40 and 250 people in the Amazonian rainforest (Ross 1993). Since the 1960s, biological anthropologist Napoleon Chagnon has studied several Yanomami villages. He has written a widely read and frequently republished ethnography about the Yanomami, subtitled *The Fierce People* (1992 [1968]) and has helped produce several classic ethnographic films about them, including *The Feast* and *The Ax Fight*.

Chagnon's writings and films have promoted a view of the Yanomami as exceptionally violent and prone to lethal warfare. According to Chagnon, about one-third of adult Yanomami males die violently, about two-thirds of all adults had lost at least one close relative through violence, and over 50 percent had lost two or more close relatives (1992:205). He has reported that one village was raided 25 times during his first 15 months of fieldwork. Although village alliances are sometimes formed, they are fragile and allies may turn against each other unpredictably.

The Yanomami world, as depicted by Chagnon, is one of danger, threats, and counterthreats. Enemies, human and supernatural, are everywhere. Support from one's allies is uncertain. All of this uncertainty leads to what Chagnon describes as the *waiteri complex*, a set of behaviors and attitudes that includes a fierce political and personal stance for men and forms of individual and group communication that stress aggression and independence. Fierceness is a dominant theme in socialization, as boys learn how to fight with clubs, participate in chest-pounding duels with other boys, and use a spear. Adult males are aggressive and hostile toward adult females, and boys learn to be aggressive toward girls from an early age.

Chagnon provides a biological, Darwinian explanation for the fierceness shown by the Yanomami. He reports that the Yanomami explain that village raids and warfare are carried out so that men may obtain wives. Although the Yanomami prefer to marry within their village, a shortage of potential brides exists because of the Yanomami practice of female infanticide. Although the Yanomami prefer to marry endogamously, taking a wife from another group is preferable to remaining a bachelor. Men in other groups, however, are unwilling to give up their women—hence the necessity for raids. Other reasons for raids are suspicion of sorcery or theft of food.

Chagnon argues that within this system, warfare contributes to reproductive success because successful warriors are able to gain a wife or more than one wife (polygyny is allowed). Thus, successful warriors will have higher reproductive rates than unsuccessful warriors. Successful warriors, Chagnon suggests, have a genetic advantage for fierceness, which they pass on to their sons, leading to a higher growth rate of groups with violent males through genetic selection for fierceness. Male fierceness, in this view, is biologically adaptive.

Marvin Harris, taking the cultural materialist perspective, says that protein scarcity and population dynamics in the area are the underlying cause of warfare (1984). The Yanomami lack plentiful sources of meat, which is highly valued. Harris suggests that when game in an area becomes depleted, pressure rises to expand into the territory of neighboring groups, thus precipitating conflict. Such conflicts in turn result in high rates of adult male mortality. Combined with the effects of female infanticide, this meat-warfare complex keeps population growth rates down to a level that the environment can support.

A third view relies on historical data. Brian Ferguson (1990) argues that the high levels of violence among the Yanomami were caused by the intensified Western presence during the preceding 100 years. Furthermore, diseases introduced from outside, especially measles and malaria, severely depopulated the Yanomami and greatly increased their fears of sorcery (their explanation for disease). The attraction to Western goods such as steel axes and guns would also

---

outside forces such as the British and Czarist Russia. The last Afghan king was murdered in a coup in 1978. When the Soviet Union invaded in 1979, no centralized ruling group existed to meet it. The Soviet Union deposed the ruling faction, set up one of its own, and then killed over 1 million people, caused 3 million to flee the country, and millions of others to be displaced internally. In spite of the lack of a central command, ethnic and sectarian differences, and being outmatched in equipment by Soviet forces, the Afghanis waged a war of resistance that eventually wore down the Soviets, who withdrew in 1989.

This case suggests that war was a more effective tool of domination in the premodern period when it settled matters more definitively (Barfield 1994). In premodern times, fewer troops were needed to maintain dominance after a conquest because continued internal revolts were less common and the main issue was defense against rivals from outside. Success in the Soviet Union's holding of Afghanistan would have required more extensive involvement and commitment, including introduction of a new economic and political system and ideology that would win over the population.

increase intergroup rivalry. Thus, Ferguson suggests that the "fierce people" are a creation of historical forces, especially contact and pressure from outsiders.

Following Ferguson's position, but with a new angle, journalist Patrick Tierney points the finger of blame at Chagnon himself (2000). Tierney maintains that it was the presence of Chagnon, with his team of coresearchers and many boxes of trade goods, that triggered a series of lethal raids due to increased competition for those very goods. Inaddition, Tierney argues that Chagnon intentionally prompted the Yanomami to act fiercely for his films and to stage raids that created aggravated intergroup hostility beyond what had originally existed.

In 2001, the American Anthropological Association established a task force to examine five topics related to Tierney's allegations that Chagnon's and others' interactions with and representations of the Yanomami may have had a negative impact on them, contributing to "disorganization" among the Yanomami. The report of the El Dorado Task Force appears on the AAA website (www.aaanet.org). The task force rejected all charges against Chagnon and instead emphasized the harmfulness of false accusations that may jeopardize future scientific research.

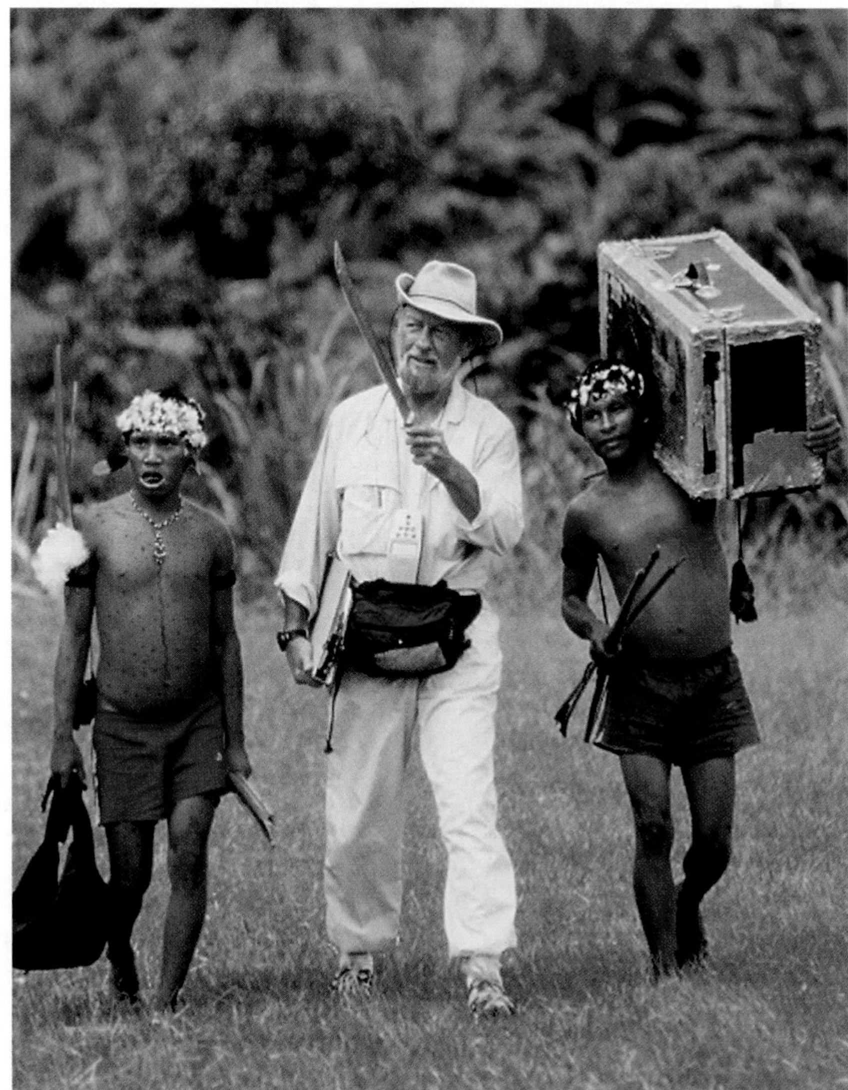

Napoleon Chagnon (center) in the field with two Yanomami men, 1995. Chagnon distributed goods such as steel axes and tobacco to the Yanomami to gain their cooperation in his research.

◆ **CRITICAL THINKING QUESTIONS**

- Which perspective presented here on Yanomami men's behavior appears most persuasive to you and why?
- What relevance does this case have to the theory that violence is a universal human trait?
- Do you think it is possible that anthropological research could have negative effects such as increased violence among the study population?

Current events show clearly that attacking and taking over a country are only the first stages in a process much more complicated than the term "regime change" implies. Afghanistan is still attempting to recover and rebuild after more than three decades of war, although its problems of state integration and security have roots that go deeper than either the Soviet invasion or the U.S. occupation (Shahrani 2002). These cultural roots include local codes of honor that value political autonomy and require vengeance for harm received, the moral system of Islam, the revitalized drug economy, and the effects of intervention from outside powers involving foreign governments and corporations, including Unocal of California, Delta Oil of Saudi Arabia, and Bridas of Argentina. The difficulty of constructing a strong state with loyal citizens in the face of these conflicting internal and external factors is great.

Cultural anthropologists, by and large, oppose war and have perhaps, therefore, avoided studying the institutions of war. Some cultural anthropologists are now doing research on topics such as the armed forces as social institutions, soldiers

Members of the Turkish army special forces hang from a helicopter with their weapons and flags in 2002 as part of the celebration of the 79th anniversary of the foundation of the Turkish Republic.

▶ *In your culture, what role do military forces play in celebrations of "statehood"?*

in the armed forces, and the effects of soldiers on the wider society. Much of this research could be termed **critical military anthropology**, the study of the military as a power structure. It takes a perspective of critique, viewing the armed forces as instruments of power and, often, repressive domination, and the process of militarization as problematic. *Militarization* refers to the intensification of labor and resources allocated to military purposes. Cultural anthropologists seek to provide insights that might lead to its control and reduction (Gusterson 2007).

The military in Bolivia (see Map 7.4 on p. 173) recruits young, male soldiers from the most powerless sections of society—indigenous farmers and poor urban dwellers (Gill 1997). Serving as the foot soldiers, they risk death in combat more than the members of more powerful social groups, and they are more likely to suffer emotional abuse from their commanding officers. Military service is an obligation of all able-bodied Bolivian men, but many middle-class and upper-class men are able to avoid serving. It is also a prerequisite for many forms of urban employment. A more subtle, underlying motivation is that army service enables marginalized, powerless boys to express bravery, competence, and patriotism and thereby earn the respect and admiration of women as responsible adult males. The army instills a heightened sense of masculinity in its soldiers through basic training, which lasts for three months and emphasizes the importance of male bonding and the link between masculinity and citizenship. A soldier who completes his service receives a *libreta militar,* or "military booklet," which documents his successful

critical military anthropology the study of the military as a power structure in terms of its roles and internal social dynamics.

A child soldier named Alfred walks to a UN disarmament camp in the Liberian city of Tubmanburg in 2004. Many countries have programs to help child soldiers adjust to life after war.

▶ *What might be the three most important challenges that child soldiers face in a postconflict situation?*

completion of duty and is used to help him obtain work in urban factories. The booklet is also useful in various transactions with the state and thus is a kind of ticket to citizenship. Better-off men simply pay a fee for the booklet. That is easy enough for them but impossible for poor men. Under President Evo Morales, it is possible for indigenous people to attend officer training (Gill 2006, personal communication).

In Israel, military service is a focal point of citizenship and nation building (Khanaaneh 2005). Service in the military, for all Jewish citizens, is also a pathway to full citizenship. Non-Jews in Israel, notably Palestinians, who constitute one-fifth of Israel's population, are normally excluded from the military. Nonetheless, about 5000 Palestinians living in Israel currently volunteer to serve in the Israeli military. Interviews with 24 Arab men and 1 Arab woman who served in various Israeli security branches—the army, border patrol, and police force—reveal the complexities and contradictions involved in their motivations and their identities as military personnel. These people are socially marginal in Israeli society because they are Arabs, and are even feared as security threats, but in their roles in the military they often gain positions of power and physical force. Joining the military is a way for non-Jews to achieve higher status through access to jobs, state land, educational subsidies, and low-interest loans. All of these entitlements are denied to non-serving Arabs.

Being able to buy state land, however, raises a stark contradiction: The state policy of taking over Arab lands often involves confiscating land of Arabs who served in the military. In one instance in 2002, 50 homes of Arab Bedu who had served were confiscated. Thus, military service enables Arabs to buy back land that was originally theirs. Other contradictions arise when Arab members of the Israeli army have to carry out operations against other Arabs. Some of the soldiers justify their role by saying that their presence makes for gentler treatment of Arabs than would otherwise be administered. Others say that they are "nationalists" and that their role is neither Zionist nor Arab.

Mahatma Gandhi (left), leader of the Indian movement for freedom from British colonial control, on his famous "Salt March" of 1930, in which he led a procession to the sea to collect salt in defiance of British law. He is accompanied by Sarojini Naidu, a noted freedom fighter.

▶ *What are your images of Gandhi and how did you come by them?*

NONVIOLENT CONFLICT

Mohandas K. Gandhi was one of the greatest designers of strategies for bringing about peaceful political change. Born in India, he studied law in London and then went to South Africa, where he worked as a lawyer serving the Indian community and evolved his primary method of civil disobedience through nonviolent resistance (Caplan 1987). In 1915, he returned to India, joined the nationalist struggle against British colonialism, and put into action his model of civil disobedience through nonviolent resistance, public fasting, and strikes.

Celibacy (abstaining from sexual relations) is a key feature of Gandhian philosophy because avoiding sex, in the Hindu view, helps maintain one's inner strength and purity (recall the lost semen complex mentioned in Chapter 6). Regardless of whether one agrees with Gandhi's support of sexual abstinence, the methods he developed of nonviolent civil disobedience have had a profound impact on the world. Martin Luther King, Jr., and his followers adopted many of Gandhi's tactics during the U.S. civil rights movement, as did members of the peace movement of the 1960s and 1970s in the United States.

Most subordinate classes throughout history have not had the luxury of open, organized political activity because of its danger. Instead, people have had to resort to indirect ways of "working" the system. Political scientist and cultural anthropologist James Scott (1985) uses the phrase *weapons of the weak* in the title of his book on rural people's resistance to domination by landlords and government through tactics other than outright rebellion or revolution. Weapons of the weak include "foot dragging," desertion, false compliance, feigned ignorance, and slander, as well as more aggressive acts such as theft, arson, and sabotage. One weapon of the weak that Scott overlooked is humor. Humor is an important part of Native American cultural resistance to domination by White society (Lincoln 1993). Instead of pitying themselves or lamenting the genocide that occurred as a result of European and Euro-American colonization, Native Americans have cultivated a sharp sense of humor. "Rez" (reservation) jokes travel like wildfire. Charlie Hill, for example, is notorious for his one-liners such as: "What did Native Americans say at Plymouth Rock?" Answer: "There goes the neighborhood" (1993:4–5). Although humor has not been the only source of strength for Native Americans, it surely must be added to the list of weapons of the weak.

Representatives of 10 NATO countries at the World Court in The Hague. This distinguished body of legal experts exhibits a clear pattern of age, gender, and ethnicity.

Culture, World Order, and World Peace

Computer-operated war missiles, email, the Internet, satellite television, and jet flights mean that the world's states are more closely connected and better able to influence each other's fate than ever before. Modern weaponry means that such influences can be more lethal and more depersonalized. In the face of these realities, politicians, academics, and the public ponder the possibilities for world peace. Anthropological research on peaceful, local-level societies shows that humans are capable of living together in peace. The question is whether people living in larger groups that are globally connected can also live in peace. This section discusses two issues related to world order and world peace.

Women near Kabul, Afghanistan, look at replicas of land mines during a mining awareness program sponsored in 2003 by the International Committee of the Red Cross (ICRC). Afghanistan is heavily mined, and rates of injury and mortality from mines are high.

▶ *Do Internet research to learn about international organizations involved in de-mining.*

INTERNATIONAL LEGAL DISPUTES

Numerous attempts have been made, over time, to create institutions to promote world peace. The United Nations is the most established and respected of such institutions. One of the UN's significant accomplishments was its creation of the International Court of Justice, also known as the World Court, located in The Hague in the Netherlands (Nader 1995). In 1946, two-thirds of the Court's judges were American or Western European. Today, the Court has many judges from developing countries.

Despite this more balanced representation, use of the World Court has declined and use of international negotiating teams for resolving disputes between countries has increased. Laura Nader (1995) analyzed this change and found that it follows a trend in the United States, beginning in the 1970s, to promote *alternate dispute resolution* (ADR). The goal was to move more cases out of the courts and to privatize dispute resolution. On the surface, ADR seems a more peaceful and more dignified option. Deeper analysis of actual cases and their resolution shows, however, that this bilateral process favors the stronger party. *Adjudication* (formal decree by a judge) would have resulted in a better deal for the weaker party than bilateral negotiation did. Thus, less powerful nations are negatively affected by the move away from the World Court.

THE UNITED NATIONS AND INTERNATIONAL PEACEKEEPING

What role might cultural anthropology play in international peacekeeping? Robert Carneiro (1994) has a pessimistic response. Carneiro says that during the long history of human political evolution from bands to states, warfare has been the major means by which political units enlarged their power and domain. Foreseeing no logical end to this process, he predicts that war will follow war until superstates become ever larger and one mega-state is the final result. He considers the United Nations powerless in dealing with the principal obstacle to world peace: state sovereignty interests. Carneiro indicts the United Nations for its lack of coercive power and its record of having resolved disputes through military intervention in only a few cases.

If war is inevitable, little hope exists that anthropological knowledge can be applied to peacemaking efforts. Despite Carneiro's views, cultural anthropologists have shown that war is not a cultural universal and that some cultures solve disputes without resorting to war. The cultural anthropological perspective of critical cultural relativism (review this concept in Chapter 1) can provide useful background on issues of conflict and prompt a deeper dialogue between parties.

Two positive points emerge. The United Nations provides, at least, an arena for airing disputes. International peace organizations may thus play a role in world peace and order by providing a forum for analysis of the interrelationships among world problems and by exposing the causes and consequences of violence. Another positive direction is the role of NGOs and grassroots organizations in promoting local and global peacemaking through initiatives that bridge group interests.

11

the BIG questions REVISITED

◆ How do different cultures maintain social control?

Legal anthropology encompasses the study of cultural variation in social order and social conflict. Early legal anthropologists approached the subject from a functionalist viewpoint that stresses how social institutions promote social cohesion and continuity. In contrast, the more recent approach of critical legal anthropology examines how law and judicial institutions serve to maintain and expand dominant power interests rather than protect marginal and less powerful people.

Systems of social order and social control vary cross-culturally and over time. Social control is the process by which people maintain an orderly group life. They do so by designing rules for proper behavior and ensuring social conformity to these rules, including ways of dealing with people who do not adhere to the rules. Legal anthropologists distinguish between norms, which are a cultural universal, and laws, which are more associated with large-scale societies. A norm is a culturally accepted standard for how people should behave that is unwritten and learned unconsciously through socialization. Enforcement is usually informal and socially regulated. A law is a binding rule created through custom or official enactment with defined forms of punishment for violation, which may include death. Laws are associated with the development of professional specialization.

All cultures have to deal with the fact that violations of norms and laws may occur. Social control in small-scale societies seeks to restore order more than to punish offenders. In small-scale societies, common forms of punishment are social shaming and shunning. States have power-related forms of punishment, including imprisonment and execution and a wide array of professional specializations involved in enacting punishment.

◆ What are cross-cultural patterns of social conflict and violence?

Ethnographic evidence on levels and forms of conflict and violence indicates that high levels of violence, especially lethal violence, are not universal. Cross-culturally, social conflict ranges from face-to-face conflicts, as among neighbors or domestic partners, to larger group conflicts between ethnic groups and states. Extensive violence is more associated with the state than with other forms of political organization.

The immediate causes of interpersonal violence range from economic debt to problems with neighborhood dogs. Many forms of social conflict involve property in one way or another. Banditry is devoted to illegal transfer of property and also may involve one's cultural identity as a person of worth. Feuding is a form of intergroup violence that may go on for decades, with revenge for harm done in the past being the motivating factor and resource issues often underlying the interpersonal enmity.

Ethnic conflict appears to be on the rise in recent decades and is more common than interstate violence. Research suggests that much ethnic conflict is also about resources such as land, water, and oil. Beyond their causes, ethnic conflicts have generated massive suffering and the forced displacement of millions of people as either refugees or internally displaced people. Revolutions are intentionally planned forms of conflict, usually violent, by subordinate groups that seek to change the status quo. Many are rural based, others are urban based, and some are a mixture of the two. War is difficult to define. The best definition is that war is conflict involving organized group action directed against another group and involving lethal force. War is associated with the emergence of the state.

◆ How does cultural anthropology contribute to world peace and order?

Many cultural anthropologists are turning their attention to global conflict and peacekeeping solutions. Key issues involve the role of cultural knowledge in global dispute resolution and how international or local organizations can help achieve or maintain peace.

Some anthropologists are pessimistic about the role of global organizations such as the United Nations in maintaining world order and world peace. Others point to evidence for hope and also look to NGOs and grassroots organizations as ways of bridging group differences.

KEY CONCEPTS

banditry, p. 274
critical legal anthropology, p. 267
critical military anthropology, p. 282
feuding, p. 275
law, p. 267
legal pluralism, p. 272
norm, p. 267
policing, p. 268
revolution, p. 277
social control, p. 267
trial by ordeal, p. 269
war, p. 278

SUGGESTED READINGS

Thomas Biolsi. *"Deadliest Enemies": Law and the Making of Race Relations on and off Rosebud Reservation.* Berkeley: University of California Press, 2001. This book examines the effects of contradictory U.S. laws about Indians within the context of the Sicangu Lakota, or Rosebud Sioux, and the non-Indians in south-central South Dakota.

Leslie Gill. *The School of the Americas: Military Training and Political Violence in the Americas.* Durham, NC: Duke University Press, 2004. Located at Fort Benning, Colorado, the School of the Americas (SOA) is a U.S. Army center that trains soldiers and police, mostly from Latin America, in counterinsurgency techniques and combat skills. Gill attended classes, accompanied students and their families on shopping trips to the mall, and examined the effects of the SOA in Colombia and Bolivia.

Daniel M. Goldstein. *The Spectacular City: Violence and Performance in Urban Bolivia.* Durham, NC: Duke University Press, 2004. Situated within the context of the increasing crime that has accompanied the consolidation of Western capitalism in Bolivia, this ethnography explores how local political activism is expressed using traditional performance genres.

Thomas Gregor, ed. *A Natural History of Peace.* Nashville: University of Tennessee Press, 1996. This book contains essays on "what is peace?" reconciliation among nonhuman primates, the psychological bases of violent and nonviolent societies, case studies of Amazonia and American Indians, and international relations.

Hugh Gusterson. *Nuclear Rites: A Weapons Laboratory at the End of the Cold War.* Berkeley: University of California Press, 1996. This ethnographic study focuses on the nuclear research community of Livermore, California. It explores the scientists' motivations to develop nuclear weapons, the culture of secrecy, and the metaphors used in nuclear research.

Susan F. Hirsch. *In the Moment of Greatest Calamity: Terrorism, Grief, and a Victim's Quest for Justice.* Princeton: Princeton University Press, 2006. The author's husband was killed in the 1998 bombing of the U.S. embassy in Kenya. In this book, Hirsch describes her experiences in Kenya in the aftermath of the bombing, her grief, and her witnessing of the bombing trials in Manhattan in 2001.

Mindie Lazarus. *Everyday Harm: Domestic Violence, Court Rites, and Cultures of Reconciliation.* Champaign-Urbana: University of Illinois Press, 2007. This book combines archival and ethnographic research in its study of the responses of law to domestic violence in Trinidad, the Caribbean.

Mahmood Mamdani. *When Victims Become Killers: Colonialism, Nativism, and the Genocide in Rwanda.* Princeton, NJ: Princeton University Press, 2001. Mamdani examines the historical context of violence from the colonial era in order to understand root causes and how ethnic labels and identities change.

Beatriz Manz. *Paradise in Ashes: A Guatemalan Journey of Courage, Terror, and Hope.* Berkeley: University of California Press, 2004. Manz traces the lives and deaths of some Guatemalan Maya villagers who left their impoverished homeland in the mountains to build a new life in the lowlands. In their new location, they became victims of state-sponsored violence. Many were murdered, and others were forced to flee into the jungle. The survivors have returned to rebuild their homes and lives.

Bruce Miller. *The Problem of Justice: Tradition and Law in the Coast Salish World.* Lincoln: University of Nebraska Press, 2001. The author compares several legal systems operating in the Northwest Coast region from Washington state to British Columbia. The effects of colonialism differ from group to group. Some are strong and independent, whereas others are disintegrating.

Carolyn Nordstrom. *Shadows of War: Violence, Power, and International Profiteering in the Twenty-First Century.* Berkeley: University of California Press, 2004. Nordstrom did fieldwork in Sri Lanka and Mozambique to reveal the shadow economy that surrounds and supports war. She focuses on informal trading networks that involve goods ranging from guns to food and the people who profit from this economy.

Jeffrey Rubin. *Decentering the Regime: Ethnicity, Radicalism and Democracy in Juchitán, Mexico.* Durham, NC: Duke University Press, 1997. Written by a political scientist who adopted the methods of cultural anthropology, this study analyzes how the Mexican state defines, represents, and relates to indigenous peoples and how indigenous peoples struggle against the state.

Jennifer Schirmer. *The Guatemalan Military Project: A Violence Called Democracy.* Philadelphia: University of Pennsylvania Press, 1998. This book is an ethnography of the Guatemalan military, documenting its role in human rights violations through extensive interviews with military officers and trained torturers.

12  COMMUNICATION

13  RELIGION

14  EXPRESSIVE CULTURE

PART IV
SYMBOLIC SYSTEMS

ANTHROPOLOGY works

Brian Craik is a federal relations and environmental impact assessment anthropologist. "Working together" is his basic principle for achieving First Nations' rights in Canada. In his current position, Craik is the director of federal relations for the Grand Council of the Crees. The Cree People, or Eeyouch or Eenouch, number over 14,000. They live in the area of eastern James Bay and southern Hudson Bay in northern Québec, Canada.

Working for over 30 years as an applied anthropologist, Craik has combined his anthropological training with advocacy skills to assist the Cree in seeking social and environmental justice.

Craik is the first anthropologist in the world to become fluent in the Cree language (Preston 2006). After earning a doctorate in anthropology at McMaster University in the early 1970s, Craik began working as a consultant for various Cree communities.

In 1974, he joined Canada's Department of Indian Affairs and Northern Development. In that role, he helped to implement the James Bay and Northern Québec Agreement (JBNQA) that was signed in 1975. The JBNQA was a benchmark settlement related to land claims issues and compensation for damages. It awarded $225 million in compensation to the James Bay Cree and the Inuit of northern Québec to be paid by Canada and Québec. The agreement defined Native rights to the land and laid out various protections to ensure the maintenance of these rights in the face of possible undesirable effects of commercial development. As part of this effort, Craik worked on the passage of the Cree/Naskapi (of Québec) Act, Canada's first Aboriginal local government act.

In 1987, he left government work to return to private consulting. In 1989, he advised the James Bay Cree on relations with the federal government and on the environmental and social issues related to the Great Whale Project. The Cree People appointed him to two of the environmental committees that reviewed the project.

Craik played a central role in the 1989–1994 campaign that stopped the Great Whale River hydroelectric project. From 1997 to 1999, he negotiated an agreement between the Crees and Canada on Canada Manpower Services, helped implement the 2002 New Relationship Agreement between the Crees and the government of Québec, and took part in the review of the Eastmain 1A–Rupert Diversion Project that it contains.

The Cree People have faced many threats to their culture and their environment. They formed the Grand Council of the Crees in 1974 in response to the James Bay Hydroelectric Project (http://www.gcc.ca/gcc/fedrelations.php). Their political mobilization was inspired by the need to "stand in the way of development projects designed to serve others" (Craik 2004).

With Craik's assistance, the Cree have developed political and economic power and skills. They now choose when to block a destructive project or when to work to change the terms of a project in order to reduce damage to their culture and gain financial benefits to support Cree development goals.

Tuareg pastoralists in Niger, West Africa, greeting each other. Tuareg men's greetings involve lengthy handshaking and close body contact.

COMMUNICATION

the BIG questions

- How do humans communicate?
- How does communication relate to cultural diversity and inequality?
- How does language change?

OUTLINE

This chapter is about human communication and language, drawing on work in both linguistic anthropology and cultural anthropology. It looks at communication with a wide-angle lens to include topics from word choice to language extinction. The chapter first discusses how humans communicate and what distinguishes human communication from that of other animals. The second section offers examples of language, microcultures, and inequality. The third section discusses language change from its origins in the distant past to contemporary concerns about language loss.

The Varieties of Human Communication

Humans can communicate with words, either spoken or signed, with gestures and other forms of body language such as clothing and hairstyle, and through methods such as telephone calls, postal mail, and e-mail.

LANGUAGE AND VERBAL COMMUNICATION

Most people are in almost constant communication—with other people, with supernaturals, or with pets. We communicate in face-to-face situations or indirectly through mail or email. **Communication** is the process of sending and receiving messages. Among humans, it involves some form of **language**, a systematic set of symbols and signs with learned and shared meanings. Language may be spoken, hand-signed, written, or conveyed through body movements, body markings and modifications, hairstyle, dress, and accessories.

TWO FEATURES OF HUMAN LANGUAGE Scholars of language, over many years, have proposed characteristics of human language that distinguish it from communication among other living beings. This section presents the two most robust of these.

First, human language has **productivity**, or the ability to create an infinite range of understandable expressions from a finite set of rules. This characteristic is a result of the rich variety of symbols and signs that humans use in their communication. In contrast, nonhuman primates have a more limited set of communicative resources. They rely on a **call system**, or a form of oral communication among nonhuman primates with a set repertoire of meaningful sounds generated in response to environmental factors. Nonhuman primates do not have the physiological capacity for speech that humans do. In captivity, however, some bonobos and chimpanzees have learned to communicate effectively with humans through sign language and by pointing to symbols on a chart. The world's most famous bonobo is Kanzi, who lives at the Great Ape Trust in Des Moines, Iowa. He can understand much of what humans say to him, and he can respond by combining symbols on a printed board. He can also play simple video games, such as Ms. Pac-Man (http://www.greatapetrust.org).

Second, human language emphasizes the feature of **displacement**, the ability to refer to events and issues beyond the immediate present. The past and the future, in this view, are considered to be *displaced domains*. They include reference to people and events that may never exist at all, as in fantasy and fiction. Some bonobos who have been raised by and live in a close relationship with humans exhibit some aspects of displacement (http://www.pbs.org). But, especially in the wild, they are far less likely to use it than humans do.

Primatologist Sue Savage-Rumbaugh, working with Kanzi, an adult male bonobo. Kanzi is involved in a long-term project about ape language. He has learned to communicate with researchers using several symbols. Some chimpanzees, bonobos, orangutans, and gorillas are also able to communicate using American Sign Language and symbols on computer keyboards.

---

communication the conveying of meaningful messages from one person, animal, or insect to another.

language a form of communication that is a systematic set of learned symbols and signs shared among a group and passed on from generation to generation.

productivity a feature of human language that offers the ability to communicate many messages efficiently.

call system a form of oral communication among nonhuman primates with a set repertoire of meaningful sounds generated in response to environmental factors.

displacement a feature of human language that allows people to talk about events in the past and future.

phoneme a sound that makes a difference for meaning in a language.

A Pirahã shelter. According to Daniel Everett, who has spent many years learning about their culture and language, the Pirahã do not lead a culturally deprived life. The Pirahã are content with their lifestyle that includes leisure activities such as playing tag and other games. In spite of their wish to remain living as they are, their reservation is not secure from outside encroachment.

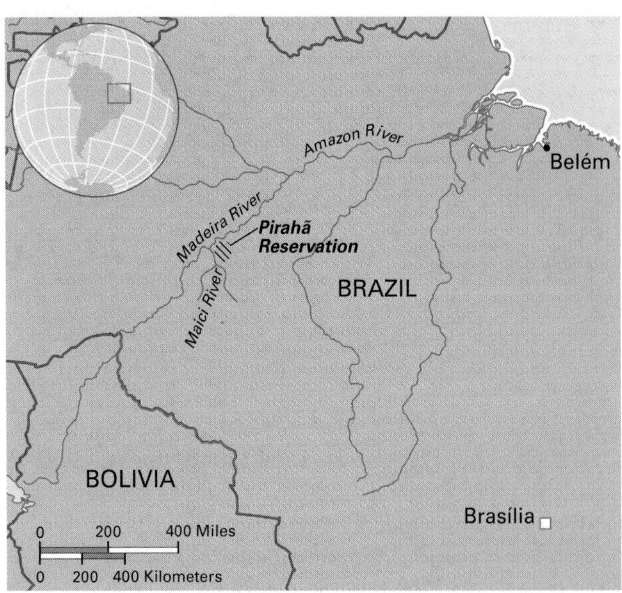

MAP 12.1 Pirahã Reservation in Brazil. Linguistic anthropologist Daniel Everett helped to define the boundaries of the Pirahã reservation in the 1980s. With support from Cultural Survival and other sources, the demarcation was legally declared in 1994.

In respect to productivity and displacement in human language, the case of language among the Pirahã (Pee-duh-hah) of Brazil raises many questions (Everett 2005, 2008) (see Map 12.1). Their language does not emphasize either productivity or displacement, though both exist to some degree. The Pirahã are a group of about 350 foragers living on a reservation in the Amazonian rainforest near the Maici River. Their language contains only three pronouns, few words associated with time, no past-tense verbs, no color terms, and no numbers other than a word that translates into English roughly as "about one." Grammar is simple, with no subordinate clauses. Kinship terms are simple and few. The Pirahã have no myths or stories and no art other than necklaces and a few rudimentary stick figures. In spite of over 200 years of regular contact with Brazilians and neighboring Indians who speak a different language, the Pirahã remain monolingual.

Since 1977, linguist Daniel Everett has lived with the Pirahã and learned their language, so it is unlikely that he has overlooked major aspects of their language. He insists that their language is in no way "primitive" or inadequate. It has extremely complex verbs and rich and varied uses of stress and intonation, referred to in linguistics as *prosody*. The Pirahã especially enjoy verbal joking and teasing, both among themselves and with researchers.

FORMAL PROPERTIES OF VERBAL LANGUAGE Human language can be analyzed in terms of its formal properties: sounds, vocabulary, and syntax (sometimes called grammar), which are the formal building blocks of all languages. But languages differ widely in which sounds are important, what words are important in the vocabulary, and how people put words together to form meaningful sentences. Learning a new language usually involves learning different sets of sounds. The sounds that make a difference for meaning in a language are called **phonemes**. The study of phonemes is called *phonetics*.

A native English-speaker learning to speak Hindi, the major language of North India, must learn to produce and recognize several new sounds. Four different "d" sounds exist. None is the same as an English "d," which is usually pronounced with the tongue placed on the ridge behind the upper front teeth (try it). One "d" in Hindi, which linguists refer to as a "dental" sound, is pronounced with the tongue pressed firmly behind the upper front teeth (try it) (see Figure 12.1). Next is a dental "d" that is also aspirated (pronounced "with air"); making this sound involves the tongue being in the same position and a puff of air expelled during pronunciation (try it, and try the regular dental "d" again with no puff of air at all). Next is what is referred to as a "retroflex" sound, made by flipping the tongue back to the central dome of the roof of the mouth (try it, with no puff of air). Finally, there is the aspirated retroflex "d" with the tongue in the center of the roof of the mouth and a puff of air. Once you can do this, try the whole series again with a "t," because Hindi follows the same pattern with this letter as with the "d." Several other sounds in Hindi require careful use of aspiration and placement of the tongue for communicating the right word. A puff of air at the wrong time can produce a serious error, such as

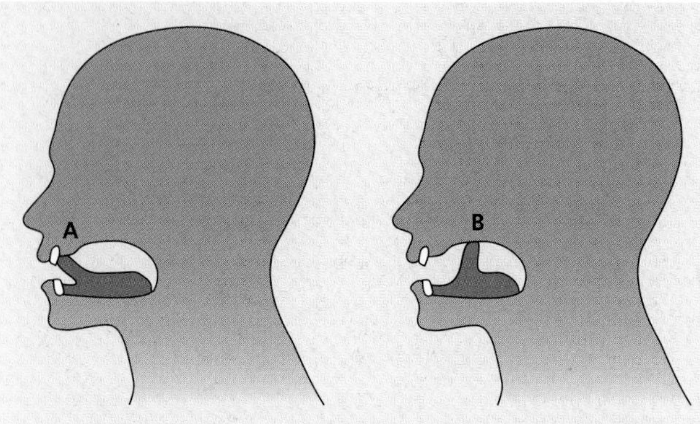

FIGURE 12.1 DENTAL AND RETROFLEX TONGUE POSITIONS. **When making a dental sound, the speaker places the tongue against the upper front teeth (position A in the diagram). When making a retroflex sound, the speaker places the tongue up against the roof of the mouth (position B in the diagram).**

- Firm, even snow that falls in mild weather
- Thickly packed snow caused by intermittent freezing/thawing and high winds
- Hard-packed snow formed by strong wind
- Dry, large-grained, water-holding snow at the deepest layers, closest to the ground, found in late winter and spring
- Snow that forms a hard layer after rain
- Ice sheet on pastures formed by rain on open ground that freezes
- A layer of frozen snow between other snow layers that acts as an ice sheet

Source: Jernsletten 1997.

FIGURE 12.2 **Kinds of "Snow" the Saami Recognize Related to Reindeer Herding.**

saying the word for "breast" when you want to say the word for "letter."

All languages have a vocabulary, or *lexicon,* which consists of all its meaningful words. Speakers combine words into phrases and sentences to create meaning. *Semantics* refers to the study of the meaning of words, phrases, and sentences. Anthropologists add the concept of **ethnosemantics**, the study of the meaning of words, phrases, and sentences in particular cultural contexts. They find that different languages classify the world in different ways and categorize even such seemingly natural things as color and disease in different ways (recall the discussion of Subanun disease categories in Chapter 7). Ethnosemantic research reveals much about how people define the world and their place in it, how they organize their social lives, and what is of value to them. *Focal vocabularies* are clusters of words that refer to important features of a particular culture. For example, many circumpolar languages have rich focal vocabularies related to snow (see Figure 12.2). In mountainous areas of Afghanistan, plentiful terms for kinds of rocks exist.

Syntax, or grammar, consists of the patterns and rules by which words are organized to make sense in a string. All languages have rules for syntax, although they vary in form. Even within the languages of contemporary Europe, syntactical variation exists. German, for example, places verbs at the end of the sentence (try composing an English sentence with its main verb at the end).

NONVERBAL LANGUAGE AND EMBODIED COMMUNICATION

Many forms of language and communication do not rely on verbal speech. Like verbal language, though, they are based on symbols and signs and have rules for their proper combination and meaning.

SIGN LANGUAGE **Sign language** is a form of communication that uses mainly hand movements to convey messages. A sign language provides a fully competent communication system for its users just as spoken language does (Baker 1999). Around the world, many varieties of sign language exist, including American Sign Language, British Sign Language, Japanese Sign Language, Russian Sign Language, and many varieties of indigenous Australian sign languages. Most sign languages are used by people who are hearing impaired as their main form of communication. Indigenous Australian sign languages, in contrast, are used by people who have the capacity for verbal communication. They switch to sign language in situations in which verbal speech is forbidden or undesirable (Kendon 1988). Verbal speech is forbidden in some sacred contexts and for widows during mourning. It is also undesirable when hunting.

Although sign languages are complete and complex languages in their own right, they are often treated as second-class. A breakthrough in recognition of the validity and communicative competence of sign languages came in 1983 when the government of Sweden recognized Swedish Sign Language as a native language. Such recognition is especially important in contexts where a person's sense of identity, and even citizenship itself, is based on the ability to speak an officially accepted language. Anthropologists work with people who are deaf to help promote public understanding of the

---

ethnosemantics the study of the meaning of words, phrases, and sentences in particular cultural contexts.

sign language a form of communication that uses mainly hand movements to convey messages.

LESSONS applied

Anthropology and Public Understanding of the Language and Culture of People Who Are Deaf

Ethnographic studies of the communication practices and wider culture of people who are deaf have great importance and practical application (Senghas and Monaghan 2002). This research demonstrates the limitations and inaccuracy of the *medical model* that construes deafness as a pathology or deficit and sees the goal as curing it. Instead, anthropologists propose the "cultural model," which views deafness simply as one possibility in the wide spectrum of cultural variation. In this view, a capital D is often used: Deaf culture.

Deafness in fact allows plenty of room for human agency. The strongest evidence of agency among people who are deaf is sign language itself, which exhibits adaptiveness, creativity, and change. This view helps to promote a nonvictim, nonpathological identity for people who are deaf and to reduce social stigma related to deafness.

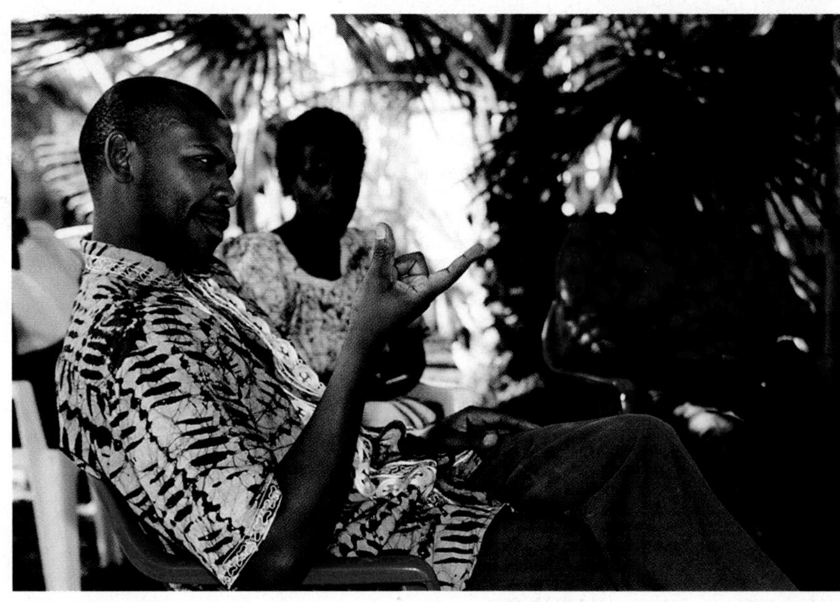

In Uganda, James Mwadha, a deaf attendee at a meeting for Action on Disability and Development (ADD), signs to others in the group. ADD seeks to promote the rights of disabled people.

Anthropologists involved in Deaf culture studies are examining topics such as how people who are deaf become bilingual—for example, fluent in both English and Japanese sign languages. Their findings are being incorporated in improved ways of teaching sign language.

◆ **FOOD FOR THOUGHT**

- Choose five words and learn the signs for them in American Sign Language and in another culture's sign language. Are they the same or different, and how might one explain the similarity or difference?

legitimacy of their language and to advocate for improved teaching of sign language (see Lessons Applied).

Gestures are movements, usually of the hands, that convey meanings. Some gestures may be universally meaningful, but most are culturally specific and often completely arbitrary. Some cultures have more highly developed gesture systems than others. Black urban youths in Pretoria and Johannesburg, South Africa, use a rich repertoire of gestures (Brookes 2004) (see Map 9.5, p. 230). Some of the gestures are widely used and recognized, but many vary by age, gender, and situation (see Figure 12.3). Men use more gestures than women do; the reason for this difference is not clear.

Greetings, an important part of communication in every known culture, often involve gestures (Duranti 1997b). They are typically among the first communicative routines that children learn, as well as tourists and anyone trying to learn a foreign language. Greetings establish a social encounter. They typically involve both verbal and nonverbal language. Depending on the context and the social relationship, many variations exist for both the verbal and the nonverbal component. Contextual factors include the degree of formality or informality. Social factors include gender, ethnicity, class, and age.

SILENCE Silence is another form of nonverbal communication. Its use is often related to social status, but in unpredictable ways. In rural Siberia, an in-marrying daughter-in-law has the lowest status in the household, and she rarely speaks (Humphrey 1978). In other contexts, silence is associated with power. In U.S. courts, lawyers speak more than anyone else, the judge speaks rarely but has more power than a lawyer, while the silent jury holds the most power (Lakoff 1990).

Silence is an important component of communication among many Native American cultures. White outsiders, including social workers, have sometimes misinterpreted

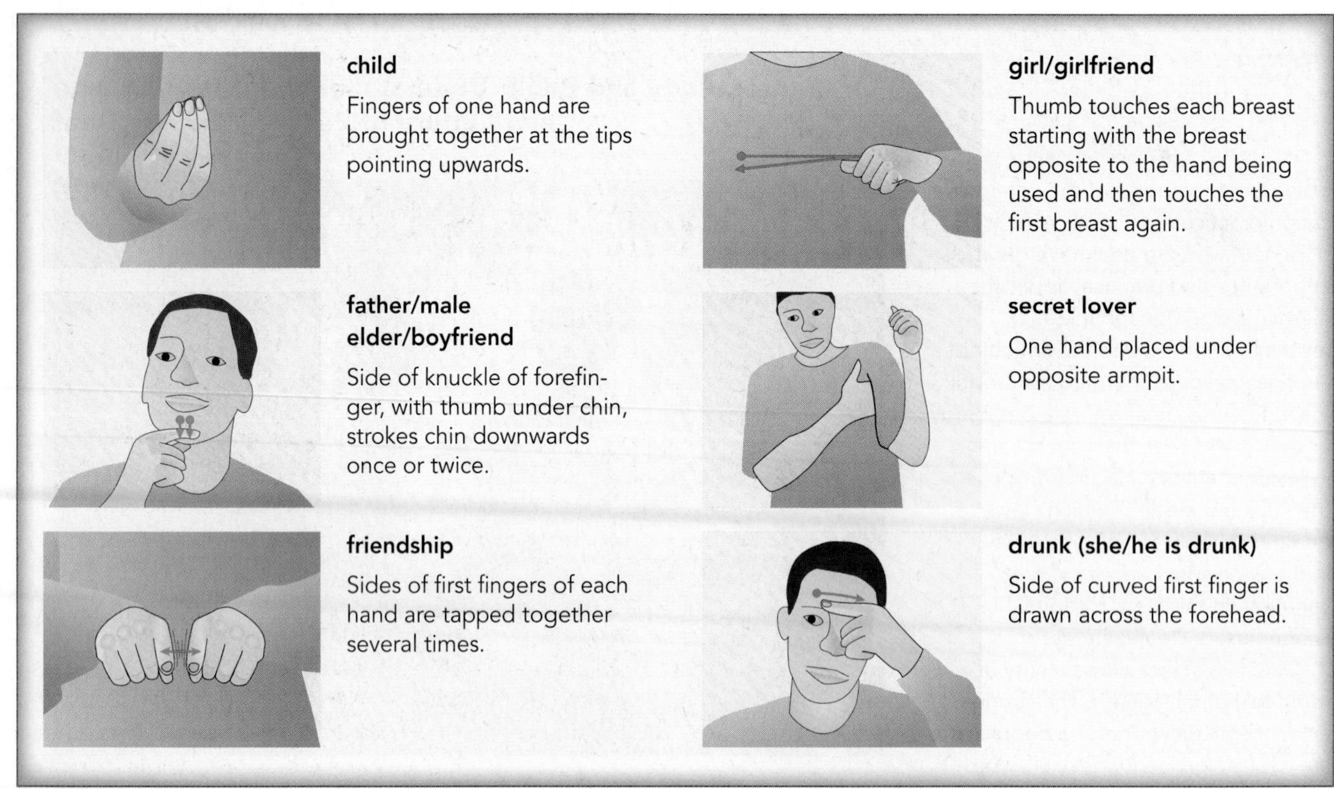

child
Fingers of one hand are brought together at the tips pointing upwards.
girl/girlfriend
Thumb touches each breast starting with the breast opposite to the hand being used and then touches the first breast again.
father/male elder/boyfriend
Side of knuckle of forefinger, with thumb under chin, strokes chin downwards once or twice.
secret lover
One hand placed under opposite armpit.
friendship
Sides of first fingers of each hand are tapped together several times.
drunk (she/he is drunk)
Side of curved first finger is drawn across the forehead.

FIGURE 12.3 **Some South African Gestures Used by a Man.**

Source: From *A Repertoire of South African Quotable Gestures*, from *The Journal of Linguistic Anthropology*, Copyright © 2004 Blackwell Publishers Ltd. Reproduced with permission of Blackwell Publishers.

this silence as a reflection of dignity or a lack of emotion or intelligence. How ethnocentric such judgments are is revealed by a study of silence among the Western Apache of Arizona (Basso 1972 [1970]) (see Map 12.2). The Western Apache use silence in four contexts:

- When meeting a stranger, especially at fairs, rodeos, or other public events. Speaking with a stranger immediately indicates interest in something such as money, work, or transportation, all possible reasons for exhibiting such bad manners.
- In the early stages of courting. Sitting in silence and holding hands for several hours is appropriate. Speaking "too soon" would indicate sexual willingness or interest.
- When parents and children meet after the child has been away at boarding school. They should be silent for about 15 minutes. It may be two or three days before sustained conversations are initiated.
- When "getting cussed out," especially at drinking parties.

An underlying similarity of all these contexts is the uncertainty, ambiguity, and unpredictability of the social relationships involved.

BODY LANGUAGE Human communication, in one way or another, often involves the body in sending and receiving messages. Beyond the mechanics of speaking, hearing, gesturing, and seeing, the body itself can function as a "text" that conveys messages. The full range of *body language* includes eye movements, posture, walking style, the way of standing and sitting, cultural *inscriptions* on the body such as tattoos and hairstyles, and accessories such as dress, shoes, and jewelry. Body language follows patterns and rules just as verbal language does. Like verbal language, the rules and meanings are learned, often unconsciously. Without learning the rules and meanings, one will commit communication errors, which are sometimes funny and sometimes serious.

Different cultures emphasize different body language channels more than others. Some are more touch oriented than others, and some use facial expressions more. Eye contact is valued during Euro-American conversations, but in many Asian contexts, direct eye contact is considered rude or perhaps a sexual invitation.

Modification of and marks on the body, clothing, and hairstyles convey messages about age, gender, sexual interest or availability, profession, wealth, and emotions. Color of clothing can send messages about a person's identity, class, gender, and more. In the United States, gender differentiation begins in the hospital nursery with the color coding of blue

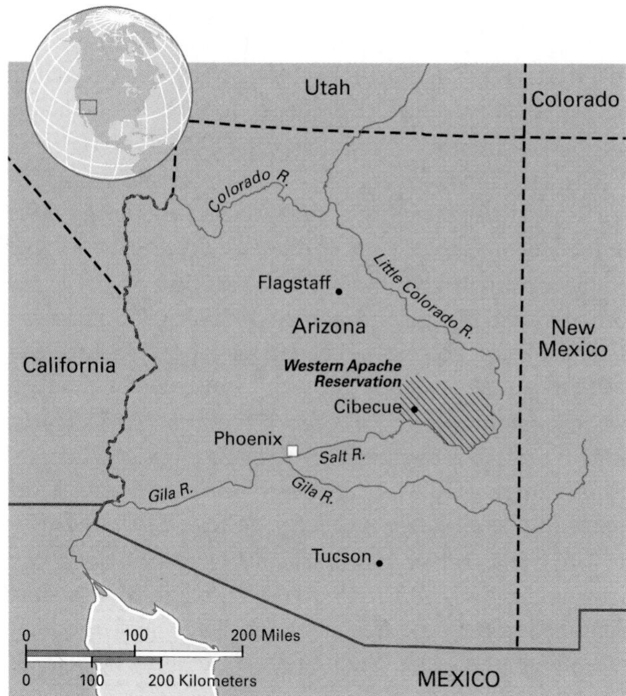

MAP 12.2 Western Apache Reservation in Arizona. Before European colonialism, the Apache lived in a wide area extending from present day Arizona to northwestern Texas. Originally foragers, they starting planting some food crops in the 1600s. After the arrival of the Spanish, the Apache gained horses from them and became skilled equestrian warriors. In the second half of the nineteenth century, the U.S. government was active in exterminating many Apache groups and forced those who survived to live on reservations in order to make way for White settlements.

for boys and pink for girls. In parts of the Middle East, public dress is black for women and white for men.

Covering or not covering various parts of the body with clothing is another culturally coded matter. Consider the different meanings of veiling/head covering in Egypt and Kuwait (MacLeod 1992). Kuwaiti women's head covering distinguishes them as relatively wealthy, leisured, and honorable, in contrast to the immigrant women workers from Asia who do not cover their heads. In contrast, the head covering in Egypt is done mainly by women from the lower and middle economic levels. For them, it is a way to accommodate conservative Islamic values while preserving their right to work outside the home. In Egypt, the head covering says, "I am a good Muslim and a good wife/daughter." In Kuwait, the headscarf says, "I am a wealthy Kuwaiti citizen." In many conservative Muslim contexts, it is important for a woman in public to cover more than her head by wearing a full-length loose garment. These rules, along with other patriarchal values, make it difficult for women in some Muslim contexts to participate in sports while in school and public domains such as the international Olympics.

In Japan, the kimono provides an elaborate coding system for gender and life-cycle stage (Dalby 2001). The

A horse race at Ascot, England, attended by members of the elite.

▶ *If you were going to the races at Ascot and wanted to be dressed properly, what should you wear?*

higher one's status, the shorter the sleeve of one's kimono. Men's kimono sleeves come in one length: short. Unmarried women's sleeve length is nearly to the ground, whereas a married woman's sleeve is nearly as short as that of a man's.

Lanita Jacobs-Huey's research on African American women's hair culture (review Chapter 3) reveals the links among women's hair, their talk about hair, and their identity (2006). She also learned about the complex linguistic terminology that Black hairstylists use to refer to various hair styling procedures. Stylists use specialized language and language correction to affirm their identities as hair-care specialists.

COMMUNICATING WITH MEDIA AND INFORMATION TECHNOLOGY

Media anthropology is the cross-cultural study of communication through electronic media such as radio, television, film, recorded music, the Internet, and print media, including newspapers, magazines, and popular literature (Spitulnik 1993). Media anthropology is an important emerging area that links linguistic and cultural anthropology (Allen 1994). Media anthropologists study the media process and content, the audience response, and the social effects of media presentations. **Critical media anthropology** asks to what degree access to media messages is liberating or controlling, and whose interests the media serve. It is especially active in examining journalism, television, advertising, and new information technology, as the following examples illustrate.

---

critical media anthropology an approach within the cross-cultural study of media that examines how power interests shape people's access to media and the contents of its messages.

(TOP) Japanese business men meet each other, bow, and exchange business cards. Bowing is an important part of nonverbal communication in Japan. (BOTTOM) The *furisode* kimono is distinguished by its fine silk material, long sleeves, elaborate colors and designs. A girl's twentieth birthday gift is typically a furisode, marking her transition to young adulthood. Only unmarried women wear furisode, so wearing one is a statement of marital availability. Fluttering the long, wide sleeves at a man is a way to express love for him.

▶ *What meanings do the styles and lengths of sleeves convey in your cultural world?*

THE POLITICS OF JOURNALISM Mark Pedelty studied war correspondents in El Salvador to learn about journalists and journalistic practices during war (1995) (see Map 7.3, p. 169). He found that the lives and identities of war correspondents are highly charged with violence and terror: "War correspondents have a unique relationship to terror . . . that combines voyeurism and direct participation. . . . They need terror to . . . maintain their cultural identity as 'war correspondents'" (1995:2). The primary job of journalists, including war correspondents, is communication of a specific sort. They gather information that is time sensitive and often brutal. Their job is to provide brief stories for the public.

A critical media anthropology perspective reveals the important role of the news agency that pays their salary or, if they are freelancers or "stringers," that buys their story. War correspondents in El Salvador, Pedelty found, write a story about the same event differently, depending on whether they are sending it to a U.S. newspaper or a European newspaper. How "accurate," then, is "the news"?

GENDER AND JAPANESE TELEVISION PROGRAMMING Most television programming in Japan presents women as housewives, performing traditional domestic roles (Painter 1996). Many Japanese women now reject such shows. In response, producers are experimenting with new sorts of dramas in which women are shown as active workers and aggressive lovers. One such show is a 10-part serial that first aired in 1992 called *Selfish Women.* The story concerns three women: an aggressive single businesswoman who faces discrimination at work, a young mother who is raising her daughter alone while her photographer husband lives with another woman, and an ex-housewife who divorced her husband because she found home life empty and unrewarding. There are several male characters, but, except for one, they are depicted as less interesting than the women.

The show's title is ironic. In Japan, men often label women who assert themselves as "selfish." The lead women in the drama use the term in a positive way to encourage each other: "Let's become even more selfish!" Although dramas like *Selfish Women* may not be revolutionary, they indicate that telerepresentations of gender in Japan are changing, largely through the agency of Japanese women.

ADVERTISING FOR LATINOS IN THE UNITED STATES Within the U.S. advertising market, one of the most sought-after segments is the Latino population, also called "the Hispanic market" in the advertising industry (Dávila 2002). Interviews with staff of 16 Latino advertising agencies and content analysis of their advertisements reveal their approach of treating Latinos as a unified, culturally specific market. The dominant theme, or trope, is that of "the family" as being the most important feature of Latino culture, in contrast to the stereotype of the Anglo population as more individualistic.

Recent milk-promotion advertisements for the Anglo population show a celebrity with a milk moustache. The Latino version shows a grandmother cooking a traditional milk-based dessert with the caption "Have you given your loved ones enough milk today?" (2002:270). In Spanish-language television and radio networks, a kind of "standard" Spanish is used, a generic form with no hint of regionalism or accent.

Latinos are, however, a highly heterogeneous population. By promoting a monolithic image of Latino culture, media messages may be contributing to identity change toward a more monolithic pattern. At the same time, they are certainly missing opportunities to tap into more specialized markets within the Latino population.

MAP 12.3 Hungary.
The Republic of Hungary has a population of around 10 million. The Roma population, variously estimated at between 450,000, and 600,000, has increased rapidly in recent years. Hungary's landscape is mainly plains with hills and low mountains to the north. One of the newest members of the European Union, Hungary has a growing economy. The main religion is Christianity, with Catholicism accounting for about half of the total; about 30 percent, however, are atheists. Magyar, the Hungarian language, is one of the few European languages that does not belong to the Indo-European language family but belongs instead to the Finno-Ugric family.

CROSSING THE DIGITAL DIVIDE IN RURAL HUNGARY

The term **digital divide** refers to social inequality in access to new and emerging information technology, especially access to up-to-date computers, the Internet, and training related to their use. Local attempts to overcome the digital divide between Hungary and countries in the European Union involve the development of the Hungarian Telecottage Association (HTA) (Wormald 2005) (see Map 12.3). The idea of the telecottage, which started in Sweden and Scotland, involves dedicating some space, such as an unused workshop or part of a house, for public use in which a computer with Internet access is provided.

The HTA, centered in Bucharest, promotes village-based Internet access in order to improve the lives of rural people through enhanced communication. Most telecottages in Hungary are located in rural communities of fewer than 5000 people. The HTA website provides announcements about funding opportunities and relevant news. Although these innovations sound highly positive, some emerging interpersonal problems exist related to who gets access first to

A satellite dish dominates the view of a village in Niger, West Africa. Throughout the world, the spread of electronic forms of communication have many and diverse social effects.

▶ *Pretend you are a cultural anthropologist doing research on communication in this village. What do you want to study in order to assess the effects of satellite communication on the people and their culture?*

digital divide social inequality in access to new and emerging information technology, notably access to up-to-date computers, the Internet, and training related to their use.

information for posting on the website and to information hoarding by some managers.

Like the Hungarian villagers, many marginalized people around the world, including indigenous people, women, and youth, realize the importance of having access to the Internet and other information and communication technologies (ICT). These technologies can help people preserve and learn their ancestral languages, record traditional agricultural and medical knowledge, and otherwise protect their culture and improve their lives (Lutz 2005, Turner 2002).

◆◆◆

Communication and Cultural Diversity and Inequality

This section presents material about the links between language and microcultures and social inequality. It begins by presenting two models of the relationship between language and culture. Examples follow about class, gender and sexuality, "race" and ethnicity, and age.

LANGUAGE AND CULTURE: TWO THEORIES

During the twentieth century, two theoretical perspectives were influential in the study of the relationship between language and culture. They are presented here as two distinct models, even though they actually overlap in real life and anthropologists tend to draw on both of them (Hill and Mannheim 1992).

The first was formulated by two early founding figures in linguistic anthropology, Edward Sapir and Benjamin Whorf. In the mid-twentieth century, they formulated an influential model called the **Sapir-Whorf hypothesis**, which says that people's language affects how they think. If a language has many words for different kinds of snow, for example, then someone who speaks that language can "think" about snow in more ways than someone can whose language has fewer "snow" terms. Among the Saami, whose traditional occupation was reindeer herding (see Culturama, p. 309), a rich set of terms exist for "snow" (review Figure 12.2, p. 294). If a language has no word for "snow," then someone who speaks that language cannot think of "snow." Thus, a language constitutes a *thought world,* and people who speak different languages inhabit different thought worlds. This catchy phrase became the basis for *linguistic determinism,* a theory stating that language determines consciousness of the world and behavior. Extreme linguistic determinism implies that the frames and definitions of a person's primary language are so strong that it is impossible to learn another language fully or, therefore, to understand another culture fully. Most anthropologists see value in the Sapir-Whorf hypothesis, but not in its extreme form.

A second model for understanding the relationship between language and culture is proposed by scholars working in the area of **sociolinguistics**, the study of how cultural and social context shapes language. These theorists support a *cultural constructionist* argument that a person's context and social position shape the content, form, and meaning of their language. Most anthropologists see value in this model and agree that language and culture are interactive: Language shapes culture and culture shapes language.

CRITICAL DISCOURSE ANALYSIS: CLASS, GENDER, INDIGENEITY, AND "RACE"

Critical discourse analysis is an emerging area that focuses on the relations of power and inequality in language (Blommaert and Bulcaen 2000). This part of the chapter looks at distinctive communication styles, or *registers,* that include variation in vocabulary, grammar, and intonation. Critical discourse analysis reveals links between language and social inequality, power, and stigma as well as agency and resistance through language.

CLASS AND ACCENT IN NEW YORK CITY William Labov launched the subfield of sociolinguistics with his classic study of accents among mainly Euro-American people of different socioeconomic classes in New York City (1966). For example, pronunciation of the consonant "r" in words such as car, card, floor, and fourth tends to be associated with upper-class people, whereas its absence ("caw," "cawd," "flaw," "fawth") is associated with lower-class people. In order to avoid the observer's paradox, Labov used informal observations of sales clerks' speech in three Manhattan department stores of different "class" levels: Saks (the highest), Macy's, and S. Klein (the lowest). Labov wanted to find out whether the clerks in the different stores spoke with different class accents. He would approach a clerk and inquire about the location of an item that he knew was on the fourth floor. The clerk would respond, and then Labov would say, "Excuse me?" in order to prompt a more emphatic repeat of the word fourth. He found that the higher-status "r" was pronounced both the first and second times by 44 percent of the employees in Saks, by 16 percent of the employees in Macy's, and by 6 percent of the employees in S. Klein.

Sapir-Whorf hypothesis a theory in linguistic anthropology that says language determines thought.

sociolinguistics a theory in linguistic anthropology that says that culture and society and a person's social position determine language.

critical discourse analysis the study of the relations of power and inequality in language.

tag question a question seeking affirmation, placed at the end of a sentence.

GENDER IN EURO-AMERICAN CONVERSATIONS Most languages contain gender differences in word choice, grammar, intonation, content, and style. Early studies of language and gender among white Euro-Americans revealed three general characteristics of female speech (Lakoff 1973):

- Politeness
- Rising intonation at the end of sentences
- Frequent use of **tag questions** (questions seeking affirmation placed at the end of sentences, such as, "It's a nice day, isn't it?")

In English, male speech, in general, is less polite, maintains a flat and assertive tone in a sentence, and does not use tag questions. Related to politeness is the fact that, during cross-gender conversations, men tend to interrupt women more than women interrupt men.

Deborah Tannen's popular book *You Just Don't Understand* (1990) shows how differences in conversational styles between white Euro-American men and women lead to miscommunication. She says that "women speak and hear a language of connection and intimacy, whereas men speak and hear a language of status and independence" (1990:42). Although both men and women use indirect response (not really answering the question), their different motivations, create different meanings embedded in their speech:

Michele: What time is the concert?
Gary: We have to be ready by seven-thirty. (1990:289)

Gary sees his role as one of protector in using an indirect response to Michele's question. He feels that he is simply "watching out for her" by getting to the real point of her question. Michele feels that Gary is withholding information by not answering her directly and is maintaining a power position. A wife's indirect response to a question from her husband is prompted by her goal of being helpful in anticipating her husband's underlying interest:

Ned: Are you just about finished?
Valerie: Do you want to have supper now? (1990:289)

Women's speech cross-culturally is not universally accommodating, subservient, and polite. In cultural contexts in which women's roles are prominent and valued, their language reflects and reinforces their position.

GENDER AND POLITENESS IN JAPANESE, AND THOSE NAUGHTY TEENAGE GIRLS Gender registers in spoken Japanese reflect gender differences (Shibamoto 1987). Certain words and sentence structures convey femininity, humbleness, and politeness. One important contrast between male and female speech is the attachment, by female speakers, of the honorific prefix "o-" to nouns (see Figure 12.4). This addition gives women's speech a more refined and polite tone.

	Male	Female
Box lunch	bentoo	obentoo
Money	kane	okane
Chopsticks	hasi	ohasi
Book	hon	ohon

Source: *Language, Gender, and Sex in Comparative Perspective,* by Susan U. Philips, Susan Steele, Chrisitne Tanz. Copyright © Cambridge University Press 1987. Reprinted with permission of Cambridge University Press.

FIGURE 12.4 Male-Unmarked and Female-Marked Nouns in Japanese

A contrasting pattern of gendered language comes from the *Kogals,* young Japanese women between 14 and 22 years of age, known for their female-centered coolness (Miller 2004). The Kogals have distinctive language, clothing, hairstyles, make-up, attitude, and activities, all of which challenge prescriptive norms for young women. Their overall style is flashy and exuberant, combining global and local elements. Heavy users of cell phones, Kogals have created an extensive set of emoticons, or "face characters," far more complex than the American smiley face. Read vertically, they include icons for "wow," "ouch," "applause," and "I can't hear you." They have also invented a unique text message code for their cell phones that uses mixed scripts such as mathematical symbols and Cyrillic (Russian) letters.

The spoken language of Kogals is a rich and quickly changing mixture of slang, some classic but much newly created. They create new words through compounds and by adding the Japanese suffix "-ru," which turns a noun into a verb, such as *maku-ru* ("go to McDonald's). They intentionally use strongly masculine language forms, openly talk about sex, and rework taboo sexual terms into new meanings. Reactions from mainstream society to Kogals are mixed, ranging from horror to fascination. No matter what, they have cultural influence and are shaking up the gender order.

"FAT TALK" AMONG EURO-AMERICAN ADOLESCENT GIRLS In the United States, Euro-American adolescent girls' conversations exhibit a high level of concern with their body weight and image (Nichter 2000). A study of 253 girls in the eighth and ninth grades in two urban high schools of

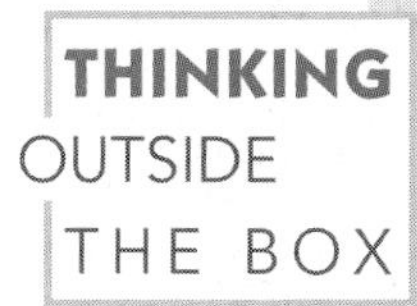

These broad generalizations about Euro-American conversational styles do not apply to all situations. What are your microcultural rules?

A Kogal in Tokyo's trendy Shibuyu district displays her cell phone that is covered with stickers. Her facial make-up and dress are characteristic of some, but not all, Kogals. Various Kogal make-up and dress styles, like their language, exist and keep changing.

the Southwest reveals the contexts and meanings of fat talk. Fat talk usually starts with a girl commenting, "I'm so fat." The immediate response from her friends is "No, you're not." Girls who use fat talk are typically not overweight and are not dieting. The weight of the girls in the study was within "normal" range, and none suffered from a serious eating disorder. Fat talk occurs frequently throughout a day. Sometimes it appears to function as a call for reinforcement from friends that the initiator is an accepted group member. In other cases, it occurs at the beginning of a meal. In this context, fat talk may function to absolve the girl from guilty feelings and to give her a sense of agency.

GAY LANGUAGE AND BELONGING IN INDONESIA

The national language of Indonesia is referred to as *bahasa Indonesia*. Many homosexual men in Indonesia speak *bahasa gay*, or "gay language" (Boellstorff 2004). Indonesia is the world's fourth largest country in terms of population, with nearly 250 million citizens living in over 6000 islands and speaking nearly 700 local languages. In spite of this cultural and linguistic diversity, bahasa gay is highly standardized.

Bahasa gay has a distinct vocabulary that plays humorously on mainstream language and provides a political commentary on mainstream life. Some of the vocabulary changes involve sound-alikes; others add a suffix to a standard word. In terms of the state's strongly heterosexual image, Indonesian gays would seem to be a clearly excluded group. Nonetheless, bahasa gay is moving into mainstream linguistic culture, where it conveys agency and freedom from official control.

CUING AMONG THE AKWESASNE MOHAWKS

Linguistic *cues* are words or phrases that preface a remark to indicate the speaker's attitude toward what is being said. Standard English cues include *maybe* and *in my opinion* (Woolfson et al. 1995). Three functions of cuing exist in Mohawk English, a version of English spoken by the Akwesasne people of the St. Lawrence River area (see Map 12.4). They are:

- The speaker's unwillingness or inability to verify the certainty of a statement
- Respect for the listener
- The inability to make statements that have to do with matters that are in the domain of religion

Frequent miscommunication occurs between the Akwesasne people and Anglo medical professionals. Analysis of doctor–patient conversations reveals the role that Akwesasne cuing plays and how it is misinterpreted by the professionals. Here is a response to a question posed by an anthropologist about the kinds of diseases Akwesasne people had in the past, with the cues italicized:

> Hmm . . . That [tuberculosis] . . . was mostly, it well . . . they always said cirrhosis. . . . *It seems* like no matter what anybody died from . . . if they drank, it was cirrhosis. *I don't know* if anybody *really* knew a long time ago what anybody really died from. Even if the doctor requested an autopsy, the people would just say no . . . you know . . . it won't be done. So *I don't think* it was . . . you know . . . it was just what the doctor thought that would go down on the death certificate. (1995:506)

The White medical practitioners misinterpret such clues as indications of indecisiveness or noncooperation. The Akwesasne speakers are following linguistic rules about truthfulness, humility, and the sacred.

AFRICAN AMERICAN ENGLISH: PREJUDICE AND PRIDE

The topic of African American English (AAE), or African American Vernacular English (AAVE), is complicated by racism of the past and present (Jacobs-Huey 2006). Scholars debate whether AAE/AAVE is a language in its own right or a dialect of English. "Linguistic conservatives" who champion standard American Mainstream English (AME) view AAE as an ungrammatical form of English that needs to be "corrected." In the current linguistic hierarchy in the United States, with

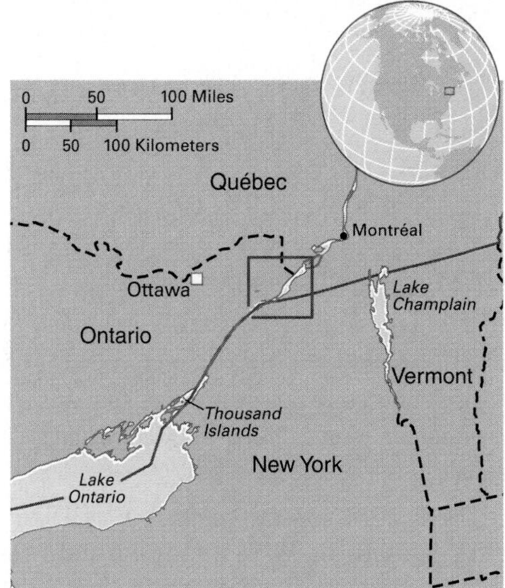

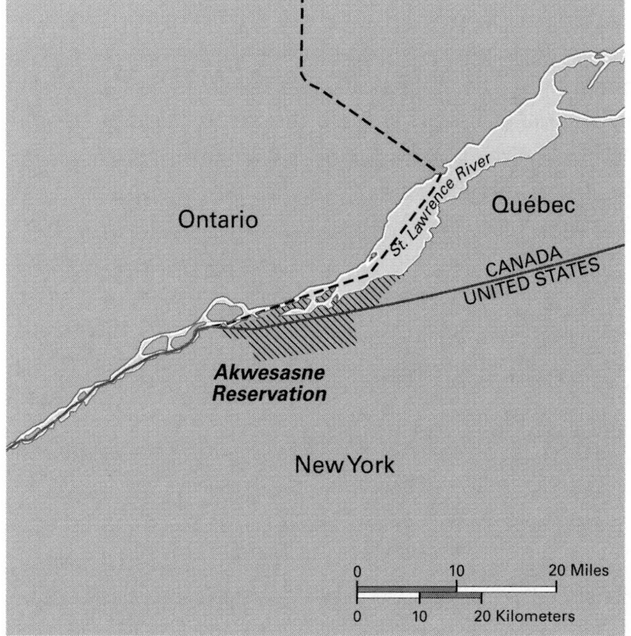

MAP 12.4 Akwesasne Territory in New York State and Ontario, Canada.
The Akwesasne Territory has an international border running through it with New York State on one side and two provinces of Canada on the other: Ontario and Québec. The Mohawk Council of Akwesasne comprises 12 District Chiefs and a Grand Chief. Since the 1960s, the Akwesasne Territory has been negatively affected by environmental pollution of the water, soil, and food supply from industries along the St. Lawrence River. In 1987, the Akwesasne formed a Task Force to restore and protect the environment and the survival of their culture.

AME at the top, speakers of AAE may be both proud of their language and feel stigmatized by those who judge AAE negatively and treat its speakers unfairly (Lanehart 1999).

African American English is a relatively new language, emerging out of slavery to develop a degree of standardization across the United States, along with many local variants. Some of its characteristic grammar results from its African roots. One of the most prominent is the use, or nonuse, of forms of the English verb "to be" (Lanehart 1999:217). In AAE, one says, "She married," which in AME means "she is married." Viewed incorrectly by outsiders as "bad" English, the sentence "She married" follows a grammatical rule in AAE. The fact that AME has its own grammar and usage rules is evident in the fact that when non-AME speakers attempt to speak it or imitate it, they often make mistakes (Jacobs-Huey 1997).

Ethnographic research among African American school-age children in a working-class neighborhood of southwest Philadelphia examined within-gender and cross-gender conversations, including *directives* (getting someone to do something), argument, he-said-she-said accusations, and storytelling (Goodwin 1990). All of these speech activities involve complex verbal strategies that are culturally embedded. In arguments, the children may bring in imaginary events as a "put-on," preceded by the cue term "psych," or use words of a song to create and maintain playfulness within an argument. Much of their arguments involve highly ritualized insults that work quickly to return an insult to the original giver. When a group of girls were practicing some dance steps and singing, a boy said, "You sound terrible." A girl responded, "We sound just like you look" (1990:183). The study revealed the importance of verbal play and art among the children. It also showed that girls often excel at verbal competitions in mixed gender settings.

Children who grow up speaking a version of AAE at home and with peer groups face a challenge in schools where they are expected to perform in AME. Just like native Spanish speakers or any non–English-speaking new immigrants, African American children are implicitly expected to become bilingual in AAE and AME. More than vocabulary and grammar are involved. Teachers should understand that African American children may have culturally distinct styles of expression that should be recognized and valued. For example, in narrative style, African American children tend to use a spiral pattern, skipping around to different topics before addressing the theme, instead of a linear style. Rather than being considered a deficiency, having AAE speakers in a classroom adds cultural diversity to those whose linguistic worlds are limited to AME.

Inspired by such findings, the Oakland School Board in California approved a resolution in 1996 to recognize *Ebonics*, or AAE, as the primary language, or vernacular, of African American students. The school developed a special teaching program, called the Bridge Program, in which AAE speakers were encouraged to learn Standard American English through a process of translation between AAE and SAE (Rickford 1997). After several months, students in the Bridge Program had progressed in their SAE reading ability much faster than African American students who were not in the program. Nevertheless, the program received so much negative publicity and raised such sensitive questions about the best way to enhance minority student learning that it was cancelled within the year.

The underlying issues of the so-called *Ebonics controversy* are still unresolved. One of the thorniest questions debated is whether AAE/AAVE/Ebonics is sufficiently distinct (either as a separate language from SAE or a vernacular form) that schools should address it in their curriculum with special programs. If so, can it be dealt with in a positive way as a rich part of Black cultural heritage? Or should it be suppressed in public schools in favor of promoting SAE? No easy answers exist. According to John Rickford, a sociolinguist at Stanford University and an expert on AAE, the Bridge Program of using AAE to teach SAE was well intentioned and demonstrated persuasively that the approach works (1997).

◆◆◆

Language Change

Languages, like the cultures of which they are a part, experience both continuity and change, and for similar reasons. Human creativity and contact lead to linguistic innovation and linguistic borrowing. War, imperialism, genocide, and other disasters may destroy languages. This section looks first at what is known about the origins of human language and provides a brief history of writing. Later sections discuss the role of European colonialism on languages, nationalism and language, world languages, and contemporary language loss and revitalization.

THE ORIGINS AND HISTORY OF LANGUAGE

As mentioned in Chapter 2, no one knows how verbal language began. Current evidence of other aspects of human cultural evolution suggests that verbal language began to develop between 100,000 and 50,000 years ago when early modern humans had both the physical and mental capacity for symbolic thinking and verbal communication. Facial expressions, gestures, and body postures were likely important features of hominin communication as they are among many nonhuman primate species today.

Early scholars of language were often misled by ethnocentric assumptions that the structure of European languages was normative and that languages with different structures were less developed and deficient. For example, they considered the Chinese language "primitive" because it lacks the kinds of verbs that European languages have. As discussed at the beginning of this chapter, the Pirahã language appears "simpler" in many ways when compared to English, as does the Pirahã culture, but both Pirahã and English have to be examined within their cultural contexts. Pirahã is a language that works for a rainforest foraging population. English works for a globalizing, technology-driven, consumerist culture. Languages of foraging cultures today can, with caution, provide insights about what foragers' language may have been like thousands of years ago. But they are not "frozen in time" examples of "stone age" language.

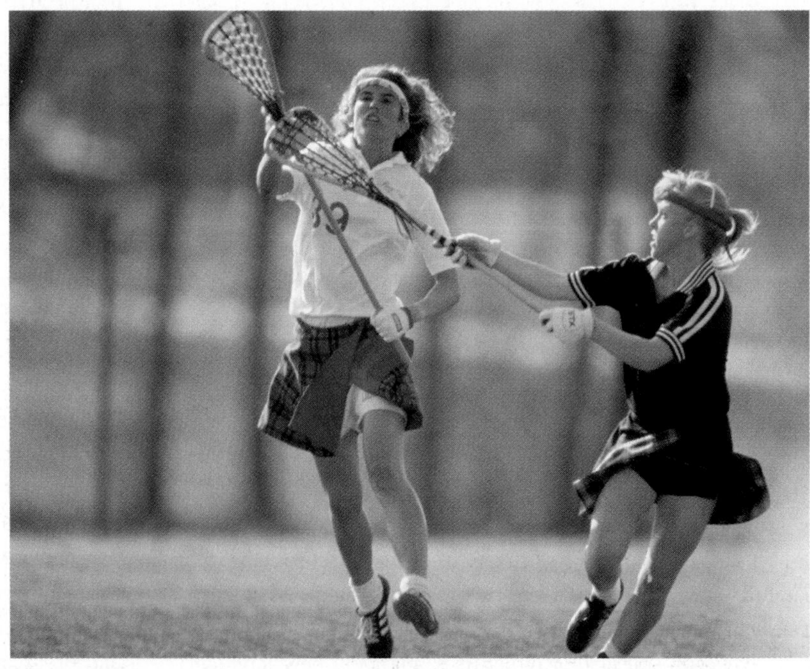

(LEFT) An African bonobo male waves branches in a display of power. (RIGHT) In the United States, women lacrosse players use sticks in a competitive sport invented by American Indians.

▶ *Threat is clearly conveyed by the bonobo's behavior. In lacrosse, are sticks also used to communicate threats?*

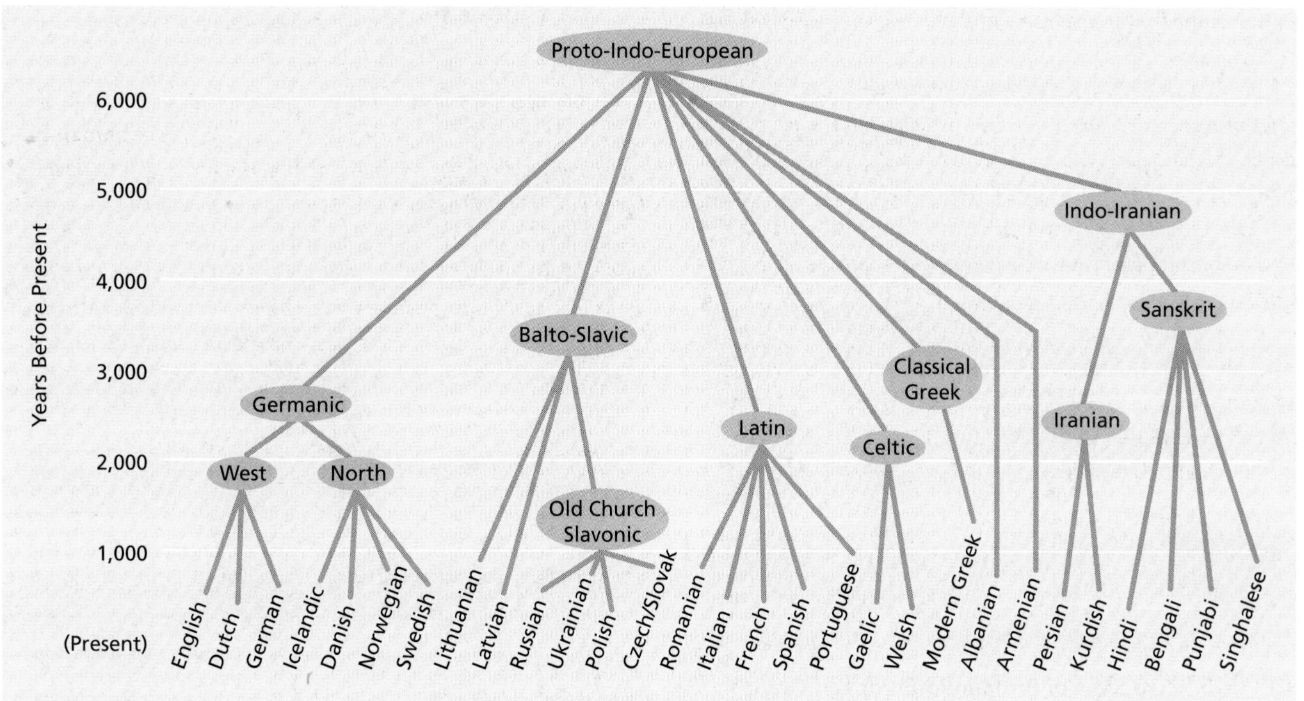

FIGURE 12.5 The Indo-European Language Family.

HISTORICAL LINGUISTICS

Historical linguistics is the study of language change through history. It relies on many specialized methods that compare shifts over time and across space in aspects of language such as phonetics, syntax, and meaning. It originated in the eighteenth century with a discovery made by Sir William Jones, a British colonial administrator working in India. During his spare time, he studied Sanskrit, a classical language of India. He noticed strong similarities among Sanskrit, Greek, and Latin in vocabulary and syntax. For example, the Sanskrit word for "father" is *pitr;* in Greek it is *patér,* and in Latin it is *pater*. This was an astounding discovery for the time, given the prevailing European mentality that placed its cultural heritage firmly in the classical Graeco-Roman world and depicted the "Orient" as completely separate from "Europe" (Bernal 1987).

Following Jones's discovery, other scholars began comparing lists of words and grammatical forms in different languages: the French *père,* the German *Vater,* the Italian *padre,* the Old English *faeder,* the Old Norse *fadhir,* the Swedish *far*. These lists allowed scholars to determine degrees of closeness and distance in their relationships. Later scholars contributed the concept of **language families,** or languages descended from a parent language (see Figure 12.5). Descendant languages that are part of the same language are referred to as *sister languages,* such as French and Spanish.

Using comparative evidence from historical and contemporary Eurasian languages, historical linguists developed a hypothetical model of the original parent language, or *proto-language,* of most Eurasian languages. It is called *Proto-Indo-European* (PIE). Linguistic evidence suggests that PIE was located in Eurasia, either north or south of the Black Sea (see Map 12.5). From its area of origin, between 6000 and 8000 years ago, PIE spread into Europe, central and eastern Asia, and South Asia, where local variants developed over the centuries.

Similar linguistic methods reveal the existence of the original parent form of the Bantu language family, Proto-Bantu (Afolayan 2000). Scholars can trace the *Bantu expansion* in Africa starting around 5000 years ago (see Map 12.6). Today, some form of Bantu language is spoken by over 100 million people in Africa, not to mention the number of people in the African diaspora worldwide. Over 600 African languages are derived from Proto-Bantu. According to linguistic analysis, the homeland of Proto-Bantu is the present-day countries of Cameroon and Nigeria, West Africa. It is likely that Proto-Bantu spread through population migration as the farming population expanded and moved, over hundreds of years, into areas occupied by indigenous foragers. Bantu cultural imperialism may have wiped out some local languages, although it is impossible to document possible extinctions. Substantial linguistic evidence, however, suggests some

---

historical linguistics the study of language change using formal methods that compare shifts over time and across space in aspects of language such as phonetics, syntax, and semantics.

language family languages descended from a parent language.

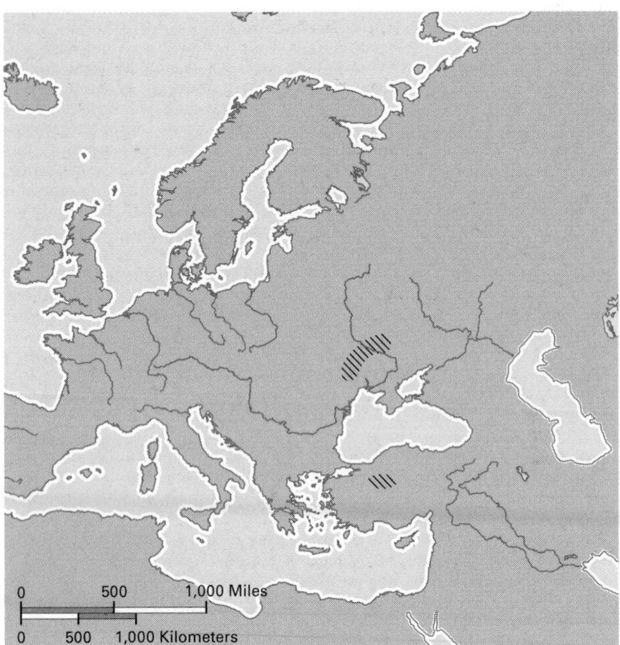

MAP 12.5 Two Sites of Proto-Indo-European Origins. Two major theories about the location of PIE exist, with the site south of the Black Sea considered to be earlier.

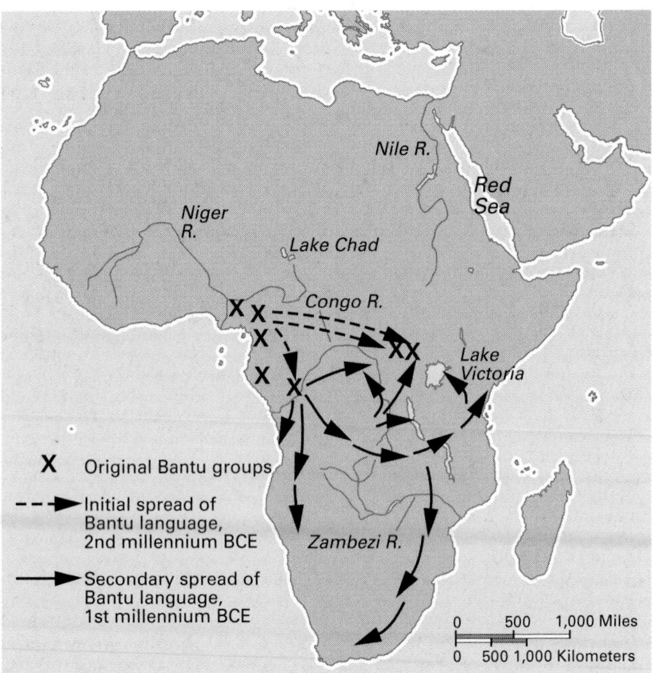

MAP 12.6 The Bantu Migrations in Africa. Linguistic evidence for the migrations of Bantu-speaking people relies on similarities between languages in parts of eastern, central, and southern Africa and languages of the original Bantu homeland in West Africa. Over 600 African languages are derived from Proto-Bantu.

interactions between the farmers and the foragers through which standard Bantu absorbed elements from local languages.

WRITING SYSTEMS

Evidence of the earliest written languages comes from Mesopotamia, Egypt, and China. The oldest writing system was in use in the fourth millennium BCE in Mesopotamia (Postgate, Wang, and Wilkinson 1995). All early writing systems used **logographs**, signs that indicate a word, syllable, or sound. Over time, some logographs retained their original meaning; others were kept but given more abstract meaning, and nonlogographic symbols were added (see Figure 12.6).

The emergence of writing is associated with the development of the state. Some scholars take writing as a key diagnostic feature that distinguishes the state from nonstate political forms because recordkeeping was such an essential task of the state. The Inca empire, centered in the Peruvian Andes, is a notable exception to this generalization. It used **khipu** (KEE-poo), or cords of knotted strings of different colors, for keeping accounts and recording events. Scholars are not quite sure how khipu worked in the past because their coding system is so complicated. Debates are ongoing as to whether khipu served as an actual language or more simply as an accounting system. Whatever is the answer, the world's largest empire in the fourteenth century relied on khipu.

Two interpretations of the function of early writing systems exist. The first says that early writing was mainly for ceremonial purposes because of its prevalence on tombs, bone inscriptions, or temple carvings. The second says that early

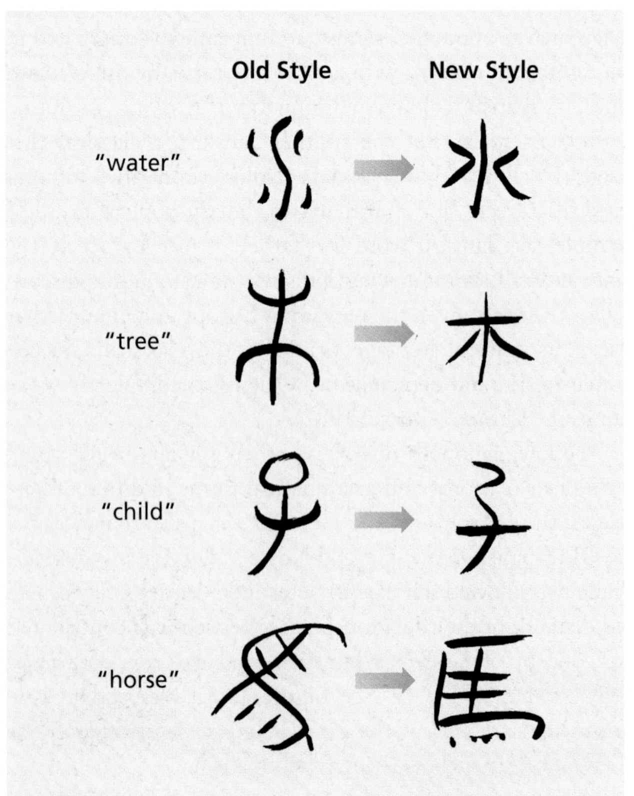

FIGURE 12.6 Logographic and Current Writing Styles in China

writing was mainly for secular use in government recordkeeping and trade. The archaeological record is biased toward durable substances such as stone. Because ceremonial writing was intended to last, it was more likely to be inscribed on stone. Utilitarian writing, in contrast, was more likely to have been done on perishable materials because people would be less concerned with permanence (consider the way you treat shopping lists). Compared to what has been preserved, more utilitarian writing and other forms of nonceremonial writing must have existed.

The scripts of much of South and Southeast Asia originated in the Aramaic system of the Middle East (Kuipers and McDermott 1996). It spread eastward to India, where it took on new forms, and continued to move into much of Southeast Asia, including Indonesia and the Philippines but excluding Vietnam. The functions of the scripts vary from context to context. Writing for recordkeeping and taxation exists but is subordinate to, and carries less status than, writing for communication with the spirits, to record medical knowledge, and for love poetry. Writing love poetry is exalted and esteemed, and sometimes done in secret. Some love songs in the Philippine highlands have strict rules regulating such matters as how many syllables may be used per line. All adolescents seek to learn the rules of writing love poetry and to be able to write it well.

COLONIALISM, NATIONALISM, AND GLOBALIZATION

European colonialism was a major force of language change. Not only did colonial powers declare their own language as the language of government, business, and education, but they often took direct steps to suppress indigenous languages and literatures. Widespread bilingualism, or competence in a language other than one's birth language, is one prominent effect of colonialism. Globalization is also having substantial and complex effects on language.

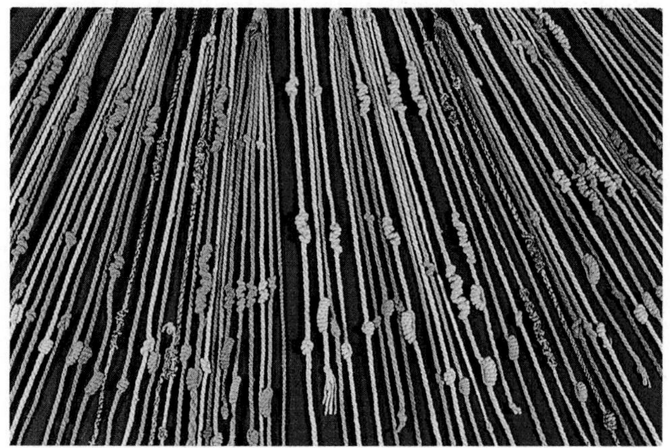

Khipu, or knotted strings, were the basis of state-level accounting in the Incan empire. The knots convey substantial information for those who could interpret their meaning.

French colonialism added another cultural layer to Arabic influences in Morocco, resulting in many bilingual and trilingual shop signs.

▶ *Where have you seen multilingualism in public use? What languages were used and why?*

EUROPEAN COLONIALISM AND CONTACT LANGUAGES Beginning in the fifteenth century, European colonialism had dramatic effects on the people with whom it came into contact, as discussed elsewhere in this book. Language change is an important part of the story of colonialism and indigenous cultures. Depending on the type and duration of contact, it resulted in the development of new languages, the decline of others, and the extinction of many, along with the people who spoke them (Silverstein 1997). Two forms of new languages prompted by European colonialism are pidgins and creoles.

A **pidgin** is a language that blends elements of at least two parent languages and that emerges when two different cultures with different languages come in contact and must communicate (Baptista 2005). All speakers have their own native language(s) but learn to speak pidgin as a second, rudimentary language. Pidgins are typically limited to specific functional domains, such as trade and basic social interactions. Many pidgins of the Western Hemisphere were the result of the Atlantic slave trade and plantation slavery. Owners needed to communicate with their slaves, and slaves from various parts of Africa needed to communicate with each other.

---

logograph a symbol that conveys meaning through a form or picture resembling that to which it refers.

khipu cords of knotted strings used during the Inca empire for keeping accounts and recording events.

pidgin a contact language that blends elements of at least two languages and that emerges when people with different languages need to communicate.

A pidgin often evolves into a **creole**, which is a language descended from a pidgin with its own native speakers, richer vocabularies, and more developed grammar. Throughout the Western Hemisphere, many localized creoles have developed in areas such as Louisiana, Haiti, Ecuador, and Suriname. Though a living reminder of the heritage of slavery, Creole languages and associated literature and music are also evidence of resilience and creativity in the African diaspora.

Pidgins are common throughout the South Pacific. Tok Pisin, the pidgin language of Papua New Guinea, consists of a mixture of English, Samoan, Chinese, and Malayan. Tok Pisin is now a creole language and recognized as one of the official languages of Papua New Guinea.

NATIONALISM AND LINGUISTIC ASSIMILATION Nationalist policies of cultural assimilation of minorities have led to suppression and loss of local dialects and the extinction of many indigenous and minority languages throughout the world. Direct policies of linguistic assimilation include declaration of a lingua franca, or standard language and rules about the language of instruction in public schools. Indirect mechanisms include discrimination in hiring on the basis of language and social stigma.

The Soviet attempt to build a USSR-wide commitment to the state after the 1930s included mass migration of Russian speakers into remote areas, where they eventually outnumbered indigenous peoples (Belikov 1994). Russian officials burned books in local languages. Many children were forcibly sent away to boarding schools, where they were taught in Russian. The indigenous Komi traditionally formed the majority population in an area around the Pechora River (see Map 12.7). Russian immigration brought in so many outsiders that the Komi were outnumbered. The Russians initiated the use of the Russian language in schools, and the Komi people became bilingual. Eventually, the Komi language was so heavily influenced by Russian that it may be extinct.

This story can be repeated for many indigenous languages of the former Soviet Union. Enforced attendance at boarding schools was also a strategy of the United States, Canada, and Australia in their attempts to assimilate indigenous peoples. Often, Christian missionaries worked to suppress indigenous languages as part of their attempts to "civilize" "pagan" peoples (see Culturama).

GLOBAL LANGUAGES Ninety-six percent of the world's population speaks 4 percent of the world's languages (Crystal 2000:14). The eight most-spoken languages are Mandarin, Spanish, English, Bengali, Hindi, Portuguese, Russian, and Japanese. Languages that are gaining widespread currency are called **global languages**, or **world languages**. Global languages are spoken worldwide in diverse cultural contexts. As they spread to areas and cultures beyond their home area and culture, they take on new, localized identities. At the same time, the "mother language" picks up words and phrases from local languages (see Figure 12.7). Global languages may act as both a form of linguistic and economic opportunity and a form of cultural imperialism.

MAP 12.7 Komi Region in Russia.
The Komi were traditionally reindeer hunters. The Komi language belongs to the Finno-Ugric language family and is closer to Finnish and Estonian than to Russian.

English is the most globalized language in history (Bhatt 2001; Crystal 2003). British English was first transplanted through colonial expansion to the present-day United States, Canada, Australia, New Zealand, South Asia, Africa, Hong Kong, and the Caribbean. English was the dominant language in the colonies, used in government and commerce and taught in schools. Over time, regional and subregional varieties of English have developed, often leading to a "New English" that a native speaker from England cannot understand at all. So many varieties of English now exist that scholars are beginning to talk of the English language family that includes American English, Spanglish, Japlish, and Tex-Mex.

ENDANGERED LANGUAGES AND LANGUAGE REVITALIZATION

The emergence of linguistic anthropology, as mentioned in Chapter 1, was prompted by the need to document disappearing indigenous languages in the United States. Today,

creole a language directly descended from a pidgin but possessing its own native speakers and involving linguistic expansion and elaboration.

global language or **world language** a language spoken widely throughout the world and in diverse cultural contexts, often replacing indigenous languages.

CULTURAMA

ʽhe Saami of Lapland, or Sapmi

he Saami (SAH-mee) are indigenous, fourth world" people who live in the orthernmost stretches of Norway, weden, Finland, and western Russia Gaski 1993). The area is called apland or Sapmi, the land of the aami. The total Saami population around 100,000 people, with the najority in Norway (Magga and kutnabb-Kangas 2001).

At the time of the earliest written ecords of 1000 years ago, all Saami unted wild reindeer, among other ınd and sea species, and may have ept some tamed reindeer for ransport (Paine 2004). Over time, erding domesticated reindeer develped and became the economic mainay. In the past few hundred years, ough, reindeer pastoralism declined being a specialization of about 0 percent of the population. Settled aami are farmers or work in trade, small-scale industry, handicrafts, services, and the professions.

Traditional Saami reindeer herding has been a family-based system. Men and women cared for the herd, and sons and daughters inherited equally the rights to the herd (Paine 2004). The value of social equality was strong, entailing both rights and privileges.

In their relationships with the modern state, the Saami have experienced discrimination, exclusion, loss of territorial rights, and cultural and linguistic repression. Specific risks to Saami cultural survival include being downwind of the prevailing winds after the 1986 Chernobyl disaster, being near the earlier Soviet atomic testing grounds in Siberia, having their ancestral territory and sacred spaces suffer environmental degradation from hydroelectric dam construction, and having grazing lands taken over for use as military training grounds (Anderson 2004).

State policies of cultural assimilatior and forced Christianization in the twentieth century marginalized the Saami language and led to language loss (Magga and Skutnabb-Kangas 2001). Several Saami languages and dialects still exist, however, and spatially distant versions are mutually unintelligible (Gaski 1993:116).

Language is of central cultural value to the Saami, and efforts to maintain it have been under way since the 1960s. Besides the Saami language, a traditional song form, the *yoik*, is of particular importance (Anderson 2005) Yoik lyrics allow a subtle system of double meanings that can camouflage political content (Gaski 1997).

Thanks to Myrdene Anderson, Purdue University, for reviewing this material.

Alcohol	Arabic, Middle East
Avocado	Nahuatl, Mexico/Central America
Banana	Mandingo, West Africa
Bogus	Hausa, West Africa
Candy	Arabic, Middle East
Caucus	Algonquin, Virginia/Delaware, North America
Chimpanzee	Bantu, West and Central Africa
Chocolate	Aztec Nahuatl, Mexico/Central America
Dungaree	Hindi, North India, South Asia
Gong	Malaysia, Southeast Asia
Hammock	Arawakan, South America
Hip/hep	Wolof, West Africa
Hurricane	Taino, Caribbean
Lime	Inca Quechua, South America
Moose	Algonquin, Virginia/Delaware, North America
Panda	Nepali, South Asia
Savannah	Taino, Caribbean
Shampoo	Hindi, North India, South Asia
Sugar	Sanskrit, South Asia
Tepee	Sioux, Dakotas, North America
Thug	Hindi, North India, South Asia
Tobacco	Arawak, South America
Tomato	Nahuatl, Mexico/Central America
Tundra	Saami, Lapland, Northern Europe
Tycoon	Japanese
Typhoon	Mandarin Chinese, East Asia
Zombie	Congo and Angola, Central and West Africa

FIGURE 12.7 Loan Words in North American English

anthropologists and other scholars, as well as descendant language communities themselves, are still concerned about the rapid loss of languages (Fishman 1991; Maffi 2005). The task of documenting declining languages is urgent. It is often accompanied by applied work to preserve and revive endangered and dying languages (see Critical Thinking).

language shift or **language decay** condition of a language in which speakers adopt a new language for most situations, begin to use their native language only in certain contexts, and may be only semi-fluent and have limited vocabulary in their native language.

language loss or decline (Walsh 2005). The general stages proceed from shift to extinction. **Language shift**, or **language decay**, is a category of language decline when speakers have limited vocabulary in their native language and more often use a new language in which they may be semifluent or fluent (Hill 2001). An intermediary stage, **language endangerment**, is judged to exist when a language has fewer than 10,000 speakers. Near-extinction is a situation in which only a few elderly speakers are still living. **Language extinction**, or language death, occurs when the language no longer has any competent users (Crystal 2000:11).

Keeping track of endangered and dying languages is difficult because no one is sure how many languages have existed in the recent past and even now (Crystal 2000). Estimates of the number of living languages today range between 5000 and 7000. Part of the explanation for the fuzzy numbers is the problem in separating languages from dialects. The largest number of languages of any world region is found on the island of New Guinea, which includes the island of New Guinea (comprising Papua New Guinea and West Papua) and several neighboring small islands (Foley 2000). Some 1000 languages exist in this area, many from completely separate language families.

Language extinction is especially acute in the Australia/Pacific region, where 99.5 percent of the indigenous languages have fewer than 100,000 speakers (Nettle and Romaine 2000:40). The situation of indigenous languages in the Americas, Siberia, Africa, and South and Southeast Asia is increasingly serious. Over half of the world's languages have fewer than 10,000 speakers, and one-fourth have fewer than 1000 speakers.

Linguistic diversity is closely tied to cultural survival and diversity. It is also closely tied to biological diversity. The

CRITICAL Thinking

Should Dying Languages Be Revived?

The Western media often carry articles about endangered biological species, such as certain frogs or birds, and the need to protect them from extinction. The reasons for concern about loss of biological species are many. One major factor is simply that biological diversity is a good thing to have on the earth. Opponents of taking special measures to protect endangered species find support for their position in a Darwinian view that progress involves competition and fitness as measured in the long-term survival of species that succeed in reproducing over time. Consider this imagined scenario: An economic development project involves building a new shopping center or airport with a massive parking lot that will bring about the extinction of a particular kind of plant. In the Darwinian view, that loss is simply the price of progress as the stronger drives out the weaker. But is it all so simple? What if that particular plant held a unique cure for cancer, and now it is gone forever? If the cure had been discovered, it would have contributed to the survival of many humans. What looks "weak" may in fact be important and valuable.

Some parallels exist between the survival of endangered biological species and endangered languages. Supporters of language preservation and revitalization point to the sheer fact of diversity on earth as a good thing, a sign of a culturally healthy planet with room for many languages. They also argue that a people's language is an intrinsic part of their culture. Without language, the culture, too, will die. They argue that dying cultures, like dying languages, are treasures lost forever to humanity.

The Darwinian view, in contrast, says that languages, like species, live in a world of competition. Language survival means that the strong and fit carry on while the weak and unfit die out. They are likely to point out that preserving linguistic heritage is useless because dying languages are part of a past that no longer exists. They resist spending public funds on language preservation and regard revitalization programs as wasteful.

◆ **CRITICAL THINKING QUESTIONS**

- Have you read or heard of an endangered biological species in the media recently? What was the species?
- Have you read or heard of an endangered language in the media lately? What was the language?
- Where do you stand on biological species preservation and on language preservation, and why?

greatest linguistic diversity is found in the same regions as the greatest biodiversity (Maffi 2005). These are areas where indigenous people live, the "keepers" of much of the world's cultural and biological heritage, including the knowledge of how to live a culturally and biologically sustainable life. Yet they are also the people, languages, and biological species most in danger of extinction in the near future.

Efforts to revive or maintain local languages face many challenges (Fishman 2001). Political opposition may come from governments that fear local identity movements. Governments are often averse to devoting financial resources to supporting minority language programs. Deciding which version of an endangered language to preserve may have political consequences at the local level (Nevins 2004). Notable achievements have been made, however, with perhaps one of the most robust examples of language maintenance occurring in French-speaking Québec.

Approaches to language maintenance and revitalization must respond to local circumstances and factors such as how serious the degree of loss is, how many living speakers there are, what version of the language should be maintained or revived, and what resources for maintenance and revitalization programs are available. Major strategies include (Walsh 2005):

- Formal classroom instruction
- Master-apprentice system in which an elder teaches a nonspeaker in a one-on-one situation
- Web-based tools and services to support language learning

Each method has both promise and pitfalls. One thing is key: It takes living communities to activate and keep alive the knowledge of a language (Maffi 2003).

12

the BIG questions REVISITED

◆ How do humans communicate?

Human communication is the sending of meaningful messages through language. Language is a systematic set of symbols and signs with learned and shared meanings. It may be spoken, hand-signed, written, or conveyed through body movements, marking, or accessories.

Human language has two characteristics that distinguish it from communicative systems of other living beings. It has productivity, or the ability to create an infinite number of novel and understandable messages, and displacement, the ability to communicate about the past, the future, and imaginary things.

Language consists of basic sounds, vocabulary, and syntax. Cross-culturally, however, languages vary substantially in the details of all three features.

Humans use many forms of nonverbal language to communicate with each other. Sign language is a form of communication that uses mainly hand movements to communicate. Silence is a form of nonverbal communication with its own cultural values and meaning. Body language includes body movements and placement in relation to other people, body modifications such as tattoos and piercing, dress, hairstyles, and odors.

Media anthropology sheds light on how culture shapes media messages and the social dynamics in media institutions. Critical media anthropology examines the power relations involved in the media.

◆ How does communication relate to cultural diversity and inequality?

In order to study language in society, anthropologists have to deal with the observer's paradox, or the difficulty of collecting data on language without affecting the object of study in the process. Translation is another challenge.

The Sapir-Whorf hypothesis emphasizes how language shapes culture. A competing model, called sociolinguistics, emphasizes how one's culture and one's position in it shape language. Each position has merit, and many anthropologists draw on both models.

Critical discourse analysis studies the relations of power and inequality in language. Language can reveal social difference and reinforce exclusion. It can also empower oppressed people, depending on the context. In mainstream North America, women's speech is generally more polite and accommodating than that of men. In Japan, gender codes emphasize politeness in women's speech, but many young Japanese women, Kogals, are creating a new linguistic style of resistance. Gay language in Indonesia is entering the mainstream as an expression of freedom from official control. Linguistic cuing among the Akwesasne Mohawks has been frequently misinterpreted by Anglo medical practitioners as a sign of indecisiveness or noncooperation. African American English (AAE) has evolved from the tragic heritage of slavery to become a standard language with many local variants.

◆ How does language change?

The exact origins of human verbal language will never be known. The discovery of language families provides insights about human history and settlement patterns. The emergence of writing can be traced to around 6000 years ago, with the emergence of the state in Mesopotamia. Scripts have spread widely throughout the world, with the Aramaic system the basis of scripts in South and Southeast Asia. The functions of writing vary from context to context. In some situations, official recordkeeping predominates, whereas in others, writing is important for courtship.

The recent history of language change has been influenced by the colonialism of past centuries and by Western globalization of the current era. Nationalist policies of cultural integration often involve the repression of minority languages and promotion of a lingua franca. Colonial contact created the context for the emergence of pidgin languages, many of which evolved into creoles. Western globalization supports the spread of English and the development of localized variants.

In the past 500 years, colonialism and globalization have resulted in the extinction of many indigenous and minority languages. Many others are in danger of dying. Applied linguistic anthropologists seek to preserve the world's linguistic diversity. They document languages and participate in designing programs for teaching dead and dying languages. A key element in language revitalization and survival is having communities use the language.

KEY CONCEPTS

call system, p. 292
communication, p. 292
creole, p. 308
critical discourse analysis, p. 300
critical media anthropology, p. 297
digital divide, p. 299
displacement, p. 292
ethnosemantics, p. 294
global language, or **world language,** p. 308
historical linguistics, p. 305
khipu, p. 306
language, p. 292
language endangerment, p. 310
language extinction, p. 310
language family, p. 305
language shift or **language decay,** p. 310
logograph, p. 306
phoneme, p. 293
pidgin, p. 307
productivity, p. 292
Sapir-Whorf hypothesis, p. 300
sign language, p. 294
sociolinguistics, p. 300
tag question, p. 301

SUGGESTED READINGS

Keith H. Basso, *Wisdom Sits in Places: Landscape and Language among the Western Apache*. Albuquerque: University of New Mexico Press, 1996. Fieldwork on the Fort Apache Indian Reservation, Arizona, reveals the importance of natural places in people's everyday life, thought, and language.

David Crystal, *English as a Global Language,* 2nd ed. New York: Cambridge University Press, 2003. This book discusses the history, current status, and future of English as a world language. It covers the role of English in international relations, the media, international travel, education, and "New Englishes."

Joshua A. Fishman, ed. *Can Threatened Languages Be Saved?* Buffalo, NY: Multilingual Matters Ltd., 2001. Seventeen case studies examine language shift and language loss and the attempts to reverse such changes.

Marjorie H. Goodwin. *He-Said-She-Said: Talk as Social Organization among Black Children*. Bloomington: Indiana University Press, 1990. A study of everyday talk among children of an urban African American community in the United States, this book shows how children construct social relationships among themselves through verbal interactions, including disputes, pretend play, and stories.

Niloofar Haeri, *Sacred Language, Ordinary People: Dilemmas of Culture and Politics in Egypt*. New York: Palgrave Macmillan, 2003. Classical Arabic is the official language of all Arab states and the language of the Qur'an, but no Arabs speak it as their mother tongue. This book uses research in Cairo to show how the state maintains its identity in people's everyday lives through classical Arabic.

Lanita Jacobs-Huey. *From the Kitchen to the Parlor: Language and Becoming in African-American Women's Hair Care*. New York: Oxford University Press, 2006. Jacobs-Huey combines childhood experiences as the daughter of a cosmetologist with multisited fieldwork in the United States and England. She finds a complex world centered on hair that relates to race, gender, religion, body esthetics, health, and verbal language.

William L. Leap. *Word's Out: Gay Men's English*. Minneapolis: University of Minnesota Press, 1996. Fieldwork among gay men in the Washington, DC, area produced this ethnography. It addresses gay men's speech as a cooperative mode of discourse, bathroom graffiti, and discourse about HIV/AIDS.

Julie Lindquist. *A Place to Stand: Politics and Persuasion in a Working-Class Bar*. New York: Oxford University Press, 2002. The author did participant observation while working as a bartender in a White, working-class bar in the U.S. Midwest. The book is an ethnography of speaking in which the bar is a site of cultural performance related to White, working-class identity.

Karen Nakamura. *Deaf in Japan: Signing and the Politics of Identity*. Ithaca, NY: Cornell University Press. 2007. This book combines archival and ethnographic data to understand ideas about modernity and Westernization.

Lisa Philips Valentine. *Making It Their Own: Ojibwe Communicative Practices*. Toronto: University of Toronto Press, 1995. This ethnography examines speech events in a small Ojibwe community in northern Ontario, Canada. It considers speech variations among speakers, code switching, multilingualism, and church music.

In Nepal, Hindus and Buddhists worship select girls thought to be the living embodiment of a goddess. This girl, who is 6 years old, lives in a special residence in Kathmandu, the capital of Nepal, with other girl goddesses, or kumaris. Kumaris appear at religious events and bless people. When a kumari reaches puberty, she returns to ordinary life and receives a monthly stipend.

RELIGION

the BIG questions

- What is religion and what are the basic features of religions?
- How do world religions illustrate globalization and localization?
- What are some important aspects of religious change in contemporary times?

OUTLINE

When studying the religious life of people of rural Greece, anthropologist Loring Danforth observed rituals in which participants walk across several yards of burning coals (1989). They do not get burned, they say, because their faith in a saint protects them. Back in the United States, Danforth met an American who regularly walks on fire as part of his New Age faith and organizes training workshops for people who want to learn how to do it. Danforth himself firewalked in a ceremony in rural Maine.

Not every anthropologist who studies religion undertakes such challenges, but they all share an interest in questions about humanity's understanding of the supernatural realm and relationships with it: Why do some religions have many gods and others just one? Why do some religions practice sacrifice? Why do some religions have more participation by women? How do religions respond to changing conditions in the political economy?

Religion has been a cornerstone topic in cultural anthropology since the beginnings of the discipline. The early focus, in the nineteenth century, was on religions of indigenous peoples living in places far from Europe. Now, anthropologists also study the religions of state-level societies and the effects of globalization on religious change.

Christian firewalkers in northern Greece by walking on hot coals. They reaffirm God's protection by not getting burned.

▶ *If you have a religious faith, are pain or other physical discomforts involved in any of the rituals?*

◆◆◆

Religion in Comparative Perspective

This section sets the stage for the chapter by discussing basic areas in the anthropology of religion, including how to define religion, theories about the origin of religion, and types of religious beliefs, rituals, and religious specialists.

WHAT IS RELIGION?

Since the earliest days of anthropology, scholars have proposed various definitions of religion. In the late 1800s, British anthropologist Sir Edward Tylor defined religion as the belief in spirits. A more comprehensive, current definition says that **religion** is beliefs and behavior related to supernatural beings and forces, parallel to our definition of culture. This definition specifically avoids linking religion with belief in a supreme deity because some religions have no concept of a supreme deity, whereas others have multiple deities.

Religion is related to, but not the same as, a people's *worldview*, or way of understanding how the world came to be, its design, and their place in it. Worldview is a broader concept and does not include the criterion of concern with a supernatural realm. An atheist has a worldview, but not a religious one.

MAGIC VERSUS RELIGION Sir Edward Tylor wrote that magic, religion, and science are alike in that they are different ways in which people have tried to explain the physical world and events in it. He considered science to be the superior, most rational of the three. Sir James Frazer, writing at about the same time as Tylor, defined **magic** as people's attempt to compel supernatural forces and beings to act in certain ways (1978 [1890]). He contrasted magic with religion, which he said is the attempt to please supernatural forces or beings. Frazer differentiated two general principles of magic:

- *The law of similarity,* the basis of imitative magic, is founded on the assumption that if person or item X is like person or item Y, then actions done to person or item X will affect person or item Y. A familiar example is a voodoo doll. If someone sticks pins into a doll X that represents person Y, then person Y will experience pain or suffering.
- *The law of contagion,* the basis of contagious magic, says that persons or things once in contact with a person can still have an effect on that person. Common items for working contagious magic include a person's hair trimmings, nail clippings, teeth, saliva, blood, fecal matter, and the placenta of a baby. In cultures where contagious magic is practiced, people are careful about disposing of their personal wastes so that no one else can get hold of them.

---

religion beliefs and behavior related to supernatural beings and forces.

magic the attempt to compel supernatural forces and beings to act in certain ways.

animism the belief in souls or "doubles."

Tylor, Frazer, and other early anthropologists supported an evolutionary model (review Chapter 1), with magic preceding religion. They evaluated magic as being less spiritual and ethical than religion and therefore more "primitive." They assumed that, in time, magic would be completely replaced by the "higher" system of religion, which would eventually be replaced by science as the most rational way of thinking. They would be surprised to see the widespread presence of magical religions in the modern world, such as the so-called Wicca, or Neo-Pagan, religion that centers on respect for the Earth, nature, and the seasonal cycle. An anthropologist who studied Wicca in the San Francisco Bay area learned about beliefs, rituals, and magical practices through participant observation (Magliocco 2004). The pentacle is an important Wicca symbol (see Figure 13.1). As of 2007, the U.S. Veterans Administration added the pentacle to its list of approved religious symbols that can be placed on the headstones of the graves of deceased veterans and their family members.

Many people turn to magical behavior in situations of uncertainty. Magic, for example, is prominent in sports (Gmelch 1997 [1971]). Some baseball players in the United States repeat actions or use charms, including a special shirt or hat, to help them win. This practice is based on the assumption that if it worked before, it may work again. In baseball, pitching and hitting involve more uncertainty than fielding, and pitchers and hitters are more likely to use magic. Magical practices are also common in farming, fishing, the military, and love.

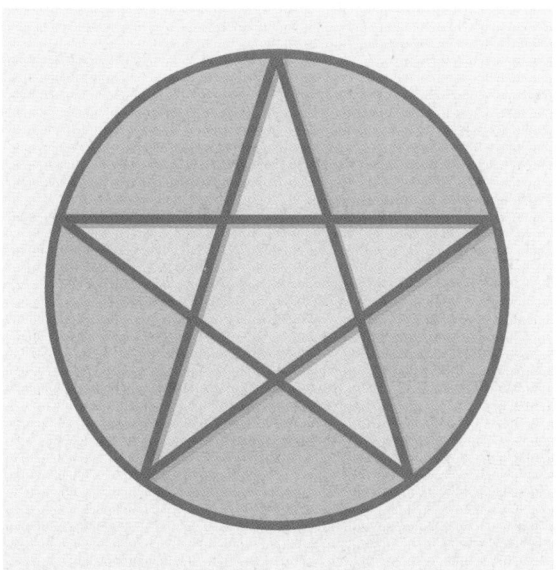

FIGURE 13.1 A Pentacle. Sometimes called a pentagram, it is a five-pointed star surrounded by a circle. An important symbol in Neo-Pagan and Wiccan religions, the pentacle is also a magical tool used for summoning energies and commanding spirits.

THEORIES OF THE ORIGIN AND FUNCTIONS OF RELIGION Many theorists adopt a functionalist approach (review Chapter 1) in explaining why religion is such a pervasive aspect of human culture. According to this view, religion provides ways of explaining and coping with universal human problems such as life and death, illness, and misfortune.

Tylor's theory was based on his assumption that early human ancestors needed to explain the difference between the living and the dead (1871). They therefore developed the concept of a soul that exists in all living things and departs from the body after death. Tylor named this way of thinking **animism**, the belief in souls or "doubles." Tylor speculated that the concept of the soul eventually became personified, and human-like deities were conceived. For Tylor, religion evolved from animism to *polytheism* (the belief in many deities) to *monotheism* (the belief in one supreme deity). Once again, this evolutionary model is proved wrong. Animistic beliefs exist in many religions, including, for example, some Christians' beliefs about visitations of the dead (Stringer 1999), and many contemporary religions are polytheistic.

Throughout the nineteenth and twentieth centuries, functionalist theories about religion continued to emerge. Karl Marx emphasized religion's role as an "opiate of the masses." He thought that religion provides a superficial form of comfort to the poor, masking the harsh realities of class inequality and thereby preventing lower-class uprisings against the rich. In contrast, French scholar Emile Durkheim, in his book *The Elementary Forms of the Religious Life* (1965 [1915]), speculated that early humans understood the benefits of social contact, and therefore they developed group symbols and rituals to maintain social continuity over time. Bronislaw Malinowski suggested that rituals reduce individual anxiety and uncertainty. For Sigmund Freud, religion is a *projective system* that expresses people's unconscious thoughts, wishes, and worries.

More recently, noted cultural anthropologist Clifford Geertz combines Durkheimian functionalism with symbolic analysis (1966). In his view, religions are primarily systems of meaning that provide people with a *model of life* (how to understand the world) and a *model for life* (how to behave in the world). Given the local orientation of early anthropologists, they did not address international questions about religion in terms of how it contributes to world peace and world conflict.

VARIETIES OF RELIGIOUS BELIEFS

Religions comprise beliefs and behavior. Scholars of religion generally address belief systems first because they appear to

THINKING OUTSIDE THE BOX

Take careful note of your daily activities and events for a week and assess them in terms of how magic, religion, or science are involved. What did you find?

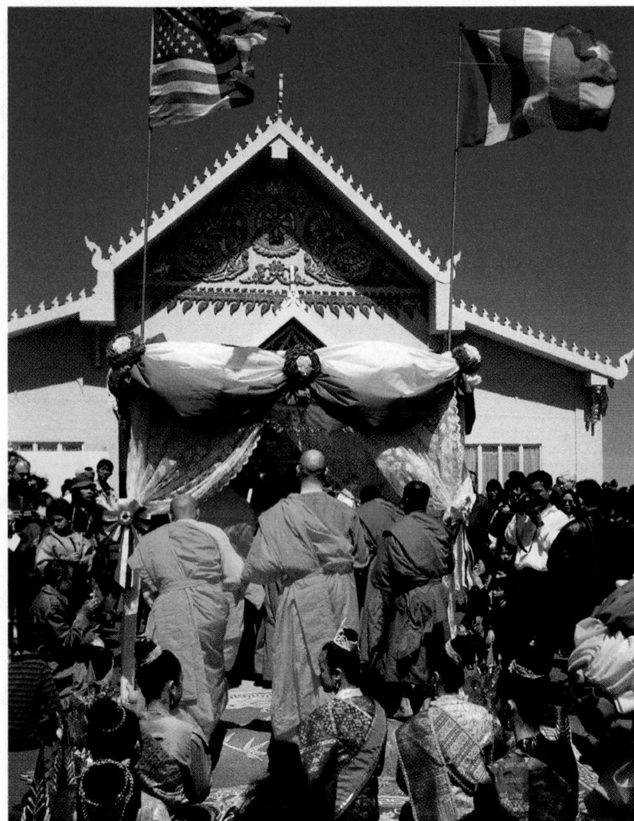

Religion provides an important source of social cohesion and psychological support for many immigrant groups, whose places of worship attract both worshippers and cultural anthropologists interested in learning how religion fits into migrants' adaptation. This is a scene at a Lao Buddhist temple in Virginia.

▶ *Learn about Buddhism in North America from the Internet.*

inform patterns of religious behavior. Religious beliefs are shared by a group, sometimes by millions of people, and are passed on through the generations. Elders teach children through songs and narratives, artists paint the stories on rocks and walls, and sculptors create images in wood and stone that depict aspects of religious belief.

HOW BELIEFS ARE EXPRESSED Beliefs are expressed and transferred over the generations in two main forms:

- **Myth**, stories about supernatural forces or beings
- **Doctrine**, direct statements about religious beliefs

A myth is a narrative that has a plot with a beginning, middle, and end. The plot may involve recurrent motifs, the smallest units of narrative. Myths convey messages about the supernaturals indirectly, through the story itself, rather than by using logic or formal argument. Greek and Roman myths, such as the stories of Zeus, Athena, Orpheus, and Persephone, are world famous. Some people would say that the Bible is a collection of myths; others would object to that categorization as suggesting that the stories are not "real" or "sacred." Myths have long been part of people's oral tradition, and many are still unwritten.

Anthropologists ask why myths exist. Malinowski said that a myth is a charter for society in that it expresses core beliefs and teaches morality. Claude Lévi-Strauss, the most famous mythologist, saw myths as functional in a philosophical and psychological way. In his view, myths help people deal with the deep conceptual contradictions between, for example, life and death and good and evil, by providing stories in which these dualities find a solution in a mediating third factor. These mythological solutions are buried within a variety of surface details in the myth. For example, many myths of the Pueblo Indians of the U.S. Southwest juxtapose grass-eating animals (vegetarians) with predators (carnivores). The mediating third character is the raven, who is a carnivore but, unlike other creatures, does not have to kill to eat meat because it is a scavenger.

A cultural materialist perspective, also functionalist, says that myths store and transmit information related to making a living and managing economic crises (Sobel and Bettles 2000). Analysis of 28 myths of the Klamath and Modoc Indians (see Map 13.1) reveals that subsistence risk is a consistent theme. The myths also describe ways to cope with hunger, such as skill in hunting and fishing, food storage, resource diversification, resource conservation, spatial mobility, reciprocity, and the role of supernatural forces. Thus, myths are repositories of knowledge related to economic survival, crisis management, and environmental conservation.

Doctrine, the other major form in which beliefs are expressed, explicitly defines the supernaturals, the world and

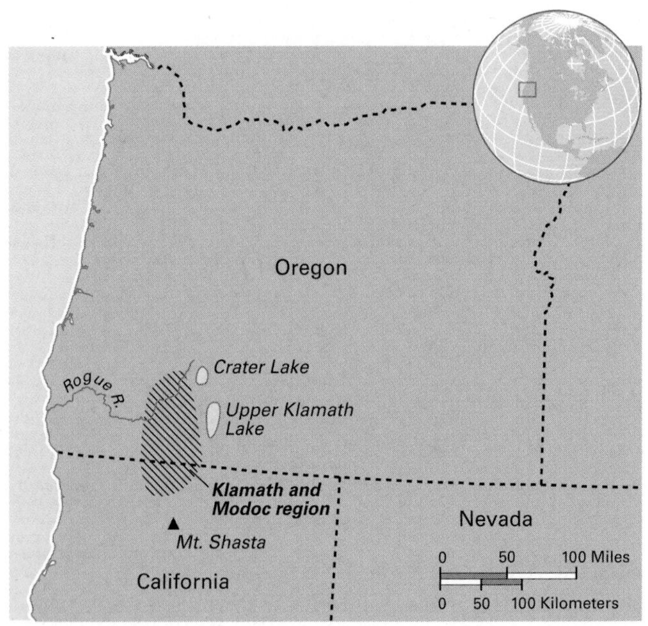

MAP 13.1 Klamath and Modoc Indian Region in Oregon and California.

(LEFT) San rock paintings in the Tsodillo Hills, northwestern Botswana. Some of the paintings date back to 800 CE. The site is sacred to the San people because important spirits come to the hills to rest. (RIGHT) A stone sculpture at Mamallapuram, southern India, dating from the eighth or ninth century, depicts the triumph of the goddess Durga (riding the lion) over the bull-headed demon Mahishasura. This site is now more popular among tourists than among Hindu devotees.

how it came to be, and people's roles in relation to the supernaturals and to other humans. Doctrine is written and formal. It is close to law because it links incorrect beliefs and behaviors with punishments. Doctrine is associated with institutionalized, large-scale religions rather with than small-scale "folk" religions.

Doctrine can and does change (Bowen 1998:38–40). Over the centuries, various popes have pronounced new doctrine for the Catholic Church. A papal declaration of 1854, made with the intent of reinvigorating European Catholicism, bestowed authenticity on the concept of the Immaculate Conception, an idea with substantial popular support.

Muslim doctrine is expressed in the Qu'ran, the basic holy text of the Islamic faith, which consists of revelations made to the prophet Muhammad in the seventh century, and in collections of Muhammad's statements and deeds (Bowen 1998:38). In Kuala Lumpur, Malaysia (see Map 8.3, p. 198), a small group of highly educated women called the Sisters in Islam regularly debate with members of the local *ulama*, religious authorities who are responsible for interpreting Islamic doctrine especially concerning families, education, and commercial affairs (Ong 1995). Debates concern such issues as polygamy, divorce, women's work roles, and women's clothing.

BELIEFS ABOUT SUPERNATURAL FORCES AND BEINGS

Supernaturals range from impersonal forces to those who look just like humans. Supernaturals can be supreme and all-powerful creators or smaller-scale, annoying spirits that take up residence in people through possession.

The term **animatism** refers to a belief system in which the supernatural is conceived of as an impersonal power. An important example is *mana*, a concept widespread throughout the South Pacific region, including Melanesia, Polynesia, and Micronesia. Mana is a force outside nature that works automatically; it is neither spirit nor deity. It manifests itself in objects and people and is associated with personal status and power, because some people accumulate more of it than others.

Some supernaturals are *zoomorphic*, deities in the shape, or partial shape, of animals. No satisfactory theory has appeared to explain why some religions develop zoomorphic deities, and for what purposes, and why others do not. Religions of classical Greece and Rome and ancient and contemporary Hinduism are especially rich in zoomorphic supernaturals. *Anthropomorphic* supernaturals, deities in the form of humans, are common but not universal. The human tendency to perceive of supernaturals in their own form was noted 2500 years ago by the Greek philosopher Xenophanes, who lived sometime between 570 and 470 BCE. He said,

> But if horses or oxen or lions had hands and could draw with their hands and accomplish such works as men, horses would draw the figures of their gods as similar to horses and the oxen as similar to oxen, and they would make the bodies of the sort which each of them had (Lesher 2001:25).

The question, though, of why some religions have anthropomorphic deities and others do not is impossible to answer.

Anthropomorphic supernaturals, like humans, can be moved by praise, flattery, and gifts. They have emotions. They

---

myth a narrative with a plot that involves the supernaturals.

doctrine direct and formalized statements about religious beliefs.

animatism a belief system in which the supernatural is conceived of as an impersonal power.

eye on the ENVIRONMENT

Eagle Protection, National Parks, and the Preservation of Hopi Indian Culture

For many generations, young men of the Hopi Indian tribe have searched each spring for golden eaglets in the cliffs of Arizona's Wupatki National Park and other parts of northeastern Arizona (Fenstemaker 2007). They bring the young eagles to the reservation and care for them until the summer when, as mature birds, they are smothered in a ceremony that the Hopi believe frees the spirits of the birds, which convey messages to their ancestors who reside in the spiritual world. This ceremony is the most important Hopi ritual, but they use golden eagle feathers in all their rituals. For the Hopi, golden eagles are their link to the spiritual world, and their ritual use is essential to the continuity of their culture.

In 1783, the Continental Congress adopted the bald eagle as the national symbol of the newly independent country. By 1940, numbers of bald eagles had dropped so low that the U.S. Congress passed the Bald Eagle Protection Act to preserve the species that had become established as the symbol of American ideals of freedom. In 1962, Congress amended the act to include golden eagles, because the young of each species are nearly indistinguishable.

In 1994, President Clinton promoted some official accommodation to Hopi beliefs about golden eagles. His administration established a repository for golden eagle feathers and other remains in Colorado. The demand is, however, higher than the supply.

The Hopi have a permit for an annual take of 40 golden eagles in northeastern Arizona, but they are excluded from Wupatki because of its status as a national park. The United States policy toward national parks follows the *Yellowstone model,* which aims to preserve the physical environment and species but excludes indigenous peoples and their cultures. This model has been applied widely throughout the world to the detriment of peoples who have, for long, successfully lived in regions that are now off limits to them for hunting, fishing, and gathering. In addition, many of these lands are sacred to them, but they are prevented from using them in traditional ways for the sake of "conservation" as defined by the government.

Anthropologists and others support environmental and species preservation, but not to the exclusion of heritage populations and cultures. They suggest that a case-by-case approach should be followed in considering exemptions to national laws. In terms of the golden eagles of Arizona, they point out that golden eagles are abundant, and the Hopi requests for the spring take are small and present no threat to the survival of the species.

Environmentalists are concerned, however, that granting exemptions will establish dangerous precedents that will, over time, destroy pristine environments and precious species. Other environmentalists counter that more eagles are killed every year by airplanes or contact with electrical wires, or they die from eating prey that contain lead bullets.

---

get annoyed if neglected. They can be loving and caring, or they can be distant and nonresponsive. Most anthropomorphic supernaturals are adults, though some are children. Supernaturals tend to have similar marital and sexual relationships as the humans who worship them do. Divine marriages are heterosexual, and in some societies male gods have multiple wives. Although many supernaturals have children, grandchildren are not prominent. In *pantheons* (collectivities of deities), a division of labor reflects specializations in human society. There may be deities of forests, rivers, the sky, wind and rain, agriculture, childbirth, disease, warfare, and marital happiness. The supernaturals have political roles and hierarchies. High gods, such as Jupiter and Juno of classical Roman religion, are all-powerful, with a range of less powerful deities and spirits below them.

In some cultures, deceased ancestors can be supernaturals. Many African, Asian, and Native American religions have a cult of the ancestors in which the living must do certain things to please the dead ancestors and may also ask for their help in time of need (see Eye on the Environment). In contemporary Japan, ancestor worship is the principal religious activity of many families. Three national holidays recognize the importance of the ancestors: the annual summer visit of the dead to their homes and the visits by the living to graves during the two equinoxes.

BELIEFS ABOUT SACRED SPACE Beliefs about sacred space probably exist in all religions, but such beliefs are more prominent in some religions than others. Sacred spaces, such as rock formations or rapids in a river, may or may not be permanently marked (Bradley 2000). Among the Saami (see Culturama in Chapter 12, p. 309), traditional religious beliefs were closely tied to sacred natural sites (Mulk 1994). The sites, often unmarked, included rock formations resembling humans, animals, or birds. The Saami sacrificed animals and fish at these sites until strong pressures from Christian missionaries forced them to repress their practices and beliefs. Many Saami today know where the sacred sites are, but they will not reveal them to outsiders.

A Kachina doll. Among the Hopi, the word "Kachina" (kuh-CHEE-nuh) refers to a spirit or "life-bringer." Uncles carve Kachina dolls for their nieces to help them learn about the many spirits that exist in the Hopi religion. Kachina dolls, especially older ones, are highly sought after by non-Indians who collect Indian artifacts.

0 25 50 Miles
0 25 50 Kilometers
Utah
Colorado
Navajo Nation
Hopi Reservation
New Mexico
Arizona
Flagstaff

MAP 13.2 Hopi Indian Reservation in Arizona. The Hopi and Navajo tribes once shared the area known as Big Mountain. U.S. Acts of Congress in 1974 and 1996 divided the area into two reservations, leaving the Hopi completely surrounded by the much larger Navajo reservation. About 7000 people live on the Hopi Reservation.

In contrast to the Yellowstone model, anthropologists advocate for a *parks and people approach,* which builds on community-based conservation that does not exclude heritage populations from continuing to enjoy the economic and religious benefits of their territory while also sharing with the wider population.

◆ **FOOD FOR THOUGHT**

- Consider how you would feel if you were told that you could no longer practice the most important annual ritual in your religion but that other people could have a touristic experience at the place where you would normally practice the ritual. For secular students, consider a secular ritual, for example, watching the Super Bowl.

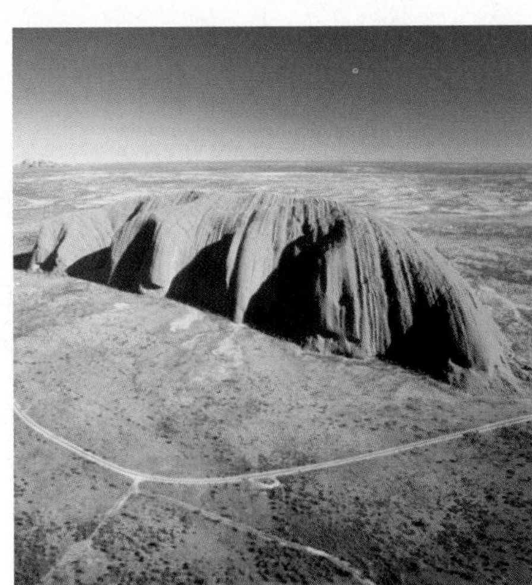

Uluru, Kata Tjuta National Park, Australia. Located roughly in the center of Australia in the Northern Territory and 280 miles south of Alice Springs, Uluru is an Aboriginal sacred site and a World Heritage Site. Tourists often want to make the arduous climb to the top, though the Anangu people who are the custodians urge people to consider other ways to enjoy the region.

Another important form of sacred space that has no permanent mark occurs in a domestic ritual conducted by Muslim women throughout the world called the *khatam quran* (kuh-RAHN), the "sealing" or reading of the holy book of the Qu'ran (Werbner 1988). Among Pakistani migrants living in the city of Manchester, northern England (see Map 13.3), the ritual involves a gathering of women who read the Qu'ran and then share a ritual meal. The reason for gathering is to give thanks or seek divine blessing. During the ritual, the otherwise nonsacred space of the house becomes sacred. A "portable" ritual such as this one is especially helpful in migrant adaptation because it can be conducted without a formally consecrated ritual space. All that is required is a place, a supportive group of kin and friends, and the Qu'ran.

Religions of the Aboriginal people of Australia are closely tied to sacred space. During a mythological past called the *Dream Time,* the ancestors walked the earth and marked out the territory belonging to a particular group. People's knowledge of where the ancestors roamed is secret. In several

MAP 13.3 England.
England is the largest of the constituent countries of the United Kingdom, and its population of 50 million accounts for 84 percent of the total. DNA analysis reveals that a majority of the English are of Germanic descent, as is their language. The terrain is mainly rolling hills, with some mountains in the north and east. London is by far the largest city, with Manchester and Birmingham competing for second place. English is the dominant language, with its diverse regional accents. Many other languages brought into the country by immigrant communities are spoken as first languages, including several South Asian languages, Polish, Greek, and Cantonese. An estimated 250,000 people speak British Sign Language. Although the Church of England is the state religion, everyone in England has the right to religious freedom.

cases that have recently been brought to the courts, Aboriginal peoples have claimed title to land that is being sought by commercial developers. Some anthropologists have provided expert testimony documenting the validity of the Aboriginal claims to their sacred space. In one such case, secret Aboriginal knowledge about a sacred place and its associated beliefs was gender specific: It belonged to women and could not be told to men. The anthropologist who was hired to support the women's claims was a woman, so the women could tell her about the sacred places, but she could not convey that knowledge in court to the male judge, a situation that demanded considerable ingenuity on the part of the anthropological consultant (see Lessons Applied).

RITUAL PRACTICES

A **ritual** is patterned behavior that is focused on the supernatural realm. Many rituals are the enactment of beliefs expressed in myth and doctrine, such as the Christian ritual of communion. Rituals are distinct from *secular rituals,* such as a sorority or fraternity initiation or a common-law wedding, which are patterned forms of behavior with no connection to the supernatural realm. Some ritual events combine sacred and secular elements. The U.S. holiday of Thanksgiving originated as a Christian sacred meal with the primary purpose of giving thanks to God for the survival of the pilgrims (Siskind 1992). Its original Christian meaning is not maintained by everyone who celebrates the holiday today. Secular features of the holiday, such as watching football, may be of greater importance than the ritual aspect of thanking God for plentiful food.

Anthropologists categorize rituals in many ways. One division is based on their timing. Regularly performed rituals are called *periodic rituals*. Many periodic rituals are performed annually to mark a seasonal milestone such as planting or harvesting or to commemorate some important event. For example, an important periodic ritual in Buddhism, or Buddha's Day, commemorates the birth, enlightenment, and death of the Buddha all on one day. On this day, Buddhists gather at monasteries, hear sermons about the Buddha, and perform rituals such as pouring water over images of the Buddha. Calendrical events such as the shortest day of the year, the longest day, the new moon, and the full moon often

A gathering of contemporary Druids at Stonehenge, England. The Druids, who claim that Stonehenge is important to their religion, are one of several groups with interests in the preservation of this World Heritage Site and access to it. Public debates concern possible changes in the location of nearby roads, the planting or removing of trees, and how close the public can get to the stones.

▶ *As a research project, learn about the various groups and preservation issues related to Stonehenge.*

---

ritual a patterned behavior that has to do with the supernatural realm.

life-cycle ritual a ritual that marks a change in status from one life stage to another; also called rite of passage.

LESSONS applied

Aboriginal Australian Women's Culture, Sacred Site Protection, and the Anthropologist as Expert Witness

A group of Ngarrindjeri (nar-en-jeer-ee) women and their lawyer hired cultural anthropologist Diane Bell to serve as a consultant to them in supporting their claims to a sacred site in southern Australia (Bell 1998). The area on Hindmarsh Island was threatened by the proposed construction of a bridge that would cross sacred waters between the mainland and the island.

The women claimed protection for the area and sought prevention of the bridge project on the basis of their secret knowledge of its sacredness, knowledge passed down in trust from mother to daughter over generations. The High Commission formed by the government to investigate their claim considered it to be a hoax perpetrated to block a project important to the country.

Helping the women prove their case to a White, male-dominated court system was a challenging task for Diane Bell, a White Australian with extensive fieldwork experience among Aboriginal women. Bell conducted research over many months to marshal evidence for the validity of the women's claims. She examined newspaper archives, early recordings of ritual songs, and oral histories of Ngarrindjeri women. She prepared reports for the courtroom about women's sacred knowledge that were general enough to avoid violating the secrecy rule that applies to women-only knowledge but detailed enough to convince the High Court judge that the women's sacred knowledge was authentic. In the end, the judge was convinced, and the bridge project was canceled in 1999.

◆ **FOOD FOR THOUGHT**

- Learn more about this case and other disputes in Australia over sacred sites, from the Internet.

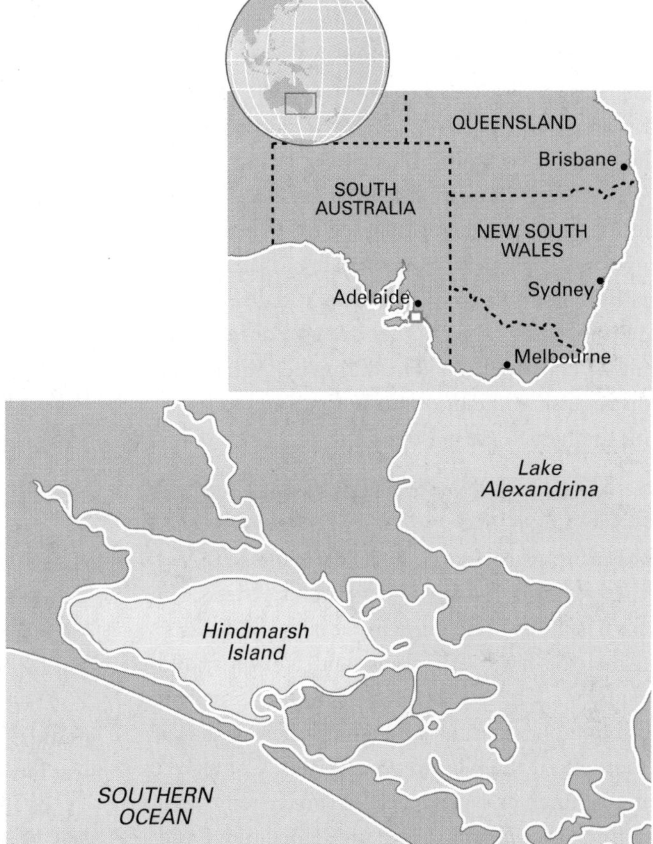

MAP 13.4 Hindmarsh Island in Southeast Australia. The Ngarrindjeri name for Hindmarsh Island is Kumarangk.

shape ritual cycles. *Nonperiodic rituals,* in contrast, occur irregularly, at unpredictable times, in response to unscheduled events such as a drought or flood, or to mark events in a person's life such as illness, infertility, birth, marriage, or death. The following material presents highlights of various ritual types.

LIFE-CYCLE RITUALS A **life-cycle ritual**, or rite of passage, marks a change in status from one life stage to another of an individual or group. Victor Turner's (1969) fieldwork among the Ndembu (en-dem-boo), horticulturalists of northwestern Zambia (see Map 11.2, p. 274) provides insights about the phases of life-cycle rituals. Turner found that among the Ndembu, and cross-culturally, life-cycle rituals have three phases: *separation, transition,* and *reintegration.*

- In the first phase, the initiate (the person undergoing the ritual) is separated physically, socially, or symbolically from normal life. Special dress may mark the separation. In many cultures of the Amazon and in East and

West Africa, adolescents are secluded for several years in separate huts or areas away from the village.

- The transition, or *liminal,* phase, is when the person is no longer in the previous status but is not yet a member of the next stage. Liminality often involves the learning of specialized skills that will equip the person for the new status.
- Reintegration, the last stage, occurs when the initiate emerges and is welcomed by the community in the new status.

Differences in the cross-cultural distribution of puberty rituals for boys and girls reflect the economic value and status of males and females (review Chapter 6). Most societies have some form of puberty ceremony for boys, but puberty ceremonies for girls are less common. In societies where female labor is important and valued, girls have elaborate, and sometimes painful, puberty rites (Brown 1978). Where their labor is not important, menarche is unmarked and there is no puberty ceremony. Puberty rites function to socialize future members of the labor force, among other things. For example, among the Bemba of northern Zambia, during her initiation a girl learns to distinguish 40 kinds of mushrooms and to know which are edible and which are poisonous.

An Apache girl's puberty ceremony. Cross-cultural research indicates that the celebration of girls' puberty is more likely to occur in cultures in which adult women have valued productive and reproductive roles.

▶ *How does this theory apply to your microcultural experience?*

PILGRIMAGE **Pilgrimage** is round-trip travel to a sacred place or places for purposes of religious devotion or ritual. Prominent pilgrimage places are Varanasi (var-uh-NAS-ee) in India (formerly called Banaras) for Hindus; Mecca in Saudi Arabia for Muslims; Bodh Gaya in India for Buddhists; Jerusalem in Israel for Jews, Christians, and Muslims; and Lourdes in France for Christians. Pilgrimage often involves hardship, with the implication that the more suffering that is involved, the more merit the pilgrim accumulates. Compared to a weekly trip to church or synagogue, pilgrimage removes a person further from everyday life, is more demanding, and therefore is potentially more transformative.

Victor Turner applied the three sequences of life-cycle rituals to pilgrimage: The pilgrim first separates from everyday life, then enters the liminal stage during the actual pilgrimage, and then returns to be reintegrated into society in a transformed state. A person who has gone on a pilgrimage often gains enhanced public status as well as spiritual benefits.

RITUALS OF INVERSION In **rituals of inversion**, normal social roles and relations are temporarily inverted. A functionalist perspective says that these rituals allow for social pressure to be released. They also provide a reminder about the propriety of normal, everyday roles and practices to which people must return once the ritual is over.

Carnival (or *carnaval* in Portuguese-speaking Brazil) is a ritual of inversion with roots in the northern Mediterranean region. It is celebrated widely throughout southern Europe and the Western Hemisphere. Carnival is a period of riotous celebration before the Christian fast of Lent. It begins at different times in different places, but always ends on Mardi Gras (or Shrove Tuesday), the day before the fasting period of Lent begins. The word "carnival," from Latin, means "flesh farewell," referring to the fact that believers give up eating meat during Lent .

In Bosa, a town in Sardegna (Sardinia), Italy (see Map 13.5), carnival involves social-role reversal and relaxing of usual social norms. Discotheques extend their hours, mothers allow their daughters to stay out late, and men and women flirt with each other in public in ways that are forbidden during the rest of the year (Counihan 1985). Carnival in Bosa has three major phases. The first is impromptu street theater and masquerades that take place over several weeks, usually on Sundays. The skits are social critiques of current events and local happenings. In the masquerades, men dress up as exaggerated women:

> Young boys thrust their padded breasts forward with their hands while brassily hiking up their skirts to reveal their thighs. . . . A youth stuffs his shirt front with melons and holds them proudly out. . . . The high school gym teacher dresses as a nun and lifts up his habit to reveal suggestive red underwear. Two men wearing nothing but bikinis, wigs, and high heels feign a stripper's dance on a table top. (1985:15)

---

pilgrimage round-trip travel to a sacred place or places for purposes of religious devotion or ritual.

ritual of inversion a ritual in which normal social roles and order are temporarily reversed.

sacrifice a ritual in which something is offered to the supernaturals.

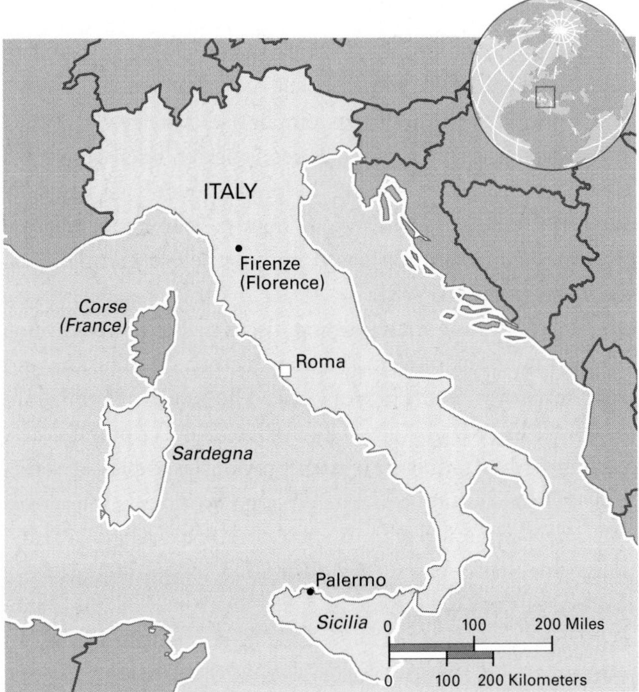

MAP 13.5 Italy.
Officially the Italian Republic, the country includes the mainland and two large islands. In 2006, Italy had the seventh highest GDP in the world. A mountain system forms the backbone of the peninsula, and the climate varies according to altitude. Its population of nearly 60 million people makes it one of the most densely populated countries in Europe. Roman Catholicism is the dominant religion. Recent waves of immigration, especially from northern Africa, have increased the number of Muslims to perhaps 1 million. The official language is standard Italian, descended from the Tuscan dialect of Firenze (Florence). Many cherished dialects of Italian exist throughout the country; people in northern border provinces speak dialects of German and French. Italy has the largest number of UNESCO World Heritage Sites of any country.

The second phase occurs on the morning of Mardi Gras, when hundreds of Bosans, mostly men, dress in black, like widows, and flood the streets. They accost passersby, shaking in their faces dolls and other objects that are maimed in some way or bloodied. They shriek at the top of their lungs as if mourning, and they say, "Give us milk, milk for our babies. . . . They are dying, they are neglected, their mothers have been gallivanting since St. Anthony's Day and have abandoned their poor children" (1985:16).

The third phase, called *Giolzi,* takes place during the evening. Men and women dress in white, wearing sheets for cloaks and pillow cases for hoods. They blacken their faces. Rushing into the street, they hold hands and chant the word "Giolzi." They storm at people, pretending to search their bodies for Giolzi and then say, "Got it!" It is not clear what Giolzi is, but whatever it is, it represents something that makes everyone happy.

SACRIFICE Many rituals involve **sacrifice**, or the offering of something for transfer to the supernaturals. Sacrifice has a long history throughout the world and is probably one of the oldest forms of ritual. It may involve killing and offering animals; making human offerings (of whole people, parts of a person's body, or bloodletting); or offering vegetables, fruits, grains, flowers, or other products. One interpretation of flowers as sacrificial offerings is that they, like vegetables and fruits, are symbolic replacements for former animal sacrifices (Goody 1993).

Spanish documents from the sixteenth century describe the Aztec practice of public sacrifice of humans and other animals to please the gods. The details are gory and involve marching thousands of human victims up to the top of a temple and then cutting out their hearts so that the blood spurts forth. Debate exists among anthropologists as to how many victims were actually sacrificed and why. Marvin Harris has argued that the numbers were large, up to 100,000 at particular sites, and that the remains of the victims were butchered and eaten by commoners (1977). His argument is that the Aztec state, through such rituals, both demonstrated its power and provided protein to the masses. In opposition to Harris, symbolic anthropologist Peggy Sanday takes an emic perspective and says that the sacrifices were necessary to please the gods and had nothing to do with maintaining the worldly power of leaders or feeding the masses (1986).

RELIGIOUS SPECIALISTS

Not all rituals require the presence of a religious specialist, or someone with extensive, formal training, but all require some level of knowledge on the part of the performer(s) about how to do them correctly. Even the daily, household veneration of an ancestor requires some knowledge gained through informal learning. At the other extreme, many rituals cannot be done without a highly trained specialist.

SHAMANS AND PRIESTS General features of the categories of shaman and priest illustrate key differences between these two types of specialists (many other specialists fit somewhere in between). A *shaman* or *shamanka* (as defined in Chapter 7) is a religious specialist who has a direct relationship with the supernaturals, often by being "called." A potential shaman may be recognized by special signs, such as the ability to go into a trance. Anyone who demonstrates shamanic abilities can become a shaman; in other words, this is an openly available role. Shamans are more often associated with nonstate societies, yet faith healers and evangelists of the United States could fit in this category (review the discussion in Chapter 7 of shamanic specialists as healers).

In states, the more complex occupational specialization in religion means that there is a wider variety of types of specialists, especially what anthropologists refer to as *priests* (not the same as the specific modern role of the Catholic priest) and promotes the development of religious hierarchies and power structures. The terms **priest** and **priestess** refer to a category of full-time religious specialists whose position is based mainly on abilities gained through formal training. A priest may receive a divine call, but more often the role is hereditary, passed on through priestly lineages. In terms of ritual performance, shamans are more involved with nonperiodic rituals. Priests perform a wider range of rituals, including periodic state rituals. In contrast to shamans, who rarely have secular power, priests and priestly lineages often do.

OTHER SPECIALISTS Many other specialized religious roles exist cross-culturally. *Diviners* are specialists who are able to discover the will and wishes of the supernaturals through techniques such as reading animal entrails. Palm readers and tarot card readers fit into the category of diviners.

Prophets are specialists who convey divine revelations usually gained through visions or dreams. They often possess charisma, an especially attractive and powerful personality, and may be able to perform miracles. Prophets have founded new religions, some long-lasting and others short-lived.

Witches use psychic powers and affect people through emotion and thought. Mainstream society often condemns witchcraft as negative. Some scholars of ancient and contemporary witchcraft differentiate between positive forms that involve healing and negative forms that seek to harm people.

World Religions and Local Variations

The term **world religion** was coined in the nineteenth century to refer to religions that were text-based, with many followers that crossed country borders and had a concern with salvation (the belief that human beings require deliverance from an imperfect world). At that time, the term referred only to Christianity, Islam, and Buddhism. It was later expanded to include Judaism, Hinduism, Confucianism, Taoism, and Shintoism. Because of the global importance of the African diaspora that began with the European colonial slave trade, a sixth category of world religions is included here that describes key elements shared among the diversity of traditional African belief systems.

For many centuries, the world religions have traveled outside their original borders through intentional attempts to expand and gain converts or through migration of believers to new locales. European colonialism was a major force that led to the expansion of Christianity through the missionary work of Protestant sects. Now, the increased rate of population migration (Chapter 15) and the expansion of television and the Internet give even greater impetus to religious movement and change. The designation of only five world religions is increasingly inappropriate, because many religions cross state boundaries and have "world" reach.

Cultural anthropologists emphasize that no world religion exists as a single, homogeneous entity. Each comprises many local variants, raising a "predicament" for centrally organized religions in terms of how to maintain a balance between standardization based on core beliefs and the local variations (Hefner 1998).

The following material first discusses the five traditional world religions in terms of their history, distribution, and basic teachings (see Figure 13.2). The world religions are presented in order by age, largely based on scriptural dates, starting with Hinduism. It then provides examples of variations in local cultural contexts. When a world religion moves into a new cultural region, it encounters local religious traditions. In many cases, the incoming religion and local religions coexist as separate traditions, either as complements or competitors, in what is called **religious pluralism**. In **religious syncretism**, elements of two or more religions blend together. It is most likely to occur when aspects of two religions form a close match with each other. For example, if a local myth involves a hero who has something to do with snakes, there may be a syncretistic link with the Catholic belief in St. Patrick, who is believed to have driven snakes out of Ireland.

Many situations of nonfit also exist. For example, Christian missionaries have had difficulty translating the Bible into some indigenous languages because of lack of matching words or concepts, and because of differing kinship and social structures. Some Amazonian groups, such as the Pirahã (review Chapter 12), have no word that corresponds with the Christian concept of "heaven" (Everett 1995, personal communication). In other cases, matrilineal

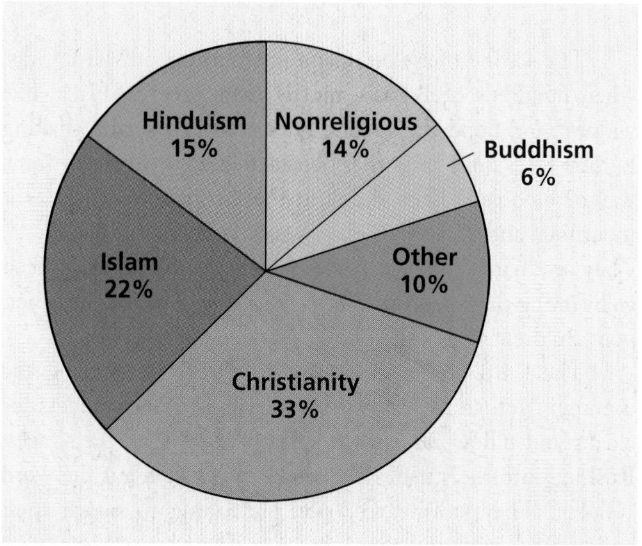

FIGURE 13.2 Population Distribution of Major World Religions

peoples have found it difficult to understand the significance of the Christian construct of "god the father."

The two world religions that emphasize proselytizing, or seeking converts, are Christianity and Islam. Their encounters with local religions have sometimes been violent, involving physical destruction of sacred places and objects (Corbey 2003). Common methods include burning, overturning, dismantling, or cutting up sacred objects, dumping them into rivers, and hiding them in caves. European Christian missionaries in the 1800s often confiscated sacred goods and shipped them to Europe for sale to private owners or museums. Both Christian and Islamic conversion efforts frequently involved the construction of their own places of worship on top of the original sacred site. Conflict between these two religions is, unfortunately, not a matter of the past only.

An early nineteenth-century painting of the Virgin of Guadalupe by Isidro Escamilla, a Mexican artist. The Virgin of Guadalupe, or Our Lady of Guadalupe, is Mexico's most popular image. Her depiction may involve syncretism with the indigenous Aztec goddess Tonantzin, part of a conscious strategy of Christian clergy to convert the Indians. Today, the Virgin of Guadalupe conveys messages of sacrifice and nurturance as well as strength and hope. She appeals to Mexican mothers, nationalists, and feminists alike.

HINDUISM

Around 920 million people in the world are Hindus. (*Note:* Population statistics for the world religions are rough averages derived from several Internet sources.) About 97 percent of all Hindus live in India, where Hinduism accounts for 80 percent of the population. The rest live throughout the world in countries such as Bangladesh, Myanmar, Pakistan, Sri Lanka, the United States, Canada, the United Kingdom, Malaysia, Fiji, Trinidad, Guyana, and Hong Kong. A Hindu is born a Hindu, and Hinduism does not actively seek converts. The core texts of Hinduism are the four Vedas, which were composed in Sanskrit in northern India between 1200 and 900 BCE. Many other scholarly texts, epics and stories, and oral traditions enrich the Hindu tradition. The two most widely-known stories are the *Mahabharata* (muh-huh-BHAR-uh-tuh), the story of a war between two patrilineages in which Krishna plays an important role, and the *Ramayana* (ruh-MY-uh-nuh), the story of King Rama and his devoted wife, Sita. Throughout India, many local stories also exist, some containing elements from pre-Vedic times.

Hinduism offers a rich polytheism and at the same time a philosophical tradition that reduces the multiplicity of deities into oneness. Deities range from being a simple stone placed at the foot of a tree to elegantly carved and painted icons of gods such as Shiva and Vishnu and the goddesses Durga and Saraswati. Everyday worship of a deity involves lighting a lamp in front of the god, chanting hymns and mantras (sacred phrases), and taking *darshan* (DAR-shun), which means seeing the deity, usually in the form of an icon (Eck 1985). These acts bring blessings to the worshipper. Local variations of worship often involve deities and rituals unknown elsewhere. For example, firewalking is an important part of goddess worship in southern and eastern India (Freeman 1981) and among some Hindu groups living outside India, notably Fiji (Brown 1984).

---

priest/priestess male or female full-time religious specialist whose position is based mainly on abilities gained through formal training.

world religion a term coined in the nineteenth century to refer to a religion that is text-based, has many followers, is regionally widespread, and is concerned with salvation.

religious pluralism when one or more religions coexist as either complementary to each other or as competitive systems.

religious syncretism the blending of features of two or more cultures, especially used in discussion of religious change.

Caste differences in beliefs and practices are also marked, even within the same village. Lower-caste deities prefer offerings of meat sacrifices and alcohol, whereas upper-caste deities prefer flowers, rice, and fruit. Yet the "unity in diversity" of Hinduism has long been recognized as real, mainly because of the shared acceptance of at least some elements of Vedic thought.

A NAYAR FERTILITY RITUAL The matrilineal Nayars (nai-ers) of Kerala, South India (see Map 16.2, p. 400), perform a nonperiodic ritual as a remedy for the curse of the serpent deities who cause infertility in women (Neff 1994). This ritual illustrates the unity of Hinduism in several ritual elements: the use of a camphor flame and incense, the importance of serpent deities, and offering flowers to the deity. Locally specific elements are related to the matrilineal cultural context of Kerala.

The all-night ritual includes, first, women painting a sacred design of intertwined serpents on the floor. Several hours of worshipping the deity follow, with the camphor flame, incense, and flowers. Music comes from drumming, cymbals, and singing. The presence of the deity is fully achieved when one of the women goes into a trance. Through her, matrilineal family members may speak to the deity and be blessed.

Among the Nayars, a woman's mother, mother's brothers, and brothers are responsible for ensuring that her desires for motherhood are fulfilled. They share her interest in continuing the matrilineage. What the women say during the trance is important. They typically draw attention to family disharmonies or neglect of the deities. This message diverts blame from the infertile woman for whom the ritual is being held. It reminds family and lineage members of their responsibilities for each other.

Celebration of Holi, a spring festival popular among Hindus worldwide. In this scene in New Delhi, a young woman sprays colored water on a young man as part of the joyous event. The deeper meaning of Holi is tied to a myth about a demon.
▶ *Is the arrival of spring ritually marked in your culture?*

HINDU WOMEN AND KARMA IN NORTHERN ENGLAND
One of Hinduism's basic concepts is *karma,* translated as "destiny" or "fate." A person's karma is determined at birth on the basis of his or her previous life and how it was conducted. The karma concept has prompted many outsiders to judge Hindus as fatalistic, lacking a sense of agency. But anthropological research on how people actually think about karma in their everyday lives reveals much individual variation from fatalism to a strong sense of being in charge of one's destiny. One study looked at women's perceptions of karma among Hindus living in the city of Leeds, northern England (Knott 1996) (see Map 13.3, p. 322). Some of the women are fatalistic in their attitudes and behavior. One woman who had a strongly fatalistic view of karma said,

> When a baby's born . . . we have a ritual on the sixth day. That's when you name the baby, you know. And on that day, we believe the goddess comes and writes your future . . . we leave a blank white paper and a pen and we just leave it [overnight]. . . . So I believe that my future—whatever happens—is what she has written for me. That tells me [that] I have to do what I can do, and if I have a mishap in between I have to accept that. (1996:24)

Another woman said that her sufferings were caused by the irresponsibility of her father and the "bad husband" to whom she had been married. She challenged her karma and left her husband: "I could not accept the karma of being with Nirmal [her husband]. If I had done so, what would have become of my children?" (1996:25). Because Hindu women's karma dictates being married and having children, leaving one's husband is a major act of resistance.

Options for women seeking support when questioning or changing their karmic roles can be religious, such as praying more and fasting, or they can be secular, such as seeking the advice of a psychological counselor or social worker. Some Hindu women in England have become counselors, working in support of other women's independence and self-confidence. They illustrate how human agency can work against traditional religious rules.

BUDDHISM

Buddhism originated in a founding figure, Siddhartha Gautama (ca. 566–486 BCE), revered as the Buddha, or Awakened One (Eckel 1995:135). It began in northern India, where the Buddha grew up. From there, it spread throughout the subcontinent, into inner Asia and China, to Sri Lanka, and on to Southeast Asia. In the past 200 years, Buddhism has spread to Europe and North America. Buddhism's popularity declined in India, and Buddhists now constitute less than 1 percent of India's population. Its global spread is matched by a great diversity of doctrine and practice, to the extent that it is difficult to point to a single essential feature other than the importance of Gautama Buddha. No single text is accepted as authoritative for all forms of Buddhism. Many Buddhists worship the Buddha as a deity, but others do not. Instead, they honor his teachings and follow the pathway he suggested for reaching *nirvana*, or release from worldly life. The total number of Buddhists worldwide is around 400 million.

Buddhism arose as a protest against Hinduism, especially caste inequality, but it retained and revised several Hindu concepts, such as karma. In Buddhism, everyone has the potential for achieving nirvana (enlightenment and the overcoming of human suffering in this life), the ultimate goal of Buddhism. Good deeds are one way to achieve a better rebirth with each incarnation, until finally, release from *samsara* (the cycle of birth, reincarnation, death, and so on) is achieved. Compassion toward others, including animals, is a key virtue. Branches of Buddhism have different texts that they consider their canon. The major division is between the Theravada Buddhism practiced in Southeast Asia and the Mahayana Buddhism of Tibet, China, Taiwan, Korea, and Japan. Buddhism is associated with a strong tradition of monasticism through which monks and nuns renounce the everyday world and spend their lives meditating and doing good works. Buddhists have many and varied annual festivals and rituals. Some events bring pilgrims from around the world to Sarnath, near Varanasi, North India, where the Buddha gave his first teaching, and to Gaya, where he gained enlightenment.

Buddhism gained an established footing in Japan in the eighth century. The city of Nara was an important early center of Buddhism. An emperor sponsored the casting of this huge bronze statue of the Buddha.

▶ *Is there a Buddhist temple where you live? If so, have you visited it? If not, find out where the nearest one is, and visit it if possible.*

LOCAL SPIRITS AND BUDDHISM IN SOUTHEAST ASIA
Wherever Buddhism exists outside India, it is never the exclusive religion of the devotees because it arrived to find established local religions already in place (Spiro 1967). In Myanmar, Buddhism and indigenous traditions coexist without one being dominant (see Map 6.7, p. 157). Indigenous beliefs remained strong because they offer a way of dealing with everyday problems. Buddhist beliefs about karma in Myanmar are similar to those in Hinduism: A person's karma is the result of previous births and determines his or her present condition. If something bad happens, the person can do little but suffer through it.

In contrast, indigenous supernaturalism says that the bad things happen because of the actions of capricious spirits called *nats*. Ritual actions, however, can combat the influence of nats. Thus, people can deal with nats but not with karma. The continuity of belief in nats is an example of human agency and creativity. Burmese people kept what was important to them from their traditional beliefs and adopted aspects of the new religion.

Buddhism became an important cultural force and the basis for social integration in Myanmar. A typical village may have one or more Buddhist monasteries and several resident monks. All boys are ordained as temporary members of the monastic order. Almost every villager observes Buddhist holy days. Nonetheless, although Buddhism is held to be the supreme truth, the spirits retain control when it comes to dealing with everyday problems such as a toothache or a monetary loss. In Myanmar, the two traditions exist in a pluralistic situation as two separate options.

Other studies of religion in Southeast Asia provide examples in which there is more thorough blending, or syncretism, of local religions with Buddhism (see Everyday Anthropology).

JUDAISM

The first Judaic religious system was defined around 500 BCE, following the destruction of the Temple in Jerusalem by the Babylonians in 586 BCE (Neusner 1995). The early writings, called the Pentateuch (pen-ta-took), established the theme of exile and return as a paradigm for Judaism that endures today. The Pentateuch is also called the Five Books of Moses, or the Torah. Followers of Judaism share in the belief in the Torah as the revelation of God's truth through Israel, a term for the "holy people." The Torah explains the relationship between the supernatural and human realms and guides people in how to carry out the worldview through appropriate actions. A key feature of all forms of Judaism is the identification of what is wrong with the present and how to escape, overcome, or survive that situation. Jewish life is symbolically interpreted as a tension between exile and return, given its foundational myth in the exile of the Jews from Israel and their period of slavery in Egypt.

everyday ANTHROPOLOGY

Tattoos and Sacred Power

Fieldwork among Shan people in northern Thailand (see Map 6.7, p. 157) reveals the importance of tattooing, a tradition shared with much of Southeast Asia (Tannenbaum 1987). Shan tattooing blends aspects of Buddhism with local spirit beliefs and even elements of Hinduism as practiced by some groups in neighboring Myanmar.

Among the Shan, three types of tattoos exist:

- Tattoos that act on other people, causing them to like or fear the bearer, and that cause the spirits to be kind
- Tattoos that act on the bearer, increasing the bearer's skill
- Tattoos that create a barrier around the person that prevents animals from biting, knives from cutting, and bullets from entering the body

Tattoos are done in two colors—red and blue/black. The first two types tend to be done in red; the third type tends to be done in blue/black. Different designs are associated with each type. For example, the two-tailed lizard is a common tattoo in the first type.

The first type of tattoo is popular among many people, because it brings health to the bearer. It is the main type among women, used for illness prevention as well as for curing an illness. A person who falls ill may get a tattoo incorporating a letter of the Shan alphabet in the design, either on the calf, around a body joint, around the mouth, or on the top of the tongue. Some of the most powerful designs in this category are placed on the back or over the heart.

The most powerful tattoo in this category, called the Five Buddha tattoo, is not allowed for women. Men who get this tattoo have to follow five Buddhist precepts at all times: refrain from killing, stealing, improper sexual behavior, lying, and intoxication. This tattoo is red, but it also includes exfoliated skin from a Buddhist monk. That makes this tattoo different from all others and makes its bearer like a monk. Whereas most tattoos in the first category cause other people to look favorably on the bearer, the Five Buddha tattoo inspires fear and awe.

Tattoos in the second category, worn by men, are all related to words. Some increase people's memory and help them on exams. Others strengthen a person's speaking ability. The most powerful tattoos in this group give a person such great verbal skills that he or she can intimidate others. They increase courage as well. One tattoo in this category is the Saraswati tattoo, which depicts, among other things, the head of Saraswati, the Hindu goddess of knowledge, on the bearer's right shoulder. To call on Saraswati for help, the person brushes his or her lips on the tattoo.

The third category of tattoos, those that provide a protective barrier, has one subset that prevents bites from insects, snakes, dogs, cats, tigers, and so on. If the person has the tattoo and gets bitten nonetheless, the tattoo helps reduce the pain. A general anti-bite tattoo is a cat on the lower arm. More powerful tattoos in this third category protect people from weapons. They seal off the body. A person should be careful not to get too many of these tattoos, however, because they seal the body off completely and therefore prevent good fortune from entering it. Someone with many of these tattoos is likely to be poor or unlucky.

The Shan people do not question why or how their tattoos work. They simply believe that they do. They blend what anthropologists classify as magic with religious beliefs from Buddhism and Hinduism, in the case of the Saraswati tattoo. Sacred power is the key that links all these beliefs together into a coherent system for the Shan.

◆ FOOD FOR THOUGHT

- What do people in your microculture do to get people to like them, to succeed on exams, and protect the body from harmful intrusions?

Judaism is monotheistic, teaching that God is one, unique, and all powerful. Humans have a moral duty to follow Jewish law, to protect and preserve life and health, and to follow certain duties, such as observing the Sabbath. The high regard for human life is reflected in the general opposition to abortion within Jewish law and in opposition to the death penalty. Words, both spoken and written, are important in Judaism. There is an emphasis on truth telling in life and on the use of established literary formulas at precise times during worship. These formulas are encoded in a *sidur,* or prayer book. Dietary patterns distinguish Judaism from other religions; for example, rules of kosher eating forbid the mixing of milk or milk products with meat.

Contemporary varieties of Judaism range from conservative Hasidism to Reform Judaism, which emerged in the early 1800s. One difference between these two perspectives concerns the question of who is Jewish. Jewish law traditionally defined a Jewish person as someone born of a Jewish mother. In contrast, reform Judaism recognizes as Jewish the offspring of a Jewish father and a non-Jewish mother. Currently, the Jewish population numbers about 15 million worldwide, with about half living in North America, a quarter in Israel, and

20 percent in Europe and Russia. Smaller populations are scattered across the globe.

WHO'S WHO AT THE KOTEL The most sacred place to all Jews is the Kotel (ko-TELL), or Western Wall in Jerusalem (see Map 13.6). Since the 1967 war, which brought Jerusalem under Israeli rule, the Kotel has been the most important religious shrine and pilgrimage site of Israel. The Kotel is located at one edge of the Temple Mount (also called Haram Sharif), an area sacred to Jews, Muslims, and Christians. According to Jewish scriptures, God asked Abraham to sacrifice his son Isaac on this hill. Later, King Solomon built the First Temple here in the middle of the tenth century BCE. It was destroyed by Nebuchadnessar (neh-boo-kud-NES-er) in 587 BCE, when the Jews were led into captivity in Babylon. Around 500 BCE, King Herod built the Second Temple on the same site. The Kotel is a remnant of the Second Temple. Jews of all varieties and non-Jews come to the Kotel in vast numbers from around the world. The Kotel plaza is open to everyone, pilgrims and tourists. The wall is made of massive rectangular stones weighing between two and eight tons each. At its base is a synagogue area partitioned into men's and women's sections.

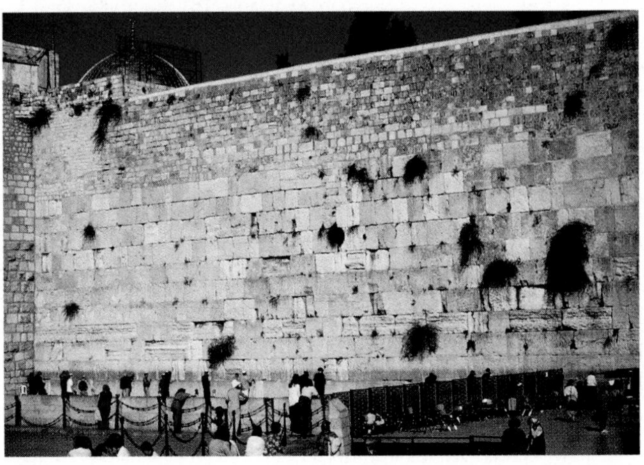

The Kotel, or Western Wall, in Jerusalem is a sacred place of pilgrimage, especially for Jews. Men pray at a section marked off on the left, women at the area on the right. Both men and women should cover their heads, and when leaving the wall area, women should take care to keep their faces toward it and avoid turning their backs to it.

▶ *Think of some behavioral rules at another sacred place you know.*

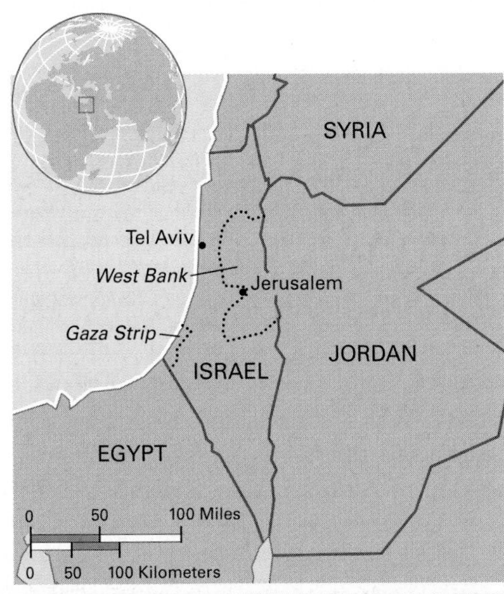

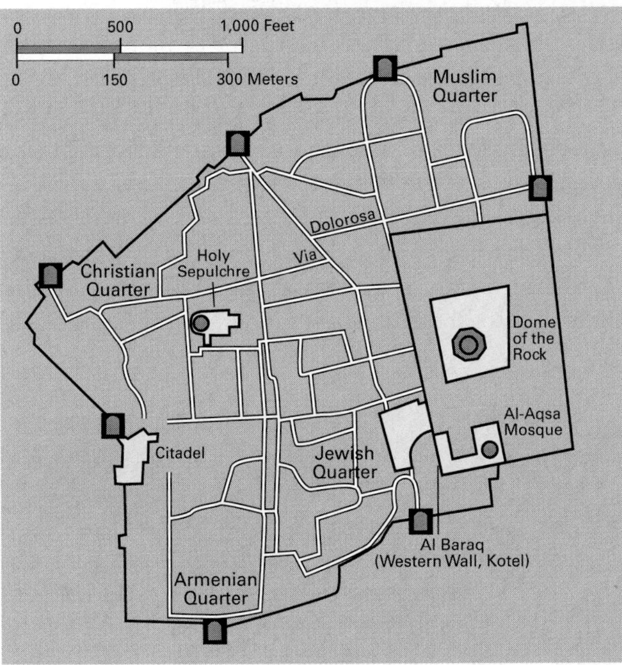

MAP 13.6 Sacred Sites in the Old City of Jerusalem, Israel.

Jerusalem is the holiest city of Judaism, the third holiest city of Islam, and holy to Christians. The section called the Old City is surrounded by walls that have been built, razed, relocated, and rebuilt over several hundred years. The Old City contains four quarters: Armenian, Christian, Jewish, and Muslim, and many sacred sites such as the Kotel and the Via Dolorosa.

This single site brings together a variety of Jewish worshippers and secular visitors. The great diversity among the visitors is evident in the various styles of dress and gesture:

> The Hasid . . . with a fur shtreimel on his head may enter the synagogue area alongside a man in shorts who utilizes a cardboard skullcap available for "secular" visitors. American youngsters in jeans may ponder Israeli soldiers of their own age, dressed in uniform, and wonder what their lot might have been if they [had been] born in another country. Women from Yemen, wearing embroidered trousers under their dresses, edge close to the Wall as do women accoutred in contemporary styles whose religiosity may have been filtered through a modern education. . . . (Storper-Perez and Goldberg 1994:321)

In spite of plaques that state the prohibition against begging, beggars offer to "sell a blessing" to visitors. They may remind visitors that it was the poor who built the wall in the first place. Another category of people is young Jewish men who, in search of prospective "born again" Jews, "hang around" looking for a "hit" (in their words). Most of the hits are young Americans who are urged to take their Jewishness more seriously and, if male, to be sure to marry a Jewish woman. Other regulars are Hebrew-speaking men who are available to organize a prayer service. One of the most frequent forms of religious expression at the Kotel is the insertion of written prayers into the crevices of the wall.

The social heterogeneity of the Jewish people is thus transcended in a single space, creating some sense of what Victor Turner (1969) called *communitas,* a sense of collective unity that bridges individual difference.

PASSOVER IN KERALA The Jews of the Kochi (ko-chee) area of Kerala, South India, have lived there for about 1000 years (Katz and Goldberg 1989) (see Map 16.2, p. 400). The Maharaja of Kochi had respect for the Jewish people, who were mainly merchants. He relied on them for external trade and contacts. In recognition of this, he allowed a synagogue, which is still standing, to be built next to his palace. Syncretism is apparent in Kochi Jewish lifestyle, social structure, and rituals. Basic aspects of Judaism are retained, along with adoption of many aspects of Hindu practices.

Three aspects of syncretism with Hinduism are apparent in Passover, one of the most important annual rituals of the Jewish faith. First, the Western/European Passover celebration is typically joyous and a time of feasting. In contrast, the Kochi version has adopted a tone of austerity and is called "the fasting feast." Second, Kochi Passover allows no role for children, whereas at a traditional ritual meal, or *seder* (say-der) children usually ask four questions as a starting point of the narrative. The Kochi Jews chant the questions in unison. (In Hinduism, children do not have solo roles in rituals.) Third, a Kochi seder stresses purity even more than standard Jewish requirements. Standard rules about maintaining the purity of kosher wine usually mean that no gentile (non-Jew) should touch it. But Kochi Jews expand the rule to say that if the shelf or table on which the wine sits is touched by a gentile, the wine is impure. This extra level of "contagion" is influenced by Hindu concepts of pollution.

CHRISTIANITY

Christianity has many ties with Judaism, from which it sprang, especially in terms of the biblical teachings of a coming savior, or *messiah* (anointed one). It began in the eastern Mediterranean in the second quarter of the first century (Cunningham 1995:240–253). Most of the early believers were Jews who took up the belief in Jesus Christ as the messiah who came to earth in fulfillment of prophesies contained in the Hebrew scriptures. Today, Christianity is the largest of the world religions, with about 2 billion adherents, roughly one-third of the world's population. It is the majority religion of Australia, New Zealand, the Philippines, Papua New Guinea, most countries of Europe and of North and South America, and about a dozen southern African countries. Christianity is a minority religion throughout Asia, but Asian Christians constitute 16 percent of the world's total Christians and are thus a significant population.

Christians accept the Bible (Old and New Testaments) as containing the basic teachings of their faith, believe that a supreme God sent His son to earth as a sacrifice for the welfare of humanity, and look to Jesus as the model to follow for moral guidance. The three largest branches of Christianity are Roman Catholic, Protestant, and Eastern Orthodox. Within each of these branches, various denominations exist.

(LEFT) The Vatican in Rome. The Vatican attracts more pilgrims/visitors each year than any religious site in the world. (RIGHT) In the nearby neighborhood, shops cater to pilgrims/visitors by offering a variety of religious and secular goods.

The greatest growth in Christianity is occurring in sub-Saharan Africa, India, Indonesia, and Eastern Europe.

PROTESTANTISM AMONG WHITE APPALACHIANS Studies of Protestantism in Appalachia describe local traditions that outsiders who are accustomed to standard, urban versions may view as "deviant." For example, some churches in rural West Virginia and North Carolina, called Old Regulars, practice three obligatory rituals: footwashing, communion (a ritual commemorating the Last Supper that Jesus had with his disciples), and baptism (Dorgan 1989). The footwashing ceremony occurs once a year in conjunction with communion, usually as an extension of the Sunday service. An elder is called to the front of the church, and he preaches for 10 to 20 minutes. A round of handshaking and embracing follows. Two deaconesses then come forward to "prepare the table" by uncovering the sacramental elements placed there earlier under a white tablecloth. The elements are unleavened bread, serving plates for the bread, cups for the wine, and a decanter or quart jar or two of wine. The deacons break the bread into pieces and the moderator pours the wine into the cups. Men and women form separate groups as the deacons serve the bread and wine. The deacons serve each other, and then it is time for the footwashing.

The moderator begins by quoting from the New Testament (John 13:4): "He riseth from supper, and laid aside his garments; and he took a towel and girded himself." The moderator takes a towel and basin from the communion table, puts water in it, and selects a senior elder and removes his shoes and socks. The moderator washes his feet slowly and attentively. Other members come forward and take towels and basins and take turns washing other's feet and having their feet washed. Soon "the church is filled with crying, shouting, and praising as these highly poignant exchanges unleash a flood of emotions" (Dorgan 1989:106). A functional interpretation of the ritual of footwashing is that it helps maintain social cohesion.

Another feature of worship in some small, Protestant churches in Appalachia, especially remote areas of rural West Virginia, involves the handling of poisonous snakes. This practice finds legitimation in the New Testament (Daugherty 1997 [1976]). According to a passage in Mark (16:15–18), "In my name shall they cast out devils; they shall speak with new tongues; they shall take up serpents; and if they drink any deadly thing, it shall not hurt them; they shall lay hands on the sick, and they shall recover." Members of "Holiness-type" churches believe that the handling of poisonous snakes is the supreme act of devotion to God. Biblical literalists, these people choose serpent handling as their way of celebrating life, death, and resurrection and of proving that only Jesus has the power to deliver them from death. Most serpent handlers have been bitten many times, but few have died.

One interpretation says that the risks of handling poisonous snakes mirror the risks of the environment. Rates of unemployment are high and many people are economically poor. The structurist view (review Chapter 1) points to the fact that serpent handling increased when local people lost their land rights to big mining and forestry companies (Tidball and Toumey 2003:4). As their lives became more economically insecure, they turned to a way of increasing their sense of stability through a dramatic religious ritual. Outsiders might ask whether such dangerous ritual practices indicate that the people are psychologically disturbed. Psychological tests indicate that members of Holiness churches are more emotionally healthy, on average, than members of mainline Protestant churches.

A celebration of the Christian holy day of Palm Sunday in Port-au-Prince, Haiti. European colonialism brought African slaves to the New World and Christianity through missionary efforts. Many forms of Christianity are now firmly established in the Caribbean region.

▶ *Discover through a website or other source what the major Christian denominations in Haiti are.*

Recent U.S. newspaper and television coverage of serpent handling sensationalizes these religious practices. In doing so, it adds a secular avenue to economic success for some of the most famous serpent handlers. One pastor, for example, got a better job offer from a coal mining company, which allowed him and his family to purchase a new house and car (Tidball and Toumey 2003:10).

THE LAST SUPPER IN FIJI Among Christians in Fiji, the image of the Last Supper is a dominant motif (Toren 1988). This scene, depicted on tapestry hangings, adorns most churches and many houses. People say, "Christ is the head of

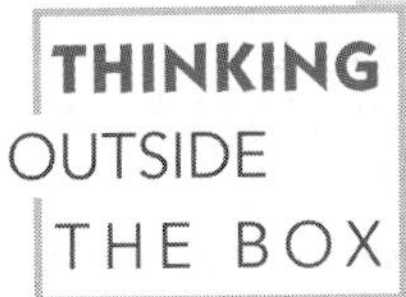

Visit the Vatican website and explore the Vatican's position on the "Da Vinci code" phenomenon.

this household, he eats with us and overhears us" (1988:697). The image's popularity is the result of its fit with Fijian notions of communal eating and kava drinking. Seating rules at such events place the people of highest status, such as the chief and others close to him, at the "above" side of the room, away from the entrance. Others sit at the "lower" end, facing the highly ranked people. Intermediate positions are located on either side of the person of honor, in ranked order.

Leonardo Da Vinci's fifteenth century painting of the Last Supper places Jesus Christ in the position of a Fijian chief, with the disciples in an ordered arrangement around him. The disciples and the viewers "face" the chief and eat and drink together, as is appropriate in Fijian society. This positioning parallels the orderly placement of Fijian people around the kava as encountered "virtually every day in the village" (1988:706). This kind of cultural fit is a clear example of religious syncretism.

ISLAM

Islam is based on the teachings of the prophet Muhammad (570–632 CE) and is thus the youngest of the world religions (Martin 1995:498–513). The Arabic word *Islam* means "submission" to the will of the one god, Allah, through which peace will be achieved. Followers of Islam, known as Muslims, believe that Muhammad was God's final prophet. Islam has several denominations with essentially similar beliefs but also distinct theological and legal approaches. The two major schools of thought are Sunni and Shi'a. About 85 percent of the total Muslim population worldwide are Sunnis, and about 15 percent are Shi'as. Sufism is a more mystical variant, with much smaller numbers of adherents. Many other subgroups exist.

The Five Pillars of Islam are profession of faith in Allah, daily prayer, fasting, contributing alms for the poor, and the *Hajj* (pilgrimage to Mecca). The five pillars are central to Sunni Islam but less so to other branches of Islam such as the Shi'as and the Sufis.

The total number of Muslims worldwide is about 1.4 billion, making it the second largest religion. Muslim-majority nations are located in northern Africa; the Middle East, including Afghanistan, Pakistan, and Bangladesh in South Asia; and several nations in Central Asia and Southeast Asia. Most of the world's Muslims (60 percent) live in South Asia or Southeast Asia. Muslims live as minorities in many other countries, including China, where they seek to maintain their religious practices (see Culturama). Although Islam originally flourished among pastoralists, only 2 percent of its adherents now are in that category.

A common and inaccurate stereotype of Islam prevalent among many non-Muslims is that it is the same no matter where it exists. This erroneously monolithic model tends to be based on an image of conservative Wahhabist Islam as practiced in Saudi Arabia. But Wahhabist Islam is only one of many varieties of Islam.

A comparison of Islam in highland Sumatra, Indonesia, and Morocco, North Africa, reveals differences that are the result of local cultural adaptations (Bowen 1992). Eid-ul-Adha (eed-ull-ah-dah), or the Feast of Sacrifice, is celebrated annually by Muslims around the world. It commemorates Ibrahim's willingness to sacrifice his son Ishmael (Isaac in Christian and Jewish traditions) to Allah. It occurs on the tenth of the last month of the year, called Pilgrimage Month, and marks the end of the Hajj. The ritual reminds Muslims of their global unity within the Islamic faith.

An important aspect of this ritual in Morocco (see Map 6.2, p. 143) involves the king publicly plunging a dagger into a ram's throat, a reenactment of Muhammad's performance of the sacrifice on the same day in the seventh century. Each male head of household follows the pattern and sacrifices a ram. The size and virility of the ram are a measure of the man's power and virility. Other men of the household stand to witness the sacrifice, while women and children are

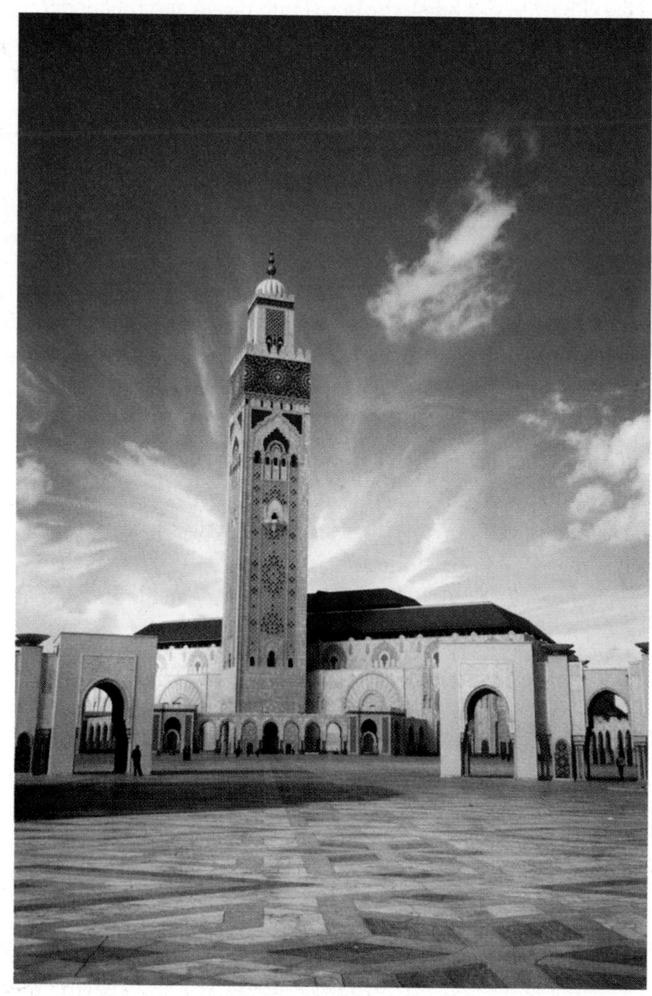

The Hassan II Mosque was built for the sixtieth birthday of Morocco's previous king, Hassan II. It is the largest religious monument in the world, after Mecca, with space for 25,000 worshippers inside and another 80,000 outside. The minaret, 210 meters in height, is the tallest in the world.

Hui Muslims of Xi'an, China

The Hui, one of China's largest designated minorities, number around 10 million people. Most live in the northwestern part of the country. The state classifies the Hui as "backward" and "feudal" in comparison to China's majority Han population. Hui residents of Xi'an (shee-ahn), however, reject the official characterization of them as less civilized and less modern than the Han majority (Gillette 2000).

About 60,000 Hui live in Xi'an, mainly in the so-called Old Muslim Area, which is dominated by small shops, restaurants, and mosques. The quality of housing and public services is inferior to that found elsewhere in the city. Parents worry that their children are not getting the best education and feel that the state is not providing adequate schooling in their neighborhood. Many Hui have taken steps to improve their houses themselves and to send their children to schools outside the district.

The Hui of Xi'an construct what they consider to be a modern and civilized lifestyle by choosing aspects of Muslim culture and Western culture. Their form of "progress" is visible in many aspects of their daily life, such as eating habits, dress styles, housing, religious practices, education, and family organization.

Being Muslim in China poses several challenges in relation to the dominant Han culture. Diet is one prominent example. The Qu'ran forbids four types of food to Muslims: animals that have not been consecrated to God and properly slaughtered, blood, pork, and alcohol (Gillette 2000:116). Three of the four rules apply to meat, and meat is the central part of a proper meal for Muslims. The Hui say that pork is especially impure. This belief differentiates the Hui clearly from other Chinese people, for whom pork is a major food item. Given the Hui belief that the kinds of food one eats affect a person's essence and behavior, they view pork eaters with disdain.

Hui residents consider alcohol even more impure than pork (Gillette 2000:167). Hui of Xi'an do not drink alcohol. They avoid using utensils that have touched alcohol and people who are drinking it. Many Hui of Xi'an, however, make a living in the restaurant business, which caters to Chinese Han and foreign tourists. Although selling alcohol boosts business, many Hui object to it. Several Hui formed the Anti-Alcohol Committee to advocate for banning the sale of alcohol in restaurants in the Hui quarter and preventing customers from bringing their own alcohol. Some areas of the market section are alcohol-free zones. Committee members say that restricting alcohol has improved the quality of life by making the neighborhood more peaceful and orderly.

In 2003, an urban development project in the Old Muslim Quarter was launched with financial support from the Norwegian government (*People's Daily* 2003). The project will widen the main street, replace "shabby" housing and infrastructure, and restore crumbling buildings of historic interest. A commercial area will be dedicated to restaurants serving Hui food in recognition of the touristic appeal of traditional Hui specialties such as baked beef and mutton, buns with beef, mutton pancake, and mutton soup. It is unclear where alcohol consumption will fit into this plan.

Thanks to Maris Boyd Gillette, Haverford College, for reviewing this material.

(LEFT) At a street stand in Xi'an, Hui men prepare and sell a noodle dish. Like Muslim men in many parts of the world, they wear a white cap.
(CENTER) Hui women in Xi'an participate in a ritual that commemorates Hui people who died in a massive conflict that spread across in northwestern China

MAP 13.7 The City of Xi'an in China. Xi'an, the capital of Shaanxi province, is one of the most economically developed cities in

absent or in the background. After the ram is killed, the men come forward and dab its blood on their faces. In some villages, women play a more prominent role before the sacrifice by daubing the ram with henna (red dye), thus sanctifying it, and using its blood afterward in rituals to protect the household. These state and household rituals are symbolic of male power in the public and private domains—the power of the monarchy and the power of patriarchy.

In Isak (EE-suk), Sumatra (see Map 8.3, p. 198), the cultural context is less patriarchal and the political structure does not emphasize monarchy. Isak is a traditionalist Muslim village where people have been Muslims since the seventeenth century. They sacrifice many kinds of animals: chickens, ducks, sheep, goats, and water buffalo. The people believe that so long as the animal's throat is cut and the meat is eaten, the sacrifice satisfies God. Most sacrifices are family affairs and receive little public notice. They are done in the back of the house. Both women and men of the household refer to it as "their" sacrifice, and there are no signs of male dominance. Women may sponsor a sacrifice, as did one wealthy woman trader who sacrificed a buffalo (the cutting was done by a man).

The Moroccan ritual emphasizes fathers and sons, whereas the Isak ritual includes attention to a wider range of kin on both the husband's and wife's side, daughters as well as sons, and even dead relatives. In Isak, the ritual carries no centralized political meanings. The differences are not due to the fact that Moroccans know the scriptures better than Sumatrans do. The Isak area has many Islamic scholars who are familiar with the scriptures and regularly discuss them with each other. Rather, the two cultural contexts, including kinship and politics, shape the ritual to local realities.

AFRICAN RELIGIONS

Many African religions are now global. In earlier centuries, they spread outside Africa through the coerced movement of people as slaves. African diaspora religions are especially prominent in the United States, the Caribbean region, and Central and South America. This section summarizes some key features of African religions and then offers two examples of African religions in the Western Hemisphere.

FEATURES OF AFRICAN RELIGIONS With its diverse geography, cultural variation, and history, Africa encompasses a wide range of religious affiliations, including many Muslims, Christians, Jews, Hindus, practitioners of indigenous religions, and people who follow some combination of these.

revitalization movement a socioreligious movement, usually organized by a prophetic leader, that seeks to construct a more satisfying situation by reviving all or parts of a religion that has been threatened by outside forces or by adopting new practices and beliefs.

A sacred altar in a local African religion in Togo, West Africa. ▶ *Can you distinguish some of the ritual elements displayed here? Are some incomprehensible to you? How would an anthropologist begin to learn about the beliefs involved in this religion?*

Indigenous African religions are difficult to typify, but some of their shared features are:

- Myths about a rupture that once occurred between the creator deity and humans
- A pantheon that includes a high god and many secondary supernaturals ranging from powerful gods to lesser spirits
- Elaborate initiation rituals
- Rituals involving animal sacrifices and other offerings, meals, and dances
- Altars within shrines as focal places where humans and deities meet
- Close links with healing

Although these features are fairly constant, African religions are rethought and reshaped locally and over time with complex and variable results (Gable 1995). In their home locations, they have been influenced by foreign religions, notably Islam and various types of Christianity. The out-migration of African peoples has brought African religions to new locations where they have been localized in their new contexts and also revitalized (Clarke 2004). Kamari Clarke's research on the Yorùbá (YOR-uh-buh) revivalist religion in the United States took her from New York City to South Carolina and Nigeria. The focal point of her fieldwork was in Ọyọ̀túnjí Village near Beaufort, South Carolina (see Map 14.3, p. 359). African American Yorùbá revivalists have created a place that reconstructs royal Yorùbá spiritual leadership and worship that helps some African Americans reconnect with their lost identity. In the words of Kamari Clarke, "Ritual initiations and rhythmic drumming echo in the endless hours of the night as residents remake their ancestral homeland outside the territory of Africa" (2004:51). The place, the rituals, and the music tie the people to Africa. Many Yorùbá-descent Americans, like other African Americans, go even further in their attempt to reconnect with their heritage. "Roots tourism" is a growing industry that provides culturally informed travel for African Americans to their places of ancestral origin in Africa.

Many religious syncretisms in North and South America combine African traditions with aspects of Christianity, indigenous Indian religions, and other traditions. Widely popular in Brazil are Afro-Brazilian religions such as *umbanda*, *santería*, and *condomblé* that appeal to people of all social classes, urban and rural, especially for providing social support and alleviation of stress (refer to photo on p. 172) (Burdick 2004).

RAS TAFARI Also called Rastafarianism, Ras Tafari is an Afro-Caribbean religion with its original roots in Jamaica. It is not known how many Rastafarians there are because they refuse to be counted (Smith 1995:23). Ras Tafari is a protest religion that shares only a few of the features of African religions just mentioned. It traces its history to several preachers of the early twentieth century who taught that Ras ("Prince") Tafari, then the Ethiopian emperor Haile Selassie, was the "Lion of Judah" who would lead Blacks to the African promised land.

Rastafarianism does not have an organized set of doctrines or written texts. Shared beliefs of the many diffuse groups in the Caribbean, the United States, and Europe include the belief that Ethiopia is heaven on earth, that Haile Selassie is a living god, and that all Blacks will be able to return to the homeland through his help. Since the death of Haile Selassie in 1975, more emphasis has been placed on pan-African unity and Black power, and less on Ethiopia.

Rastafarianism is particularly strong in Jamaica, where it is associated with reggae music, dreadlocks, and *ganja* (marijuana) smoking. Variations within the Rastafarian movement in Jamaica range from beliefs that one must fight oppression to the position that living a peaceful life brings victory against evil.

Directions of Religious Change

All religions have mythologies and doctrines that provide for continuity in beliefs and practices. Yet no religion is frozen and unchanging. Cultural anthropologists have traced the resurgence of religions that seemed to be headed toward extinction through colonial forces, and they have documented the emergence of new religions. Likewise, they are observing the contemporary struggle of once-suppressed religions in socialist states to find a new position in the postsocialist world. Religious *icons* (images, pictures, or other forms of representations), once a prominent feature in Russian Orthodox churches, had been removed and placed in museums. The churches want them back.

Bob Marley, legendary reggae artist and Rastafarian, performing at the Roxy Theater in Hollywood, California, in 1979. Marley died in 1981 at the age of 36, but he is still the most revered reggae musician. He launched the global spread of Jamaican music. Reggae is a genre of Jamaican music associated with Rastafarianism. Its songs address poverty, social injustice, love, and sexuality.

Indigenous people's beliefs about the sacredness of their land are an important part of their attempts to protect their territory from encroachment and development by outside commercial interests. The world of religious change offers these examples, and far more, as windows into wider cultural change.

REVITALIZATION MOVEMENTS

Revitalization movements are socioreligious movements that seek to bring about positive change through reestablishing a religion that has been threatened by outside forces or through adopting new practices and beliefs. Such movements often arise in the context of rapid cultural change and appear to represent a way for people to try to make sense of their changing world and their place in it. One such movement that emerged as a response of Native Americans to the invasion of their land by Europeans and Euro-Americans was the Ghost Dance movement (Kehoe 1989). In the early 1870s, a shaman named Wodziwob of the Paiute (pie-yoot) tribe in California declared that the world would soon be destroyed and then renewed: Native Americans, plants, and animals

THINKING OUTSIDE THE BOX

Learn about Ọ̀yọ̀túnjí Village from the Web. What goes on there? Do people live there? If you went to visit, where would you stay, what would you eat, and what would you do?

A Ghost Dance shirt of the Arapaho Indians of the Plains region, with painted designs of birds, turtle, and stars. These specially decorated garments were believed to protect the wearer from the White man's bullets.

would come back to life. He instructed people to perform a circle dance, known as the Ghost Dance, at night.

The movement spread to other tribes in California, Oregon, and Idaho but ended when the prophet died and his prophecy was unfulfilled. A similar movement emerged in 1890, led by another Paiute prophet, Wovoka, who had a vision during a total eclipse. His message was the same: destruction, renewal, and the need to perform circle dances in anticipation of the impending event. The dance spread widely and had various effects. Among the Pawnee, it provided the basis for a cultural revival of old ceremonies that had fallen into disuse. The Sioux altered Wovoka's message and adopted a more overtly hostile stance toward the government and White people. Newspapers began to carry stories about the "messiah craze," referring to Wovoka. Ultimately, the government took action against the Sioux, killing Chief Sitting Bull and Chief Big Foot and about 300 Sioux at Wounded Knee. In the 1970s, the Ghost Dance was revived again by the American Indian Movement, an activist organization that seeks to advance Native American rights.

Cargo cults are a type of revitalization movement that emerged in much of Melanesia (see Map 10.2, p. 247) and in New Zealand among the Māori people (review Culturama, Ch. 11, p. 273), in response to Western influences. Most prominent in the first half of the nineteenth century, cargo cults emphasize the acquisition of Western trade goods, or cargo in local terms. Typically, a prophetic leader emerges with a vision of how the cargo will arrive. In one instance, the leader predicted that a ship would come, bringing not only cargo but also the people's dead ancestors. Followers set up tables for the expected guests, complete with flower arrangements.

Later, after World War II and the islanders' experiences of aircraft arrivals bringing cargo, the mode of anticipated arrival changed to planes. Once again, people would wait expectantly for the arrival of the plane. Cargo cults emerged as a response to the disruptive effects of new goods being suddenly introduced into indigenous settings. The outsiders imposed a new form of exchange system that emphasized the importance of Western goods and suppressed the importance of indigenous valuables such as shells and pigs. This transformation undermined traditional patterns of gaining status through the exchange of indigenous goods. Cargo cult leaders sought help, in the only way they knew, in obtaining Western goods so that they could acquire social status in the new system.

CONTESTED SACRED SITES

Religious conflict often becomes focused on sacred sites. One place of recurrent conflict is Jerusalem, where many religions and sects within religions compete for control of sacred terrain. Three major religions claim they have primary rights: Islam,

John Frum Movement supporters stand guard around one of the cult's flag poles at Sulphur Bay village, on Tanna Island, Vanuatu, in the region of Melanesia.

▶ *Does this scene remind you of anything from your culture?*

cargo cult a form of revitalization movement that emerged in Melanesia and New Zealand following World War II in response to Western and Japanese influences.

After the Chinese takeover of Tibet, many Tibetans became refugees, including the revered head of Tibetan Buddhism, the Dalai Lama. Buddhism, founded in India as a protest against Hinduism, is a minority religion in its homeland. It has millions of followers elsewhere, from Scotland to San Francisco.

Judaism, and Christianity. Among the Christians, several different sects vie for control of the Church of the Holy Sepulchre (see Map 13.6, p. 331). In India, frequent conflicts over sacred sites occur between Hindus and Muslims. Hindus claim that Muslim mosques have been built on sites sacred to Hindus. On some occasions, the Hindus have destroyed the mosques. Many conflicts that involve secular issues surrounding sacred sites also exist worldwide. In the United States, White racists have burned African American churches. In Israel, some Jewish leaders object to archaeological research because the ancient Jewish burial places should remain undisturbed.

A similar situation exists among indigenous populations in the Western Hemisphere. Their sacred sites and burial grounds have often been destroyed for the sake of urban growth, petroleum and mineral extraction, and recreational sports. Resistance to such destruction is growing, with indigenous people finding creative ways to protect, restore, and manage their heritage.

RELIGIOUS FREEDOM AS A HUMAN RIGHT

According to a United Nations Declaration, freedom from religious persecution is a universal human right. Yet violations of this right by countries and by competing religions are common. Sometimes people who are persecuted on religious grounds can seek and obtain sanctuary in other places or nations. Thousands of Tibetan Buddhist refugees, including their leader the Dalai Lama, fled Tibet after it was taken over by the Chinese. Several Tibetan communities have been established in exile in India, the United States, and Canada, where the Tibetan people attempt to keep their religion, language, and heritage alive.

The post-9/11 policy enactments in the United States related to its campaign against terrorism are seen by many as dangerous steps against constitutional principles of personal liberty—specifically, as infringements on the religious rights of practicing Muslims. The prevalent mentality in the U.S. government, and in much of the general populace, links the whole of Islam with terrorism and thereby stigmatizes all Muslims as potential terrorists. Many anthropologists (for example, Mamdani 2002) have spoken out against the inaccuracy and indecency of labeling an entire religion dangerous and putting all its members under the shadow of suspicion.

Religions are often the focal point of conflict and dissension and the source of conflict resolution. As an integral part of the heritage of humanity, they can be better understood from a cross-cultural and contextualized perspective. Such understanding is essential for building a more secure and peaceful future.

13

the BIG questions REVISITED

◆ What is religion and what are the basic features of religions?

Early cultural anthropologists defined religion in contrast to magic and suggested that religion was a more evolved form of thinking about the supernatural realm. They collected information on religions of non-Western cultures and constructed theories about the origin and functions of religion. Since then, ethnographers have described many religious systems and documented a rich variety of beliefs, forms of ritual behavior, and types of religious specialists. Beliefs are expressed in either myth or doctrine and often are concerned with defining the roles and characteristics of supernatural beings and how humans should relate to them.

Religious beliefs are enacted in rituals that are periodic or nonperiodic. Some common rituals worldwide are life-cycle rites, pilgrimage, rituals of inversion, and sacrifice. Rituals are transformative for the participants.

Many rituals require the involvement of a trained religious specialist such as a shaman/shamanka or priest/priestess. Compared to the situation in states, religious specialist roles in nonstate contexts are fewer, less than full-time, less formalized and carry less secular power. In states, religious specialists are often organized into hierarchies, and many specialists gain substantial secular power.

◆ How do world religions illustrate globalization and localization?

The five so-called world religions are based on texts and generally agreed-on teachings and beliefs shared by many people around the world. In order of historic age, they are Hinduism, Buddhism, Judaism, Christianity, and Islam. Christianity has the largest number of adherents, with Islam second and Hinduism third. Due to accelerated global population migration in the past few centuries, many formerly local religions now have a worldwide membership. African diaspora religions are particularly prominent in the Western Hemisphere, with a variety of syncretistic religions attracting many adherents.

As members of the world religions have moved around the world, religious beliefs and practices have become contextualized into localized variants. When a new religion moves into a culture, it may be blended with local systems (syncretism), may coexist with indigenous religions in a pluralistic fashion, or may take over and obliterate the original beliefs.

◆ What are some important aspects of religious change in contemporary times?

Religious movements of the past two centuries have often been prompted by colonialism and other forms of social contact. In some instances, indigenous religious leaders and cults have arisen in the attempt to resist unwanted outside forces of change. In other cases, they evolve as ways of incorporating selected outside elements. Revitalization movements, such as the Ghost Dance movement in the United States Plains region, look to the past and attempt to recover lost and suppressed religious beliefs and practices.

Issues of contemporary importance include the increasing amount of conflict surrounding sacred sites, hostilities related to the effects of secular power interests on religious institutions and spaces, and religious freedom as a human right.

KEY CONCEPTS

animatism, p. 319
animism, p. 317
cargo cult, p. 338
doctrine, p. 318
life-cycle ritual, p. 323
magic, p. 316
myth, p. 318
pilgrimage, p. 324
priest/priestess, p. 326
religion, p. 316
religious pluralism, p. 326
religious syncretism, p. 326
revitalization movement, p. 337
ritual, p. 322
ritual of inversion, p. 324
sacrifice, p. 325
world religion, p. 326

SUGGESTED READINGS

Paulo Apolito. *The Internet and the Madonna: Religious Visionary Experience on the Web.* Antony Shugaar, trans. Chicago: University of Chicago Press, 2003. This book traces the Christian cult of Mary as it has developed and grown through the medium of the World Wide Web.

Diane Bell. *Ngarrindjeri Wurruwarrin: A World That Is, Was, and Will Be.* North Melbourne, Australia: Spinifex, 1998. This ethnography describes Ngarrindjeri women's struggles to protect their sacred land from encroachment by developers. It includes the women's voices, the perspective of the Australian government, the media, and disputes among anthropologists.

Janet Bennion. *Desert Patriarchy: Mormon and Mennonite Communities in the Chihuahua Valley.* Tucson: University of Arizona Press, 2004. The ethnographer, raised in a Mormon family, reports on her fieldwork among Mormons in a desert region in Mexico.

Karen McCarthy Brown. *Mama Lola: A Vodou Priestess in Brooklyn.* Berkeley: University of California Press, 1991. This life story of Mama Lola, a voodoo practitioner, is set within an ethnographic study of a Haitian community in New York City.

Sondra L. Hausner. *Wandering with Sadhus: Ascetics in the Hindu Himalayas.* Bloomington: Indiana University Press, 2008. This ethnographic study explores the interactions of Hindu ascetics in northern India with ordinary households and considers how they are part of the public community in spite of their commitment to solitary religious practices.

Klara Bonsack Kelley and Harris Francis. *Navajo Sacred Places.* Bloomington: Indiana University Press, 1994. The authors report on the results of a research project undertaken to learn about Navajo cultural resources, especially sacred sites, and the stories associated with them in order to help protect these places.

Melvin Konner. *Unsettled: An Anthropology of the Jews.* New York: Penguin Compass, 2003. A biological anthropologist is the author of this cultural history of the Jewish people and their religion. It extends from the origins of Judaism among pastoralists in the Middle East through enslavement in the Roman Empire, to the Holocaust and the creation of Israel.

J. David Lewis-Williams and D. G. Pearce. *San Spirituality: Roots, Expression, and Social Consequences.* New York: AltaMira Press, 2004. This book examines the interplay of cosmology, myth, ritual, and art among the San people of southern Africa.

Charlene Makley. *The Violence of Liberation: Gender and Tibetan Buddhist Revival in Post-Mao China.* Berkeley: University of California Press, 2007. Makley combines archival research with fieldwork in a Buddhist monastery in Tibet. She describes the incorporation of the region of Labrang into China.

Fatima Mernissi. *Beyond the Veil: Male–Female Dynamics in Modern Muslim Society.* Bloomington: Indiana University Press, revised edition, 1987. The author considers how Islam perceives female sexuality and regulates it on behalf of the social order.

Todd Sanders. *Beyond Bodies: Rainmaking and Sense Making in Tanzania.* Toronto: University of Toronto Press, 2008. This study of rainmaking rituals among the Inhanzu of central Tanzania reveals ideas about gender roles and relations.

Maureen Trudelle Schwarz. *Blood and Voice: Navajo Women Ceremonial Practitioners.* Tucson: University of Arizona Press, 2003. Contemporary Navajo women are increasingly taking on the ritual role of ceremonial Singer, formerly the domain of men. This book describes how women gain sacred knowledge and explains how they overcome the tradition that only men can be Singers.

Stephen Selka. *Religion and the Politics of Ethnic Identity in Bahia, Brazil.* Gainesville: University Press of Florida, 2008. This study shows how Catholicism, evangelical Protestantism, and the traditional Brazilian religion of Candomblé shape the discourse of race and identity in northeastern Brazil.

Katharine L. Wiegele. *Investing in Miracles: El Shaddai and the Transformation of Popular Catholicism in the Philippines.* Honolulu: University of Hawai'i Press, 2005. This book examines the widespread popularity in the Philippines of a charismatic businessman who became a preacher, Brother Mike. He appears at huge outdoor rallies and uses mass media to spread his message of economic prosperity within a Catholic framework.

Brazilian country music singer Inaia performs at the opening ceremony of the Barretos Rodeo in Berretos in the Brazilian state of São Paolo.

EXPRESSIVE CULTURE

the BIG questions

- How is culture expressed through art?
- What do play and leisure activities reveal about culture?
- How is expressive culture changing in contemporary times?

OUTLINE

In 2006, the Louvre in Paris, one of the most famous art museums in the world, opened a new museum in the shadow of the Eiffel Tower to display so-called tribal art of Africa, Asia, the South Pacific, and the Americas. This project reflects the interest of France's former president, Jacques Chirac, in non-Western art. It is also an example of the growing role of cultural anthropologists in helping museums provide contextual information for objects that are displayed, because Maurice Godelier, a specialist on Papua New Guinea, was closely involved in planning the exhibits (Corbey 2000). The new museum elevates "tribal" objects to the level of art, rather than placing them in a museum of natural history as is the practice in the United States. It does, however, segregate "tribal" art in a museum physically separate from the Louvre with all its "classic" treasures. This long-standing conceptual division, beginning in the European Enlightenment, links the West with "civilization" and non-Western peoples with that which is "uncivilized."

This chapter considers a vast area of human behavior and thought called **expressive culture**, or behavior and beliefs related to art, leisure, and play (definitions of these terms are provided later). It starts with a discussion of theoretical perspectives on cross-cultural art and how anthropologists study art and expressive culture. The second section considers the topics of play and leisure cross-culturally. The last section provides examples of change in expressive culture.

◆◆◆

Art and Culture

Compared to questions raised in art history classes you may have taken, cultural anthropologists have a rather different view of art and how to study it. Their findings, here as in other cultural domains, stretch and subvert Western concepts and categories and prompt us to look at art within its context. Thus, anthropologists consider many products, practices, and processes to be art. They also study the artist and the artist's place in society. In addition, they ask questions about how art, and expressive culture more generally, is related to microcultural variation, inequality, and power. They question how cross-cultural art is to be selected and put on display in museums.

WHAT IS ART?

Are ancient rock carvings art? Is subway graffiti art? An embroidered robe? A painting of a can of Campbell's soup? Philosophers, art critics, anthropologists, and art lovers have all struggled with the question of What is art? The issue of how to define art involves more than mere word games. The way art is defined affects the manner in which a person values and treats artistic creations and those who create art (see Critical Thinking).

Anthropologists propose broad definitions of art to take into account emic definitions cross-culturally. One definition says that **art** is the application of imagination, skill, and style to matter, movement, and sound that goes beyond the purely practical (Nanda 1994:383). Such skill can be applied to many substances and activities and the product can be considered art—for example, a beautifully presented meal, a well-told story, or a perfectly formed basket. In this sense, art is a human universal, and no culture can be said to lack artistic activity completely, although the Pirahã (review Chapter 12) appear to have very little art, no matter how broadly defined. The anthropological study of art considers the products of such human skill as well as the process of making art, variations in art and its preferred forms cross-culturally, and the way culture constructs and changes artistic traditions.

Within the general category of art, subcategories exist, sometimes denoting eras such as Paleolithic or modern art.

Painting walls has a long heritage, going back at least to prehistoric cave paintings discovered in Europe and Australia. (LEFT) Grafitti in New York City in the 1980s. (CENTER) A mural in west Belfast, Northern Ireland, where the Irish Republican Army and its opponents frequently displayed their positions in large wall paintings. (RIGHT) Albetina Mahalangu paints a wall with Ndebele designs in South Africa.

▶ *How do these images help you rethink the possible motivations and meanings of prehistoric cave paintings?*

CRITICAL thinking

Probing the Categories of Art

Probably every reader of this book, at one time or another, has looked at an object in an art museum or in an art book or magazine and exclaimed, "But that's not art!" As a critical thinking research project on "what is art," visit two museums, either in person or on the Internet. One of these should be a museum of either fine art or modern art. The other should be a museum of natural history. In the former, examine at least five items on display. In the latter, examine several items on display that have to do with human cultures (that is, skip the bugs and rocks).

Take notes on all the items that you are examining. Then answer the following questions.

◆ CRITICAL THINKING QUESTIONS

- What is it?
- What contextual explanation does the museum provide about the object?
- Was the object intended as a work of art or as something else?
- In your opinion, is it art or not, and why or why not?
- Compare your notes on the objects in the two types of museums. What do your notes tell you about categories of art?

Other subcategories are based on the medium of expression, such as graphic or plastic arts (painting, drawing, sculpture, weaving, basketry, and architecture); decorative arts (interior design, landscaping, gardens, costume design, and body adornment such as hairstyles, tattooing, and painting); performance arts (music, dance, and theater); and verbal arts (poetry, writing, rhetoric, and telling stories and jokes). All these are Western, English-language categories.

A long-standing distinction in the Western view exists between *fine art* and *folk art*. This distinction is based on a Western-centric judgment that defines fine art as rare, expensive art produced by artists usually trained in the Western classical tradition. This is the kind of art that is included in college courses called Fine Arts. The implication is that all other art is less than fine and is more appropriately called folk art, ethnic art, primitive art, or crafts. Characteristics of Western fine art are as follows: The product is created by a formally schooled artist, it is made for sale on the market, it is clearly associated with a particular artist, its uniqueness is valued, and it is not primarily utilitarian but is rather "art for art's sake." In contrast, all the rest of the world's art that is non-Western and nonclassical is supposedly characterized by the opposite features:

- It is created by an artist who has not received formal training.
- It is not produced for the market.
- The artist is anonymous and does not sign or individually claim the product.
- It is made primarily for everyday use, such as food procurement, processing, or storage; in ritual; or in war.

Closer examination of these two categories is in order. All cultures have art, and all cultures have a sense of what makes something art versus non-art. The term *esthetics* refers to socially agreed-upon notions of quality (Thompson 1971). Before anthropologists proved otherwise, Western art experts considered that esthetics either did not exist or was poorly developed in non-Western cultures. We now know that esthetic principles, or established criteria for artistic quality, exist everywhere, whether or not they are written down and formalized. **Ethno-esthetics** refers to culturally specific definitions of what art is.

The set of standards concerning wood carving in West Africa illustrates the importance of considering cross-cultural variation in the criteria for art (Thompson 1971). Among the Yorúbà of Nigeria, esthetic guidelines for wood carving include these:

- Figures should be depicted midway between complete abstraction and complete realism so that they resemble "somebody," but no one in particular (portraiture in the Western sense is considered dangerous).
- Humans should be depicted at their optimal physical peak, not in infancy or old age.
- Line and form should have clarity.
- The sculpture should have the quality of luminosity achieved through a polished surface and the play of incisions and shadows.
- The piece should exhibit symmetry.

Some anthropological studies have documented intracultural differences in esthetic standards as well as cross-cultural variation. For example, an anthropologist showed computer-generated graphics to the Shipibo (shih-PEE-bo) Indians of the Peruvian Amazon and learned that the men liked the

expressive culture behavior and beliefs related to art, leisure, and play.

art the application of imagination, skill, and style to matter, movement, and sound that goes beyond what is purely practical.

ethno-esthetics culturally specific definitions of what art is.

Yorúbà wood carving follows esthetic principles that require clarity of line and form, a polished surface that creates a play of light and shadows, symmetry, and the depiction of human figures that are neither completely abstract nor completely realistic.

▶ *Have you seen African sculptures that follow these principles? Visit an African art museum on the Web for further exploration.*

abstract designs, whereas the women thought they were ugly (Roe, in Anderson and Field 1993). If you are wondering why this difference would exist, consider the interpretation of the anthropologist: Shipibo men are the shamans and take hallucinogenic drugs that may give them familiarity with more "psychedelic"/abstract images.

STUDYING ART IN SOCIETY

The anthropological study of art seeks to understand not only the products of art but also who makes it and why, the role of art in society, and its wider social meanings. Franz Boas was the first anthropologist to emphasize the importance of studying the artist in society. Functionalism (review Chapter 1) was the most important theory informing anthropological research on art in the first half of the twentieth century. Anthropologists wrote about how paintings, dance, theater, and songs serve to socialize children into the culture, provide a sense of social identity and group boundaries, and promote healing. Art may legitimize political leaders and enhance efforts in war through body painting, adornment, and magical decorations on shields and weapons. Art may also serve as a form of social control, as in African masks worn by dancers who represent deities visiting humans to remind them of the moral order. Art, like language, can be a catalyst for political resistance or a rallying point for ethnic solidarity in the face of oppression.

The anthropology of art relies on a range of methods in data gathering and analysis. The basic method is participant observation which is supplemented by collecting and

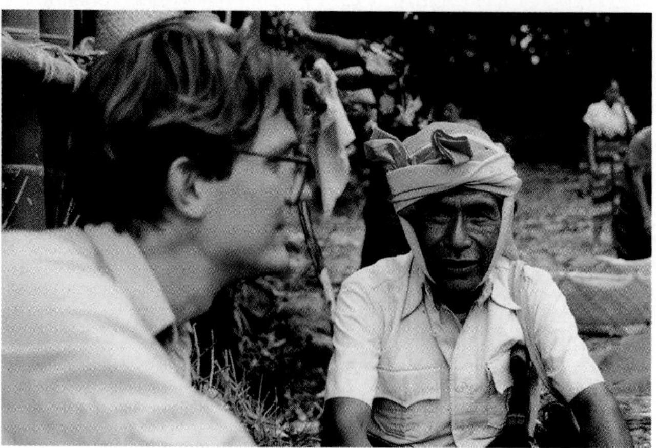

Expressive culture in Sumba, Indonesia. A woman weaves ikat (IH-kut) cloth on a bamboo loom. (TOP) Ikat is a style of weaving that uses a tie-dye process on either the warp or weft before the threads are woven that will create a design in the final product. Double ikat is when both warp and weft threads are tie-dyed before weaving. The motif on this piece of ikat is the Tree of Life flanked by roosters. (BOTTOM) Linguistic anthropologist Joel Kuipers interviews a ritual speaker who is adept at verbal arts performance.

▶ *What is a form of verbal art in your culture?*

analyzing oral or written material such as video and tape recordings. Thus, strong ties often exist between cultural and linguistic anthropologists in the study of art.

Many anthropologists have become apprentices in an artistic tradition. For John Chernoff, learning to play African drums was an important part of building rapport during his fieldwork in Ghana and an essential aspect of his ability to gain an understanding of the importance of music in Ghanaian society (1979). His book, *African Rhythm and African Sensibility* is one of the first reflexive ethnographies (recall Chapter 3), taking into account the position and role of the ethnographer and how they shape what the ethnographer learns. Reading the introduction to his book is the best way to become convinced that fieldwork in cultural anthropology is far more than simply gathering the data you think you need for the project you have in mind, especially if your project concerns processes of creativity and expression.

Chernoff argues that only by relinquishing a scientific approach can a researcher learn about creativity and how it is related to society. As one of his drumming teachers said, "The heart sees before the eyes." Chernoff had to do more than practice participant observation. His heart had to participate too. During his early months in the field, Chernoff often found himself wondering why he was there. To write a book? To tell people back in the United States about Ghana? No doubt many of the Ghanaians he met wondered the same thing, especially given that his early efforts at drumming were pretty bad, although he did not realize it because he always drank copious amounts of gin before playing. Eventually, he became the student of a master drummer and went through a formal initiation ceremony. For the ceremony, he had to kill two chickens himself and eat parts of them in a form that most North Americans will never see in a grocery store. Still, he was not playing well enough. He went through another ritual to make his wrist "smart" so that it would turn faster, like a cat chasing a mouse. For that ritual, he had to go into the bush, 10 miles outside town, and collect ingredients. The ritual worked. Having a cat's hand was a good thing, but anthropologically it was more important to Chernoff that he had begun to gain an understanding of drumming in its social and ritual contexts.

Chernoff learned about Ghanaian family life and how it is connected to individual performers and to rituals that have to do with music. He also grew to see where his performance fell short and what he needed to do to improve. He gained great respect for the artists who taught him and admiration for their striving for respect. Chernoff's personality was an important ingredient of the learning process. He comments, "I assumed that I did not know what to do in most situations. I accepted what people told me about myself and what I should be doing. . . . I waited to see what people would make of me. . . . By staying cool I learned the meaning of character" (1979:170).

FOCUS ON THE ARTIST In the early twentieth century, Franz Boas urged his students to go beyond the study of the products of art and study the artists. One role of the anthropologist, he said, is to add to the understanding of art by studying art from the artist's perspective. Ruth Bunzel's (1972 [1929]) research with Native American potters in the U.S. Southwest is a classic example of this tradition. While undergoing training as an apprentice potter, she paid attention to the variety of pot shapes and motifs and asked individual potters about their design choices. One Zuni potter commented, "I always know the whole design before I start to paint" (1972:49). A Laguna potter said, "I made up all my designs and never copy. I learned this design from my mother. I learned most of my designs from my mother" (1972:52). Bunzel discovered the importance of both past traditions and individual agency.

The social status of artists is another aspect of the focus on the artist. Artists may be revered and wealthy as individuals or as a group, or they may be stigmatized and economically marginal. In ancient Mexico, goldworkers were highly respected. In Native American groups of the Pacific Northwest coast, male carvers and painters had to be initiated into a secret society, and they had higher status than other men. Often a gender division exists. Among the Navajo of Arizona, women weave and men do silversmithing. In the Caribbean, women of African descent are noted for their carvings of *calabashes* (large gourds). In the contemporary United States, most famous and successful graphic artists are men, although the profession includes many women. Depending on the genre, race/ethnicity/indigeneity is another factor shaping success as an artist.

As with other occupations, the performing arts are more specialized in state-level societies. Generally, among free-ranging foragers, little specialization exists. Artistic activity is open to all, and artistic products are shared equally by all. Some

Kanye West performs on the main stage at the 2006 Coachella Valley Music and Arts Festival in Indio, California.
▶ *Do your parents or grandparents know who Kanye West is?*

everyday ANTHROPOLOGY

The Invisible Hands That Craft Souvenirs

Tourists who buy arts and crafts souvenirs rarely learn much about the people who actually made the items. Yet they probably have some mental image of, for example, a village potter sitting at the wheel or a silversmith hammering at a piece of metal in a quaint workshop. Souvenir shops come in different varieties, from street stalls that sell a few items such as embroidered clothing or "ethnic" jewelry to national emporiums that offer a wide range of arts and crafts. An upscale store of the latter category in Israel, called Maskit, caters mainly to tourists (Shenhav-Keller 1993:183). Ethnographic study shows how the sellers "put Israeli society on display via its souvenirs." It also reveals how certain artists and craftspeople are selectively rendered invisible.

The tourist artifact, or souvenir, can be analyzed like a "text" that contains social messages. Looking at souvenirs this way reveals what both marketeers and tourists choose to preserve, value, and exchange (Clifford 1988:221). In the Maskit stores, three central themes in Israeli society are expressed in the choice and presentation of souvenirs: Israel's attitudes toward its ancient and recent past, its view of its religion and culture, and its approach to Arab Israelis and Palestinians. Shelly Shenhav-Keller (1993) conducted participant observation in the original Maskit store in Tel Aviv and interviewed Jewish Israeli, Arab Israeli, and Palestinian artists and artisans whose products were sold there.

Maskit, the Israel Center for Handicrafts, was founded by Ruth Dayan (then the wife of Moshe Dayan) as a Ministry of Labor project in 1954. Its purpose was "to encourage artisans to continue their native crafts in the new surrounding . . . to retain and safeguard the ancient crafts" (Shenhav-Keller 1983:183). Maskit was a success, and a chain of shops was eventually opened. As its status increased, Maskit came to be perceived as an "ambassador of Israel." Dignitaries who traveled from Israel abroad were loaded with gifts from the shop. Official visitors to Israel were given Maskit gifts.

The shop had two floors. The top floor, where the entrance was located, had five sections: fashion (women's clothing, wedding gowns, and dresses with three different styles of Arab embroidery); jewelry; ritual articles (candlesticks, goblets, incense burners); decorative items; and books. The larger lower floor had five thematic sections: the Bar-Mitzvah Corner with prayer books and other ritual items; the children's corner (clothing, games, toys, and T-shirts); the embroidery section (tablecloths, linens, pillow covers, wallets, eyeglass cases); the carpet section; and a large area for ceramics, glassware, and copperware.

Over the years, changes have occurred in who produces the art sold in Maskit. The amount of Jewish ethnic art has declined as the older artists have aged and their children have not taken up the craft. Many of the original Jewish Israeli artists gained eminence and opened their own shops. Those who continue to supply Maskit specialize in ceramics, jewelry, carpet design, and ritual articles. These pieces are considered to have the status of art and may be displayed as an "individual collection" within the store. To make up for the decline in objects made by Jewish Israelis, Maskit has turned to Arab artists and craftsmakers.

After the 1967 Six-Day War, Arab Israeli and Palestinian craftsmanship became increasingly available with the incorporation of new areas within Israel, including the Occupied Territories. Most of the Arabs absorbed into the souvenir industry became hired laborers in factories and workshops owned by Maskit or by Israeli artisans who sold their works to Maskit as "Israeli." Maskit provides no information about the artistic role of Israeli Arabs or Palestinians in creating its products. The carpets, for example, are presented simply as hand-woven "Israeli" carpets, even though Arab Israelis wove them.

◆ FOOD FOR THOUGHT

- Do you know of another example in which something attributed to one ethnic group or culture is actually produced by people of a different group?

people may be especially appreciated as singers, storytellers, or carvers. With increasing social complexity and a market for art, specialized training is required to produce certain kinds of art, and the products are sought after by those who can afford them. Class differences in artistic styles and preferences emerge along with the increasingly complex division of labor.

MICROCULTURES, ART, AND POWER Art forms and styles, like language, are often associated with microcultural groups' identity and sense of pride. For example, the Berbers of highland Morocco are associated with woolen carpets, Maya Indians with woven and embroidered blouses, and the Inuit of Alaska with small stone carvings of figurines. Cultural anthropologists provide many examples of linkages between various microcultural dimensions and power issues. In some instances, more powerful groups appropriate the art forms of less powerful groups. In others, forms of art are said to be expressive of resistance. One study reveals how political interests in Israel take ownership of ethnic artistic expression (see Everyday Anthropology).

An example of how gender relations are played out in expressive culture comes from a study of male strip dancing in Florida (Margolis and Arnold 1993). Advertisements in the media tell women that seeing a male strip dancer is "their chance," "their night out." Going to a male strip is marketed as a time of reversal of traditional gender roles in which men are dominant and women submissive. Are gender roles actually reversed in a male stripper bar? The short answer is no. Women customers are treated like juveniles. As they stand in line waiting for the show to open, the manager instructs them on how to tip. They are symbolically dominated by the dancers, who take on various roles such as lion tamers. The *dive-bomb* is further evidence of women's subordinate position. The dive-bomb is a form of tipping the dancer in which the woman customer gets on her hands and knees and tucks a bill held between her teeth into the dancer's g-string. The interpretation of all this behavior is that, rather than reversing the gender hierarchy, it reinforces it.

Not all forms of popular art and performance are mechanisms of social control and hierarchy maintenance. In the United States, for example, hip-hop and urban Black youths' verbal arts and rap music can be seen as a form of protest through performance (Smitherman 1997). Their lyrics report on their experience of economic oppression, the danger of drugs, and men's disrespect for women. The global spread of hip-hop and related music is another example of social resistance through song and performance.

PERFORMANCE ARTS

The performance arts include music, dance, theater, rhetoric (speech-making), and narrative (storytelling). One important area has developed its own name: **ethnomusicology**, the cross-cultural study of music. Ethnomusicologists study a range of topics, including the form of the music itself, the social position of musicians, how music interacts with other domains of culture such as religion or healing, and change in musical traditions. This section provides examples about music and gender in Malaysia, music and globalization in Brazil, and theater and society in India.

MUSIC AND GENDER AMONG THE TEMIAR OF MALAYSIA An important topic for ethnomusicologists is gender differences in access to performance roles in music (for ideas about research on this topic, see Figure 14.1). A cultural materialist perspective would predict that in cultures where gender roles are relatively egalitarian, access to and meanings in music will tend to be egalitarian. This is the case among the Temiar, a group of foragers of highland Malaysia (see Map 8.3, p. 198). Their musical traditions emphasize balance and complementarity between males and females (Roseman 1987).

Among the Temiar, kinship and marriage rules are flexible and open. Marriages are based on the mutual desires of the partners. Descent is bilineal (review Chapter 8), and marital residence follows no particular rule after a period of bride service. Marriages often end in separation, and serial monogamy is common. Men have a slight edge over women in political and ritual spheres. They are typically the village leaders, and they are the spirit mediums who sing the songs that energize the spirits. Historical records, however, indicate that women were spirit mediums in the past.

If you were doing an ethnographic study of gender roles in musical performance, the following questions would be useful in starting the inquiry. But they would not exhaust the topic. Can you think of questions that should be added to the list?

1. Are men and women equally encouraged to use certain instruments and repertoires?
2. Is musical training available to all?
3. Do male and female repertoires overlap? If so, how, when and for what reasons?
4. Are the performances of men and women public, private, or both? Are women and men allowed to perform together? In what circumstances?
5. Do members of the culture give equal value to the performances of men and women? On what criteria are these evaluations based, and are they the same for men and women performers?

Source: From "Power and Gender in the Musical Experiences of Women," pp. 224–225 by Carol E Robertson in *Women and Music in Cross-Cultural Perspective*, ed. by Ellen Koskoff. Copyright © 1987. Reprinted by permission of the Greenwood Publishing Group, Inc. Westport, CT.

FIGURE 14.1 Five Ethnographic Questions about Gender and Music

Although men singers are the nodes through which the songs of the spirits enter the community, women's performance role is significant and the male spirit-medium role is not of greater importance or status. The distinction between male leader and female chorus is blurred through overlap between phrases and repetition. The performance is one of general community participation with integrated male and female roles, as in Temiar society in general.

COUNTRY MUSIC AND GLOBALIZATION IN BRAZIL Linguistic anthropologist Alexander Dent studies the growing popularity of *música sertaneja* (MOO-see-kah ser-tah-NAY-shah) Brazilian country music (2005). Música sertaneja draws heavily on U.S. country music, but it is significantly localized within Brazilian contexts. Brazilian performers creatively use North American country music songs, such as "Achy Breaky Heart" to convey messages that make sense in the Brazilian context about gender relationships, intimacy, the family, the past, and the importance of the countryside. In their performances and recordings, they use an American genre to critique American-driven processes such as extreme capitalism and globalization and to critique the Brazilian adoption of such Western ways.

ethnomusicology the cross-cultural study of music.

(LEFT) Many forms of theater combine the use of facial makeup, masks, and costumes to transform an actor into someone (or something) else. This Kathakali dancer is applying makeup before a performance in Kerala, South India. (RIGHT) A new use for classical dance-drama in India is for raising social awareness about problems such as excessive dowries and female infanticide. Street theater groups go into neighborhoods and act out skits, drawing members of the audience into dialogue with them.

A prominent feature of Brazilian country music is performance by a *dupla,* two brothers. The "brothers" (who may or may not be biological brothers) emphasize their similarity by cutting their hair the same way and wearing similar clothes. Musically, they blend their voices, with neither voice dominating the other. When performing, they sing part of a song with their arms over each other's shoulders and gaze at each other affectionately. The dupla and their music emphasize kinship and caring as important aspects of Brazilian tradition that should be preserved.

THEATER AND MYTH IN SOUTH INDIA **Theater** is a type of enactment that seeks to entertain through movement and words related to dance, music, parades, competitive games and sports, and verbal art (Beeman 1993). Cross-culturally, strong connections exist among myth, ritual, and performance.

One theatrical tradition that offers a blend of mythology, acting, and music is the Kathakali (kuh-tuh-kal-lee) ritual dance-drama of southern India (Zarrilli 1990). Stylized hand gestures, elaborate makeup, and costumes contribute to the attraction of these performances, which dramatize India's great Hindu epics, especially the Mahabharata (review Chapter 13) and the Ramayana. Costumes and makeup transform the actor into one of several well-known characters from Indian mythology. The audience easily recognizes the basic character types at their first entrance by the performers' costumes and makeup. Six makeup types exist to depict characters ranging from the most refined to the most vulgar. Kings and heroes have green facial makeup, reflecting their refinement and moral uprightness. Vulgar characters are associated with black facial makeup and occasionally black beards. With their black faces dotted with red and white, they are the most frightening of the Kathakali characters.

theater a form of enactment, related to other forms such as dance, music, parades, competitive games and sports, and verbal art, that seeks to entertain through acting, movement, and sound.

ARCHITECTURE AND DECORATIVE ARTS

Like all art forms, architecture is interwoven with other aspects of culture. Architecture may reflect and protect social rank and class differences as well as gender, age, and ethnic differences (Guidoni 1987). Decorative arts—including interior decoration of homes and buildings, and external design features such as gardens—likewise reflect people's social position and "taste." Local cultures have long defined preferred standards in these areas of expression, but global influences from the West and elsewhere, such as Japan and other non-Western cultures, have been adopted and adapted by other traditions.

ARCHITECTURE AND INTERIOR DESIGN Foragers, being highly mobile, build dwellings as needed and then abandon them (refer to the photo on p. 91 of Ju/'hoansi shelter). Having few personal possessions and no surplus goods, they need no permanent storage structures. The construction of dwellings does not require the efforts of groups larger than the family unit. Foragers' dwellings are an image of the family and not of the wider society. The dwellings' positioning in relation to each other reflects the relations among families.

More elaborate shelters and greater social cohesiveness in planning occur as foraging is combined with horticulture, as in the semipermanent settlements in the Amazon rainforest. People live in the settlement part of the year but break up into smaller groups that spread out into a larger area for foraging. Important decisions concern location of the site in terms of weather, availability of drinking water, and defensibility. The central plaza must be elevated for drainage, and drainage channels dug around the hearths. The overall plan is circular. In some groups, separate shelters are built for extended family groups; in others, they are joined into a continuous circle with connected roofs. In some cases, the headman has a separate and larger shelter.

Pastoralists have designed ingenious portable structures such as the North American teepee and the Mongolian *ger*, or yert. The teepee is a conical tent made with a framework of four wooden poles tied at the top with thongs, to which are joined other poles to complete the cone. This frame is then covered with buffalo hide. A ger is also a circular, portable dwelling, but its roof is flatter. The covering is made of cloth. This lightweight structure is easy to set up, take down, and transport, and it is adaptable to all weather conditions. Encampments are often arranged the teepees or gers in several concentric circles. Social status was the structuring principle, and the council of chiefs and the head chief were located in the center.

With the development of the state, urban areas grew and showed the effects of centralized planning and power, for example, in grid-style street planning rather than haphazard street placement. The symbolic demonstration of the power, grandeur, and identity of states was and is expressed architecturally through the construction of impressive urban monuments: temples, administrative buildings, memorials, and museums.

Interior decoration of domestic dwellings also became more elaborate. In settled agricultural communities and urban centers where permanent housing is the norm, decoration is more likely to be found in homes. Wall paintings, sculptures, and other features distinguish the homes of wealthier individuals. Research on interior decoration in contemporary Japan involved studying the contents of home decorating magazines and doing participant observation within homes (Rosenberger 1992). Findings reveal how people incorporate and localize selected aspects of Western decorating styles.

Home decorating magazines target middle- and upper-class Japanese housewives who seek to express their status through new consumption styles. A trend is the abandonment of three features of traditional Japanese design: *tatami, shoji,* and *fusuma.* Tatami are 2-inch-thick mats that are about 3 feet wide and 6 feet long. A room's size is measured in terms of the number of tatami mats it holds. Shoji are the sliding screen doors of tatami rooms, one covered with glass and the other with translucent rice paper often printed with a design of leaves or waves. Fusuma are sliding wall panels made of thick paper; they are removable so that rooms can be enlarged for gatherings. The tatami room usually contains a low table in the center, with pillows for seating on the floor. A special alcove may contain a flower arrangement, ancestors' pictures, and a Buddhist altar. Futons are stored in closets around the edges and brought out at night for sleeping.

In distancing themselves from the old style, "modern" Japanese housewives make several changes. The kitchen has a central rather than marginal location and is merged with a space called the DK (dining-kitchen) or LDK (living-dining-kitchen), with wood, tile, or carpeting on the floor. Western products such as carpeting and curtains (instead of the fusuma, the tatami, and shoji) are used to cover surfaces and to separate rooms. The LDK has a couch, dining set, VCR, stereo, and an array of small items on display such as Western-style teapots, cuckoo clocks, and knick-knacks.

These design choices accompany deeper social changes that involve new aspirations about marriage and family relationships. Home decorating magazines promote the idea that the modern style brings with it happier children with better grades and closer husband–wife ties. Tensions exist, however, between these ideals and the realities of middle- and upper-class life in Japan. Women feel compelled to work either part time or full time to be able to contribute income for satisfying their new consumer needs. Yet Japanese women are discouraged from pursuing careers and are urged to devote more time to domestic pursuits, including home decorating and child care, in order to provide the kind of life portrayed in the magazines. Children are in the conflicting position of being indulged as new consumer targets, while the traditional value of self-discipline still holds. Husbands are in the conflicting position of needing to be more attentive to wife and home, whereas the corporate world calls them for a "7–11" working day. Furthermore, the Western image of the happy nuclear family contains no plan for the aged. The wealthiest Japanese families manage to satisfy both individualistic desires and

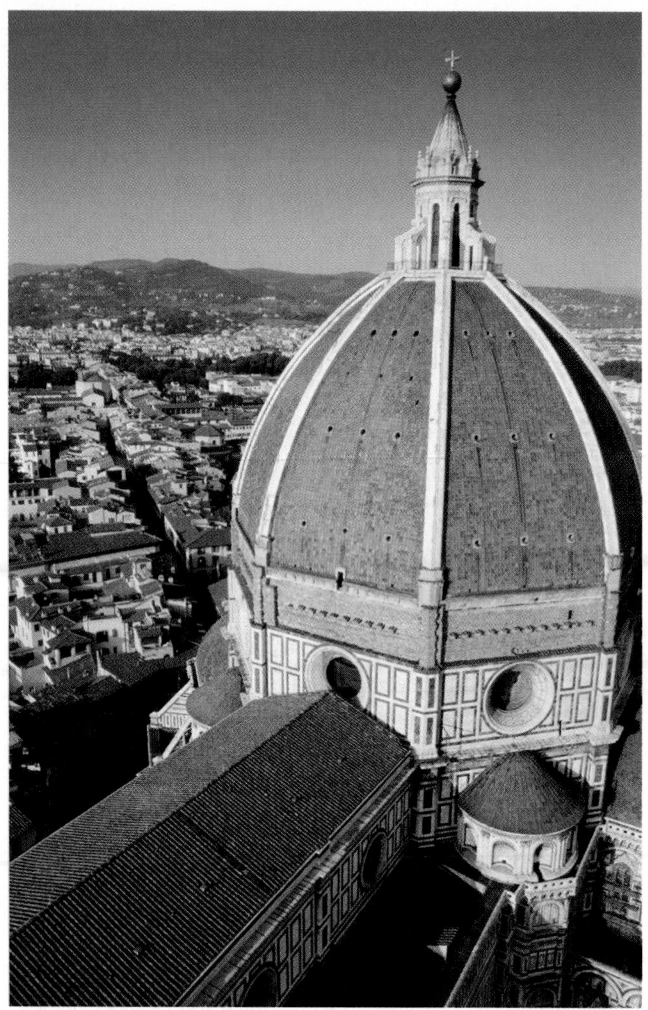

(LEFT) The Duomo in Florence, Italy. The Duomo, or Cathedral of Santa Maria del Fiore, was begun in 1296. Its massive dome, designed by architect and sculptor Filippo Brunelleschi, was not completed until 1436. The goal was to surpass in height and beauty all other edifices. It still physically dominates the city of Florence and also attracts many tourists from around the world. (RIGHT) Burj Dubai, or Dubai Tower, in Dubai, United Arab Emirates, is currently the tallest building in the world. Its immense height signals the importance of Dubai in the modern world and, more generally, the success and prosperity of the Middle East.

filial duties because they can afford a large house in which they dedicate a separate floor for the husband's parents, complete with tatami mats. Less wealthy people have a more difficult time dealing with these conflicting values.

GARDENS AND FLOWERS Gardens for use, especially for food production, are differentiated from gardens for decorative purposes. The concept of the decorative garden is not a cultural universal. Circumpolar peoples cannot construct gardens in the snow, and highly mobile pastoralists have no gardens because they are on the move. The decorative garden is a product of state-level societies, especially in the Middle East, Europe, and Asia (Goody 1993). Within these contexts, variation exists in what are considered to be the appropriate contents and design of a garden. A Japanese garden may contain no blooming flowers, focusing instead on the shape and placement of trees, shrubs, stones, and bodies of water.

Elite Muslim culture, with its core in the Middle East, has long been associated with formal decorative gardens. A garden, enclosed with four walls, is symbolically equivalent to the concept of "paradise." The Islamic garden pattern involves a square design with symmetrical layout, fountains, waterways, and straight pathways, all enclosed within walls. Islamic gardens often surrounded the tombs of prominent people. India's Taj Mahal (refer to the photo on p. 203), built by a Muslim emperor, follows this pattern, with one modification: The tomb is placed at one edge of the garden rather than in the center. The result is a dramatic stretch of fountains and flowers leading from the main gate to the monument.

heterotopia a new situation formed from elements drawn from multiple and diverse contexts.

museum an institution that collects, preserves, interprets, and displays objects on a regular basis.

The contents of a personal garden, like a dinner menu with all its special ingredients or a collection of souvenirs from around the world with all their memories and meanings, makes a statement about its owner's identity and status. For example, in Europe during the height of colonialism, imperial gardens contained specimens from remote corners of the globe, collected through scientific expeditions. Such gardens are created through the collection and placement of plants from many parts of the world. The cultural practice of creating a new situation formed from elements drawn from multiple and diverse contexts is called **heterotopia** (Foucault 1970). Heterotopias can be constructed in architecture, cuisine, dress, and more. In the case of these gardens, the heterotopic message conveyed the owner's worldliness and intellectual status.

Cut flowers are now important economic products. They provide income for gardeners throughout the world, and they are also exchange items. In France, women receive flowers from men more than any other kind of gift (Goody 1993:316). In much of the world, special occasions require gifts of flowers: In the West, as well as in East Asia, funerals are times for displays of flowers. Ritual offerings to the deities in Hinduism are often flowers such as marigolds woven into a chain or necklace.

Flowers are prominent motifs in Western and Asian secular and sacred art, but less so in African art (Goody 1993). Some possible reasons for this variation include ecological and economic factors. Eurasia's more temperate environment possesses a greater variety of blooming plants than Africa's does. Sheer economic necessity in developing countries of Africa limits the amount of space that can be used for decorative purposes. In wealthy African kingdoms, prominent luxury goods include fabrics, gold ornaments, and wooden carvings rather than flowers. This pattern of production is changing with globalization, however. Many African countries now grow flowers for export to the world market.

An early morning scene in the city of Den Haag (The Hague), in the Netherlands. Dutch people buy, on average, a dozen bouquets of cut flowers per year. Because raising and transporting cut flowers is energy intensive, it is important to consider alternate gifts.

▶ *How often do you buy cut flowers per year, and what are the occasions? What alternatives exist that are less costly to the environment?*

MUSEUMS AND CULTURE

This section considers the concept of the museum and the debates about the role of museums in exhibiting and representing culture. Museum studies, in anthropology, include anthropologists who work in museums helping to prepare exhibits and anthropologists who study museums—what they choose to display and how they display it—as important sites of culture itself.

WHAT IS A MUSEUM? A **museum** is an institution that collects, preserves, interprets, and displays objects on a regular basis (Kahn 1995:324). Its purpose may be esthetic or educational. The idea of gathering and displaying objects goes back at least to the Babylonian kings of the sixth century BCE who ruled in what is now Iraq (Maybury-Lewis 1997a). The word comes from a Greek word referring to a place where the *muses* (spirits who inspire thought and creativity) congregate, or a place to have philosophical discussions or see artistic performances. In Europe, it came to denote a place where art objects were housed and displayed. Ethnographic and science museums came later, inspired by Europe's emerging interests in exploration in the 1500s and the accompanying scientific urge to gather specimens from around the world and classify them into an evolutionary history.

The Western concept of the museum and its several forms diffused throughout the world through colonialism. Many museums in developing countries still bear a strong colonial imprint and fail to connect with local people's interests (Fogelman 2008). In spite of these problems, such museums play an important role in preserving aspects of culture that would otherwise have been lost forever. A recent program through the European Economic Community (EEC) supports the remodeling and expansion of national museums throughout Africa. In 2008, the revamped Kenya National Museum, funded by the EEC, opened with great fanfare. Its prominent attractions include original fossils of early hominins and a garden displaying healing plants found in the country, organized by species and providing information on their uses.

THE POLITICS OF EXHIBITS Within anthropology, the subfield of *museum anthropology* is concerned with studying how and why museums choose to collect and display

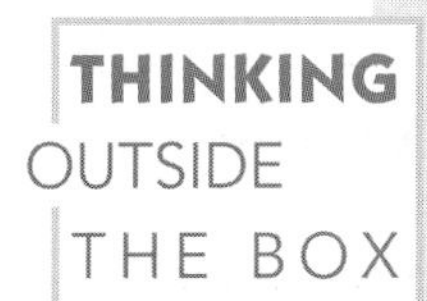

Think of some occasions in your cultural world in which cut flowers play a role, and what that role is.

(LEFT) A display of African artifacts collected by British colonial-era explorers and early anthropologists, shown with minimal labels and context, at the Powell-Cotton Museum in Kent, southeast England. This museum is moving toward exhibits that provide more context while preserving some of its "colonialist" exhibits as examples of their time. (RIGHT) In Port Blair, the Andaman Islands, the Anthropological Museum is a small building containing some artifacts, but mainly photographs of the indigenous people. The so-called Jarawa, shown here, are the most well-known and feared group for their false reputation as being cannibals. The Jarawa photographs are the museum's main attraction.

particular objects (Ames 1992, A. Jones 1993). Museum anthropologists are at the forefront of debates about who gets to represent whom, the ownership of particular objects, and the public-service role of museums versus possible elitism. One issue is whether objects from non-Western cultures should be exhibited, like Western art objects, with little or no ethnographic context (Clifford 1988, Watson 1997).

Most anthropologists support the need for context, and not just for non-Western objects but for all objects on display. For example, a museum label of Andy Warhol's hyperrealistic painting of a can of Campbell's soup should include information on the social context in which such art was produced and some background on the artist. The anthropological view that all forms of expressive culture are context bound and are better understood and appreciated within their social context is, however, still rare among Western art historians and critics (Best 1986).

Another contentious issue concerns who should have control of objects in museums that were acquired through colonialism and neocolonialism. The issue of **repatriation**, or returning objects to their original peoples, is a matter of international and intranational concern. In the United States and Canada, many Native American groups have lobbied successfully for the return of ancestral bones, grave goods, and potlatch goods. In 1990, the United States passed the *Native American Graves Protection and Repatriation Act (NAGRPA)* after two decades of lobbying by Native American groups (Bray 1996; Rose, Green, and Green 1996). This act requires universities, museums, and federal agencies in the United States to inventory their archaeological holdings in preparation for repatriating skeletons to their Native American descendant communities. Estimates of the number of Native American skeletons in museums in the United States (not including Hawai'i) range from 14,000 to 600,000. Unknown numbers of other items are being inventoried for possible repatriation, a process that is stretching slender museum budgets (Watson 1997).

The breakup of the former Soviet Union prompted claims from several newly independent states seeking to retrieve artistic property that originated in their locale and had been taken to Soviet national museums in Moscow and St. Petersburg. Ukraine, for example (see Map 14.1), has asked for the return of about 2 million art objects from Russia (Akinsha 1992a).

Another disputed area about art in Russia concerns the state and the church. The Soviet state put many icons (images of the Christian deities, Mary, and Jesus) and other religious objects in museums and turned churches into museums. The Russian Orthodox Church has campaigned for the return of church property. Churches ask that all sacred objects of the church, church buildings, and masterpieces of church art confiscated by the state after 1917 be returned to the ownership of the Russian Orthodox Church (Akinsha 1992b). Art historians and museum officials worry that the churches lack the resources and the experience to care for these treasures. Another complication comes from occasional threats of theft and violence to museums by those who seek the return

repatriation returning art or other objects from museums to the people with whom they originated.

MAP 14.1 Ukraine.
Ukraine became independent after the collapse of the Soviet Union in 1991. It is mostly fertile plains, or steppes, crossed by rivers. Since independence and privatization, the economy has been unstable, with high inflation rates. Related to the economic crisis, sex trafficking of women became a major problem, infant mortality rates rose, and the birth rate fell. The total population is around 50 million and declining. Ukrainian is the official language, though many people speak Russian, especially in the south and east. Many people speak a mixture of both languages. Government policy promotes the increased use of the Ukrainian language. The dominant religion is Eastern Orthodox Christianity. The tradition of coloring Easter eggs began in Ukraine in pre-Christian times.

of icons to churches and monasteries. In response, some museums have removed some pieces from display.

◆◆◆

Play, Leisure, and Culture

This section considers the area of expressive culture related to what people do for "fun." It is impossible to draw a clear line between the concepts of *play* or *leisure* and art or performance, however, because they often overlap. For example, a person could paint watercolors in her leisure time, yet simultaneously be creating a work of art. In most cases, though, play and leisure can be distinguished from other activities by the fact that they have no direct, utilitarian purpose for the participant (Huizinga as summarized in Hutter 1996):

- Play is unnecessary activity.
- Play is outside of ordinary life.
- Play is closed and limited in terms of time.
- Play has rules.
- Play may contain chance and tension.

Leisure activities often overlap with play, but many leisure activities, such as reading or lying on a beach, would not be considered play because they lack rules, chance, and tension. Within the broad category of play and leisure activities, several subcategories exist, including varieties of games, hobbies, and recreational travel. Although play and leisure, and their subcategories, may be pursued from a nonutilitarian perspective, they are often situated in a wider context of commercial and political interests. The Olympic Games are a good example of such complexities. China's hosting of the 2008 summer Olympics was a major opportunity for China to demonstrate its status as a world leader.

Cultural anthropologists study play and leisure within their cultural contexts as part of social systems. They ask, for example, why some leisure activities involve teams rather than individuals; what the social roles and status of people involved in particular activities are; what the goals of the games are and how they are achieved; how much danger or violence is involved; how certain activities are related to group identity; and how such activities link or separate different groups within or between societies or countries.

GAMES AND SPORTS AS A CULTURAL MICROCOSM

Games and sports, like religious rituals and festivals, can be interpreted as reflections of social relationships and cultural ideals. In Clifford Geertz's terms, they are both *models of a culture,* depicting basic ideals, and *models for a culture,* socializing people into certain values and ideals (1996). American football can be seen as a model for corporate culture in its clear hierarchy with leadership vested in one person (the quarterback) and its goal of territorial expansion by taking over areas from the competition.

A comparison of baseball as played in the United States and in Japan reveals core values about social relationships in each country (Whiting 1979). These differences emerge clearly when U.S. players are hired by Japanese teams. The U.S. players bring with them an intense sense of individualism, which promotes the value of "doing your own thing."

Two extreme sports. (LEFT) Tony Stewart, driver of the No. 20 Home Depot Chevrolet, makes a pit stop during the NASCAR NEXTEL Cup Series at Bristol Meyer Speedway in Tennessee. (RIGHT) Clearing a stone platform over 6 feet high, a young man from Nias, Indonesia, participates in the sport of *fahombe*. Formerly a method of training warriors to leap over walls of enemy villages during a raid and of demonstrating a man's readiness to marry, fahombe is now a popular sport in several islands off Sumatra.

This pattern conflicts with a primary value that influences the playing style in Japan: ***wa***, meaning discipline and self-sacrifice for the good of the group. In Japanese baseball, players must seek to achieve and maintain team harmony. Japanese baseball players have a negative view of extremely individualistic, egotistical plays and strategies.

SPORTS AND SPIRITUALITY: MALE WRESTLING IN INDIA In many contexts, sports are closely tied to religion and spirituality. Asian martial arts, for example, require forms of concentration much like meditation, leading to spiritual self-control. Male wrestling in India, a popular form of entertainment at rural fairs and other public events, involves a strong link with spiritual development and asceticism (Alter 1992).

In some ways these wrestlers are just like other members of Indian society. They go to work, and they marry and have families, but their dedication to wrestling involves important differences. A wrestler's daily routine is one of self-discipline. Every act—defecation, bathing, comportment, devotion—is integrated into a daily regimen of discipline. Wrestlers come to the *akhara* (AKH-uh-ruh), equivalent to a gymnasium, early in the morning for practice under the supervision of a guru or other senior akhara member. They practice moves with different partners for two to three hours. In the early evening, they return for more exercise. In all, a strong young wrestler will do around 2000 push-ups and 1000 deep-knee bends a day in sets of 50 to 100.

The wrestler's diet is strictly defined. Most wrestlers are mainly vegetarian. Although they avoid alcohol and tobacco, they do consume *bhang* a beverage made of blended milk, spices, almonds, and concentrated marijuana. In addition to regular meals, wrestlers consume large quantities of milk, *ghee* (clarified butter), and almonds. These substances are sources of strength, because according to traditional dietary principles, they help to build up the body's semen.

Several aspects of the wrestler's life are similar to those of a Hindu *sanyasi* (sun-YAH-see) or holy man, who renounces life in the normal world. The aspiring sanyasi studies under a guru and learns to follow a strict routine of discipline and meditation called yoga, and he adheres to a restricted diet to achieve control of the body and its life force. Both wrestler

Wrestlers in a village in northern India. They follow a rigorous regimen of dietary restrictions and exercise in order to keep their bodies and minds under control.

▶ *Think of another sport that emphasizes dietary restrictions.*

---

wa Japanese word meaning discipline and self-sacrifice for the good of the group.

blood sport a form of competition that explicitly seeks to bring about a flow of blood, or even death, of human–human contestants, human–animal contestants, or animal–animal contestants.

and sanyasi roles focus on discipline to achieve a controlled self. Therefore, in India, wrestling does not involve the "dumb jock" stereotype that it sometimes does in North America. Rather, wrestlers have respect because their sport requires perfected physical, spiritual, and moral health.

PLAY, PLEASURE, AND PAIN Many leisure activities combine pleasure and pain. Serious injuries can result from mountain climbing, horseback riding, or playing touch football in the backyard. A more intentionally dangerous category of sports is **blood sports**, competition that explicitly seeks to bring about a flow of blood or even death. Blood sports may involve human contestants, humans contesting against animal competitors, or animal–animal contestants (Donlon 1990). In the United States and Europe, professional boxing is an example of a popular blood sport that few, if any, anthropologists have studied so far. Cultural anthropologists have looked at the use of animals in blood sports such as cockfights and bullfights. These sports are variously interpreted as providing sadistic pleasure, as offering vicarious self-validation (usually of males) through the triumph of their representative pit bulls or fighting cocks, and as the triumph of culture over nature in the symbolism of bullfighting.

Even the seemingly pleasurable leisure experience of a Turkish bath can involve discomfort and pain. One phase involves scrubbing the skin vigorously several times with a rough natural sponge, a pumice stone, or a piece of cork wood wrapped in cloth (Staats 1994). The scrubbing removes layers of dead skin and opens the pores so that the skin will be beautiful. In Turkey, an option for men is a massage that can be quite violent, involving deep probes of leg muscles, cracking of the back, and being walked on by the often weighty masseur. In Ukraine, being struck repeatedly on one's bare skin with birch branches is the final stage of the bath. Violent scrubbing, scraping, and beating of the skin, along with radical temperature changes in the water, are combined with valued social interaction at the bathhouse.

Many international tourists seek "cultural tourism" so that they can participate in what is presented to them as a "traditional" cultural context. Safari tour groups in Africa, as in this visit to Maasailand, combine sightings of exotic wildlife and contact with Maasai people.

▶ *Go to the Web to learn about cultural tourism opportunities among the Maasai.*

Laotians attend a cockfight on the outskirts of Vientiane, capital of the Lao People's Democratic Republic. Officials of the World Health Organization are concerned that this sport may be one cause of the spread of avian or bird flu in Southeast Asia.

LEISURE TRAVEL

Anthropologists who study leisure travel, or tourism, often comment that their research is dismissed as trivial and based on "hanging out" at beautiful beaches or at five-star hotels. Research on tourism, however, can involve as much conflict and danger as anthropological study of any other topic. Violence is not unknown in tourist destinations, and tourist sites are increasingly the focus of violence. Even when the research site is peaceful, anthropological investigation of tourism involves the same amount of effort as any other fieldwork.

Tourism is now one of the major economic forces in the world, and it has dramatic effects on people and places in tourist destination areas. A large percentage of worldwide tourism involves individuals from Europe, North America, and Japan traveling to less industrialized countries. Ethnic tourism, cultural tourism, and ecotourism are attracting increasing numbers of travelers. They are often marketed as

THINKING OUTSIDE THE BOX

In your cultural world, what are some examples of leisure activities that combine pleasure and pain? As a research project, conduct some informal interviews with participants to learn why they are attracted to such activities.

providing a view of "authentic" cultures. Images of indigenous people figure prominently in travel brochures and advertisements (Bruner 2005).

Tourist promotional literature often presents a "myth" of other peoples and places and offers travel as a form of escape to a mythical land of wonder. Research on Western travel literature shows that from the time of the earliest explorers to the present, it has been full of *primitivist* images about indigenous peoples who are portrayed as having static or "stone age" traditions, largely unchanged by the forces of Western colonialism, nationalism, economic development, and even tourism. Tourists often seek to find the culture that the tourist industry defines rather than gaining a genuine, more complicated, and perhaps less photogenic view of it. For the tourist, obtaining these desired cultural images through mass tourism involves packaging the "primitive" with the "modern" because most tourists want comfort and convenience along with their "authentic" experience. Thus, advertisements minimize the foreignness of the host country, noting, for example, that English is spoken and that the destination is remote yet accessible, while simultaneously promoting primitivist and racist imagery.

The strains between accuracy in presenting a cultural experience, sensationalism, and social stigma emerge clearly in research on tourism in the coal-mining region of Appalachia in Virginia (LaLone 2003). Mary LaLone pinpoints some of the challenges in representing Appalachian culture with accuracy and dignity in relation to responding to marketing demands of tourists. For example, in portraying people's everyday lives, accuracy says that it is right to show people wearing shoes and using indoor plumbing, whereas tourists may expect and want to see displays of "hillbilly life" that emphasize poverty, shoelessness, outhouses, feuding, and "moonshining" (producing and consuming illicit alcohol). LaLone suggests that cultural anthropologists may help find a way toward heritage interpretation and presentation that provides a more complex view so that hosts retain their dignity, accuracy is maintained, and tourists learn more than they expected.

The anthropology of tourism has focused on the impact of global and local tourism on indigenous peoples and places. Such studies are important in exposing the degree to which tourism helps or harms local people and local ecosystems. For example, the formation of Amboseli National Park in Kenya (see Map 6.5, p. 153) reduced the access of the Maasai to traditional water resources for their herds (Honadle 1985, as summarized in Drake 1991). The project staff promised benefits (such as shares of the revenues from the park) to the Maasai if they stayed off the reserve, but most of the benefits never materialized. In contrast, in Costa Rica local people were included in the early planning stages of the Guanacaste National Park (see Map 14.2), they play a greater role in the park management system, and they share some of the benefits.

Local people with long-standing rights to land, water, and other resources often attempt to exercise agency and take an active role in transforming the effects of tourism to their advantage and designing and managing tourist projects (Natcher, Davis, and Hickey 2005; Miller 2009). The Gullah people of South Carolina are one such example (see Culturama). The last section of this chapter provides others.

High-end tourism in Costa Rica.

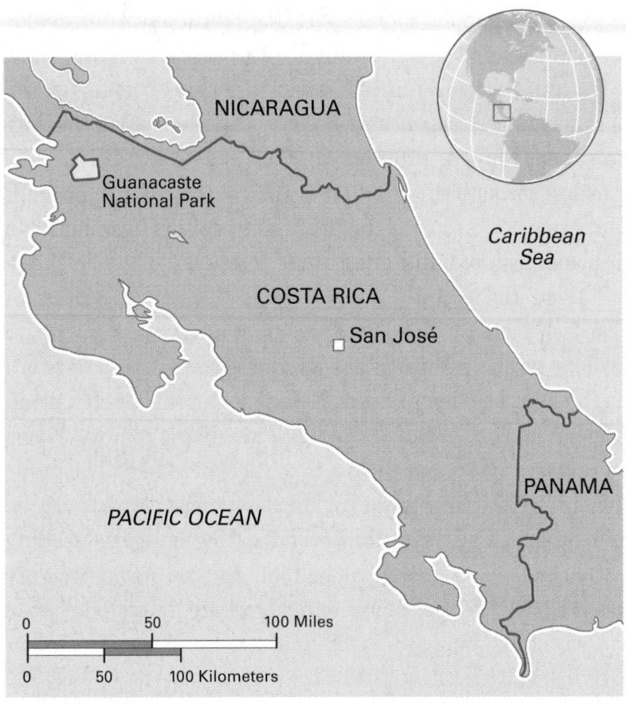

MAP 14.2 Costa Rica.

The Republic of Costa Rica was the first country in the world to constitutionally abolish its army, and it has largely escaped the violence that its neighbors have endured. Agriculture is the basis of the economy with tourism, especially ecotourism, playing an increasing role. Most of the 4 million inhabitants of Costa Rica are descended from Spanish colonialists. Less than 3 percent are Afro-Costa Ricans, and less than 2 percent, or around 50,000, are indigenous people. Seventy-five percent of the people are Roman Catholic and 14 percent Protestant. The official language is Spanish.

CULTURAMA

The Gullah of South Carolina

The Gullah (goo-luh) culture in South Carolina stretches along the coast, going inland about thirty miles (National Park Service 2005). The Gullah are descended from African slaves originating in West and Central Africa. In the early eighteenth century, Charleston, South Carolina, was the location of the largest trans-Atlantic slave market on the coast of British North America.

The enslaved people brought with them many forms of knowledge and practice. Rice was a central part of their African heritage and identity. They knew how to plant it in swamps, harvest it, and prepare it. Gullah ancestors in colonial South Carolina were influential in developing tidal irrigation methods of rice growing, using irrigation and management of the tides to increase yields compared to yields from rainfall-dependent plantings.

Experts at net fishing, the Gullah made handwoven nets that are masterpieces of folk art. Their textile arts include a form of quilting, or sewing strips of cloth together into a larger piece. Gullah women combined their African quilting styles with those of Europeans to form new styles and patterns. Many quilts tell a story in their several panels.

Gullah cuisine combines African elements such as rice, yams, peas, okra, hot peppers, peanuts, watermelon, and sesame seeds with European ingredients, and Indian foods such as corn, squash, tomatoes, and berries (National Park Service 2005). Popular dishes are stews of seafood and vegetables served over rice. Rice is the cornerstone of the meal, and the family rice pot is a treasured possession passed down over the generations.

Gullah culture in South Carolina has become a major tourist attraction, including music, crafts, and cuisine. If there is a single item that tourists identify with the Gullah, it is sweetgrass baskets. Basketmaking, once common among all Gullah people in South Carolina, is now a specialized activity. In South Carolina it is thriving in the Charleston area largely due to a combination of tourist demand and the creativity of local artists. Both men and women "sew" the baskets. They sell them in shops in Charleston's historic center and along Highway 17.

As the success of the basketmakers has grown and the popularity of the baskets increased, so too has the need for sweetgrass. Sweetgrass baskets, thus, are a focal point of conflict between Gullah cultural producers and local economic developers who are destroying the land on which the sweetgrass grows. Because tourism in low country South Carolina is increasingly dependent on cultural tourism, some planners are trying to find ways to devote land to growing sweetgrass.

The story of the Gullah of South Carolina begins with their rich African cultural heritage through their suffering as slaves, to racism and social exclusion, and to their current situation in which their expressive culture is a key factor in the state economy.

(LEFT) The hands of Charleston artist Mary Jackson are shown making a sweetgrass basket. (CENTER) Drummers at the Gullah Festival in Beaufort (BO-fert). The Festival celebrates the cultures and accomplishments of the Gullah people.

MAP 14.3 The Gullah Region of South Carolina. The heartland of Gullah culture is in the low country area of South Carolina, Georgia, and Florida, and on the Sea Islands.

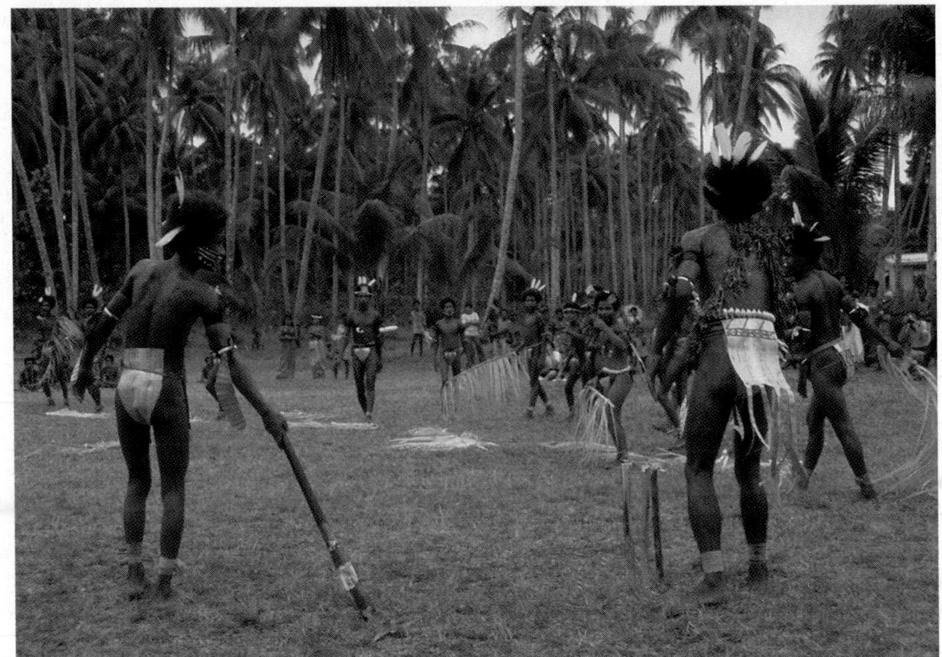

In the Trobriand Islands, British missionaries, in the late nineteenth century, tried to substitute their game of cricket for intertribal rivalries and warfare. It did not take long, however, for the Trobriand people to transform British rules and style to Trobriand ways.

▶ *If you wanted to watch a cricket match, what would be the closest place for you to go?*

◆◆◆

Change in Expressive Culture

Nowhere are forms and patterns of expressive culture frozen in time. Much change is influenced by Western culture through globalization, but influence does not occur in only one direction. African musical styles have transformed the U.S. musical scene since the days of slavery. Japan has exerted a strong influence on upper-class garden styles in the United States. Cultures in which tradition and conformity have been valued in pottery making, dress, or theater find themselves having to make choices about whether to innovate, and if so, how. Many contemporary artists (including musicians and playwrights) from Latin America to China are fusing ancient and "traditional" motifs and styles with more contemporary themes and messages.

Changes occur through the use of new materials and technology and through the incorporation of new ideas, tastes, and meanings. These changes often accompany other aspects of social change, such as colonialism, global tourism, or political transitions.

COLONIALISM AND SYNCRETISM

Western colonialism had dramatic effects on the expressive culture of indigenous peoples. In some instances, colonial disapproval of particular art forms and activities resulted in their extinction. For example, when colonialists banned head-hunting in various cultures, this change also meant that body decoration, weapon decoration, and other related expressive activities were abandoned. This section provides an example of how colonial repression of indigenous forms succeeded, but only temporarily.

In the Trobriand Islands of Papua New Guinea (see Culturama box, on p. 359), British administrators and missionaries sought to eradicate the frequent tribal warfare as part of a pacification process. One strategy was to replace it with intertribal competitive sports (Leach 1975). In 1903, a British missionary introduced the British game of cricket in the Trobriands as a way of promoting a new morality, separate from the warring traditions. As played in England, cricket involves particular rules of play and a proper look of pure white uniforms. In the early stages of the adoption of cricket in the Trobriands, the game followed the British pattern closely. As time passed and the game spread into more parts of the islands, it developed localized and syncretized versions.

Throughout the Trobriands, the islanders merged cricket into indigenous political competition between big-men (Foster 2006). Big-men leaders urged their followers to increase production in anticipation of a cricket match because matches were followed by a redistributive feast (review the discussion of moka in Chapter 10). The British missionaries discouraged traditional magic in favor of Christian beliefs, but the Trobriand Islanders brought war-related magic into cricket. For example, they use spells against the opponent team, and they decorate bats like war weapons. Weather magic is important. If things are not going well, a ritual

---

material cultural heritage sites, monuments, buildings, and movable objects considered to have outstanding value to humanity. Also called cultural heritage.

specialist may use a spell to bring rain and force cancellation of the game.

Over time, the Trobrianders stopped wearing the crisp white uniforms and instead painted their bodies and adorned themselves with feathers and shells. The teams announced their entry into the host village with songs and dances, praising their team in contrast to the opposition. Syncretism in notable in team songs and dances which draw on Western elements such as the famous entry song of the "P-K" team. P-K is the name of a Western chewing gum. The P-K team chose its name because the stickiness of gum is like the ability of their bat to hit the ball. Other teams incorporated sounds and motions of airplanes, objects that they first saw during World War II. The songs and dances are explicitly sexual and enjoyed by all, in spite of Christian missionary attempts to suppress the "immoral" aspects of Trobriand culture, which included sexual metaphors about large yams in songs and thrusting hip movements in dances, among other things.

The Trobrianders also changed some of the rules of play. The home team should always win, but not by too many runs. In this way, guests show respect to the hosts. Winning is not the major goal. The feast after the match is the climax, in which hosts demonstrate their generosity to their guests, establishing the requirement for the next match and feast.

TOURISM'S COMPLEX EFFECTS

Global tourism has had varied effects on indigenous arts. Often, tourist demand for ethnic arts and souvenirs has led to mass production of sculpture or weaving or jewelry of a lesser quality than was created before the demand. Tourists' interests in seeing an abbreviated form of traditionally long dance or theater performances has led to the presentation of "cuts" rather than an entire piece. As a result, some scholars say that tourism leads to the decline in quality and authenticity of indigenous arts.

Tourist support for indigenous arts, however, is often the sole force maintaining them, because local people in a particular culture may themselves be more interested in foreign music, art, or sports. Vietnamese water puppetry is an ancient performance mode, dating back at least to the Ly Dynasty of 1121 (Contreras 1995). Traditionally, water puppet shows took place in the spring during a lull in the farm work, or at special festival times. The stage for this performance art is either a small natural pond or an artificial water tank, with a backdrop that hides the puppeteers from the audience. They operate wooden puppets with bamboo poles, wires, and strings to make the puppets glide over the water as if on their own. Since the 1980s, water puppetry has grown in popularity among Vietnamese people and international tourists (Foley 2001). It has spread from its core area in the Red River Delta in the northern part of the country to being nationwide and from being a seasonal performance to being year-round.

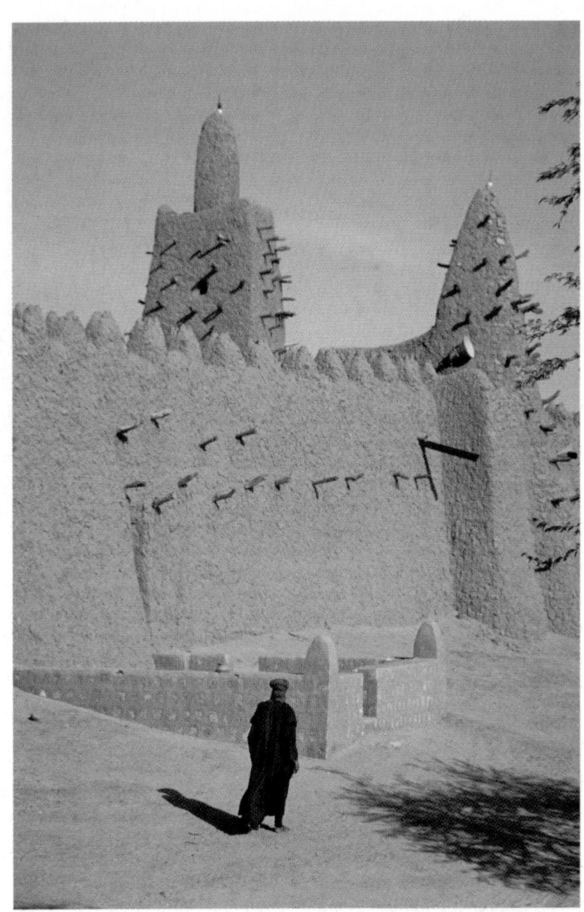

The Grande Mosque in Timbuktu, Mali. Built from mud, the mosque dates from the fourteenth century.

A more complicated situation exists in the growth of belly dancing as an essential touristic performance in Istanbul, Turkey (Potuoğlu-Cook 2006). International and Turkish tourists associate belly dancing with the Ottoman past, and it is increasingly available in various venues including classical concerts, restaurants, and nightclubs in Istanbul and other major cities (see Map 14.4). In spite of Muslim values about female modesty, commercial interests are promoting this performance mode. Even middle-class housewives are taking belly dancing lessons, a sign that a formerly stigmatized and lower-class activity is gentrifying. The rising popularity of belly dancing is evidence of Turkey's growing cosmopolitanism.

One positive result of global tourism is the growing international and local support for preservation of **material cultural heritage**, which includes sites, monuments and

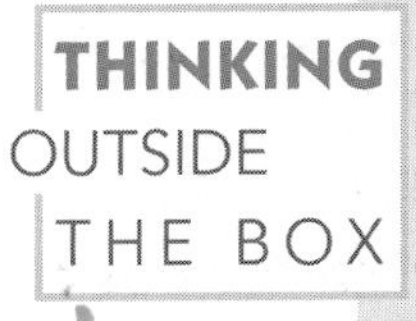

Explore at least three sites by using UNESCO's interactive map of World Heritage Sites at http://whc.unesco.org/en/254 (Google Earth is required, but is available free). Follow up by looking at photographs for each site at http://ourplaceworldheritage.com.

MAP 14.4 **Turkey.**

Turkey straddles two continents, with most of its territory being in Asia. Its largest city, Istanbul, is located in the European part. The capital city, Ankara, is located in the Asian part, called Anatolia. Turkey's culture is a blend between East and West. Its population is over 70 million. Under the leadership of Mustafa Kamal Atatürk, a constitutional, representative political system was established in 1923, following the break-up of the Ottoman Empire after World War I. Turkish is the only official language in the country. It is also widely spoken in countries once part of the Ottoman Empire, including Albania, Bosnia-Herzegovina, the Republic of Macedonia, Greece, Romania, and Serbia. Over 2 million Turkish-speaking immigrants live in Germany. Islam is the overwhelmingly predominant religion with 99 percent of the people Muslim. Of these, 75 percent are Sunni, 20 percent Shia, and 5 percent Sufi. According to the constitution, Turkey is a secular state, so there is no official state religion. The most popular sport is football (soccer). The most serious internal security issue is the Kurdish quest for greater cultural autonomy and rights.

A belly dancer performing in Istanbul, Turkey. Belly dancing may have originated in Egypt. In Turkey, it is influenced by Egyptian styles and also by Roma traditions, and many prominent contemporary Turkish belly dancers are Roma. Turkish belly dancing is distinguished by its highly energetic and athletic style and the adept use of *zils*, or finger cymbols.

buildings, and movable objects considered of outstanding world value in terms of history, art, and science (Cernea 2001). UNESCO proposed the basic definition of material cultural heritage in 1972. Since then, several hundred locations worldwide have been placed on its World Heritage List and receive some financial support for preservation. Many other invaluable sites are lost, and will be lost in the future, through destructive engineering projects, urbanization, war, looting, private collecting, and climate change.

Applied anthropologists are involved in promoting improved stewardship of material cultural heritage. Some are motivated by a desire to preserve the record of humanity for future generations, or for science. Others see that material cultural heritage, especially in poorer countries, can promote improvements in human welfare, and they endorse forging a link between material cultural heritage and sustainable development (see Lessons Applied).

In 2003, UNESCO ratified a new policy aimed at protecting **intangible cultural heritage**, or **living heritage** manifested in oral traditions, languages, performing arts, rituals and festive events, knowledge and practices about nature and the universe, and craftmaking (http://portal.unesco.org/culture). Support for this policy is based on the understanding that intangible culture provides people with a sense of identity and continuity, promotes respect for cultural diversity and human creativity, is compatible with human rights promotion, and supports sustainable development. Through this initiative, member countries of the United Nations are to make lists of valuable forms of intangible culture and take steps to preserve them. This policy has stimulated discussion and debate among cultural anthropologists who see culture as more than a list of traits, highly contextualized, always changing, and not amenable to being managed or preserved through policy mandates (Handler 2003).

Cultural anthropologists point to the fact that the preservation of expressive culture sometimes occurs as a form of resistance to outside development forces. One example of this phenomenon is the resurgence of the hula, a traditional

intangible cultural heritage UNESCO's view of culture as manifested in oral traditions, languages, performing arts, rituals and festive events, knowledge and practices about nature and the universe, and craftmaking. Also called living heritage.

LESSONS applied

A Strategy for the World Bank on Cultural Heritage

With headquarters in Washington, DC, and offices throughout the world, the World Bank is an international organization funded by member nations that works to promote and finance economic development in poor countries. Even though most of its permanent professional staff are economists, the Bank has begun to pay more attention to noneconomic factors that affect development projects.

A major move in that direction occurred in 1972 when the Bank hired its first anthropologist, Michael Cernea. For three decades, Cernea has drawn attention to the cultural dimensions of development, especially in terms of the importance of local participation in development projects and people-centered approaches to project-forced resettlement (when, for example, large dams are being planned). His most recent campaign is to convince top officials at the World Bank that the Bank should become involved in supporting cultural heritage projects as potential pathways to development.

The World Bank already has in place a "do no harm" rule when it approves and financially supports construction projects. Cernea agrees that a "do no harm" rule is basic to preventing outright destruction, but it is a passive rule and does nothing to provide resources to preserve sites. But Cernea wants to move beyond its "do no harm" rule and has written a strategy for it that is active, not passive. The strategy has two major objectives:

- The World Bank should support cultural heritage projects that promote poverty reduction and cultural heritage preservation by creating employment and generating capital from tourism.
- The projects should emphasize the educational value to local people and international visitors on the grounds that cultural understanding promotes value for goodwill and relations at all levels—local, state, and international.

Cernea offers two suggestions for better management of cultural heritage projects: (1) selectivity in site selection on the basis of the impact in reducing poverty and (2) building partnerships for project planning and implementation among local, national, and international institutions.

◆ FOOD FOR THOUGHT

- On the Internet, find the UNESCO World Heritage Site that is nearest to where you live. What does the site contain, and what can you learn about its possible or potential role in generating income for the local people?

Hawai'ian dance (Stillman 1996). Beginning in the early 1970s, the *Hawai'ian Renaissance* grew out of political protest, mainly against American colonialism. Hawai'ian youth began speaking out against encroaching development that was displacing indigenous people from their land and destroying their natural resources. They launched a concerted effort to revive the Hawai'ian language, the hula, and canoe paddling, among other things. Since then, hula schools have proliferated, and hula competitions among the islands are widely attended by local people and international tourists.

The 1990s saw the inauguration of the International Hula Festival in Honolulu, which attracts competitors from around the world. Although the hula competitions have helped ensure the survival of this ancient art form, some Hawai'ians voice concerns. First, they feel that allowing non-Hawai'ians to compete is compromising the quality of the dancing. Second, the format of the competition violates traditional rules of style and presentation, which require more time than is allowed, so important dances have to be cut. Third, for Hawai'ians, hula has close ties to religious beliefs and stories about the deities (Silva 2004). Performing hula in a mainly secular format is offensive to the gods and violates the true Hawai'ian way.

Another approach to cultural heritage preservation that is not top-down is "people-first" cultural heritage projects (Miller 2009). These are projects designed by the people whose culture is to be preserved, designed for their benefit, and managed by them. A growing number of examples worldwide demonstrate the value of people-first cultural heritage preservation as having strong positive, measurable effects. One major area of impact is on the very survival of a culture through territorial entitlements, community security, poverty reduction, improved mental health, and educating youth in traditional knowledge. Other important domains where *people-first cultural heritage preservation* has demonstrable positive effects include minority rights, conflict prevention and resolution, and environmental conservation and sustainability.

An example of people-first heritage preservation with implications for territorial entitlements and cultural survival is the Waanyi Women's History Project, Northern Queensland, Australia (Smith, Morgan, and van der Meer 2003) (see Map 5.4, p. 124). This is a case of a community-driven project devoted to archiving cultural heritage and to establishing local community management. The "community" is a group of Waanyi women who value their family history as heritage.

Classical dancers perform in Thailand. The intricate hand motions, with their impact augmented by metal finger extenders, have meanings that accompany the narrative being acted out. International tourism is a major support for such performance arts in Thailand.

▶ *Learn about UNESCO's recent declaration about intangible cultural heritage, and speculate on what it may mean for the preservation of particular cultural forms.*

The traditional way of maintaining this heritage has been to pass it on verbally from mother to daughter. The women were interested in having a written record of their history and documentation of sites and places of significance to Waanyi women. They hired an anthropologist consultant to collect and record their narratives. An interesting feature of this case, which contrasts with traditional academic research, is that the knowledge generated cannot be published. The role of the researcher is limited to supporting the aspirations of the Waanyi women.

The project had positive effects in providing a new source of income and thus reducing material deprivation and entitlement insecurity through the formal recognition of Waanyi custodial rights and the establishment of a National Park. It generated new sources of cash income for some Waanyi women through employment in the National Park as "cultural rangers" responsible for conservation of women's sites. This project is a clear case of a community-initiated and community-controlled heritage project. It involved concern for, and recognition of, community interests and goals. It produced benefits to the local people in terms of firmer entitlement to the land, new sources of income, skill acquisition, and pride.

POST-COMMUNIST TRANSITIONS

Major changes have occurred in the arts in the states of the former USSR for two reasons: loss of state financial support and removal of state controls over subject matter and creativity. A new generation of talented young artists has appeared (Akinsha 1992c:109). They are looking for something new and different. Art for art's sake, independent from the socialist project, is now possible. Many of the new artists find inspiration in nostalgia for the popular culture of the 1950s and 1960s, such as a pack of Yugoslav chewing gum, or the cover of a Western magazine. Commercial galleries are springing up, and a museum of modern art in Moscow opened in 1999. Classical music is thriving, and Russian opera and ballet groups are performing worldwide.

Theater in China is passing through a transition period with the recent development of some features of capitalism. Since the beginning of the People's Republic in 1949, the arts have gone through different phases, from being suppressed as part of the old feudal tradition to being revived under state control. China's theater companies have experienced financial crises in recent times (Jiang 1994). Steep inflation means that actors can no longer live on their pay. Theater companies are urging their workers to find jobs elsewhere, such as making movies or videos, but this is not an option for provincial troupes. As of the 1990s, local audience preferences changed: "People are fed up with shows that 'educate,' have too strong a political flavor, or convey 'artistic values.' They no longer seem to enjoy love stories, old Chinese legends, or Euro-American theater. Most of the young people prefer nightclubs, discos, or karaokes. Others stay at home watching TV" (1994:73). The new materialism in China means that young people want to spend their leisure time having fun. For the theater, too, money now comes first. One trend is toward the production of Western plays.

For example, Harold Pinter's *The Lover* was an immediate success when it was performed in Shanghai in 1992 (Jiang 1994). In explaining its success, sex is a big part of the answer.

The topic of sex was taboo in China for a long time and censored in theater and films. The producers of the play warned parents not to bring children with them, fueling speculation about a possible sex scene. Although *The Lover* contains only hints of sexuality, by Chinese standards it was bold. The actress's alluring dress had seldom, if ever, been seen by Chinese theatergoers in the early 1990s. There was also bold language: talk about female breasts, for example. Another feature was the play's focus on private life, interiority, and individual thoughts and feelings. This emphasis corresponds with a new focus on and cultivation of private lives in China. Change in the performing arts in China thus is being shaped both by changes in the local political economy and by globalization. As of the first decade of the twenty-first century, China's new (mainly urban) cultural revolution is moving in directions that no one would have predicted even a decade ago.

14

the BIG questions REVISITED

◆ How is culture expressed through art?

Cultural anthropologists choose a broad definition of art that takes into account cross-cultural variations. In the anthropological perspective, all cultures have some form of art and a concept of what is good art. Ethnographers document the ways in which art is related to many aspects of culture: economics, politics, human development and psychology, healing, social control, and entertainment. Art may serve to reinforce social patterns, and it may also be a vehicle of protest and resistance.

In state societies, especially in Europe, people began collecting art worldwide and placing it in museums a few hundred years ago. Later, ethnographic museums were established in Europe as the result of scientific and colonialist interest in learning about other cultures. Anthropologists study museum displays as a reflection of cultural values as well as sites where perceptions and values are formed. Many indigenous and formerly colonized people are reclaiming objects from museums as part of their cultural heritage.

◆ What do play and leisure activities reveal about culture?

Anthropological studies of play and leisure examine these activities within their cultural context. Cultural anthropologists view games as cultural microcosms, both reflecting and reinforcing dominant social values. Sports and leisure activities, although engaged in for nonutilitarian purposes, are often tied to economic and political interests. In some contexts, sports are related to religion and spirituality.

Tourism is a rapidly growing part of the world economy with vast implications for culture. Anthropologists who study tourism examine the impact of tourism on local cultures and questions of authenticity in the touristic experience. Tourism companies often market "other" cultures to appeal to the consumers, a phenomenon that perpetuates stereotypes and denigrates the "host" culture. Cultural anthropologists work with the tourism industry and local people to find better ways of representing culture that are more accurate, less stigmatizing to the host culture, and more informative for tourists. Local groups are actively seeking ways to share in the benefits of large-scale tourism and conservation projects and contribute to cultural and environmental sustainability.

◆ How is expressive culture changing in contemporary times?

Major forces of change in expressive culture include Western colonialism, contemporary tourism, and globalization in general. As with other kinds of cultural change through contact, expressive culture may reject, adopt, and adapt new elements. Cultural resistance and syncretism are increasingly frequent, as exemplified in the Trobriand Islanders' co-optation and re-creation of cricket as a performative event leading up to a traditional feast.

In some cases, outside forces have led to the extinction of local forms of expressive culture. In others, outside forces have promoted continuity or the recovery of practices that had been lost. The rising popularity of belly dancing among the middle and upper class of Istanbul is partly inspired by the demand for its performance by international tourists, Resistance to colonialism and neocolonialism has often inspired cultural revitalization, as in the Hawai'ian Renaissance and community projects in Australia.

Post-communist states, in the past few decades, have reacted to freedom of expression and the privatization of art in various ways. Artists find new subject matter and audiences have more options.

KEY CONCEPTS

art, p. 344
blood sports, p. 357
ethno-esthetics, p. 345
ethnomusicology, p. 349
expressive culture, p. 344
heterotopia, p. 353
intangible cultural heritage, p. 362
material cultural heritage, p. 361
museum, p. 353
repatriation, p. 354
theater, p. 350
wa, p. 356

SUGGESTED READINGS

Eduardo Archetti. *Football, Polo and the Tango in Argentina*. New York: Berg, 1999. An Argentinean anthropologist examines expressive culture in Buenos Aires and how it is related to elite tastes, gender, and international competitiveness.

Edna G. Bay, ed. *Asen, Ancestors, and Vodun: Tracing Change in African Art.* Champaign-Urbana: University of Illinois Press, 2008. Focusing on southern Benin, this book documents the rise and decline of the sculptural production of *asen*, metal art objects created to honor the spirits of ancestors and vodun deities.

Jennifer Loureide Biddle. *Breasts, Bodies, Canvas: Central Desert Art as Experience.* Seattle: University of Washington Press, 2008. This study of artists in Australia's Central Desert draws on fieldwork among the Walpiri people.

Kevin K. Birth. *Bacchanalian Sentiments: Musical Experiences and Political Counterpoints in Trinidad.* Durham, NC: Duke University Press, 2008. The author explores links among several Trinidadian musical styles and political consciousness on the island.

Tara Browner. *Heartbeat of the People: Music and Dance of the Northern Pow-Wow.* Urbana: University of Illinois Press, 2002. An ethnomusicologist of Choctaw heritage uses archival research on the pow-wow and participant observation to show how elements of the pow-wow in North America have changed.

Shirley F. Campbell. *The Art of Kula*. New York: Berg, 2002. The author focuses on designs painted on kula canoes and finds that kula art and its associated male ideology linked to the sea competes with female ideology and symbolism linked to the earth.

Michael M. Cernea. *Cultural Heritage and Development: A Framework for Action in the Middle East and North Africa.* Washington, DC: The World Bank, 2001. Following an overview of cultural heritage projects and possibilities in the Middle East and North Africa, Cernea presents a strategy to reduce poverty with high-impact cultural heritage projects.

Michael Chibnik. *Carving Tradition: The Making and Marketing of Oaxacan Wood Carvings*. Austin: University of Texas Press, 2003. Chibnik examines the production of and international trade in Oaxacan wood carvings. Wood carving is not an indigenous art form in Oaxaca but was developed to appeal to tourists.

Louise Meintjes. *Sound of Africa! Making Music Zulu in a South African Studio*. Durham, NC: Duke University Press, 2003. A South African anthropologist reveals the connections among music, culture, and state building. Focused on one studio in Johannesburg, this ethnography describes the roles of artists, sound engineers, emcees, and producers.

Laura Miller. *Beauty Up: Selling and Consuming Body Aesthetics in Japan*. Berkeley: University of California Press, 2006. The author, a linguistic anthropologist, examines the diversity of Japanese personal beauty practices for both males and females. She links eyelid surgery, body hair removal, and beauty products to a wider context of body esthetics.

Debra L. Klein. *Yorùbá Bàtà Goes Global: Artists, Culture Brokers, and Fans.* Chicago: University of Chicago Press, 2007. The author describes the musical traditions of southwestern Nigeria, which are declining at home while being embraced internationally.

Alaina Lemon. *Between Two Fires: Gypsy Performance and Romani Memory from Pushkin to Post-Socialism*. Durham, NC: Duke University Press, 2000. This book examines how theater in Moscow both liberates Roma in Russia and reinforces their status as stigmatized outsiders.

Beverly B. Mack. *Muslim Women Sing: Hausa Popular Song*. CD included. Bloomington: Indiana University Press, 2004. This ethnography provides an intimate portrait of the life and art of Hausa women singers in northern Nigeria. It shows how Hausa women exercise agency and creativity through music and dance.

Roger Magazine. *Golden and Blue Like My Heart: Masculinity, Youth, and Power among Soccer Fans in Mexico City.* Tucson: University of Arizona Press, 2007. This book is an ethnography of fan clubs devoted to the Pumas, one of the most popular soccer teams in Mexico City.

Fiona Magowan. *Melodies in Mourning: Music and Emotion in Northern Australia.* Albuquerque, NM: School of American Research Press, 2007. Through study of music and ritual life, this book focuses on women's experiences and child socialization among the Yolngu, an Aboriginal people of Arnhem Land in Australia's Northern Territory.

Jay R. Mandle and Joan D. Mandle. *Caribbean Hoops: The Development of West Indian Basketball.* Amsterdam: Gordon and Breach Publishers, 1994. This book describes and analyzes the emergence of (mainly men's) basketball as a popular sport in several Caribbean nations and explores regional differences within the Caribbean.

PART V
CONTEMPORARY CULTURAL CHANGE

ANTHROPOLOGY works

Mamphela Ramphele's life story moves from her birth in 1947 in rural South Africa to growing up in a context of racial apartheid and gender discrimination, to adulthood and achievement as a political activist, medical doctor, anthropologist, teacher, university administrator, mother, and now one of the four managing directors of the World Bank.

As a child, Ramphele saw the injustices of apartheid inflicted on her family when the government retaliated against her relatives who worked for social equality. This experience spurred her on to political activism while she was still pursuing her education. Speaking of her school years, Ramphele says that although she knew she was intelligent, she had a difficult time overcoming the sense of inferiority that apartheid instilled in Black people.

In the early 1970s, Ramphele completed her medical studies at the University of Natal in South Africa. At the same time, she became an activist working for social justice. She founded the South Africa's Black Consciousness movement to abolish segregation and repression at a time when the White government was engaged in some of the most brutal activities against Black South Africans in its history.

As a consequence of her activism, she was censured under the Terrorism Act. Exiled for six years to Northern Transvaal, Ramphele worked there with the rural poor, setting up community health programs.

In the 1980s, after her release, she became a research fellow with the South African Development Research Unit at the University of Cape Town and earned a doctorate in anthropology. Her dissertation, *A Bed Called Home: Life in the Migrant Labour Hostels of Cape Town*, was later published as a book. In 1996, Ramphele was elected as vice-chancellor of the University of Cape Town, the first Black and the first woman in the position.

Since 2000, Ramphele has been working with the World Bank, where she is the first South African to hold a position as managing director. She oversees human development activities in the areas of education; health, nutrition, and population; and social protection. She also monitors and guides the World Bank's relationships with client governments in strengthening socioeconomic support programs. She has worked to reduce child mortality, eradicate polio, and reduce the prevalence of HIV/AIDS, TB, and malaria.

In 2001, the South African Women for Women organization awarded Ramphele a Woman of Distinction Award that recognizes her "energetic leadership, her commitment to excellence, and her continuing dedication to transforming the lives of those around her."

The Marsh Arab people suffered under the rule of Saddam Hussein from government projects that drained their marshes and political repression. Many who fled the country as refugees are now returning and plans are under way for restoring some of the marshes.

PEOPLE ON THE MOVE

OUTLINE

the BIG questions

- What are the major categories of migration?
- What are examples of the new immigrants in the United States and Canada?
- How do anthropologists contribute to migration policies and programs?

The current generation of North American youth will move more times during their lives than previous generations. College graduates are likely to change jobs an average of eight times during their careers, and these changes are likely to require relocation.

Environmental, economic, familial, and political factors are causing population movements worldwide at seemingly all-time high levels. Research in anthropology shows, however, that frequent moves during a person's life and mass movements have occurred throughout human evolution. Foragers, horticulturalists, and pastoralists relocate frequently as a normal part of their lives.

Migration is the movement of a person or people from one place to another. Its causes are linked to major aspects of life such as providing for one's food or for marriage. It often has profound effects on a person's economic and social status, for better or worse, as well as health, language, religious identity, and education.

Thus, migration is of great interest to many academic subjects and professions. Historians, economists, political scientists, sociologists, and scholars of religion, literature, art, and music have studied migration. The professions of law, medicine, education, business, architecture, urban planning, public administration, and social work have specialties that focus on the process of migration and the period of adaptation following a move. Experts working in these areas share with anthropologists an interest in such issues as the kinds of people who migrate, causes of migration, processes of migration, health and psychosocial adaptations to new locations, and implications for planning and policy.

Cultural anthropologists do research on many issues related to migration. They study how migration is related to economic and reproductive systems, health and human development over the life cycle, marriage and household formation, politics and social order, and religion and expressive culture. Because migration affects all areas of human life, this topic pulls together the material in preceding chapters of this book.

Three tendencies characterize research on migration in cultural anthropology:

- Fieldwork experience in more than one location in order to understand the places of origin and destination.
- Combination of macro and micro perspectives. Studying migration challenges the traditional fieldwork focus on one village or neighborhood, creating the need to take into account national and global economic, political, and social forces.
- Involvement in applied work. Many opportunities exist for anthropologists to contribute their knowledge and insights to improve government policies and programs related to migration. Anthropologists assist efforts to address the situation of people forced to move by war, environmental destruction, and massive building projects such as dams.

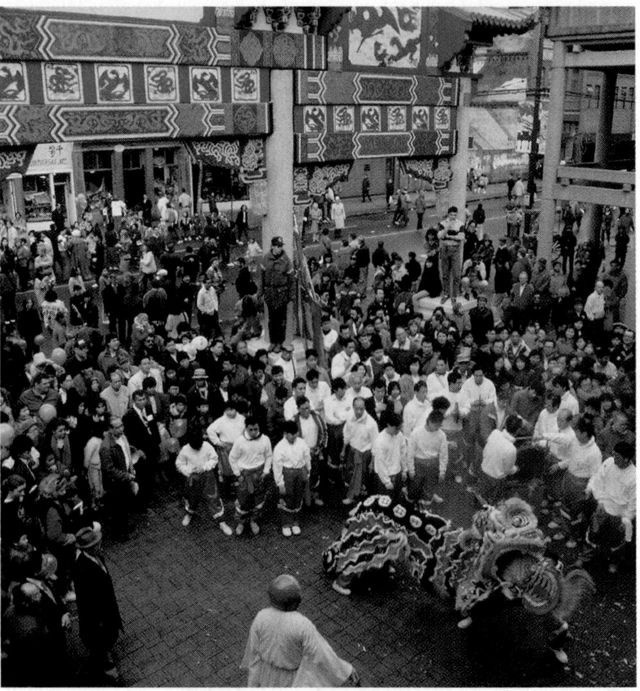

(LEFT) The Chinatown Cultural Plaza in Honolulu, Hawai'i. Ninety-five percent of Chinese Americans in Hawai'i live in Honolulu. (RIGHT) Chinese Canadians also mainly live in urban areas such as Vancouver and Toronto. In Vancouver, they constitute about 16 percent of the population. Vancouver's Chinatown is a vibrant tourist site and a place where Chinese Canadians reaffirm their cultural heritage, as in the celebration shown here of Chinese New Year.

▶ *When does Chinese New Year take place, and how is the date determined?*

This chapter first presents information on the most important categories of migrants and the opportunities and challenges they face. The second section provides descriptions of several examples of immigrants to the United States and Canada. The last section considers urgent issues related to migration, such as human rights and risk assessment and prevention programs.

◆◆◆

Categories of Migration

Migration and its effects on people come in many forms. It varies in terms of the distance involved, the purpose of the move, whether the move was forced or a matter of choice, and the migrant's status in the new destination. Microcultures play an important role in migration and its consequences for the migrant, as the rest of this chapter will document.

CATEGORIES BASED ON SPATIAL BOUNDARIES

This section reviews the basic features of three categories of population movement defined in terms of the spatial boundaries crossed:

- **Internal migration**, movement within country boundaries
- **International migration**, movement across country boundaries
- **Transnational migration**, movement in which a person regularly moves back and forth between two or more countries and forms a new cultural identity transcending a single geopolitical unit

INTERNAL MIGRATION Rural-to-urban migration was the dominant form of internal population movements in most countries during the twentieth century. A major reason why people migrate to urban areas is the availability of work. According to the **push–pull theory** of labor migration, rural areas are unable to support population growth and rising expectations about the quality of life (*the push factor*). Cities (*the pull factor*), in contrast, attract people, especially youth, for employment and lifestyle reasons. According to this theory, rural people weigh the costs and benefits of rural versus urban life and then decide to go or stay. This theory is related to the approach in anthropology that emphasizes human agency, or choice (review Chapter 1). Many instances of urban migration, however, are shaped by structural forces that are beyond the control of the individual, such as war or poverty.

INTERNATIONAL MIGRATION International migration has grown in volume and significance since 1945 and especially since the mid-1980s. Nearly 2 percent of the world's population lives outside of their home countries, or around 100 million people, including both legal and undocumented immigrants. Migrants who move for work-related reasons constitute most of the people in this category. The driving forces behind this trend are economic and political changes that affect labor demands and human welfare (see Critical Thinking).

The major destination countries of early international immigration are the United States, Canada, Australia, New Zealand, and Argentina. The immigration policies that these countries applied in the early twentieth century are labeled "White immigration" because they explicitly limited non-White immigration (Ongley 1995). In the 1960s, Canada made its immigration policies less racially discriminatory and more focused on skills and experience. The "White Australia" policy formally ended in 1973. In both the Canadian and Australian cases, a combination of changing labor needs and interest in improving their international image prompted the reforms.

During the 1980s and the 1990s, the United States, Canada, and Australia experienced large-scale immigration from new sources, especially from Asia, and—to the United States—from Latin America and the Caribbean. These trends continue in the twenty-first century.

The classic areas of outmigration of northern, western, and southern Europe are now, instead, receiving many immigrants, including refugees from Africa and the Middle East. International migration flows in the Middle East are complex, with some countries, such as Turkey, experiencing substantial movements both in and out. Millions of Turkish people immigrated to Germany in the later decades of the twentieth century. Turkey, in turn, has received many Iraqi and Iranian Kurdish refugees (review Culturama, Chapter 10, p. 257). Several million Palestinian refugees live in Jordan and Lebanon. Israel has attracted Jewish immigrants from Europe, northern Africa, the United States, and Russia.

TRANSNATIONAL MIGRATION Transnational migration is increasing along with other aspects of globalization. It is important to recall, however, that rising rates of transnational migration are related to the creation of state boundaries in recent centuries. Pastoralists with extensive seasonal herding routes were "transnational" migrants long before state boundaries cut across their pathways.

---

migration the movement of a person or people from one place to another

internal migration population movement within country boundaries.

international migration population movement across country boundaries.

transnational migration a form of population movement in which a person regularly moves between two or more countries and forms a new cultural identity transcending a single geopolitical unit.

push–pull theory an explanation for rural-to-urban migration that emphasizes people's incentives to move based on a lack of opportunity in rural areas (the "push") compared to urban areas (the "pull").

CRITICAL thinking

Haitian Cane Cutters in the Dominican Republic: A Case of Structure or Human Agency?

The circulation of male labor from villages in Haiti (see Map 16.3, p. 404) to work on sugar estates in the neighboring Dominican Republic is the oldest and perhaps largest continuing population movement within the Caribbean region (Martínez 1996). Beginning in the early twentieth century, Dominican sugarcane growers began to recruit Haitian workers, called **braceros**, agricultural laborers permitted entry to a country to work for a limited time. Between 1852 and 1986, an agreement between the two countries' governments regulated and organized the labor recruitment. Since then, recruitment has become a private matter, with men crossing the border on their own or with recruiters working in Haiti without official approval.

Many studies and reports have addressed this system of labor migration. Two competing perspectives exist:

- View 1, the structurist position: The bracero system is neo-slavery and a clear violation of human rights.
- View 2, the human agency position: Braceros are not slaves because they migrate voluntarily.

View 1

Supporters of this position point to interviews with Haitian braceros in the Dominican Republic that indicate, they say, a consistent pattern of labor rights abuses. Haitian recruiters approach poor men, and boys as young as 7 years old, and promise them easy, well-paid employment in the Dominican Republic. Those who agree to go are taken to the frontier on foot and then either transported directly to a sugar estate in the Dominican Republic or turned over to Dominican soldiers for a fee for each recruit and then passed on to the sugar estate. Once there, the workers are given only one option for survival: cutting sugarcane, for which even the most experienced workers can earn only about US$2 a day. Working and living conditions on the estates are bad. The cane cutters are coerced into working even if they are ill, and working hours start before dawn and extend into the night. Many estate owners prevent Haitian laborers from leaving by having armed guards patrol the estate grounds at night. Many of the workers say that they cannot save enough from their meager wages to return home.

View 2

According to this view, reports of coercion are greatly exaggerated and miss the point that most Haitian labor migrants cross the border of their own volition. On the basis of his fieldwork in Haiti, cultural anthropologist Samuel

An Iraqi girl carries her sister at a camp for internally displaced persons (IDPs) near Falluja in 2004. Well over 2 million people in Iraq are IDPs. Some IDPs live in the same city but in a different neighborhood because they fear their former neighbors.

Much contemporary transnational migration is motivated by economic factors. The spread of the global corporate economy is the basis for the growth of one category of transnational migrants nicknamed "astronauts," businesspeople who spend most of their time flying among different cities as investment bankers or corporate executives. At the lower end of the income scale are transnational migrant laborers who spend substantial amounts of time working in different places and whose movements depend on the demand for their labor.

An important feature of transnational migration is how it affects a migrant's identity, sense of citizenship, and entitlements. Constant movement among different places weakens the sense of having one home and promotes instead a sense of belonging to a diffuse community of similar transnational migrants whose lives "in between" locations take on a new transnational cultural reality.

As a response to the increased rate of transnational migration and the growth of overseas diaspora populations (review definition in Chapter 9), many "sending" countries (countries that are the source of emigrants) are redefining themselves as *transnational countries*. A transnational country is a country with a substantial proportion of its population living outside the country boundaries (Glick Schiller and Fouron 1999). Examples are Haiti, Colombia, Mexico, Brazil,

A Haitian migrant laborer. It is a matter of debate how much choice such a laborer has in terms of whether he will migrate to the neighboring Dominican Republic for short-term work, cutting cane, given the fact that he cannot find paid work in Haiti.

Martínez comments that "Recruitment by force in Haiti seems virtually unheard of. On the contrary, if this is a system of slavery, it may be the first in history to turn away potential recruits" (1996:20). Some recruits have even paid bribes to recruiters in order to be hired. Most people, even young people, are aware of the terrible working conditions in the Dominican Republic, so they are exercising informed choice when they decide to migrate. Repeat migration is common and is further evidence of free choice. The major means of maintaining labor discipline and productivity on the sugar estates is not force but wage incentives, especially piecework. The life histories of braceros show that many of them move from one estate to another, thus discrediting the view that the estates are "concentration camps."

Martínez does, however, raise the issue of how free the "choice" to migrate to the Dominican Republic really is, given the extreme poverty in which many Haitians live. In Haiti, few work opportunities exist, and the prevailing wage for rural workers is US$1 a day. Thus, the poor are not truly free to choose to work in their home country: Labor migration to the Dominican Republic becomes a necessity.

In this view, what looks like a free choice to participate in the bracero system is actually "illusory" or structured choice. It is based on the unavailability of the option to work for a decent wage in Haiti and on the forced, or structured, choice to work in the Dominican Republic.

◆ **CRITICAL THINKING QUESTIONS**

- What are the comparative strengths of View 1 and View 2?
- What does each perspective support in terms of policy recommendations?
- How does the concept of structured choice change those policy recommendations?

the Dominican Republic, Portugal, Greece, and the Philippines. These countries grant continuing citizenship to emigrants and their descendants in order to foster a sense of belonging and willingness to continue to send **remittances**, or transfers of money or goods from a migrant to his or her family back home. Remittances are an increasingly large, though difficult to quantify, proportion of the global economy and often a large part of a country's economy. For example, at least 60 percent of the gross domestic product of the small Pacific island country of Tonga comes from remittances from members of the Tongan diaspora (Lee 2003:32) (see Map 15.1). India is the country that receives the largest total amount of remittances.

A debate that crosses the social sciences is about the effects of remittances on the welfare of the people and the development of the countries to which they are sent (Binford 2003). The major issue is whether remittances go into long-term investments that raise people's quality of life or are used for short-term consumption purposes. The term "investment," though, is difficult to define. Is taking a child to a clinic for a vaccination a short-term expenditure or an investment? Semantic quibbles aside, most experts agree that, overall, remittances are important in helping families maintain their health and welfare and in promoting local development through donations to build schools, roads, and clinics.

CATEGORIES BASED ON REASON FOR MOVING

Migrants are also categorized on the basis of their reason for relocating. The spatial categories just discussed overlap with these categories. An international migrant, for example, may also be a person who moved for employment reasons. Migrants experience different kinds of spatial change and, at the same time, have various reasons for moving.

LABOR MIGRANTS Many thousands of people migrate each year to work for a specific period of time. They do not intend to establish permanent residence and are often explicitly barred from doing so. This form of migration, when legally contracted, is called *wage labor migration*. The period of work may be brief or it may last several years, as among rural Egyptian men who go to the Gulf countries to work for an average period of four years (Brink 1991).

bracero an agricultural laborer who is permitted entry to a country to work for a limited time.

remittance transfer of money or goods by a migrant to his or her family in the country of origin.

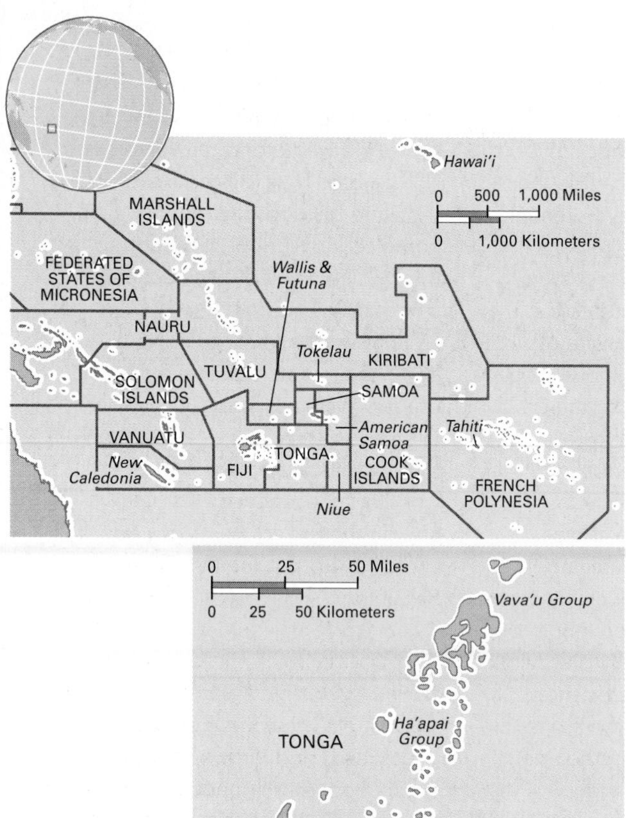

MAP 15.1 Tonga.
The Kingdom of Tonga is an archipelago of 169 islands, nicknamed by Captain Cook as the Friendly Islands on the basis of his reception there. A constitutional monarchy, Tonga has great reverence for its king, stemming from a tradition of the sacred paramount chief. The current king, who has reigned since 1965, is Taufa'ahau Tupou IV. Before him, Queen Salote Tupou II reigned from 1918 to 1965. The population is around 113,000, with two-thirds living on the main island, Tongatapu. Rural Tongans are small-scale farmers. Most Tongans are ethnically Polynesian, and Christianity is by far the dominant religion. Languages are Tongan and English. Many Tongans have emigrated, and remittances are a major part of the economy.

Asian women are the fastest-growing category among the world's more than 35 million migrant workers (http://www.ilo.org). Over 1.5 million Asian women are working abroad. Most are in domestic service jobs, and some work as nurses and teachers. Major sending countries are Indonesia, the Philippines, Sri Lanka, and Thailand. Main receiving countries are Saudi Arabia and Kuwait, and, to a lesser degree, Hong Kong, Japan, Taiwan, Singapore, Malaysia, and Brunei. Such women are usually alone and are not allowed to marry or have a child in the country where they are temporary workers. International migrant workers are sometimes illegally recruited and have no legal protection in their working conditions.

Circular migration is a regular pattern of population movement between two or more places. It may occur within or between countries. Internal circular migrants include, for example, female domestic workers throughout Latin America and the Caribbean. These women have their permanent residence in the rural areas, but they work for long periods of time in the city for better-off people. They may leave their children in the care of grandparents in the country, sending remittances for the children's support.

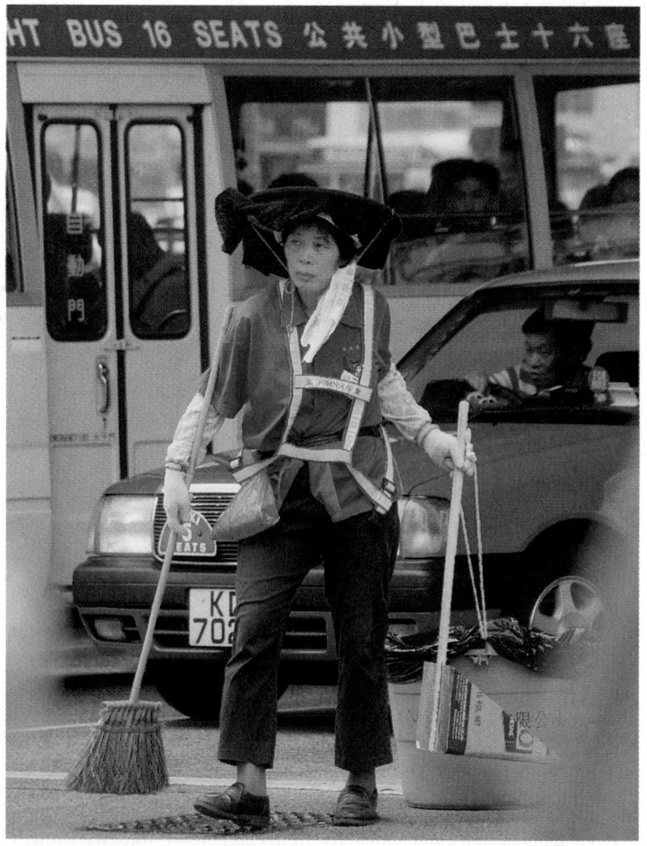

Hakka women of rural southern China are touristically defined by their "lamp shade" hats. This Hakka woman migrated to Hong Kong for work and wears a traditional Hakka woman's hat as she pursues an urban lifestyle.

circular migration a regular pattern of population movement between two or more places, either within or between countries.

displaced person someone who is forced to leave his or her home and community or country.

refugee someone who is forced to leave his or her home, community, or country.

internally displaced person someone who is forced to leave his or her home and community but who remains in the same country.

development-induced displacement (DID) forced migration due to development projects, such as dam building.

As construction of the massive Three Gorges Dam project proceeds in China, residents of a village that will be flooded by the dam collect their belongings from their homes as the bulldozers arrive.

▶ *Do research so that you can present a 5-minute briefing on the social and environmental implications of the Three Gorges Dam to the people in the "affected" areas.*

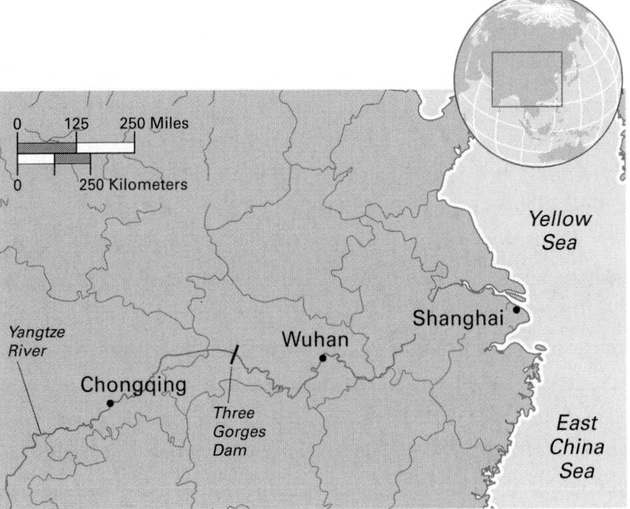

MAP 15.2 Site of Three Gorges Dam in China.
The Three Gorges Dam, the world's biggest dam, is one of several projects that are transforming China's environment. It will operate at full capacity in 2009. The dam will create a vast reservoir upstream to Chongqing. Engineers believe the dam will solve problems of annual flooding of the Yangtze River, the world's third largest river, and generate immense amounts of power. Environmentalists point to the downsides, which include the decline of many important fish species, destabilizing slopes, and eroding islands in the Yangtze River delta. Cultural anthropologists are concerned about the forced migration of over 1 million people from 13 major cities and 140 villages, and the loss of rural farming livelihoods as land is flooded. Archaeologists decry the loss of unknown numbers of prehistoric and historic sites now buried under water. Others mourn the loss of one of the most beautiful places in the world with its "gumdrop" mountains and breathtaking vistas that have inspired artists for centuries.

DISPLACED PERSONS **Displaced persons** are people who are evicted from their homes, communities, or countries and forced to move elsewhere (Guggenheim and Cernea 1993). Colonialism, slavery, war, persecution, natural disasters, and large-scale mining and dam building are major causes of population displacement.

Refugees are internationally displaced persons. Many refugees are forced to relocate because they are victims or potential victims of persecution on the basis of their race, religion, nationality, ethnicity, gender, or political views (Camino and Krulfeld 1994). Refugees constitute a large and growing category of displaced persons. An accurate count of all categories of refugees globally is unavailable, but it probably exceeds 10 million people, meaning that about one of every 500 people is a refugee (Lubkemann 2002). One-fourth of the world's refugees are Palestinians.

Women and children form the bulk of refugees and are vulnerable to abuse in refugee camps, including rape and children trading sex for food (Martin 2005). Some case studies shed some more positive light (Burton 2004). Refugee women from El Salvador, for example, learned to read and write in the camps and found positive role models in the "internationalist" workers and their vision of social equality.

Internally displaced persons (IDPs) are people who are forced to leave their home and community but who remain within their country. They are the fastest-growing category of displaced people. Estimates are that the number of IDPs is double that of refugees, over 20 million people (Cohen 2002). Africa is the continent with the most IDPs, and within Africa, Sudan (see Map 16.7, p. 412) is the country with the highest number (around 4.5 million). Many IDPs, like refugees, live for extended periods in camps with miserable conditions and no access to basic supports such as health care and schools. Because IDPs do not cross country boundaries, they do not come under the purview of the United Nations or any other international body. These institutions have limited authority over problems within countries. Several people have taken up the cause of IDPs and worked to raise international awareness of the immensity of the problem. Such efforts have led to the formal definition of IDPs and to legal recognition of their status.

Political violence is a major cause of people becoming IDPs. But other factors come into play, including natural disasters and, ironically, development projects (discussed in Chapter 16). Large dam construction, mining, and other projects have displaced millions in the past several decades. Dam construction alone is estimated to have displaced around 80 million people since 1950 (Worldwatch Institute 2003). Forced migration due to development projects is called **development-induced displacement (DID)**. Depending on a country's policy, people displaced by development may or may not be compensated financially for the loss of their homes and homeland. Even with monetary compensation, it is rarely possible to replace the life one had and the local knowledge that made life livable.

Mega-dam projects, or dam construction projects that involve costs in the billions of dollars and affect massive areas of land and huge numbers of people, are now attracting the attention of concerned people worldwide who support local resistance to massive population displacement. One of the most notorious cases is India's construction of a series of high dams in its Narmada River Valley, which cuts across the middle of the country from the west coast. This massive project involves relocating hundreds of thousands of people. The relocation is against the residents' wishes, and government compensation to the "oustees" for the loss of their homes, land, and livelihood is completely inadequate. Thousands of people in the Narmada Valley have organized protests over the many years of construction, and international environmental organizations have lent support. Celebrated Indian novelist Arundhati Roy joined the cause by learning everything she could about the 20 years of government planning for the Narmada dam projects, interviewing people who have been relocated, and writing a passionate statement in opposition to the project called *The Cost of Living* (1999). A man who was displaced and living in a barren resettlement area tells how he used to pick fruit in the forest, 48 kinds. In the resettlement area, he and his family have to purchase all their food, and they cannot afford any fruit at all (1999:54–55).

Governments promote mega-dam projects as important to the state's interest. The uncalculated costs, however, are high for the local people who are displaced. The benefits are skewed toward corporate profits, energy for industrial plants, and water for urban consumers who can pay for it.

The manner in which displaced persons are relocated affects how well they will adjust to their new lives. Displaced persons in general have little choice about when and where they move, and refugees typically have the least choice of all. The Maya people of Guatemala suffered horribly during years of state violence and genocide. Many became refugees, relocating to Mexico and the United States. Others fit in the category of internally displaced persons (see Culturama).

Cultural anthropologists have done substantial research with refugee populations, especially those related to war and other forms of violence and terror (Camino and Krulfeld 1994, Hirschon 1989, Manz 2004). They have discovered some key factors that ease or increase relocation stresses. One critical factor is the extent to which the new location resembles or differs from the home place in features such as climate, language, and food (Muecke 1987). Generally, the more different the places of origin and destination are, the greater the adaptational demands and stress. Other key factors are the refugee's ability to get a job commensurate with his or her training and experience, the presence of family members, and whether people in the new location are welcoming or hostile to the refugees.

INSTITUTIONAL MIGRANTS **Institutional migrants** are people who move into a social institution, either voluntarily or involuntarily. They include monks and nuns, the elderly, prisoners, and boarding school or college students. This section considers examples of students and soldiers within the category of institutional migrants.

Student adjustment is similar to many other forms of migration, especially in terms of risks for mental stress (see Everyday Anthropology). International students face serious challenges of spatial and cultural relocation. They are at greater risk of adjustment stress than are local students. Many international students report mental health problems, depending on age, marital status, and other factors. Spouses who accompany international students also suffer the strains of dislocation.

Soldiers are often sent on long-distance assignments for lengthy periods of time. Their destination may have negative physical and mental health effects on them, in addition to the fact that they may face combat. During the British and French colonial expansion, thousands of soldiers were assigned to tropical countries (Curtin 1989). Colonial soldiers faced new diseases in their destination areas. Their death rates from disease were twice as high as those of soldiers who stayed home, with two exceptions—Tahiti and Hawai'i—where soldiers experienced better health than soldiers at home.

As noted in Chapter 11, military anthropology is an emerging specialty in cultural anthropology, but still a small one. Anthropologists have published little about the effects of military migration on people in the military and local people. One matter is clear, however: Military people on assignment need more in-depth training about how to communicate with local people and about the importance of respecting local people's cultures. A pocket-size handbook on Iraqi etiquette used by some U.S. troops in Iraq provides limited guidelines (Lorch 2003). It says, for example, that one should avoid arguments and should not take more than three cups of coffee or tea if one is a guest. Also, one should not use the "thumbs up" gesture because its meaning is obscene, and one should not sit with one's feet on a desk because that is rude. Such basics are helpful, but they do little to provide more in-depth cultural awareness that can make all the difference in conflict and postconflict situations.

Soldiers during wartime are trained primarily to seek out and destroy the enemy, not to engage in cross-cultural

---

institutional migrant someone who moves into a social institution (such as a school or prison), voluntarily or involuntarily.

CULTURAMA

The Maya of Guatemala

The term *Maya* refers to a diverse range of indigenous people who share elements of a common culture and speak varieties of the Mayan language. (*Note:* The adjective includes a final *n* only when referring to the language.) Most Maya people live in Mexico and Guatemala, with smaller populations in Belize and the western parts of Honduras and El Salvador. Their total population in Mexico and Central America is about 6 million people.

In Guatemala, the Maya live mainly in the western highlands. The Spanish treated the Maya as subservient, exploited their labor, and took their land. Descendants of a formerly rich and powerful civilization, most Maya now live in poverty and lack basic human rights.

The Maya in Guatemala suffered years of genocide during the 36-year civil war. During the war, about 200,000 Maya "disappeared" and were brutally murdered by government military forces (Manz 2004:3). Many more were forcibly displaced from their homeland, with around 250,000 Maya today living as IDPs (Fitigu 2005). Thousands left the country as refugees, fleeing to Mexico and the United States.

Beatriz Manz tells a chilling story of one group of K'iche' Maya and their struggle to survive during the war (2004). Manz began her fieldwork in 1973 among the Maya living in the rural areas near the highland town of Santa Cruz del Quiché in the province of El Quiché. The Maya farmed small plots, growing maize and other food items, but found it increasingly difficult to grow enough food for their families. An American Catholic priest came to them with an idea for a new settlement, over the mountains to the east, in Santa María Tzejá.

Several Maya from the highlands decided to establish a new village. They divided land into equal-size plots so that everyone had enough to support their families. Over time, more settlers came from the highland village. They cleared land for houses, farms, workshops, and a school.

In the late 1970s, their lives were increasingly under surveillance by the Guatemalan military, who suspected the village of harboring insurgents. In the early 1980s, the military began taking village men away. These men were never seen alive again. In 1982, a brutal attack left the village in flames and survivors fleeing into the jungle. Some went to Mexico, where they lived in exile for years, and others migrated as refugees to the United States. The peace accords of 1996 officially ended the bloodshed. Many of the villagers returned and began to rebuild.

Thanks to Beatriz Manz, University of California at Berkeley, for reviewing this material.

(LEFT) Maya women pray in a church 55 miles southeast of Guatemala City in 2003. The coffins contain the remains of the victims of a 1982 massacre inside the church. (CENTER) Maya women are active in market trade.

MAP 15.3 Guatemala. Within the Republic of Guatemala, Maya Indians constitute about 40 percent of the country's population of 14.6 million.

everyday ANTHROPOLOGY

Stress among Boarding School Girls in Madagascar

Ethnographic research conducted among adolescent boarding school children in Ambanja, a town in Madagascar, showed that girls experience more adjustment strains than boys (Sharp 1990). Ambanja is a booming migrant town characterized by **anomie**, an individual's feeling of alienation and isolation due to the breakdown of traditional values about identity and social relationships, often due to rapid social change. Boarding school children in this town constitute a vulnerable group because they have left their families and come alone to the school.

Many of the boarding school girls, between the ages of 13 and 17, experienced bouts of spirit possession. Local people say that the prettiest girls are the ones who become possessed. The data on possession patterns showed, instead, that possession is correlated with a girl's being unmarried and pregnant. Many of these schoolgirls become the mistresses of older men, who shower them with expensive gifts such as perfume and gold jewelry. Such girls attract the envy of both other girls and schoolboys, who are being passed over in favor of adult men. Thus, the girls have little peer support among their schoolmates. If a girl becomes pregnant, school policy requires that she be expelled. If the baby's father refuses to help her, she faces severe hardship. Her return home will be a great disappointment to her parents.

Within this context, a girl's spirit possession may be understood as an expression of distress. Through the spirits, girls act out their difficult position between country and city and between girlhood and womanhood.

◆ **FOOD FOR THOUGHT**

- Consider the patterns of psychological stress among college students and their possible gender dimensions. How do these patterns of stress differ from or resemble the situation described here?

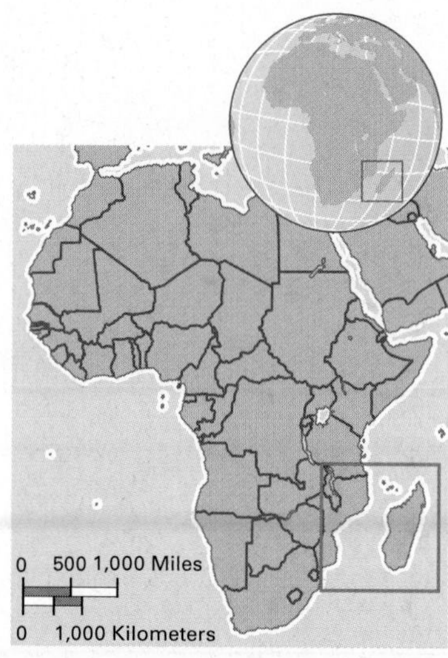

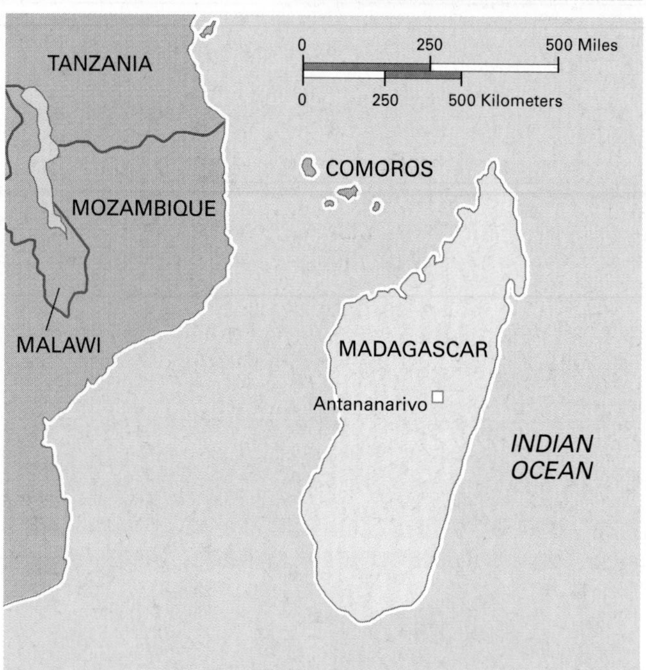

MAP 15.4 Madagascar.
The Republic of Madagascar includes the main island of Madagascar and several much smaller islands off its coast. It is the home of 5 percent of the world's plant and animal species, of which 80 percent are unique to Madagascar. The terrain varies from highlands to lowlands, rain forests, and deserts. The economy is reliant on tourism, especially ecotourism, and mining is increasing. The total population is 18 million. DNA analysis reveals that the population is a mixture of Malay and East African heritage. The primary language is Malagasy, which shares about 90 percent of its vocabulary with a language in southern Borneo. About half the people practice traditional religions related to ancestors, and most others are Catholics or Protestants.

United States marines wearing gas masks as protection from oil fumes during the 1990–1991 Gulf War. Many poorly understood illnesses afflict veterans of "Desert Storm," including skin conditions, neurological disorders, chronic fatigue, and psychological-cognitive problems.

▶ *Do research to learn about current medical thinking on the causes of Gulf War illnesses.*

communication. As mentioned in Chapter 11, winning a war in contemporary times often hinges on what the conquerors do following the outright conflict, and that often means keeping troops stationed in foreign contexts for a long time. Such extended assignments take a heavy toll on military personnel's mental health and appear to be linked to high rates of suicide, interpersonal violence, stress-based acts of violence against people in the occupied country, and major readjustment problems when returning home.

◆◆◆

The New Immigrants to the United States and Canada

The term **new immigrant** refers to a person who moved internationally since the 1960s. The category of new immigrants worldwide includes rapidly increasing proportions of refugees, most of whom are destitute and desperate for asylum. Three trends characterize the new international migration in the twenty-first century:

- Globalization: More countries are involved in international migration, leading to increased cultural diversity in sending and receiving countries.
- Acceleration: Growth in numbers of migrants has occurred worldwide.
- Feminization: Women are a growing percentage of international migrants to and from all regions and in all types of migration; some forms exhibit a majority of women.

In the United States, the category of new immigrants refers to people who arrived following the 1965 amendments to the Immigration and Naturalization Act. This change made it possible for far more people from developing countries to enter, especially if they were professionals or trained in some desired skill. Later, the *family reunification* provision allowed permanent residents and naturalized citizens to bring in close family members. Most of the new immigrants in the United States are from Asia, Latin America, and the Caribbean, although increasing numbers are from Eastern Europe, especially Russia.

The United States offers two kinds of visas for foreigners: immigrant visas (also called residence visas) and nonimmigrant visas for tourists and students (Pessar 1995:6). An immigration visa is usually valid indefinitely and allows its holder to be employed and to apply for citizenship. A nonimmigrant visa is issued for a limited time period and usually bars its holder from paid employment. Some immigrants are granted visas because of their special skills in relation to labor market needs, but most are admitted under the family unification provision.

THE NEW IMMIGRANTS FROM LATIN AMERICA AND THE CARIBBEAN

Since the 1960s, substantial movements of the *Latino population* (people who share roots in former Spanish and Portuguese colonies in the Western Hemisphere) have occurred, mainly to the United States. Latinos are about 10 percent of the U.S. population, excluding the population of Puerto Rico.

In the United States as a whole, and in some cities, such as Los Angeles, Miami, San Antonio, and New York, Latinos are the largest minority group. Within the category of Latino new immigrants, the three largest subgroups are Mexicans, Puerto Ricans, and Cubans. Large numbers also come from the Dominican Republic, Colombia, Ecuador, El Salvador, Nicaragua, and Peru.

Mexico is by far the major source of foreign-born immigrants to the United States (http://www.migrationinformation.org). Over 11 million foreign-born Mexicans live in the United States, a number that doubled from 1995 to 2006. Most live in the traditional destination states of California, Texas, and Illinois. Increasing numbers of immigrants from Mexico are settling in new destination states such as Georgia and North Carolina. Mexico is also the major source of unauthorized immigration into the United States. Due to the large number

---

anomie breakdown of traditional values associated with rapid social change.

new immigrant international migrant who has moved since the 1960s.

(LEFT) Latino immigrants studying English in a program in Virginia. (RIGHT) A Dominican Day parade in New York City.

▶ *Learn about an ethnic festival or event that is being held in the near future. Attend it and observe what signs and symbols of ethnicity are displayed, who attends, and what major messages about identity are conveyed.*

of out-migrants, many rural areas in Mexico are left with mainly elderly people and their grandchildren until the Christmas holidays when migrant workers return to join their families for a week or two.

CHAIN MIGRATION OF DOMINICANS The Dominican Republic has ranked among the top 10 source countries of immigrants to the United States since the 1960s (Pessar 1995) (see Map 16.3, p. 404), and Dominicans are one of the fastest-growing immigrant groups in the United States. They live in clusters in a few states, with their highest concentration in New York State.

Patricia Pessar conducted fieldwork in the Dominican Republic and with Dominican immigrants living in New York City. She studied the dynamics of departure (such as getting a visa), the process of arrival, and adaptation. Like most anthropologists who work with immigrant groups, she became involved in helping many of her participants: "Along the way I also endeavored to repay people's help by brokering for them with institutions such as the Immigration and Naturalization Service, social service agencies, schools, and hospitals" (1995:xv).

Within New York City, Washington Heights is the heart of the Dominican community. Unlike many other new immigrant groups, Dominicans are mainly middle and upper class. Although most left their homeland in search of a better life, many hope to return to the Dominican Republic, saying that in New York "there is work but there is no life."

For Dominican immigrants, as for many other immigrant groups, the *cadena*, or chain, links one immigrant to another. **Chain migration** is a form of population movement in which a first wave of migrants comes, which then attracts relatives and friends to join them in the destination place. Most Dominicans who are legal immigrants have sponsored other family members. Thus, many Dominicans have entered the United States through the family unification provision. The policy, however, defines a family as a nuclear unit (review Chapter 8) and excludes important members of Dominican extended families such as cousins and ritual kin (*compadres*). To overcome this barrier, some Dominicans use a technique called the *business marriage*. In a business marriage, an individual seeking to migrate pays a legal immigrant or citizen a fee, perhaps $2000, to contract a "marriage." He or she then acquires a visa through the family unification provision. A business marriage does not involve cohabitation or sexual relations; it is meant to be broken.

In New York City, most Dominicans work in manufacturing industries, including the garment industry. They are more concentrated in these industries than any other ethnic group. Recent declines in manufacturing jobs in New York City, and the redefining of better positions into less desirable ones, have therefore disproportionately affected them. Dominicans also work in retail and wholesale trade, another sector that has declined since the late 1960s. Others have established their own retail businesses, or *bodegas*. Many bodegas are located in unsafe areas and some owners have been assaulted or killed. Declining economic opportunities for Dominicans are aggravated by the arrival of even newer immigrants, especially from Mexico and Central America, who are willing to accept lower wages and worse working conditions.

---

chain migration population movement in which a first wave of migrants comes and then attracts relatives and friends to join them in the destination.

Although many middle-class and upper-class Dominican migrants secured fairly solid employment in the United States on their arrival, they have declined economically since then. Dominicans have the highest poverty rate in New York City of 37 percent, compared with a city average of 17 percent. Wages are higher for men than women. Poverty is concentrated among women-headed households with young children, and women are more likely than men to be on public assistance.

On the other hand, Dominican women in the United States are more often regularly employed than they would be in the Dominican Republic. This pattern upsets a patriarchal norm in which the nuclear family depends on male earnings and female domestic responsibilities. A woman's earning power means that husband–wife decision making is more egalitarian. A working Dominican woman is likely to obtain more assistance from the man in doing household chores. All of these changes help explain why more Dominican men are eager to return to the Dominican Republic than women are. As one man said, "Your country is a country for women; mine is for men" (1995:81).

SALVADORANS: ESCAPING WAR TO STRUGGLE WITH POVERTY Salvadorans are the fourth largest Latino population in the United States, numbering around 1,200,000 people in 2006 (http://www.migrationinformation.org). The civil war in El Salvador, which began in 1979 and continued for a decade, was the major stimulus for Salvadoran emigration (Mahler 1995) (see Map 15.5). By 1984, one-fourth of its population were either refugees or IDPs (Burton 2004). Most of the refugees came to the United States. About half of all Salvadorans in the United States live in California, especially Los Angeles (Baker-Christales 2004), with another large percentage in the Washington, DC, area. Many also settled around New York City, including some 60,000 who moved to suburban areas of Long Island.

Middle-class and upper-class Salvadorans obtained tourist or even immigration visas relatively easily. The poor, however, were less successful and many entered the United States illegally as *mojados* ("wet-backs"), or undocumented immigrants. Like Mexican illegal immigrants, Salavadorans

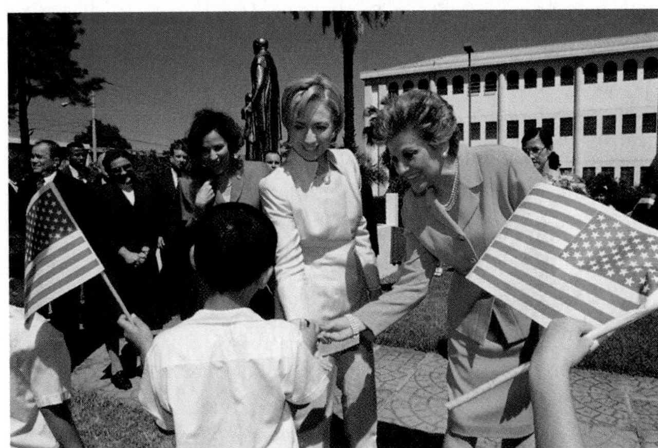

Hillary Clinton visits an orphanage in El Salvador in 1998. Many children were orphaned because their parents were killed during the civil war of the 1980s. Others were abducted by the Salvadoran military and still have not been reunited with their parents, over two decades later.

▶ *What can and should governments do to ensure children's safety and rights during war?*

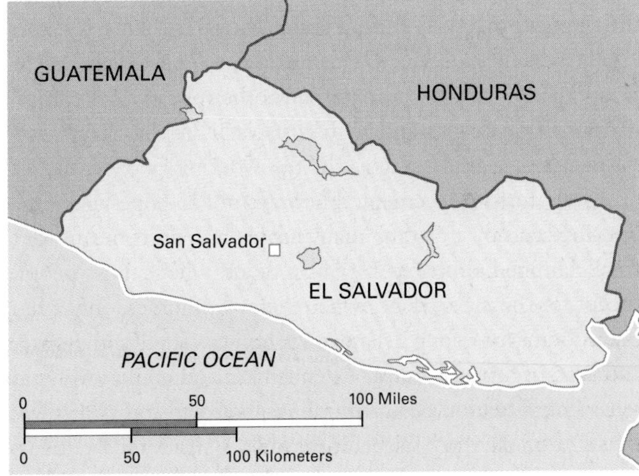

MAP 15.5 El Salvador.

The Republic of El Salvador in recent times has tended to emphasize one or two major export crops, with coffee being dominant. Coffee growing requires high-altitude land, and coffee production has displaced many of the indigenous people. The country's total population is nearly 7 million. About 90 percent are mestizo, 9 percent European descent (mostly Spanish), and 1 percent indigenous. The dominant language is Spanish, although some indigenous people speak Nahuat, a dialect of Nahuatl. Eighty-three percent of the people are Roman Catholic, and Protestants are 15 percent and growing in number.

use the term mojado to describe their journey. The Salvadorans, though, had to cross three rivers instead of one. These three crossings are a prominent theme of their escape stories, which are full of physical and psychological hardship, including hunger, arrests, and women being beaten and raped along the way. Once they arrive, things are still not easy, especially in the search for work and housing. Lack of education and marketable skills limit the job search. For undocumented immigrants, getting a decent job is even harder. These factors make it more likely that Salvadorans will work in the informal sector (review Chapter 4), where they are easy targets for economic exploitation.

Salvadorans living on Long Island receive low wages and labor in poor conditions. Their jobs involve providing services to better-off households. Men do outside work, such as gardening, landscaping, construction, and pool cleaning. Women work as nannies, live-in maids, house cleaners, restaurant workers, and caregivers for the elderly. The Salvadorans often hold down more than one job—for example, working at a McDonald's in the morning and cleaning houses in the afternoon. Men's pride prevents them from taking lowly ("female") jobs such as washing dishes. Women are more flexible and hence are more likely than men to find work. For the poorest of Salvadoran refugees, even exploitative jobs may be an economic improvement compared to back home, where they could not support their families at all.

The Salvadorans were attracted to Long Island by its thriving informal economy, a sector where checking for visas was less likely to occur. Unfortunately, the cost of living on Long Island is higher than in many other places. The combination of low wages and high costs of living has kept most Salvadorans in the category of the working poor, with few prospects for improvement. They attempt to cope with high housing costs by crowding many people into units meant for a small family. Compared to El Salvador, where most people except for the urban poor owned their own homes, only a few Salvadorans on Long Island own homes. Residential space and costs are shared among extended kin and nonkin who pay rent. This situation causes intrahousehold tension and stress. In spite of all these difficulties, most Salvadorans evaluate their experience in the United States positively.

THE NEW IMMIGRANTS FROM EAST ASIA

The new immigrants to the United States and Canada from East Asia tend to be considered "model" immigrants because their children do well in school and become economically successful. The two examples here, however, present a more complex picture of struggle to achieve.

KOREANS: ECONOMIC ACHIEVEMENT AND POLITICAL IDENTITY In 1962, the South Korean government began encouraging massive emigration (Yoon 1993). This policy change was motivated by perceived population pressure and an interest in gaining remittances from persons working abroad. Before 1965, most Korean immigrants were wives of U.S. servicemen and children being adopted by American parents. After 1965, most immigrants were members of nuclear families or family members being unified with earlier "pioneer" migrants already in the United States. During the peak years of 1985 and 1987, more than 35,000 Koreans immigrated to the United States annually, making South Korea the largest immigrant source nation after Mexico and the Philippines.

Korean Americans clean up the debris from attacks on their businesses after the Los Angeles riots of May 1992

Many of the migrants were displaced North Koreans who had fled their homeland to South Korea to avoid communist rule between 1945 and 1951. They had difficulty gaining an economic foothold in South Korea. When the opportunity arose to emigrate to the United States or South America, they were more willing to do so than many established South Koreans. In 1981, North Koreans constituted only 2 percent of the population of South Korea, but they were 22 percent of the Korean population of Los Angeles. Most of these immigrants were entrepreneurial, Christian, and middle class. In the 1990s, the number of lower-class migrants increased, and many lower-class Korean immigrants moved to Los Angeles (Sonenshein 1996). Whites constitute 47 percent of the population, Latinos account for 47 percent,

Blacks 11 percent, and Asian Americans 10 percent (http://www.laalmanac.com/population).

In the area of Los Angeles called South Central—a low-income section of the city shared by Blacks, Latinos, and Korean Americans—Blacks are the most politically active group. Their views are liberal, and they are mainly Democrats. A wide gap separates Black politics from interests of the Korean Americans. Although the Korean Americans are arguably exploited by larger economic interests, especially in their role as small shop owners, within South Central they are seen by other local people as exploitative. One issue over which conflict exists, especially between Blacks and Korean Americans, is liquor store ownership. Over the years, many bank branches, large grocery stores, and movie theaters have left South Central. The gap was filled by stores in which the most valuable commodity sold is liquor. In South Central there are far more liquor licenses per square mile than in the rest of Los Angeles County. Given this background, it is perplexing that no one foresaw the 1992 riots in which thousands of Korean businesses were damaged, including 187 liquor stores. (The Latino population also suffered severe losses. One-third of all deaths resulting from the riot were Latinos.) For the Koreans, one outcome was an increased sense of ethnic unity and political awareness. As of 2006, South Central is becoming increasingly populated by Latinos as members of other ethnic groups move to the suburbs.

CHANGING PATTERNS OF CONSUMPTION AMONG HONG KONG CHINESE Research on how international migrants change their behavior in the new destination have addressed, among other things, the question of whether different consumption patterns emerge and, if so, how, why, and what effects such changes have on other aspects of their culture.

A Canadian study examined consumption patterns among four groups: Anglo-Canadians, new Hong Kong immigrants (who had arrived within the previous seven years), long-time Hong Kong immigrants, and Hong Kong residents (Lee and Tse 1994). Since 1987, Hong Kong has been the single largest source of migrants to Canada. The new immigrant settlement pattern in Canada is one of urban clustering. The Hong Kong Chinese have developed their own shopping centers, television and radio stations, newspapers, and country clubs. Because of generally high incomes, Hong Kong immigrants have greatly boosted Canadian buying power.

For most migrants, however, the move brought a lowered economic situation, reflected in consumption patterns. New immigrants may have to reduce spending on entertainment and expensive items. Primary needs of the new immigrants in the 1990s included items that only about half of all households owned: TVs, car, family house, VCR, carpets, and microwave oven. Items in the second-needs category were dining room set, barbecue stove, deep freezer, and dehumidifier. Long-time immigrants owned more secondary products.

At the same time, businesses in Canada have responded to Hong Kong immigrant tastes by providing Hong Kong–style restaurants, Chinese branch banks, and travel agencies. Supermarkets offer specialized Asian sections. Thus, traditional patterns and ties are maintained to some extent. Two characteristics of Hong Kong immigrants distinguish them from other groups discussed in this section: their relatively secure economic status and their high level of education. Still, in Canada, they often have a difficult time finding suitable employment. Some have named Canada "Kan Lan Tai," meaning a difficult place to prosper, a fact that leads many to become "astronauts," or transnational migrants.

THE NEW IMMIGRANTS FROM SOUTHEAST ASIA

Most of the new immigrants from Southeast Asia came to North America as refugees. Compared to better-off voluntary migrants, their adjustment has involved not only learning a new language and culture but recovering from the stress of war and dealing with painful memories.

THREE PATTERNS OF ADAPTATION AMONG THE VIETNAMESE Over 125 million refugees left Vietnam during and after the wartime 1970s. Most relocated to the United States, but many others went to Canada, Australia, France, Germany, and Britain (Gold 1992). Vietnamese immigrants in the United States constitute the nation's third largest Asian American minority group. Three distinct subgroups are the 1975-era elite, the "boat people," and the ethnic Chinese. Although they interact frequently, they have retained distinct patterns of adaptation.

The first group, the 1975-era elite, avoided many of the traumatic elements of flight. They were U.S. employees and members of the South Vietnamese government and military. They left before having to live under the communists, and they spent little time in refugee camps. Most came with intact families and received generous financial assistance from the United States. Using their education and English language skills, most found good jobs quickly and adjusted rapidly.

The boat people began to enter the United States after the outbreak of the Vietnam–China conflict of 1978. Mainly

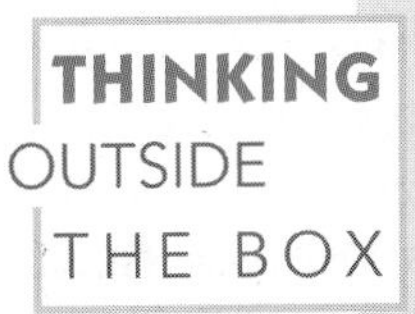

Find a detailed map that shows the geography of the United States, Mexico, and Central America, including El Salvador. Trace a possible overland migration route to the United States and find the three rivers that Salvadoran refugees had to cross.

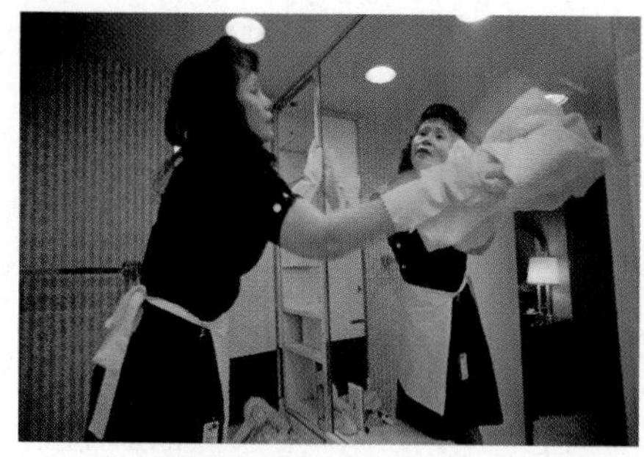

(LEFT) A Vietnamese American maid working in the Hilton Hotel in Washington, DC. (CENTER) A Vietnamese American woman in New Orleans prays before a crucifix. (RIGHT) Vietnamese American college students have fun in a Hollywood nightclub.
▶ *What do these three images tell you about the lives of Vietnamese immigrants in the United States?*

of rural origin, they had lived for three years or more under communism. Their exit, either by overcrowded and leaky boats or on foot through Cambodia, was dangerous and difficult. Over 50 percent died on the way. Those who survived faced many months in refugee camps in Thailand, Malaysia, the Philippines, or Hong Kong before being admitted to the United States. Because many more men than women escaped as boat people, these refugees are less likely to have arrived with intact families. They were less well educated than the earlier wave, with half lacking competence in English. They faced the depressed U.S. economy of the 1980s. By the time of their arrival, the U.S. government had severely reduced refugee cash assistance and had canceled other benefits. These refugees had a much more difficult time adjusting to life in the United States than the 1975-era elite.

The ethnic Chinese, a distinct and socially marginalized class of entrepreneurs in Vietnam, arrived in the United States mainly as boat people. Most have had a difficult time in the United States because they lacked a Western-style education. They were also sometimes subject to discrimination from other Vietnamese in the United States.

The general picture of first-generation Vietnamese adjustment in the United States shows high rates of unemployment, welfare dependency, and poverty. Interviews with Vietnamese refugees in southern California reveal generational change and fading traditions among youth. Vietnamese teenagers in southern California, for example, have adopted the lifestyle of low-income U.S. teenagers. Their Euro-American friends are more important to them than their Vietnamese heritage is. Given social variations and regional differences in adaptation throughout the United States, however, generalizations about Vietnamese Americans must be made with extreme caution.

KHMER REFUGEES' INTERPRETATION OF THEIR SUFFERING In the late 1970s, over 150,000 people from Cambodia came to the United States as refugees of the Pol Pot regime (Mortland 1994). They survived years of political repression, a difficult escape, and time in refugee camps before arriving in the United States.

Most Khmer refugees were Buddhist when they lived in Cambodia. They have attempted to understand, within the Buddhist framework of karma (review Chapter 13), why they experienced such disasters. According to their beliefs, good actions bring good to the individual, family, and community; bad actions bring bad. Thus, many Khmer Buddhists blame themselves for the suffering they endured under the Pol Pot regime, thinking that they did something wrong in a previous life. Self-blame and depression characterize many Khmer refugees (Ong 2003). Others feel that Buddhism failed, and so they turn in large numbers to Christianity (including Mormonism), the dominant faith of the seemingly successful Americans.

Recently, a resurgence of Khmer Buddhism has occurred among some refugees from Cambodia living in North America. Many temples have been constructed, and they sponsor rituals and traditional celebrations that are widely attended. These reviving Buddhists have mixed reactions to Christianity. Some accept it as a complementary religion to Buddhism, whereas others reject it as a threat to Buddhism and their cultural identity.

Changing interpretations of identity, including religion, arise over time with the new generations and altered circumstances. It is difficult to say what the future holds for either the Cambodian adults who are still trying to make sense of their suffering or for their children, the new generation (Ong 2003).

THE NEW IMMIGRANTS FROM SOUTH ASIA

Like the new immigrants from East Asia, many of the new immigrants from South Asia (India, Pakistan, Bangladesh, Sri Lanka, and Nepal) are voluntary migrants who have done well in North America, either as upper class professionals, small business owners, or employed in various occupations. Like the children of East Asian immigrants, those of South Asian immigrants tend to be high academic achievers.

HINDUS OF NEW YORK CITY MAINTAIN THEIR CULTURE With the 1965 change in legislation in the United States, a first wave of South Asian immigrants dominated by male professionals from India arrived (Bhardwaj and Rao 1990). Members of this first wave settled primarily in eastern and western cities. Subsequent immigrants from India were less well educated and less wealthy. They tend to be concentrated in New York and New Jersey. New York City has the largest population of South Asian Indians in the United States, with about one-eighth of the total number of South Asians in the United States (Mogelonsky 1995).

Members of the highly educated first wave are concentrated in professional fields such as medicine, engineering, and management (Helweg and Helweg 1990). One of the major immigrant groups in Silicon Valley, California, is South Asian Indians. Members of the less educated, later wave find work in family-run businesses or service industries. Indians dominate some trades, such as convenience stores. They have penetrated the ownership of budget hotels and motels and operate nearly half of the total number of establishments in this niche. More than 40 percent of New York City's licensed cab drivers are Indians, Pakistanis, or Bangladeshis (Mogelonsky 1995).

The South Asian Indian population in the United States is one of the better-off immigrant groups and is considered an immigrant success story. They place high value on their children's education and urge them to pursue higher education in fields such as medicine and engineering. They tend to have few children and invest heavily in their schooling and social advancement.

A continuing concern of many members of the first wave is the maintenance of Hindu cultural values in the face of patterns prevalent in mainstream U.S. culture, such as dating, premarital sex, drinking, and drugs (Lessinger 1995). The Hindu population supports the construction of Hindu temples that offer Sunday school classes for young people and cultural events as a way of passing on the Hindu heritage to the next generation. They attempt to appeal to the youth by accommodating to their lifestyles and preferences in terms of things like the kind of food served after rituals. Vegetarian pizza is now a common temple menu item for the young people.

Hindu worshippers at the Geeta Temple in Elmhurst, Queens, pass their hands over a camphor lamp flame as a blessing. Queens, one of the five boroughs of New York City, is one of the most ethnically diverse communities in the world.

Another challenge for Hinduism in the United States and Canada is to establish temples that offer ritual diversity that speaks to Hindus of many varieties. In New York City, the growth of one temple shows how its ritual flexibility helped it to expand. The Ganesha Temple was founded in 1997 under leadership from Hindus from southern India. Temple rituals at first were the same as those conducted in southern Indian temples. Over the years, though, in order to widen its reach, the temple expanded its rituals to include those that would appeal to Hindus from other regions of India. The congregation has grown, and the physical structure has expanded to provide for this growth. The daily and yearly cycle has become more elaborate and more varied than what one would find at a typical Hindu temple in southern India. The Ganesha temple in New York City is an important pilgrimage destination for Hindus from throughout India.

THE NEW IMMIGRANTS FROM THE FORMER SOVIET UNION

The breakup of the Soviet Union into 15 separate countries spurred the movement of over 9 million people throughout Eastern Europe and Central Asia. Many, of Slavic descent, lived in Central Asia during the existence of the Soviet Union and seek to return to their homelands. Another large category includes people who were forcibly relocated to Siberia or Central Asia. Since 1988, refugees from the former Soviet Union have been one of the largest refugee nationalities to enter the United States (Littman 1993, cited in Gold 1995).

SOVIET JEWS FLEE PERSECUTION Many of the refugees from the former Soviet Union are Soviet Jews. Although most Soviet Jews live in Israel, since the mid-1960s, over 300,000 have settled in the United States, especially in California (Gold 1995). Several features characterize the experience of Soviet Jewish refugees in the United States. First, their origins in the Soviet Union accustomed them to the fact that the government controlled most aspects of life and provided many public services, including jobs, housing, day care, and health care. In their new locations, they had to find ways of meeting these needs in a market economy. Second, Soviet Jews, as "White Europeans," become members of the "racial" majority group. Their high level of education places them in the elite of new immigrant groups. Third, they have access to established and prosperous communities of American Jews, which provides them with sponsors when they arrive. Most other new immigrant groups do not have these advantages.

Soviet Jewish immigrants, however, face several challenges. Many have a difficult time finding a job commensurate with their education and previous work in the Soviet Union. Throughout the United States, many Soviet Jewish

LESSONS applied

Studying Pastoralists' Movements for Risk Assessment and Service Delivery

Pastoralists are often vulnerable to malnutrition as a consequence of climate changes, fluctuations in food supply, and war and political upheaval. Because of their spatial mobility, they are difficult to reach with relief aid during a crisis. Cultural anthropologists are devising ways to gather and manage basic information about pastoralists' movements and nutritional needs in order to provide improved service delivery (Watkins and Fleisher 2002). The data required for such proactive planning include the following:

- Information on the number of migrants and the size of their herds in a particular location and at a particular time. Such data can inform planners about the level of services required for public health programs, educational programs, and veterinary services. This information can be used to assess the demand on particular grazing areas and water sources and is therefore important in predicting possible future crises.
- Information on patterns of migratory movements. This information can enable planners to move services to where the people are rather than expecting people to move to the services. Some nongovernmental organizations, for example, are providing mobile banking services and mobile veterinary services. Information about pastoralist movements can be used as an early warning to prevent social conflicts that might result if several groups arrived in the same place at the same time. And conflict resolution mechanisms can be put in place more effectively if conflict does occur.

The data collection involves interviews with pastoralists, often with one or two key participants, whom the anthropologists select for their specialized knowledge. Interviews cover topics such as the migratory paths followed (both typical and atypical), population levels, herd sizes, and the nutritional and water requirements of people and animals. Given the complex social systems of pastoralists, the data gathering must also include group leadership, decision-making practices, and concepts about land and water rights.

In January 2004, more than 50,000 Russian immigrants to Israel returned to Russia. Motivations for the move back include the difficult living conditions for many Russian immigrants in Israel, violence, and the improving economic situation in Russia. Nonetheless, people from Russia continue to migrate to Israel, and they now number over one million people, about 13 percent of the population.

▶ *Learn how many people left Russia after the break-up of the Soviet Union in 1989 and where they went.*

lifeboat mentality a view that seeks to limit enlarging a particular group because of perceived resource constraints.

immigrants remain unemployed or work at menial jobs far beneath their qualifications. This pattern is especially true for women. They were employed professionals in the Soviet Union but can find no work in the United States other than house cleaning or babysitting. Another major challenge involves marriage options. Cultural norms promote intraethnic marriage. The number in the U.S. marriage pool is small.

◆◆◆

Migration Politics, Policies, and Programs in a Globalizing World

The major questions related to migration politics, policies, and programs concern state and international policies of inclusion and exclusion of particular categories of people. The human rights of various categories of migrants vary dramatically. Migrants of all sorts, including long-standing migratory groups such as pastoralists and horticulturalists, seek to find ways of protecting their lifestyles, maintaining their health, and creating security for future.

PROTECTING MIGRANTS' HEALTH

Health risks to migrants are many and varied, depending on the wide variety of migrant types and destinations. One group

In 2006, women of eastern Kenya, after three years of drought, search out increasingly scarce pasture for their declining herd of goats. As they walk through a dust storm, clouds and a rainbow in the distance are signs that rain is coming. Heavy rains did come in the next few days, but the pastoralists in the region, like these women, had lost most of their animals during the drought and were dependent on food aid and other forms of humanitarian assistance for survival. Global climate change is linked to increasingly severe swings in climatic conditions in this region.

The anthropologists organize this information into a computerized database, linking the ethnographic data with other data collected and managed through what is called a *geographic information system* (GIS), which includes data on the environment and climate information from satellites. The anthropologists then construct various scenarios and assess the relative risks that they pose to the people's health. Impending crises can be foreseen, and warning can be provided to governments and international aid agencies.

◆ **FOOD FOR THOUGHT**

- The tracking system described here remains outside the control of the pastoralists themselves. How might it be managed so that they can participate more meaningfully and gain greater autonomy?

of migrants of special concern are those whose livelihoods depend on long-standing economic systems requiring spatial mobility, such as foragers, horticulturalists, and pastoralists. The frequency in recent decades of drought and food shortages in the Sahel region of Africa (see Map 16.6, p. 411) is prompting research by cultural anthropologists to learn how to prevent such situations through better monitoring and enhanced provision of services (see Lessons Applied).

INCLUSION AND EXCLUSION

National policies that set quotas on the quantity and types of immigrants who are welcome and that determine how they are treated are largely dictated by political and economic interests. Even in the cases of seemingly humanitarian quotas, governments undertake a cost–benefit analysis of how much will be gained and how much will be lost. Governments show their political support or disapproval of other governments through their immigration policies. One of the most obvious economic factors affecting policy is labor flow. Cheap, including illegal, immigrant labor is used around the world to maintain profits for businesses and services for the better-off. Flows of such labor undermine labor unions and the status of established workers.

State immigration policies are played out in local communities. In some instances, local resentments are associated with a so-called **lifeboat mentality**, a view that seeks to limit enlarging a particular group because of perceived resource constraints. This perspective may be part of the explanation for many recent outbreaks of hostility throughout the world where, instead of host populations being gracious and sharing what they have, they seek to drive out the immigrants who seek a better way of life, and act to protect their own entitlements.

Labor immigrants are not always the subject of resentment, as a study of Palermo, Italy, shows (Cole 1996). The number of immigrants has grown substantially in southern Italy since the early 1980s. In the city of Palermo, Sicilia (see Map 13.5, p. 325), with a total population of 1 million people, nearly 30,000 immigrants are from Africa, Asia, and elsewhere. Does working-class racism exist among the working class in Palermo? Two conditions seem to predict that it would: large numbers of foreign immigrants and a high rate of unemployment. So far, however, instead of expressing racist condemnation of the immigrants, working-class residents of Palermo accept the immigrants as fellow poor people. One critical factor may be the lack of competition for jobs because Palmeritans and immigrants occupy different economic niches. African immigrant men work in less desirable jobs in bars and restaurants, as building cleaners, or as street vendors. African and Asian women work as domestic servants in the better-off neighborhoods. Sicilians do refer to immigrants by certain racial/ethnic names, but these seem to be used interchangeably and imprecisely. For example, a common term for

Memorials to illegal border crossers on the Mexico side of a fence along the US-Mexico border. US-built barriers along its border with Mexico have existed for decades. Recent increases in illegal crossings and a closed-border policy prompted President George W. Bush to push for the Secure Fence Act of 2007 which authorized the construction of 700 additional miles of fencing. Human rights supporters say that the fences simply push immigrants to attempt to cross into the United States in more desolate and dangerous areas, adding to the mortality rate of illegal immigrants.

▶ *The World Trade Organization supports the free trade of goods between countries. Where does it stand, if at all, on the free movement of labor between countries?*

all immigrants, Asian or African, is *turchi,* which means "Turks," but it can also be applied teasingly to a Sicilian. In a questionnaire given to schoolchildren, the great majority agreed with the statement that "a person's race is not important." Although the tolerance among Palermo's working class may be only temporary and may change to resentment if economic conditions change or the numbers of immigrants increase, it nonetheless suggests that working class racism against immigrants is not inevitable.

Recent politically conservative trends in the United States have succeeded in reversing earlier more progressive immigration policies. Police raids in areas thought to have many undocumented migrants have brought mass expulsion. This lifeboat mentality of exclusiveness is held mainly by the dominant White majority and others who have achieved the "American dream" and resent competition from outsiders.

MIGRATION AND HUMAN RIGHTS

Several questions arise about migration and human rights. One of the most basic is whether migration is forced or voluntary (review Critical Thinking, this chapter). Forced migration itself may be considered a violation of a person's human rights. Another issue is whether members of a displaced group have a guaranteed **right of return**, or a refugee's ability to return to and live in his or her homeland. The right of return has been considered a basic human right in the West since the time of the signing of the Magna Carta. It is included in the United Nations General Assembly Resolution 194 passed in 1948 and was elevated by the UN in 1974 to an "inalienable right."

The right of return is a pressing issue for the hundreds of thousands of Palestinians who fled or were driven from their homes during the 1948 war. They went mainly to Jordan, the West Bank/East Jerusalem, Gaza, Lebanon, Syria, and other Arab states. Jordan and Syria have granted Palestinian refugees rights equal to those of their citizens. In Lebanon, where estimates of the number of Palestinian refugees range between 200,000 and 600,000, the government refuses them such rights (Salam 1994). Israel favors the lower number because it makes the problem seem less severe. The Palestinians favor the higher number to highlight the seriousness of their plight. The Lebanese government also favors the higher number to emphasize its burden in hosting so many refugees. Palestinians know that they are not welcome in Lebanon, but they cannot return to Israel because Israel denies them the right of return. Israel responds to the

---

right of return United Nations guaranteed right of a refugee to return to his or her home country to live.

Palestinians' claims by saying that their acceptance of Jewish immigrants from Arab countries constitutes an equal exchange.

The right of return can be considered, just as validly, within states even though most have no policy close to that of the UN. Indigenous people's rights to their ancestral lands are a prominent case in point (to be discussed in Chapter 16).

Another stark instance of internal displacement and loss of rights to home comes from the 2005 hurricanes in New Orleans and the coastal counties of Mississippi and Louisiana. The "racial" lines of displacement are nowhere clearer than in the statistics for the city of New Orleans (Lyman 2006). Before Hurricane Katrina, the population of New Orleans was 54 percent White, 36 percent Black, and 6 percent Latino. In 2006, the population was 68 percent White and 21 percent Black, with no change in the Latino percentage. The causes for the *differential displacement* of the Black population are one problem. The fact that many Black people still have little chance of returning to their homes—*differential resettlement*—and rebuilding their lives is another.

15

the BIG questions REVISITED

◆ What are the major categories of migration?

Migrants are classified as internal, international, or transnational. Another category is based on the migrants' reason for moving. On this dimension, migrants are classified as labor migrants, institutional migrants, or displaced persons. People's adjustment to their new situations depends on the degree of voluntarism involved in the move, the degree of cultural and environmental difference between the place of origin and the destination, and how closely expectations about the new location are met, especially in terms of making a living and establishing social ties.

Displaced persons are one of the fastest-growing categories of migrants. Refugees fleeing from political persecution or warfare face serious adjustment challenges because they often leave their home countries with few material resources and frequently have experienced much psychological suffering. The number of internally displaced persons is growing even faster than the number of refugees. Dams and other large-scale development projects result in thousands of people becoming IDPs. Internally displaced persons do not fall under the purview of international organizations such as the United Nations, but their situation is attracting the attention of a global consortium of governments and nongovernmental organizations.

◆ What are examples of the new immigrants in the United States and Canada?

Worldwide, the "new immigrants" are contributing to growing transnational connections and to the formation of increasingly multicultural populations within states. In the United States, the new immigrants from Latin America, especially Mexico, are the fastest-growing category. In the United States, members of most refugee immigrant groups tend to have jobs at the lower end of the economic scale. Jewish refugees from the Soviet Union experience a major gap in what their employment was like in Russia versus their limited options in the United States. Immigrants from East and South Asia, who are more likely than others to have immigrated to the United States voluntarily, have achieved greater levels of economic success than most other new immigrant groups.

Immigrant groups throughout the world may face discrimination in their new destinations, although the degree to which it occurs varies with the level of perceived resource competition from residents. Immigrants from India in Canada experience discriminatory practices that differ on the basis of their gender.

◆ How do anthropologists contribute to migration policies and programs?

Anthropologists have studied national and international migration policies and practices in terms of social inclusion and exclusion. Fieldwork in particular contexts reveals a range of patterns between local residents and immigrants. Working-class resentment among local people against immigrants is not universal and varies with the overall amount and type of employment available.

Anthropologists examine possible infringements of human rights on migrants, especially in terms of the degree of voluntarism in their move and the conditions they face in the destination area. Another human rights issue related to migration is the right of return. The UN proclaimed the right of return for internationally displaced populations. Most countries, however, have no such policy. Internally displaced persons, including the evacuees from the 2005 hurricanes in the United States, have no guarantee that they can return to their home area.

Cultural anthropologists find many roles in applied work related to migration. Gathering data on migratory movements of traditionally mobile people, such as pastoralists, can help make humanitarian aid programs more timely and effective.

KEY CONCEPTS

anomie, p. 380
bracero, p. 374
chain migration, p. 382
circular migration, p. 376
development-induced displacement (DID), p. 377
displaced person, p. 377
institutional migrant, p. 378
internal migration, p. 373
internally displaced person (IDP), p. 377
international migration, p. 373
lifeboat mentality, p. 389
migration, p. 372
new immigrant, p. 381
push–pull theory, p. 373
refugee, p. 377
remittance, p. 375
right of return, p. 390
transnational migration, p. 373

SUGGESTED READINGS

Rogaia Mustafa Abusharaf. *Wanderings: Sudanese Migrants and Exiles in North America*. Ithaca, NY: Cornell University Press, 2002. Abusharaf provides historical background on the first wave of Sudanese migration to the United States and Canada, information on various Sudanese groups who have migrated, and an interpretation of Sudanese identity in North America.

Beth Baker-Cristales. *Salvadoran Migration to Southern California: Redefining El Hermano Lejano*. Gainesville: University of Florida Press, 2004. This book provides a history of Salvadoran migration to the United States and a detailed description of the lives of Salvadoran migrants in Los Angeles, home to about half of all Salvadorans in the United States.

Jeffrey H. Cohen. *The Culture of Migration in Southern Mexico*. Austin: University of Texas Press, 2004. Migration is a way of life for many individuals and entire families in the Mexican state of Oaxaca. Some migrants go to other parts of Mexico and others to the United States. Cohen discusses outmigration in 12 communities and its effects on the people who remain.

Sheba Mariam George. *When Women Come First: Gender and Class in Transnational Migration*. Berkeley: University of California Press, 2005. This book traces the experiences of women nurses from Kerala, India, who migrate to work in the United States, the effects on their marriages, and how husbands adapt through active involvement in religion.

Farha Ghannam. *Remaking the Modern: Space, Relocation, and the Politics of Identity in a Global Cairo*. Berkeley: University of California Press, 2002. As part of a plan to modernize Cairo, the government relocated low-income residents from what valuable real estate in downtown Cairo to public housing outside the city. Ghannam explores how the displaced people deal with the loss of social networks and the stigma of living in public housing.

Julianne Hammer. *Palestinians Born in Exile: Diaspora and the Search for a Homeland*. Austin: University of Texas Press, 2004. In the decade following the 1993 Oslo Peace Accords, 100,000 diasporic Palestinians moved to the West Bank and Gaza. This ethnography documents the experiences of young adults and their adjustment to the move.

Josiah McC. Heyman. *Finding a Moral Heart for U.S. Immigration Policy: An Anthropological Perspective*. Washington, DC: American Ethnological Society, Monograph Series, Number 7, 1998. This critique finds that current U.S. immigration policy is basically anti-immigrationist. The author suggests steps toward a more inclusive policy.

Helen Morton Lee. *Tongans Overseas: Between Two Shores*. Honolulu: University of Hawai'i Press, 2003. This book about Tongan migrants in Melbourne uses participant observation and analysis of messages on a Tongan Internet forum called Kava Bowl as well as email interviews with people who participate in Kava Bowl.

Ann Aurelia López. *The Farmworkers' Journey*. Berkeley: University of California Press, 2007. Interviews conducted over a 10-year period document the lives of farm workers who migrate from west-central Mexico to central California.

Martin F. Manalansan IV. *Global Divas: Filipino Gay Men in the Diaspora*. Durham, NC: Duke University Press, 2004. This book is based on the life narratives of 50 Filipino gay men in New York City and participant observation in homes, bars, hospitals, restaurants, and the Gay Pride Parade.

Ann V. Millard and Jorge Chapa, with others. *Apple Pie and Enchiladas: Latino Newcomers in the Rural Midwest*. Austin: University of Texas Press, 2004. Many Latinos migrate to the rural Midwest in the United States to work in food-processing plants and small factories. The authors explore relations between the local Anglos and the immigrants.

Karen Richman. *Migration and Vodou*. Gainesville: University of Florida Press, 2005. This book and its accompanying CD reveal the innovative ways that Haitian migrants in South Florida maintain their religious traditions and familial connections. .

Archana B. Verma. *The Making of Little Punjab in Canada: Patterns of Immigration*. Thousand Oaks, CA: Sage Publications, 2002. Verma describes the historical connections between Hindu migrants from a village in India's northern state of Punjab, to Vancouver Island, British Columbia. Strong family and kinship ties continue to link the migrants to their home area.

A traditional custodian from the Ngarrindjeri nation in South Australia holds a box containing four skulls of Australian Aborigines at a ceremony at Manchester University, England, 2003. The skulls were returned, after 100 years in England, to a sacred keeping place.

PEOPLE DEFINING DEVELOPMENT

the BIG questions

- What is development and the approaches to achieving it?
- How has development affected indigenous people and women and how are they redefining development?
- What are urgent issues in development?

We have had many visitors to Walpole Island since the French "discovered us" in the seventeenth century in our territory, Bkejwanong. In many cases, these visitors failed to recognize who we were and to appreciate our traditions. They tried to place us in their European framework of knowledge, denying that we possessed our indigenous knowledge. They attempted to steal our lands, water, and knowledge. We resisted. They left and never came back. We continued to share our knowledge with the next visitors to our place. . . . It was a long-term strategy that has lasted more than three hundred years. (Dr. Dean Jacobs, Executive Director of Walpole Island First Nation, from his Foreword in VanWynsberghe 2002:ix)

These are the words of a leader of the Walpole Island First Nation, located in southern Ontario, Canada (see Map 16.1). They, along with many other indigenous groups worldwide, have begun to take strong action in recent decades to protect their culture and its natural environment. The Walpole Island First Nation organized itself and successfully fought to control industrial waste that was polluting its water and land. In the process, the people have regained their pride and cultural integrity.

The subfield of development anthropology looks at how culture and "development" interact to improve people's lives and reduce poverty. Thus, it has a strong applied component as well as a critical component that asks hard questions about the causes of poverty. This chapter's first section considers concepts related to change and development and the approaches to development. The second section focuses on development in relation to indigenous peoples and women. The third section looks at urgent issues in development and what cultural anthropology can contribute to them.

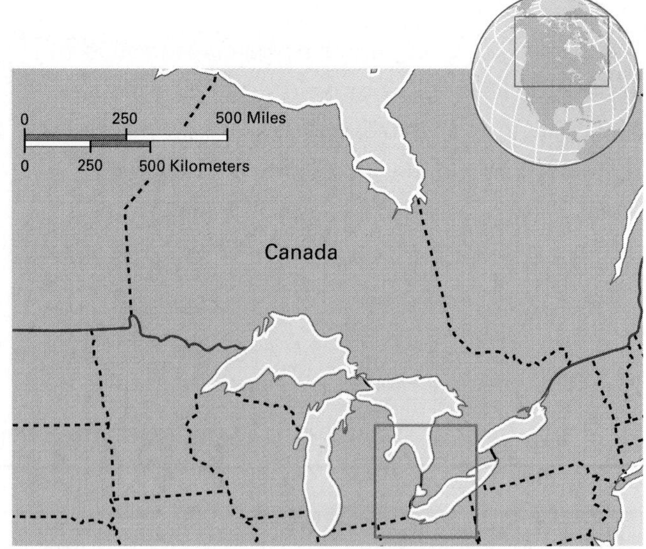

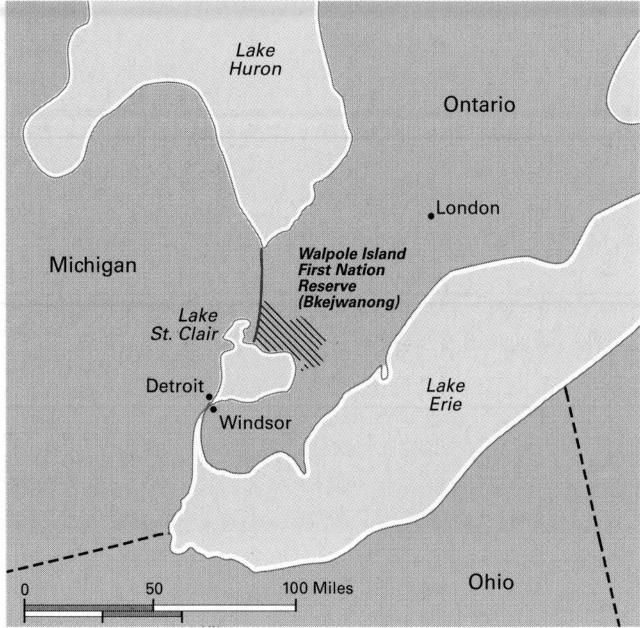

MAP 16.1 Walpole Island Reservation in Southern Ontario, Canada.

Defining Development and Approaches to It

This chapter focuses on the topic of contemporary cultural change as shaped by **development**, or directed change to improve human welfare. A major focus of development efforts is preventing or reducing poverty. Poverty is extremely difficult to define, but one workable definition says that **poverty** is the lack of tangible and intangible assets that contribute to life and the quality of life. Some approaches to poverty reduction focus on *basic needs* such as access to decent food, water, housing, and clothing, factors without which a person may die or certainly fail to thrive. More expanded definitions include access to things such as education and personal security (freedom from fear). Development experts in Paris, Rome, and Washington, DC, spend much time discussing how to measure poverty rates, how to assess whether poverty is increasing or decreasing and why, and what kinds of policies and programs are best to reduce poverty. More locally, real people in real places experience poverty and attempt to deal with it.

development directed change to achieve improved human welfare.

poverty the lack of tangible and intangible assets that contributing to life and the quality of life.

invention discovery of something new.

diffusion the spread of culture through contact.

acculturation a form of cultural change in which a minority culture becomes more like the dominant culture.

assimilation a form of culture change in which a culture is thoroughly acculturated, or decultured, and is no longer distinguishable as having a separate identity.

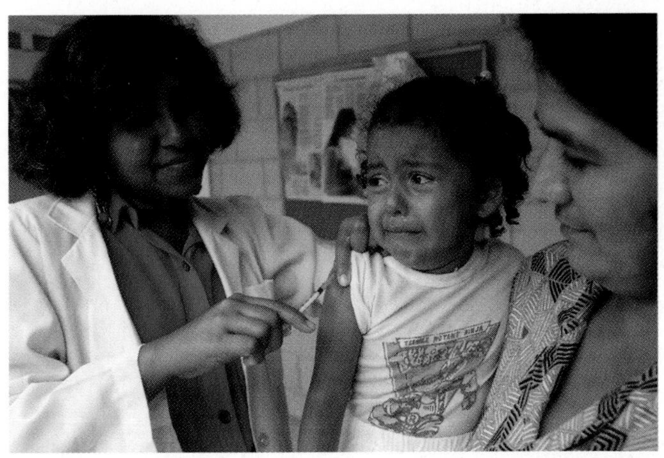

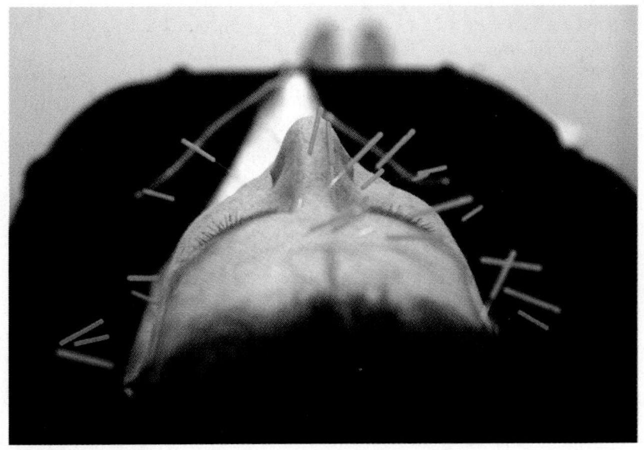

(LEFT) A doctor administering polio vaccine in Ecuador. The Pan American Health Organization (PAHO) established a plan in 1985 for eradicating the polio virus from the Americas by 1990. (RIGHT) A patient rests with acupuncture needles on her face during a "face lift" treatment (to remove wrinkles and make the individual look younger) in New York City. This acupuncture procedure, based in traditional Chinese medicine, follows the theory that the face is where the essence of yin and the energy of yang meet. It seeks to adjust imbalances in yin and yang by inserting needles at particular places in the face.

▶ *Do research to find out whether traditional Chinese acupuncture had a specialization in "face lifting." If not, can you learn when, where, and why did this specialization emerge?*

TWO PROCESSES OF CULTURAL CHANGE

Two basic processes underlie all cultural change. The first is **invention**, the discovery of something new. The second is **diffusion**, the spread of culture through contact.

INVENTION Most inventions evolve gradually through experimentation and accumulation of knowledge, but some appear suddenly. Examples of technological inventions that have created cultural change include the printing press, gunpowder, the polio vaccine, and satellite communication. Conceptual innovations, such as Jeffersonian democracy, are also inventions. Many inventions bring about positive cultural change, but not all inventions have positive social outcomes. Inventions inspired by a socially positive goal may have mixed or unintended negative consequences (see Critical Thinking).

DIFFUSION Diffusion is logically related to invention because new discoveries are likely to spread. Diffusion can occur in several ways. First, in mutual borrowing, two societies that are roughly equal in power exchange aspects of their culture. Second, diffusion sometimes involves a transfer from a dominant culture to a less powerful culture. This process may occur through force or, more subtly, through education or marketing processes that promote adoption of new practices and beliefs. Third, a more powerful culture may appropriate aspects of a less powerful culture, through cultural imperialism. Last, a less powerful and even oppressed cultural group often provides sources of cultural change in a dominant culture.

Changes in a minority culture that make it more like the dominant culture are referred to as **acculturation**. In extreme cases, a culture becomes so thoroughly acculturated that it is **assimilated**, or *decultured*—that is, it is no longer distinguishable as having a separate identity. In the most extreme cases, the impact on the minority culture is that it becomes extinct. These processes parallel degrees of language change resulting from contact with dominating cultures and languages. Such changes have occurred among many indigenous people as the result of globalization and the introduction of new technology (see Lessons Applied, p. 401). Other responses to acculturative influences include partial acceptance of something new with localization and syncretism, as in the case of the game of cricket in the Trobriands (Chapter 14), or rejection and resistance.

THEORIES AND MODELS OF DEVELOPMENT

This part of the section reviews theories and models of development and the various kinds of the institutions involved in development. It then examines development projects.

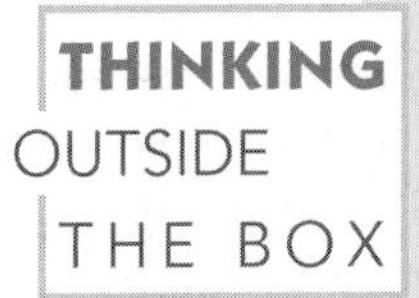

Choose two inventions made in your lifetime and assess how they affect your everyday activities, social interactions, and ways of thinking.

CRITICAL thinking

The Green Revolution and Social Inequality

Agricultural scientists of the 1950s, inspired by the laudable goal of eliminating world hunger, developed genetic variations of wheat, rice, and corn that would be resistant to pests and drought and provide abundant yields. The seeds of these *high-yielding varieties* (*HYVs*) were promoted to farmers throughout the developing world as part of the Green Revolution. The goal of the Green Revolution of the mid-twentieth century was to feed the planet by boosting production of food crops per acre. In most places where Green Revolution agricultural practices were adopted, grain production did increase. Was world hunger conquered? The answer is no, because world hunger is not merely a problem of production. It also involves distribution.

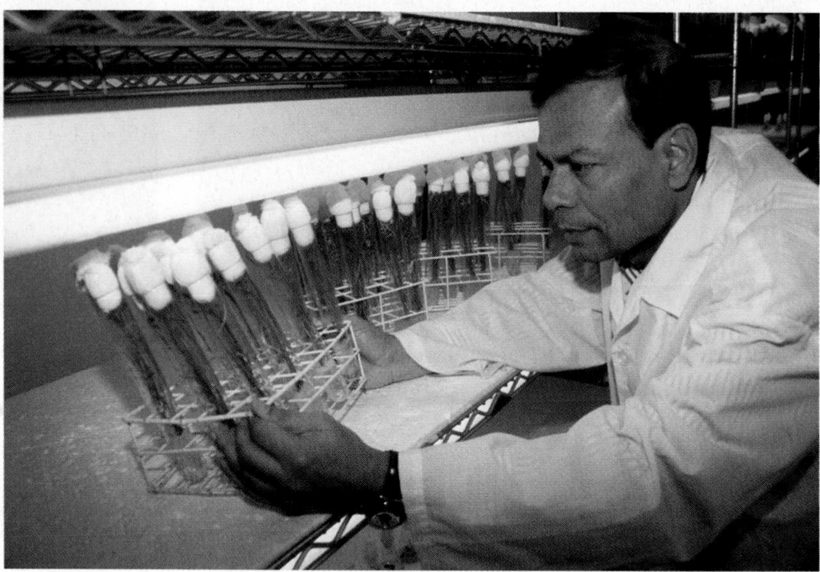

Dr. Swapan Datta, chief biotechnologist at the International Rice Research Institute in Manila, the Philippines, is responsible for assimilating "Golden Rice" into Asian varieties.

Analyses of the social impact of the Green Revolution in India reveal that one of its results was to increase the inequality between the rich and the poor (Frankel 1971). How did this happen? The answer lies in the fact that Green Revolution agriculture requires three expensive inputs:

- Purchase of seeds each year, because HYV seeds are hybridized and cannot be harvested from the crop and used the next year
- Heavy application of commercial fertilizers
- Dependable irrigation sources

Farmers who had success with HYV seeds were those who were already better off than others. They were selected to adopt the new seeds because they could afford the costly inputs. Small farmers who tried planting HYV seeds but could not provide the inputs experienced crop failure, went deeper into debt, and had to sell their land.

Larger, better-off farmers took advantage of these new openings in the land market to buy land and expand their holdings. With the acquisition of tractors and other mechanized equipment, they became even more productive. Small farmers, unable to compete, continued to be squeezed out financially. They became hired day laborers, dependent on seasonal employment by large farmers, or they migrated to cities and joined the urban underclass.

Looking at the Green Revolution from a critical thinking perspective reveals a framework of economic interests and benefits that exist, regardless of the original intentions of the HYV seed inventors or the program promoters. The following are the big winners:

- Companies that manufacture and sell HYV seeds
- Companies that manufacture and sell chemical fertilizers (largely petroleum-based)
- Companies that manufacture and sell mechanized farm equipment
- Wealthier farmers who could afford the inputs and the risks and were able to increase their land holdings by buying land from small farmers who failed
- The scientists who gained funding for their research and world fame for their discoveries.

The big losers are the small farmers who lost their land and were forced to move to cities and take up low-pay wage work.

Some unanswered questions are: Did malnutrition in India decline as a result of the adoption of Green Revolution farming? Was the problem of world hunger solved? The simple answer to both questions is no, but one has to wonder what would have happened if HYV grains had not been discovered. These questions are complicated. They are also extremely timely given contemporary debates about the potential of genetically modified foods to "solve world hunger."

◆ CRITICAL THINKING QUESTIONS

- Is it likely that the original innovators of HYV grains considered what social transformations might occur in developing countries' agriculture as a result of their invention?
- Would they have been likely to stop their research if they had realized that it would lead to the "rich getting richer and the poor getting poorer"?
- How does the example of the Green Revolution of the 1970s shed light on current debates about genetically modified food?

Canadian Prime Minister Stephen Harper, center (standing), officially apologizes for more than a century of abuse and culture loss related to Indian boarding schools at a ceremony in the House of Commons on Parliament Hill in Ottawa, Canada, in June 2008. From the 19th century to the 1970s, more than 150,000 aboriginal children were required to attend state-funded Christian schools as part of a program to assimilate them into the Canadian state.

No single view of development or how to achieve it exists. Debates about these issues are heated and involve experts from many disciplines, governments, and local people worldwide. Five theories or models of development are presented here. They differ in these respects:

- The definition of development
- The goal of development
- Measures of development
- Attention to environmental and financial sustainability

MODERNIZATION **Modernization** is a form of change marked by economic growth through industrialization and market expansion, political consolidation through the state, technological innovation, literacy, and options for social mobility. It originated in Western Europe in the beginning of the seventeenth century with the emerging emphasis on secular rationality and scientific thinking as the pathways to progress (Norgaard 1994). Given the insights of rationality and science, modernization is thought to spread inevitably throughout the world and lead to improvement in people's lives everywhere. The major goals of modernization are material progress and individual betterment.

Supporters and critics of modernization are found in both rich and poor countries. Supporters claim that the benefits of modernization (improved transportation, electricity, biomedical health care, and telecommunications) are worth the costs to the environment and society.

Others take a critical view and regard modernization as problematic because of its focus on ever-increasing consumption levels and heavy use of nonrenewable resources. Many cultural anthropologists are critical of Westernization and modernization because their research shows how modernization often brings environmental ruin, increases social inequality, destroys indigenous cultures, and reduces global cultural and biological diversity. In spite of strong cautionary critiques from anthropologists, environmentalists, and others about the negative effects of modernization, most countries worldwide have not slowed their attempts to achieve it. Some governments and citizen groups, however, are promoting lifestyles that rely less on nonrenewable resources and include concern for protecting the environment.

GROWTH-ORIENTED DEVELOPMENT Development as "induced" change, brought about through applying modernization theory in so-called developing countries, emerged after World War II. At that time, the United States began

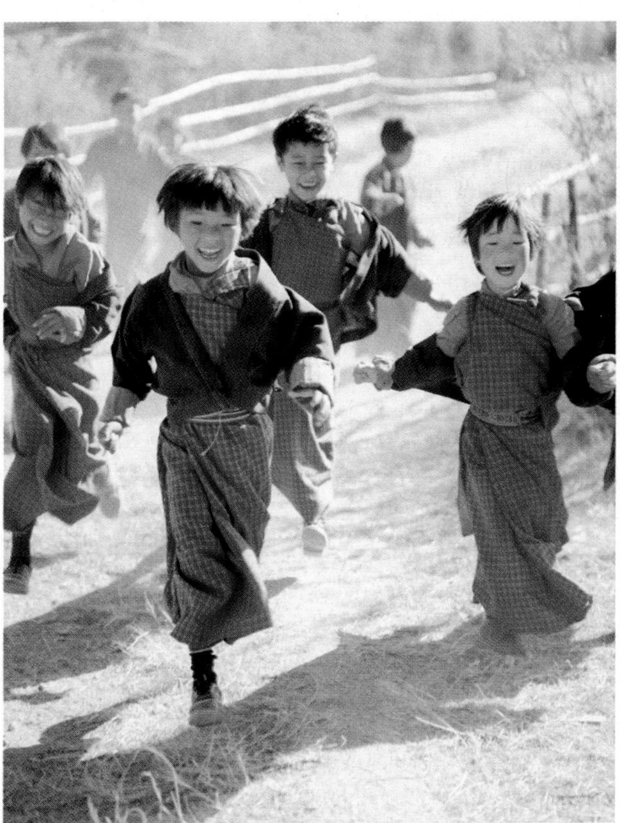

School girls in Bhutan. The government of Bhutan rejects the Western concept of the Gross Domestic Product (GDP) as the best measure of a country's success and instead uses a measure called Gross Domestic Happiness (GDH).

▶ *Go to the Internet to learn more about Bhutan and the government's aspirations for its people.*

modernization a model of change based on belief in the inevitable advance of science and Western secularism and processes including industrial growth, consolidation of the state, bureaucratization, market economy, technological innovation, literacy, and options for social mobility.

to expand its role as a world leader, and development aid was part of its international policy agenda. International development, as defined by major Western development institutions, is similar to modernization in terms of its goals. The process emphasizes economic growth as the most crucial element. According to growth-oriented development theory, investments in economic growth will, through the *trickle-down effect,* lead to improved human welfare through the gradual increase of wealth among the less well-off.

Promoting economic growth in developing countries includes two strategies:

- Increasing economic productivity and trade through modernized agriculture and manufacturing and participation in world markets.
- Reducing government expenditures on public services such as schools and health in order to reduce debt and reallocate resources to increase productivity. This strategy, called *structural adjustment,* has been promoted by the World Bank since the 1980s.

Measures to assess the achievement of development through this model include the rate of growth of the economy, especially the *gross domestic product,* or *GDP.*

DISTRIBUTIONAL DEVELOPMENT Distributional development contrasts with growth-oriented development in its emphasis on social equity in benefits, especially in terms of increased income, literacy, and health. It rejects the trickle-down process as ineffective in reaching less well-off people. Its position is based on evidence that growth-oriented strategies, applied without concern for distribution, actually increase social inequality. In this view, the growth model ensures that "the rich get richer and the poor get poorer."

The distributional approach opposes structural adjustment policies because they further undermine the welfare of the poor by removing the few entitlements they had in the form of services. Advocates of the distributional model see the need for benevolent governments to ensure equitable access to crucial resources in order to enhance the ability of the poor to provide for their own needs (Gardner and Lewis 1996).

Although conservative, "neoliberal" economists argue that redistribution is neither realistic or feasible, supporters of the distributive approach point to cases in the model that have worked. As an example, anthropological research in a village in central Kerala, a state in southern India (see Map 16.2), assessed whether redistribution was an effective development strategy (Franke 1993). The findings showed the answer to be

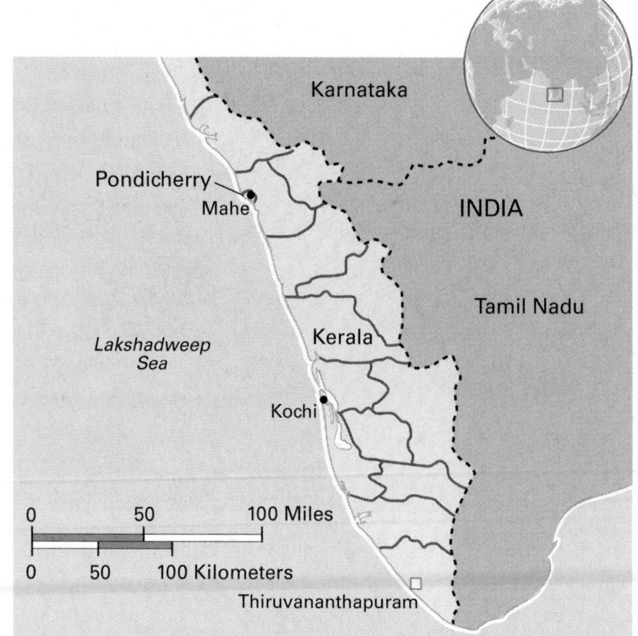

MAP 16.2 Kerala, South India.
With a population of 30 million, Kerala's living standard, literacy, and health are high compared to the rest of India. It comprises 14 districts and three historical regions: Travancore in the south, Kochi in the central part, and Malabar in the north. Long a socialist democracy, Kerala now allows the free market and foreign direct investment to play larger roles. A major tourist destination due to its tropical ecology and cultural features such as dramatic martial arts and theater, Kerala also hosts a growing Ayurvedic health tourism industry along its coast.

positive. Even though Kerala's per capita income is the lowest of any state in India, it has the highest social indicators in the country in health and literacy.

Government attention to distribution in Kerala came about through democratic channels, including demonstrations and pressure on the government by popular movements and labor unions. These groups forced the state to reallocate land ownership, which alleviated social inequality somewhat. In other instances, people pressured government leaders to improve village conditions by providing school lunches for poor children, increasing school attendance by dalit children (review Chapter 9), and investing in school facilities. Through public action, Nadur village became a better place to live for many people.

HUMAN DEVELOPMENT Another alternative to the growth-first model is called *human development,* the strategy that emphasizes investing in human welfare. The United Nations adopted the phrase "human development" to emphasize the need for improvements in human welfare in terms of health, education, and personal security and safety. In this model, investments in improving human welfare will lead to economic development. The reverse is not invariably true: The level of economic growth of a country (or region within

---

social impact assessment a study conducted to gauge the potential social costs and benefits of particular innovations before change is undertaken.

LESSONS applied

The Saami, Snowmobiles, and the Need for Social Impact Analysis

How might adoption of a new belief or practice benefit or harm a particular culture and its various members? Although often difficult to answer, this question must always be asked. A classic study of the snowmobile disaster among a Saami group in Finland offers a careful response to this question in a context of rapid technological diffusion (Pelto 1973). In the 1950s, the Saami of Finland (review Culturama, Chapter 12, p. 309) had an economy based on reindeer herding, which provided most of their diet.

Besides supplying meat, reindeer had other important economic and social functions. They were used as draft animals, especially hauling wood for fuel. Their hides were made into clothing and their sinews used for sewing. Reindeer were key items of exchange, both in external trade and internal gift giving. Parents gave a child a reindeer to mark the appearance of the child's first tooth. When a couple became engaged, they exchanged a reindeer with each other to mark the commitment.

By the 1960s, all this had changed because of the introduction of the snowmobile. Previously, people herded the reindeer herds on skis. The use of snowmobiles for herd management had several results. The herds were no longer kept domesticated for part of the year, during which they became tame. Instead, they were allowed to roam freely all year and thus became wilder.

Snowmobiles allowed herders to cover larger amounts of territory at roundup time, and sometimes several roundups occurred instead of one. Herd size declined dramatically. The reasons for the decline included the stress inflicted on the reindeer by the extra distance traveled during roundups, the multiple roundups instead of a single one, and the fear aroused by the noisy snowmobiles. Roundups were held at a time when the females were near the end of their pregnancy, another factor inducing reproductive stress. As the number of snowmobiles increased, the number of reindeer decreased.

Introduction of snowmobiles for herding also increased young men's dominance in herding (Larsson 2005). Before the snowmobiles, reindeer herding was a family operation. Although men did more of the long-distance herding, women also worked closely with the herd. Since snowmobiles were adopted, parents have steered their sons toward herding and their daughters toward education and a professional career. Two rationales for such gender tracking are that driving a snowmobile is difficult due to its heaviness, and the driver may get stuck somewhere. The use of snowmobiles also changed the age pattern of reindeer herding in favor of youth over age; thus, older herders were squeezed out.

Another change involved a new dependence on the outside through the cash economy. Cash is needed in order to purchase a snowmobile, buy gasoline, and pay for parts and repairs. This delocalization of the economy created social inequality, which had not existed before. Other social and economic repercussions include:

- The cash cost of effective participation in herding exceeded the resources of some families, who had to drop out of participation in herding.
- The snowmobile pushed many Saami into debt.
- Dependence on cash and indebtedness forced many Saami to migrate to cities for work.

Pertti Pelto, the anthropologist who first documented this case, calls these transformations a disaster for Saami culture. He offers a recommendation for the future: Communities confronting the adoption of new technology should have a chance to weigh evidence on the pros and cons and make an informed judgment. Pelto's work is one of the early warnings from anthropology about the need for **social impact assessments**, studies that gauge the potential social costs and benefits of particular innovations before change is undertaken.

A Saami herder riding a skidoo in northern Norway leads his herd.

◆ FOOD FOR THOUGHT

- Speculate about what the Saami might have done if they had been able to consider a social impact assessment of the effects of snowmobiles on their culture.

a country) is not necessarily correlated with its level of human development, as is clear from the case of Kerala. Thus, in this view, economic growth is neither an end in itself nor even a necessary component of development as measured in human welfare. Economic resources, combined with distributive policies, are a strong basis for attaining high levels of human development.

SUSTAINABLE DEVELOPMENT *Sustainable development* refers to forms of improvement that do not destroy nonrenewable resources and are financially supportable over time. Advocates of sustainable development argue that the economic growth of wealthy countries has been and still is costly in terms of the natural environment and people whose lives depend on fragile ecosystems. They say that such growth cannot be sustained at even its present level, not to mention projected demands as more countries become industrialized.

In 1992, the UN Conference on Environment and Development, better known as the Rio Earth Summit, established goals for global actions to ensure the well-being of the planet and its people. Since then, follow-up international meetings have occurred, producing more agreements and updated plans. Countries vary in terms of how much they support Earth Summit goals, and they differ in the degree to which they implement policies to which they have agreed. As of 2009, increased concern globally about the environment is generating new ideas about energy generation, such as through windmills, and ways that consumers can reduce their use of nonrenewable fuels.

INSTITUTIONAL APPROACHES TO DEVELOPMENT

Cultural anthropologists are increasingly aware of the importance of examining the institutions, organizations, and specialists involved in development policy making, programs, and projects. With this knowledge, cultural anthropologists have a better chance of shaping development policies and programs. Institutional research includes studying the management systems of large-scale institutions, such as the World Bank, and of small-scale organizations in diverse settings. Topics include behavior within the institutions, social interactions with the "client population," and institutional discourse. This section first describes some large development institutions and then some smaller organizations.

LARGE-SCALE DEVELOPMENT INSTITUTIONS Two major types of large-scale development institutions exist. First are the *multilateral institutions*—those that include several countries as "donor" members. Second are the *bilateral institutions*—those that involve only two countries: a "donor" and a "recipient."

social capital the intangible resources existing in social ties, trust, and cooperation.

The largest multilaterals are the United Nations and the World Bank. Each is a vast and complex social system. The United Nations, established in 1945, includes over 160 member states. Each country contributes money according to its ability, and each has one vote in the General Assembly. Several UN agencies exist, fulfilling a range of functions, such as the United Nations Development Programme (UNDP), Food and Agriculture Organization (FAO), World Health Organization (WHO), United Nations Children's Fund (UNICEF), United Nations Educational, Scientific, and Cultural Organization (UNESCO), and United Nations High Commissioner for Refugees (UNHCR).

The World Bank is supported by contributions from over 150 member countries. Founded in 1944, the Bank is dedicated to promoting the concept of economic growth worldwide. Its main strategy is to promote international investment through loans. The World Bank is guided by a Board of Governors made up of the finance ministers of member countries. The World Bank system assigns each country a number of votes based on the size of its financial commitment. The economic superpowers, therefore, dominate.

The World Bank system includes the International Bank for Reconstruction and Development (IBRD) and the International Development Association (IDA). Both are administered at the World Bank headquarters in Washington, DC. They lend for similar types of projects and often in the same country, but their loan conditions differ. The IBRD provides loans to poor countries that are generally regarded as "bad risks" on the world commercial market. Thus, the IBRD is a source of interest-bearing loans to countries that otherwise would not be able to borrow. The IBRD has recorded a profit every year of its existence. Most of its loans support large infrastructure projects such as roads and dams. The IDA is the "soft-loan" side of the World Bank. It provides interest-free loans (although there is a 0.75 percent annual service charge) and a flexible repayment schedule averaging between 35 and

World Bank headquarters in Washington, DC. The World Bank employs over 8000 people. It employs over 2000 people internationally.

40 years (Rich 1994). These concessional loans are granted to the poorest countries.

Prominent bilateral institutions include the Japan International Cooperation Agency (JICA), the United States Agency for International Development (USAID), the Canadian International Development Agency (CIDA), Britain's Department for International Development (DfID), the Swedish Agency for International Development (SIDA), and the Danish Organization for International Development (DANIDA). These agencies vary in terms of the total size of their aid programs, the types of programs they support, and the proportion of aid disbursed as loans that have to be repaid with interest compared to aid disbursed as grants that do not require repayment. The USAID tends to give more loans than grants, compared to other bilaterals.

Loans and grants also differ in terms of whether they are *tied* or *untied*. Tied loans and grants require that a certain percentage of project expenditures go for goods, expertise, and services originating in the donor country. For example, a tied loan to a certain country for road construction would require allocation of a designated percentage of the funds to donor country construction companies, airfare for donor country road experts, and in-country expenses for donor country experts, such as hotels, food, and local transportation. When loans or grants are untied, the recipient country may decide freely how to use the funds. The USAID offers more tied than untied aid, whereas countries such as Sweden, the Netherlands, and Norway tend to give untied aid.

Another difference among the bilaterals is the proportion of their total aid that goes to the poorest countries. The United Kingdom's DfID sends more than 80 percent of its aid to the poorest countries, whereas most of U.S. foreign aid dollars go to Egypt and Israel. Emphasis on certain types of aid also varies from one bilateral institution to another. Cuba has long played a unique role in bilateral aid. Cuba has concentrated on aid for training health-care providers and promoting preventive health care (Feinsilver 1993). Its development assistance goes to socialist countries, including many in Africa and, in Latin America, Venezuela and Bolivia.

The USAID has funded many development projects worldwide, such as this improved road in rural Bangladesh. Proceeds from the toll gate will help pay for maintenance of the road. The rickshaws are parked while their drivers pay their toll. The large white vehicle belongs to USAID and was being used by American researchers.

▶ *What kinds of user fees have you paid in the past few months? Did you think the fees were fair?*

GRASSROOTS APPROACHES Many countries have experimented with *grassroots approaches* to development, or locally initiated, small-scale projects. This alternative to the top-down development pursued by the large-scale agencies described in the previous section is more likely to be culturally appropriate, supported through local participation, and successful.

During the 1970s, for example, Kenya (see Map 6.5, p. 153) sponsored a national program whereby the government committed itself to providing teachers if local communities would build schools (Winans and Haugerud 1977). This program was part of Kenya's promotion of *harambee*, or self-help, in improving health, housing, and schooling. Local people's response to the schooling program especially was overwhelmingly positive. They turned out in large numbers to build schools, fulfilling their part of the bargain. They built so many schools that the government found it difficult to hold up its end of the bargain: paying the teachers' salaries. This program shows that self-help movements can be highly successful in mobilizing local participation if the target is valued.

The term **social capital** refers to the intangible resources of social ties, trust, and cooperation. Many local grassroots organizations around the world use social capital to provide basic social needs (see Culturama).

Religious organizations sponsor a wide variety of grassroots development projects. In the Philippines, the Basic Ecclesiastical Community (BEC) movement is based on Christian teachings and follows the model of Jesus as a supporter of the poor and oppressed (Nadeau 2002) (see Map 7.2, p. 166). The BECs seek to follow the general principles of liberation theology, which blends Christian principles of compassion and social justice, political consciousness raising among the oppressed, and communal activism. In the rural areas, several BECs have successfully built trust among

THINKING OUTSIDE THE BOX

Visit the website of one of the multilateral development organizations and one bilateral organization to learn about their goals, programs, and internship opportunities. For current information on territorial rights of indigenous peoples, consult the websites of Cultural Survival (www.cs.org) and Survival International (www.survival-international.org).

The Peyizan yo of Haiti

Haiti and the Dominican Republic share the island of Hispaniola. Following the island's discovery by Columbus in 1492, Spanish colonialists exterminated the island's indigenous Arawak Indians. In 1697, the French took control of what is now Haiti and instituted an exceptionally cruel system of African plantation slavery. In the late 1700s, the half million slaves revolted. In what is the only successful slave revolution in history, they ousted the French and established the first Black republic in the Western Hemisphere.

Haiti's population of over 8 million people occupies a territory somewhat smaller than the state of Maryland in the United States (www.unfpa.org). The land is rugged, hilly, or mountainous. Over 90 percent of the forests have been cleared. Haiti is the poorest country in the Western Hemisphere. Extreme inequality exists between the urban elite, who live in the capital city of Port-au-Prince, and everyone else.

The people in the countryside are the *peyizan yo* (the plural form of *peyizan*), a Creole term for small farmers who produce for their own use and for the market (Smith 2001). Many also participate in small-scale marketing. Most peyizan yo in Haiti own their land. They grow vegetables, fruits (especially mangoes), sugarcane, rice, and corn.

Accurate health statistics are not available, but even rough estimates show that Haiti has the highest prevalence level of HIV/AIDS of any country in the region. Medical anthropologist Paul Farmer emphasizes the role of colonialism in the past and global structural inequalities now in causing these high rates (1992).

Colonial plantation owners grew fabulously rich from this island. It produced more wealth for France than all of France's other colonies combined and more than the 13 colonies in North America produced for Britain. Why is Haiti so poor now? Colonialism launched environmental degradation by clearing forests. After the revolution, the new citizens carried with them the traumatic history of slavery. Now, neocolonialism and globalization are leaving new scars. For decades, the United States has played, and still plays, a powerful role in supporting conservative political regimes.

In contrast to these structural explanations, some people point to problems with the Haitian people: They cannot work together and they lack a vision of the future. In contrast to these views, Jennie Smith's ethnographic research in southwestern Haiti sheds light on life and perspectives on development of the peyizan yo (2001). She found many active social organizations with functions such as labor sharing to help each member get his or her field planted on time and cost sharing to help pay for health care or funerals. The peyizan yo had clear opinions about their vision for the future, including relative economic equality, political leaders with a sense of social service, *respe* (respect), and access of citizens to basic social services.

Thanks to Jennie Smith-Pariola, Berry College, for reviewing this material.

(LEFT) A woman repays her loan at a small-scale savings and loan business in rural Haiti. Many of the credit union members use their loans to set up small businesses. (CENTER) Food riots erupted in Port au Prince in 2008, and a soldier in the UN peacekeeping forces was shot dead. The Haitian Senate dismissed the standing Prime Minister.

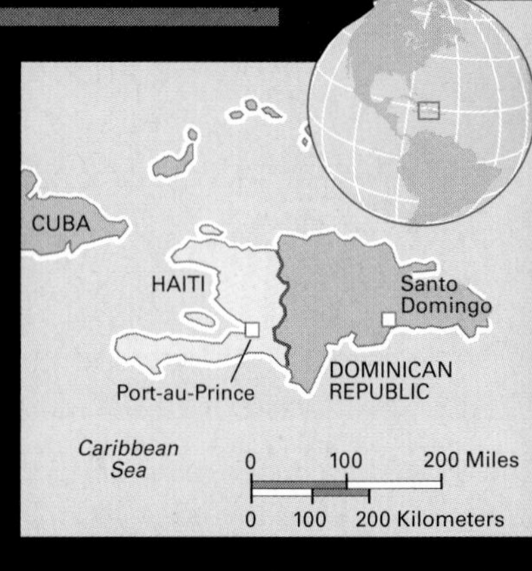

MAP 16.3 Haiti. The Republic of Haiti occupies one-third of the Caribbean island of Hispaniola.

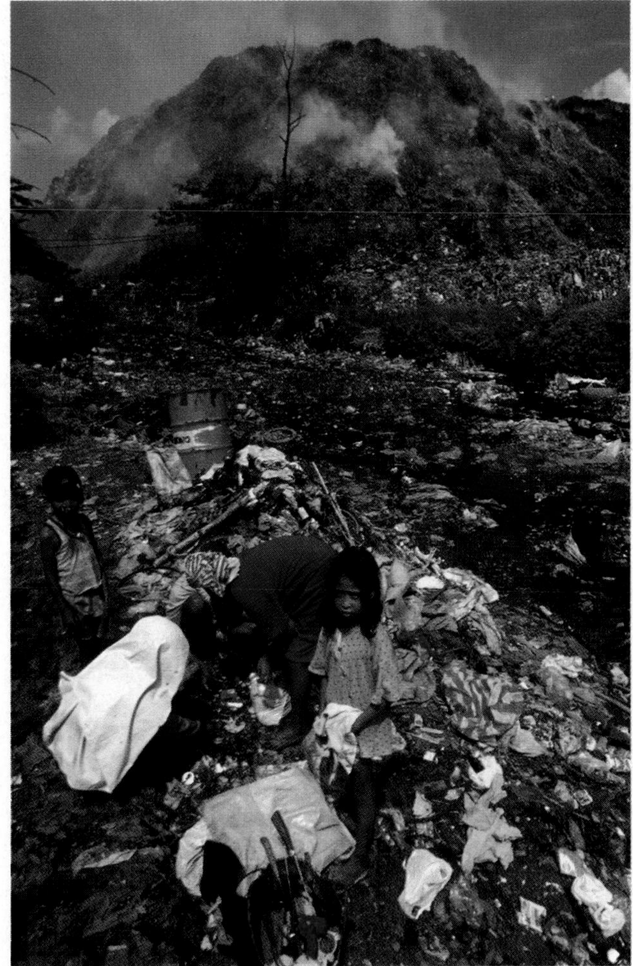

Scavenging for a livelihood in an urban dump in the Philippines.

▶ *What kind of an entitlement is this?*

group members and leaders and developed people's awareness of the excesses of global capitalism and the dangers of private greed and accumulation. Part of their success is due to the fact that members were able to pursue new economic strategies outside the constraints of capitalism, such as organic farming, that require little capital input.

A BEC in Cebu City, on the Island of Cebu, the Philippines, however, was unsuccessful. It faced the challenge of organizing people who make a living scavenging in a nearby city dump. Both adults and children scavenge for materials that are then sorted and sold for recycling, such as plastic. They work for 14 hours a day, seven days a week. It is an organized operation, with district officials monitoring the dump. Customary arrangements among the scavengers regulate their work areas. Scavenging requires no formal education and few tools, just a basket and a steel hook, and a kerosene lantern for nighttime work. Scavengers earn more than other nonskilled laborers in the city. In the BEC meetings, the scavengers found little on which to build solidarity. Instead, they bickered with each other and complained about each other to the leaders. The sheer poverty of the people was so great that communal values could not compete against their daily economic struggle. In cases of extreme poverty with limited or no options for alternative forms of income generation, government programs may be required to complement faith-based, grassroots initiatives.

Beginning with the Reagan administration's push toward privatization in the 1980s in the United States and a similar trend in the United Kingdom, the U.S. government sought to reduce direct financial support for international development and to encourage *privatization* of development assistance. Since then, many hundreds of *nongovernmental organizations* (*NGOs*) have emerged. A number of NGOs are focused on a particular issue, such as girls' education, HIV/AIDS prevention, human rights, or refugee relief. Some, however, are larger umbrella organizations with substantial projects covering many domains. Others, unfortunately, are only fronts that receive funding from government and nongovernment sources but do no actual work.

THE DEVELOPMENT PROJECT

Development institutions, whether they are large multilaterals or local NGOs, implement their goals through the **development project**, a set of activities designed to put development policies into action. For example, suppose a government sets a policy of increased agricultural production by a certain percent within a designated period. A development project to achieve the policy goal might be the construction of irrigation canals that would supply water to a targeted number of farmers.

ANTHROPOLOGISTS AND THE DEVELOPMENT PROJECT CYCLE Although details vary between organizations, all development projects have a **project cycle**, or the full process of a project from initial planning to completion (Cernea 1985). The project cycle includes five basic steps from beginning to end (see Figure 16.1).

Since the 1970s, applied anthropologists have been involved in development projects. Early on, they were hired primarily to do project evaluations, to determine whether the project had achieved its goals. Their research shows that projects were often dismal failures (Cochrane 1979). Three major reasons for the project failures are:

- The project did not fit the cultural and environmental context.

---

development project a set of activities designed to put development policies into action.

project cycle the steps of a development project from initial planning to completion: project identification, project design, project appraisal, project implementation, and project evaluation.

Project identification	Selecting a project to fit a particular purpose
Project design	Preparing the details of the project
Project appraisal	Assessing the project's budgetary aspects
Project implementation	Putting the project in place
Project evaluation	Assessing whether the project goals were fulfilled

FIGURE 16.1 The Development Project Cycle

- The project benefits did not reach the target group, such as the poor or women; instead, project benefits went to elites or some other less needy group.
- The intended beneficiaries were worse off after the project than before it.

One factor underlying these three problems is poor project design. The projects were designed by bureaucrats, usually Western economists, who lived in cities far from the project site with no firsthand experience of the lives of the target population. These experts applied a universal formula ("one size fits all") to all situations (Cochrane 2009). The cultural anthropologists who evaluated the projects, in contrast, knew the local people and context and were therefore shocked by the degree of nonfit between the projects and the people.

Applied anthropologists gained a reputation in development circles as troublemakers—people to be avoided by those who favored a move-ahead approach to getting projects funded and implemented. Applied anthropologists are still considered a nuisance by many development policy makers and planners, but sometimes, at least, a necessary nuisance. On a more positive note, through persistent efforts they have made progress in gaining a role earlier in the project cycle, at the stages of project identification and design.

CULTURAL FIT Review of many development projects over the past few decades reveals the importance of **cultural fit**, or taking the local culture into account in project design (Kottak 1985). A glaring case of nonfit between a project and its target population is a project intended to improve nutrition and health in some South Pacific islands by promoting increased milk consumption (Cochrane, author's class lecture notes, 1974). The project involved the transfer of large quantities of powdered milk from the United States to an island community. The local people, however, were lactose intolerant (unable to digest raw milk), and they all soon had diarrhea. They stopped drinking the milk and used the powder to whitewash their houses. Beyond wasting resources, inappropriately designed projects result in the exclusion of the intended beneficiaries. Two examples are when a person's signature is required but the people do not know how to write, and when photo identification cards are requested from Muslim women, whose faces may not be shown in public.

Applied anthropologists can provide insights about how to achieve cultural fit in order to enhance project success. Anthropologist Gerald Murray played a positive role in redesigning a costly and unsuccessful reforestation project supported by USAID in Haiti (1987). Since the colonial era in Haiti (see Map 16.3, p. 404), deforestation has been dramatic, with an estimated 50 million trees cut annually. Some of the deforestation is driven by the market demand for wood for construction and for charcoal in the capital city of Port-au-Prince. Another reason is that the peyizan yo, or small farmers, need cleared land for growing crops and grazing their goats. The ecological consequences of so much clearing, however, are extensive soil erosion and declining fertility of the land.

In the 1980s, USAID sent millions of tree seedlings to Haiti, and the Haitian government urged rural people to plant them. The peyizan yo, however, refused to plant the seedlings on their land and instead fed them to their goats. Murray, who had done his doctoral dissertation on rural Haitian land tenure practices, was called on by USAID to diagnose the problem and suggest an alternative approach. He advised that the kind of seedling promoted be changed from fruit trees, in which the peyizan yo saw little benefit because they are not to be cut, to fast-growing trees such as eucalyptus that could be cut as early as four years after planting and sold in Port-au-Prince. The peyizan yo quickly accepted this plan because it would yield profits in the foreseeable future. The cultural nonfit was that USAID wanted trees to stay in place for many years, but the peyizan yo viewed trees as things that were meant to be cut in the short term.

THE ANTHROPOLOGICAL CRITIQUE OF DEVELOPMENT PROJECTS The early decades of development anthropology were dominated by what I call **traditional development anthropology**. In traditional development anthropology, the anthropologist takes on a role of helping to make development policies and programs work better. It is the "add an anthropologist and stir" approach to development. Like good applied anthropology in any domain, traditional

cultural fit a characteristic of informed and effective project design in which planners take local culture into account; opposite of one-size-fits-all project design.

traditional development anthropology an approach to international development in which the anthropologist accepts the role of helping to make development work better by providing cultural information to planners.

critical development anthropology an approach to international development in which the anthropologist takes on a critical-thinking role and asks why and to whose benefit particular development policies and programs are pursued.

developmental anthropology does work. For example, an anthropologist familiar with a local culture can provide information about what kinds of consumer goods would be desired by the people or what might persuade people to relocate with less resistance. The anthropologist may act as a *cultural broker*, or someone who uses knowledge of both donor culture and recipient culture to devise a workable plan.

Concern exists among many anthropologists about development projects that have negative effects on local people and their environments. For example, comparison of the welfare of local inhabitants of the middle Senegal River valley (see Map 16.4), before and after the construction of a large dam, shows that people's level of food insecurity increased after the dam was built (Horowitz and Salem-Murdock 1993). Before the dam, periodic flooding of the plain provided for a dense population supporting itself with agriculture, fishing, forestry, and herding. After the dam was constructed, water was released less often. The people downstream lacked sufficient water for their crops, and fishing was no longer a dependable source of food. At other times, dam managers released a large flood of water, damaging farmers' crops. Many downstream residents have had to leave the area due to the effects of the dam; they are victims of development-induced displacement (review Chapter 15). Downstream people now have high rates of schistosomiasis, a severely debilitating disease caused by parasites, because the disease spreads quickly in the slow-moving water below the dam.

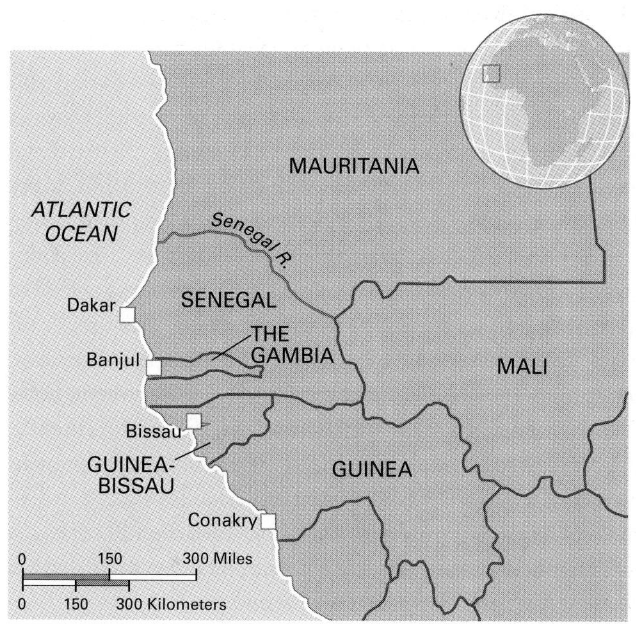

MAP 16.4 Senegal.
The Republic of Senegal is mainly rolling sandy plains of the western Sahel. Senegal's economy has been struggling. Social inequality is extreme, and urban unemployment is high. Its population is over 11 million, of which 70 percent live in rural areas. Of the many ethnic groups, the Wolof are the largest. Islam is the major religion, practiced by 94 percent of the population, with Christians 4 percent. Sufi brotherhoods are the organizing principle of Islam in Senegal.

Other "dam stories" document the negative effects of dam construction on local people, including the destruction of their economy, social organization, sacred space, sense of home, and the environment (Loker 2004). Such mega-projects force thousands, even millions, of people in the affected area to cope with the changes in one way or another. Many leave; others stay and try to replace what they have lost by clearing new land and rebuilding. Most end up in situations far worse than where they lived originally.

The growing awareness of the negative effects of many supposedly positive development projects has led to the emergence of what I call **critical development anthropology**. In this approach, the anthropologist takes on a critical-thinking role. The question is not What can I do to make this project successful? Instead, the anthropologist asks, Is this a good project from the perspective of the local people and their environment? If the answer is yes, then an applied anthropologist can take a supportive role. If the answer is no, then the anthropologist can intervene with this information, taking on the role of either a whistle-blower to stop the project, or an advocate promoting ideas about how to change the project in order to mitigate harm. In the case of the Senegal River dam project, applied anthropologists worked in collaboration with engineers and local people to devise an alternative management plan for the water flow in which regular and controlled amounts of water were released. In many other cases, the process is less positive, with planners ignoring the anthropologist's advice (Loker 2000).

Development and Indigenous People and Women

This section considers two categories of people who are increasingly taking an active role in redefining development in their own terms: indigenous people and women. Although they are overlapping categories, this section presents material about them separately for purposes of illustration.

INDIGENOUS PEOPLE AND DEVELOPMENT

Indigenous peoples have been victimized by many aspects of growth-oriented development, as they were by colonialism before it. But now many indigenous groups are redefining development and taking development into their own hands.

As noted in Chapter 1, indigenous people are usually a numerical minority in the states that control their territory. The United Nations distinguishes between indigenous peoples and other minority groups such as African Americans, the Roma,

In the southern part of Madagascar, there is pressure to grow more rice, which means irrigating more land. The expansion of intensive rice cultivation will bring the death of many baobab trees and threaten the habitats of wild animal species, including lemurs.

▶ *Assume you have just been appointed as Madagascar's Minister of People, Nature, and Development. What do you want your research staff to brief you about during your first month of service?*

and Tamils of Sri Lanka. It is more useful to view all "minority" groups as forming a continuum from purely indigenous groups to minority/ethnic groups that are not geographically original to a place but share many problems with indigenous peoples as a result of displacement and living within a more powerful majority culture (Maybury-Lewis 1997b).

Indigenous peoples differ from most minorities in that they tend to occupy remote areas and often areas rich in natural resources. Remoteness has, to some extent, protected them from outsiders. Now, however, governments, international business, conservationists, and tourists increasingly recognize that the lands of these people contain valuable natural resources, such as gas in the circumpolar region, gold in Papua New Guinea and the Amazon, sapphires in Madagascar, hydroelectric potential in large rivers throughout the world, and cultural attractions.

Accurate statistics on indigenous populations do not exist. Several reasons account for this lack of information (Kennedy and Perz 2000). First, no one agrees about whom to count as indigenous. Second, some governments do not bother to conduct a census of indigenous people. If they do, they may undercount indigenous people in order to downplay recognition of their existence. Third, it is often physically difficult, if not impossible, to carry out census operations in indigenous areas. The indigenous people of North Sentinel Island in India's Andaman Islands remain uncounted because Indian officials cannot land on the island without being shot with arrows (Singh 1994) (see Map 4.2, p. 94).

Rough estimates of the total population of indigenous people worldwide range between 300 million and 350 million people, or about 5 percent of the world's population (Hughes 2003). The greatest numbers are in Asia, including Central Asia, South Asia, East Asia, and Southeast Asia. Canada's First Nation population is under 2 million. The Indian population in the United States numbers around 1 million.

INDIGENOUS PEOPLE AS VICTIMS OF COLONIALISM AND DEVELOPMENT Like colonialism, contemporary global and state political and economic interests often involve takeover and control of indigenous people's territory. Over the past several hundred years, many indigenous groups and their cultures have been exterminated as a result of contact with outsiders. In addition to death and population decline through contagious disease, slavery, warfare, and other forms of violence have threatened their survival. With colonialism, indigenous people have experienced wholesale attacks as outsiders sought to take over their land by force, prevented them from practicing their traditional lifestyle, and integrated them into the colonial state as marginalized subjects. The loss of economic, political, and expressive autonomy have had devastating physical and psychological effects on indigenous peoples. Reduction in the biodiversity of their natural environment is directly linked to impoverishment, despair, and overall cultural decline (Maffi 2005, Arambiza and Painter 2006). These processes are common worldwide, creating unforeseen new risks for indigenous people's welfare.

In Southeast Asia (see Map 6.7, p. 157), states use policies of "planned resettlement" that displace indigenous people, or "hill tribes," in the name of progress (Evrard and Goudineau 2004). Development programs for the hill tribes in Thailand, for example, reveal the links among international interests, state goals, and the well-being of the hill tribes (Kesmanee 1994). The hill tribes include groups such as the Karen, Hmong, Mian, Lahu, Lisu, and Akha. They total about half a million people. International pressures are applied to have the hill tribes replace cultivation of opium with other cash crops. International aid agencies therefore sponsor alternative agricultural projects and tourism. The Thai government, however, is more concerned with political stability and security in the area, given its strategic location. It promotes development projects such as roads and markets to establish links between the highlands and the lowlands. Either way, the hill tribes are the target of outsiders' interests, and they therefore have a challenge in promoting their own agenda.

Efforts to find viable substitute crops for opium have been unsuccessful, especially among the Hmong, who are most dependent on opium as a cash crop. Alternative crops require heavy use of fertilizers and pesticides, which are costly to the farmers and greatly increase environmental pollution, and such crops are less lucrative for the farmers. Logging companies have gained access to the hills and have done far more damage to the forests than the highlanders' horticultural practices. Increased penetration of the hill areas by lowlanders and international tourists have promoted the increase in the highlands of HIV/AIDS rates, illegal trafficking of girls and boys for sex work, and opium addiction.

The Thai government, like neighboring Laos, has attempted to relocate highland horticulturalists to the plains through various resettlement schemes. Highlanders who opt for relocation find the lowland plots to be unproductive due to poor soil quality. Relocated highlanders find that their quality of life and economic status decline in the lowlands. Yet another new risk for the resettlers in Thailand and Laos is that they are now heavy consumers of methamphetamines, an addictive euphoria-inducing compound with serious negative side effects such as rapid weight loss, tooth decay, diarrhea, nausea, and agitation (Lyttleton 2004). Overall, 50 years of so-called "development" have been disastrous for Southeast Asia's hill peoples.

INDIGENOUS PEOPLE AND TERRITORIAL ENTITLEMENTS

Throughout their history of contact with the outside world, indigenous peoples have actively sought to resist the negative effects of "civilization." Since the 1980s, more effective and highly organized forms of protest have become prominent. Indigenous groups now hire lawyers and other experts as consultants in order to reclaim and defend their territorial rights, gain self-determination, and secure protection from outside risks. Many indigenous people have themselves become trained as lawyers, researchers, and advocates. Conflicts range from lawsuits to attempts at secession (Stidsen 2006).

This section provides an overview on the status of indigenous people's territorial rights claims. Within each large world region, country-by-country variation exists in legal codes and adherence to such codes that may exist.

LATIN AMERICA Few Latin American countries provide legal protection against encroachment on the land of indigenous groups. Nicaragua, Peru, Colombia, Ecuador, Bolivia, and Brazil have taken the lead in enacting policies that legitimize indigenous rights to land and demarcating and titling indigenous territories (Stocks 2005). A wide gap often exists, however, between policy and actual protection. Despite the efforts, increasing numbers of Indians throughout the entire region of Latin America have been forced off their land in the past few decades, through poverty, violence, and environmental degradation due to encroachment by logging companies, mining operations, ranch developers, and others.

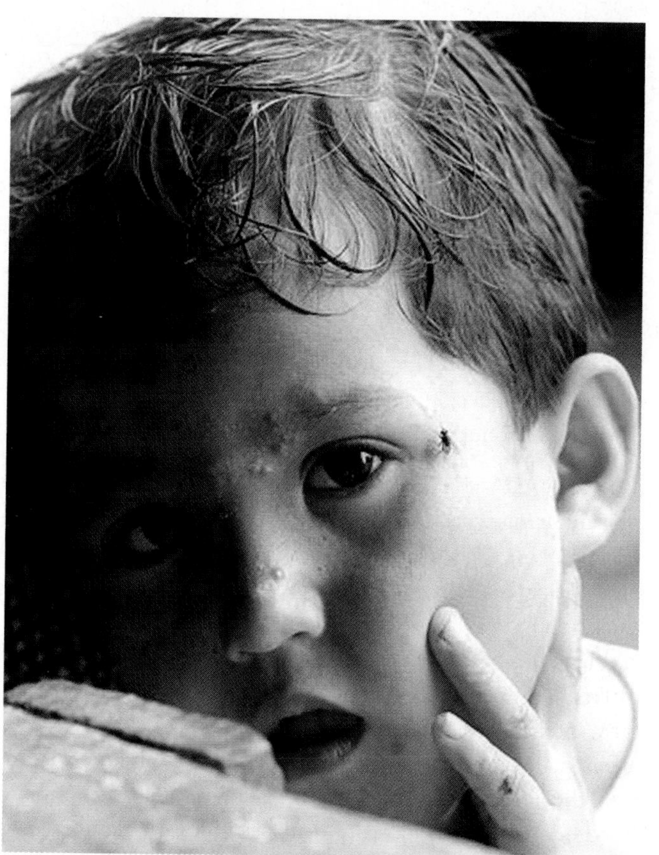

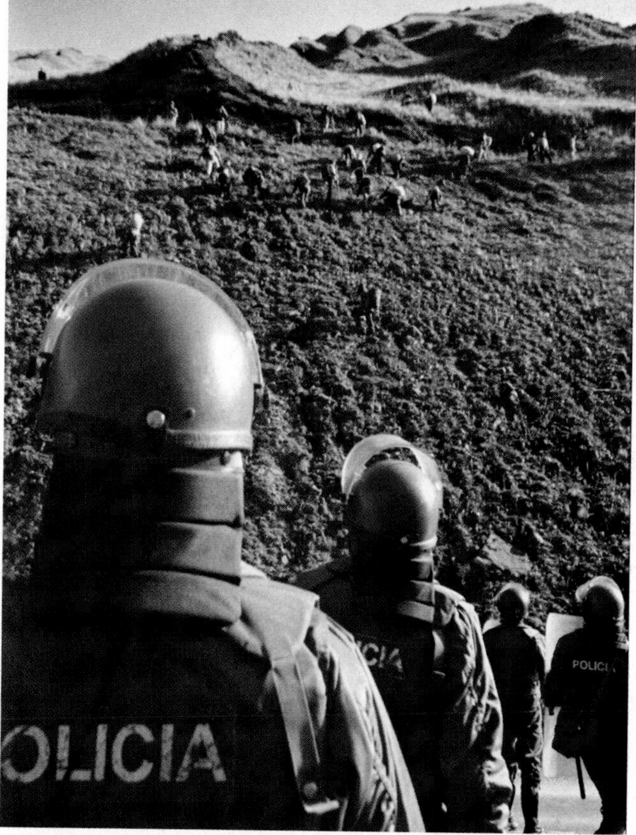

(LEFT) In Colombia, a 5-year-old boy has blisters on his face caused by the herbicide sprayed on coca farms from planes working for Plan Colombia, financed by the U.S. war on cocaine. (RIGHT) Bolivian security forces confront coca farmers during a protest march to the capital city of La Paz, and the farmers scatter to avoid arrest. The farmers were protesting the U.S.-backed coca eradication plan that affects their livelihoods. This photograph was taken before President Evo Morales was elected. His policy allows coca farmers to grow a small amount of coca for traditional consumption.

MAP 16.5 Nunavut Province, Canada.
Created in 1999, Nunavut is the newest and largest of Canada's provinces. It is also the least populated, with 30,000 people. About 85 percent of the people are First Nations peoples, mainly Inuit. Official languages are Inuktitut, Inuinnagtun, English, and French. The landscape is mainly Arctic tundra. The award-winning movie, *Atanarjuat (The Fast Runner)*, was produced by Inuit filmmakers and filmed in Nunavut.

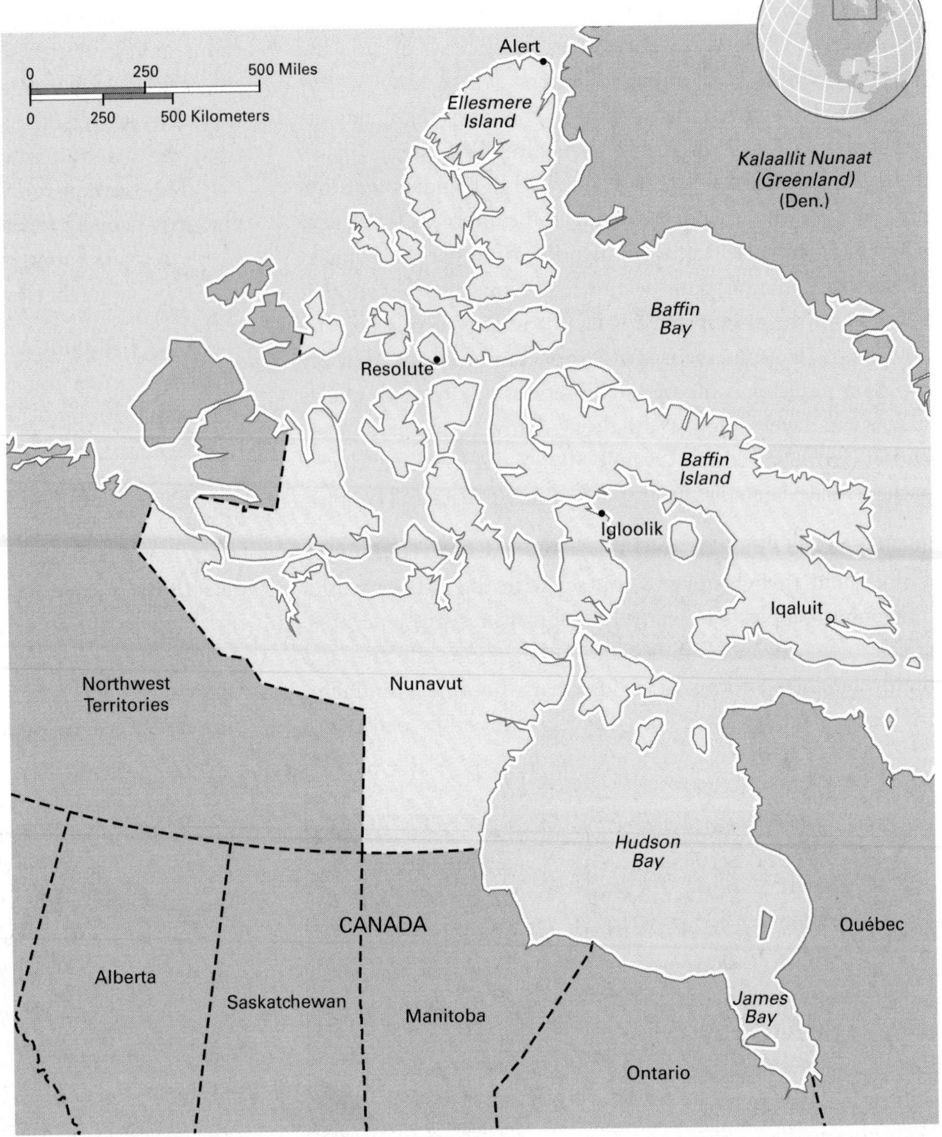

In response, many migrate to cities and seek wage labor. Those who remain face extreme poverty, malnutrition, and personal and group insecurity.

A surge of political activism by indigenous people has occurred since the 1990s, sometimes involving physical resistance. Violence continues to erupt between indigenous groups and state-supported power structures, especially in the southern Mexican state of Chiapas (see Map 6.3, p. 144). In 2005, participants at the First Symposium on Isolated Indigenous Peoples of the Amazon created a group called the International Alliance for the Protection of Isolated Indigenous Peoples. The group seeks to make the relevant state governments aware of the current endangered situation of many indigenous peoples. They demand their right to isolation, if that is their choice, and to protection from unwelcome outside contact and encroachment. In 2008, the International Alliance of Forest Peoples formed to push for indigenous people's participation in global climate change talks and to devise a plan whereby wealthy countries would compensate developing countries for conserving tropical forests (Barrionuevo 2008).

CANADA In Canada, the law distinguishes between two different types of Native Peoples and their land claims (Plant 1994). Specific claims concern problems arising from previous agreements or treaties, and comprehensive claims are those made by Native Peoples who have not been displaced and have made no treaties or agreements. Most of the former claims have led to monetary compensation. In the latter category, interest in oil and mineral exploration has prompted governments to negotiate with indigenous people in an effort to have the latter's native claims either relinquished or redefined. In some provinces, especially British Columbia, claims affect most of the province. The Nunavut land claim was settled, granting about 25,000 Inuit access to a vast tract of land, including subsurface rights (Jensen 2004) (see Map 16.5).

ASIA In Asia, most countries have been reluctant to recognize the territorial rights of indigenous people (Plant 1994).

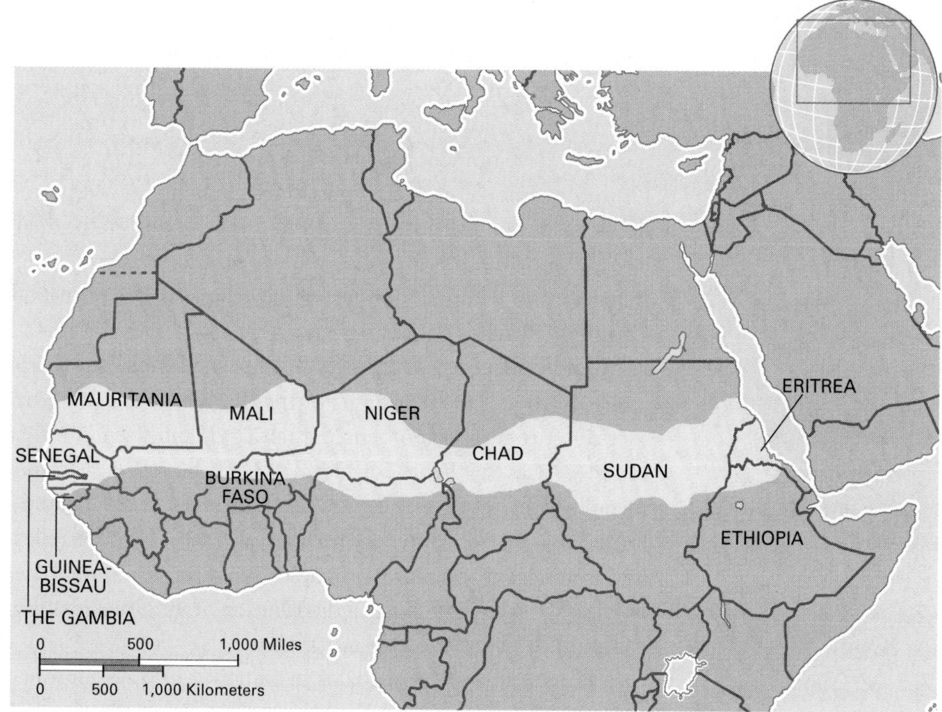

MAP 16.6 Sahel Region. The word *sahel* comes from the Arabic for "shore" or "border," referring in this case to the area between the Sahara desert and the more fertile regions to the south. Primarily savanna, the region has been the home to many rich kingdoms that controlled Saharan trade routes. Most people make their living from pastoralism and semisedentary cattle raising. The region has recently experienced several major droughts, leading to widespread death of herd animals, widespread human starvation and malnutrition, and forced population displacement.

In Bangladesh, the Chittagong Hill Tracts in the southeast is being massively encroached upon by settlers from the crowded plains region (see Map 9.1, p. 219). Encroachers now occupy the most fertile land, and the indigenous people are endangered in many ways. A large hydroelectric dam built in 1963 displaced 100,000 hill dwellers because they could no longer practice horticulture in the flooded areas. A few received some financial compensation, but most did not. Tribal opposition groups began emerging, and conflict, although suppressed in the world news, has been ongoing for decades.

In Thailand, no legal recognition of hill tribes' land rights exists, whereas in Laos and Vietnam, some land has been allocated to indigenous communities (Jensen 2004:5). Sites of active contestation with the state over land and resources in the Asia-Pacific region include the Moros of the southern Philippines (see Map 7.2, p. 166) and the people of Western Papua, the western part of the island of New Guinea controlled by Indonesia (see Map 1.3, p. 19). In some cases, indigenous people's fight for secession from the state continues to cost many lives, mainly of indigenous peoples.

AFRICA In Africa, political interests of state governments in establishing and enforcing territorial boundaries have created difficulties for indigenous peoples, especially mobile populations such as foragers and pastoralists. Many formerly autonomous pastoralists of the Sahel region (see Map 16.6) have been transformed into refugees living in terrible conditions. The Tuareg, for example, have traditionally lived and herded in a territory that now crosses five different countries: Mali, Niger, Algeria, Burkina Faso, and Libya (Childs and Chelala 1994).

Because of political conflict in the region, thousands of Tuareg people live in exile in Mauritania, and their prospects are grim. Resistance movements spring up, but states act to suppress them. The people of southern Sudan and Darfur have been living in violence for many years (see Map 16.7, p. 412). They have been subject to genocide and violent displacement for global and local political and economic reasons, not the least of which involves the rich deposits of oil in the southern part of the country (Warren 2001) As mentioned in the Culturama in Chapter 1 (p. 23), South Africa has established more protective legislation for San peoples than have Namibia or Botswana.

AUSTRALIA AND NEW ZEALAND The picture is also mixed in Australia and New Zealand, with more progress in Australia in terms of legal recognition of Aboriginal territorial rights. Urban development, expansion of the non-Aboriginal population, road building, mineral extraction, and international tourism are some of the major threats to both livelihood and protection of sacred space. Aboriginal activism has seen some notable successes in achieving what is referred to as native title (Colley 2002). A key turning point in Australia occurred through the efforts of Eddie Koiko Mabo (mah-bo), from the Torres Strait Islands (see Map 5.4, p. 124). He and his group, the Miriam people, took their claim of rights to their traditional land and water to the High Court, contesting the principle of *terra nullius,* or "empty land." Colonialists and neocolonialist developers use terra nullius to justify territorial takeovers, claiming that no one lives in a particular place

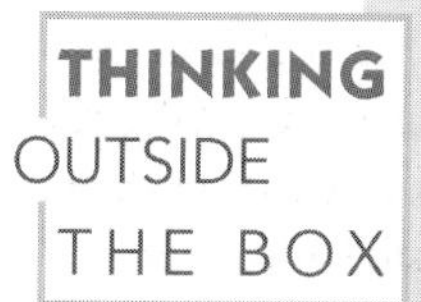

Formulate your definition of development and sketch out its pros and cons for one or more cultures that you have learned about in this book.

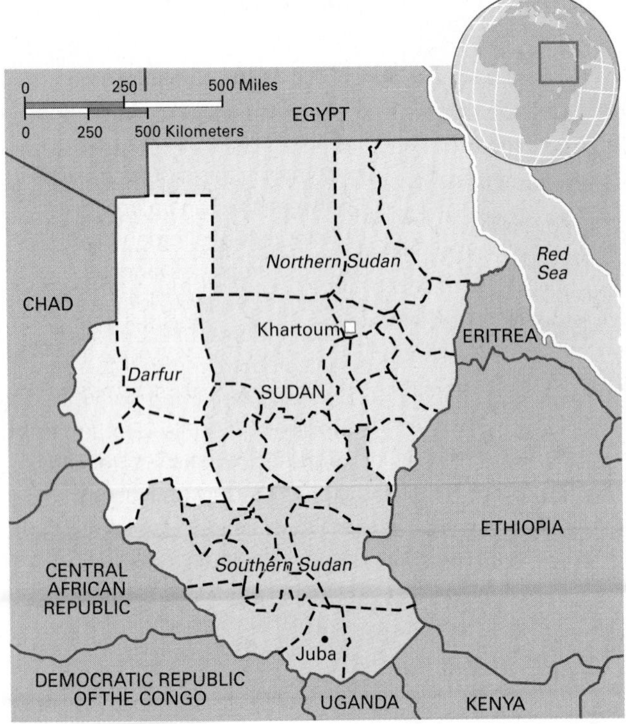

MAP 16.7 Sudan.
The Republic of Sudan gained its independence from Britain in 1956 but, unlike other former British colonies, did not join the Commonwealth. The year before independence, a civil war began between the north and south. In 2005, a treaty granted southern Sudan the status of an autonomous region for six years to be followed by a referendum. In 2003, conflict erupted in the Darfur region. Sudan and neighboring Chad are also having conflicts. Most of the economy depends on agriculture, although oil production and trade have increased. The population of 37 million includes two ethnic groups: Arabs with Nubian roots and non-Arab Black Africans. Arabic is the dominant language of the north. Most Sudanese also speak local, tribal languages. Sunni Islam is the dominant religion (70 percent) in the north, with indigenous religions also important (25 percent). Christianity (5 percent) is practiced mainly in the south.

because there is no evidence of property ownership or agriculture or permanent structures. This claim justified colonial takeover of large parts of the world occupied by foragers, horticulturalists, and pastoralists. In this landmark case, Mabo convinced the High Court of the legitimacy of the Miriams' claim in 1992 and set a precedent for a series of future land claims by indigenous peoples of Australia.

ORGANIZING FOR CHANGE Many indigenous peoples have formed organizations for change in order to promote development from within. In Ethiopia, for example, several NGOs organized by local people have sprung up since the 1990s (Kassam 2002). One organization in the southern region is especially noteworthy because it seeks to provide a model of development based on the oral folk traditions of the Oromo people. This model combines elements of Western-defined "development" with Oromo values and traditional laws. It provides an approach that is culturally appropriate, transforming external notions of development in terms of Oromo lifeways.

The indigenous Oromo NGO is called *Hundee,* which refers to "roots," or the origins of the Oromo people, and, by extension, to all Oromo people, their land, and their culture. Hundee uses a theory of development based in Oromo metaphors of fertility and growth. It involves gradual transformation like the spirals in the horn of a ram. Hundee relies on Oromo legal and moral principles about the communal use of natural resources and the redistribution of wealth across the community to provide a social safety net.

Hundee's long-term goal is to empower Oromo communities to be self-sufficient. It takes the view that the Oromo culture is a positive force for social and economic change rather than a barrier. Hundee members use a participatory approach in all their endeavors. They consult with traditional legal assemblies to identify needs and then to shape projects to address those needs. Specific activities include the establishment of a credit association and a grain bank to help combat price fluctuations and food shortages. The Oromo feel that these are elements of *good development,* as distinguished from the outsiders' *bad development* that has inflicted hunger and dependency on the Oromo people.

In many cases, indigenous people's development organizations link formerly separate groups in response to external threats (Perry 1996:245–246). In Australia, several indigenous groups are joined in regional coalitions and pan-Australian organizations that have been successful in land claim cases. In Canada, the Grand Council of the Cree collaborates with other northern groups over land issues and opposition to a major hydroelectric dam project (Coon Come 2004, Craik 2004, and see Anthropology Works, p. 289). In southern Africa, separate San groups joined together to claim a share in the profits of commercial marketing of hoodia as a diet pill (review Culturama, Chapter 1, p. 23). Indigenous groups are taking advantage of new technology and media to build and maintain links with each other over large areas.

Although it is tempting to see hope in the newly emerging forms of resistance, self-determination, and organizing among indigenous peoples, such hope cannot be generalized to all indigenous groups. Many are making progress in asserting their claims and their economic status is improving, but many others are suffering extreme political and economic repression and possible extinction.

---

male bias in development the design and implementation of development projects with men as beneficiaries and without regard to their impact on women's roles and status.

WOMEN AND DEVELOPMENT

The category of women contrasts with that of indigenous peoples because women, as a group, do not have a recognized territory associated with them. But the effects of colonialism, and now international development, on women are similar to their effects on indigenous people: Women have often lost economic entitlements and political power in their communities. Matrilineal kinship, for example, which keeps property in the female line (review Chapter 8), is in decline throughout the world. Westernization and modernization are frequently the cause of this change. Another factor that has had a pervasive negative effect on women's status is the **male bias in development**, or the design and implementation of development projects with men as beneficiaries and without regard to their impact on women's roles and status.

THE MALE BIAS IN DEVELOPMENT In the 1970s, researchers began to notice and write about the fact that development projects were male biased (Boserup 1970, Tinker 1976). Many projects completely bypassed women as beneficiaries, targeting men for such initiatives as growing cash crops and learning about new technology. This male bias in development contributed to increased gender inequality by giving men greater access to new sources of income and by depriving women of their traditional economic roles. The development experts' image of a farmer, for example, was male, not female.

Women's projects were typically focused on the domestic domain—for example, infant feeding practices, child care, and family planning. This emphasis led to the *domestication of women* worldwide, meaning that their lives became more focused on the domestic domain and more removed from the public domain (Rogers 1979). For example, agricultural projects bypassed female horticulturalists, who were taught to spend more time in the house bathing their babies, and political leadership projects focused on men and left women out even in contexts where women traditionally had public political roles.

The male bias in development also contributed to project failure. In the West African country of Burkina Faso (see Map 16.6, p. 411), a reforestation project included men as the sole participants, whose tasks would include planting and caring for the trees. Cultural patterns there, however, dictate that men do not water plants; women do. The men planted the seedlings and left them. Excluding women from the project ensured its failure. Exclusion of women from development continues to be a problem in spite of many years of work attempting to place and keep women's issues on the development agenda.

Inclusion of women's knowledge, concerns, and voices has brought new and important issues to the fore, redefining development to fits women's needs. One such issue is gender-based violence. This issue has gained attention even among the large multilateral organizations, where experts realize that women cannot participate in a credit program, for example, if they fear that their husbands will beat them for leaving the house. The United Nations Commission on the Status of Women drafted a declaration in opposition of violence against women that was adopted by the General Assembly in 1993 (Heise, Pitanguy, and Germain 1994). Article 1 of the declaration states that violence against women includes "any act of gender-based violence that results in, or is likely to result in, physical, sexual or psychological harm or suffering to women, including threats of such acts, coercion or arbitrary deprivations of liberty, whether occurring in public or private life" (Economic and Social Council 1992). This definition cites women as the focus of concern but also includes girls (see Figure 16.2).

Programs that target violence against girls and women tend to deal with their effects rather than the causes, often with disastrous results. For example, programs may seek to increase personal security of women and girls in refugee camps

Prebirth	Sex-selective abortion, battering during pregnancy, coerced pregnancy
Infancy	Infanticide, emotional and physical abuse, deprivation of food and medical care
Girlhood	Child marriage, genital mutilation, sexual abuse by family members and strangers, rape, deprivation of food and medical care, child prostitution
Adolescence	Dating and courtship violence, forced prostitution, rape, sexual abuse in the workplace, sexual harassment
Adulthood	Rape and partner abuse, partner homicide, sexual abuse in the workplace, sexual harassment
Old Age	Abuse and neglect of widows, elder abuse

Source: Adapted from Heise, Pitanguy, and Germain 1994:5.

FIGURE 16.2 Violence against Girls and Women throughout the Life Cycle.

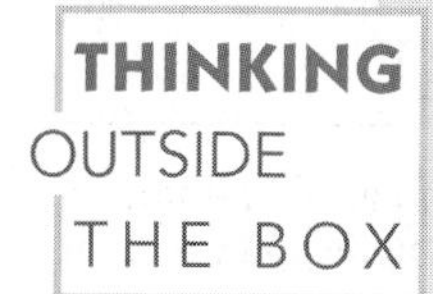

What lessons might SMW be able to share with programs that seek to prevent wife abuse in other countries (recall the case of wife abuse in Kentucky presented in Chapter 8, p. 209).

Grameen Bank, a development project in Bangladesh to provide small loans to poor people, is one of the most successful examples of improving human welfare through microcredit, or small loans. Professor Mohammed Yunnus (center) founded Grameen Bank and continues to be a source of charismatic leadership for it.

▶ *How does the success of Grameen Bank cause you to question your previous image of Bangladesh?*

by augmenting the number of guards at the camp when, in fact, the guards are often guilty of abusing refugee women and girls (Martin 2005).

WOMEN'S ORGANIZATIONS FOR CHANGE In many countries, women have improved their status and welfare through forming organizations, which are sometimes part of their traditional culture and sometimes a response to outside inspiration. These organizations range from mothers' clubs that help provide for communal child care to credit organizations that give women an opportunity to start their own businesses. Some are local and small scale; others are global, such as Women's World Banking, an international organization that grew out of credit programs for poor working women that started in India and Bangladesh.

A community-based credit system in rural Mozambique, southern Africa (see Map 9.5, p. 230), provides loans to help farm women buy seeds, fertilizers, and supplies (Clark 1992). When the loan program began, 32 farm families in one village formed themselves into seven solidarity groups, each with an elected leader. The woman-headed farmer groups managed irrigation efficiently and conferred on how to minimize the use of pesticides and chemical fertilizers. Through their efforts, the women quadrupled their harvests and paid off their loans. They then turned their attention to getting additional loans to improve their herds and to buy a maize (corn) mill. In spite of poverty, violent military conflict, the lack of government resources, and a drought, the organization helped many women farmers to improve their lives.

In another case, an informal system of social networks emerged to help support poor Maya women vendors in San Cristóbal, Chiapas, Mexico (Sullivan 1992) (see Map 6.3, p. 144). Many of the vendors who work in the city square have fled from the highlands because of long-term political conflict there. They manufacture and sell goods to tourists, earning an important portion of household income. In the city, they find social support in an expanded network that helps compensate for the loss of support from the extensive godparenthood system (review Chapter 8) of the highlands. The vendors' new networks include relatives, neighbors, church members, and other vendors, regardless of their religious, political, economic, or social background.

These networks first developed in response to a series of rapes and robberies that began in 1987. Because the offenders were persons of power and influence, the women did not dare to press charges. Mostly single mothers and widows, they adopted a strategy of self-protection. First, they began to gather during the slow period each afternoon. Second, they always travel in groups. Third, they carry sharpened corset bones and prongs: "If a man insults one of them, the group surrounds him and jabs him in the groin" (39–40). Fourth, if a woman is robbed, the other women surround her, comfort her, and help contribute something toward compensating her for her loss. The mid-afternoon gatherings developed into support groups that provide financial assistance, child care, medical advice, and training in job skills. The groups have publicly demonstrated against city officials' attempts to prevent them from continuing their vending. Through their efforts, they have succeeded in bringing greater security into their lives.

A last example of women's empowerment and personal risk reduction through organized efforts comes from Kazakhstan, Central Asia (see Map 11.4, p. 277). In response to widespread domestic violence of husbands against wives, an NGO called the Society of Muslim Women (SMW) defines domestic violence as a problem that the Islamic faith should address at the grassroots level (Snajdr 2005). The organization declines to work with the police and civic activists, who provide secular responses that involve criminalization of the offense, arrest of offenders, and other public procedures. Instead, SMW views domestic violence as a private matter that should be dealt with using Islamic and Kazakhi values. Its three approaches are counseling and shelter for abused women and couples' mediation. SMW's guiding principle is to find a way, if possible, to rebuild the family, something that may sound conservative, and even dangerous, in a situation where wife abuse is reported to occur in four out of five marriages. Yet, without funding or professional training, SMW members have provided support for countless women. They

In the town of San Cristóbal de las Casas, the capital city of Chiapas state in Mexico, a Maya vendor sells her goods. The city is located near the Tzotzil Maya communities of Chamula and Zinacantan.

▶ *Review the discussion in Chapter 4 of change among family farmers, of Zinacantan, Chiapas, Mexico.*

help the women overcome isolation by offering shelter, which conforms to the Kazakhi custom of hospitality and the Muslim virtue of patience. SMW support gives the spouses time to think about their relationship and shifts blame from the victims by invoking Islamic values of familial commitment and gender equality. Nationalist rhetoric shifts blame about men's alcoholism from the individual to the Russian occupation. Thus SMW works within the bounds of Kazakh culture and uses Kazakh culture for positive outcomes within those bounds.

◆◆◆

Urgent Issues in Development

This chapter opened with a vignette about the people of Walpole Island Reservation in Canada and their ongoing attempt to recover from the damage that colonialism and neocolonialism have wreaked on their culture and natural environment. In spite of much progress of local people and women in redefining development to improve their lives rather than the lives of external groups such as international businesses and neocolonial states, the bulk of "development" money still goes for mega-projects that do more for people who already have resources than for the poor.

As discussed earlier in this chapter, development projects are the main mechanism through which development institutions implement their goals. They are typically designed by outsiders, often with little local knowledge, and they follow a universal, one-size-fits-all pattern. They range from mega-projects such as massive dams to small projects, with the former being much more damaging to local people than the latter. The so-called beneficiaries or target population are often not consulted at all about projects that will affect their community. Critics of such externally imposed and often damaging initiatives refer to such actions as **development aggression**, the imposition of development projects and policies without the free, prior, and informed consent of the affected people (Tauli-Corpuz 2005). Such development violates the human rights of local people, including their right to pursuing a livelihood in their homeland and to preventing environmental destruction of their territory. It also contributes nothing to poverty prevention or alleviation.

LIFE PROJECTS AND HUMAN RIGHTS

Moving beyond critique, indigenous people, women, and others who are victimized by development aggression are redefining what should be done to improve their lives or protect them from further decline. They propose the concept of the life project rather than the development project. A **life project** is local people's vision of the direction they want to take in life, informed by their knowledge, history, and context, and how to achieve that vision.

Life projects can be considered a human right and thus in accord with the UN's Declaration of Human Rights that was ratified in 1948. Development that leads to environmental degradation, including loss of biological diversity, air

---

development aggression the imposition of development projects and policies without the free, prior, and informed consent of the affected people.

life project local people's definition of the direction they want to take in life, informed by their knowledge, history, and context.

eye on the ENVIRONMENT

Oil, Environmental Degradation, and Human Rights in the Nigerian Delta

During the British colonial era, Nigeria provided wealth for the Crown through the export of palm oil (Osha 2006). In the postcolonial era of globalization, a different kind of oil dominates the country's economy: petroleum. Starting in the 1950s, with the discovery of vast petroleum reserves in Nigeria's Delta Region (see Map 16.8), several European and American companies have explored for, drilled, and exported crude oil to the extent that Nigeria occupies an important position in the world economy. But the local people have gained few economic benefits from the oil industry and instead have reaped major losses in their agricultural and fishing livelihoods due to environmental pollution. The people of the delta are poorer now than in the 1960s. In

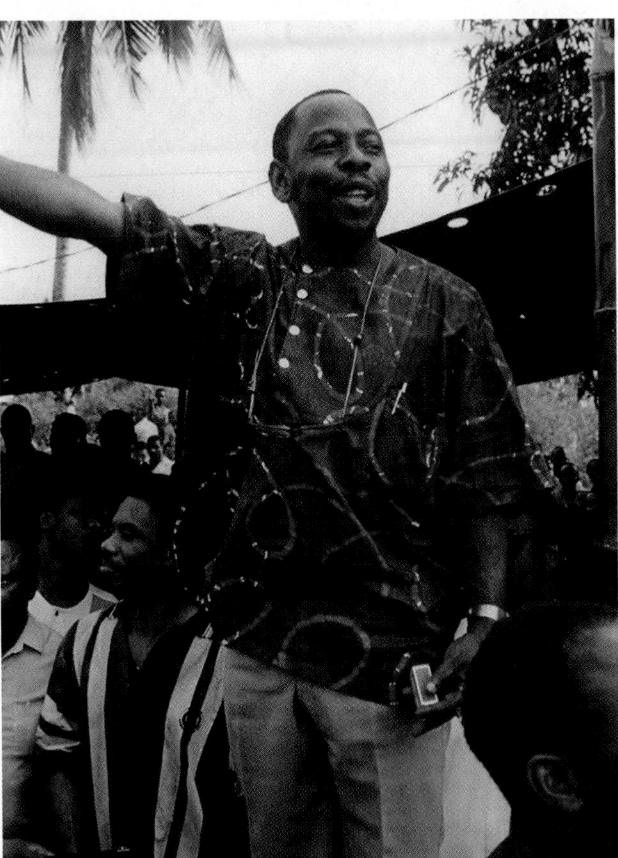

(LEFT) A farmer walks through an oil-soaked field. About 500,000 Ogoni people live in Ogoniland, a deltaic region in southern Nigeria. The fertility of the Niger delta has supported farming and fishing populations at high density for many years. Since Shell discovered oil there in 1958, 100 oil wells were constructed in Ogoniland and countless oil spills have occurred. (RIGHT) Ogoni author and Nobel prizewinner Ken Saro-Wiwa founded the Movement for Survival of Ogoni People (MOSOP) in 1992 to protest Shell's actions in Ogoniland and the Nigerian government's indifference. In 1995, he was arrested, tried for murder under suspicious circumstances, and executed by hanging. Shell has denied any role in his death.

addition to economic loss, they have lost personal security. Many have become victims of the violence that has increased in the region since the 1990s due to state and corporate repression of a local resistance movement. Many others have become IDPs (review Chapter 15), leaving the delta region to escape the pervasive violence.

One of the most negatively affected groups are the Ogoni people who live in the southeastern portion of the delta. Ogoni author and Nobel prizewinner Ken Saro-Wiwa founded the Movement for Survival of the Ogoni People (MOSOP) in 1992 to protest Shell's actions in Ogoniland and the Nigerian government's militarized repression in the region. In 1995, he and eight other Ogoni activists were arrested and tried under suspicious circumstances, and then executed by hanging.

In a 1992 speech to the United Nations Working Group on Indigenous Populations, Saro-Wiwa eloquently points to the connections between resource extraction, the environment, and Ogoni human and cultural rights:

> Environmental degradation has been a lethal weapon in the war against the indigenous Ogoni people. . . . Oil exploration has turned Ogoni into a wasteland: lands, streams, and creeks are totally and continually polluted; the atmosphere has been poisoned, charged as it is with hydrocarbon vapors, methane, carbon monoxide, carbon dioxide, and soot emitted by gas which has been flared 24 hours a day for 33 years in close proximity to human habitation. . . . All one sees and feels around is death. (quoted in Sachs 1996:13–16)

Many social scientists agree with Saro-Wiwa that such forms of development violate human and cultural rights because they undermine a people's way of life and threaten its continued existence (Johnston 1994).

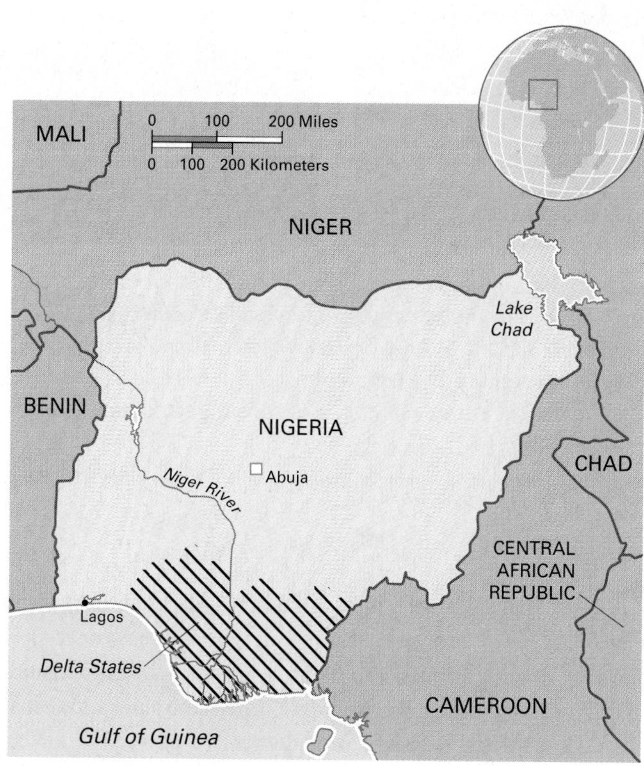

MAP 16.8 Nigeria and the Niger Delta.
Nigeria is the most populous country in Africa, with over 140 million people. It has over 250 ethnic groups, with the largest being the Fulani, Hausa, Yorúbà, and Igbo. Nigerians speak over 500 languages; English is the official language. Nigeria is Africa's biggest petroleum producer, with an average of 2 million barrels a day extracted in the Niger Delta. The Niger Delta comprises 7.5 percent of Nigeria's landmass, but its population of 31 million accounts for 22 percent of the population. The Niger Delta's petroleum industry supports a high economic growth rate for the country, making it one of the fastest growing economies in the world. Yet little of this wealth filters back to the local people of the Delta, who bear the brunt of the environmental and cultural damage caused by the petroleum industry. Oil spills are a frequent problem. Traditional economic pursuits such as fishing have been negatively affected. One of the world's richest wetlands and richest areas of cultural diversity, with over 40 ethnic groups, is endangered by large-scale petroleum mining that benefits people in the capital city and in other countries.

◆ **FOOD FOR THOUGHT**

- Explore on the Internet the concept of corporate social responsibility and be prepared to discuss its relationship to the Ogoni situation.

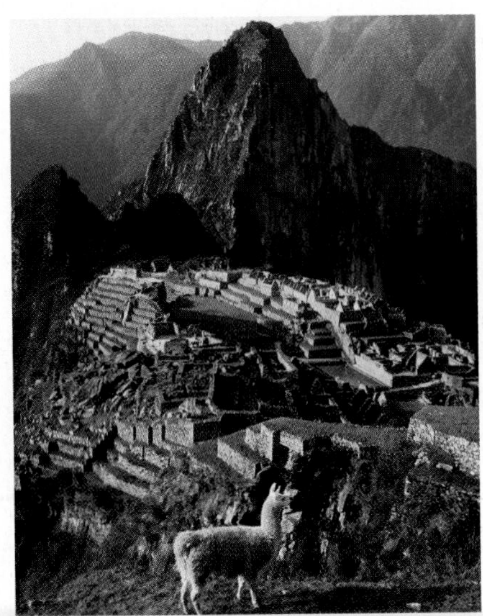

These World Heritage sites, and many more, have both benefited from the designation and now suffer from the problems created by too many tourists. (LEFT) Located high in the Peruvian Andes, the fifteenth-century palace complex at Machu Picchu (mah-choo pee-choo) was designated a World Heritage Site in 1983. (CENTER) Angkor Wat, which means "Temple City," was designated a World Heritage Site in 1993. It was built in the twelfth century as a Hindu temple, but later additions to it were Buddhist. (RIGHT) Gondolas on the Grand Canal, Venice, Italy. Venice, or Venezia in Italian, is considered to be one of the world's most beautiful cities. It was designated a World Heritage site in 1987.

▶ *Plan a trip to one of these sites and learn whether "green" options exist for accommodations, or if the sites otherwise promote ways to lessen the damage from excess numbers of tourists.*

and water pollution, deforestation, and soil erosion, is a human rights abuse. Many examples exist worldwide of how rich natural resources are improperly exploited to the gain of a few and the detriment of many, turning a blessing into what is now considered a curse (see Eye on the Environment).

The major extractive industries of mining, oil, and gas are driven by the profit motive to the extent that they are disinclined to take local people's interests and environmental concerns seriously. An **extractive industry** is a business that explores for, removes and processes, and sells minerals, oil, and gas that are found on or beneath the earth's surface and are nonrenewable. The many tragic cases of local violence around the world where local people seek to prevent or remove an extractive industry project from their land, however, have given a wake-up call to some companies. Rio Tinto, one of the largest mining companies in the world, seeks to use cultural anthropology expertise to find ways to treat "affected peoples" more fairly and to do a better job of ensuring that environmental "mitigation" will occur once a mine is closed (Cochrane 2008). What drives extractive industries to continue to explore for gold, drill for oil, and cut down trees? What drives countries to build mega-dams and mega-highways? The demand lies with all of us, in our consumerist lifestyle that requires diamonds for engagement rings, gold and platinum for computers and gold and copper for cell phones, electrical power for air conditioning, and fuel to transport us, our food and water, and everything else we buy. Entire mountains in West Virginia are being leveled to provide coal to power the air conditioning used in Washington, DC. Forests in Brazil and Papua New Guinea are taken down so we can read the newspaper. Corn is being harvested to move vehicles rather than to feed people, and millions of gallons of water are being used to process minerals such as aluminum rather than being available for human drinking, bathing, and swimming, or for fish and water fowl. It will take a lot to turn this pattern around from destructive projects to life projects.

extractive industry a business that explores for, removes and processes, and sells minerals, oil, and gas that are found on or beneath the earth's surface and are nonrenewable.

CULTURAL HERITAGE AND DEVELOPMENT: LINKING THE PAST AND PRESENT TO THE FUTURE

Chapter 14 discussed the potential of cultural heritage, both tangible and nontangible, in creating employment opportunities for local people through cultural tourism. This section goes more deeply into the complicated connections between cultural heritage and improving people's welfare from a life project perspective.

The connection of cultural heritage tourism to development is a double-edged sword, with both benefits and costs (Bauer 2006). Promoting cultural heritage through tourism requires expansion of supportive infrastructure such as roads

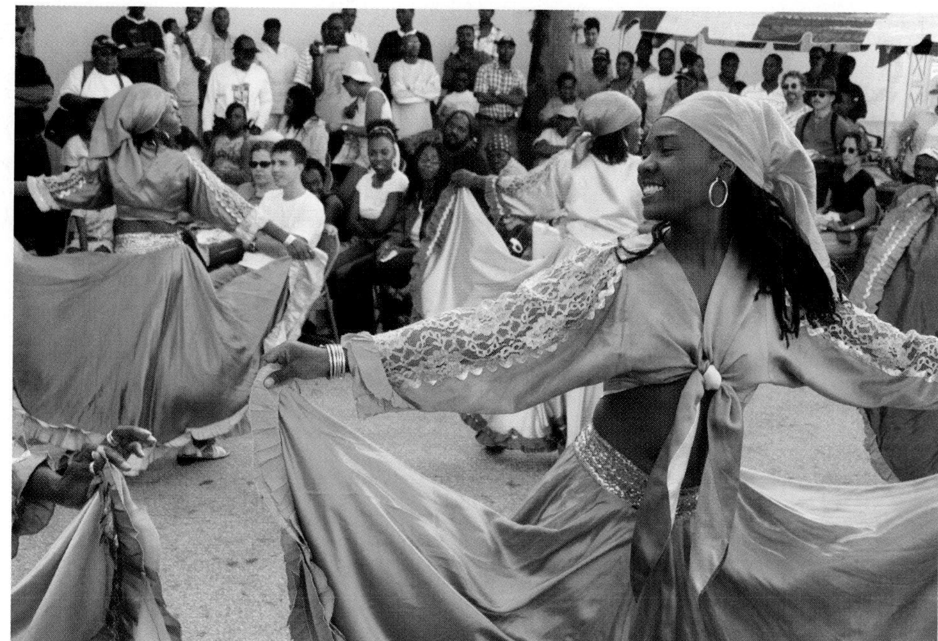

Haitian dancers perform on Discover Miami Day at Miami's Little Haiti Caribbean Marketplace. Haitian culture in Miami is an increasingly popular tourist attraction in North America.

and hotels and electricity, provision of food and other supplies for tourists, and labor to provide services for tourists. Thus, although generating revenue, such tourism can preserve and protect cultural heritage, but the presence of the tourism industry and the tourists themselves may damage and even destroy it. Such famous World Heritage Sites as Machu Picchu in Peru and Angkor Wat in Cambodia are physically suffering the strains of huge numbers of tourists. Venice, the world's most touristed city, is also a World Heritage Site. Given its particular attraction as a city of canals, it is also at particular risk of overload and environmental degradation from the ever-increasing number of tourist boats in the canals, not to mention the massive amount of solid and liquid trash that tourists leave behind (David and Marvin 2004). Although tourist promotional literature for Venice shows a romantic scene of a couple in a gondola or sitting along in the Piazza San Marco, the reality is that the couple would be surrounded by crowds of tourists and heckled by ambitious local entrepreneurs.

A growing area related to cultural heritage preservation is intellectual property rights law or cultural property rights law. Lawyers worldwide are increasingly involved in providing legal definitions and protections of rights to various forms of cultural knowledge and behavior. The legalization of culture is another double-edged sword: On one hand, laws may help people, such as the San of southern Africa, to gain a share of the profits from the hoodia plant. On the other hand, legalization of culture can transform much of everyday life into a legal battle. For thousands of years, the San had full and unquestioned entitlement to hoodia and its benefits. They did not need to hire international lawyers.

Everything from website addresses that may use tribal names to the designation of what is or is not champagne can now become grounds for litigation. And money, you can be sure, is involved from the start to the finish, as is the more difficult to quantify sense of identity of people who define themselves in relation to a place, a product, or a taste.

CULTURAL ANTHROPOLOGY AND THE FUTURE

Over the next several years, culture as defined and understood and argued about—will be a major factor in international, regional, and local development and change. Determining how cultural anthropologists can contribute more effectively to a better future for humanity is a challenge for a field with its intellectual roots in studying what is rather than what might be. But just as local people everywhere are redefining development and reclaiming their culture, so also are they helping to redefine the theory, practice, and application of cultural anthropology. Although we live in a time of war, it is also a time of hope, in which insights and strength often come from those with the least in terms of material wealth but with cultural wealth beyond measure.

16

the BIG questions REVISITED

◆ What is development and what are the approaches to achieving it?

Several theories or models of development exist, including modernization, growth-oriented development, distributional development, human development, and sustainable development. They differ in terms of how they define development and how to achieve it.

Institutional approaches to development, whether pursued by large-scale or grassroots organizations, tend to rely on the development project as a vehicle of local change. Cultural anthropologists have been hired as consultants on development projects, typically at the end of the project cycle to provide evaluations. Anthropologists have pushed for involvement earlier in the project so that their cultural knowledge can be used in project planning to avoid common errors. A one-size-fits-all project design often results in failed projects because of a lack of cultural fit.

In traditional development anthropology, anthropological knowledge contributes to development projects by adding insights that will make a project work. In critical development anthropology, anthropological knowledge may suggest that the most socially beneficial path is either to stop the project or to redesign it.

◆ How has development affected indigenous people and women?

Indigenous people and women have been affected by international development in various ways, often negatively. They are taking an increasingly active role in redefining development to better suit their vision of the future.

Colonialism, neocolonialism, and globalization have had negative effects on indigenous peoples and women worldwide in terms of declines in their entitlements and standard of living. Often, such losses are tied to environmental degradation and violence. Indigenous peoples throughout the world suffer from lack of secure claim to their ancestral territories. They seek social recognition of territorial claims from state governments and protection from encroachment. Some governments are responding to their claims; others are not. Establishing organizations has been a major source of strength for promoting indigenous people's rights.

Western development planning and projects have long suffered from a male bias in project design. Excluding women from projects serves to domesticate women and often results in failed projects. Women are stating their needs and visions for the future, and thus redefining development in ways that are helpful to them. They have added the issue of violence against women and girls to the policy agenda of development institutions worldwide, including the large multilateral organizations.

◆ What are urgent issues in development?

Three urgent issues, as informed by cultural anthropology and the views and voices of people themselves, are the redefinition of development projects as life projects or people-centered projects, the relationship between human rights and development, and the role of cultural heritage in development. Indigenous people, women, and others adversely affected by certain forms of development are promoting a new kind of development that is people centered and that enhances the life projects that people define for themselves.

The concept of the life project is a human right and a right to live in one's cultural world without encroachment, threat, and discrimination. Cultural anthropologists contribute insights from different cultures about perceptions of basic human and cultural rights, and this knowledge, linked to advocacy, may be able to help prevent human/cultural rights abuses in the future.

People's cultural heritage can be a path toward improved welfare, but it is a double-edged sword. Promoting cultural tourism can protect culture but can also lead to damage and destruction. An emerging area is the legalization of cultural heritage through intellectual property rights law, another double-edged sword.

Culture is a central issue of our time, and local people are working with cultural anthropologists to address the challenges of an increasingly globalized, insecure, but exciting world.

KEY CONCEPTS

acculturation, p. 397
assimilation, p. 397
critical development anthropology, p. 407
cultural fit, p. 406
development, p. 396
development aggression, p. 415
development project, p. 405
diffusion, p. 397
extractive industry, p. 418
invention, p. 397
life project, p. 415
male bias in development, p. 413
modernization, p. 399
poverty, p. 396
project cycle, p. 405
social capital, p. 403
social impact assessment, p. 401
traditional development anthropology, p. 406

SUGGESTED READINGS

Mario Blaser, Harvey A. Feit, and Glenn McRae, eds. *In the Way of Development: Indigenous Peoples, Life Projects and Globalization.* New York: Zed Books, 2004. The authors are indigenous leaders, social activists, and anthropologists. Topics include the environment, women's status, social justice, participation, and dealing with mega-development projects.

Glynn Cochrane. *Festival Elephants and the Myth of Global Poverty.* Boston: Pearson, 2008. Over 40 years of experience in international development inform this memoir and critique. Cochrane argues that no single form of global poverty exists but that poverty is local and must be addressed with local solutions.

Ann Frechette. *Tibetans in Nepal: The Dynamics of International Assistance among a Community in Exile.* New York: Bergahn Books, 2002. This book explores how a long history of international assistance to refugees has affected individual and community identity and values. Focusing on Tibetans in Nepal, Frechette shows how aid complicates exiled Tibetans' attempts to define and maintain a sense of community.

Dorothy L. Hodgson. *Once Intrepid Warriors: Gender, Ethnicity, and the Cultural Politics of Maasai Development.* Bloomington: Indiana University Press, 2004. This ethnography shows how Maasai identity and gender connect with development and globalization to shape Maasai life today.

Gideon M. Kressel. *Let Shepherding Endure: Applied Anthropology and the Preservation of a Cultural Tradition in Israel and the Middle East.* Albany: SUNY Press, 2003. This book presents a case study of the Bedu of the Negev, southern Israel. It discusses how globalization is encroaching on herders to their great detriment. The author lays out an applied anthropology program for reconstituting and promoting pastoralism.

William Loker. *Changing Places: Environment, Development, and Social Change in Rural Honduras.* Durham, NC: Carolina Academic Press, 2004. Loker uses qualitative and quantitative data to assess the social and environmental effects of a large dam in the El Cajón region of Honduras.

Mark Moberg. *Citrus, Strategy, and Class: The Politics of Development in Southern Belize.* Iowa City: University of Iowa Press, 1992. Moberg compares the involvement of two villages in Belize in the global citrus market. He describes the formation of a rural class and the increasing dependency of rural Belize on the global market.

David Mosse. *Cultivating Development: An Ethnography of Aid Policy and Practice.* Ann Arbor, MI: Pluto Press, 2005. Mosse uses his experience as a development worker in India to analyze and critique how the structure of aid shapes the actions of development workers. The subject matter is policy making and projects viewed from a critical ethnographic perspective.

Richard J. Perry. *From Time Immemorial: Indigenous Peoples and State Systems.* Austin: University of Texas Press, 1996. Perry provides a comparative review of the history and status of indigenous peoples of Mexico, the United States, Canada, and Australia. Topics covered are state policies, state violence, resistance of the indigenous people, and efforts at self-determination.

Joanne Rappaport. *Intercultural Utopias: Public Intellectuals, Cultural Experimentation, and Ethnography.* Durham, NC: Duke University Press, 2005. The author draws on collaborative research in Colombia with indigenous activists. She documents the country's complex indigenous political movement with a focus on the southwestern Cauca region and its long history of indigenous mobilization and ethnic pluralism.

John Sherry. *Land, Wind and Hard Words: A Story of Navajo Activism.* Albuquerque: University of New Mexico Press, 2002. This book presents the story of the community-based activists of a Navajo environmental organization called Diné CARE that seeks to protect Navajo forests from logging.

Jennie M. Smith. *When the Hands Are Many: Community Organization and Social Change in Rural Haiti.* Ithaca, NY: Cornell University Press, 2001. Fieldwork in southwest Haiti reveals how poor rural people use social organizing and expressive culture to unite in resistance to the larger forces that impoverish them.

John van Willigen. *Anthropology in Action: A Source Book on Anthropological Practice.* Boulder, CO: Westview Press, 1991. This book first provides brief overviews of ethics, publications, and professional organizations in applied anthropology. Case studies follow, arranged alphabetically by topic, from "Agriculture" to "Women in Development."

PHOTO CREDITS

Chapter 1: Page 4, © Rob Howard/CORBIS All Rights Reserved; **Page 6,** © Lindsay Hebberd/CORBIS All Rights Reserved; **Page 7,** J. A. English-Lueck, Cofounder Silicon Valley Cultures Project; **Page 8,** AP/Wide World Photos; **Page 8,** Photo by Richard Gould; **Page 9,** Barbara Miller; **Page 11,** © Spooner/Redmond-Callow/Gamma Press; **Page 11,** © Frans Lanting/CORBIS All Rights Reserved; **Page 13,** © Bettmann/CORBIS; **Page 13,** Courtesy of the Library of Congress; **Page 15,** Patricia Tovar; **Page 16,** University of Florida News & Public Affairs Archives; **Page 16,** © Laura Pedrick/The New York Times/Redux Pictures; **Page 17,** © Michael Newman/PhotoEdit; **Page 18,** Philip Gould/CORBIS; **Page 20,** Barbara Miller; **Page 22,** Barbara Miller; **Page 23,** Stan Washburn/AnthroPhoto; **Page 23,** Louise Gubb/CORBIS; **Page 24,** © Bob Krist/CORBIS All Rights Reserved; **Page 26,** © CRDPHOTO/CORBIS; **Page 27,** © Jack Fields/CORBIS; **Page 27,** AP/Wide World Photos

Chapter 2: Page 32, © John Reader/Science Photo Library/Photo Researchers, Inc; **Page 34,** © Cyril Ruoso/Minden Pictures; **Page 37,** © Theo Allofs/zefa/Corbis; **Page 37,** © Jim Tuten/Animals Animals; **Page 38,** © Minden Pictures; **Page 38,** © Frans Lanting/Minden Pictures; **Page 39,** © Heather Angel/Natural Visions; **Page 41,** © Patrick Robert/CORBIS All Rights Reserved; **Page 42,** Donald Johanson/Institute of Human Origins; **Page 43,** © 2004 Frans Lanting; **Page 44,** © Lowell Georgia/CORBIS; **Page 44,** Werner Forman/Art Resource, NY; **Page 45,** © Mick Tsikas/epe/CORBIS; **Page 48,** Sally McBrearty; **Page 48,** American Museum of Natural History; **Page 50,** Réunion des Musées Nationaux/Art Resource; **Page 50,** © Erich Lessing/Art Resource, NY; **Page 50,** © Réunion des Musées Nationaux/Art Resource, NY; **Page 50,** © Jacka Photography; **Page 52,** © Yann Arthus-Bertrand/CORBIS; **Page 53,** © Adam Woolfitt/CORBIS All Rights Reserved; **Page 54,** © Nik Wheeler/CORBIS; **Page 54,** © The Granger Collection, New York; **Page 55,** Dave Rudkin © Dorling Kindersley, Courtesy of the Birmingham Museum and Art Galleries; **Page 56,** © Bettmann/CORBIS; **Page 57,** © Otis Imboden Jr./National Geographic Image Collection

Chapter 3: Page 60, © Tronick/Anthro-Photo File; **Page 62,** A. R. Radcliffe-Brown, The Andaman Islanders. Cambridge: Cambridge University Press, 1964 [1922]; **Page 63,** Lanita Jacobs-Huey; **Page 64,** © Philippe Issac/Godong/CORBIS All Rights Reserved; **Page 64,** © Kazuyoshi Nomachi/CORBIS All Rights Reserved; **Page 64,** © Wolfgang Kumm/epa/CORBIS All Rights Reserved; **Page 66,** Pearson Education; **Page 67,** Irven Devore/AnthroPhoto; **Page 67,** © Albrecht G. Schaefer/CORBIS; **Page 68,** Jennifer Robertson; **Page 70,** Liza Dalby; **Page 71,** Isabel Balseiro; **Page 74,** © Mel Konner/AnthroPhoto; **Page 74,** Gananath Obeyesekere; **Page 75,** Michael Horowitz; **Page 77,** © Atlantide Phototravel/CORBIS All Rights Reserved; **Page 78,** © Catherine Karnow/CORBIS All Rights Reserved; **Page 81,** © Danny Gawlowski; **Page 81,** © Danny Hoffman

Chapter 4: Page 86, © Colin McPherson/CORBIS All Rights Reserved; **Page 88,** © Joel Savishinsky; **Page 89,** Barbara Miller; **Page 91,** © Irven DeVore/AnthroPhoto; **Page 93,** Joel Savishinsky; **Page 93,** © Charles O. Cecil; **Page 94,** Pankaj Sekhsaria; **Page 94,** Pankaj Sekhsaria; **Page 95,** Stock Montage, Inc./Historical Pictures Collection; **Page 97,** Elliott Fratkin; **Page 97,** Barbara Miller; **Page 99,** © Jeremy Horner/CORBIS; **Page 101,** © Morton Beebe/CORBIS; **Page 102,** Barbara Miller; **Page 103,** © David Longstreath/AP Wide World; **Page 105,** © Reuters/Megan Lewis/Archive Photos; **Page 106,** © Adrian Arbib/CORBIS

Chapter 5: Page 110, © Luca Da Ros/CORBIS All Rights Reserved; **Page 114,** Barbara Miller; **Page 115,** © Kim Newton/Woodfin Camp & Associates; **Page 115,** Barbara Miller; **Page 115,** © Sean Sprague/Stock Boston, LLC; **Page 117,** © Shannon Stapleton/CORBIS; **Page 118,** Edward Keller III; **Page 118,** Stephanie Kuykendal/CORBIS; **Page 121,** © David Austen/Stock Boston LLC; **Page 122,** © Charles O. Cecil; **Page 123,** © Charles O. Cecil; **Page 125,** J. Marshall—Tribaleye Images/Alamy; **Page 127,** Barbara Miller; **Page 127,** Bob Krist/CORBIS; **Page 129,** © Miguel Gandert/CORBIS All Rights Reserved; **Page 131,** © Wilson Melo/CORBIS; **Page 132,** Barbara Miller; **Page 133,** © Vickie Jensen; **Page 133,** © Vickie Jensen

Chapter 6: Page 136, © William Coupon/CORBIS; **Page 140,** © David & Peter Turnley/CORBIS; **Page 140,** Barbara Miller; **Page 141,** © Victor Tonelli/ReutersCORBIS; **Page 143,** © Stephanie Dinkins/Photo Researchers, Inc.; **Page 144,** © Barry Iverson/Woodfin Camp & Associates; **Page 145,** © Reza; Webistan/CORBIS; **Page 146,** Barbara Miller; **Page 146,** © Brian Snyder/Reuters/CORBIS; **Page 148,** © Bettmann/CORBIS; **Page 148,** Nancy Scheper-Hughes; **Page 151,** © Napoleon A. Chagnon/AnthroPhoto; **Page 151,** © Bill Varie/CORBIS; **Page 153,** © Robert Caputo/National Geographic Image Collection; **Page 153,** Abigail Adams; **Page 156,** © The National Anthropological Archive/Smithsonian Institution; **Page 157,** © Kim Kyung-Hoon/Reuters/CORBIS; **Page 158,** Barry Hewlett; **Page 159,** © Orjan F. Ellingvag/Dagbladet Naringsliv/Corbis

Chapter 7: Page 162, © Kevin Fleming/CORBIS; **Page 164,** © AFP/CORBIS; **Page 166,** © Janet Jarman/CORBIS All Rights Reserved; **Page 170,** Barbara Miller; **Page 170,** Mary Beth Mills; **Page 171,** © Irven DeVore/AnthroPhoto; **Page 172,** © Ricardo Azoury/CORBIS; **Page 174,** © Ed Kashi/CORBIS; **Page 174,** CORBIS; **Page 175,** © Peter Menzel/Stock Boston, LLC; **Page 179,** © Lara Jo Regan/Getty Images; **Page 180,** © Sean Sprague/Stock Boston, LLC; **Page 180,** Barbara Miller; **Page 181,** Royalty Free/CORBIS; **Page 181,** © Pawel Kopczynski/Reuters/CORBIS All Rights Reserved; **Page 184,** © CDC/PHIL/CORBIS

Chapter 8: Page 190, © CORBIS; **Page 195,** © Norbert Schiller/The Image Works; **Page 195,** © Chris Lisle/CORBIS; **Page 198,** © Wolfgang Kachler/CORBIS; **Page 198,** © Lindsay Hebberd/CORBIS; **Page 199,** Deanne Fitzmaurice/San Francisco Chronicle/CORBIS; **Page 202,** © Rick Smolan/Stock Boston, LLC; **Page 203,** Jack Heaton; **Page 204,** Deborah Pellow; **Page 205,** © Thomas L. Kelly/Woodfin Camp & Associates; **Page 206,** © Keren Su/Stock Boston, LLC; **Page 206,** Barbara Miller; **Page 207,** © Barry Lewis/Alamy; **Page 208,** © David Wells/The Image Works; **Page 211,** © Noboro Komine/Photo Researchers, Inc.; **Page 212,** Matthew Amster; **Page 212,** Matthew Amster

Chapter 9: Page 216, © Tiz/CORBIS SYGMA; **Page 220,** © David Lees/CORBIS All Rights Reserved; **Page 220,** © Stephanie Maze/Woodfin Camp & Associates; **Page 222,** © Phil Schermeister/CORBIS; **Page 222,** © Bob Daemmrich/Stock Boston, LLC; **Page 224,** © Jerome Sessini/In Visu/CORBIS; **Page 224,** © Charles & Josette Lenars/CORBIS; **Page 224,** © Royalty-Free/CORBIS; **Page 226,** © Wolfgang Kaehler; **Page 228,** © Matthew Cavanaugh/EPA/CORBIS All Rights Reserved; **Page 228,** Barbara Miller; **Page 229,** © David G. Houser/CORBIS; **Page 230,** © Gideon Mendel/CORBIS; **Page 232,** David Z. Scheffel; **Page 232,** David Z. Scheffel; **Page 234,** Barbara Miller; **Page 234,** Barbara Miller; **Page 236,** Courtesy of Stuart Kirsch; **Page 237,** © Peter Menzel/Stock Boston, LLC

Chapter 10: Page 240, © Henning Cristoph/DAS FOTOARCHIV/Peter Arnold; **Page 243,** Chunghee Sarah Soh; **Page 245,** © Roger De La Harpe/Gallo Images/CORBIS All Rights Reserved; **Page 246,** © Hank Wittemore/CORBIS SYGMA; **Page 248,** © Kal Muller/Woodfin Camp & Associates; **Page 248,** © Tobias Bernhard/zefa/CORBIS All Rights Reserved; **Page 249,** Christie's Images/CORBIS; **Page 249,** © Bettmann/CORBIS All Rights Reserved; **Page 250,** © David Turnley/CORBIS All Rights Reserved; **Page 250,** © George Tiedemann/GT Images/CORBIS All Rights Reserved; **Page 250,** © Bettmann/CORBIS All Rights Reserved; **Page 251,** © Laszio Balogh/Reuters/CORBIS All Rights Reserved; **Page 252,** © Reuters NewMedia Inc./CORBIS; **Page 252,** AP Photo/J. Scott Applewhite; **Page 256,** Republic of South Africa; **Page 257,** blickwinkel/Alamy; **Page 257,** Ed Kashi/CORBIS; **Page 260,** © David Van Der Veen/epa/CORBIS All Rights Reserved; **Page 260,** © Faleh Kheiber/Reuters/Corbis; **Page 260,** © Stan Honda/Getty Images; **Page 261,** © Alex Grimm/Reuters/CORBIS

Chapter 11: Page 264, © Wang Ying/Xinhua Press/CORBIS All Rights Reserved; **Page 266,** © Todd Gipstein/CORBIS All Rights Reserved; **Page 266,** © Luis Galdamez/Reuters/CORBIS All Rights Reserved; **Page 266,** © Alex de la Rosa/Reuters/CORBIS All Rights Reserved; **Page 268,** © Paul Solomon/Woodfin Camp & Associates; **Page 270,** Barbara Miller; **Page 270,** © EPA/CORBIS; **Page 272,** © Giry Daniel/CORBIS SYGMA; **Page 273,** Ross Setford/Getty Images; **Page 273,** © Robert Harding World Imagery/CORBIS; **Page 274,** Cornelia Mayer Herzfeld; **Page 276,** AFP/CORBIS; **Page 276,** © Bettmann/CORBIS; **Page 279,** © Fehim Demir/epa/CORBIS All Rights Reserved; **Page 281,** © Antonio Mari; **Page 282,** © Reuters/CORBIS; **Page 282,** © Emmanuel Tobey/Reuters/Corbis; **Page 283,** © Bettmann/CORBIS; **Page 284,** © Reuters NewMedia Inc./CORBIS; **Page 284,** © Reuters/Fred Ernst

Chapter 12: Page 290, © Charles O. Cecil; **Page 292,** © Frans Lanting/Minden Pictures; **Page 293,** Daniel Everett; **Page 295,** © Penny Tweedie/CORBIS; **Page 297,** © Olympia/PhotoEdit; **Page 298,** © 2004 Getty Images; **Page 298,** © Around the World in a Viewfinder/Alamy Images; **Page 299,** Barbara Miller; **Page 302,** © Charles O. Cecil; **Page 304,** Eriko Sugita/Reuters/CORBIS; **Page 304,** © Gallo Images/CORBIS; **Page 307,** © Paul A. Souders/CORBIS All Rights Reserved; **Page 307,** © M. Vautier, Anthropological & Archaeological Museum, Lima, Peru/Woodfin Camp & Associates; **Page 309,** Barbara Miller; **Page 309,** © Anders Ryman/Alamy; **Page 310,** © Bryan and Cherry Alexander Photography/Alamy

Chapter 13: Page 314, © Viviane Moos/CORBIS All Rights Reserved; **Page 316,** © Loring Danforth; **Page 318,** Ruth Krulfeld; **Page 319,** © Galen Rowell/CORBIS; **Page 319,** Simon Hiltebeitel; **Page 321,** © Bob Rowan/Progressive Images/CORBIS All Rights Reserved; **Page 321,** © Bob Rowan; Progressive Image/CORBIS; **Page 322,** © Adam Wolfitt/CORBIS; **Page 324,** © CORBIS; **Page 327,** © Brooklyn Museum of Art/CORBIS; **Page 328,** © AFP/CORBIS; **Page 329,** Jack Heaton; **Page 331,** Barbara Miller; **Page 332,** Barbara Miller; **Page 332,** Barbara Miller; **Page 333,** Edward Keller III; **Page 334,** Jack Heaton; **Page 335,** Eddie Gerald/Alamy; **Page 335,** Maris Boyd Gillette; **Page 336,** © Gerd Ludwig/Woodfin Camp & Associates; **Page 337,** © Michael Ochs Archives/CORBIS All Rights Reserved; **Page 338,** © Visual Arts Library [London]/Alamy; **Page 338,** Lamont Lindstrom; **Page 339,** AP/Wide World Photos

Chapter 14: Page 342, © Douglas Engle/CORBIS; **Page 344,** © Joseph Sohm/Visions of America/CORBIS All Rights Reserved; **Page 344,** © Paul McErlane/epa/CORBIS All Rights Reserved; **Page 344,** © Lindsay Hebberd/CORBIS All Rights Reserved; **Page 346,** © Bowers Museum of Cultural Art/CORBIS All Rights Reserved; **Page 346,** Joel Kuipers; **Page 346,** Lindsay Hebberd/CORBIS; **Page 347,** © Lucas Jackson/Reuters/CORBIS; **Page 350,** Roshani Kothari; **Page 350,** Barbara Miller; **Page 352,** Andrew Ward/Life File; **Page 352,** © epa/CORBIS All Rights Reserved; **Page 353,** Barbara Miller; **Page 354,** Barbara Miller; **Page 354,** Barbara Miller; **Page 356,** © George Tiedemann/GT Images/CORBIS; **Page 356,** © Lindsay Hebberd/CORBIS; **Page 356,** © CORBIS. All Rights Reserved.; **Page 357,** © Vincent Gautier/epa/CORBIS All Rights Reserved; **Page 357,** © Betty Press/ Woodfin Camp & Associates; **Page 358,** © Jay Dickman/CORBIS All Rights Reserved; **Page 359,** © Karen Kasmauski/CORBIS; **Page 359,** © Bob Krist/CORBIS; **Page 360,** © Wolfgang Kaehler/CORBIS; **Page 361,** © David Sutherland/CORBIS All Rights Reserved; **Page 362,** © Nik Wheeler/CORBIS All Rights Reserved; **Page 364,** © Dallas and John Heaton/CORBIS

Chapter 15: Page 370, © Nik Wheeler/CORBIS; **Page 372,** © Annie Griffiths Belt/CORBIS; **Page 372,** © Jon Hicks/CORBIS All Rights Reserved; **Page 374,** EdwardKeller III; **Page 375,** © Omar Khodor/Reuters/CORBIS All Rights Reserved; **Page 376,** Hans Blossey/Das Fotoarchiv/Peter Arnold; **Page 377,** © Gilles Sabrié/CORBIS; **Page 379,** © Reuters/CORBIS; **Page 379,** © Tibor Bogár/CORBIS; **Page 381,** © David Leeson/The Image Works; **Page 382,** © David H. Wells/CORBIS; **Page 382,** © Stephen Ferry/Getty Images; **Page 383,** © Yuri Cortez/CORBIS; **Page 384,** © David Young-Wolff/PhotoEdit; **Page 386,** © Karen Kasmauski/CORBIS All Rights Reserved; **Page 386,** © Bob Sacha/CORBIS All Rights Reserved; **Page 386,** © David Butow/CORBIS All Rights Reserved; **Page 387,** © James Leynse/CORBIS; **Page 388,** © David H. Wells/CORBIS; **Page 389,** Gideon Mendel/CORBIS; **Page 390,** © Diane Cook and Len Jenshel/CORBIS All Rights Reserved

Chapter 16: Page 394, © Reuters/CORBIS; **Page 397,** © Jeremy Horner/CORBIS; **Page 397,** © Shannon Stapleton/Reuters/CORBIS All Rights Reserved; **Page 398,** © Pallava Bagla/CORBIS; **Page 399,** © Fred Chartrand/The Canadian Press/AP Wide World; **Page 399,** © Bryan & Cherry Alexander Photography; **Page 401,** Rob Howard/CORBIS; **Page 402,** © Wim Wiskerke/Alamy; **Page 403,** Barbara Miller; **Page 404,** © Gideon Mendel/CORBIS; **Page 404,** © Orlando Barria/epa/CORBIS All Rights Reserved; **Page 405,** Jeremy Horner/Alamy Images; **Page 408,** © Robb Kendrick/Aurora & Quanta Productions; **Page 409,** © Reuters/CORBIS; **Page 409,** © George Philipas/Alamy; **Page 414,** © Robert Nickelsberg/Getty Images; **Page 415,** © Philippe Giraud/Goodlook/CORBIS; **Page 416,** © CORBIS. All Rights Reserved; **Page 416,** © CORBIS; **Page 418,** © Robert E. Barber; **Page 418,** © Angelo Cavalli/zefa/CORBIS All Rights Reserved; **Page 418,** © Bob Krist/CORBIS All Rights Reserved; **Page 419,** © Jeff Greenberg/Alamy

GLOSSARY

acculturation a form of cultural change in which a minority culture becomes more like the dominant culture.

Acheulian tradition a toolkit of *H. erectus*, used from 1.7 million years ago to 300,000 years ago, and characterized by handaxes.

achieved position a person's standing in society based on qualities that the person has gained through action.

adolescence a culturally defined period of maturation from the time of puberty until adulthood that occurs in some but not all cultures.

age set a group of people close in age who go through certain rituals, such as circumcision, at the same time.

agency the ability of humans to make choices and exercise free will even within dominating structures.

agriculture a mode of livelihood that involves growing crops with the use of plowing, irrigation, and fertilizer.

amazon a person who is biologically female but takes on a male gender role.

Anatomically Modern Humans (AMH) or ***Homo sapiens*** or **modern humans** the species to which modern humans belong and also referred to by that term; first emerged in Africa between 300,000–160,000 years ago and then spread throughout the Old and New Worlds.

animatism a belief system in which the supernatural is conceived of as an impersonal power.

animism the belief in souls or "doubles."

anomie the breakdown of traditional values associated with rapid social change.

anthropogenic caused by humans.

anthropology the study of humanity, including prehistoric origins and contemporary human diversity.

applied anthropology or **practicing anthropology** or **practical anthropology** the use of anthropological knowledge to prevent or solve problems or to shape and achieve policy goals.

applied medical anthropology the application of anthropological knowledge to furthering the goals of health care providers.

archaeology or **prehistory** the study of past human cultures through their material remains.

archaic *Homo* a category of several extinct hominin species that lived from 2.4 million years to 19,000 years ago and is characterized by different stone tool traditions, depending on the species.

art the application of imagination, skill, and style to matter, movement, and sound that goes beyond what is purely practical.

artifact a portable object made or modified by humans.

ascribed position a person's standing in society based on qualities that the person has gained through birth.

assimilation a form of culture change in which a culture is thoroughly acculturated, or decultured, and is no longer distinguishable as having a separate identity.

australopithecines a category of several extinct hominin species found in Africa that lived between 4.5 and 3 million years ago.

authority the ability to take action based on a person's achieved or ascribed status or moral reputation.

balanced exchange a system of transfers in which the goal is either immediate or eventual equality in value.

band the political organization of foraging groups, with minimal leadership and flexible membership.

banditry a form of aggressive conflict that involves socially patterned theft, usually practiced by a person or group of persons who are socially marginal and who may gain a mythic status.

berdache a blurred gender category, usually referring to a person who is biologically male but who takes on a female gender role.

big-man or **big-woman system** a form of political organization midway between tribe and chiefdom involving reliance on the leadership of key individuals who develop a political following through personal ties and redistributive feasts.

bilineal descent a kinship system in which a child is recognized as being related by descent to both parents.

biological anthropology or **physical anthropology** the study of humans as biological organisms, including evolution and contemporary variation.

biological determinism a theory that explains human behavior and ideas mainly as shaped by biological features such as genes and hormones.

bipedalism upright locomotion on two feet.

blood sport a form of competition that explicitly seeks to bring about a flow of blood, or even death, of human–human contestants, human–animal contestants, or animal–animal contestants.

bracero an agricultural laborer who is permitted entry to a country to work for a limited time.

brachiation arboreal travel, using the forelimbs to swing from branch to branch, that is distinct to apes.

brideprice or **bridewealth** the transfer of cash and goods from the groom's family to the bride's family and to the bride.

brideservice a form of marriage exchange in which the groom works for his father-in-law for a certain period of time before returning home with the bride.

call system a form of oral communication among nonhuman primates with a set repertoire of meaningful sounds generated in response to environmental factors.

cargo cult a form of revitalization movement that emerged in Melanesia and New Zealand following World War II in response to Western and Japanese influences.

cash crop a plant grown primarily for sale rather than for one's own use.

caste system a form of social stratification linked with Hinduism and based on a person's birth into a particular group.

chain migration a population movement in which a first wave of migrants comes and then attracts relatives and friends to join them in the destination.

chiefdom a political unit of permanently allied tribes and villages under one recognized leader.

circular migration a regular pattern of population movement between two or more places, either within or between countries.

civil society the collection of interest groups that function outside the government to organize economic and other aspects of life.

class a way of categorizing people on the basis of their economic position in society, usually measured in terms of income or wealth.

Clovis culture New World population characterized by the Clovis point with the earliest site dated to 11,000 years ago in the Southwest United States.

collaborative research an approach to learning about culture that involves anthropologists working with members of the study population as partners and participants rather than as "subjects."

communication the conveying of meaningful messages from one person, animal, or insect to another.

community healing healing that emphasizes the social context as a key component and which is carried out within the public domain.

consumerism a mode of consumption in which people's demands are many and infinite and the means of satisfying them are insufficient and become depleted in the effort to satisfy these demands.

consumption fund a category of a personal or household budget used to provide for consumption needs and desires.

couvade customs applying to the behavior of fathers during and shortly after the birth of their children.

creole a language directly descended from a pidgin but possessing its own native speakers and involving linguistic expansion and elaboration.

critical development anthropology an approach to international development in which the anthropologist takes on a critical-thinking role and asks why and to whose benefit particular development policies and programs are pursued.

critical discourse analysis the study of the relations of power and inequality in language.

critical legal anthropology an approach within legal anthropology that examines how law and judicial systems serve to maintain and expand dominant power interests rather than protecting marginal and less powerful people.

critical media anthropology an approach within the cross-cultural study of media that examines how power interests shape people's access to media and the contents of its messages.

critical medical anthropology approach within medical anthropology involving the analysis of how economic and political structures shape people's health status, their access to health care, and the prevailing medical systems that exist in relation to them.

critical military anthropology the study of the military as a power structure in terms of its roles and internal social dynamics.

Cro-Magnons the first modern humans in Europe, dating from 40,000 years ago.

cross-cousin the offspring of either one's father's sister or one's mother's brother.

cultural anthropology or **social anthropology** the study of living peoples and their cultures, including variation and change.

cultural constructionism a theory that explains human behavior and ideas mainly as shaped by learning.

cultural fit a characteristic of informed and effective project design in which planners take local culture into account; opposite of one-size-fits-all project design.

cultural materialism a theoretical position that takes material features of life, such as the environment, natural resources, and mode of production, as the bases for explaining social organization and ideology.

cultural relativism the perspective that each culture must be understood in terms of the values and ideas of that culture and should not be judged by the standards of another.

culture people's learned and shared behavior and beliefs.

culture shock persistent feelings of uneasiness, loneliness, and anxiety that often occur when a person has shifted from one culture to a different one.

culture-specific syndrome a collection of signs and symptoms that is restricted to a particular culture or a limited number of cultures.

dalit the preferred name for the socially defined lowest groups in the Indian caste system, meaning "oppressed" or "ground down."

deductive approach (to research) a research method that involves posing a research question or hypothesis, gathering data related to the question, and then assessing the findings in relation to the original hypothesis.

demographic transition the change from the agricultural pattern of high fertility and high mortality to the industrial pattern of low fertility and low mortality.

descent the tracing of kinship relationships through parentage.

development directed change to achieve improved human welfare.

development aggression the imposition of development projects and policies without the free, prior, and informed consent of the affected people.

development project a set of activities designed to put development policies into action.

development-induced displacement (DID) forced migration due to development projects, such as dam building.

diaspora population a dispersed group of people living outside their original homeland.

diffusion the spread of culture through contact.

digital divide social inequality in access to new and emerging information technology, notably access to up-to-date computers, the Internet, and training related to their use.

disease in the disease/illness dichotomy, a biological health problem that is objective and universal.

disease of development a health problem caused or increased by economic development activities that affect the environment and people's relationship with it.

displaced person someone who is forced to leave his or her home and community or country.

displacement a feature of human language that allows people to talk about events in the past and future.

doctrine direct and formalized statements about religious beliefs.

domestication the process by which human selection causes changes in the genetic material of plants and animals.

dowry the transfer of cash and goods from the bride's family to the newly married couple and to the groom's family.

ecological/epidemiological approach an approach within medical anthropology that considers how aspects of the natural environment and social environment interact to cause illness.

economic system the linked processes of livelihood, consumption, and exchange.

emic insiders' perceptions and categories, and their explanations for why they do what they do.

endogamy marriage within a particular group or locality.

entitlement a culturally defined right to life-sustaining resources.

ethnicity a shared sense of identity among a group based on a heritage, language, or culture.

ethnocentrism judging other cultures by the standards of one's own culture rather than by the standards of that particular culture.

ethno-esthetics culturally specific definitions of what art is.

ethno-etiologies culturally specific causal explanations for health problems and suffering.

ethnography a firsthand, detailed description of a living culture, based on personal observation.

ethnomedicine the study of cross-cultural health systems.

ethnomusicology the cross-cultural study of music.

ethnosemantics the study of the meaning of words, phrases, and sentences in particular cultural contexts.

etic an analytical framework used by outside analysts in studying culture.

evolution an inherited and cumulative change in the characteristics of a species, population, or culture.

exogamy marriage outside a particular group or locality.

expected reciprocity exchange of approximately equally valued goods or services, usually between people roughly equal in social status.

expressive culture behavior and beliefs related to art, leisure, and play.

extended household a coresidential group that comprises more than one parent–child unit.

extensive strategy a form of livelihood involving temporary use of large areas of land and a high degree of spatial mobility.

extractive industry a business that explores for, removes, processes, and sells minerals, oil, and gas that are found on or beneath the earth's surface and are nonrenewable.

faction a politically oriented group with strong lateral ties to a leader.

family a group of people who consider themselves related through a form of kinship, such as descent, marriage, or sharing.

family farming a form of agriculture in which farmers produce mainly to support themselves and also produce goods for sale in the market system; formerly called *peasant farming*.

female genital cutting term used for a range of genital cutting procedures, including the excision of part or all of the clitoris, excision of part or all of the labia, and sometimes infibulation, the stitching together of the vaginal entry.

fertility the rate of births in a population, or the rate of population increase in general.

feuding long-term, retributive violence that may be lethal between families, groups of families, or tribes.

fieldwork research in the field, which is any place where people and culture are found.

foraging obtaining food available in nature through gathering, hunting, or scavenging.

formal sector salaried or wage-based work registered in official statistics.

fossil the preserved remains of a plant or animal of the past.

functionalism the theory that a culture is similar to a biological organism, in which parts work to support the operation and maintenance of the whole.

gender culturally constructed and learned behaviors and ideas attributed to males, females, or blended genders.

gender pluralism the existence within a culture of multiple categories of femininity, masculinity, and blurred genders that are tolerated and legitimate.

generalized reciprocity exchange involving the least conscious sense of interest in material gain or thought of what might be received in return.

globalization the increased and intensified international ties related to the spread of Western, especially United States, capitalism that affect all world cultures.

global language or **world language** a language spoken widely throughout the world and in diverse cultural contexts, often replacing indigenous languages.

great apes a category of large and tailless primates that includes orangutans, gorillas, chimpanzees, bonobos, and humans.

groomprice the transfer of cash and goods, often large amounts, from the bride's family to the groom's family.

Hawthorne effect research bias due to participants changing their behavior to conform to expectations of the researcher.

heterotopia a new situation formed from elements drawn from multiple and diverse contexts.

hijra a term used in India to refer to a blurred gender role in which a person, usually biologically male, takes on female dress and behavior.

historical linguistics the study of language change using formal methods that compare shifts over time and across space in aspects of language such as phonetics, syntax, and semantics.

historical trauma the intergenerational transfer of the negative effects of colonialism from parents to children.

holism the perspective in anthropology that cultures are complex systems that cannot be fully understood without paying attention to their different components, including economics, social organization, and ideology.

hominins a category of primates that includes modern humans and extinct species of early human ancestors that are more closely related to humans than to living chimpanzees and bonobos.

horticulture a mode of livelihood based on growing domesticated crops in gardens, using simple hand tools.

household a group of people, who may or may not be related by kinship, who share living space.

humoral healing healing that emphasizes balance among natural elements within the body.

illness in the disease/illness dichotomy, culturally shaped perceptions and experiences of a health problem.

incest taboo a strongly held prohibition against marrying or having sex with particular kin.

indigenous knowledge (IK) local understanding of the environment, climate, plants, and animals.

indigenous people groups who have a long-standing connection with their home territory that predates colonial or outside societies that prevail in that territory.

inductive approach (to research) a research approach that avoids hypothesis formation in advance of the research and instead takes its lead from the culture being studied.

industrial capital agriculture a form of agriculture that is capital-intensive, substituting machinery and purchased inputs for human and animal labor.

industrialism/informatics a mode of livelihood in which goods are produced through mass employment in business and commercial operations and through the creation and movement of information through electronic media.

infanticide the killing of an infant or child.

influence the ability to achieve a desired end by exerting social or moral pressure on someone or some group.

informal sector work that is not officially registered, and sometimes illegal.

informed consent an aspect of fieldwork ethics requiring that the researcher inform the research participants of the intent, scope, and possible effects of the study and seek their consent to be in the study.

in-kind taxation a system of mandatory noncash contributions to the state.

institutional migrant someone who moves into a social institution (such as a school or prison), voluntarily or involuntarily.

intangible cultural heritage UNESCO's view of culture as manifested in oral traditions, languages, performing arts, rituals and festive events, knowledge and practices about nature and the universe, and craftmaking; also called living heritage.

intensive strategy a form of livelihood that involves continuous use of the same land and resources.

internal migration population movement within country boundaries.

internally displaced person someone who is forced to leave his or her home and community but who remains in the same country.

international migration population movement across country boundaries.

interpretive anthropology or **interpretivism** the view that cultures can be understood by studying what people think about, their ideas, and the meanings that are important to them.

interview a research technique that involves gathering of verbal data through questions or guided conversation between at least two people.

invention the discovery of something new.

khipu the cords of knotted strings used during the Inca empire for keeping accounts and recording events.

kinship system the predominant form of kin relationships in a culture and the kinds of behavior involved.

knuckle-walking a form of nonhuman primate terrestrial travel that involves walking flat-footed while supporting the upper body on the front of fingers bent beyond the knuckle.

kula a trading network, linking many of the Trobriand Islands, in which men have long-standing partnerships for the exchange of everyday goods such as food as well as highly valued necklaces and armlets.

language a form of communication that is a systematic set of learned symbols and signs shared among a group and passed on from generation to generation.

language endangerment condition of a language when it has fewer than 10,000 speakers.

language extinction condition of a language in which speakers abandon it in favor of a new language to the extent that the native language loses functions and no longer has competent users.

language family languages descended from a parent language.

language shift or **language decay** condition of a language in which speakers adopt a new language for most situations, begin to use their native language only in certain contexts, and may be only semi-fluent and have limited vocabulary in their native language.

law a binding rule created through enactment or custom that defines right and reasonable behavior and is enforceable by threat of punishment.

legal pluralism a situation in which more than one way exists of defining acceptable and unacceptable behavior and ways to deal with the latter.

leveling mechanism an unwritten, culturally embedded rule that prevents an individual from becoming wealthier or more powerful than anyone else.

life project local people's definition of the direction they want to take in life, informed by their knowledge, history, and context.

lifeboat mentality a view that seeks to limit enlarging a particular group because of perceived resource constraints.

life-cycle ritual a ritual that marks a change in status from one life stage to another; also called rite of passage.

linguistic anthropology the study of human communication, including its origins, history, and contemporary variation and change.

localization the transformation of global culture by local cultures into something new.

logograph a symbol that conveys meaning through a form or picture resembling that to which it refers.

magic the attempt to compel supernatural forces and beings to act in certain ways.

male bias in development the design and implementation of development projects with men as beneficiaries and without regard to their impact on women's roles and status.

market exchange the buying and selling of commodities under competitive conditions in which the forces of supply and demand determine value.

marriage a union between two people (usually), who are likely to be, but are not necessarily, coresident, sexually involved with each other, and procreative.

material cultural heritage the sites, monuments, buildings, and movable objects considered to have outstanding value to humanity; also called cultural heritage.

matrescence motherhood, or the cultural process of becoming a mother.

matriarchy a society in which women are dominant in terms of economics, politics, and ideology.

matrifocality a household pattern in which a female (or females) is the central, stable figure around whom other members cluster.

matrilineal descent a kinship system that highlights the importance of women by tracing descent through the female line, favoring marital residence with or near the bride's family, and providing for property to be inherited through the female line.

mechanical solidarity social bonding among groups that are similar.

medicalization labeling a particular issue or problem as medical and requiring medical treatment when, in fact, that issue or problem is economic or political.

medical pluralism the existence of more than one health system in a culture, or a government policy to promote the integration of local healing systems into biomedical practice.

menarche the onset of menstruation.

menopause the cessation of menstruation.

mestizaje literally, racial mixture; in Central and South America, indigenous people who are cut off from their Indian roots, or literate and successful indigenous people who retain some traditional cultural practices.

microculture a distinct pattern of learned and shared behavior and thinking found within larger cultures.

migration the movement of a person or people from one place to another.

minimalism a mode of consumption that emphasizes simplicity, is characterized by few and finite consumer demands, and involves an adequate and sustainable means to achieve them.

mode of consumption the dominant pattern, in a culture, of using things up or spending resources in order to satisfy demands.

mode of exchange the dominant pattern, in a culture, of transferring goods, services, and other items between and among people and groups.

mode of livelihood the dominant way of making a living in a culture.

mode of reproduction the predominant pattern of fertility and mortality in a culture.

modernization a model of change based on belief in the inevitable advance of science and Western secularism and processes including industrial growth, consolidation of the state, bureaucratization, market economy, technological innovation, literacy, and options for social mobility.

moka a strategy for developing political leadership in highland Papua New Guinea that involves exchanging gifts and favors with individuals and sponsoring large feasts where further gift giving occurs.

money a medium of exchange that can be used for a variety of goods.

monogamy marriage between two people.

Mousterian tradition the toolkit of the Neanderthals characterized by the predominance of small, light, and more specialized flake tools such as points, serapers, and awls.

multisited research fieldwork conducted in more than one location in order to understand the behaviors and ideas of dispersed members of a culture or the relationships among different levels such as state policy and local culture.

museum an institution that collects, preserves, interprets, and displays objects on a regular basis.

myth a narrative with a plot that involves the supernaturals.

nation a group of people who share a language, culture, territorial base, political organization, and history.

natural selection the process by which organisms better adapted to the environment reproduce more effectively compared with less well-adapted forms.

Neolithic Revolution the period of rapid transformation in technology, related to plant and animal domestication, which includes tools such as sickle blades and grinding stones.

new immigrant an international migrant who has moved since the 1960s.

norm a generally agreed-upon standard for how people should behave, usually unwritten and learned unconsciously.

nuclear household a domestic unit containing one adult couple (married or partners), with or without children.

Oldowan tradition the oldest hominin toolkit, characterized by core tools and flake tools.

organic solidarity social bonding between and among groups with different abilities and resources.

parallel cousin the offspring of either one's father's brother or one's mother's sister.

participant observation the basic fieldwork method in cultural anthropology that involves living in a culture for a long period of time while gathering data.

pastoralism a mode of livelihood based on keeping domesticated animals and using their products, such as meat and milk, for most of the diet.

patrescence fatherhood, or the cultural process of becoming a father.

patrilineal descent a kinship system that highlights the importance of men in tracing descent, determining marital residence with or near the groom's family, and providing for inheritance of property through the male line.

personality an individual's patterned and characteristic way of behaving, thinking, and feeling.

phoneme a sound that makes a difference for meaning in a language.

phytotherapy healing through the use of plants.

pidgin a contact language that blends elements of at least two languages and that emerges when people with different languages need to communicate.

pilgrimage round-trip travel to a sacred place or places for purposes of religious devotion or ritual.

placebo effect or **meaning effect** a positive result from a healing method due to a symbolic or otherwise nonmaterial factor.

policing the exercise of social control through processes of surveillance and the threat of punishment related to maintaining social order.

political organization the existence of groups for purposes of public decision making and leadership, maintaining social cohesion and order, protecting group rights, and ensuring safety from external threats.

polyandry a marriage of one wife with more than one husband.

polygamy a marriage involving multiple spouses.

polygyny a marriage of one husband with more than one wife.

potlatch a grand feast in which guests are invited to eat and to receive gifts from the hosts.

poverty the lack of tangible and intangible assets that contributing to life and the quality of life.

power the capacity to take action in the face of resistance, through force if necessary.

priest/priestess a male or female full-time religious specialist whose position is based mainly on abilities gained through formal training.

primary group a social group in which members meet on a face-to-face basis.

primates an order of mammals that includes modern humans.

productivity a feature of human language that offers the ability to communicate many messages efficiently.

project cycle the steps of a development project from initial planning to completion: project identification, project design, project appraisal, project implementation, and project evaluation.

pronatalism an ideology promoting many children.

puberty a time in the human life cycle that occurs universally and involves a set of biological markers and sexual maturation.

pure gift something given with no expectation or thought of a return.

push–pull theory an explanation for rural-to-urban migration that emphasizes people's incentives to move based on a lack of opportunity in rural areas (the "push") compared to urban areas (the "pull").

qualitative data non-numeric information.

quantitative data numeric information.

questionnaire a formal research instrument containing a pre-set series of questions that the anthropologist asks in a face-to-face setting, by mail, or by email.

"race" a classification of people into groups on the basis of supposedly homogeneous and largely superficial biological traits such as skin color or hair characteristics.

rainforest an environment, found at mid-latitudes, of tall, broadleaf evergreen trees, with annual rainfall of 400 centimeters (or 60 inches) and no dry season.

rapport a trusting relationship between the researcher and the study population.

redistribution a form of exchange that involves one person collecting goods or money from many members of a group, who then, at a later time and at a public event, "returns" the pooled goods to everyone who contributed.

refugee someone who is forced to leave his or her home, community, or country.

religion beliefs and behavior related to supernatural beings and forces.

religious pluralism when one or more religions coexist as either complementary to each other or as competitive systems.

religious syncretism the blending of features of two or more cultures, especially used in discussion of religious change.

remittance the transfer of money or goods by a migrant to his or her family in the country of origin.

repatriation returning art or other objects from museums to the people with whom they originated.

revitalization movement a socioreligious movement, usually organized by a prophetic leader, that seeks to construct a more satisfying situation by reviving all or parts of a religion that has been threatened by outside forces or by adopting new practices and beliefs.

revolution a political crisis prompted by illegal and often violent actions of subordinate groups that seek to change the political institutions or social structure of a society.

right of return the United Nations guaranteed right of a refugee to return to his or her home country to live.

ritual a patterned behavior that has to do with the supernatural realm.

ritual of inversion a ritual in which normal social roles and order are temporarily reversed.

sacrifice a ritual in which something is offered to the supernaturals.

Sapir-Whorf hypothesis a theory in linguistic anthropology that says language determines thought.

savanna an environment that consists of open plains with tall grasses and patches of trees.

secondary group people who identify with each other on some basis but may never meet with one another personally.

sedentism a lifestyle associated with residence in permanent villages, towns, and cities, generally linked with the emergence of farming.

segmentary model a type of political organization in which smaller units unite in the face of external threats and then disunite when the external threat is absent.

sex ratio the number of males per 100 females in a population.

shaman/shamanka a male or female healer who have a direct relationship with the supernaturals.

sign language a form of communication that uses mainly hand movements to convey messages.

social capital the intangible resources existing in social ties, trust, and cooperation.

social control the processes that maintain orderly social life, including informal and formal mechanisms.

social group a cluster of people beyond the domestic unit who are usually related on grounds other than kinship.

social impact assessment a study conducted to gauge the potential social costs and benefits of particular innovations before change is undertaken.

social stratification the hierarchical relationships between different groups as though they were arranged in layers, or "strata."

sociality a preference for living in groups and interacting regularly with members of the same species.

sociolinguistics a theory in linguistic anthropology that says that culture and society and a person's social position determine language.

somatization the process through which the body absorbs social stress and manifests symptoms of suffering; also called embodiment.

status a person's position, or standing, in society.

stem household a coresidential group that comprises only two married couples related through males, commonly found in East Asian cultures.

structural suffering the human health problems caused by such economic and political situations as war, famine, terrorism, forced migration, and poverty.

structurism a theoretical position concerning human behavior and ideas that says large forces such as the economy, social and political organization, and the media shape what people do and think.

susto a fright/shock disease; a culture-specific syndrome found in Spain and Portugal and among Latino people wherever they live; symptoms include back pain, fatigue, weakness, and lack of appetite.

symbol an object, word, or action with culturally defined meaning that stands for something else; most symbols are arbitrary.

tag question a question seeking affirmation, placed at the end of a sentence.

tell a human-made mound resulting from the accumulation of successive generations of house construction, reconstruction, and trash.

theater a form of enactment, related to other forms such as dance, music, parades, competitive games and sports, and verbal art, that seeks to entertain through acting, movement, and sound.

toponymy the naming of places.

trade the formalized exchange of one thing for another according to set standards of value.

traditional development anthropology an approach to international development in which the anthropologist accepts the role of helping to make development work better by providing cultural information to planners.

transnational migration a form of population movement in which a person regularly moves between two or more countries and forms a new cultural identity transcending a single geopolitical unit.

trial by ordeal a way of determining innocence or guilt in which the accused person is put to a test that may be painful, stressful, or fatal.

tribe a political group that comprises several bands or lineage groups, each with similar language and lifestyle and occupying a distinct territory.

unbalanced exchange a system of transfers in which one party seeks to make a profit.

unilineal descent a kinship system that traces descent through only one parent, either the mother or the father.

Upper Paleolithic the period of modern human occupation in Europe and Eurasia (including the Middle East) from 45,000–40,000 years ago to 12,000 years ago, characterized by microlithic tools and prolific cave art and portable art.

use rights a system of property relations in which a person or group has socially recognized priority in access to particular resources such as gathering, hunting, and fishing areas and water holes.

wa a Japanese word meaning discipline and self-sacrifice for the good of the group.

war an organized and purposeful group action directed against another group and involving lethal force.

Western biomedicine (WBM) a healing approach based on modern Western science that emphasizes technology for diagnosing and treating health problems related to the human body.

world religion a term coined in the nineteenth century to refer to a religion that is text-based, has many followers, is regionally widespread, and is concerned with salvation.

youth gang a group of young people, found mainly in urban areas, who are often considered a social problem by adults and law enforcement officials.

REFERENCES

Abélès, Marc. 1991. *Quiet Days in Burgundy: A Study of Local Politics.* Trans. Annella McDermott. New York: Cambridge University Press.

Abu-Lughod, Lila. 1993. *Writing Women's Worlds: Bedouin Stories.* Berkeley: University of California Press.

Adams, Abigail E. 2002. Dyke to Dyke: Ritual Reproduction at a U.S. Men's Military College. In *The Best of Anthropology Today* (pp. 34–42). Jonathan Benthall, ed. New York: Routledge.

Adams, Robert McC. 1981. *Heartland of Cities.* Chicago: University of Chicago Press.

Adams, Vincanne. 1988. Modes of Production and Medicine: An Examination of the Theory in Light of Sherpa Traditional Medicine. *Social Science and Medicine* 27:505–513.

Afolayan, E. 2000. Bantu Expansion and Its Consequences. In *African History before 1885* (pp. 113–136). T. Falola, ed. Durham, NC: Carolina Academic Press.

Agar, Michael and Heather Schacht Reisinger. 2003. Going for the Global: The Case of Ecstasy. *Human Organization* 62(1):1–11.

Ahern, Laura. 2001. *Invitations to Love: Literacy, Love Letters, and Social Change in Nepal.* Ann Arbor: University of Michigan Press.

Ahmadu, Fuambai. 2000. Rites and Wrongs: An Insider/Outside Reflects on Power and Excision. In *Female "Circumcision" in Africa: Culture, Controversy, and Change* (pp. 283–312). Bettina Shell-Duncan and Ylva Hernlund, eds. Boulder, CO: Lynne Reiner Publishers.

Akinsha, Konstantin. 1992a. Whose Gold? *ARTNews* 91(3):39–40.

———. 1992b. Russia: Whose Art Is It? *ARTNews* 91(5):100–105.

———. 1992c. After the Coup: Art for Art's Sake? *ARTNews* 91(1):108–113.

Algaze, Guillermo. 2001. Initial Social Complexity in Southwestern Asia: The Mesopotamian Advantage. *Current Anthropology* 42:199–233.

Allen, Catherine J. 2002. *The Hold Life Has: Coca and Cultural Identity in an Andean Community.* Washington, DC: Smithsonian Institution Press.

Allen, Susan. 1994. What Is Media Anthropology? A Personal View and a Suggested Structure. In *Media Anthropology: Informing Global Citizens* (pp. 15–32). Susan L. Allen, ed. Westport, CT: Bergin & Garvey.

Alonso, Ana María. 2004. Conforming Disconformity: "Mestizaje," Hybridity, and the Aesthetics of Mexican Nationalism. *Cultural Anthropology* 19:459–490.

Alter, Joseph S. 1992. The Sannyasi and the Indian Wrestler: Anatomy of a Relationship. *American Ethnologist* 19(2):317–336.

Ambrose, Stanley, Jane Buikstra, and Harold W. Krueger. 2003. Status and Gender Differences in Diet at Mound 72, Cahokia, Revealed by Isotope Analysis of Bone. *Journal of Anthropological Archaeology* 22:217–236.

Ames, Michael. 1992. *Cannibal Tours and Glass Boxes: The Anthropology of Museums.* Vancouver: University of British Columbia Press.

Amster, Matthew H. 2000. It Takes a Village to Dismantle a Longhouse. *Thresholds* 20:65–71.

Ancrenaz, Marc, Olivier Gimenez, Laurentius Ambu, Karine Ancrenaz, Patrick Andau, Benoît Goossens, John Payne, Azri Sawang, Augustine Tuuga, and Isabelle Lackman-Ancrenaz. 2005. Aerial Surveys Give New Estimates for Orangutans in Sabah, Malaysia. *PloS Biology* 3(1):e3. www.plosbiology.org.

Anderson, Benedict. 1991 [1983]. *Imagined Communities: Reflections on the Origin and Spread of Nationalism.* New York: Verso.

Anderson, Myrdene. 2004. Reflections on the Saami at Loose Ends. In *Cultural Shaping of Violence: Victimization, Escalation, Response* (pp. 285–291). Myrdene Anderson, ed. West Lafayette, IN: Purdue University Press.

Anderson, Richard L. and Karen L. Field. 1993. Chapter Introduction. In *Art in Small-Scale Societies: Contemporary Readings* (p. 247). Richard L. Anderson and Karen L. Fields, eds. Englewood Cliffs, NJ: Prentice-Hall.

Anglin, Mary K. 2002. *Women, Power, and Dissent in the Hills of Carolina.* Chicago: University of Illinois Press.

Appadurai, Arjun. 1986. Introduction: Commodities and the Politics of Value. In *The Social Life of Things: Commodities in Cultural Perspective* (pp. 3–63). Arjun Appadurai, ed. New York: Cambridge University Press.

Applbaum, Kalman D. 1995. Marriage with the Proper Stranger: Arranged Marriage in Metropolitan Japan. *Ethnology* 34(1): 37–51.

Arambiza, Evelio and Michael Painter. 2006. Biodiversity Conservation and the Quality of Life of Indigenous People in the Bolivian Chaco. *Human Organization* 65:20–34.

Attwood, Donald W. 1992. *Raising Cane: The Political Economy of Sugar in Western India.* Boulder, CO: Westview Press.

Awe, Bolanle. 1977. The Iyalode in the Traditional Yoruba Political System. In *Sexual Stratification: A Cross-Cultural View* (pp. 144–160). Alice Schlegel, ed. New York: Columbia University Press.

Baker, Colin. 1999. Sign Language and the Deaf Community. In *Handbook of Language and Ethnic Identity* (pp. 122–139). Joshua A. Fishman, ed. New York: Oxford University Press.

Baker-Christales, Beth. 2004. *Salvadoran Migration to Southern California: Redefining El Hermano Lejano.* Gainesville: University of Florida Press.

Baptista, Marlyse. 2005. New Directions in Pidgin and Creole Studies. *Annual Review of Anthropology* 34:34–42.

Barfield, Thomas J. 1993. *The Nomadic Alternative.* Englewood Cliffs, NJ: Prentice-Hall.

———. 1994. Prospects for Plural Societies in Central Asia. *Cultural Survival Quarterly* 18 (2&3):48–51.

———. 2001. Pastoral Nomads or Nomadic Pastoralists. In *The Dictionary of Anthropology* (pp. 348–350). Thomas Barfield, ed. Malden, MA: Blackwell Publishers.

Barkey, Nanette, Benjamin C. Campbell, and Paul W. Leslie. 2001. A Comparison of Health Complaints of Settled and Nomadic Turkana Men. *Medical Anthropology Quarterly* 15: 391–408.

Barlett, Peggy F. 1980. Reciprocity and the San Juan Fiesta. *Journal of Anthropological Research* 36:116–130.

———. 1989. Industrial Agriculture. In *Economic Anthropology* (pp. 253–292). Stuart Plattner, ed. Stanford, CA: Stanford University Press.

Barnard, Alan. 2000. *History and Theory in Anthropology.* New York: Cambridge University Press.

———. 2004. Coat of Arms and Body Politic: Khoisan Imagery and South African National Identity. *Ethnos* 69:5–22.

Barnard, Alan and Anthony Good. 1984. *Research Practices in the Study of Kinship.* New York: Academic Press.

Barrionuevo, Alexei. 2008. Amazon's "Forest People" Seek a Role in Striking Global Climate Agreements. *New York Times.* April 5:6.

Barth, Frederik. 1993. *Balinese Worlds.* Chicago: University of Chicago Press.

Basso, Keith. H. 1972 [1970]. "To Give Up on Words": Silence in Apache Culture. In *Language and Social Context* (pp. 67–86). Pier Paolo Giglioni, ed. Baltimore: Penguin Books.

Bauer, Alexander A. 2006. Heritage Preservation in Law and Policy: Handling the Double-Edged Sword of Development. Paper presented at the International Conference on Cultural Heritage and Development, Bibliothèca Alexandrina, Alexandria, Egypt, January.

Beals, Alan R. 1980. *Gopalpur: A South Indian Village. Fieldwork Edition.* New York: Holt, Rinehart and Winston.

Beatty, Andrew. 1992. *Society and Exchange in Nias.* New York: Oxford University Press.

Beck, Lois. 1986. *The Qashqa'i of Iran.* New Haven, CT: Yale University Press.

———. 1991. *Nomad: A Year in the Life of a Qashqa'i Tribesman in Iran.* Berkeley: University of California Press.

Beeman, William O. 1993. The Anthropology of Theater and Spectacle. *Annual Review of Anthropology* 22:363–393.

Belikov, Vladimir. 1994. Language Death in Siberia. *UNESCO Courier* 1994(2):32–36.

Bell, Diane. 1998. *Ngarrindjeri Wurruwarrin: A World That Is, Was, and Will Be.* North Melbourne, Australia: Spinifex.

Bernal, Martin. 1987. *Black Athena: The Afroasiatic Roots of Classical Civilization.* New Brunswick, NJ: Rutgers University Press.

Berreman, Gerald D. 1979 [1975]. Race, Caste, and Other Invidious Distinctions in Social Stratification. In *Caste and Other Inequities: Essays on Inequality* (pp. 178–222). Gerald D. Berreman, ed. New Delhi: Manohar.

Best, David. 1986. Culture Consciousness: Understanding the Arts of Other Cultures. *Journal of Art & Design Education* 5(1&2):124–135.

Bestor, Theodore C. 2004. *Tsukiji: The Fish Market at the Center of the World.* Berkeley: University of California Press.

Beyene, Yewoubdar. 1989. *From Menarche to Menopause: Reproductive Lives of Peasant Women in Two Cultures.* Albany: State University of New York Press.

Bhardwaj, Surinder M. and N. Madhusudana Rao. 1990. Asian Indians in the United States: A Geographic Appraisal. In *South Asians Overseas: Migration and Ethnicity* (pp. 197–218). Colin Clarke, Ceri Peach, and Steven Vertovec, eds. New York: Cambridge University Press.

Bhatt, Rakesh M. 2001. World Englishes. *Annual Review of Anthropology* 30:527–550.

Bilharz, Joy. 1995. First among Equals? The Changing Status of Seneca Women. In *Women and Power in Native North America* (pp. 101–112). Laura F. Klein and Lillian A. Ackerman, eds. Norman: University of Oklahoma Press.

Billig, Michael S. 1992. The Marriage Squeeze and the Rise of Groomprice in India's Kerala State. *Journal of Comparative Family Studies* 23:197–216.

Billman, Brian R. 2002. Irrigation and the Origins of the Southern Moche State on the North Coast of Peru. *Latin American Antiquity* 13:371–400.

Binford, Leigh. 2003. Migrant Remittances and (Under) Development in Mexico. *Critique of Anthropology* 23:305–336.

Blackwood, Evelyn. 1995. Senior Women, Model Mothers, and Dutiful Wives: Managing Gender Contradictions in a Minangkabau Village. In *Bewitching Women: Pious Men: Gender and Body Politics in Southeast Asia* (pp. 124–158). Aihwa Ong and Michael Peletz, eds. Berkeley: University of California Press.

Blau, Peter M. 1964. *Exchange and Power in Social Life.* New York: Wiley.

Bledsoe, Caroline H. 1983. Stealing Food as a Problem in Demography and Nutrition. Paper presented at the annual meeting of the American Anthropological Association.

Blim, Michael. 2000. Capitalisms in Late Modernity. *Annual Review of Anthropology* 29:25–38.

Blok, Anton. 1972. The Peasant and the Brigand: Social Banditry Reconsidered. *Comparative Studies in Society and History* 14(4):494–503.

Blommaert, Jan and Chris Bulcaen. 2000. Critical Discourse Analysis. *Annual Review of Anthropology* 29:447–466.

Blood, Robert O. 1967. *Love Match and Arranged Marriage.* New York: Free Press.

Bodenhorn, Barbara. 2000. "He Used to Be My Relative." Exploring the Bases of Relatedness among the Inupiat of Northern Alaska. In *Cultures of Relatedness: New Approaches to the Study of Kinship* (pp. 128–148). Janet Carsten, ed. New York: Cambridge University Press.

Boellstorff, Tom. 2004. Gay Language and Indonesia: Registering Belonging. *Journal of Linguistic Anthropology* 14:248–268.

Bogart, Stephanie L. and Jill D. Pruetz. 2008. Ecological Context of Savanna Chimpanzee (*Pan troglodytes verus*) Termite Fishing at Fongoli, Senegal. *American Journal of Primatology* 70:605–612.

Borovoy, Amy. 2005. *The Too-Good Wife: Alcohol, Codependency, and the Politics of Nurturance in Postwar Japan.* Berkeley: University of California Press.

Boserup, Ester. 1970. *Woman's Role in Economic Development.* New York: St. Martin's Press.

Bourdieu, Pierre. 1984. *Distinction: A Social Critique of the Judgement of Taste.* Trans. Richard Nice. Cambridge, MA: Harvard University Press.

Bourgois, Philippe I. 1995. *In Search of Respect: Selling Crack in El Barrio.* New York: Cambridge University Press.

Bowen, John R. 1992. On Scriptural Essentialism and Ritual Variation: Muslim Sacrifice in Sumatra. *American Ethnologist* 19(4):656–671.

———. 1998. *Religions in Practice: An Approach to the Anthropology of Religion.* Boston: Allyn and Bacon.

Bradley, Richard. 2000. *An Archaeology of Natural Places.* New York: Routledge.

Brana-Shute, Rosemary. 1976. Women, Clubs, and Politics: The Case of a Lower-Class Neighborhood in Paramaribo, Suriname. *Urban Anthropology* 5(2):157–185.

Brandes, Stanley H. 1985. *Forty: The Age and the Symbol.* Knoxville: University of Tennessee Press.

———. 2002. *Staying Sober in Mexico City.* Austin: University of Texas Press.

Brave Heart, Mary Yellow Horse. 2004. The Historical Trauma Response among Natives and Its Relationship to Substance Abuse. In *Healing and Mental Health for Native Americans: Speaking in Red* (pp. 7–18). Ethan Nebelkopf and Mary Phillips, eds. Walnut Creek, CA: AltaMira Press.

Bray, Tamara L. 1996. Repatriation, Power Relations and the Politics of the Past. *Antiquity* 70:440–444.

Brewis, Alexandra and Mary Meyer. 2004. Marital Coitus across the Life Course. *Journal of Biosocial Science* 37(4):499–518.

Brink, Judy H. 1991. The Effect of Emigration of Husbands on the Status of Their Wives: An Egyptian Case. *International Journal of Middle East Studies* 23:201–211.

Brodkin, Karen. 2000. Global Capitalism: What's Race Got to Do with It? *American Ethnologist* 27:237–256.

Brookes, Heather. 2004. A Repertoire of South African Quotable Gestures. *Journal of Linguistic Anthropology* 14:186–224.

Brooks, Alison S. and Patricia Draper. 1998 [1991]. Anthropological Perspectives on Aging. In *Anthropology Explored: The Best of AnthroNotes* (pp. 286–297). Ruth Osterweis Selig and Marilyn R. London, eds. Washington, DC: Smithsonian Press.

Broude, Gwen J. 1988. Rethinking the Couvade: Cross-Cultural Evidence. *American Anthropologist* 90(4):902–911.

Brown, Carolyn Henning. 1984. Tourism and Ethnic Competition in a Ritual Form: The Firewalkers of Fiji. *Oceania* 54:223–244.

Brown, Judith K. 1975. Iroquois Women: An Ethnohistoric Note. In *Toward an Anthropology of Women* (pp. 235–251). Rayna R. Reiter, ed. New York: Monthly Review Press.

———. 1978. The Recruitment of a Female Labor Force. *Anthropos* 73(1/2):41–48.

———. 1999. Introduction: Definitions, Assumptions, Themes, and Issues. In *To Have and To Hit: Cultural Perspectives on Wife Beating,* 2nd ed. (pp. 3–26). Dorothy Ayers Counts, Judith K. Brown, and Jacquelyn C. Campbell, eds. Urbana: University of Illinois Press.

Brown, Peter, T. Sutikna, M. J. Morwood, R. P. Soejono, Jatmiko, E. Wayhu Saptomo, and Rokus Awe Due. 2004. A New Small-Bodied Hominin from the Late Pleistocene of Flores, Indonesia. *Nature* 431:1055–1061.

Brown, Nathan. 1990. Brigands and State Building: The Invention of Banditry in Modern Egypt. *Comparative Studies in Society and History* 32(2):258–281.

Browner, Carole H. 1986. The Politics of Reproduction in a Mexican Village. *Signs: Journal of Women in Culture and Society* 11(4): 710–724.

Browner, Carole H. and Nancy Ann Press. 1995. The Normalization of Prenatal Diagnostic Screening. In *Conceiving the New World Order: The Global Politics of Reproduction* (pp. 307–322). Faye D. Ginsberg and Rayna Rapp, eds. Berkeley: University of California Press.

———. 1996. The Production of Authoritative Knowledge in American Prenatal Care. *Medical Anthropology Quarterly* 10(2): 141–156.

Brumfiel, Elizabeth M. 1994. Introduction. In *Factional Competition and Political Development in the New World* (pp. 3–14). Elizabeth M. Brumfiel and John W. Fox, eds. New York: Cambridge University Press.

Bruner, Edward M. 2005. *Culture on Tour: Ethnographies of Travel.* Chicago: University of Chicago Press.

Brunet, Michel, F. Guy, D. Pilbeam, H. T. Mackaye, A. Likius, D. Ahounta, et al. 2002. A New Hominid from the Upper Miocene of Chad, Central Africa. *Nature* 418:145–151.

Bunzel, Ruth. 1972 [1929]. *The Pueblo Potter: A Study of Creative Imagination in Primitive Art.* New York: Dover Publications.

Burdick, John. 2004. *Legacies of Liberation: The Progressive Catholic Church in Brazil at the Turn of a New Century.* Burlington, VT: Ashgate Publishers.

Burton, Barbara. 2004. The Transmigration of Rights: Women, Movement and the Grassroots in Latin American and Caribbean Communities. *Development and Change* 35:773–798.

Call, Vaughn, Susan Sprecher, and Pepper Schwartz. 1995. The Incidence and Frequency of Marital Sex in a National Sample. *Journal of Marriage and the Family* 57:639–652.

Cameron, Mary M. 1995. Transformations of Gender and Caste Divisions of Labor in Rural Nepal: Land, Hierarchy, and the Case of Women. *Journal of Anthropological Research* 51:215–246.

Camino, Linda A. and Ruth M. Krulfeld, eds. 1994. *Reconstructing Lives, Recapturing Meaning: Refugee Identity, Gender and Culture Change.* Basel: Gordon and Breach Publishers.

Cancian, Frank. 1989. Economic Behavior in Peasant Communities. In *Economic Anthropology* (pp. 127–170). Stuart Plattner, ed. Stanford, CA: Stanford University Press.

Caplan, Pat. 1987. Celibacy as a Solution? Mahatma Gandhi and Brahmacharya. In *The Cultural Construction of Sexuality* (pp. 271–295). Pat Caplan, ed. New York: Tavistock Publications.

———. 2000. "Eating British Beef with Confidence": A Consideration of Consumers' Responses to BSE in Britain. In *Risk Revisited* (pp. 184–203). Pat Caplan, ed. Sterling, VA: Pluto Press.

Carneiro, Robert L. 1994. War and Peace: Alternating Realities in Human History. In *Studying War: Anthropological Perspectives* (pp. 3–27). S. P. Reyna and R. E. Downs, eds. Langhorne, PA: Gordon and Breach Science Publishers.

Carstairs, G. Morris. 1967. *The Twice Born.* Bloomington: Indiana University Press.

Carsten, Janet. 1995. Children in Between: Fostering and the Process of Kinship on Pulau Langkawi, Malaysia. *Man* (n.s.) 26:425–443.

Carter, William E., José V. Morales, and Mauricio P. Mamani. 1981. Medicinal Uses of Coca in Bolivia. In *Health in the Andes* (pp. 119–149). Joseph W. Bastien and John M. Donahue, eds. Washington, DC: American Anthropological Association.

Cátedra, María. 1992. *This World, Other Worlds: Sickness, Suicide, Death, and the Afterlife among the Vaqueiros de Alzada of Spain.* Chicago: University of Chicago Press.

Cernea, Michael M. 1985. Sociological Knowledge for Development Projects. In *Putting People First: Sociological Variables and Rural Development* (pp. 3–22). Michael M. Cernea, ed. New York: Oxford University Press.

———. 2001. *Cultural Heritage and Development: A Framework for Action in the Middle East and North Africa.* Washington, DC: The World Bank.

Chagnon, Napoleon. 1992. *Yanomamö,* 4th ed. New York: Harcourt Brace Jovanovich.

Chalfin, Brenda. 2004. *Shea Butter Republic: State Power, Global Markets, and the Making of an Indigenous Commodity.* New York: Routledge.

———. 2008. Cars, the Customs Service, and Sumptuary Rule in Neoliberal Ghana. *Comparative Studies in Society and History* 50:424–453.

Chanen, Jill Schachner. 1995. Reaching Out to Women of Color. *ABA Journal* 81(May):105.

Charters, Claire. 2006. An Imbalance of Powers: Maori Land Claims and an Unchecked Parliament. *Cultural Survival Quarterly* 30(1):32–35.

Chavez, Leo R. 1992. *Shadowed Lives: Undocumented Immigrants in American Society.* New York: Harcourt Brace Jovanovich.

Checker, Melissa. 2005. Polluted Promises: *Environmental Racism and the Search for Justice in a Southern Town.* New York: New York University Press.

———. 2007. "But I Know It's True": Environmental Risk Assessment, Justice, and Anthropology. *Human Organization* 66:112–124.

Chernoff, John Miller. 1979. *African Rhythm and African Sensibility: Aesthetics and African Musical Idioms.* Chicago: University of Chicago Press.

Childs, Larry and Celina Chelala. 1994. Drought, Rebellion and Social Change in Northern Mali: The Challenges Facing Tamacheq Herders. *Cultural Survival Quarterly* 18(4):16–19.

Chin, Elizabeth. 2001. *Purchasing Power: Black Kids and American Consumer Culture.* Minneapolis: University of Minnesota Press.

Chiñas, Beverly Newbold. 1992. *The Isthmus Zapotecs: A Matrifocal Culture of Mexico.* New York: Harcourt Brace Jovanovich.

Clark, Gracia. 1992. Flexibility Equals Survival. *Cultural Survival Quarterly* 16:21–24.

Clarke, Maxine Kumari. 2004. *Mapping Yorùbá Networks: Power and Agency in the Making of Transnational Communities.* Durham, NC: Duke University Press.

Clay, Jason W. 1990. What's a Nation: Latest Thinking. *Mother Jones* 15(7):28–30.

Clifford, James. 1988. *The Predicament of Culture: Twentieth Century Ethnography, Literature and Art.* Cambridge, MA: Harvard University Press.

Cochrane, D. Glynn. 1979. *The Cultural Appraisal of Development Projects.* New York: Praeger Publishers.

———. 2009. *Festival Elephants and the Myth of Global Poverty.* Boston: Pearson.

Cohen, Mark Nathan. 1989. *Health and the Rise of Civilization.* New Haven, CT: Yale University Press.

Cohen, Roberta. 2002. Nowhere to Run, No Place to Hide. *Bulletin of the Atomic Scientists* November/December:36–45.

Cohn, Bernard S. 1971. *India: The Social Anthropology of a Civilization.* New York: Prentice-Hall.

Cole, Douglas. 1991. *Chiefly Feasts: The Enduring Kwakiutl Potlatch.* Aldona Jonaitis, ed. Seattle: University of Washington Press/New York: American Museum of Natural History.

Cole, Jeffrey. 1996. Working-Class Reactions to the New Immigration in Palermo (Italy). *Critique of Anthropology* 16(2):199–220.

Colley, Sarah. 2002. *Uncovering Australia: Archaeology, Indigenous People and the Public.* Washington, DC: Smithsonian Institution Press.

Colson, Elizabeth. 1995. The Contentiousness of Disputes. In *Understanding Disputes: The Politics of Argument* (pp. 65–82). Pat Caplan, ed. Providence, RI: Berg Publishers.

Comaroff, John L. 1987. Of Totemism and Ethnicity: Consciousness, Practice and Signs of Inequality. *Ethnos* 52(3–4): 301–323.

Contreras, Gloria. 1995. Teaching about Vietnamese Culture: Water Puppetry as the Soul of the Rice Fields. *The Social Studies* 86(1):25–28.

Coon Come, Matthew. 2004. Survival in the Context of Mega-Resource Development: Experiences of the James Bay Crees and the First Nations of Canada. In *In the Way of Development: Indigenous Peoples, Life Projects and Globalization* (pp. 153–165). Mario Blaser, Harvey A. Feit, and Glenn McRae, eds. New York: Zed Books in Association with the International Development Research Centre.

Corbey, Raymond. 2000. *Arts premiers* in the Louvre. *Anthropology Today* 16:3–6.

———. 2003. Destroying the Graven Image: Religious Iconoclasm on the Christian Frontier. *Anthropology Today* 19:10–14.

Cornia, Giovanni Andrea. 1994. Poverty, Food Consumption, and Nutrition During the Transition to the Market Economy in Eastern Europe. *American Economic Review* 84(2):297–302.

Counihan, Carole M. 1985. Transvestism and Gender in a Sardinian Carnival. *Anthropology* 9(1&2):11–24.

Craik, Brian. 2004. The Importance of Working Together: Exclusions, Conflicts and Participation in James Bay, Quebec. In *In the Way of Development: Indigenous Peoples, Life Projects and Globalization* (pp. 166–186). Mario Blaser, Harvey A. Feit, and Glenn McRae, eds. Zed Books in Association with the International Development Research Centre.

Crowe, D. 1996. *A History of the Gypsies of Eastern Europe and Russia.* New York: St. Martin's Press.

Crystal, David. 2000. *Language Death.* New York: Cambridge University Press.

———. 2003. *English as a Global Language,* 2nd ed. New York: Cambridge University Press.

Cunningham, Lawrence S. 1995. Christianity. In *The HarperCollins Dictionary of Religion* (pp. 240–253). Jonathan Z. Smith, ed. New York: HarperCollins.

Curtin, Philip D. 1989. *Death by Migration: Europe's Encounter with the Tropical World in the Nineteenth Century.* New York: Cambridge University Press.

Dalby, Liza Crihfield. 1998. *Geisha,* 2nd ed. New York: Vintage Books.

———. 2001. *Kimono: Fashioning Culture.* Seattle: University of Washington Press.

Daly, Martin, and Margo Wilson. 1984. A Sociobiological Analysis of Human Infanticide. In *Infanticide: Comparative and Evolutionary Perspectives* (pp. 487–582). Glen Hausfater and Sarah Blaffer Hrdy, eds. New York: Aldine.

Danforth, Loring M. 1989. *Firewalking and Religious Healing: The Anestenaria of Greece and the American Firewalking Movement.* Princeton, NJ: Princeton University Press.

Dannhaeuser, Norbert. 1989. Marketing in Developing Urban Areas. In *Economic Anthropology* (pp. 222–252). Stuart Plattner, ed. Stanford, CA: Stanford University Press.

Daugherty, Mary Lee. 1997 [1976]. Serpent-Handling as Sacrament. In *Magic, Witchcraft, and Religion* (pp. 347–352). Arthur C. Lehmann and James E. Myers, eds. Mountain View, CA: Mayfield Publishing.

Dávila, Arlene. 2002. Culture in the Ad World: Producing the Latin Look. In *Media Worlds: Anthropology on New Terrain* (pp. 264–280). Faye D. Ginsburg, Lila Abu-Lughod, and Brian Larkin, eds. Berkeley: University of California Press.

Davis, Robert C. and Garry R. Marvin. 2004, *Venice, the Tourist Maze: A Cultural Critique of the World's Most Touristed City.* Berkeley: University of California Press.

Davis, Susan Schaefer and Douglas A. Davis. 1987. *Adolescence in a Moroccan Town: Making Social Sense.* New Brunswick: Rutgers University Press.

Davis-Floyd, Robbie E. 1987. Obstetric Training as a Rite of Passage. *Medical Anthropology Quarterly* 1:288–318.

———. 1992. *Birth as an American Rite of Passage.* Berkeley: University of California Press.

de Athayde Figueiredo, Mariza and Dando Prado. 1989. The Women of Arembepe. *UNESCO Courier* 7:38–41.

de la Cadena, Marisol. 2001. Reconstructing Race: Racism, Culture and Mestizaje in Latin America. *NACLA Report on the Americas* 34:16–23.

de Waal, Frans B. M. and Frans Lanting. 1997. *Bonobo: The Forgotten Ape.* Berkeley: University of California Press.

Dent, Alexander Sebastian. 2005. Cross-Culture "Countries": Covers, Conjuncture, and the Whiff of Nashville in *Música Sertaneja* (Brazilian Commercial Country Music). *Popular Music and Society* 28:207–227.

Devereaux, George. 1976. *A Typological Study of Abortion in Primitive Societies: A Typological, Distributional, and Dynamic Analysis of the Prevention of Birth in 400 Preindustrial Societies.* New York: International Universities Press.

Diamond, Jared. 1994 [1987]. The Worst Mistake in the History of the Human Race. In *Applying Cultural Anthropology: A Reader* (pp. 105–108). Aaron Podolefsky and Peter J. Brown, eds. Mountain View, CA: Mayfield Publishing.

DiFerdinando, George. 1999. Emerging Infectious Diseases: Biology and Behavior in the Inner City. In *Urbanism, Health, and Human Biology in Industrialised Countries* (pp. 87–110). Lawrence M. Schell and Stanley J. Ulijaszek, eds. New York: Cambridge University Press.

digim'Rina, Linus. 2006. Personal communication.

Dikötter, Frank. 1998. Hairy Barbarians, Furry Primates and Wild Men: Medical Science and Cultural Representations of Hair in China. In *Hair: Its Power and Meaning in Asian Cultures* (pp. 51–74). Alf Hiltebeitel and Barbara D. Miller, eds. Albany: State University of New York Press.

Dillehay, Thomas. 2000. *The Settlement of the Americas: A New Prehistory.* New York: Basic Books.

Divale, William T. and Marvin Harris. 1976. Population, Warfare and the Male Supremacist Complex. *American Anthropologist* 78:521–538.

Doi, Yaruko and Masami Minowa. 2003. Gender Differences in Excessive Daytime Sleepiness among Japanese Workers. *Social Science and Medicine* 56:883–894.

Donlon, Jon. 1990. Fighting Cocks, Feathered Warriors, and Little Heroes. *Play & Culture* 3:273–285.

Dorgan, Howard. 1989. *The Old Regular Baptists of Central Appalachia: Brothers and Sisters in Hope.* Knoxville: University of Tennessee Press.

Douglas, Mary. 1966. *Purity and Danger: An Analysis of Concepts of Pollution and Taboo.* New York: Penguin Books.

Drake, Susan P. 1991. Local Participation in Ecotourism Projects. In *Nature Tourism: Managing for the Environment* (pp. 132–155). Tensie Whelan, ed. Washington, DC: Island Press.

Dreifus, Claudia. 2000. Saving the Orangutan, Preserving Paradise. *New York Times*, March 21:D3.

Duany, Jorge. 2000. Nation on the Move: The Construction of Cultural Identities in Puerto Rico and the Diaspora. *American Ethnologist* 27:5–30.

Duranti, Alessandro. 1994. *From Grammar to Politics: Linguistic Anthropology in a Western Samoan Village.* Berkeley: University of California Press.

———. 1997a. *Linguistic Anthropology.* New York: Cambridge University Press.

———. 1997b. Universal and Culture-Specific Properties of Greetings. *Journal of Linguistic Anthropology* 7:63–97.

Durkheim, Emile. 1965 [1915]. *The Elementary Forms of the Religious Life.* New York: Free Press.

———. 1966 [1895]. *On the Division of Labor in Society.* Trans. G. Simpson. New York: Free Press.

Durrenberger, E. Paul. 2001. Explorations of Class and Class Consciousness in the U.S. *Journal of Anthropological Research* 57:41–60.

Earle, Timothy. 1993. The Evolution of Chiefdoms. In *Chiefdoms, Power, Economy, and Ideology* (pp. 1–15). Timothy Earle, ed. New York: Cambridge University Press.

Eck, Diana L. 1985. *Darsán: Seeing the Divine Image in India,* 2nd ed. Chambersburg, PA: Anima Books.

Eckel, Malcolm David. 1995. Buddhism. In *The HarperCollins Dictionary of Religion* (pp. 135–150). Jonathan Z. Smith, ed. New York: HarperCollins.

Economic and Social Council. 1992. *Report of the Working Group on Violence against Women.* Vienna: United Nations. E/CN.6/WG.2/1992/L.3.

Eickelman, Dale F. 1981. *The Middle East: An Anthropological Perspective.* Englewood Cliffs, NJ: Prentice-Hall.

Ember, Carol R. 1983. The Relative Decline in Women's Contribution to Agriculture with Intensification. *American Anthropologist* 85(2):285–304.

Englund, Harri. 1998. Death, Trauma and Ritual: Mozambican Refugees in Malawi. *Social Science and Medicine* 46(9):1165–1174.

Ennis-McMillan, Michael C. 2001. Suffering from Water: Social Origins of Bodily Distress in a Mexican Community. *Medical Anthropology Quarterly* 15(3):368–390.

Erickson, Barbra. 2007. Toxin or Medicine? Explanatory Models of Radon in Montana Health Mines. *Medical Anthropology Quarterly* 21:1–21.

Escobar, Arturo. 2002. Gender, Place, and Networks: A Political Ecology of Cyberculture. In *Development: A Cultural Studies Reader* (pp. 239–256). Susan Schech and Jane Haggis, eds. Malden, MA: Blackwell Publishers.

Estrin, Saul. 1996. Co-Operatives. In *The Social Science Encyclopedia* (pp. 138–139). Adam Kuper and Jessica Kuper, eds. New York: Routledge.

Etienne, Mona and Eleanor Leacock, eds. 1980. *Women and Colonization: Anthropological Perspectives.* New York: Praeger.

Evans-Pritchard, E. E. 1951. *Kinship and Marriage among the Nuer.* Oxford: Clarendon.

Everett, Daniel L. 1995. Personal communication.

———. 2005. Cultural Constraints on Grammar and Cognition in Pirahã: Another Look at Design Features in Human Language. *Current Anthropology* 46:621–634, 641–646.

———. 2008. *Don't Sleep, There Are Snakes: Life and Language in the Amazonian Jungle.* New York: Knopf Publishing Group.

Evrard, Olivier and Yves Goudineau. 2004. Planned Resettlement, Unexpected Migrations and Cultural Trauma in Laos. *Development and Change* 35:937–962.

Ewing, Katherine Pratt. 2000 Legislating Religious Freedom: Muslim Challenges to the Relationship between "Church" and "State" in Germany and France. *Daedalus* 29:31–53.

Fabrega, Horacio, Jr. and Barbara D. Miller. 1995. Adolescent Psychiatry as a Product of Contemporary Anglo-American Society. *Social Science and Medicine* 40(7):881–894.

Farmer, Paul. 1992. *AIDS and Accusation: Haiti and the Geography of Blame.* Berkeley: University of California Press.

———. 2005. *Pathologies of Power: Health, Human Rights and the New War on the Poor.* Berkeley: University of California Press.

Feinsilver, Julie M. 1993. *Healing the Masses: Cuban Health Politics at Home and Abroad.* Berkeley: University of California Press.

Feldman, Gregory. 2003. Breaking Our Silence on NATO. *Anthropology Today* 19:1–2.

Fenstemeker, Sarah. 2007. Conservation Clash and the Case for Exemptions: How Eagle Protection Conflicts with Hopi Cultural Preservation. *International Journal of Cultural Property* 14:315–328.

Fischer, Edward F. 2001. *Cultural Logics and Global Economies: Maya Identity in Thought and Practice.* Austin: University of Texas Press.

Fisher, James. 1990. *Sherpas: Reflections on Change in Himalayan Nepal.* Berkeley: University of California Press.

Fishman, Joshua A. 1991. *Reversing Language Shift: Theoretical and Empirical Foundations of Assistance to Threatened Languages.* Clevedon, UK: Multilingual Matters Ltd.

———., ed. 2001. *Can Threatened Languages Be Saved? Reversing Language Shift, Revisited: A 21st Century Perspective*. Buffalo, NY: Multilingual Matters Ltd.

Fitchen, Janet M. 1990. How Do You Know If You Haven't Listened First? Using Anthropological Methods to Prepare for Survey Research. *The Rural Sociologist* 10(2):15–22.

Fitigu, Yodit. 2005. Forgotten People: Internally Displaced Persons in Guatemala. www.refugeesinternational.org/content/article/detail/6344.

Fogelman, Arianna. 2008. Colonial Legacy in African Museology: The Case of the Ghana National Museum. *Museum Anthropology* 31:19–27.

Foley, Kathy. 2001. The Metonymy of Art: Vietnamese Water Puppetry as Representation of Modern Vietnam. *The Drama Review* 45(4):129–141.

Foley, William A. 2000. The Languages of New Guinea. *Annual Review of Anthropology* 29:357–404.

Foreign Policy. 2008. The Failed States Index 2008. Foreign Policy July/August:64–73.

Foster, George M. and Barbara Gallatin Anderson. 1978. *Medical Anthropology*. New York: Alfred A. Knopf.

Foster, Helen Bradley and Donald Clay Johnson, eds. 2003. *Wedding Dress across Cultures*. New York: Berg.

Foster, Robert J. 2002. *Materializing the Nation: Commodities, Consumption, and Media in Papua New Guinea*. Bloomington: Indiana University Press.

———. 2006. From Trobriand Cricket to Rugby Nation: The Mission of Sport in Papua New Guinea. *The International Journal of the History of Sport* 23(5):739–758.

Foucault, Michel. 1970. *The Order of Things: An Archaeology of the Human Sciences*. New York: Random House.

———. 1977. *Discipline and Punish: The Birth of the Prison*. New York: Pantheon Books.

Fox, Robin. 1995 [1978]. *The Tory Islanders: A People of the Celtic Fringe*. Notre Dame: University of Notre Dame Press.

Frake, Charles O. 1961. The Diagnosis of Disease among the Subanun of Mindanao. *American Anthropologist* 63:113–132.

Franke, Richard W. 1993. *Life is a Little Better: Redistribution as a Development Strategy in Nadur Village, Kerala*. Boulder, CO: Westview Press.

Frankel, Francine R. 1971. *India's Green Revolution: Economic Gains and Political Costs*. Princeton, NJ: Princeton University Press.

Fratkin, Elliot. 1998. *Ariaal Pastoralists of Kenya: Surviving Drought and Development in Africa's Arid Lands*. Boston: Allyn and Bacon.

Fratkin, Elliot, Kathleen Galvin, and Eric A. Roth, eds. 1994. *African Pastoralist Systems: An Integrated Approach*. Boulder, CO: Westview Press.

Frazer, Sir James. 1978 [1890]. *The Golden Bough: A Study in Magic and Religion*. New York: Macmillan.

Freedman, Diane C. 1986. Wife, Widow, Woman: Roles of an Anthropologist in a Transylvanian Village. In *Women in the Field: Anthropological Experiences* (pp. 333–358). Peggy Golde, ed. Berkeley: University of California Press.

Freeman, James A. 1981. A Firewalking Ceremony That Failed. In *Social and Cultural Context of Medicine in India* (pp. 308–336). Giri Raj Gupta, ed. New Delhi: Vikas Publishing.

French, Howard W. 2006. In a Richer China, Billionaires Put Money on Marriage. *The New York Times* January 24:A4.

Frieze, Irene et al. 1978. *Women and Sex Roles: A Social Psychological Perspective*. New York: W. W. Norton.

Furst, Peter T. 1989. The Water of Life: Symbolism and Natural History on the Northwest Coast. *Dialectical Anthropology* 14:95–115.

Gable, Eric. 1995. The Decolonization of Consciousness: Local Skeptics and the "Will to Be Modern" in a West African Village. *American Ethnologist* 22(2):242–257.

Gage-Brandon, Anastasia J. 1992. The Polygyny-Divorce Relationship: A Case Study of Nigeria. *Journal of Marriage and the Family* 54:282–292.

Galdikas, Biruté. 1995. *Reflections of Eden: My Years with the Orangutans of Borneo*. Boston: Little, Brown.

Gale, Faye, Rebecca Bailey-Harris, and Joy Wundersitz. 1990. *Aboriginal Youth and the Criminal Justice System: The Injustice of Justice?* New York: Cambridge University Press.

Gardner, Katy and David Lewis. 1996. *Anthropology, Development and the Post-Modern Challenge*. Sterling, VA: Pluto Press.

Garland, David. 1996. Social Control. In *The Social Science Encyclopedia* (pp. 780–783). Adam Kuper and Jessica Kuper, eds. Routledge: New York.

Gaski, Harald. 1993. The Sami People: The "White Indians" of Scandinavia. *American Indian Culture and Research Journal* 17:115–128.

———. 1997. Introduction: Sami Culture in a New Era. In *Sami Culture in a New Era: The Norwegian Sami Experience* (pp. 9–28). Harald Gaski, ed. Seattle: University of Washington Press.

Geertz, Clifford. 1966. Religion as a Cultural System. In *Anthropological Approaches to the Study of Religion* (pp. 1–46). Michael Banton, ed. London: Tavistock.

Gilbert, M. Thomas P., Dennis L. Jenkins, Anders Götherstrom, Nuria Naveran, Juan J. Sanchez, Michael Hofreiter, Philip Francis Thomsen, Jonas Binladen, Thomas F. G. Higham, Robert M. Yohe, II, Robert Parr, Linda Scott Cummings, Eske Willerslev. 2008. DNA from Pre-Clovis Human Coprolites in Oregon, North America, *Science* 320(5877):786–780.

Gill, Lesley. 1997. Creating Citizens, Making Men: The Military and Masculinity in Bolivia. *Cultural Anthropology* 12:527–550.

———. 2006. Personal communication.

Gillette, Maris Boyd. 2000. *Between Mecca and Beijing: Modernization and Consumption among Urban Chinese Families*. Stanford: Stanford University Press.

Gilligan, Ian. 2007. Neanderthal Extinction and Modern Human Behavior: The Role of Climate Change and Clothing. *World Archaeology* 39:499–514.

Gilman, Antonio. 1991. Trajectories towards Social Complexity in the Later Prehistory of the Mediterranean. In *Chiefdoms: Power, Economy and Ideology* (pp. 146–168). Timothy Earle, ed. New York: Cambridge University Press.

Ginsberg, Faye D. and Rayna Rapp. 1991. The Politics of Reproduction. *Annual Review of Anthropology* 20:311–343.

Glick Schiller, Nina and Georges E. Fouron. 1999. Terrains of Blood and Nation: Haitian Transnational Social Fields. *Ethnic and Racial Studies* 22:340–365.

Gmelch, George. 1997 [1971]. Baseball Magic. In *Magic, Witchcraft, and Religion* (pp. 276–282). Arthur C. Lehmann and James E. Myers, eds. Mountain View, CA: Mayfield Publishing.

Godelier, Maurice. 1971. "Salt Currency" and the Circulation of Commodities among the Baruya of New Guinea. In *Studies in Economic Anthropology* (pp. 52–73). George Dalton, ed. Anthropological Studies No. 7. Washington, DC: American Anthropological Association.

Godoy, Ricardo, Victoria Reyes-García, Tomás Huanca, William R. Leonard, Vincent Valdez, Cynthia Valdés-Galicia, and Dakun

Zhao. 2005. Why Do Subsistence-Level People Join the Market Economy? Testing Hypotheses of Push and Pull Determinants in Bolivian Amazonia. *Journal of Anthropological Research* 61:157–178.

Gold, Stevan J. 1992. *Refugee Communities: A Comparative Field Study.* Newbury Park: Sage Publications.

———. 1995. *From the Workers' State to the Golden State: Jews from the Former Soviet Union in California.* Boston: Allyn and Bacon.

Goldstein, Melvyn C. and Cynthia M. Beall. 1994. *The Changing World of Mongolia's Nomads.* Berkeley: University of California Press.

Goldstein-Gidoni, Ofra. 2003. Producers of "Japan" in Israel: Cultural Appropriation in a Non-Colonial Context. *Ethnos* 68(3): 365–390.

Goldstone, Jack. 1996. Revolutions. In *The Social Science Encyclopedia* (pp. 740–743). Adam Kuper and Jessica Kuper, eds. New York: Routledge.

González, Nancie L. 1970. Toward a Definition of Matrifocality. In *Afro-American Anthropology: Contemporary Perspectives* (pp. 231–244). Norman E. Whitten, Jr. and John F. Szwed, eds. New York: Free Press.

Goodwin, Marjorie H. 1990. *He-Said-She-Said: Talk as Social Organization among Black Children.* Bloomington: Indiana University Press.

Goody, Jack. 1993. *The Culture of Flowers.* New York: Cambridge University Press.

Goossens, Benoît, Lounès Chikhi, Marc Ancrenaz, Isabelle Lackman-Ancrenaz, Patrick Andau, and Michael W. Bruford. 2006. Genetic Signature of Anthropogenic Population Collapse in Orangutans. *PloS Biology* 4(2):e25. www.plosbiology.org.

Graeber, David. 2004. Fragments of an Anarchist Anthropology. *Paradigm* 14. Chicago: Prickly Paradigm Press.

Greenhalgh, Susan. 2008. *Just One Child: Science and Policy in Deng's China.* Berkeley: University of California Press.

Gregg, Jessica L. 2003. *Virtually Virgins: Sexual Strategies and Cervical Cancer in Recife, Brazil.* Stanford: Stanford University Press.

Gregor, Thomas. 1982. No Girls Allowed. *Science* 82.

Gremillion, Helen. 1992. Psychiatry as Social Ordering: Anorexia Nervosa, a Paradigm. *Social Science and Medicine* 35(1):57–71.

Grenier, Guillermo J., Alex Stepick, Debbie Draznin, Aileen LaBorwit, and Steve Morris. 1992. On Machines and Bureaucracy: Controlling Ethnic Interaction in Miami's Apparel and Construction Industries. In *Structuring Diversity: Ethnographic Perspectives on the New Immigration* (pp. 65–94). Louise Lamphere, ed. Chicago: University of Chicago Press.

Grinker, Roy Richard. 1994. *Houses in the Rainforest: Ethnicity and Inequality among Farmers and Foragers in Central Africa.* Berkeley: University of California Press.

Gross, Daniel R. 1984. Time Allocation: A Tool for the Study of Cultural Behavior. *Annual Review of Anthropology* 13:519–558.

Gruenbaum, Ellen. 2001. *The Female Circumcision Controversy: An Anthropological Perspective.* Philadelphia: University of Pennsylvania Press.

Guggenheim, Scott E. and Michael M. Cernea. 1993. Anthropological Approaches to Involuntary Resettlement: Policy, Practice, and Theory. In *Anthropological Approaches to Resettlement: Policy, Practice, and Theory* (pp. 1–12). Michael M. Cernea and Scott E. Guggenheim, eds. Boulder, CO: Westview Press.

Gugler, Josef. 1988. The Urban Character of Contemporary Revolutions. In *The Urbanization of the Third World* (pp. 399–412). Josef Gugler, ed. New York: Oxford University Press.

Guidoni, Enrico. 1987. *Primitive Architecture.* Trans. Robert Erich Wolf. New York: Rizzoli.

Günes-Ayata, Ayse. 1995. Women's Participation in Politics in Turkey. In *Women in Modern Turkish Society: A Reader* (pp. 235–249). Sirin Tekeli, ed. London: Zed Books.

Gusterson, Hugh. 2007. *Anthropology and Militarism.* Annual Review of Anthropology 36:155–175.

Hacker, Andrew. 1992. *Two Nations: Black and White, Separate, Hostile, Unequal.* New York: Ballantine Books.

Haddix McCay, Kimber. 2001. Leaving Your Wife and Your Brothers: When Polyandrous Marriages Fall Apart. *Evolution and Human Behavior* 22:47–60.

Hamabata, Matthews Masayuki. 1990. *Crested Kimono: Power and Love in the Japanese Business Family.* Ithaca, NY: Cornell University Press.

Handler, Richard. 2003. Cultural Property and Cultural Theory. *Journal of Social Archaeology* 3:353–365.

Harragin, Simon. 2004. Relief and Understanding of Local Knowledge: The Case of Southern Sudan. In *Culture and Public Action* (pp. 307–327). Vijayendra Rao and Michael Walton, eds. Stanford, CA: Stanford University Press.

Harris, Marvin. 1974. *Cows, Pigs, Wars and Witches: The Riddles of Culture.* New York: Random House.

———. 1975. *Culture, People, Nature: An Introduction to General Anthropology,* 2nd ed. New York: Thomas Y. Crowell.

———. 1977. *Cannibals and Kings: The Origins of Culture.* New York: Random House.

———. 1984. Animal Capture and Yanomamo Warfare: Retrospect and New Evidence. *Journal of Anthropological Research* 40(10):183–201.

———. 1993. The Evolution of Human Gender Hierarchies. In *Sex and Gender Hierarchies* (pp. 57–80). Barbara D. Miller, ed. New York: Cambridge University Press.

Hart, C. W. M., Arnold R. Pilling, and Jane C. Goodale. 1988. *The Tiwi of North Australia.* New York: Holt, Rinehart and Winston.

Hart, Gillian. 2002. *Disabling Globalization: Places of Power in Post-Apartheid South Africa.* Berkeley: University of California Press.

Harper, Krista. 2005. "Wild Capitalism" and "Ecocolonialism": A Tale of Two Rivers. *American Ethnologist* 107:221–233.

Hastrup, Kirsten. 1992 Anthropological Visions: Some Notes on Visual and Textual Authority. In *Film as Ethnography* (pp. 8–25). Peter Ian Crawford and David Turton, eds. Manchester: University of Manchester Press.

Hawn, Carleen. 2002. Please Feedback the Animals. *Forbes* 170(9):168–169.

Haynes, Gary. 2002. *The Early Settlement of North America: The Clovis Era.* New York: Cambridge University Press.

Hefner, Robert W. 1998. Multiple Modernities: Christianity, Islam, and Hinduism in a Globalizing Age. *Annual Review of Anthropology* 27:83–104.

Heise, Lori L., Jacqueline Pitanguy, and Adrienne Germain. 1994. Violence against Women: The Hidden Health Burden. *World Bank Discussion Papers No. 255.* Washington, DC: The World Bank.

Helweg, Arthur W. and Usha M. Helweg. 1990. *An Immigrant Success Story: East Indians in America.* Philadelphia: University of Pennsylvania Press.

Henshaw, Anne. 2006. Pausing along the Journey: Learning Landscapes, Environmental Change, and Toponymy amongst the Sikusilarmiut. *Arctic Anthropology* 43(1):52–66.

Herzfeld, Michael. 1985. *The Poetics of Manhood: Contest and Identity in a Cretan Mountain Village.* Princeton, NJ: Princeton University Press.

Hewlett, Barry S. 1991. *Intimate Fathers: The Nature and Context of Aka Pygmy Paternal Care.* Ann Arbor: University of Michigan Press.

Hill, Jane H. 2001. Dimensions of Attrition in Language Death. In *On Biocultural Diversity: Linking Language, Knowledge, and the Environment* (pp. 175–189). Luisa Maffi, ed. Washington, DC: Smithsonian Institution Press.

Hill, Jane H. and Bruce Mannheim. 1992. Language and World View. *Annual Review of Anthropology* 21:381–406.

Hiltebeitel, Alf. 1988. *The Cult of Draupadi: Mythologies from Gingee to Kuruksetra.* Chicago: University of Chicago Press.

Hirschon, Renee. 1989. *Heirs of the Catastrophe: The Social Life of Asia Minor Refugees in Piraeus.* New York: Oxford University Press.

Hoberg, E. P., N. L. Lalkire, A. de Queroz, and A. Jones. 2001. Out of Africa: Origins of the Taenia Tapeworms. *Proceedings of the Royal Society of London, Series B* 268:718–787.

Hobsbawm, Eric J. 1969. *Bandits,* 2nd ed. New York: Delacorte Press.

Hodge, Robert W. and Naohiro Ogawa. 1991. *Fertility Change in Contemporary Japan.* Chicago: University of Chicago Press.

Hodgson, Dorothy L. 2004. *Once Intrepid Warriors: Gender, Ethnicity, and the Cultural Politics of Maasai Development.* Bloomington: Indiana University Press.

Hoffman, Danny and Stephen Lubkemann. 2005. Warscape Ethnography in West Africa and the Anthropology of "Events." *Anthropological Quarterly* 78:315–327.

Holland, Dorothy C. and Margaret A. Eisenhart. 1990. *Educated in Romance: Women, Achievement, and College Culture.* Chicago: University of Chicago Press.

Hopkins, Nicholas S. and Sohair R. Mehanna. 2000. Social Action against Everyday Pollution in Egypt. *Human Organization* 59:245–254.

Hornbein, George and Marie Hornbein. 1992. *Salamanders: A Night at the Phi Delt House.* Video. College Park: Documentary Resource Center.

Horowitz, Irving L. 1967. *The Rise and Fall of Project Camelot: Studies in the Relationship between Social Science and Practical Politics.* Boston: MIT Press.

Horowitz, Michael M. and Muneera Salem-Murdock. 1993. Development-Induced Food Insecurity in the Middle Senegal Valley. *GeoJournal* 30(2):179–184.

Horst, Heather and Daniel Miller. 2005. From Kinship to Link-Up: Cell Phones and Social Networking in Jamaica. *Current Anthropology* 46:755–764, 773–778.

Howell, Nancy. 1979. *Demography of the Dobe !Kung.* New York: Academic Press.

———. 1986. Feedbacks and Buffers in Relation to Scarcity and Abundance: Studies of Hunter-Gatherer Populations. In *The State of Population Theory: Forward from Malthus* (pp. 156–187). David Coleman and Roger Schofield, eds. New York: Basil Blackwell.

———. 1990. *Surviving Fieldwork: A Report of the Advisory Panel on Health and Safety in Fieldwork.* Washington, DC: American Anthropological Association.

Hublin, Jean-Jacques. 2000. Modern–Nonmodern Hominid Interactions: A Mediterranean Perspective. In *The Geography of Neanderthals and Modern Humans in Europe and the Greater Mediterranean* (pp. 157– 182). Ofer Bar-Yosef and David Pilbeam, eds. Cambridge, MA: Harvard University, Peabody Museum of Archaeology and Ethnology, Peabody Museum Bulletin 8.

Hughes, Charles C. and John M. Hunter. 1970. Disease and "Development" in Africa. *Social Science and Medicine* 3:443–493.

Hughes, Lotte. 2003. *The No-Nonsense Guide to Indigenous Peoples.* London: Verso.

Hunte, Pamela A. 1985. Indigenous Methods of Fertility Regulation in Afghanistan. In *Women's Medicine: A Cross-Cultural Study of Indigenous Fertility Regulation* (pp. 44–75). Lucile F. Newman, ed. New Brunswick, NJ: Rutgers University Press.

Hutchinson, Sharon E. 1996. *Nuer Dilemmas: Coping with Money, War, and the State.* Berkeley: University of California Press.

Hutter, Michael. 1996. The Value of Play. In *The Value of Culture: On the Relationship between Economics and the Arts* (pp. 122–137). Arjo Klamer, ed. Amsterdam: Amsterdam University Press.

Illo, Jeanne Frances I. 1985. Who Heads the Household? Women in Households in the Philippines. Paper presented at the Women and Household Regional Conference for Asia, New Delhi.

Ingman, M. H., H. Kaessmann, S. Pääbo, and U. Gyllensten. 2000. Mitochondrial Genome Variation and the Origin of Modern Humans. *Nature* 408:708–713.

Inhorn, Marcia C. 2003. Global Infertility and the Globalization of New Reproductive Technologies: Illustrations from Egypt. *Social Science and Medicine* 56:1837–1851.

———. 2004. Middle Eastern Masculinities in the Age of New Reproductive Technologies: Male Infertility and Stigma in Egypt and Lebanon. *Medical Anthropology Quarterly* 18(2): 162–182.

International Classification of Diseases. Geneva: World Health Organization.

IUCN/SSC Conservation Breeding Specialist Group. 2004. *Orangutan: Population and Habitat Viability Assessment: Final Report.* Apple Valley, MN: IUCN/SSC Conservation Breeding Specialist Group. www.cbsg.org.

Jacobs-Huey, Lanita. 1997. Is There an Authentic African American Speech Community: Carla Revisited. *University of Pennsylvania Working Papers in Linguistics* 4(1):331–370.

———. 2002. The Natives Are Gazing and Talking Back: Reviewing the Problematics of Positionality, Voice, and Accountability among "Native" Anthropologists. *American Anthropologist* 104:791–804.

———. 2006. *From the Kitchen to the Parlor: Language and Becoming in African American Women's Hair Care.* New York: Oxford University Press.

Jaeggi, Adrian V., Maria A. van Noordwijk, and Carel P. van Schaik. 2008. Begging for Information: Mother-Offspring Food Sharing among Wild Bornean Orangutans. *American Journal of Primatology* 70:544–541.

Janes, Craig R. 1995. The Transformations of Tibetan Medicine. *Medical Anthropology Quarterly* 9(1):6–39.

Jankowski, Martín Sánchez. 1991. *Islands in the Street: Gangs and American Urban Society.* Berkeley: University of California Press.

Jenkins, Gwynne. 2003. Burning Bridges: Policy, Practice, and the Destruction of Midwifery in Rural Costa Rica. *Social Science and Medicine* 56:1893–1909.

Jenkins, Gwynne L. and Marcia C. Inhorn. 2003. Reproduction Gone Awry: Medical Anthropology Perspectives. *Social Science and Medicine* 56:1831–1836.

Jensen, Marianne Wiben, ed. Elaine Bolton, trans. 2004. Land Rights: A Key Issue. *Indigenous Affairs* 4.

Jiang, David W. 1994. Shanghai Revisited: Chinese Theatre and the Forces of the Market. *The Drama Review* 38(2):72–80.

Jinadu, L. Adele. 1994. The Dialectics of Theory and Research on Race and Ethnicity in Nigeria. In *"Race," Ethnicity and Nation: International Perspectives on Social Conflict* (pp. 163–178). Peter Ratcliffe, ed. London: University College of London Press.

Johanson, Donald C. 2004. Lucy, Thirty Years Later: An Expanded View of *Australopithecus afarensis. Journal of Anthropological Research* 60(44):465–486.

Johnson, Walter R. 1994. *Dismantling Apartheid: A South African Town in Transition.* Ithaca, NY: Cornell University Press.

Johnson-Hanks, Jennifer. 2002. On the Limits of Life Stages in Ethnography: Toward a Theory of Vital Conjectures. *American Anthropologist* 104:865–880.

Johnston, Barbara Rose. 1994. Environmental Degradation and Human Rights Abuse. In *Who Pays the Price? The Sociocultural Context of Environmental Crisis* (pp. 7–16). Barbara Rose Johnston, ed. Washington, DC: Island Press.

Jones, Anna Laura. 1993. Exploding Canons: The Anthropology of Museums. *Annual Review of Anthropology* 22:201–220.

Joralemon, Donald. 1982. New World Depopulation and the Case of Disease. *Journal of Anthropological Research* 38:108–127.

Jordan, Brigitte. 1983. *Birth in Four Cultures,* 3rd ed. Montreal: Eden Press.

Joseph, Suad. 1994. Brother/Sister Relationships: Connectivity, Love, and Power in the Reproduction of Patriarchy in Lebanon. *American Ethnologist* 21:50–73.

Jourdan, Christine. 1995. Masta Liu. In *Youth Cultures: A Cross-Cultural Perspective* (pp. 202–222). Vered Amit-Talai and Helena Wulff, eds. New York: Routledge.

Judd, Ellen. 2002. *The Chinese Women's Movement: Between State and Market.* Stanford, CA: Stanford University Press.

Kahn, Miriam. 1995. Heterotopic Dissonance in the Museum Representation of Pacific Island Cultures. *American Anthropologist* 97(2):324–338.

Karan, P. P. and Cotton Mather. 1985. Tourism and Environment in the Mount Everest Region. *Geographical Review* 75(1):93–95.

Kassam, Aneesa. 2002. Ethnodevelopment in the Oromia Regional State of Ethiopia. In *Participating in Development: Approaches to Indigenous Knowledge* (pp. 65–81). Paul Sillitoe, Alan Bicker, and Johan Pottier, eds. ASA Monographs No. 39. New York: Routledge.

Katz, Nathan and Ellen S. Goldberg. 1989. Asceticism and Caste in the Passover Observances of the Cochin Jews. *Journal of the American Academy of Religion* 57(1):53–81.

Katz, Richard. 1982. *Boiling Energy: Community Healing among the Kalahari Kung.* Cambridge, MA: Harvard University Press.

Kaul, Adam. 2004. The Anthropologist as Barman and Tour-Guide: Reflections on Fieldwork in a Touristed Destination. *Durham Anthropology Journal* 12:22–36.

Kawamura, S. 1959. The Process of Subculture Propagation among Japanese Macaques. *Primates* 2:43–60.

Kehoe, Alice Beck. 1989. *The Ghost Dance: History and Revitalization.* Philadelphia: Holt.

Keiser, R. Lincoln. 1986. Death Enmity in Thull: Organized Vengeance and Social Change in a Kohistani Community. *American Ethnologist* 13(3):489–505.

Kelly, Patty. 2008. *Lydia's Open Door: Inside Mexico's Most Modern Brothel.* Berkeley: University of California Press.

Kendon, A. 1998. Parallels and Divergences between Warlpiri Sign Language and Spoken Warlpiri: Analyses of Spoken and Signed Discourse. *Oceania* 58:239–254.

Kennedy, David P. and Stephen G. Perz. 2000. Who Are Brazil's Indígenas? Contributions of Census Data Analysis to Anthropological Demography of Indigenous Populations. *Human Organization* 59:311–324.

Kerns, Virginia. 1999. Preventing Violence against Women: A Central American Case. In *To Have and To Hit: Cultural Perspectives on Wife Beating,* 2nd ed. (pp. 153–168). Dorothy Ayers Counts, Judith K. Brown, and Jacquelyn C. Campbell, eds. Urbana: University of Illinois Press.

Kesmanee, Chupinit. 1994. Dubious Development Concepts in the Thai Highlands: The Chao Khao in Transition. *Law & Society Review* 28:673–683.

Khanaaneh, Rhoda. 2005. Boys or Men? Duped or "Made"? Palestinian Soldiers in the Israeli Military. *American Ethnologist* 32:250–275.

Kirsch, Stuart. 2002. Anthropology and Advocacy: A Case Study of the Campaign against the Ok Tedi Mine. *Critique of Anthropology* 22:175–200.

Klima, Alan. 2002. *The Funeral Casino: Meditation, Massacre, and Exchange with the Dead in Thailand.* Princeton: Princeton University Press.

Knott, Kim. 1996. Hindu Women, Destiny and Stridharma. *Religion* 26:15–35.

Kolenda, Pauline M. 1978. *Caste in Contemporary India: Beyond Organic Solidarity.* Prospect Heights, IL: Waveland Press.

Kondo, Dorinne. 1997. *About Face: Performing "Race" in Fashion and Theater.* New York: Routledge.

Konner, Melvin. 1989. Homosexuality: Who and Why? *New York Times Magazine.* April 2:60–61.

Kottak, Conrad Phillip. 1985. When People Don't Come First: Some Sociological Lessons from Completed Projects. In *Putting People First: Sociological Variables and Rural Development* (pp. 325–356). Michael M. Cernea, ed. New York: Oxford University Press.

———. 1992. *Assault on Paradise: Social Change in a Brazilian Village.* New York: McGraw-Hill.

Kovats-Bernat, J. Christopher. 2002. Negotiating Dangerous Fields: Pragmatic Strategies for Fieldwork amid Violence and Terror. *American Anthropologist* 104:1–15.

Kramer, Jennifer. 2005. Personal communication.

Krantzler, Nora J. 1987. Traditional Medicine as "Medical Neglect": Dilemmas in the Case Management of a Samoan Teenager with Diabetes. In *Child Survival: Cultural Perspectives on the Treatment and Maltreatment of Children* (pp. 325–337). Nancy Scheper-Hughes, ed. Boston: D. Reidel.

Kraybill, Donald B. and Steven M. Nolt. 2004. *Amish Enterprise: From Plows to Profits,* 2nd ed. Baltimore, MD: Johns Hopkins University Press.

Kroeber, A. L. and Clyde Kluckhohn. 1952. *Culture: A Critical Review of Concepts and Definitions.* New York: Vintage Books.

Kuipers, Joel C. 1991. Matters of Taste in Weyéwa. In *The Varieties of Sensory Experience: A Sourcebook in the Anthropology of the Senses* (pp. 111–127). David Howes, ed. Toronto: University of Toronto Press.

Kuipers, Joel C. and Ray McDermott. 1996. Insular Southeast Asian Scripts. In *The World's Writing Systems* (pp. 474–484). Peter T. Daniels and William Bright, eds. New York: Oxford University Press.

Kumar, Krishna. 1996. Civil Society. In *The Social Science Encyclopedia* (pp. 88–90). Adam Kuper and Jessica Kuper, eds. New York: Routledge.

Kuwayama, Takami. 2004. *Native Anthropology: The Japanese Challenge to Western Academic Hegemony.* Melbourne: Trans Pacific Press.

Labov, William. 1966. *The Social Stratification of English in New York City.* Washington, DC: Center for Applied Linguistics.

Lacey, Marc. 2002. Where 9/11 News Is Late, But Aid Is Swift. *New York Times* June 3:A1, A7.

Ladányi, János. 1993. Patterns of Residential Segregation and the Gypsy Minority in Budapest. *International Journal of Urban and Regional Research* 17(1):30–41.

Laderman, Carol. 1988. A Welcoming Soil: Islamic Humoralism on the Malay Peninsula. In *Paths to Asian Medical Knowledge* (pp. 272–288). Charles Leslie and Allan Young, eds. Berkeley: University of California Press.

LaFleur, William. 1992. *Liquid Life: Abortion and Buddhism in Japan.* Princeton, NJ: Princeton University Press.

Lakoff, Robin. 1973. Language and Woman's Place. *Language in Society* 2:45–79.

———. 1990. *Talking Power: The Politics of Language in Our Lives.* New York: Basic Books.

LaLone, Mary B. 2003. Walking the Line between Alternative Interpretations in Heritage Education and Tourism: A Demonstration of the Complexities with an Appalachian Coal Mining Example. In *Signifying Serpents and Mardi Gras Runners: Representing Identity in Selected Souths* (pp. 72–92). Southern Anthropological Proceedings, No. 36. Celeste Ray and Luke Eric Lassiter, eds. Athens: University of Georgia Press.

Lane, Sandra D., Robert H. Keefe, Robert A. Rubenstein, Brooke A. Levandowski, Michael Freedman, Alan Rosenthal, Donald A. Cibula, and Maria Czerwinski. 2004. Marriage Promotion and Missing Men: African American Women in a Demographic Double Bind. *Medical Anthropology Quarterly* 18:405–428.

Lanehart, Sonja L. 1999. African American Vernacular English. In *Handbook of Language and Ethnic Identity* (pp. 211–225). Joshua A. Fishman, ed. New York: Oxford University Press.

Larsen, Ulla and Marida Hollos. 2003. Women's Empowerment and Fertility Decline among the Pare of Kilimanjaro Region, Northern Tanzania. *Social Science and Medicine* 57:1099–1115.

Larsen, Ulla and Sharon Yan. 2000. Does Female Circumcision Affect Infertility and Fertility? A Study of the Central African Republic, Côte d'Ivoire, and Tanzania. *Demography* 37:313–321.

Lassiter, Luke Eric, Hurley Goodall, Elizabeth Campbell, and Michelle Natasya Johnson. 2004. *The Other Side of Middletown: Exploring Muncie's African American Community.* Walnut Creek, CA: AltaMira Press.

Lawler, Andrew. 2001. Writing Gets a Rewrite. *Science* 292:2418–2420.

Leakey, Louis S. B., P. V. Tobias, and J. R. Napier. 1964. A New Species of the Genus *Homo* from Olduvai Gorge. *Nature* 202:7–9.

Lederer, Edith. 2006. Record Number of Women in Politics. *Guardian Weekly,* March 10–15:9.

Lee, Gary R. and Mindy Kezis. 1979. Family Structure and the Status of the Elderly. *Journal of Comparative Family Studies* 10:429–443.

Lee, Helen Morton. 2003. *Tongans Overseas: Between Two Shores.* Honolulu: University of Hawai'i Press.

Lee, Richard B. 1969. Eating Christmas in the Kalahari. *Natural History,* December 14–22, 60–63.

———. 1979. *The !Kung San: Men, Women, and Work in a Foraging Society.* New York: Cambridge University Press.

Lee, Wai-Na and David K. Tse. 1994. Becoming Canadian: Understanding How Hong Kong Immigrants Change Their Consumption. *Pacific Affairs* 67(1):70–95.

Lempert, David. 1996. *Daily Life in a Crumbling Empire.* 2 volumes. New York: Columbia University Press.

Lepowsky, Maria. 1990. Big Men, Big Women, and Cultural Autonomy. *Ethnology* 29(10):35–50.

Lesher, James H., trans. 2001. *Xenophanes of Colophon: Fragments.* Toronto: University of Toronto Press.

Lessinger, Johanna. 1995. *From the Ganges to the Hudson: Indian Immigrants in New York City.* Boston: Allyn and Bacon.

Levine, Robert, Suguru Sato, Tsukasa Hashimoto, and Jyoti Verma. 1995. Love and Marriage in Eleven Cultures. *Journal of Cross-Cultural Psychology* 26:554–571.

Levinson, David. 1989. *Family Violence in Cross-Cultural Perspective.* Newbury Park, CA: Sage Publications.

Lévi-Strauss, Claude. 1967. *Structural Anthropology.* New York: Anchor Books.

———. 1968. *Tristes Tropiques: An Anthropological Study of Primitive Societies in Brazil.* New York: Atheneum.

———. 1969 [1949]. *The Elementary Structures of Kinship.* Boston: Beacon Press.

Levy, Jerrold E., Eric B. Henderson, and Tracy J. Andrews. 1989. The Effects of Regional Variation and Temporal Change in Matrilineal Elements of Navajo Social Organization. *Journal of Anthropological Research* 45(4):351–377.

Lincoln, Kenneth. 1993. *Indi'n Humor: Bicultural Play in Native America.* New York: Oxford University Press.

Lindenbaum, Shirley. 1979. *Kuru Sorcery: Disease and Danger in the New Guinea Highlands.* Mountain View, CA: Mayfield Publishing.

Linnekan, Jocelyn. 1990. *Sacred Queens and Women of Consequence: Rank, Gender, and Colonialism in the Hawaiian Islands.* Ann Arbor: University of Michigan Press.

Lock, Margaret. 1993. *Encounters with Aging: Mythologies of Meno pause in Japan and North America.* Berkeley: University of California Press.

Loker, William. 2000. Sowing Discord, Planting Doubts: Rhetoric and Reality in an Environment and Development Project in Honduras. *Human Organization* 59:300–310.

———. 2004. *Changing Places: Environment, Development, and Social Change in Rural Honduras.* Durham, NC: Carolina Academic Press.

Long, Susan Orpett. 2005. *Final Days: Japanese Culture and Choice at the End of Life.* Honolulu: University of Hawai'i Press.

Lorch, Donatella. 2003. Do Read This for War. *Newsweek* 141(11):13.

Low, Setha M. 1995. Indigenous Architecture and the Spanish American Plaza in Mesoamerica and the Caribbean. *American Anthropologist* 97(4):748–762.

Lubkemann, Stephen C. 2002. Refugees. In *World at Risk: A Global Issues Sourcebook* (pp. 522–544). Washington, DC: CQ Press.

———. 2005. Migratory Coping in Wartime Mozambique: An Anthropology of Violence and Displacement in "Fragmented Wars." *Journal of Peace Research* 42:493–508.

Lutz, Ellen L. 2005. The Many Meanings of Technology: A Message from our Executive Editor. *Cultural Survival Quarterly* 29(2):5.

Lyman, Rick. 2006. Reports Reveal Hurricanes' Impact on Human Landscape. *New York Times,* May 6, p. A16.

Lyttleton, Chris. 2004. Relative Pleasures: Drugs, Development and Modern Dependencies in Asia's Golden Triangle. *Development and Change* 35:909–935.

MacCormack, Sabine. 2001. Cuzco, Another Rome? In *Empires: Perspectives from Archaeology and History* (pp. 419–435). Susan E. Alcock, Terence N. D'Altroy, Kathleen D. Morrison, and Carla M. Sinopoli, eds. New York: Cambridge University Press.

MacLeod, Arlene Elowe. 1992. Hegemonic Relations and Gender Resistance: The New Veiling as Accommodating Protest in Cairo. *Signs: The Journal of Women in Culture and Society* 17(3):533–557.

Macnair, Peter. 1995. From Kwakiutl to Kwakwa ka'wakw. In *Native Peoples: The Canadian Experience,* 2nd ed. (pp. 586–605). R. Bruce Morrison and C. Roderick Wilson, eds. Toronto: McClelland & Stewart.

Maffi, Luisa. 2005. Linguistic, Cultural, and Biological Diversity. *Annual Review of Anthropology* 34:599–617.

Magga, Ole Henrik and Tove Skutnabb-Kangas. 2001. The Saami Languages: The Present and the Future. *Cultural Survival Quarterly* 25(2):26–31.

Magliocco, Sabina. 2004. *Witching Culture: Folklore and Neo-Paganism in America.* Philadelphia: University of Pennsylvania Press.

Mahler, Sarah J. 1995. *Salvadorans in Suburbia: Symbiosis and Conflict.* Boston: Allyn and Bacon.

Major, Marc R. 1996. No Friends but the Mountains: A Simulation on Kurdistan. *Social Education* 60(3):C1–C8.

Makepeace, James M. 1997. Courtship Violence as Process: A Developmental Theory. In *Violence between Intimate Partners: Patterns, Causes, and Effects* (pp. 29–47). Albert P. Cardarelli, ed. Boston: Allyn and Bacon.

Malinowski, Bronislaw. 1929. *The Sexual Life of Savages.* New York: Harcourt, Brace & World.

———. 1961 [1922]. *Argonauts of the Western Pacific.* New York: E. P. Dutton & Co.

———. 1962 [1926]. *Crime and Custom in Savage Society.* Paterson, NJ: Littlefield, Adams & Co.

Mamdani, Mahmoud. 1972. *The Myth of Population Control: Family, Caste, and Class in an Indian Village.* New York: Monthly Review Press.

Manz, Beatriz. 2004. *Paradise in Ashes: A Guatemalan Journey of Courage, Terror, and Hope.* Berkeley: University of California Press.

March, Kathryn S. and Rachell L. Taqqu. 1986. *Women's Informal Associations in Developing Countries: Catalysts for Change?* Boulder, CO: Westview Press.

Marcus, George. 1995. Ethnography in/of the World System: The Emergence of Multi-Sited Ethnography. *Annual Review of Anthropology* 24:95–117.

Marcus, Joyce. 1998. The Peaks and Valleys of Ancient States: An Extension of the Dynamic Model. In *Archaic States* (pp. 59–94). Gary M. Feinman and Joyce Marcus, eds. Santa Fe, NM: School of American Research Press.

Margolis, Maxine L. and Marigene Arnold. 1993. Turning the Tables? Male Strippers and the Gender Hierarchy in America. In *Sex and Gender Hierarchies* (pp. 334–350). Barbara D. Miller, ed. New York: Cambridge University Press.

Marshall, Fiona and Elisabeth Hildebrand. 2002. Cattle before Crops: The Beginnings of Food Production in Africa. *Journal of World Prehistory* 16:99–143.

Marshall, Robert C. 1985. Giving a Gift to the Hamlet: Rank, Solidarity and Productive Exchange in Rural Japan. *Ethnology* 24:167–182.

Martin, Richard C. 1995. Islam. In *The HarperCollins Dictionary of Religion* (pp. 498–513). Jonathan Z. Smith, ed. New York: HarperCollins.

Martin, Sarah. 2005. *Must Boys Be Boys? Ending Sexual Exploitation and Abuse in UN Peacekeeping Missions.* Washington, DC: Refugees International.

Martínez, Samuel. 1996. Indifference with Indignation: Anthropology, Human Rights, and the Haitian Bracero. *American Anthropologist* 98(1):17–25.

Masquelier, Adeline. 2005. The Scorpion's Sting: Youth, Marriage and the Struggle for Social Maturity in Niger. *Journal of the Royal Anthropological Institute* 11:59–83.

Maybury-Lewis, David. 1997a. Museums and Indigenous Cultures. *Cultural Survival Quarterly* 21(1):3.

———. 1997b. *Indigenous Peoples, Ethnic Groups, and the State.* Boston: Allyn and Bacon.

McCallum, Cecilia. 2005. Explaining Caesarean Section in Salvador da Bahia, Brazil. *Sociology of Health and Illness* 27(2):215–242.

McCallum, Cecilia and Ana Paula dos Reis. 2005. Childbirth as Ritual in Brazil: Young Mothers' Experiences. *Ethnos* 70(3):335–360.

McDonald, James H. 2005. The Narcoeconomy in Small-Town, Rural Mexico. *Human Organization* 64:115–125.

McElroy, Ann and Patricia K. Townsend. 1996. *Medical Anthropology in Ecological Perspective,* 3rd ed. Boulder, CO: Westview Press.

McGrew, William. 2004. *The Cultured Chimpanzee: Reflections on Cultural Primatology.* New York: Cambridge University Press.

Mead, Margaret. 1928 [1961]. *Coming of Age in Samoa: A Psychological Study of Primitive Youth for Western Civilization.* New York: Dell Publishing.

Meador, Elizabeth. 2005. The Making of Marginality: Schooling for Mexican Immigrants in the Rural Southwest. *Anthropology and Education Quarterly* 36(2):149–164.

Meigs, Anna S. 1984. *Food, Sex, and Pollution: A New Guinea Religion.* New Brunswick, NJ: Rutgers University Press.

Mencher, Joan P. 1974. The Caste System Upside Down, or The Not-So-Mysterious East. *Current Anthropology* 15(4):469–493.

Mernissi, Fatima. 1987. *Beyond the Veil: Male-Female Dynamics in Modern Muslim Society.* Revised edition. Bloomington: Indiana University Press.

Merry, Sally Engle. 1992. Anthropology, Law, and Transnational Processes. *Annual Review of Anthropology* 21:357–379.

Michaelson, Evelyn Jacobson and Walter Goldschmidt. 1971. Female Roles and Male Dominance among Peasants. *Southwestern Journal of Anthropology* 27:330–352.

Michaud, Catherine M., W. Scott Gordon, and Michael R. Reich. 2005. *The Global Burden of Disease Due to Schistosomiasis.* Cambridge: Harvard School of Public Health, Harvard Center for Population and Development Studies, Schistosomiasis Research Program Working Paper Series. Volume 14, Number 1.

Miller, Barbara D. 1993. Surveying the Anthropology of Sex and Gender Hierarchies. In *Sex and Gender Hierarchies* (pp. 3–31). Barbara D. Miller, ed. New York: Cambridge University Press.

———. 1997 [1981]. *The Endangered Sex: Neglect of Female Children in Rural North India,* 2nd ed. New Delhi: Oxford University Press.

———. 2009. Putting People First in Cultural Heritage Advocacy. In *Cultural Heritage Policies and Issues in Global Perspective.* George S. Smith and Phyllis Messenger, eds. Gainesville: University of Florida Press.

Miller, Barbara D. and Showkat Hayat Khan. 1986. Incorporating Voluntarism into Rural Development in Bangladesh. *Third World Planning Review* 8(2):139–152.

Miller, Bruce G. 1994. Contemporary Native Women: Role Flexibility and Politics. *Anthropologica* 36:57–72.

Miller, Daniel, ed. 2001. *Car Cultures.* New York: Berg.

Miller, Laura. 2004. Those Naughty Teenage Girls: Japanese Kogals, Slang, and Media Assessments. *Journal of Linguistic Anthropology* 14:225–247.

———. 2006. *Beauty Up: Exploring Contemporary Japanese Body Aesthetics.* Berkeley: University of California Press.

Mills, Mary Beth. 1995. Attack of the Widow Ghosts: Gender, Death, and Modernity in Northeast Thailand. In *Bewitching*

Women, Pious Men: Gender and Body Politics in Southeast Asia (pp. 44–273). Aihwa Ong and Michael G. Peletz, eds. Berkeley: University of California Press.

Milton, Katherine. 1984. The Role of Food-Processing Factors in Primate Food Choice. In *Adaptations for Foraging in Nonhuman Primates: Contributions to an Organismal Biology of Prosimians, Monkeys, and Apes* (pp. 249–279). P. S. Rodman and J. G. H. Cant, eds. New York: Columbia University Press.

———. 1992. Civilization and Its Discontents. *Natural History* 3(92):37–92.

Miner, Horace. 1965 [1956]. Body Ritual among the Nacirema. In *Reader in Comparative Religion: An Anthropological Approach* (pp. 414–418). William A. Lessa and Evon Z. Vogt, eds. New York: Harper & Row.

Mines, Mattison. 1994. *Public Faces, Private Voices: Community and Individuality in South India.* Berkeley: University of California Press.

Mintz, Sidney. 1985. *Sweetness and Power: The Place of Sugar in Modern History*. New York: Viking.

Miyazawa, Setsuo. 1992. *Policing in Japan: A Study on Making Crime.* Frank G. Bennett, Jr. with John O. Haley, trans. Albany: State University of New York Press.

Moberg, Mark. 1991. Citrus and the State: Factions and Class Formation in Rural Belize. *American Ethnologist* 18(20):215–233.

Modell, Judith S. 1994. *Kinship with Strangers: Adoption and Interpretations of Kinship in American Culture.* Berkeley: University of California Press.

Moerman, Daniel. 2002. *Meaning, Medicine and the "Placebo" Effect.* New York: Cambridge University Press.

Mogelonsky, Marcia. 1995. Asian-Indian Americans. *American Demographics* 17(8):32–39.

Montgomery, Heather. 2001. *Modern Babylon: Prostituting Children in Thailand.* New York: Bergahn Books.

Moore, A. M. T., G. C. Hillman, and A. J. Legge. 2000. *Village on the Euphrates: The Excavation of Abu Hureyra.* Oxford: Oxford University Press.

Moore, John H. 1999. *The Cheyenne.* Malden, MA: Blackwell Publishers.

Moore, Molly. 2008. In France, Prisons Filled with Muslims. *Washington Post* April 29:A1, A4.

Morris, Rosalind. 1994. Three Sexes and Four Sexualities: Redressing the Discourses on Gender and Sexuality in Contemporary Thailand. *Positions* 2:15–43.

Mortland, Carol A. 1994. Khmer Buddhism in the United States: Ultimate Questions. In *Cambodian Culture Since 1975: Homeland and Exile* (pp. 72–90). May M. Ebihara, Carol A. Mortland, and Judy Ledgerwood, eds. Ithaca, NY: Cornell University Press.

Morwood, M. J., R. P. Soejono, R. G. Roberts, T. Sutikna, C. S. M. Turney, K. E. Westaway, et al. 2004. Achaeology and Age of a New Hominin from Flores in Eastern Indonesia. *Nature* 431:1087–1091.

Mukerjee, Madhusree. 2005. Lessons on Island Living. Samar: South Asian Magazine for Action and Reflection. www.samarmagazine.org/archive/article.

Mullings, Leith. 2005. Towards an Anti-Racist Anthropology: Interrogating Racism. *Annual Review of Anthropology* 34: 667–693.

Murdock, George Peter. 1965 [1949]. *Social Structure.* New York: Free Press.

Murphy, Yolanda and Robert F. Murphy. 1985. *Women of the Forest.* New York: Columbia University Press.

Murray, Gerald F. 1987. The Domestication of Wood in Haiti: A Case Study of Applied Evolution. In *Anthropological Praxis: Translating Knowledge into Action* (pp. 233–240). Robert M. Wulff and Shirley J. Fiske, eds. Boulder, CO: Westview Press.

Myerhoff, Barbara. 1978. *Number Our Days.* New York: Simon and Schuster.

Myers, James. 1992. Nonmainstream Body Modification: Genital Piercing, Branding, Burning, and Cutting. *Journal of Contemporary Ethnography* 21(3):267–306.

Nadeau, Kathleen M. 2002. *Liberation Theology in the Philippines: Faith in a Revolution*. Westport: Praeger.

Nader, Laura. 1972. Up the Anthropologist—Perspectives Gained from Studying Up. In *Reinventing Anthropology* (pp. 284–311). Dell Hymes, ed. New York: Vintage Books.

———. 1995. Civilization and Its Negotiations. In *Understanding Disputes: The Politics of Argument* (pp. 39–64). Pat Caplan, ed. Providence, RI: Berg Publishers.

———. 2001. Harmony Coerced Is Freedom Denied. *The Chronicle of Higher Education.* July 13:B1.

Nag, Moni. 1972. Sex, Culture and Human Fertility: India and the United States. *Current Anthropology* 13:231–238.

———. 1983. Modernization Affects Fertility. *Populi* 10:56–77.

Nag, Moni, Benjamin N. F. White, and R. Creighton Peet. 1978. An Anthropological Approach to the Study of the Economic Value of Children in Java and Nepal. *Current Anthropology* 19(2):293–301.

Nanda, Serena. 1990. *Neither Man nor Woman: The Hijras of India.* Belmont, CA: Wadsworth.

Natcher, David C., Susan Davis, and Clifford G. Hickey. 2005. Co-Management: Managing Relationships, Not Resources. *Human Organization* 64:240–250.

National Park Service. 2005. *Low Country Gullah Culture: Special Resource Study and Final Environmental Impact Statement*. Atlanta: NPS Southeast Regional Office. www.nps.gov.

Neff, Deborah L. 1994. The Social Construction of Infertility: The Case of the Matrilineal Nayars in South India. *Social Science and Medicine* 39(4):475–485.

Nettle, Daniel and Suzanne Romaine. 2000. *Vanishing Voices: The Extinction of the World's Languages*. New York: Oxford University Press.

Neusner, Jacob. 1995. Judaism. In *The HarperCollins Dictionary of Religion* (pp. 598–607). Jonathan Z. Smith, ed. New York: HarperCollins.

Nevins, M. Eleanor. 2004. Learning to Listen: Confronting Two Meanings of Language Loss in the Contemporary White Mountain Apache Speech Community. *Journal of Linguistic Anthropology* 14:269–288.

Newman, Lucile. 1972. *Birth Control: An Anthropological View.* Module No. 27. Reading, MA: Addison-Wesley.

———, ed. 1985. *Women's Medicine: A Cross-Cultural Study of Indigenous Fertility Regulation.* New Brunswick, NJ: Rutgers University Pres.

Ngokwey, Ndolamb. 1988. Pluralistic Etiological Systems in Their Social Context: A Brazilian Case Study. *Social Science and Medicine* 26:793–802.

Nichter, Mark. 1992. Of Ticks, Kings, Spirits and the Promise of Vaccines. In *Paths to Asian Medical Knowledge* (pp. 224–253). Charles Leslie and Allan Young, eds. Berkeley: University of California Press.

———. 1996. Vaccinations in the Third World: A Consideration of Community Demand. In *Anthropology and International Health: Asian Case Studies* (pp. 329–365). Mark Nichter and Mimi Nichter, eds. Amsterdam: Gordon and Breach Publishers.

Nordstrom, Carolyn. 1997. *A Different Kind of War Story.* Philadelphia: University of Pennsylvania Press.

Norgaard, Richard B. 1994. *Development Betrayed: The End of Progress and the Coevolutionary Revisioning of the Future.* New York: Routledge.

Obeyesekere, Gananath. 1981. *Medusa's Hair: An Essay on Personal Symbols and Religious Experience.* Chicago: University of Chicago Press.

Ochoa, Carlos M. 1991. *The Potatoes of South America: Bolivia.* Trans. Donald Nugent. New York: Cambridge University Press.

Ochs, Elinor. 1993. Indexing Gender. In *Sex and Gender Hierarchies* (pp. 146–169). Barbara D. Miller, ed. New York: Cambridge University Press.

O'Hara, Sean J. and Phyllis C. Lee. 2006. High Frequency of Post-coital Penis Cleaning in Budongo Chimpanzees. *Folia Primatologica* 77:353–358.

O'Higgins, Paul and Sarah Elton. 2007. Walking on Trees. *Science* 316:1292–1294.

Ohnuki-Tierney, Emiko. 1980. Shamans and Imu: Among Two Ainu Groups. In *The Culture-Bound Syndromes* (pp. 91–110). Ronald C. Simons and Charles C. Hughes, eds. Dordrecht: D. Reidel Publishing.

———. 1994. Brain Death and Organ Transplantation: Cultural Bases of Medical Technology. *Current Anthropology* 35(3): 233–242.

Oliver-Smith, Anthony. 2002. Theorizing Disasters: Nature, Power, and Culture. In *Catastrophe and Culture: The Anthropology of Disaster* (pp. 23–47). Anthony Oliver-Smith and Susannah Hoffman, eds. Sante Fe, NM: School of American Research Press.

Olsen, Teresa, Gabrielle M. Maxwell, and Allison Morris. 1995. Maori and Youth Justice in New Zealand. In *Popular Justice and Community Regeneration: Pathways of Indigenous Reform* (pp. 45–65). Kayleen M. Hazlehurst, ed. Westport, CT: Praeger.

Ong, Aihwa. 1995. State versus Islam: Malay Families, Women's Bodies, and the Body Politic in Malaysia. In *Bewitching Women, Pious Men: Gender and Body Politics in Southeast Asia* (pp. 159–194). Aihwa Ong and Michael G. Peletz, eds. Berkeley: University of California Press.

———. 2003. *Buddha Is Hiding: Refugees, Citizenship, the New America.* Berkeley: University of California Press.

Ongley, Patrick. 1995. Post-1945 International Migration: New Zealand, Australia and Canada Compared. *International Migration Review* 29(3):765–793.

Ortner, Sherry. 1999. *Life and Death on Mt. Everest: Sherpas and Himalayan Mountaineering.* Princeton, NJ: Princeton University Press.

Osha, Sanya. 2006. Birth of the Ogoni Protest Movement. *Journal of Asian and African Studies* 41:13–38.

Pääbo, Svante. 2003. The Mosaic That Is Our Genome. *Nature* 421:409-412.

Paine, Robert. 2004. Saami Reindeer Pastoralism: Quo Vadis? *Ethnos* 69:23–42.

Pappas, Gregory. 1989. *The Magic City: Unemployment in a Working-Class Community.* Ithaca, NY: Cornell University Press.

Parry, Jonathan P. 1996. Caste. In *The Social Science Encyclopedia* (pp. 76–77). Adam Kuper and Jessica Kuper, eds. New York: Routledge.

Pasquino, Gianfranco. 1996. Democratization. In *The Social Science Encyclopedia* (pp. 173–174). Adam Kuper and Jessica Kuper, eds. Routledge: New York.

Patterson, Thomas C. 2001. *A Social History of Anthropology in the United States.* New York: Berg.

Pauketat, Timothy R. 2004. *Ancient Cahokia and the Mississippians.* New York: Cambridge University Press.

Peacock, James L. and Dorothy C. Holland. 1993. The Narrated Self: Life Stories in Process. *Ethos* 21(4):367–383.

Pedelty, Mark. 1995. *War Stories: The Culture of Foreign Correspondents.* New York: Routledge.

Peletz, Michael. 1987. The Exchange of Men in 19th-Century Negeri Sembilan (Malaya). *American Ethnologist* 14(3): 449–469.

———. 2006. Transgenderism and Gender Pluralism in Southeast Asia since Early Modern Times. *Current Anthropology* 47(2): 309–325, 333–340.

Pelto, Pertti. 1973. *The Snowmobile Revolution: Technology and Social Change in the Arctic.* Menlo Park, CA: Cummings.

People's Daily. 2003. Xi'an Protects Oldest Residential Area. April 9.

Peregrine, Peter N., ed. 1992. *Mississippian Evolution: A World System Perspective.* Madison, WI: Prehistory Press.

Perin, Constance. 1988. *Belonging in America: Reading between the Lines.* Madison: University of Wisconsin Press.

Perry, Richard J. 1996. *From Time Immemorial: Indigenous Peoples and State Systems.* Austin: University of Texas Press.

Pessar, Patricia R. 1995. *A Visa for a Dream: Dominicans in the United States.* Boston: Allyn and Bacon.

Petryna, Adriana, Andrew Lakoff, and Arthur Kleinman, eds. 2007. *Global Pharmaceuticals: Ethics, Markets, Practices.* Durham, NC: Duke University Press.

Pew Center. 2008. One in 100: Behind Bars in America. www.pewcenteronthestates.org

Plant, Roger. 1994. *Land Rights and Minorities.* London: Minority Rights Group.

Plattner, Stuart. 1989. Markets and Marketplaces. In *Economic Anthropology* (pp. 171–208). Stuart Plattner, ed. Stanford, CA: Stanford University Press.

Poirier, Sylvie. 1992. "Nomadic" Rituals: Networks of Ritual Exchange between Women of the Australian Western Desert. *Man* 27:757–776.

Pollock, Susan. 1999. *Ancient Mesopotamia: The Eden That Never Was.* Cambridge: Cambridge University Press.

Population Reference Bureau. 2005. *2005 World Population Data Sheet.* Washington, DC: Population Reference Bureau.

Posey, Darrell Addison. 1990. Intellectual Property Rights: What Is the Position of Ethnobiology? *Journal of Ethnobiology* 10:93–98.

Potter, Jack M. 1976. *Thai Peasant Social Structure.* Chicago: University of Chicago Press.

Potter, Sulamith Heins. 1977. *Family Life in a Northern Thai Village: A Study in the Structural Significance of Women.* Berkeley: University of California Press.

Potuoğlu-Cook, Öykü. 2006. Beyond the Glitter: Belly Dance and Neoliberal Gentrification in Istanbul. *Cultural Anthropology* 21:633–660.

Pratt, Jeff. 2007. Food Values: The Local and the Authentic. *Critique of Anthropology* 27:285–300.

Price, David. 2003. Personal communication, response to "Six Questions Survey," author's files, Washington, DC.

Pruetz, J. D., S. J. Fulton, L. F. Marchant, W. C. McGrew, M. Schiel, and M. Walker. 2008. Arboreal Nesting as an Anti-Predator Adaptation by Savanna Chimpanzees (*Pan troglodytes verus*) in Southeastern Senegal. *American Journal of Primatology* 70:393–401.

Psychology Today. 1995. Child Support. 28:16.

Purdum, Elizabeth D. and J. Anthony Paredes. 1989. *Facing the Death Penalty: Essays on Cruel and Unusual Punishment.* Philadelphia: Temple University Press.

Quilter, Jeffrey. 2002. Moche Politics, Religion, and Warfare. *Journal of World Prehistory* 16:145–195.

Quintana-Murci, L. O., O. Semino, G. Bandelt, K. Passarino, K. McElreavey, and S. Santachiara-Benerecetti. 1999. Genetic Evidence of an Early Exit of Homo sapiens sapiens from Africa through Eastern Africa. *Nature Genetics* 23:437–441.

Raheja, Gloria Goodwin. 1988. *The Poison in the Gift: Ritual, Presentation, and the Dominant Caste in a North Indian Village.* Chicago: University of Chicago Press.

Ramesh, A., C. R. Srikumari, and S. Sukumar. 1989. Parallel Cousin Marriages in Madras, Tamil Nadu: New Trends in Dravidian Kinship. *Social Biology* 36(3/4):248–254.

Ramphele, Mamphela. 1996. Political Widowhood in South Africa: The Embodiment of Ambiguity. *Daedalus* 125(1):99–17.

Raphael, Dana. 1975. Matrescence: Becoming a Mother: A "New/Old" *Rite de Passage.* In *Being Female: Reproduction, Power and Change* (pp. 65–72). Dana Raphael, ed. The Hague: Mouton Publishers.

Rathje, William and Cullen Murphy. 1992. *Rubbish! The Archaeology of Garbage.* New York: Harper & Row.

Reid, Russell M. 1992. Cultural and Medical Perspectives on Geophagia. *Medical Anthropology* 13:337–351.

Reiner, R. 1996. Police. In *The Social Science Encyclopedia* (pp. 619–621). Adam Kuper and Jessica Kuper, eds. New York: Routledge.

Rende Taylor, Lisa. 2005. Dangerous Trade-Offs: The Behavioral Ecology of Child Labor and Prostitution in Rural Northern Thailand. *Current Anthropology* 46:411–423, 428–431.

Reyna, Stephen P. 1994. A Mode of Domination Approach to Organized Violence. In *Studying War: Anthropological Perspectives* (pp. 29–65). S. P. Reyna and R. E. Downs, eds. Langhorne, PA: Gordon and Breach Science Publishers.

Rich, Bruce. 1994. *Mortgaging the Earth: The World Bank, Environmental Impoverishment, and the Crisis of Development.* Boston: Beacon Press.

Richmond, Brian G. and William L. Jungers. 2008. *Orrorin tugenensis* Femoral Morphology and the Evolution of Hominin Bipedalism. *Science* 319(5870):1662–1665.

Rickford, John. 1997. Unequal Partnership: Sociolinguistics and the African American Speech Community. *Language in Society* 26:161–198.

Robertson, Jennifer. 1991. *Native and Newcomer: Making and Remaking a Japanese City.* Berkeley: University of California Press.

Rogers, Barbara. 1979. *The Domestication of Women: Discrimination in Developing Societies.* New York: St. Martin's Press.

Rosaldo, Renato. 1980. *Ilongot Headhunting 1883–1974: A Study in Society and History.* Stanford, CA: Stanford University Press.

Roscoe, Will. 1991. *The Zuni Man-Woman.* Albuquerque: University of New Mexico Press.

Rose, Jerome C., Thomas J. Green, and Victoria D. Green. 1996. NAGPRA Is Forever: Osteology and the Repatriation of Skeletons. *Annual Review of Anthropology* 25:81–103.

Roseman, Marina. 1987. Inversion and Conjuncture: Male and Female Performance among the Temiar of Peninsular Malaysia. In *Women and Music in Cross-Cultural Perspective* (pp. 131–149). Ellen Koskoff, ed. New York: Greenwood Press.

Rosenberger, Nancy. 1992. Images of the West: Home Style in Japanese Magazines. In *Re-Made in Japan: Everyday Life and Consumer Taste in a Changing Society* (pp. 106–125). James J. Tobin, ed. New Haven, CT: Yale University Press.

Rosenblatt, Paul C., Patricia R. Walsh, and Douglas A. Jackson. 1976. *Grief and Mourning in Cross-Cultural Perspective.* New Haven, CT: HRAF Press.

Ross, Marc Howard. 1993. *The Culture of Conflict: Interpretations and Interests in Comparative Perspective.* New Haven, CT: Yale University Press.

Roy, Arundhati. 1999. *The Cost of Living.* New York: Modern Library.

Rubel, Arthur J., Carl W. O'Nell, and Rolando Collado-Ardon. 1984. *Susto: A Folk Illness.* Berkeley: University of California Press.

Rubin, Gayle. 1975. The Traffic in Women: Notes on the "Political Economy" of Sex. In *Toward an Anthropology of Women* (pp. 157–210). Rayna R, Rapp, ed. New York: Monthly Review Press.

Sachs, Aaron. 1996. Dying for Oil. *WorldWatch* June:10–21.

Sahlins, Marshall. 1963. Poor Man, Rich Man, Big Man, Chief. *Comparative Studies in Society and History* 5:285–303.

Saitoti, Tepilit Ole. 1986. *The Worlds of a Maasai Warrior.* New York: Random House.

Salam, Nawaf A. 1994. Between Repatriation and Resettlement: Palestinian Refugees in Lebanon. *Journal of Palestine Studies* 24:18–27.

Salamandra, Christa. 2004. *A New Old Damascus: Authenticity and Distinction in Urban Syria.* Bloomington: Indiana University Press.

Sanday, Peggy Reeves. 1973. Toward a Theory of the Status of Women. *American Anthropologist* 75:1682–1700.

———. 1990. *Fraternity Gang Rape: Sex, Brotherhood, and Privilege on Campus.* New York: New York University Press.

———. 1996. *A Woman Scorned: Date Rape on Trial.* New York: Doubleday.

———. 2002. *Women at the Center: Life in a Modern Matriarchy.* Ithaca, NY: Cornell University Press.

Sanders, Douglas E. 1999. Indigenous Peoples: Issues of Definition. *International Journal of Cultural Property* 8:4–13.

Sanders, William B. 1994. *Gangbangs and Drive-Bys: Grounded Culture and Juvenile Gang Violence.* New York: Aldine de Gruyter.

Sanjek, Roger. 1990. A Vocabulary for Fieldnotes. In *Fieldnotes: The Making of Anthropology* (pp. 92–138). Roger Sanjek, ed. Ithaca, NY: Cornell University Press.

———. 2000. Keeping Ethnography Alive in an Urbanizing World. *Human Organization* 53:280–288.

Sant Cassia, Paul. 1993. Banditry, Myth, and Terror in Cyprus and Other Mediterranean Societies. *Comparative Studies in Society and History* 35(4):773–795.

Sargent, Carolyn F. 2005. Counselling Contraception for Malian Migrants in Paris: Global, State and Personal Politics. *Human Organization* 64:147–156.

Sault, Nicole L. 1985. Baptismal Sponsorship as a Source of Power for Zapotec Women of Oaxaca, Mexico. *Journal of Latin American Lore* 11(2):225–243.

Savishinsky, Joel S. 1974. *The Trail of the Hare: Life and Stress in an Arctic Community.* New York: Gordon and Breach.

———. 1991. *The Ends of Time: Life and Work in a Nursing Home.* New York: Bergin & Garvey.

Schaft, Kai and David L. Brown. 2000. Social Capital and Grassroots Development: The Case of Roma Self-Governance in Hungary. *Social Problems* 47(2):201–219.

Scheffel, David Z. 2004. Slovak Roma on the Threshold of Europe. *Anthropology Today* 20(1):6–12.

Scheper-Hughes, Nancy. 1992. *Death without Weeping: The Violence of Everyday Life in Brazil.* Berkeley: University of California Press.

Schlegel, Alice. 1995. A Cross-Cultural Approach to Adolescence. *Ethos* 23(1):15–32.

Schlegel, Alice and Herbert Barry III. 1991. *Adolescence: An Anthropological Inquiry.* New York: Free Press.

Scott, James C. 1985. *Weapons of the Weak: Everyday Forms of Peasant Resistance.* New Haven, CT: Yale University Press.

———. 1998. *Seeing Like a State: How Certain Schemes to Improve the Human Condition Have Failed.* New Haven, CT: Yale University Press.

Scrimshaw, Susan. 1984. Infanticide in Human Populations: Societal and Individual Concerns. In *Infanticide: Comparative and Evolutionary Perspectives* (pp. 463–486). Glenn Hausfater and Sarah Blaffer Hrdy, eds. New York: Aldine.

Scudder, Thayer. 1973. The Human Ecology of Big Dam Projects: River Basin Development and Resettlement. *Annual Review of Anthropology* 2:45–55.

Semaw, Seleshi, M. J. Rogers, J. Quade, P. Renne, R. F. Butler, M. Dominguez-Rodrigo, et al. 2003. 2.6-Million-Year-Old Stone Tools and Associated Bones from OGS-6 and OGS-7, Gona, Ethiopia. *Journal of Human Evolution* 45:169–177.

Sen, Amartya. 1981. *Poverty and Famines: An Essay on Entitlement and Deprivation.* New York: Oxford University Press.

Senghas, Richard J. and Leila Monaghan. 2002. Signs of Their Times: Deaf Communities and the Culture of Language. *Annual Review of Anthropology* 31:69–97.

Sentumbwe, Nayinda. 1995. Sighted Lovers and Blind Husbands: Experience of Blind Women in Uganda. In *Disability and Culture* (pp. 159–173). Benedicte Ingstad and Susan Reynolds, eds. Berkeley: University of California Press.

Senut, Brigitte, M. Pickford, D. Gommery, P. Mein, K. Cheboi, and Y. Coppens. 2001. First Hominid from the Miocene (Lukeino Formation, Kenya). *Comptes Rendus de l'Academie des Sciences, Paris* 332:137–144.

Shachtman, Tom. 2006. *Rumspringa: To Be or Not to Be Amish.* New York: North Point Press.

Shahrani, Nazif M. 2002. War, Factionalism, and the State in Afghanistan. *American Anthropologist* 104:715–722.

Shanklin, Eugenia. 2000. Representations of Race and Racism in American Anthropology. *Current Anthropology* 41(1):99–103.

Shapiro, Thomas M. 2004. *The Hidden Cost of Being African American.* New York: Oxford University Press.

Sharff, Jagna Wojcicka. 1995. "We Are All Chickens for the Colonel": A Cultural Materialist View of Prisons. In *Science, Materialism, and the Study of Culture* (pp. 132–158). Martin F. Murphy and Maxine L. Margolis, eds. Gainesville: University of Florida Press.

Sharp, Lesley. 1990. Possessed and Dispossessed Youth: Spirit Possession of School Children in Northwest Madagascar. *Culture, Medicine and Psychiatry* 14:339–364.

Shenhav-Keller, Shelly. 1993. The Israeli Souvenir: Its Text and Context. *Annals of Tourism Research* 20:182–196.

Shibamoto, Janet. 1987. The Womanly Woman: Manipulation of Stereotypical and Nonstereotypical Features of Japanese Female Speech. In *Language, Gender, and Sex in Comparative Perspective* (pp. 26–49). Susan U. Philips, Susan Steel, and Christine Tanz, eds. New York: Cambridge University Press.

Shipton, Parker. 2001. Money. In *The Dictionary of Anthropology* (pp. 327–329). Malden, MA: Blackwell Thomas Barfield, ed.

Shore, Bradd. 1998. Status Reversal: The Coming of Age in Samoa. In *Welcome to Middle Age! (And Other Cultural Fictions)* (pp. 101–138). Richard A. Shweder, ed. Chicago: University of Chicago Press.

Short, James F. 1996. Gangs. In *The Social Science Encyclopedia* (pp. 325–326). Adam Kuper and Jessica Kuper, eds. New York: Routledge.

Shostak, Marjorie. 1981. *Nisa: The Life and Times of a !Kung Woman.* Cambridge, MA: Harvard University Press.

Shu-Min, Huang. 1993. A Cross-Cultural Experience: A Chinese Anthropologist in the United States. In *Distance Mirrors: America as a Foreign Culture* (pp. 39–45). Philip R. DeVita and James D. Armstrong, eds. Belmont, CA: Wadsworth.

Shweder, Richard A. 2003. *Why Do Men Barbecue? Recipes for Cultural Psychology.* Cambridge, MA: Harvard University Press.

Sidnell, Jack. 2000. *Primus inter pares:* Storytelling and Male Peer Groups in an Indo-Guyanese Rumshop. *American Ethnologist* 27:72–99.

Silva, Noenoe K. 2004. *Aloha Betrayed: Native Hawaiian Resistance to American Colonialism.* Durham, NC: Duke University Press.

Silverstein, Michael. 1997. Encountering Language and Languages of Encounter in North American Ethnohistory. *Journal of Linguistic Anthropology* 6:126–144.

Singh, K. S. 1994. *The Scheduled Tribes. Anthropological Survey of India, People of India, National Series Volume III.* Delhi: Oxford University Press.

Siskind, Janet. 1992. The Invention of Thanksgiving: A Ritual of American Nationality. *Critique of Anthropology* 12(2):167–191.

Skocpol, Theda. 1979. *States and Social Revolutions: A Comparative Analysis of France, Russia, and China.* New York: Cambridge University Press.

Smith, Bruce D. 1998. *The Emergence of Agriculture.* New York: Scientific American Library.

Smith, Jennie M. 2001. *When the Hands Are Many: Community Organization and Change in Rural Haiti.* Ithaca, NY: Cornell University Press.

Smith, Jonathan Z., ed. 1995. *The HarperCollins Dictionary of Religion.* New York: HarperCollins.

Smith, Laurajane, Anna Morgan, and Anita van der Meer. 2003. Community-Driven Research in Cultural Heritage Management: The Waanyi Women's History Project. *International Journal of Heritage Studies* 9(1):65–80.

Smitherman, Geneva. 1997. "The Chain Remain the Same": Communicative Practices in the Hip Hop Nation. *Black Studies* 28(1):3–25.

Snajdr, Edward. 2005. Gender, Power, and the Performance of Justice: Muslim Women's Responses to Domestic Violence in Kazakhstan. *American Ethnologist* 32:294–311.

Sobel, Elizabeth and Gordon Bettles. 2000. Winter Hunger, Winter Myths: Subsistence Risk and Mythology among the Klamath and Modoc. *Journal of Anthropological Archaeology* 19:276–316.

Soh, Chunghee Sarah. 1993. *Women in Korean Politics,* 2nd ed. Boulder, CO: Westview Press.

Solomon, Maui and Leo Watson. 2001. The Waitungi Tribunal and the Māori Claim to the Cultural and Intellectual Heritage Rights Property. *Cultural Survival Quarterly* 24(4):46–50.

Sonenshein, Raphael J. 1996. The Battle over Liquor Stores in South Central Los Angeles: The Management of an Interminority Conflict. *Urban Affairs Review* 31(6):710–737.

Spilde Contreras, Kate. 2006. Indian Gaming in California Brings Jobs and Income to Areas that Need It Most. Indian Gaming. www.indiangaming.com/regulatory/view/?id=35.

Spiro, Melford. 1967. *Burmese Supernaturalism: A Study in the Explanation and Reduction of Suffering.* Englewood Cliffs, NJ: Prentice-Hall.

Spitulnik, Deborah. 1993. Anthropology and Mass Media. *Annual Review of Anthropology* 22:293–315.

Srinivas, M. N. 1959. The Dominant Caste in Rampura. *American Anthropologist* 1:1–16.

Staats, Valerie. 1994. Ritual, Strategy or Convention: Social Meaning in Traditional Women's Baths in Morocco. *Frontiers: A Journal of Women's Studies* 14(3):1–18.

Stack, Carol. 1974. *All Our Kin: Strategies for Survival in a Black Community.* New York: Harper & Row.

Stephen, Lynn. 1995. Women's Rights Are Human Rights: The Merging of Feminine and Feminist Interests among El Salvador's Mothers of the Disappeared (CO-MADRES). *American Ethnologist* 22(4):807–827.

Stidsen, Sille, comp. and ed. Elaine Bolton, trans. 2006. *The Indigenous World 2006.* Rutgers, NJ: Transaction Books.

Stillman, Amy Ku'uleialoha. 1996. Hawaiian Hula Competitions: Event, Repertoire, Performance and Tradition. *Journal of American Folklore* 109(434):357–380.

Stivens, Maila, Cecelia Ng, and Jomo K. S., with Jahara Bee. 1994. *Malay Peasant Women and the Land.* Atlantic Highlands, NJ: Zed Books.

Stocks, Anthony. 2005. Too Much for Too Few: Problems of Indigenous Land Rights in Latin America. *Annual Review of Anthropology* 34:85–104.

Stoler, Ann Laura. 1985. *Capitalism and Confrontation in Sumatra's Plantation Belt, 1870–1979.* New Haven, CT: Yale University Press.

Storper-Perez, Danielle and Harvey E. Goldberg. 1994. The Kotel: Toward an Ethnographic Portrait. *Religion* 24:309–332.

Strathern, Andrew. 1971. *The Rope of Moka: Big-Men and Ceremonial Exchange in Mount Hagen, New Guinea.* London: Cambridge University Press.

Straughan, B. and W. Schuler. 1991. The Secrets of Ancient Tiwanaku Are Benefiting Today's Bolivia. *Smithsonian* 12:38–47.

Strier, Karen B. 2007. *Primate Behavioral Ecology,* 3rd ed. Boston: Allyn and Bacon.

Stringer, Chris B. 2000. Coasting Out of Africa. *Nature* 405:24–26.

Stringer, Martin D. 1999. Rethinking Animism: Thoughts from the Infancy of Our Discipline. *Journal of the Royal Anthropological Institute* 5:541–556.

Sullivan, Kathleen. 1992. Protagonists of Change: Indigenous Street Vendors in San Cristobal, Mexico, Are Adapting Tradition and Customs to Fit New Life Styles. *Cultural Survival Quarterly* 16:38–40.

Sundar Rao, P. S. S. 1983. Religion and Intensity of In-breeding in Tamil Nadu, South India. *Social Biology* 30(4):413–422.

Sussman, Robert W. and Paul A. Garber. 2004. Rethinking Sociality: Cooperation and Aggression among Primates. In *The Origins and Nature of Sociality* (pp. 161–190). Robert W. Sussman and Audrey R. Chapman, eds. New York: Aldine de Gruyter.

Suttles, Wayne. 1991. The Traditional Kwakiutl Potlatch. In *Chiefly Feasts: The Enduring Kwakiutl Potlatch* (pp. 71–134). Aldona Jonaitis, ed. Washington, DC: American Museum of Natural History.

Tannen, Deborah. 1990. *You Just Don't Understand: Women and Men in Conversation.* New York: Morrow.

Tannenbaum, Nicola B. 1987. Tattoos: Invulnerability and Power in Shan Cosmology. *American Ethnologist* 14:693–711.

Tauli-Corpuz, Victoria. 2005. Indigenous Peoples and the Millennium Development Goals. Paper submitted to the Fourth Session of the UN Permanent Forum on Indigenous Issues, New York City, May 16–27. www.tebtebba.org.

Taussig, Michael. 2004. *My Cocaine Museum.* Chicago: University of Chicago Press.

Te Pareake Mead, Aroha. 2004. He Paua, He Korowai, me Nga Waahi Tapu. *Cultural Survival Quarterly* 28(1):61–64.

Thomas, Frédéric, Francois Renaud, Eric Benefice, Thierry de Meeüs, and Jean-François Guegan. 2001. International Variability of Ages at Menarche and Menopause: Patterns and Main Determinants. *Human Biology* 73(2):271–290.

Thompson, Nile R. and C. Dale Sloat. 2004. The Use of Oral Literature to Provide Community Health Education on the Southern Northwest Coast. *American Indian Culture and Research Journal* 28(3):1–28.

Thompson, Robert Farris. 1971. Aesthetics in Traditional Africa. In *Art and Aesthetics in Primitive Societies* (pp. 374–381). Carol F. Jopling, ed. New York: E. P. Dutton.

Thorpe, S. K. S., R. L. Holder, and R. H. Crompton. 2007. Origin of Human Bipedalism as an Adaptation for Locomotion on Flexible Branches. *Science* 316:1328–1331.

Tishkoff, Sarah A. and B. C. Verrelli. 2003. Patterns of Human Genetic Diversity. *Annual Review Genomics and Human Genetics* 4:293–340.

Tice, Karin E. 1995. *Kuna Crafts, Gender, and the Global Economy.* Austin: University of Texas Press.

Tidball, Keith G. and Christopher P. Toumey. 2003. Signifying Serpents: Hermeneutic Change in Appalachian Pentecostal Serpent Handling. In *Signifying Serpents and Mardi Gras Runners: Representing Identity in Selected Souths* (pp. 1–18). Southern Anthropological Society Proceedings, No. 36. Celeste Ray and Luke Eric Lassiter, eds. Athens: University of Georgia Press.

Tierney, Patrick. 2000. *Darkness in El Dorado: How Scientists and Journalists Devastated the Amazon.* New York: W. W. Norton.

Tiffany, Walter W. 1979. New Directions in Political Anthropology: The Use of Corporate Models for the Analysis of Political Organizations. In *Political Anthropology: The State of the Art* (pp. 63–75). S. Lee Seaton and Henri J. M. Claessen, eds. New York: Mouton.

Tinker, Irene. 1976. The Adverse Impact of Development on Women. In *Women and World Development* (pp. 22–34). Irene Tinker and Michele Bo Bramsen, eds. Washington, DC: Overseas Development Council.

Tooker, Elisabeth. 1992. Lewis H. Morgan and His Contemporaries. *American Anthropologist* 94(2):357–375.

Toren, Christina. 1988. Making the Present, Revealing the Past: The Mutability and Continuity of Tradition as Process. *Man* (n.s.) 23:696–717.

Toth, Nick and K. Schick. 1993. Early Stone Industries and Inferences Regarding Language and Cognition. In *Tools, Language and Cognition in Human Evolution* (pp. 346–362). Kathleen Gibson and Tim Ingold, eds. New York: Cambridge University Press.

Traphagan, John W. 2000. The Liminal Family: Return Migration and Intergenerational Conflict in Japan. *Journal of Anthropological Research* 56:365–385.

Trelease, Murray L. 1975. Dying among Alaskan Indians: A Matter of Choice. In *Death: The Final Stage of Growth* (pp. 33–37). Elisabeth Kübler-Ross, ed. Englewood Cliffs, NJ: Prentice-Hall.

Trotter, Robert T. II. 1987. A Case of Lead Poisoning from Folk Remedies in Mexican American Communities. In *Anthropological Praxis: Translating Knowledge into Action* (pp. 146–159). Robert M. Wulff and Shirley J. Fiske, eds. Boulder, CO: Westview Press.

Trouillot, Michel-Rolph. 1994. Culture, Color, and Politics in Haiti. In *Race* (pp. 146–174). Steven Gregory and Roger Sanjek, eds. New Brunswick, NJ: Rutgers University Press.

———. 2001. The Anthropology of the State in the Age of Globalization. *Current Anthropology* 42:125–133, 135–138.

Turner, Victor W. 1969. *The Ritual Process: Structure and Anti-Structure.* Chicago: Aldine.

Tylor, Edward Burnett. 1871. *Primitive Culture: Researchers into the Development of Mythology, Philosophy, Religion, Art, and Custom.* 2 volumes. London: J. Murray.

Uhl, Sarah. 1991. Forbidden Friends: Cultural Veils of Female Friendship in Andalusia. *American Ethnologist* 18(1):90–105.

United Nations Environment Programme. 2002. *Impact of Global Warming on Mountain Areas Confirmed by UNEP-Backed Mountaineers.* News Release.

Uphoff, Norman T. and Milton J. Esman. 1984. *Local Organizations: Intermediaries in Rural Development.* Ithaca, NY: Cornell University Press.

Ury, William L. 1990. Dispute Resolution Notes from the Kalahari. *Negotiation Journal* 63:229–238.

VanWynsberghe, Robert M. 2002. *AlterNatives: Community, Identity, and Environmental Justice on Walpole Island.* Boston: Allyn and Bacon.

Vekua, A., D. Lordkipanidze, G. P. Rightmire, J. Agusti, R. Ferring, G. Maisuradze, et al. 2002. A New Skull of Early *Homo* from Dmanisi, Georgia. *Science* 297:85–89.

Vellinga, Marcel. 2004. *Constituting Unity and Difference: Vernacular Architecture in a Minangkabau Village.* Leiden: KITLV Press.

Veltmeyer, Henry and James Petras. 2002. The Social Dynamics of Brazil's Rural Landless Workers' Movement: Ten Hypotheses on Successful Leadership. *Canadian Review of Sociology and Anthropology* 39:79–96.

Wainwright, Elsina. 2003. Responding to State Failure: The Case of Australia and the Solomon Islands. *Australian Journal of International Affairs* 57:485–498.

Wallerstein, Immanuel. 1979. *The Capitalist World-Economy.* New York: Cambridge University Press.

Walmsley, Roy. 2007. Prison Planet. *Foreign Policy* May/June: 30–31.

Walsh, Michael. 2005. Will Indigenous Languages Survive? *Annual Review of Anthropology* 34:293–315.

Ward, Martha C. 1989. Once Upon a Time. In *Nest in the Wind: Adventures in Anthropology on a Tropical Island* (pp. 1–22). Martha C. Ward, ed. Prospect Heights, IL: Waveland Press.

Warren, Carol A. B. 1988. *Gender Issues in Field Research. Qualitative Research Methods, Volume 9.* Newbury Park, CA: Sage Publications.

Warren, D. Michael. 2001. The Role of the Global Network of Indigenous Knowledge Resource Centers in the Conservation of Cultural and Biological Diversity. In *Biocultural Diversity: Linking Language, Knowledge and the Environment* (pp. 446–461). Washington, DC: Smithsonian Institution Press.

Waters, Michael R. and Thomas W. Stafford, Jr. 2007. Redefining the Age of Clovis: Implications for the Peopling of the Americas. *Science* 315:1122–1126.

Watkins, Ben and Michael L. Fleisher. 2002. Tracking Pastoralist Migration: Lessons from the Ethiopian Somali National Regional State. *Human Organization* 61:328–338.

Watson, James, L., ed. 1997. *Golden Arches East: McDonald's in East Asia.* Stanford, CA: Stanford University Press.

Watson, Rubie S. 1986. The Named and the Nameless: Gender and Person in Chinese Society. *American Ethnologist* 13(4):619–631.

Weatherford, J. 1981. *Tribes on the Hill.* New York: Random House.

Websdale, Neil. 1995. An Ethnographic Assessment of the Policing of Domestic Violence in Rural Eastern Kentucky. *Social Justice* 22(1):102–122.

Webster, Gloria Cranmer. 1991. The Contemporary Potlatch. In *Chiefly Feasts: The Enduring Kwakiutl Potlatch* (pp. 227–250). Aldona Jonaitis, ed. Washington, DC: American Museum of Natural History.

Weine, Stevan M. et al. 1995. Psychiatric Consequences of "Ethnic Cleansing": Clinical Assessments and Trauma Testimonies of Newly Resettled Bosnian Refugees. *American Journal of Psychiatry* 152(4):536–542.

Weiner, Annette B. 1976. *Women of Value, Men of Renown: New Perspectives in Trobriand Exchange.* Austin: University of Texas Press.

———. 1988. *The Trobrianders of Papua New Guinea.* New York: Holt, Rinehart and Winston.

Werbner, Pnina. 1988. "Sealing the Koran": Offering and Sacrifice among Pakistani Labour Migrants. *Cultural Dynamics* 1:77–97.

Whitehead, Tony Larry. 1986. Breakdown, Resolution, and Coherence: The Fieldwork Experience of a Big, Brown, Pretty-talking Man in a West Indian Community. In *Self, Sex, and Gender in Cross-Cultural Fieldwork* (pp. 213–239). Tony Larry Whitehead and Mary Ellen Conway, eds. Chicago: University of Illinois Press.

Whiten, A., J. Goodall, W. C. McGrew, T. Nishida, V. Reynolds, Y. Sugiyama, et al. 1999. Cultures in Chimpanzees. *Nature* 399:682–685.

Whiting, Beatrice B. and John W. M. Whiting. 1975. *Children of Six Cultures: A Psycho-Cultural Analysis.* Cambridge, MA: Harvard University Press.

Whiting, Robert. 1979. You've Gotta Have "Wa." *Sports Illustrated* September 24:60–71.

Whyte, Martin King. 1993. Wedding Behavior and Family Strategies in Chengdu. In *Chinese Families in the Post-Mao Era* (pp. 189–216). Deborah Davis and Stevan Harrell, eds. Berkeley: University of California Press.

Wikan, Unni. 1977. Man Becomes Woman: Transsexualism in Oman as a Key to Gender Roles. *Man* 12(2):304–319.

———. 1982. *Behind the Veil in Arabia: Women in Oman.* Chicago: University of Chicago Press.

———. 2000. Citizenship on Trial: Nadia's Case. *Daedalus* 129:55–76.

Williams, Brett. 1984. Why Migrant Women Feed Their Husbands Tamales: Foodways as a Basis for a Revisionist View of Tejano Family Life. In *Ethnic and Regional Foodways in the United States: The Performance of Group Identity* (pp. 113–126). Linda Keller Brown and Kay Mussell, eds. Knoxville: University of Tennessee Press.

Wilson, Richard. 1995. *Maya Resurgence in Guatemala: Q'eqchi' Experiences.* Norman: University of Oklahoma Press.

Winans, Edgar V. and Angelique Haugerud. 1977. Rural Self-Help in Kenya: The Harambee Movement. *Human Organization* 36:334–351.

Wolf, Charlotte. 1996. Status. In *The Social Science Encyclopedia* (pp. 842–843). Adam Kuper and Jessica Kuper, eds. New York: Routledge.

Wolf, Eric R. 1969. *Peasant Wars of the Twentieth Century.* New York: Harper & Row.

Woolfson, Peter, Virginia Hood, Roger Secker-Walker, and Ann C. Macaulay. 1995. Mohawk English in the Medical Interview. *Medical Anthropology Quarterly* 9(4):503–509.

World Bank. 2003. *Roma Poverty Remains Key Hurdle to Shared Prosperity in Central and Eastern Europe.* Washington, DC: The World Bank. www.worldbank.org/roma.

Worldwatch Institute. 2003. *Vital Signs 2003: The Trends That Are Shaping Our Future.* Washington, DC: Worldwatch Institute/W. W. Norton.

Wormald, Tom. 2005. Visions of the Future: Technology and the Imagination in Hungarian Civil Society. *Anthropology Matters* 7(1):1–10. http://www.anthropologymatters.com.

Wrangham, Richard and Dale Peterson. 1996. *Demonic Males: Apes and the Origins of Human Violence.* New York: Houghton Mifflin Company.

Wu, David Y. H. 1990. Chinese Minority Policy and the Meaning of Minority Culture: The Example of Bai in Yunnan, China. *Human Organization* 49(1):1–13.

www.greatapetrust.org/bonobo/meet/kanzi.php.

www.npr.org.

Xizhe, Peng. 1991. *Demographic Transition in China: Fertility Trends since the 1980s.* New York: Oxford University Press.

Yamamoto, Shinya, Gen Yamakoshi, Tatyana Humle, and Tetsuro Matsuzawa. 2008. Invention and Modification of a New Tool Use Behavior: Ant-Fishing in Trees by a Wild Chimpanzee (*Pan troglodytes verus*) at Bossou, Guinea. *American Journal of Primatology* 70:699-–702.

Yoon, In-Jin. 1993. *The Social Origins of Korean Immigration to the United States from 1965 to the Present.* Papers of the Program on Population, Number 121. Honolulu: East-West Center.

Young, Biloine Whiting and Melvin L. Fowler. 2000. *Cahokia: The Great Native American Metropolis.* Urbana: University of Illinois Press.

Zabusky, Stacia E. 1995. *Launching Europe: An Ethnography of European Cooperation in Space Science.* Princeton, NJ: Princeton University Press.

Zaidi, S. Akbar. 1988. Poverty and Disease: Need for Structural Change. *Social Science and Medicine* 27:119–127.

Zarrilli, Phillip B. 1990. Kathakali. In *Indian Theatre: Traditions of Performance* (pp. 315–357). Farley P. Richmond, Darius L. Swann, and Phillip B. Zarrilli, eds. Honolulu: University of Hawaii Press.

Zeder, Melinda A. 2006. Central Questions in the Domestication of Plants and Animals. *Evolutionary Anthropology* 15:105–117.

Sources for "Anthropology in the Real World"

Part I: Susan Squires

American Breakfast & the Mother-in-Law: How an Anthropologist Created Go-Gurt. National Association for the Practice of Anthropology. (2003–2004). www.practicinganthropology.org/learn/index.cfm?print=1storyid=4.

Boss, Shira J. (2 January 2001). Anthropologists on the Job. *The Christian Science Monitor.* http://csmonitor.com/cgi-bin/durableRedirect.pl?/durable/2001/01/02/fp9sl-csm.shtml.

Squires, Susan. Ph.D., Research Director, Tactics LLC. (2004). Southwestern Anthropological Association. www2.sjsu.edu/depts/anthropology/swaa/pages/PgSquares.html.

Walsh, Sharon. (23 May 2001). Corporate Anthropology: Dirt-Free Research. CNN.com/CAREER. www.cnn.com/2001/CAREER/dayonthejob/05/23/corp.anthropologist.idg/.

Part II: Lara Tabac

Lara Tabac. (29 September 2003). Slate. http://slate.msn.com/id/2088748/entry/2088987/.

Part III: Fredy Peccerelli

AAAS Human Rights Action Network. American Association for the Advancement of Science. (21 March 2002). http://shr.aaas.org/news/050204_peccerelli.html.

Black, Richard. Guatemala Rights Scientist Honoured. BBC. (15 February 2004). http://news.bbc.co.uk/go/pr/fr/-/2/hi/science/nature/3489743.stm.

Digging for Truth in Guatemala. American Association for the Advancement of Science Public Release. (14 February 2004). www.eurekalert.org/pub_releases/2004-02/aaft-dft020504.php.

Elton, Catherine. (27 March 2002). Despite Threats, Guatemalan Scientists Dig for the Truth. *The Christian Science Monitor.* www.csmonitor.com/2002/0327/pO8s01-woam.html.

Peccerelli, Fredy. (2004). Executive Director of the Guatemalan Forensic Anthropology Foundation Speaks at AAAS. American Association for the Advancement of Science. http://shr.aaas.org/news/050204_peccerelli.html.

Part IV: Brian Craik

Craik, Brian. (2004). The Importance of Working Together: Exclusions, Conflicts and Participation in James Bay, Quebec. IDRC Books Online. www.idrc.ca/en/ev-64530-201-1-DO_TOPIC.html.

Grand Council of the Crees website. (7 August 2006). www.gcc.ca/gcc/fedrelations.php.

Preston, Richard J. (12 May 2006). Reflections on Becoming an Applied Anthropologist. The 2006 Weaver-Tremblay Lecture, presented at the Canadian Anthropology Section/Société Canadien Anthropologie, Concordia University, Montreal. www.socsci.mcmaster.ca/anthro/emplibrary/prestonawardreflection.

Part V: Mamphela Ramphele

Across Boundaries. (21 April 1997). Online NewsHour: Zair: End of an Era. 1999, MacNeil-Lehrer Productions. www.pbs.org/newshur/bb/africa/april97/ramph_4-21.html.

New Vice-Chancellor Appointed. (10 December 1996). University of Capetown Department of Development and Public Affairs. web.uct.ac.za/depts/dpa/news/ramphele.html.

Ramphele, Mamphela. Dr. Mamphela Ramphele's Biography. www.sahistory.org.za/pages/people/ramphele-m.html.

INDEX

Italicized page numbers indicate photos, figures, or maps.